Creating Business Value and Competitive Advantage With Social Entrepreneurship

N. Oyku Iyigun
Istanbul Commerce University, Turkey

A volume in the Advances in Business Strategy and Competitive Advantage (ABSCA) Book Series

IGI Global
DISSEMINATOR OF KNOWLEDGE

Published in the United States of America by
IGI Global
Business Science Reference (an imprint of IGI Global)
701 E. Chocolate Avenue
Hershey PA, USA 17033
Tel: 717-533-8845
Fax: 717-533-8661
E-mail: cust@igi-global.com
Web site: http://www.igi-global.com

Library of Congress Cataloging-in-Publication Data

Names: Iyigun, N. Oyku, 1981- editor.
Title: Creating business value and competitive advantage with social entrepreneurship / N. Oyku Iyigun, editor.
Description: Hershey : Business Science Reference, [2018]
Identifiers: LCCN 2017051835| ISBN 9781522556879 (hardcover) | ISBN 9781522556886 (ebook)
Subjects: LCSH: Social entrepreneurship. | Value.
Classification: LCC HD60 .C7394 2018 | DDC 658.4/08--dc23 LC record available at https://lccn.loc.gov/2017051835

This book is published in the IGI Global book series Advances in Business Strategy and Competitive Advantage (ABSCA) (ISSN: 2327-3429; eISSN: 2327-3437)

British Cataloguing in Publication Data
A Cataloguing in Publication record for this book is available from the British Library.

For electronic access to this publication, please contact: eresources@igi-global.com.

Advances in Business Strategy and Competitive Advantage (ABSCA) Book Series

Patricia Ordóñez de Pablos
Universidad de Oviedo, Spain

ISSN:2327-3429
EISSN:2327-3437

Mission

Business entities are constantly seeking new ways through which to gain advantage over their competitors and strengthen their position within the business environment. With competition at an all-time high due to technological advancements allowing for competition on a global scale, firms continue to seek new ways through which to improve and strengthen their business processes, procedures, and profitability.

The **Advances in Business Strategy and Competitive Advantage (ABSCA) Book Series** is a timely series responding to the high demand for state-of-the-art research on how business strategies are created, implemented and re-designed to meet the demands of globalized competitive markets. With a focus on local and global challenges, business opportunities and the needs of society, the **ABSCA** encourages scientific discourse on doing business and managing information technologies for the creation of sustainable competitive advantage.

Coverage

- Joint Ventures
- Resource-Based Competition
- Small and Medium Enterprises
- Strategy Performance Management
- Strategic alliances
- Competitive Strategy
- Cost Leadership Strategy
- Business Models
- Outsourcing
- Adaptive Enterprise

IGI Global is currently accepting manuscripts for publication within this series. To submit a proposal for a volume in this series, please contact our Acquisition Editors at Acquisitions@igi-global.com or visit: http://www.igi-global.com/publish/.

The Advances in Business Strategy and Competitive Advantage (ABSCA) Book Series (ISSN 2327-3429) is published by IGI Global, 701 E. Chocolate Avenue, Hershey, PA 17033-1240, USA, www.igi-global.com. This series is composed of titles available for purchase individually; each title is edited to be contextually exclusive from any other title within the series. For pricing and ordering information please visit http://www.igi-global.com/book-series/advances-business-strategy-competitive-advantage/73672. Postmaster: Send all address changes to above address.

Titles in this Series

For a list of additional titles in this series, please visit: www.igi-global.com/book-series

Ethical Standards and Practice in International Relations
F. Sigmund Topor (Keio University, Japan)
Information Science Reference • copyright 2018 • 364pp • H/C (ISBN: 9781522526506) • US $195.00 (our price)

Applications of Conscious Innovation in Organizations
Jesus Enrique Portillo Pizana (Tecnológico de Monterrey University, Mexico) Sergio Ortiz Valdes (Tecnológico de Monterrey University, Mexico) and Luis Miguel Beristain Hernandez (Tecnológico de Monterrey University, Mexico)
Business Science Reference • copyright 2018 • 296pp • H/C (ISBN: 9781522540236) • US $205.00 (our price)

Business Strategies and Advanced Techniques for Entrepreneurship 4.0
Jose Manuel Saiz-Alvarez (Tecnológico de Monterrey, Mexico)
Business Science Reference • copyright 2018 • 231pp • H/C (ISBN: 9781522549789) • US $195.00 (our price)

Ethics and Decision-Making for Sustainable Business Practices
Ionica Oncioiu (Titu Maiorescu University, Romania)
Business Science Reference • copyright 2018 • 308pp • H/C (ISBN: 9781522537731) • US $215.00 (our price)

Handbook of Research on Entrepreneurial Ecosystems and Social Dynamics in a Globalized World
Luísa Cagica Carvalho (Universidade Aberta, Portugal & Universidade de Évora, Portugal)
Business Science Reference • copyright 2018 • 601pp • H/C (ISBN: 9781522535256) • US $345.00 (our price)

Start-Up Enterprises and Contemporary Innovation Strategies in the Global Marketplace
Rajagopal (EGADE Business School, Tecnologico de Monterrey, Mexico) and Ramesh Behl (International Management Institute Bhubaneswar, India)
Business Science Reference • copyright 2018 • 341pp • H/C (ISBN: 9781522548317) • US $235.00 (our price)

Global Practices in Knowledge Management for Societal and Organizational Development
Neeta Baporikar (Namibia University of Science and Technology, Namibia & University of Pune, India)
Business Science Reference • copyright 2018 • 475pp • H/C (ISBN: 9781522530091) • US $240.00 (our price)

Exploring the Global Competitiveness of Agri-Food Sectors and Serbia's Dominant Presence Emerging Research...
Svetlana Ignjatijević (University of Business Academy in Novi Sad, Serbia) and Drago Cvijanović (University of Kragujevac, Serbia)
Business Science Reference • copyright 2018 • 193pp • H/C (ISBN: 9781522527626) • US $165.00 (our price)

IGI Global
DISSEMINATOR OF KNOWLEDGE

701 East Chocolate Avenue, Hershey, PA 17033, USA
Tel: 717-533-8845 x100 • Fax: 717-533-8661
E-Mail: cust@igi-global.com • www.igi-global.com

Table of Contents

Detailed Table of Contents

Preface

What business entrepreneurs are to the economy, social entrepreneurs are to social change. They are the driven, creative individuals who question the status quo, exploit new opportunities, refuse to give up, and remake the world for the better. David Bornstein (2007)

David Bornstein is a journalist and the author of the famous book, 'How to Change the World: Social Entrepreneurs and the Power of New Ideas'. Up to now, he has written three books on 'social entrepreneurship' and he is one of the co-founders of the Solutions Journalism Network. I have always been inspired by his outstanding vision for change.

According to the World Population Prospects Report, the world population stands at 7.3 billion (UN, 2017). With the growth in population, the demand to address social needs is also increasing – particularly problems such as inadequate education and healthcare systems, environmental threats, poverty, homelessness, unemployment, hunger and high crime rates. Approximately 1.2 billion people live in extreme poverty (which forces them to live in environments without access to decent shelter, clean water or sanitation), 101 million children under the age of five are underweight, and more than a million people die from AIDS-related causes each year (Kickul & Lyons, 2016; Singh, 2016). In an age of rising environmental and social concerns, it has become necessary for the business world to pay special attention to sustainability issues, as well as social needs. Social entrepreneurship has become a global movement over the last 40 years.

Creating Business Value and Competitive Advantage With Social Entrepreneurship sheds light on the wide spectrum of social entrepreneurship addressing different aspects of how social entrepreneurship can be beneficial for the global economy as a whole. It also demonstrates the difficulties posed in trying to engage in social entrepreneurship for a change on a global level (Munshi, 2010). This book is an essential reference source for professionals, scholars and researchers in various fields including psychology, sociology, economics and management.

This book examines the broad topic of social entrepreneurship by looking at relevant theoretical frameworks and fundamental terms, focusing on creating business value, exploring social entrepreneurship and promotion of social entrepreneurship. Social entrepreneurs creatively contribute to the welfare of marginalized members of society by availing affordable products and services. The objective of this book is to discuss the concept of social entrepreneurship and provide some theoretical lenses by addressing both theory and research, to suggest practical solutions, to engage scholars and practitioners across disciplines and to debate various methods and approaches of enacting programs for social change. Specifically, this book aims to exhibit research that builds a broad, inclusive framework with 28 authors from 5 different countries and different disciplinary backgrounds, addressing the key issues of 'value creation and 'social innovation' in social entrepreneurship.

Chapter 1 starts the discussion by explaining the context of social entrepreneurship and its background. It continues by exploring the related terms and characteristics of social entrepreneurship. The purpose of this chapter is to review and extend the current literature by providing insight about social entrepreneurship in the spectrum of entrepreneurship through value creation. In conclusion, this chapter suggests implications for social entrepreneurs and scholars and discusses social entrepreneurship in the spectrum of entrepreneurship, with value creation focusing at the bottom of the pyramid.

Chapter 2 explores entrepreneurship from a sociological perspective. The aim of this chapter is to create a sociological perspective on social entrepreneurship to contribute to social order and welfare rather than commercial entrepreneurship serving the purpose of individual or organizational interest in an economic sense. In the context of sociological perspective, the concepts of social problem, social benefit, social mission and vision, social value, social capital and finally social change and transformation and their relation with social entrepreneurship are examined.

Chapter 3 highlights the different definitions of social entrepreneurs and examines three main typologies -social bricoleurs, social constructionists, and social engineers- and their characteristics. This chapter also investigates the personality traits and motivation factors of social entrepreneurs. The distinctive personality traits of social entrepreneurs have a direct impact on their intention to build a social venture and sustain it. Social entrepreneurs are motivated by existent opportunities in their environment. They deeply concentrate on social problems and recognize each problem as an opportunity to help others or to create social value.

Chapter 4 is based on in-depth interviews with four participants to get a better understanding of the individual and behavioral factors of social entrepreneurs. The interviews showed that the social entrepreneurial potential encompasses entrepreneurial motivations and psychological, social, managerial competencies which include dimensions such as self-motivation, self-efficacy, risk-taking, strategic planning capacity, innovation capacity, social capital capacity, leadership capacity, resilience, and conflict management.

Chapter 5 examines the concepts of social innovation, social entrepreneurship, corporate social responsibility, corporate social entrepreneurship and new product development. This chapter argues that social entrepreneurs can utilize the customer development process when working on a novel solution to create social and economic value. Social entrepreneurs can team up with companies for creating sustainable solutions for the society. The conclusion briefly describes possible weaknesses, limitations and challenges for social innovation and social entrepreneurship.

Chapter 6 proposes an alternate view to social entrepreneurship emphasizing that for-profit and non-profit entrepreneurship are in essence not different. It then discusses the latest trends in the commercial entrepreneurship world together with implications for social entrepreneurship. The Lean Startup phenomenon (Ries, 2011) and closely related concepts, namely; customer development philosophy, business model innovation, value proposition design and Jobs-to-be-Done Theory are explored with implications for social entrepreneurship.

Chapter 7 starts off the discussion on the ways of creating competitive advantage with social entrepreneurship by determining the instruments that social enterprises can apply. This chapter develops the concepts of social entrepreneurship and competitive advantage within their common framework and it proposes shared value, social intrapreneurship, strategic partnership, differentiation and recruiting talents as instruments for social entrepreneurs to achieve competitive advantage. It also explores various cases as examples. The chapter concludes by proposing a measurement framework that focuses on the interaction between business and social impact.

Chapter 8 highlights the importance of good management and investment in human resources for social enterprises' survival in the competitive environment of social economy. Among the management practices, human resources management acts as a tool for gaining competitive advantage and it builds mutual trust between the staff and the organization. This chapter examines the human resources management practices and challenges in social entrepreneurship such as recruitment, career management, training, and compensation and performance management.

Chapter 9 describes an international career model of five different forms of expatriate social entrepreneurs or "social expat-preneurs" within the broader international career construct of self-initiated expatriates. This chapter provides vivid examples of each form of social expat-preneurs such as predeparture, transitioned, retired senior, avocation-driven, and social expat-intrapreneur and it ends by outlining benefits to host countries and examines the importance of further research.

Chapter 10 begins with the notion of performance management; it focuses on the concept of social impact in order to deeply examine the measurement of performance in social enterprises. The chapter argues the importance of measuring social impact, a crucial process in social investment. and discusses which measurement method to choose. It then introduces the classification of methods in various forms and continues by explaining the most frequently used social impact measurement methods including cost effectiveness and cost benefit analyses, social accounting and auditing, SROI, balanced scorecard, SIMPLE, benefit-cost ratio, BACO ratio, expected return metric, cost per impact and blended value. The conclusion focuses on the overall perspective of the subject, critical areas to pay attention to and limitations.

Chapter 11 focuses on the relation between social networks and social entrepreneurship. This chapter argues that social networks are crucial in social entrepreneurship and social entrepreneurs rely on different compositions of social networks in different stages of the entrepreneurial process. Drawing from the network approach in entrepreneurship, this chapter continues by exploring the theoretical framework including conceptualizations of social entrepreneurship and social networks. This chapter discusses utilizing social networks in social entrepreneurship, by reflecting possible characteristics of network usage and composition through the life cycle of social enterprises.

Chapter 12 explores the link between social entrepreneurship and economic growth. Entrepreneurship has been of interest to academics and practitioners for a few decades and accepted as one of the important factors that play an essential role in advancing economic development. This chapter argues that social entrepreneurship should improve the well-being of individuals by generating social value. Satisfying social needs that embrace both social and economic aspects will also affect economic well-being in a positive manner. This chapter also claims that social entrepreneurship is an important catalyzer of economic well-being and economic growth.

Chapter 13 introduces the concept of entrepreneurial leadership which offers potential contributions to economic and social wealth and explains the theoretical framework of social entrepreneurial leadership and the characteristics of social entrepreneurial leaders. This chapter presents a study on the similarities between social entrepreneurial leadership and other leadership styles such as ethical, transformative, authentic, sustainable, and servant leadership. The conclusion reflects on the various understandings of social entrepreneurial leadership and how social entrepreneurial leaders can be characterized as the primary actors for a better world.

Chapter 14 attempts to explore the initiated engagement between cooperative and competitive concern among the firms with increasing popularity to achieve the certain objectives like motivating the sense to growing the business with entrepreneurship. This chapter discusses that attracting growing numbers of cooperative and competitive alliances should be strengthened in order to gain feedback and insights into performance value in social entrepreneurship. This chapter provides significant insights by exploring the key role of strategies to give the beneficial feedback to perform continuous improvement in social entrepreneurship.

Chapter 15 investigates the injustices and inadequacies in transferring public support to social problems. This chapter raises fundamental problems that have hampered social entrepreneurship and prevented further development, and it develops a number of solution proposals. This chapter also includes proposals for future research, explains various researches from different disciplines and discusses their unique character in terms of their synthesis. In conclusion, this chapter stresses the importance of social networks, social co-operatives, joint investments and economic policies in light of basic theories and doctrine of management and organization.

Chapter 16 identifies how a social entrepreneur, individually, has potential to cause social change. An Ashoka Fellow from Turkey is profiled, in order to provide information about the process of value creation. This chapter looks at important issues to be addressed such as gender inequality and violence against women and examines the selected fellow who empowers women by creating social value and advancing social change in Turkey.

Chapter 17 examines small third sector social enterprises' perspective in gaining access to public services contracts. The UK government aims to increase the role of social enterprise as a vehicle to deliver public services directly to citizens and local communities in areas such as housing, welfare-to-work, education, health and social care. This chapter looks at small third sector social enterprises' experiences by conducting face-to-face interviews with managers and chief executive officers. Empirical evidence suggests that some procurement policies and processes are impacting small third sector social enterprises' organizational development, growth, management and staff career development. The chapter helps to explain the challenges facing small third sector social enterprises in the changing context of the public services procurement process.

The growth of critical social issues worldwide has revealed that existing businesses, governments and NGOs will not be enough to solve these problems. Researchers have equated charitable contributions, financial success and business creation with the social role of entrepreneurship. As our discussion makes clear, the role of social entrepreneurship is much larger, more profound and more impactful than traditional views would suggest (Zahra, Newey, & Li, 2014). As Emerson (2003) suggests, we need new metrics, new conceptions of the fundamental value proposition that are not simply a "quid pro quo" trade-off between two competing goals perceived to be locked in a zero-sum battle. One of the best alternatives for addressing these problems is likely to be a new form of entrepreneurial organization where social value is not merely a byproduct of entrepreneurial activity but an intended primary outcome. As argued by Yunus (2011), the world needs another kind of business to make the structure of capitalism complete. We refer to such social entrepreneurial organizations as hybrid ventures, which embody a different approach to addressing social issues (Wilson & Post, 2013).

In the twenty-first century, social entrepreneurship still faces what we describe as multi-dimensional challenges especially during the inception and growth phases of these organizations. For this reason, this book adopts a multidisciplinary and international approach to look at the processes that foster social entrepreneurship in terms of value creation and competitive advantage. The selection of chapters presented and the research agenda developed will lead to further theory development and extension of the emerging research topic. The way in which social businesses are designed is complex, connected to their mission, design, legal and capital structures, strategies and operational principles. Through their business models designed for people, planet and profits, social businesses therefore appear to potentially offer powerful, sustainable solutions to some of the world's problems (Wilson & Post, 2013). As Kofi Annan, former UN Secretary General stated at the World Economic Forum in Davos in 1999:

Let us choose to unite the power of markets with the strength of universal ideas. Let us choose to reconcile the creative forces of private entrepreneurship with the needs of the disadvantaged and the requirements of the future generations.

N. Oyku Iyigun
Istanbul Commerce University, Turkey

REFERENCES

Bornstein, D. (2007). *How to change the world: social entrepreneurs and the power of new idea.* Oxford University Press.

Emerson, J. (2003). The Blended Value Proposition: Integrating Social and Financial Returns. *California Management Review*, *45*(4), 35–51. doi:10.2307/41166187

Kickul, J., & Lyons, T. S. (2016). *Understanding Social Entrepreneurship: The Relentless Pursuit of Mission in an Ever Changing World (2nd ed.).* New York: Routledge.

Munshi, N. V. (2010). Value Creation, Social Innovation, and Entrepreneurship in Global Economies. *Journal of Asia-Pacific Business*, *11*(3), 160–165. doi:10.1080/10599231.2010.500569

Singh, A. (2016). *The Process of Social Value Creation: A Multiple-Case Study on Social Entrepreneurship in India.* Springer. doi:10.1007/978-81-322-2827-1

United Nations, Department of Economic and Social Affairs, Population Division. (2017). *World Population Prospects: The 2017 Revision.* Author.

Wilson, F., & Post, J. E. (2013). Business Models for People, Planet (&Profits): Exploring the Phenomena of Social Business, A Market-Based Approach to Social Value Creation. *Small Business Economics*, *40*(3), 715–737. doi:10.100711187-011-9401-0

Yunus, M. (2011). *Building Social Business: The New Kind of Capitalism that Serves Humanity's Most Pressing Needs.* New York: Public Affairs.

Zahra, S. A., Newey, L. R., & Li, Y. (2014). On the Frontiers: The Implications of Social Entrepreneurship for International Entrepreneurship. *Entrepreneurship Theory and Practice*, *38*(1), 137–158. doi:10.1111/etap.12061

Acknowledgment

Coming together is a beginning; keeping together is progress; working together is success. Henry Ford

First and foremost, I would like to thank the 28 authors from 5 different countries who have come together, kept together and worked together by contributing 17 original chapters to this book. All of these chapters explore interesting aspects of "social entrepreneurship" and will benefit the readers –specifically scholars and entrepreneurs–, who would like to explore this issue in detail.

I gratefully acknowledge the distinguished members of the Editorial Advisory Board, whose advice and presence have made this volume possible. I also acknowledge Oguzhan Aygoren, Ph.D. (Bogazici University) and Jason D'Mello, Ph.D. (Loyola Marymount University) for their kind support. It is impossible not to state the contributions made by the professional staff of the publisher, IGI Global.

I gratefully acknowledge Professor David Choi, Ph.D. (Loyola Marymount University Fred Kiesner Center for Entrepreneurship) and Professor Charles Vance, Ph.D. (Loyola Marymount University College of Business Administration) for their invaluable support and perspectives on this book. I also gratefully acknowledge Professor Julie Feldman-Abe, Ph.D. (Mount Saint Mary's University) and Professor Meric Keskinel, Ph.D. (West Los Angeles College) for their continuous guidance and constructive insights. I would also like to thank my family, who kept me sane and encouraged me all the time. Without you, I would not have done half of this.

This book was finalized while on sabbatical during 2017-fall term at the College of Business Administration, Loyola Marymount University in Los Angeles, USA. In conclusion, I acknowledge my sending institution, namely Istanbul Commerce University for providing me time and support to focus on my academic work.

Necla Oyku Iyigun
Istanbul Commerce University, Turkey

Introduction

The field of social entrepreneurship is growing rapidly and attracting increased attention from many industries. Social entrepreneurship is attracting growing amounts of talent, money and attention. The term itself is referenced frequently by academicians and public officials and is popular on university campuses and voluntary organizations. This book examines the broad topic of social entrepreneurship by looking at relevant theoretical frameworks and fundamental terms, focuses on creating business value, exploring social entrepreneurship and promotion of social entrepreneurship. Social entrepreneurs creatively contribute towards the welfare of marginalized members of society by availing affordable products and services. The objective of this book is to discuss the concept of social entrepreneurship and provide some theoretical lens by addressing both theory and research, to suggest practical solutions, to engage scholars and practitioners across disciplines and to debate about various methods and approaches of enacting programs of social change.

N. Oyku Iyigun
Istanbul Commerce University, Turkey

Chapter 1
Context of Social Entrepreneurship and Background:
Definitions, Related Terms, and Characteristics

N. Öykü İyigün
Istanbul Commerce University, Turkey

ABSTRACT

Social entrepreneurship has been the subject of considerable interest in the literature. It has become a global phenomenon by addressing the basic needs of humans, which are neglected, and enriching communities and societies. This chapter introduces the context of social entrepreneurship and its background; it continues by exploring the related terms and characteristics of social entrepreneurship. Over the years, social entrepreneurship has emerged as a distinctive context by integrating the resourcefulness of traditional entrepreneurship with the compelling drive to address social problems. Social entrepreneurship needs to be properly defined and it requires a theoretical framework that links it to the theory of entrepreneurship. The purpose of this chapter is to review and extend the current literature by providing insight about social entrepreneurship in the spectrum of entrepreneurship through value creation. As a result, this chapter suggests implications for social entrepreneurs and boundaries for social entrepreneurship.

DOI: 10.4018/978-1-5225-5687-9.ch001

Social entrepreneurship starts with an entrepreneur who has a novel idea, an innovative product or service, a creative approach to solving a perceived problem, a new business model, and a previously untried approach to product or service delivery (Makhlouf, 2011).

INTRODUCTION

Social entrepreneurship has gained popularity in the development of societies because entrepreneurship is seen as a process that can serve as a catalyst for social change (Urban & Teise, 2015; Abu-Saifan, 2012). The concept of entrepreneurship has a long history in the academic and business world. Entrepreneurship can be defined as a process of doing something new and different for the purpose of creating wealth for the individual and adding value to society by bringing forth ideas previously unimagined. The most obvious example of entrepreneurship is the starting of new businesses. Entrepreneurs are seen as the self-made business people of today, creating their own wealth rather than inheriting it (Beaver & Jennings, 2005). Nowadays, entrepreneurship and small businesses are the basics of economy, responsible for breakthrough innovations that influence the growth of free market economy and its general performance (Iyigun & Keskin, 2016).

Governments due to their scarce resources cannot fully reach the developmental goals like economic prosperity, employment and welfare of citizens, especially in the developing countries. With a shift from the welfare approach to the democratic approach in most of the developed and developing countries, governments have given primary importance to market-driven models of welfare, which created a major change in the approach to development of people and communities with a greater emphasis on 'self-help' (Singh, 2016). Many philanthropic efforts have fallen far short of expectations and major social sector institutions are often viewed as inefficient and ineffective (Dees, 1998). Non-governmental organizations (NGOs) are now facing financial problems due to constantly decreasing supply of donations, grants and government subsidies. Thus, by the end of twentieth century, to enhance the social wealth by addressing basic human needs or by solving local problems, social entrepreneurship emerged as a complementary part of commercial entrepreneurship (Santos, 2012).

Social entrepreneurship can be defined as *entrepreneurial and innovative activity with an embedded social purpose* (Austin, Stevenson, & Wei-Skillern, 2006). Social entrepreneurs are seen as change agents by creating social value through continuous innovation, adaption and learning (Day & Jean-Denis, 2016). Social entrepreneurship has grown into a global movement that is bringing solutions to many of the world's problems and transforming the way we think about social change. The increasing recognition of the contribution made by social entrepreneurs to a nation's social, economic, cultural and environmental wealth yielded social entrepreneurship to be identified as an innovative way of tackling unmet socioeconomic needs (Iyigun & Yalcintas, 2017).

This chapter aims to present the context of social entrepreneurship in the spectrum of entrepreneurship through value creation. With this perspective, antecedents, characteristics and boundaries of social entrepreneurship will be discussed in light of social change.

BACKGROUND

According to the World Population Prospects Report, the world population stands at 7.3 billion (UN 2017). With the growth in population, the demand to address for social needs is also increasing – particularly the problems such as inadequate education and healthcare systems, environmental threats, poverty, homelessness, unemployment, hunger and high crime rates. Approximately 1.2 billion people live in extreme poverty (which forces them to live in environments without access to decent shelter, clean water or sanitation), 101 million children under the age of five are underweight, and more than a million people die from AIDS-related causes each year (Kickul & Lyons, 2016; Singh, 2016).

The free market economy and economic growth based on efficiency have failed to provide the basic conditions for living that has resulted in the rise of social and ecological degradation, persistent misery, irreversible environmental losses, vulnerabilities, social inequalities and economic and socio-cultural damage (Barki, Comini, Cunliffe, Hart, & Rai, 2015; de Paula & Cavalcanti, 2000). Moreover, during crisis situations, governments and NGOs have also failed to provide timely and effective solutions.

Social entrepreneurship focuses on pursuing innovative solutions to social problems by combining the passion of a social mission with an image of business-like discipline, innovation and determination (Dees, 1998). Social entrepreneurs are being evaluated as "change agents" in terms of societal benefits that result from their actions. Through the entrepreneurial spirit, social entrepreneurs often act boldly regardless of resources available in order to create social value (Galvin & Iannotti, 2015). In other words, social entrepreneurship is the field in which entrepreneurs tailor their activities to be directly tied with the ultimate goal of creating social value by acting with little or no intention to gain personal profit (Abu-Saifan, 2012).

THE CONCEPT OF SOCIAL ENTREPRENEURSHIP

Joseph Banks first introduced the term social entrepreneur in 1972 in his work titled 'The Sociology of Social Movements', where he used the term to describe the need to use managerial skills to address not only social problems but also business challenges. Social entrepreneurship practices proliferated further in the 1980s with the establishment of organizations like The Ashoka Foundation, i.e., organization that supports social entrepreneurs around the world (Ebrashi, 2013). Ashoka identifies the world's leading social entrepreneurs through an intensive search process and selects them based on the criteria of creativity, originality, entrepreneurial quality, ethical fiber, and social impact. With these qualities, Ashoka Fellows are serving as role models to other change-makers around the world. Currently the Fellows network includes more than 3,300 of the world's leading social entrepreneurs, spread across 93 countries (The Ashoka Foundation, 2017).

Social entrepreneurs have applied innovative business models and integrated the resourcefulness of traditional entrepreneurship with the compelling drive to address social problems by improving adverse social conditions, especially in under-developed and emerging economies where scarcity of resources and corruption limit the attention given to serious social needs (Carroll, Burke, & Carroll, 2010; Zahra, Gedajlovic, Neubaum, & Shulman, 2009). According to Dees (1998), social entrepreneurs play the role of change agents in the social sector by:

adopting a mission to create and sustain social value, recognizing and pursuing new opportunities to serve that mission, acting boldly without being limited by the current resources and exhibiting accountability for the outcomes created.

Another definition of a social entrepreneur by Abu-Saifan (2012) could be summarized as:

a mission-driven individual who uses a set of entrepreneurial behaviors to deliver a social value to the less privileged through an entrepreneurially oriented entity that is financially independent, self-sufficient or sustainable.

Vision is viewed as a key competency of social entrepreneurs, which has been characterized as consisting of actionable ideas for effecting social change (Waddock & Steckler, 2016). Social entrepreneurs play an important role in promoting initiatives and building social capital to address economic and social challenges (Urban & Teise, 2015).

Social entrepreneurship emphasizes social change and innovation in solving social problems over profit seeking. Yet more, there is general agreement that social entrepreneurship involves pattern-breaking change or innovation (Light, 2008). Social entrepreneurship has also been viewed as

Table 1. Definitions and descriptions of social entrepreneurship and social entrepreneurs

Source	Definition
Leadbetter (1997)	Social entrepreneurs are entrepreneurial, innovative and transformatory individuals who are also leaders, storytellers, people managers, visionary opportunists and alliance builders. They recognize a social problem, organize, create and manage a venture to make social change. The use of entrepreneurial behavior for social ends rather than for profit objectives, or alternatively, that the profits generated from market activities are used for the benefit of a specific disadvantaged group.
Thake and Zadek (1997)	Social entrepreneurs are driven by a desire for social justice. They seek a direct link between their actions and an improvement in the quality of life for the people with whom they work and those that they seek to serve. They aim to produce solutions which are sustainable financially, organizationally, socially and environmentally.
Bornstein (1998)	A social entrepreneur is a path breaker with a powerful new idea who combines visionary and real-world problem-solving creativity, has a strong ethical fiber and is totally possessed by his/her vision for change
Dees (1998)	Social entrepreneurs play the role of change agents in the social sector by: 1) Adopting a mission to create and sustain social value (not just private value); 2) Recognizing and relentlessly pursuing new opportunities to serve that mission; 3) Engaging in a process of continuous innovation, adaptation and learning; 4) Exhibiting a heightened sense of accountability to the constituencies served for the outcomes created.
Reis (1999) - Kellogg Foundation	Social entrepreneurs create social value through innovation and leveraging financial resources for social, economic, and community development.
Thompson et al. (2000)	Social entrepreneurs are people who realize where there is an opportunity to satisfy some unmet need that the state welfare system will not/cannot meet and who gather together the necessary resources (generally people, often volunteers, money and premises) and use these to make a difference.
Fowler (2000)	Social entrepreneurship is the creation of viable socio-economic structures, relations, institutions, organizations and practices that yield and sustain social benefits.
Brinkerhoff (2001)	Individuals constantly looking for new ways to serve their constituencies and add value to existing services. A social entrepreneur is someone who takes reasonable risk on behalf of the people their organizations serves.
Mort et al. (2002)	A multidimensional construct involving the expression of entrepreneurially virtuous behavior to achieve the social mission. The ability to recognize social value creating opportunities and key decision-making characteristics of innovation, proactiveness and risk-taking.
Drayton (2002)	A major change agent, one whose core values center on identifying, addressing and solving societal problems.

continued on following page

Table 1. Continued

Source	Definition
Alford et al. (2004)	Creates innovative solutions to immediate social problems and mobilizes the ideas, capacities, resources and social arrangements required for social transformations.
Harding (2004)	Entrepreneurs motivated by social objectives to instigate some form of new activity or venture.
Shaw (2004)	The work of community, voluntary and public organizations as well as private firms working for social rather than only profit objectives.
Said School (2005)	A professional, innovative and sustainable approach to systematic change that resolves social market failures and grasps opportunities.
Fuqua School (2005)	The art of simultaneously pursuing both a financial and a social return on investment (the double bottom line).
Schwab Foundation (2005)	Applying practical, innovative and sustainable approaches to benefit society in general, with an emphasis on those who are marginalized and poor.
NYU Stern (2005)	The process of using entrepreneurial and business skills to create innovative approaches to social problems. These non-profit and for profit ventures pursue the double bottom line of social impact and financial self-sustainability or profitability.
MacMillan (2005) - Wharton Center	Process whereby the creation of new business enterprise leads to social wealth enhancement so that both society and the entrepreneur benefits.
Tan et al. (2005)	Making profits by innovation in the face of risk with the involvement of a segment of society and where all or part of the benefits accrue to that same segment of society.
Mair and Marti (2006a)	A process of creating value by combining resources in new ways. Intended primarily to explore and exploit opportunities to create social value by stimulating social change or meeting social needs.
Predo and McLean (2006)	Social entrepreneurship is exercised where some person/group aim(s) at creating social value, shows a capacity to recognize and take advantage of opportunities, employ innovation, accept an above average degree of risk and are unusually resourceful in pursuing their social venture.
Martin and Osberg (2007)	Social entrepreneurship is the: 1) identification a stable yet unjust equilibrium which the excludes, marginalizes or causes suffering to a group which lacks the means to transform the equilibrium; 2) identification of an opportunity and developing a new social value proposition to challenge the equilibrium and; 3) forging a new, stable equilibrium to alleviate the suffering of the targeted group through imitation and creation of a stable ecosystem around the new equilibrium to ensure a better future for the group and society.
Chell (2007)	Social entrepreneurship is a model that involves pro-social motives, which emphasizes social outcomes at the expense of a surplus. To survive this enterprise requires grant-aid. The alternative model is one where outcomes involve social benefits on the one hand, and wealth generation that is used to invest in the business and help to assure its sustainability.
Mair and Schoen (2007)	Social entrepreneurship is an initiative that addresses social needs and/or catalyzes social transformation. Economic value creation is a necessary but not sufficient condition.
Tracey and Philips (2007)	Social entrepreneurs establish their organizations for a social purpose. Social entrepreneurship involves building organizations that have the capacity to be both commercially viable and socially constructive.
Zahra et al. (2008)	Social entrepreneurship encompasses the activities and processes undertaken to discover, define and exploit opportunities in order to enhance social wealth by creating new ventures or managing existing organizations in an innovative manner.
Ashoka Foundation (2012)	Social entrepreneurs are individuals with innovative solutions to society's most pressing social problems. They are both visionaries and ultimate realists concerned with the practical implementation of their vision above all else.
Santos (2012)	Social entrepreneurship is the pursuit of sustainable solutions to neglected problems with positive externalities. It is also an innovative process having predominant focus on value creation as opposed to value capture.
El Ebrashi (2013)	Social entrepreneurship focuses on achieving a social mission, which is clear in the context and outcomes of the social component. NGOs, private businesses or cooperatives could be social enterprises. To measure the social impact of the organization is important.
Lumpkin et al. (2013)	Social entrepreneurship is a social value creation process in which resources are combined in new ways to meet social needs, stimulate social change or create new organizations regardless of the presence or absence of profit motive.
Wilson and Post (2013)	Social entrepreneurship is involved with entrepreneurial organizations which join the social purpose traditionally associated with the non-profit sector, and the economic rationality and market-based approaches traditionally associated with for-profit firms.
Chahine (2016)	Social entrepreneurship is the act of pioneering new methods, processes, products and services that address social and environmental challenges through the creation of new organizations or initiatives.

innovative, social value creating activity that can occur within the non-profit, business or government sectors (Austin, Stevenson, & Wei-Skillern, 2006).

The process associated with social entrepreneurship could be described as being "embedded" in a matrix of institutions that provides the opportunity for such a process while the individual is effected by a configuration of motivations, cognitions and capital that comprise the entrepreneurial agency required to take part in the process (Grimes, McMullen, Vogus, & Miller, 2013).

Table 1 presents some definitions and descriptions of social entrepreneurship or social entrepreneurs in the literature. When examining the definitions, it is apparent that the main driver of social entrepreneurship is the social problem being addressed and the ultimate goal of a social entrepreneur is to fulfill his/her social mission through designing revenue-generating strategies to directly serve the mission to deliver social value (Goyal, & Sergi, 2015; Abu-Saifan, 2012; Zahra, Gedajlovic, Neubaum, & Shulman, 2009).

As is seen from the Table 1, most of the definitions above embrace both not-for-profit and for-profit ventures. There is significant diversity among organizational types. There are at least four main categories including: 1) traditional charities and NGOs; 2) not-for-profit social entrepreneurships; 3) for-profit social entrepreneurships and 4) traditional businesses (Choi & Gray, 2010). However, it could be claimed that organizations might not neatly fit into one category or another (Gray, 2016). Regardless of the country and governance mechanisms, the definition of social entrepreneurship includes four elements: addressing a social need, focusing on the creation of social value, emphasizing social impact and acknowledging that the means to attain the social mission can include purely philanthropic, hybrid, or market-oriented mechanisms (Beugre, 2017).

The literature highlights social orientation and socio-economic orientation as two important typologies to better understand social entrepreneurship conceptualization. Social orientation relates social entrepreneurship to the social change perspective where the focus is on designing and implementing the innovation driven value creation process with the social mission. According to this typology, the organizational resources, structure, processes and metrics are designed and implemented on the basis of the social impact in terms of beneficiaries and outreach. Socio-economic orientation relates to focus on designing and implementing the innovative self-sustainable business models for fulfillment of the social needs. According to this typology, the organizational resources, structure, processes and metrics are designed and implemented to follow an innovative (market-based) approach towards value creation and delivery at the bottom of the pyramid (Goyal, Sergi, & Jaiswal, 2015).

THEORETICAL FRAMEWORK AND RELATED TERMS

In the current business environment, businesses are expected to be profitable while promoting social responsibility and satisfying their stakeholders. Social entrepreneurship has been accepted as a business model exhibiting a continuum of objectives ranging from a purely social mission through combinations of social and profit motives (Burga & Rezania, 2016).

As is well known, entrepreneurs are one of the main actors in the economy that transform natural capital into man-made capital (Malovics, Nagypal, & Kraus, 2008). According to Groot and Dankbaar (2014), every entrepreneurial action results in some measure of intended/unintended social innovation, regardless of whether the entrepreneurs in question are considered social or not (though every entrepreneur has social impacts – sometimes negative). Social innovation is considered an important element to meet the challenges (including environmental degradation, climate change, high levels of immigration, poverty and social exclusion, terrorist attacks, and etc.) that societies are facing today.

Social Entrepreneurship in the Spectrum of Entrepreneurship

The concept of entrepreneurship has been around for more than 200 years. One of the early French writers on entrepreneurship was Jean-Baptiste Say, who noted that:

the entrepreneur shifts economic resources out of an area of lower productivity and into an area of higher productivity and greater yield (Say, 1971).

Say's definition implies that the entrepreneurs create value. The study of entrepreneurship in the contemporary sense started with Schumpeter's definition by continuing on the path set by Say (Beugre, 2017). He defined entrepreneurs as:

innovators, who use a process of shattering the status quo of the existing products and services to set up new products, new services (Schumpeter, 1965).

Entrepreneurship involves three main elements such as opportunities, enterprising individuals and resourcefulness (Iyigun, 2015). Entrepreneurial opportunities could be defined as *the situations in which new goods, services, raw materials and organizing methods can be introduced and sold at greater than their production cost* and can be found in a person's network and as a result, a network rich in entrepreneurial opportunities surrounds a person motivated to be an entrepreneur (Beugre, 2017; Dorin & Alexandru, 2014).

Traditional entrepreneurship is based on the discovery of opportunities, innovation and the creation of new businesses and it is associated with the pursuit of commercial objectives and perhaps in conflict with ethical behavior. In contrast, social entrepreneurship is focused on *the innovative use of resources to explore and exploit opportunities that meet a social need in a sustainable manner* that presents a more ethical entrepreneurial activity with an explicit social change agenda (Haugh & Talwar, 2016). At this point sustainable development could be explained as the growth of society in a direction with an increasing or at least ongoing supply of resources, including financial, physical, environmental and human resources (Chahine, 2016). The outcomes of social entrepreneurship are different from traditional entrepreneurship and measurement of those outcomes is also different. Social entrepreneurs target market failures, related to externalities, public goods and distributional equity whereas traditional entrepreneurs seek for discovering a fit between certain needs and resources (Ebrashi, 2013). Of course, there are instances when these two intersect and the delineation is not so clear.

A social business requires a strong adherence to the mission to have a social impact (Yunus, 2011). That's why social entrepreneurship involves the application of business practices in the pursuit of a social or environmental mission by bringing the mindset, principles, strategies, tools and techniques of entrepreneurship to the social sector (Kickul & Lyons, 2016). Social entrepreneurship incorporates goals of revenue generation, social awareness and environmental considerations through a deliberate decision of integrating social consciousness into the business model (Burga & Rezania, 2016; Dees, 1998). In other words, social entrepreneurship carries the concept of enterprise that utilizes a business structure to achieve a goal with adding a social component (Caslin III., Sachet, & Shevinsky, 2016).

Entrepreneurship and social entrepreneurship have many similarities. However social entrepreneurship's emphasis on social mission and social needs alongside a market-based approach separates it in terms of maximizing shareholder value. As a result of these distinctions, the social entrepreneurship literature points to the theoretical importance of founder motivations, especially compassion that creates a distinct motivated reasoning process which complements traditional theories of entrepreneurship (Grimes, McMullen, Vogus, & Miller, 2013). Social entrepreneurship embodies the enterprising spirit of the private sector and uses the power of economic markets to generate and deliver solutions to problems. Social entrepreneurship is often referred to as value-based, involving empathy, judgement and morality (Kickul & Lyons, 2016). Moreover social entrepreneurship refers to ventures targeting underserved populations, decreasing the gap between those who have access to social services and those who do not (Chahine, 2016).

Although traditional and social entrepreneurs look for opportunities in new markets and they both need to return capital to investors, one of the most important differences between them could be explained by the 'reason for existence'. An entrepreneur seeks to deliver a bottom-line profit for serving a market in a better or more efficient manner -financial profit-, whereas a social entrepreneur has a triple bottom line to consider including people, planet and profit -social impact- (Haber, 2016; Chahine, 2016).

Undoubtedly, social entrepreneurship involves new social value creation (Austin, Stevenson, & Wei-Skillern, 2006). Traditional value creation and social value creation are different from each other in terms of primary goals. In traditional entrepreneurship, maximizing profitability by taking advantage of an opportunity gap in the market is the primary goal; whereas in social entrepreneurship value creation is generated from the organization's mission to solve societal issues (Light, 2008). Bill Drayton, Founder of Ashoka explains: *Social entrepreneurs are not content just to give a fish or teach how to fish. They will not rest until they have revolutionized the fishing industry.* In other words, a systematic change yielding long-term benefits is the focus of social entrepreneurs and a social or environmental mission lies at the core of social entrepreneurship.

Consideration of ethical values and equity in traditional entrepreneurial practices, attention to the social consequences of the entrepreneurial activity, the need for global evaluations of the equitable distribution of economic and social outcomes and the consideration of institutional implications for achieving global outcomes from traditional entrepreneurship could be referred as "global sustainable well-being" which could be found at the core of social entrepreneurship (Zahra, Newey, & Li, 2014).

Figure 1. Social entrepreneurship's spectrum

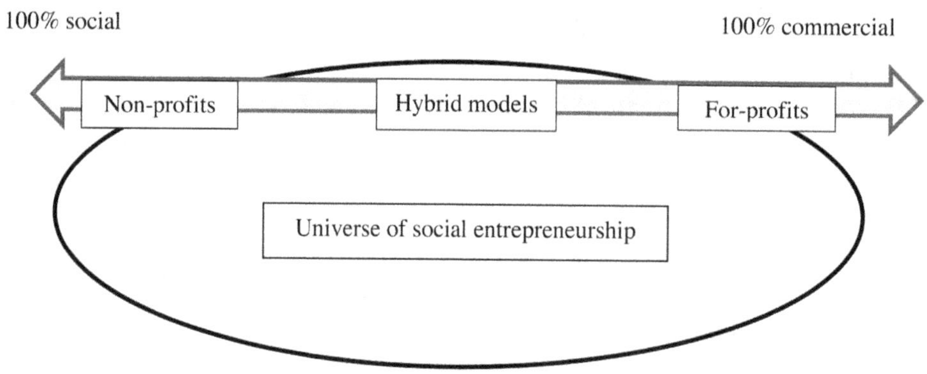

Figure 1 shows the spectrum of social entrepreneurship. As is seen from the figure, social entrepreneurship occupies the space between old-school commerce and old-school charity. In many societies around the world, there is a huge gap between social purpose organizations and businesses, and social entrepreneurship aims to fill that gap (Chahine, 2016).

As is seen from the figure, this new form of hybrid models merges the social purpose traditionally associated with non-profits with the economic purpose and market-based methods traditionally associated with for-profits. Hybrid models differ from traditional entrepreneurial ventures in terms of priorities, a focus on employees and customers, and a holistic approach to value creation (Wilson & Post, 2013).

One of the crucial factors in traditional and social entrepreneurship is networking. A social entrepreneur cannot be successful without bringing people and organizations together to focus on a problem, supplying resources from a variety of places to implement solutions, communicating the outcomes effectively (Kickul & Lyons, 2016). Global organizations are also important in the evolving web of relations and exchanges across borders, affecting traditional international entrepreneurship and *international social ventures" that could be defined as the social ventures, which have international missions* (Zahra, Newey, & Li, 2014). In other words, international social ventures is a new type of international ventures with a distinct mission to create solutions to societal challenges across the globe (Fardig & Hakansson, 2014).

Figure 2 shows the intersection of traditional international entrepreneurship and social entrepreneurship. As is seen from the figure, international social ventures seek for social concerns on a global scale. International social ventures could be counted as international in scope, and entrepreneurial in their orientation to financial, social and environmental opportunities. And they have a greater balance of earned versus contributed income that differentiates them from non-profits. International social ventures are different from traditional entrepreneurial ventures in pursuing financial profitability to make a sustainable social impact, which shows the emphasis on social impact whereas entrepreneurial ventures don't invest in social impact as a core business (Zahra, Newey, & Li, 2014).

Social innovation could be referred to as *innovative activities and services that are motivated by the goal of meeting a social need* that lead to system-level social change. Social innovation could be found

Figure 2. Intersection of international entrepreneurship and social entrepreneurship

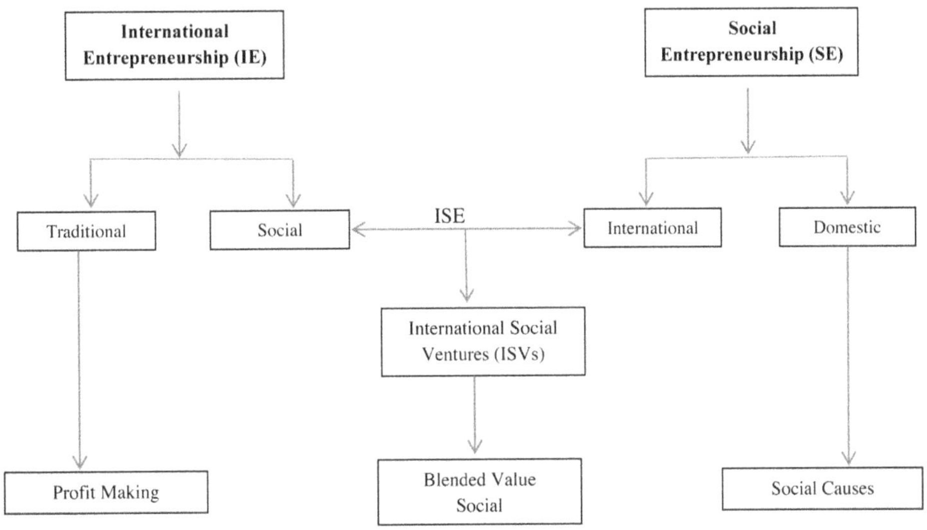

in social entrepreneurship, which tends to be a disruptive type of innovation. Social entrepreneurship is perceived as a radical social innovation at a system level brought about by social innovators who are specifically interested in solving social issues (Munshi, 2010).

Social Entrepreneurship at the Bottom of the Pyramid

The developing and under-developed economies account for more than 80% of the global population. The majority of the population living across these economies could be described as the "uncertain, informal, rural and heterogeneous segment" lying at the bottom of the socio-economic pyramid. This socio-economic segment is recognized as "base of pyramid" (BoP) and represents 4 billion people (60% of the global population) who are poor, live and transact in an informal market ecosystem for the fulfillment of the basic social needs. These people earn less than 8 dollars per person per day. This BoP segment faces persistent poverty and a huge demand-supply gap regarding the formal market ecosystem for the fulfillment of its primary needs (Goyal & Sergi, 2015). It could be argued that the BoP segment offers an opportunity for global organizations to design and implement inclusive business models for solving the problems like energy, healthcare, education, water, sanitation, information, finance, housing and transportation (Goyal & Sergi, 2015).

In recent years, social media has enabled a level of interconnectivity, which has made the world smaller. The Great Convergence changed people's sense of geography, community and responsibility. Problems seemed no longer 'over there' in some far away land and it made it easy for groups of like-minded people to band together with a sense of purpose and action. The Great Convergence was able to bring the current situation of the troubled world and thus, it opened the door to the era of social entrepreneurship which mostly relies on technology and social media to thrive. In other words, the Great Convergence makes it possible to envision an entire reboot of capitalism in a way that lifts people up, solves problems and promotes lasting change, which is called Capitalism 2.0, and its engine is social entrepreneurship (Haber, 2016). Social entrepreneurship considers the BoP segment as a customer and integrates social and economic value creation with the philosophy of "Serve and Survive at the BoP" (Goyal & Sergi, 2015).

With the end of the Cold War, the former Soviet Union and its allies, as well as China, India and Latin America opened their closed markets to foreign investment and this transformation has offered new growth opportunities for businesses. Friedman (1962) -one of the most well-known Neo-classical economists- defined the role of business as:

There is one and only one social responsibility of business to use its resources and engage in activities to increase its profits so long as it stays within the rules of the game, which is to say, engages in open and free competition, without deception or fraud.

As understood from Friedman's definition, other stakeholders such as the environment, employees, customers and the communities deserve no direct or primary consideration. Businesses have been using outsourcing as a choice to externalize their social and ecologic damages caused by production because of the tremendous increase in productivity and profitability (Schüz, 2012). The poverty challenge affecting the BoP segment shows the complexity of the BoP market despite the extensive presence and philanthropic efforts of the traditional institutions like NGOs, government and corporate social responsibility (CSR) initiatives of the commercial enterprises. At this point, a new economic model called "Doughnut", as

Figure 3. The Doughnut Model of social and planetary boundaries

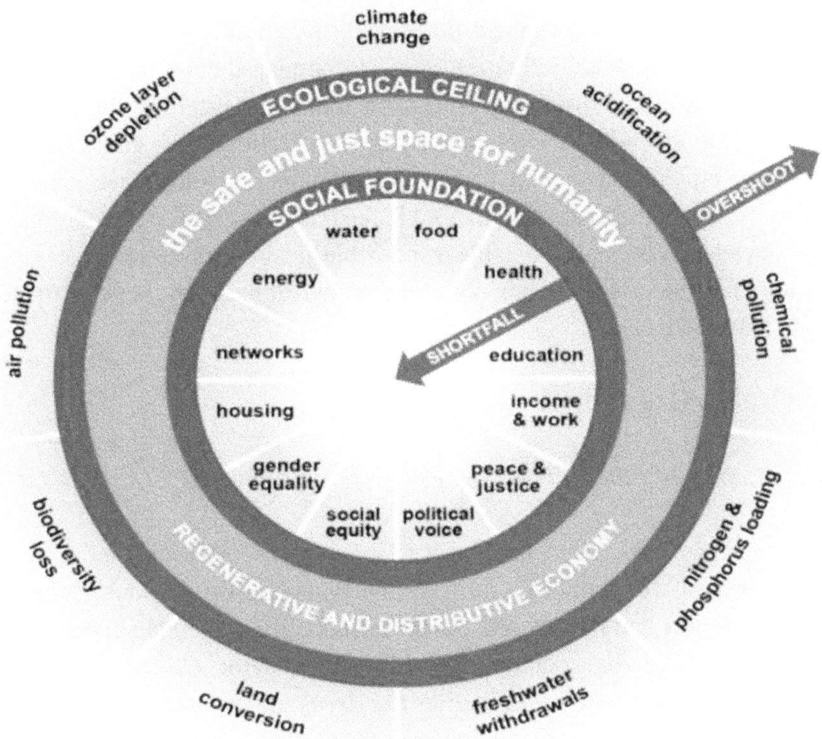

displayed in Figure 3, could be the panacea for ending inequality. This Doughnut model could be the compass that we need for creating a safe 21st century (Raworth, 2017b).

Figure 3 shows the Doughnut of social and planetary boundaries, which is a serious approach to framing the challenge of meeting the needs of all within the means of the planet. It acts as a compass for human progress. As is seen in the figure, the hole at the Doughnut's center shows the proportion of people worldwide falling short on life's essentials including food, water, healthcare and political freedom of expression – and a big part of humanity's challenge is to get everyone out of that hole. At the same time, however, we cannot afford to be overshooting the Doughnut's outer crust if we are to safeguard the Earth's life-giving systems like a stable climate, healthy oceans and a protective ozone layer, on which all our wellbeing fundamentally depends (Raworth, 2017b). The environmental ceiling consists of nine planetary boundaries, beyond which lie unacceptable environmental degradation and potential tipping points in Earth systems. The twelve dimensions of the social foundation are derived from internationally agreed minimum social standards, as identified by the world's governments in the Sustainable Development Goals in 2015. Between social and planetary boundaries lies an environmentally safe and socially just space in which humanity can thrive (Raworth, 2017a).

According to Prahalad and Hart (2002), the real source of market opportunities is not the wealthy few in the developing world, or the emerging middle-income consumers. It is the billions of poor who are joining the market economy for the first time. At this point, it could be claimed that all the businesses should look at globalization through a new lens of Capitalism 2.0 or inclusive capitalism (Haber, 2016; Prahalad & Hart, 2002).

Capitalism 2.0 could be defined as the replacement of capitalism by an alternative business model which ensures the more equitable distribution of wealth among the world's population while eliminating the practices that has led to virtual collapse of the banking system in the global recession (Baker, 2013). Inclusive capitalism could be explained by the broad movement gaining momentum in market economies for a more ethical and socially inclusive capitalism that allows everyone's talents to flourish for shared prosperity. By making capitalism more inclusive, consumers' expectations for more ethically sourced and produced goods, more socially responsible businesses and politicians promoting social equality and mitigating the effects of business on the environment could be realized (Lagarde, 2014; Dacin, Dacin, & Tracey, 2011).

Focusing on Value Creation

We never know the worth of water till the well is dry. Thomas Fuller

Sustainability could be defined as an "ideal" that business and society in general should strive for while creating value in terms of economic, social and environmental dimensions including societal values of justice, integrity, respect and mutual prosperity. Sustainability agenda addresses the implications of ecological dependency and global social impacts of local behaviors (Moon, 2007).

Sustainable development could be defined as *the development that meets the needs of the present without compromising the ability of future generations to meet their own needs.* Sustainable development could be explained as:

a process of change in which the exploitation of resources, the direction of investments, the orientation of technological development, and institutional change are made consistent with future as well as present needs (Bruntland, 1987).

In other words, the view is that it is impossible for a business to achieve its sustainable survival without creating value to its employees, shareholders, customers, society and all of its stakeholders because of the new dimensions of competition such as environmental and societal success. With this perspective, a business could not be successful by focusing only its short-term based economic performance, neglecting environmental and societal performance (Iyigun, 2014). Like biological systems, social systems like businesses can only survive in the long run, when they cooperate with other systems such as stakeholders to find their ecologic niche. A business needs physical resources including financial capital, raw materials and buildings. A business also needs social resources such as suppliers, employees and customers. Ultimately a business needs mental resources including ideas, inventions and strategies. All of these resources are to provide products and services all of which represent their ecologic niche by pursuing "enlightened self-interest" to take on responsibility that creates stakeholders' trust, assuring low-transaction costs and being open to cooperate long-term. A business acts responsibly, when it is able to take responsibility for the consequences of its actions such as economically (being profitable to shareholders (referred as self-preservation)), socially (getting along well with all stakeholders (referred

Figure 4. The Triple Corporate Responsibility

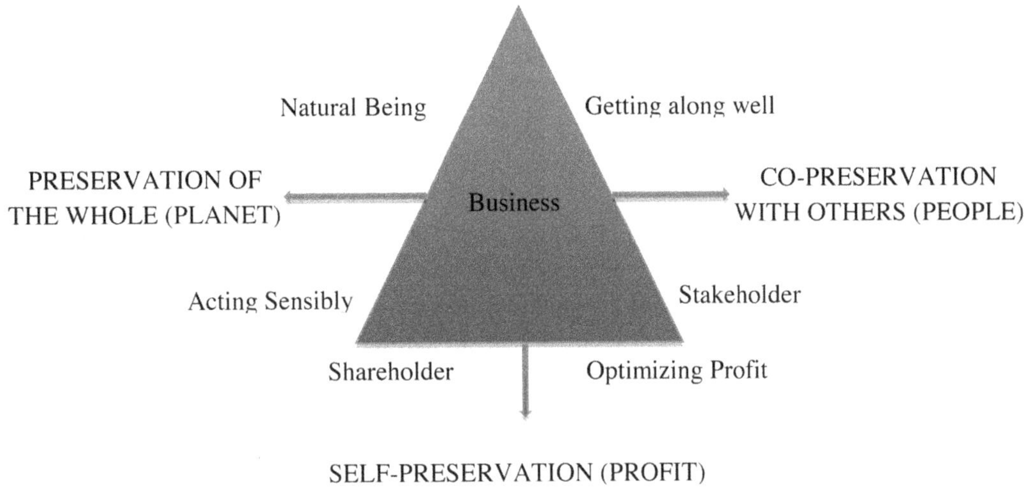

as co-preservation)) and ecologically (acting sensibly and respectfully towards nature or being (referred as preservation of the whole)) (Schüz, 2012).

Figure 4 shows the CSR's connection to sustainability. CSR represents the social (co-preservation) dimension of corporate responsibility. The model suggests that ecologic dimension (preservation of the whole planet) should be treated differently from the social dimension, which asks for ethical reflection. As is seen from the figure, the model tackles the root causes in order to improve behavior (Schüz, 2012).

Social entrepreneurship could be identified as a form of social service, which is a path toward positive social change to improve the conditions, livelihoods and standard of living of populations and ecosystems. Positive social change comes through multiple pathways that include advocacy, lobbying, awareness campaigns, policy papers, research, teaching, legislative changes, etc. Social entrepreneurship is one of these pathways, which is characterized by the application of business methods (Chahine, 2016). Social entrepreneurship can act as a "learning laboratory" for observing how social value can be generated through social innovations that achieve the intended impact and for learning how to scale them (Dees, 2011).

Social entrepreneurship extends the field of traditional entrepreneurship in defining well-being as a multidimensional concent that includes, financial, social and environmental wealth creation. Another significant related concept in social entrepreneurship could be referred as "blended value". Blended value suggests that *organizations pursue blends of financial, social and environmental values, but the difference lies in how much value is created and destroyed across the types in different business models*. Focusing on blended value, with its holistic blending of different value types, could create an opportunity for international entrepreneurship research to make substantial intellectual as well as societal contributions specifically bringing greater research focus to the creation and distribution of blends of value (Zahra, Newey, & Li, 2014).

In other words, blended value could be used as a framework for advancing a vision of value creation that is based upon a unified, holistic understanding of value that is integrated. The focus of blended value seeks how to maximize the total value creation potential and performance of all kind of organizations (nonprofit, for-profit, hybrid) and how best to maximize the total performance of capital (Emerson,

2003). The idea of merging social and economic value creation within the same organizational structure goes beyond trade-offs or balancing acts; rather it involves innovative and entrepreneurial approaches.

CONCLUSION

The growth of critical social issues worldwide has revealed that existing businesses, governments and NGOs will not be enough to solve these problems. One of the best alternatives for addressing these problems is likely to be a new form of entrepreneurial organization where social value is not merely a byproduct of entrepreneurial activity but an intended primary outcome. As argued by Yunus (2011), the world needs another kind of business to make the structure of capitalism complete. We refer such social entrepreneurial organizations as hybrid ventures, which embody a different approach to addressing social issues (Wilson & Post, 2013).

In the 21st century, social entrepreneurship still faces what we describe as multi-dimensional challenges especially during the inception and growth phases of organizations with this focus. These multi-dimensional challenges or tensions that they have to balance include BoP market imperfections; socio-economic dilemma (which relates to the ethical dilemma in the balance between social mission and economic returns); informal market setup (which involves the dominance of the informal market ecosystem especially at the BoP); resource mobilization (which is linked to the limited availability of capital and skilled labor); characteristics of offerings (such as the need for identification, design and delivery of the offerings); assessment (which is related to making a right choice of impact assessment framework for the socio-economic performance); organizational misconfiguration (which is associated with making the right choice of organizational structure and processes including stakeholders); and lastly scalability dilemma (which is the need for maintaining the social relevance while increasing the growth and impact) (Goyal & Sergi, 2015).

As Emerson (2003) suggests, we need new metrics, new conceptions of the fundamental value proposition that are not simply a "quid pro quo" trade-off between two competing goals perceived to be locked in a zero-sum battle. Instead, we should advance the framework of blended value proposition that integrates the greatest maximization of social, environmental and economic value within a single business, investment opportunity and community. To be able to build a good commercial infrastructure for BoP, which is a resource and management intensive challenge, we should re-work how to create buying power, to reshape aspirations, to improve accessibility and to solve local problems. As Prahalad & Hart (2002) argue, innovation in one leverages innovation in others. Not only businesses but also NGOs, local and state governments, international actors and communities should work together. Undoubtedly, most of the businesses especially those operating internationally could be able to transfer knowledge from one market to another with their global resources.

The intersection of social entrepreneurship and traditional entrepreneurship creates an important opportunity to revisit our conceptions of the entrepreneurship field. This intersection highlights the fruitful dialogue that can occur between the social and financial goals of entrepreneurship (Zahra, Newey, & Li, 2014). It could be claimed that the social role of entrepreneurship (like charitable contributions, financial success and business creation) should be much larger and more impactful to capture the contributions to social, environmental and economic wealth creation with a focus on blended value creation and triple corporate responsibility. These contributions could make entrepreneurs catalysts and social change agents for a better world. Moreover, it should be noted that social entrepreneurs would try new business methods and approaches to solve the world's social problems in an efficient and sustainable manner.

This chapter conducts a review of the existent scholarly literature and it demonstrates the difficulties posed in trying to engage in social entrepreneurship for a major social change. The market economy focuses on economic returns as a basis for success, whereas social entrepreneurship highlights the importance of targeting the BoP markets congruent with the literature. This shows the need for a shift from an economic growth focus towards socio-economic outcomes as the basis for designing the business models (Goyal & Sergi, 2015). This chapter extends the current literature by providing an insight about social entrepreneurship in the spectrum of entrepreneurship through value creation with the lens of blended value and triple corporate responsibility and by suggesting implications for social entrepreneurs and scholars.

ACKNOWLEDGMENT

I gratefully acknowledge Professor David Choi, Ph.D. for his invaluable support and helpful feedback on this chapter. I also gratefully acknowledge Professor Julie Feldman-Abe, Ph.D. and Professor Meric Keskinel, Ph.D. for their guidance, constructive insights and feedback on this chapter. This chapter was written while on sabbatical during 2017-fall term at the College of Business Administration, Loyola Marymount University in Los Angeles.

REFERENCES

Abu-Saifan, S. (2012, February). Social Entrepreneurship: Definition and Boundaries. *Technology Innovation Management Review*, 22-27.

Austin, J., Stevenson, H., & Wei-Skillern, J. (2006). Social and Commercial Entrepreneurship: Same, Different, or Both? *Entrepreneurship Theory and Practice*, *30*(1), 1–22. doi:10.1111/j.1540-6520.2006.00107.x

Baker, M. J. (2013). Capitalism 2.0 and Social Business. *Social Business: An Interdisciplinary Journal*, *3*(4), 297–310. doi:10.1362/204440813X13875569153984

Barki, E., Comini, G., Cunliffe, A., Hart, S., & Rai, S. (2015). Social Entrepreneurship and Social Business: Retrospective and Prospective Research. *RAE-Revista de Administração de Empresas*, *55*(4), 380–384. doi:10.1590/S0034-759020150402

Beugre, C. (2017). *Social Entrepreneurship: Managing the Creation of Social Value*. New York: Routledge.

Bruntland Commission. (1987). *Our Common Future-Towards Sustainable Development*. World Commission on Economic Developmet (WCED). Retrieved from http://www.un-documents.net/our-common-future.pdf

Burga, R., & Rezania, D. (2016). Stakeholder Theory in Social Entrepreneurship: A Descriptive Case Study. *Journal of Global Entrepreneurship*, *6*(4), 1–15.

Carroll, N., Burke, M., & Carroll, M. (2010). A Case of Social Entrepreneurship: Tackling Homelessness. *Journal of Business Case Studies*, *6*(5), 83–95.

Caslin, M. J., III, Sachet, M., & Shevinsky, E. (2016). An Overview of Structural Options and Issues. In T. S. Lyons (Ed.), Social Entrepreneurship: How Businesses can transform Society? Santa Barbara, CA: Praeger.

Chahine, T. (2016). *Introduction to Social Entrepreneurship*. Boca Raton, FL: CRC Press - Taylor & Francis Group. doi:10.1201/b19475

Choi, D. Y., & Gray, E. R. (2010). *Values-Centered Entrepreneurs and Their Companies: How a New Brand of Entrepreneurs Build Profitably Companies and Make a Positive Contribution to Society*. New York: Routledge.

Dacin, M. T., Dacin, P. A., & Tracey, P. (2011). Social entrepreneurship: A critique and future directions. *Organization Science*, *22*(5), 1203–1213. doi:10.1287/orsc.1100.0620

Day, S. W., & Jean-Denis, H. (2016). Resource Based View of Social Entrepreneurship: Putting the Pieces Together. *Journal of Strategic Innovation and Sustainability*, *11*(2), 59–69.

De Paula, G. O., & Cavalcanti, R. N. (2000). Ethics: Essence for Sustainability. *Journal of Cleaner Production*, *8*, 119–117.

Dees, J. G. (1998). *The Meaning of Social Entrepreneurship*. Palo Alto, CA: Stanford University.

Dees, J. G. (2011). Social Ventures as Learning Laboratories. *Tennessee's Business*, *20*(1), 3–5.

Dorin, C. & Alexandru, G. S. (2014). Dynamics of the Entrepreneurship Concept. Literature Review. *Annals of the University of Oradea,* 445-446.

Ebrashi, R. E. (2013). Social Entrepreneurship Theory and Sustainable Social Impact. *Social Responsibility Journal*, *9*(2), 188–209. doi:10.1108/SRJ-07-2011-0013

Emerson, J. (2003). The Blended Value Proposition: Integrating Social and Financial Returns. *California Management Review*, *45*(4), 35–51. doi:10.2307/41166187

Fardig, K., & Hakansson, M. (2014). *The Internalization of Social Enterprises: Mapping patterns in the Internationalization Process of Social Entrepreneurs*. Uppsala University Department of Business Studies Master Thesis Spring Semester 2014.

Friedman, M. (1962). *Capitalism and Freedom*. Chicago: University of Chicago Press.

Galvin, M. D., & Iannotti, L. (2015). Social Enterprise and Development: The KickStart Model. *Voluntas*, *26*(2), 421–441. doi:10.100711266-013-9424-z

Goyal, S., & Sergi, B. S. (2015). Social Entrepreneurship and Sustainability – Understanding the Context and Key Characteristics. *Journal of Security and Sustainability Issues*, *4*(3), 269–278. doi:10.9770/jssi.2015.4.3(7)

Goyal, S., Sergi, B. S., & Jaiswal, M. P. (2015). Understanding the Challenges and Strategic Actions of Social Entrepreneurship at the Base of the Pyramid. *Management Decision*, *54*(2), 418–440. doi:10.1108/MD-11-2014-0662

Gray, E. R. (2016). For-Profit Social Entrepreneurship. In T. S. Lyons (Ed.), Social Entrepreneurship: How Businesses can transform Society? Santa Barbara, CA: Praeger.

Grimes, M. G., McMullen, J. S., Vogus, T. J., & Miller, T. J. (2013). Studying the Origins of Social Entrepreneurship: Compassion and the Role of Embedded Agency. *Academy of Management Review*, *38*(3), 460–463. doi:10.5465/amr.2012.0429

Groot, A., & Dankbaar, B. (2014). Does Social Innovation Require Social Entrepreneurship? *Technology Innovation Management Review*, *4*(12), 17–26.

Haber, J. (2016). *The Business of Good: Social Entrepreneurship and the New Bottom-Line*. US: Entrepreneur Press.

Iyigun, N. O. (2014). Corporate Social Responsibility and Ethics in Management in light of Sustainable Development. In U. Akkucuk (Ed.), Handbook of Research on Developing Sustainable Value in Economics, Finance and Marketing. Hershey, PA: IGI Global.

Iyigun, N. O. (2015). What could Entrepreneurship do for Sustainable Development? A Corporate Social Responsibility-Based Approach. *Procedia: Social and Behavioral Sciences*, *195*, 1226–1231. doi:10.1016/j.sbspro.2015.06.253

Iyigun, O., & Keskin, M. (2016). Is Franchising an Efficient Tool for Entrepreneurship in the Knowledge Economy? In M. H. Bilgin & H. Danis (Eds.), *Entrepreneurship, Business and Economics:* Vol. 1. *Proceedings of the 15th Eurasia Business and Economics Society Conference* (pp. 33-43). Springer International Publishing. 10.1007/978-3-319-27570-3_4

Iyigun, O., & Yalcintas, M. (2017). Social Entrepreneurship as a Tool for Creating Competitive Advantage: A Theoretical Approach. *Turkish Journal of Entrepreneurship*, *1*(1), 91–101.

Kickul, J., & Lyons, T. S. (2016). *Understanding Social Entrepreneurship: The Relentless Pursuit of Mission in an Ever Changing World (2nd ed.)*. New York: Routledge.

Light, P. C. (2008). *The Search for Social Entrepreneurship*. Washington, DC: Brookings Institution.

Makhlouf, H. H. (2011). Social Entrepreneurship: Generating Solutions to Global Challenges. *International Journal of Management and Information Systems*, *15*(1), 1–8.

Malovics, G., Nagypal, N., & Kraus, S. (2008). The Role of Corporate Social Responsibility in Strong Sustainability. *Journal of Socio-Economics*, *37*(3), 907–918. doi:10.1016/j.socec.2006.12.061

Moon, J. (2007). The Contribution of Corporate Social Responsibility to Sustainable Development. *Sustainable Development*, *15*(5), 296–306. doi:10.1002d.346

Munshi, N. V. (2010). Value Creation, Social Innovation, and Entrepreneurship in Global Economies. *Journal of Asia-Pacific Business*, *11*(3), 160–165. doi:10.1080/10599231.2010.500569

Prahalad, C. K., & Hart, S. (2002). The Fortune at the Bottom of the Pyramid. *Strategy and Competition, 26*(1), 1–14.

Raworth, K. (2017a). *What on Earth is the Doughnut?* Retrieved from https://www.kateraworth.com/doughnut/

Raworth, K. (2017b). *Meet the Doughnut: The New Economic Model that could Help End Ineqaulity.* World Economic Forum. Retrieved from https://www.weforum.org/agenda/2017/04/the-new-economic-model-that-could-end-inequality-doughnut?utm_content=bufferd48ac&utm_medium=social&utm_source=facebook.com&utm_campaign=buffer

Santos, F. M. (2012). A Positive Theory of Social Entrepreneurship. *Journal of Business Ethics, 111*(3), 335–351. doi:10.100710551-012-1413-4

Say, J. B. (1971). *A Treatise of Political Economy or the Production, Distribution and Consumption of Wealth* (4th ed.). New York: Augustus M. Kelley.

Schumpeter, J. A. (1965). Economic Theory and Entrepreneurial History. In H. G. Aitken (Ed.), Explorations in Enterprise. Cambridge, MA: Harvard University Press. doi:10.4159/harvard.9780674594470.c5

Schüz, M. (2012). Sustainable Corporate Responsibility – The Foundation of Successful Business in the New Millenium. *Central European Business Review, 1*(2), 7–15. doi:10.18267/j.cebr.12

Singh, A. (2016). *The Process of Social Value Creation: A Multiple-Case Study on Social Entrepreneurship in India.* Springer. doi:10.1007/978-81-322-2827-1

The Ashoka Foundation. (n.d.). Retrieved from https://www.ashoka.org/en/focus/social-entrepreneurship

United Nations, Department of Economic and Social Affairs, Population Division. (2017). *World Population Prospects: The 2017 Revision.* Author.

Urban, B., & Teise, H. (2015). Antecedents to Social Entrepreneurship Intentions: An Empirical Study in South Africa. *Management Dynamics, 24*(2), 36–52.

Waddock, S., & Steckler, E. (2016). Visionaries and Wayfinders: Deliberate and Emergent Pathways to Vision in Social Entrepreneurship. *Journal of Business Ethics, 133*(4), 719–734. doi:10.100710551-014-2451-x

Wilson, F., & Post, J. E. (2013). Business Models for People, Planet (&Profits): Exploring the Phenomena of Social Business, A Market-Based Approach to Social Value Creation. *Small Business Economics, 40*(3), 715–737. doi:10.100711187-011-9401-0

Yunus, M. (2011). *Building Social Business: The New Kind of Capitalism that Serves Humanity's Most Pressing Needs.* New York: Public Affairs.

Zahra, S. A., Gedajlovic, E., Neubaum, D. O., & Shulman, J. M. (2009). A Typology of Social Entrepreneurs: Motives, Search Processes and Ethical Challenges. *Journal of Business Venturing, 24*(5), 519–532. doi:10.1016/j.jbusvent.2008.04.007

Zahra, S. A., Newey, L. R., & Li, Y. (2014). On the Frontiers: The Implications of Social Entrepreneurship for International Entrepreneurship. *Entrepreneurship Theory and Practice*, *38*(1), 137–158. doi:10.1111/etap.12061

ADDITIONAL READING

Bewayo, E. D., & Portes, L. S. V. (2016). Environmental Factors for Social Entrepreneurship Success: Comparing Four Regions. *American Journal of Management*, *16*(4), 39–56.

Chandra, Y. (2016). A Rhetoric-Orientation View of Social Entrepreneurship. *Social Enterprise Journal*, *12*(2), 161–200. doi:10.1108/SEJ-02-2016-0003

Chell, E., Spence, L. J., Perrini, F., & Harris, J. D. (2016). Social Entrepreneurship and Business Ethics: Does Social Equal Ethical? *Journal of Business Ethics*, *133*(4), 619–625. doi:10.100710551-014-2439-6

Clark, C., & Brennan, L. (2016). Social Entrepreneurship: A Global Model for Evaluating Long-Term Impact. *International Journal of Entrepreneurship*, *20*(1), 1–15.

Gawell, M. (2013). Social Entrepreneurship – Innovative Challengers or Adjustable Followers? *Social Enterprise Journal*, *9*(2), 203–220. doi:10.1108/SEJ-01-2013-0004

Haugh, H. M., & Talwar, A. (2014). Linking Social Entrepreneurship and Social Change: The Mediating Role of Empowerment. *Journal of Business Ethics*, *133*(4), 643–658. doi:10.100710551-014-2449-4

Korsgaard, S. (2011). Opportunity Formation in Social Entrepreneurship. *Journal of Enterprising Communities: People and Places in the Global Economy*, *5*(4), 265–285. doi:10.1108/17506201111177316

Mercader, V. (2017). Influence of Social Entrepreneurship in Organizations, Family and Society: Causes and Solutions for Success. *American Journal of Management*, *17*(2), 65–85.

Mody, M., Day, J., Sydnor, S., & Jaffe, W. (2015). Examining the Motivations for Social Entrepreneurship using Max Weber's Typology of Rationality. *International Journal of Contemporary Hospitality Management*, *28*(6), 1094–1114. doi:10.1108/IJCHM-05-2014-0238

Mulloth, B., Kickul, J. R., & Gundry, L. K. (2016). Driving Technology Innovation through Social Entrepreneurship at Prezi. *Journal of Small Business and Enterprise Development*, *23*(3), 753–767. doi:10.1108/JSBED-08-2015-0111

Naem, M. (2014). Social Entrepreneurship: An Effective Mode of Promoting Public Private Partnership in Middle East. *Asia Pacific Journal of Management & Entrepreneurship Research*, *3*(2), 5–28.

Omorede, A. (2014). Exploration of Motivational Drivers towards Social Entrepreneurship. *Social Enterprise Journal*, *10*(3), 239–267. doi:10.1108/SEJ-03-2013-0014

Parris, D. L., & Mclnnis-Bowers, C. V. (2014). Social Entrepreneurship Questioning the Status Quo: Waste as a Resource. *Journal of Economic Issues*, *48*(2), 359–365. doi:10.2753/JEI0021-3624480209

Roundy, P. T. (2014). Doing Good by Telling Stories: Emotion in Social Entrepreneurship Communication. *Journal of Small Business Strategy*, *24*(2), 41–68.

Stecker, M. J. (2014). Revolutionizing the Nonprofit Sector through Social Entrepreneurship. *Journal of Economic Issues*, *48*(2), 349–358. doi:10.2753/JEI0021-3624480208

Tasavori, M., Ghauri, P. N., & Zaefarian, R. (2016). Entering the Base of the Pyramid Market in India: A Corporate Social Entrepreneurship Perspective. *International Marketing Review*, *33*(4), 555–579. doi:10.1108/IMR-03-2014-0085

KEY TERMS AND DEFINITIONS

Bottom/Base of the Pyramid (BoP): The population living in developing and under-developed economies is described as "uncertain, informal, rural and heterogeneous segment" lying at the bottom of the socio-economic pyramid. This socio-economic segment is recognized as "base of pyramid" (BoP) and represents 4 billion (60% of the global population) people, who are poor, live and transact in an informal market ecosystem for the fulfillment of the basic social needs.

Corporate Social Responsibility (CSR): Commitment by business to behave ethically and contribute to economic development while improving the quality of life of the workforce, their families, as well as of the local community and society.

Social Entrepreneurship: Social entrepreneurship can be defined as an entrepreneurial and innovative activity with an embedded social purpose of change.

Sustainability: A normative notion about how individuals should act towards nature and how they are responsible for the other and the future.

Sustainable Development: It describes the responsibilities of business in terms of creating economic, social and environmental value. It is the development that meets the needs of the present without compromising the ability of future generations' needs.

Chapter 2
Social Value and Sociological Perspective on Social Entrepreneurship

Abdullah Yilmaz
Selcuk University, Turkey

Hande Ulukapi Yilmaz
Selcuk University, Turkey

ABSTRACT

The needs of communities are endless and unlimited like the needs of individuals. Societies have to meet their reasonable set of unlimited needs to sustain their continuity. Otherwise, social problems become unsolvable and these problems that become unsolvable can be sources of other problems. In this sense, social enterprises are the institutions that have emerged in order to meet the needs of the society and to solve the problems. The close relation of social enterprises with society and social structure and the "social" expression in the concept make it necessary to look at social entrepreneurship from a sociological perspective. In this direction, the aim of this chapter is intended to create a sociological perspective on social entrepreneurship that aims to contribute to social order and welfare rather than commercial entrepreneurship serving the purpose of individual or organizational interest in economic sense. In the context of sociological perspective, social problem, social benefit, social mission and vision, social value, social capital, and finally, social change and transformation concepts and their relation with social entrepreneurship are examined.

INTRODUCTION

Unlike an entrepreneur who organizes, manages, and assumes the risks of an enterprise (Merriam-Webster, 2017), social entrepreneurs are seen as *people who have vision for social change and who have financial resources to support their ideas* (Schuyler, 1998). Social entrepreneurs have gained the trust of the society by acting in a sensitive and realistic way to remedy the problem realizing the problems of the society they are in and being disturbed by the situation (Betil, 2010). Compared to traditional entre-

DOI: 10.4018/978-1-5225-5687-9.ch002

preneurship, social entrepreneurship is based on the concept of social welfare and goodness, a concept that is more than individual welfare. Social entrepreneurship is a concept that needs to be emphasized due to it closely influences human life.

Social entrepreneurship resembles traditional entrepreneurship in terms of seeking opportunities for solutions creation, creating systems and new approaches (Williams & K'nife, 2012). However, the main difference between the two concepts is that in social entrepreneurship activities, the preoccupation of creating and maintaining social value is the forefront rather than financial concerns. In this context, Trivedi and Stokols (2011) have touched on four main differences in distinguishing social entrepreneurs from commercial entrepreneurs. The authors ranged these differences as 1) emphasis on social goals contrary to economic gains; 2) social activist role played by the social entrepreneur; 3) entrepreneurship and innovation elements; 4) the use of economic profits as a means of solving a social problem rather than a purpose. While financial outputs such as profitability are primarily considered in the preliminary plan in the success of commercial enterprises, social benefits are more in the preliminary plan in success criteria rather than financial gains in social enterprises. Even if financial profitability is included in targets in social entrepreneurship, the relevant return is transferred to the necessary points in line with social mission and targets rather than the use of business owners (Görün & Kara, 2010).

At this point, it is possible to express the mission from five different perspectives, which is put onto social entrepreneurship concept by the word "social" that is in the social entrepreneurship vocabulary group (Kümbül Güler, 2008): The expression "social" requires the initiatives, in the framework of the problems social entrepreneurship looks for solutions, firstly to be aimed at realizing social goals. Secondly, the phrase "Social" in the concept expresses that it should be given importance inasmuch as social capital is thought to bring along physical and financial capital. Thirdly, as a requirement of the "social" expression, instead the basic mission of the established organization is to be making profit, it needs to be for social benefit in the direction of a social purpose, it needs to be integrated to reinvestment for social benefit even if it gains profit. Fourthly, social entrepreneurs should use their energy and opportunities in the direction of community progress and development, acting with the awareness that they are entrepreneurs of the society. Finally, as a requirement of the word "social", social entrepreneurship should be positioned on the social sector that will be located between the public and private sectors. In this context, the next section will include an assessment of social entrepreneurship from a sociological perspective.

THE CONCEPT OF SOCIAL ENTREPRENEURSHIP FROM THE SOCIOLOGICAL PERSPECTIVE

When literature related to the concept of social entrepreneurship is searched, the concept seems to be in the field of interest of, primarily business management and behavioral intelligence, approximately 25 different disciplines such as sociology, psychology, psychiatry, geography, ethics, ergonomics, accounting, technology, public administration, tourism and law (Gonçalves, Carrara, & Schmittel, 2016). The close relationship of social entrepreneurship with the society, which creates solutions to social problems by creating social value by putting the social mission at the focal point and aims at realizing a social transformation, has attracted the attention of sociology discipline as a requirement of the interdisciplinary nature of the concept as well (Mengü, 2016a).

Studies on the sociological bases of entrepreneurship in the literature have increased after 1980. Because entrepreneurship is a type of social and cultural activity, it has a power to influence social structure and relationships, and the increasing importance of entrepreneurial people as a social class required sociological approach to entrepreneurship (Aytaç & İlhan, 2007). The science of sociology focuses on the social environment in which entrepreneurial personality emerges, social processes affecting entrepreneurship and social processes influenced by entrepreneurship, the social environment in which the entrepreneur is trained, social effects, cultural legitimacy systems and the creative aspect of entrepreneurship in social construction, and thus, it goes into the path of dimensioning entrepreneurship as socially, culturally and politically (Aytaç, 2006).

While the approaches which look at the entrepreneurship concept from psychological and behavioral perspectives, focus on the attitudes and behaviors of entrepreneurs regarding to their preferences to produce added-value in economic sense; sociological approaches often emphasize the importance of social structures and variables on personal decisions and, at the same time, they argue that a tendency in which personal qualities are influential comes to the forefront as the only determining factor in entrepreneurship theory. This tendency, which has been on the frontline in entrepreneurship theory until recently, ignores the importance of social factors that are effective in deciding for entrepreneurship action (Thornton, 1999; Aytaç & İlhan, 2007).

Numerous scientists such as Weber, Schumpeter, Auster and Aldrich, Storey, Lyon, Werbner, Reynolds, Hofstede stated that on-profit elements are also motive sources apart from personal, behavioral and economic elements in the formation of entrepreneurial action. When we look at these non-profit factors, they dwelled on religion, status, social structure, historical conditions, gender, race, ethnicity, education, social/environmental and etc. characteristics (Verheul, Wennekers, Audretsch, & Thurik, 2001; Aytaç, 2006). Similarly, sociologists, who try to explain entrepreneurial action from a sociological perspective, argue that opportunities are effective in the entrepreneurial process. In fact, entrepreneurial individuals are those who attempt to undertake the role of catalyst even with the smallest mark they see, not expecting the opportunities in their environment. For entrepreneurial success, if it is deemed that ideas, opportunities, resources, skills, motivation, etc. are necessary, as well as factors such as social environment, family, education, age, gender, origin, race; the social structures and situations to which entrepreneurs are exposed will closely influence the entrepreneurship process and its success (Bridge, O'Neill, & Cromie, 1998; Thornton, 1999).

Dees (1998) argues that, considers social entrepreneurs as individuals who play the role of change agent in society, there must be five factors in order to form a social enterprise:

- Setting a mission to create and sustain social value, not just personal values,
- To serve this mission, to recognize the new opportunities and to pursue these opportunities,
- To be engaged with continuous innovation, adaptation and learning processes,
- To be brave without being restricted by the resources available,
- To demonstrate responsibility for accountability to the society.

It is understood that Dees states social enterprises as a process to create a social value and benefit and to establish a social mission in order to make this social benefit sustainable, to follow the opportunities boldly with the awareness of social responsibility in line with this mission, continuous innovation, to be engaged with integration and learning processes.

In this respect, to examine the concepts of social benefit, social mission and vision, social value, social capital and finally social change and transformation in the context of sociological perspective is seen useful for the better understanding of the subject, which we can describe as social entrepreneurship dimensions.

Social Problem

The concept of social problem, which is an integral part of social life, refers to social situations, processes, arrangements or attitudes that are undesirable and perceived as negative, which threaten the continuity of social cohesion, laws, legislations, order and moral standards, the stability and future of social institutions, economic welfare and individual freedoms (Jamrozik & Nocella, 1998).

For a problem to be regarded as a "social problem"; it is necessary to be a presence of an active group and seeing the incident as a problem, that the problem influences many individuals, occurs due to individual, sociological or socio-psychological factors and having such results, try to solve the problem with mass activities. At this point, social entrepreneurships can produce solutions to this problem by recognizing a social problem that the general public cannot recognize, without the need for a consensus of an effective group, and they can also work on individual endeavours without the need for mass activities in solving the problem. What is important here is that the social impact of individual or small efforts is to spread more, expand and ensure sustainability over time (Kümbül Güler, 2010). The social effect can be defined as the result of a change in the outcome of an activity or a result of an action / activity / project / program on different people in general terms ("Social Impact," 2017).

Globalization, rapid changes and developments in the world bring social problems in its wake such as poverty, as well as unemployment, violations of human rights, environmental/ecological problems, housing, education, health, etc. (Glancey & McQuaid, 2000), gender inequality, child and maternal deaths, spread of diseases HIV/AIDS etc., and technology/internet dependence brought by the information/communication age.

The problems that arise in different areas of social structure and the social anxieties, depending on the pace of the increase in these problems, activate the individuals to develop solutions to existing problems. Different and varied social problems oblige the solutions to be developed to be creative and to have a rich content. Every institution that forms a society needs to show interest in social problems and produce solutions for social development and progress. States that undertake an important mission in identification and resolution of social problems are sometimes insufficient to meet all social needs. This situation necessitates the existence of alternative or supplementary forms in solving social problems and meeting the related needs (Koçak & Kavi, 2014; Coşkun, 2015). At this point, it is known that non-profit and profit-oriented private sector organizations try to solve social problems in their own right or in cooperation and solidarity with central and local authorities (Ağca & Böyükaslan, 2016). In this context, the concept of social entrepreneurship comes to the forefront at the point of finding social problems and solving these problems and thus as an enterprise activity required to achieve sustainable social development (Koçak & Kavi, 2014; Coşkun, 2015). At the focal point of social entrepreneurship, there is addressing social needs of society, finding solutions to social problems or effort to minimize the effects of social problems.

Korosec and Berman (2006) define social entrepreneurs as individuals who attempt to identify, address and solve important social problems in their communities. Robinson (2006) describes social entrepreneurship as a process of identifying a particular social problem, finding ways to address the problem, evaluating the created social effect, business model and sustainability of enterprise, and creating an organization that pursues social profit oriented or an organization that does not pursue business oriented profit.

Social entrepreneurs are defined as individuals, groups, organizations or organizational associations that point to important social problems, and are aimed at achieving sustainable and profound change through innovative ideas in Light (2008)'s definition of social entrepreneur. The point that Light (2008) stands at the most is social problems. According to him, one of the most important and determining features of social entrepreneur is to find sustainable solutions for existing social problems. In this sense, according to Denizalp (2009), social entrepreneur is the one who addresses the problems with an incredible approach or with an approach that hasn't been even dared till that day, recognizing the social disruptions that arise in the society in which he lives; the one who is creative, insistent, sensitive, making a difference with his realistic attitudes and wins the trust of the society.

Bornstein and Davis (2010) defined social entrepreneurship as a process that people have established or transformed into institutions to produce sophisticated solutions to social problems such as poverty, illness, ignorance, environmental degradation, human rights violations and bribery, and thus, to offer a more liveable life to many people. According to Sivathanu and Bhise (2013), this process is possible by bringing innovations, skills and opportunities together to produce practical solutions for social problems. Social entrepreneurs who wish to create social value focus on complex social problems by identifying new services and new products or combining proven practices and innovation.

As we tried to explain above, inspiration of social entrepreneurs, point of origin is social problems in society. Social entrepreneurs are people who act to produce solutions to social problems through identifying them. Just as a commercial entrepreneur sets up new industries, social entrepreneurs approach social problems with innovative solutions and apply these solutions on a large scale. However, the main distinction between social entrepreneurs and commercial entrepreneurs is that they are passionate and creative in solving social problems and creating social value (Dees, 1998; Bhawe, Jain, & Gupta, 2006).

Social entrepreneurship undertakes the task of catalysts (Kümbül Güler, 2011) in solving many important social and environmental problems (Glancey & McQuaid, 2000) by bringing dynamism to the economic. Social entrepreneurship, rather than focusing on urgent problems and solving them, should provide a permanent and sustainable solution for social problems in a wider social system and assessing the problem as a whole with other interdependent problems (Kümbül Güler, 2010). In this context, a social entrepreneur is expected to invest resources and opportunities in "social" problems (Trivedi & Stokols, 2011).

Finally, it is worthwhile to mention some of the common features that social entrepreneurs seeking solutions to social problems should pay attention to. These are; it is necessary to respond to a real need, to manage it by a reliable and effective management cadre, to have an opportunity to reproduce economically when a good model is created, to have sources of income that will cover the periodic costs of the project and project outcomes and benefits should be measured and shared with transparency (Argüden, 2005).

The next step in the identification of social problems in society where we can call the inspiration source of social enterprises or the exit point of enterprise is the social benefit through the solution of related social problems.

Social Benefit

Social entrepreneurs acting with the motto: The selfish endings you serve cannot take you further than you, but the endings you serve for all can allow you reach even to eternity[1] aim to create collective benefit with the projects they sign.

When social entrepreneurship is considered as motivating the sensitivity to social problems through the use of entrepreneurship principles in the direction of *creating social benefit* (Mengü, 2016b), *social benefit* can be defined as benefiting from the positive outputs of a social enterprise, activity or movement that is planned and implemented through material or spiritual aspects in such a way to enhance the well-being of the target group (Seyyar, 2005).

The concept "social" means that one of the aims of the social entrepreneur must be "social benefit". According to Fowler (2000), social entrepreneurship creates socio-economic structures, relations, institutions, organizations and applications that provide and sustain social benefit. According to Austin et al. (2006), social entrepreneurship is the identification, evaluation and use of opportunities that will result in social benefits. Austin et al. (2006), who argue that social entrepreneurship is the opposite of commercial entrepreneurship, explained the reason for this stating that while commercial entrepreneurship results in profit, social entrepreneurship results in social benefits.

The main focus of social entrepreneurs is to maximize benefits for their communities and their surroundings, rather than maximizing their profits. Rather than short-term gains, they emphasize long-term sustainability and focus on maximizing the benefits for society and the environment, applying innovative approaches to the main challenges the world faces (Zamantılı Nayır & Karataş Gümüştaş, 2017). In this context, Gonçalves et al. (2016) underscored that it is an indisputable fact that social enterprises provide sustainable, fair and comprehensive benefits to social development.

The social benefit, which becomes meaningful with the element of social value creation, involves two situations; the first is the social benefit revealed by the solution of the social problem and the second is the social benefit which is the result of the social development and the change it creates. The mission focused on creating social value, and social entrepreneur who mobilizes its motivation using various forms of capital put an impact on the solution of the social problem and this impact is made visible by social benefit component. Social benefit component has importance in the context of the targeted results, from the aspect that it includes that created social value comes into being in society and it is the supplementary of the components defining the social entrepreneurship in the field (Mengü, 2016b).

In order to create social benefits, being voluntary, self-sacrificing and altruistic underlie on the basis of the characteristics that motivate the social entrepreneur. In other words, altruist reasons such as personal participation are also important in social entrepreneurship, as well as moral responsibility and ethical motives (Mair & Marti, 2006). In this direction, Tan et al. (2005) specified that altruism discussed in the context of social entrepreneurship can be seen in the following six different behaviors of the social entrepreneur:

- The person who attempts to innovatively profit society alone, in a way that involves that society, at risk of personal loss.
- The person who attempts to innovatively profit society alone, in a way that involves that society, at risk of foregoing personal profit.
- The person who attempts to innovatively profit society by profiting himself, in a way that involves that society, at risk of incurring personal loss.

- The person who attempts to innovatively profit society by profiting himself, in a way that involves that society, at risk of foregoing personal profit.
- The person who attempts to innovatively profit himself by profiting society, in a way that involves that society, at risk of personal loss.
- The person who attempts to innovatively profit himself by profiting society, in a way that involves that society, at risk of foregoing personal profit.

Social entrepreneurship creates positive spillover effects across the society from top to bottom through self-organization in order to benefit others. Organizations created by social entrepreneurs are mostly aimed at increasing the participation of the poor to the society and overcoming social exclusion. Social entrepreneurs who deal with multifaceted problems and collaborate with various stakeholders are transforming into intermediaries that overcome the existing social obstacles and create new bonds (Estrin, Mickiewicz, & Stephan, 2013).

The social entrepreneur, who aims to create social benefit through the solution of social problems in society, should determine a social vision and a mission for himself/herself or for the organization within the framework of the related objective at this stage.

Social Mission and Vision

Mission and vision are direct representations that reflect an organization's spirit and beliefs. As well as they include the service area, the receivers and the results to be achieved, these are the elements that show whether this organization can be regarded as a social initiative. At the same time, the concept of mission on its own; contains three components of social entrepreneurship: Innovation, entrepreneurship and social change (Perrini & Vurro, 2006).

Many researchers point out that social mission is the basic dimension of the concept of social entrepreneurship (Mort, Weerawardena, & Carnegıe, 2003). In this regard, it is the mission of the social entrepreneur who has entrepreneurial powers and intuitions and who seeks to create value by using the principles of entrepreneurship, original, effective and meaningful, which he uses in the direction of the means (Mengü, 2016a). The primary mission of social entrepreneurship is to create social values by using business models to solve social problems (Dacin, Dacin, & Matear, 2010). Social value creation mission is one of the most important concepts for social entrepreneurship (Hervieux, Gedajlovic, & Turcotte, 2010). In this sense, a social entrepreneur can be described as a person who creates a mission to create and sustain social value.

Dees defines social entrepreneurship, which he argues it is a special kind of entrepreneurship, as entrepreneurs who have missions. Social entrepreneurs are people who have a mission to create and maintain social values and who are in a continuous innovation and learning process, who pursue new opportunities, not limited with the limited resources available to serve this mission (Dees, Emerson, & Economy, 2001). It is stated that social entrepreneurs have social mission because they are collective-sensitive legal entities, they are catalysts to social problems and they put social values at the center of their actions in order to create social benefits (Mengü, 2016a). In this sense, social mission play an explicit and fundamental role for social entrepreneurial organizations (Dees, 1998).

Social mission clearly affects how social entrepreneurs perceive and evaluate opportunities. The basic criterion for social entrepreneurs is not to create wealth by making profit but it is the effect that will be made through they take on (Dees, 1998). However, the social entrepreneur, who puts the social mission at the center of his activity, can also maintain his profitability that he will instrumentalize with social benefit while using his commercial activities as a means to realize his social missions (Ersen, Kaya, & Meydanoğlu, 2010; Mengü, 2016a).

The basic mission of social entrepreneurs is to create social change and social values by producing solutions to social problems rather than pursuing profitability. But the main purpose of commercial entrepreneurs is to make profit. While the mission of commercial entrepreneurship is self-interest, the mission of social entrepreneurship is social interest (Rennie, 2006; Özdevecioğlu & Cingöz, 2009).

Social entrepreneurs have a social vision and, for social benefit maximization, work on subjects of collective action, to consider social needs and to identify factors related to these needs (Hasan, 2005). Social entrepreneurs focus their visions on activities that will bring collective value (Sastre-Castillo, Peris-Ortiz, & Danvila-Del Valle, 2015), they come up with a social vision that embraces a sense of necessity and destiny in meeting basic human needs. In other words, the social vision means believing that social entrepreneurship is the fate of signing services to serve society and to create social benefits. Social vision sees the opportunities beyond what is present, and transforms the social entrepreneur into a change agent. Commitment to social issues develops with an emotional tendency and a sense of responsibility to a social problem. For this reason, social entrepreneurs take the way of meeting the social needs by seeing them that public and private sectors cannot reach (Koe Hwee Nga & Shamuganathan, 2010).

A social entrepreneur who aims at achieving social benefit through the solution of social problems and who determines the social vision and mission in this aim is the person who creates social capital to realize this vision and mission.

Social Capital

Given that there are entrepreneurs who have two different perspectives in the world, while the first one is an entrepreneur who aims to maximize profits; the second one is the type of entrepreneur who is not interested in profit maximization, committed to making a difference in the world, wants to offer better chances to others in life, aims to create sustainable commercial enterprises and to support such enterprises to achieve this goal (Yunus, 2006). A commercial or social entrepreneur is in search of a capital that will provide him/her with returns (Austin J., Stevenson, H., & Wei-Skillern, J., 2006). It is possible to mention four types of capital generated by entrepreneurs in this quest: Financial, aesthetic and social capital (Thompson, Alvy, & Lees, 2000). While financial capital means tangible assets such as plant, equipment, in addition to financial assets, money etc. (Luthans, Luthans, & Luthans, 2004); aesthetic capital includes factors such as music, art and architecture. Both provide emotions that make people feel good and have an influence on the physical environment (Thompson, 2002).

Estrin et al. (2013) underline that social entrepreneurship creates a social capital, as well as it has direct effects on social needs. For social entrepreneurs, social capital, which is more preliminary than the others, shortly is the ability of people to work with groups and organizations in a common purpose and unity (Fukuyama, 1995). As well as social capital is a concept that is commonly used in social sciences, it can be thought as creation of social networks, sustaining them and performing the norms of behavior to maintain these networks (Cope, Jack, & Rose, 2007). With the shortest definition, social capital is the answer to the question "who do you know?" (Luthans, Luthans, & Luthans, 2004). Social capital undertakes a task of "bonding" that brings together people who know each other, or a "bridging" task by bringing together people who don't know each other at all (Hasan, 2005; Estrin, Mickiewicz, & Stephan, 2013).

It is possible to mention three main components of social capital, which can also be expressed as values, norms and network types that may influence the development of outputs. These are structure, attitude and culture. The structure, from these components, dwells on relationships and networks. The attitudes points to human relations such as mutual behavior patterns and trust. And finally, the culture contains values that are accepted in a society (Hasan, 2005).

Social capital, a vital component of the emergence of social entrepreneurship, represents the most valuable ones of relationships within a network. Because social capital is a concept that makes big differences in the effort of reaching larger networks and resources and survival (Miller & Wesley, 2010). Social entrepreneurs, who share their resources in communication with other people, always earn more than they can alone. Thus, the network is supported by social capital, which is an intangible asset (Cope, Jack, & Rose, 2007). At this point, it is also necessary to mention the concept of "trust", which is an important concept in the strengthening of social capital. So much so that, social capital provides the foundation of trust that allows collective action among members of a society. While individuals provide the trust of other individuals by using their social capital on the one hand, they have the idea of trusting or not trusting others on the other hand. Hereby, trust-based social capital encourages mutual benefit sharing with social actions and outputs (Hasan, 2005).

Strengthening social capital can be possible through the increase of social entrepreneurs who are seeking solutions to the social problems of society in their fields. Social entrepreneur is the one who goes over the problems with a creative and courageous approach to tackle the problems instead of feeling uncomfortable and keeping silent, realizing the social problems that arise in the society in which he/she lives, who is a man of struggle, sensitive, makes a difference with their realistic attitudes and win the trust of the society. Social entrepreneur is the person with the vision and determination that can continue to work until the whole system is transformed (Betil, 2010).

As some profit-oriented organizations can produce social capital as well as financial and environmental capital, some others destroy other types of capital, being in the first place social capital, because of the financial capital they are too focused on. But it is a fact that the lack of financial capital can limit social entrepreneurship activity by limiting the social entrepreneurs' ability to create social capital. As an entrepreneurial behavior, with the development of social relations and the establishment of networks; bringing along trust, visibility, reputation and cooperation provides financial capital for more social capital creation (Thompson, 2000).

The basic mission of a social entrepreneur who seeks to acquire social capital in order to reach the social vision and realize the social mission is to create social value. At this point, it is worth mentioning the concept of "social value" which is one of the key elements of social entrepreneurship.

Value and Social Value

As well as focusing on organizational forms in entrepreneurship, when social entrepreneurship is concerned, the forms of organizations used lose importance, the social and environmental impact of entrepreneurship come to the forefront more (Young, 2006). Gibb (1987), who puts forward that a number of values, attitudes and beliefs affect entrepreneurial behavior of entrepreneurial cultures, argues that entrepreneurs differ from others by these values and beliefs. It is necessary to deepen the concept of social value which we often pronounce in defining the concept of social entrepreneurship.

The concept of value is one of the topics frequently discussed in the social sciences literature, notably in sociology, philosophy, psychology and anthropology. The interest of social sciences to values stems from the fact that many social scientists think that values have a key role in explaining human and group behavior (Yazıcı, 2014). So much so that, values are regarded as the most important criteria that give meaning to socio-cultural elements of the society. For this reason, behavior patterns of people and groups constitute the starting point of sociological studies (Özensel, 2003).

Sociology discipline argues that there is a relationship between entrepreneurship and social structure or factors. From this point of view, we confront with value, social value, events or situations (religion, social conditions, education system, etc.) as factors that direct social entrepreneurship (Aytaç & İlhan, 2007). While sociology is using the value concept in defining and describing the phenomenon (social relations, norms, institutions, groups, etc.) it is interested in; on the other hand, it has taken it as its duty to examine the description of values, the way they occur, their interactions with social phenomena, theories and processes, typologies and the various systems that these types comprise, value conflicts encountered in certain concrete situations (Yazıcı, 2014).

According to sociologists, value is *a concept that describes the preferred one among certain known actions and behavior options either explicitly or implicitly by a certain person or a group* (Yazıcı, 2014). In short, values, which can be defined as "generalized abstract criteria", which is beneficial to a person or group, which determines the desired and liked; from this point of view, finds meaning at the degree of importance transferred to it, rather than itself (Aksan, 2016).

Value (Merriam-Webster, 2017) is not only a concept that can be pronounced for economic purposes unlike *the cost of a good or service that can be measured by money*. According to Bozeman (2007), value is a complex set of objects characterized by cognitive and emotional elements, and appears to have the potential to act because it is part of the individual's self-definition. The heterogeneity of culture, values, identities and interests is the main reason for changing social goals besides being characteristics of societies (Cho, 2006).

Value is the generalized moral principles and beliefs that reflect the common feelings, thoughts, goals and interests of a social group or society, which are acknowledged and approved by a majority of its members to ensure their existence, unity, functioning and continuation. In another definition, value is expressed as standards, beliefs or moral principles that are accepted by a person or a social group. From these definitions, it is understood that values is *reinforcing and encircling* principles and beliefs, which give guidance to the people in their lives, lead their preferences, both make societies distinguished and provide the unity of the societies (Yazıcı, 2014). As an important part of social life, social entrepreneurs use this reinforcing and encircling aspect of value to analyze social life.

According to Fichter (2001), values, from the basic concepts used in explaining and interpreting social life, is criterions for measuring the importance of group or community, people, behavioral models, their goals and other socio-cultural objects. Fichter argues that the place of a value depends on its prevalence in society where it is accepted and on the attributed importance. According to him,

the behavioral pattern with the highest social value is, at the same time, the value that is most widely obeyed and has the most social pressure on it (Fichter, 2001).

According to Felicio et al. (2013), social value is the necessary goods and services provided by organizations in the direction of social goals such as encouraging the development of a community, defending more inclusive and fairer politics or dealing with social problems. Similarly, Certo and Miller (2008) described social value as providing long-term services such as food, shelter, education and health etc. needed by people belong to a society. In this context, it is possible to list four basic characteristics of the value concept as follows (Yumuş, 2017):

- Values are phenomena that hold a society together.
- Values are the criteria upon which both individuals and society meet their social needs.
- Values are related to the consciousness, emotion and excitement of people and societies.
- Values are influential in motivating individual behaviors.

In social structure, there is a bi-directional interaction between social values and social units such as institutions, customs, traditions, family, economy, education and teaching. These units both express values and they gain strength from social values as well. Hence, "values" have a great proposition in our daily lives. Because values affect the norms, and rules and norms are revealed by the effects of values in society (Özkalp, 2003). However, any model and approach that ignores social values and cultural values will be insufficient to explain the social processes that are happening (Özensel, 2003). In support of this view, Emerson (2003) underlines that value is a phenomenon that cannot easily be separated from economic, social and cultural elements (Young, 2006). According to Aytaç (2002), who deals with social values that is a concept which cannot be considered apart from cultural elements as customs and traditions, social values have three basic qualities: They have a continuity feature, they do not have the obligation to follow reason and logic, they have qualifications that forces people to comply with them (Yazıcı, 2014).

Besides these qualifications, values that are of important building blocks of society have many functions. Fichter (2001) lists these functions as follows:

- Values serve as tools in the evaluation of people and groups. This allows the formation of a social stratification system. In addition, values help people in their neighborhood to know where they are located.
- Through values, people concentrate their attention on useful, material cultural objects. Sometimes although an object is not considered "the best" for a person or group of people, but the fact that a social value is attributed to that object leads to people trying to reach that object.
- Values are also influential on societal ideal behaviors and thinking. Values determine the course of socially acceptable behavior in society. In this way, individuals know what kind of attitude they should exhibit when performing their thoughts and actions.
- Values guide individuals in determining the roles they will choose in social life and demonstrate appropriate behavior to those roles. In this way, the individuals themselves realize that the responsibilities required of the roles and the expectations of the relevant role are shaped and carried out for some purposes.
- Values function as a control means of communities. They encourage individuals to obey the rules and to exhibit correct behavior. They prevent the conduct of unwanted behavior by the community. By virtue of values, individuals know that they will have feelings of shame and guilt when what behavior they exhibit.
- Values are of the strengths that best reinforce feelings of solidarity and perception. Through common values, social solidarity and supportive behaviors among the individuals are exhibited, and the permanence of the solidarity is ensured.

The most important function of social values is to provide social solidarity. Hence, the functions of social values most effectively occur during the periods of dissolution and depression of societies. Values that suggest social solidarity ad emphasize the importance of family, solidarity, friendship become more important in this process. The more necessary and important is the cement which holds the iron, sand, lime and other materials used in the constructing of a building together, the more necessary and important are social values in understanding, functioning and survival of social institutions (Yazıcı, 2014). Nevertheless, although in any society the values have a function of providing solidarity and integration on the persons, these values sometimes can be a source of some social problems. From this point of view, values are also the source of social conflicts. 'Generation conflict' of the generations adopting different values is the best example of this situation (Özensel, 2003). As understood from the information given thus far, the concept of value and social value are concepts that are undeniably important in the formation and development of societies. From this point of view, Social entrepreneurs who serve the society are in a strong relationship with the concept of value and social value.

When some of the social entrepreneurship definitions cited in the literature are examined, it is possible to understand how social value is a critical concept for social entrepreneurship. Sharir and Lerner (2006) stated that social entrepreneurs acted as a change agent to create and maintain social value without being limited with the available resources. Peredo and McLean (2006), who emphasized the desire to be useful to the society in somehow on the basis of social entrepreneurship, stated that this is another way of giving voice to that increasing "social value" is aimed in order to contribute to the social welfare in the community in which social entrepreneur is. As Austin et al. (2006) defined social entrepreneurship as non-profit organizations, an innovative, social value-creating activity that can take place inside or outside the business or government sectors; Chell (2007) emphasized that the social entrepreneur is a person who consciously collects resources and uses the capital in his / her environment to create social value. In summary; *the basic meaning expressed by the concept of "social" is the important emphasis* (Dees, 1998) that is made by the initiative activity on the purpose of social value creation in social entrepreneurship that can be defined as the activities that are:

focused on solving social problems, that make opportunities for creating a systematic social value to maximize social effectiveness and to achieve change, strategy-focused, innovative, and effective activities (Nicholls, 2006; Smith & Stevens, 2010).

As can be seen, the common point in all definitions of social entrepreneurship is that the driving force forming the basis of social entrepreneurship is the fact to create social value instead of personal wealth. In this direction, social entrepreneurs, acting with sensitivity to social problems, have to keep the construction of social value at the solution point in the forefront. At this point according to Smith-Hunter and College (2008) there are eight variables for constructing social value:

- Social networks of entrepreneurs,
- Dedication to the success of the enterprise,
- Capital in the establishment phase,
- Social acceptance of the idea of enterprise,
- Integration of the enterprise team,

- Formation of companies within the public sector that are not for profit in the long term,
- Ability to serve to be afloat in market tests,
- Administrative experience of entrepreneurs.

On the construction of social value, a key element in the formation of social entrepreneurship, it is understood that Smith-Hunter and College (2008) has emphasized the importance of community adoption of enterprise idea and being sustainable in addition to basic requirements such as enterprise capital of entrepreneurs, social networks, managerial experience, service skills and teamwork.

On the other hand Light (2005), Mair and Marti (2006) and Zahra et al. (2008), who emphasize the importance of creating social value in social entrepreneurship, specify the concept of social entrepreneurship as activities which reduces social problems and facilitates social transformation. Social entrepreneurship contains activities that reduce related issues and facilitate social change and transformations by producing innovative and creative solutions to social problems that are especially related to poverty, education, environmental problems, women, children, elderly people, disabled etc. (Alvord, Brown, & Letts, 2004; Aslan, Araza, & Bulut, 2012). At this point, from the perspective of social entrepreneurship, it is possible to rank the five conspicuous features of value as follows (Young, 2006):

- Firstly, value is a subjective concept in terms of one's interest in life experiences. It is closely related to the construction, consumption and effects of social values.
- The second characteristic is that social values are debatable among stakeholders.
- The third characteristic is that social values are conditional and open to re-evaluation. Ad commercial values change and updated over time, social value can also be redefined. But the problem is that there is no certainty in the determination of social value. What seems worthwhile for a generation can be considered worthless for another generation.
- According to another characteristic, social value is to bring together things that are not measurable by a single measure.
- Finally, when social issues are concerned, it is not possible to separate values from each other. The formation process of value affects all participants.

In summary; Young (2006), while describing value or social value in the context of social entrepreneurship, he stated that values are subjective concepts that people experience throughout their lives, they can be discussed only by stakeholders in society, social values may change and become worthless over time, their being adopted by society is not an easy process, and these values have an integral structure that cannot be separated from each other. These characteristics of social value will be the guide for social entrepreneurs whose basic mission is to create and sustain social value.

Santos (2012) emphasizes that a social entrepreneur who is focused on creating social value must be a person who can transform the relevant value into a reproducible and sustainable process, in addition to creating social value. Agafonow (2014) notes that this action can only be carried out by a social entrepreneur, who emphasizes the social goal. While the aforementioned form of action may occur only as a reflection of the social consciousness of the social entrepreneur, Antoni (2016) states that this situation can be understood and explained in the context of voluntary and organized individual behavior rather than rational and selfish individual behavior (Mengü, 2016a). As Barendsen and Gardner (2004) say, those entrepreneurs, who can exhibit this voluntary and altruistic behavior, appear to consist of those who have witnessed events that often left bad memories in their past, maintained their lives in difficult living conditions, know the challenges of life and feel themselves responsible individuals towards the society.

Prabhu (1999) argues that social entrepreneurs tend to this area because of the need to respect the statutory and social values of individuals. Social value, as the whole of social, cultural, scientific etc. elements created by a society with common effort, is acquired as capital by social entrepreneurs to get rid of malfunction in society. In this sense, social value is an important concept in envisaging the role that social entrepreneurs play in society and the contributions they make to the society (Young, 2006).

Value creation is at the heart of all types of entrepreneurship. Both commercial and social entrepreneurs aim to create value as entrepreneurs (Alvarez & Barney, 2007). Social entrepreneurship is considered differently from commercial entrepreneurship in terms of the type of produced value. While commercial entrepreneurs are interested in economic values, social entrepreneurs care social value. Besides, social entrepreneurs are separated from commercial entrepreneurs with the aim of creating social value (Nicholls, 2006; Smith & Stevens, 2010). The main objective of your social entrepreneurship is to create social value for the public good; whereas commercial entrepreneurship aims to create profitable operations that generate private profits. In other words, on the basis of social entrepreneurship lies the motivation to create social value rather than increasing the wealth or profit of people or stakeholders (Austin, Stevenson, & Wei-Skillern, 2006). However, it would be wrong to say that social entrepreneurs are not completely related to economic values. That is to say, while creating social value is a priority focus for social entrepreneurs, economic or financial value creation is a requirement for sustainability and continuity of the enterprise, but it is the second plan (Smith-Hunter & College, 2008).

According to Santos (2009), while social entrepreneurship is a search for creating social value like social welfare, commercial entrepreneurship is a structure that captures social value because commercial entrepreneurship cares individual and organizational profit. At this point, social value creation can be regarded as a characteristic feature of social entrepreneurs and it can be said that the organizations of social entrepreneurs build their mission, vision, policies and procedures on strategies of creating social value (Di Domenico, Haugh, & Tracey, 2010).

As the necessity of these adopted mission, vision, policies and procedures, an analogue of the contribution of economic value created by entrepreneurship to economic development is carried out by social entrepreneurs in the context of social development through social values they create. In this sense, social entrepreneurs, who provide systematic and continuous solutions together with optimistic views on social congestion, make a direct contribution to the distance society receives in social development (Denizalp, 2009). Nevertheless, accepting that social values are created only by non-profit-making organizations and that they are unique to these organizations is a view that can be an obstacle for the development of the concept of social entrepreneurship. Because profit-oriented organizations, as well, have to create social value in order to survive and remain legitimate. Having the goal of profit is not that it will not create social value. Commercial entrepreneurs can also serve a social purpose, social change and transformation, indirectly by providing social benefits through the products and services they produce or the business opportunities they provide (Besler, 2010). In other words, it should not be overlooked that economic value contributes to the social value while bringing the results to the benefit of society (Emerson, 2003; Santos, 2009).

At this point, while referring to the concept of value from the perspective of entrepreneurship in terms of both "economic" and "social" sense, it is useful to refer to the concept of "blended value". Because the concept of blended value, proposed by Emerson is a concept that includes both social and economic values, considered to be important building blocks for social entrepreneurship (Emerson & Twersky, 1996; Certo & Miller, 2008).

Social problems such as poverty, unemployment (Kök & Mert, 2016), ignorance, environmental destruction, human rights violations (Bornstein & Davis, 2010), integration of minorities, drug addiction (Sastre-Castillo, 2015), occured as a result of every subject being cast into commercial affairs, have led people to look at life from a social window. The point of view of social entrepreneurship can be handled as in Table 1 in today's world, which is faced with countless problems that just mentioned (Kök & Mert, 2016).

As seen in Table 1, while initiatives in which social value is the primary driver are considered as non-profit organizations, the initiatives that are driving economic value are called commercial. While social enterprises are separated as profit-oriented or non-profit enterprises, they are also called as socially responsible businesses that separate some of their profits for social projects. The above-mentioned blended value conceptualized by Emerson appears to be a concept that guides social entrepreneurship.

If we define the concept of value as the outcome that is revealed by entrepreneurs at the end of entrepreneurship process; it can be said that all entrepreneurs who aim for profits or do not aim for profit are aiming to create economic, social and environmental values. When it comes to social entrepreneurship, what we are aiming for impact investing is the value we produce as a blended value. In summary, contrary to the pressure on the top, the blended value emerges as a reaction to the idea that value is only economic or just social. The blended value is seen as a composition of economic, social and environmental values. This composition refers to a new and stronger structure rather than the aggregation of individual parts (Bugg-Levine & Emerson, 2011).

After all these explanations on the concepts of value and social value; it is obvious that it is extremely important to explore and identify opportunities to create social value, to determine the ways to reach these opportunities, and to have the potential to realize these opportunities and to reach new resources in creating social value, hence, in social entrepreneurship (Besler, 2010).

The social entrepreneur who is trying to create social value for the solution of social problems is basically focusing on sustainable and systematic social change and transformation. At this point, it is worth mentioning the concept of social change and transformation.

Social Change and Transformation

The tremendous innovations and progress that humanity has made in science and technology in the last century have led to positive and negative changes and transformations of societies not only in these areas

Table 1. The relationship between social entrepreneurship and value

Non-Profit Traditional Charities	Social Enterprise			Socially Responsible Organizations	Commercial Organizations
No income.	Non-Profit leverage structuring: First aid is help.	Non-Profit hybrid structuring: Help and income generation.	Social Enterprise: income generation and income generation.	Distribution of the profits between social-oriented projects or corporate social responsibility projects.	Generating income at the highest level.

Source: (Kök & Mert, 2016)

but also in their lifestyles, social and cultural structures, economic systems and activities. In this respect, the concept of social change has also become one of the important topics addressed in recent years. Especially, with the increase of industrialization and therefore urbanization, the changes and problems that have taken place in the life of the individual and the society have caused this subject to be seriously considered by the researchers (Özdemir, 2011).

It can be said that in the modern world society is never stationary and that social, political and cultural changes are frequent across the society. Change can be initiated by governments, legal or administrative movements, organized citizens in social movements, movements from one culture to another (e.g. migration), or by planned or unplanned outcomes of technology. Some of the most dramatic social changes in modern times began with inventions such as motor cars, antibiotics, television and computers. Alteration also may come out with environmental factors such as drought, famine, and changes in economic or political advantage (Marshall, 2003). For this reason, today's theories of social change deal with events in a broad perspective ranging from global society to the family as a short and long-lasting, narrow and broad dimension. Sociologists also address changes that affect norms, values, behaviours, cultural meanings, and social relationships. In this context, it can be said that the concept of social change, in the simplest sense, expresses the change that can be observed in society structure (Erkal, 2006).

It is known that change is a visible change in any situation, event, or field in a specific time period. For this reason, when it is called "change," all beings must come to mind; when "social change" is mentioned, only human being must come to mind. Social change, which expresses the differentiation of the network of social relations that make up the structure of society and the institutions that determine them, redounds up worldviews through beliefs and values, norms such as patterns of thought, emotion and action (Arslantaş, 2008).

Ginsberg (1956) describes social change as a change in the social structure, that is, the change occurs in the size of the society, in the composition between the pieces or balance, or in the form of its organization (Kongar, 1995). Within this scope, when considering the elements in the social structure, social change can be stated as change in social relations and interactions (Yılmaz, 2014). However, every change that occurs in society cannot be defined as social change. According to the generally accepted view in the social sciences, the changes in the social system that cause the consequences of the functioning of the system and of the structure elements and their functioning, or of the relative importance of these structural elements are defined as social change. In other words, important and lasting changes in social relations can be characterized as social change (Dönmezer, 1989).

Parsons (1961) puts the concept of social change in terms of structure a triple separation: Change in social values, institutional change and change in people. Change in social values manifests itself as important structural changes. Social values are the general managers of attitudes and movements, and they have an important influence on social roles and relationships. In general, changes in the system of values of society take place in very long periods. Within the society, changes in statutes, roles and their norms and other organizational forms are institutional changes. The changes that occur in those who take positions and roles within the social system are the changes over the persons. These changes are not seen as structural changes. On the contrary, changes in rules and resources on the choice of the people who will assume social status and roles affect the structure of the social system and are regarded as structural changes in this respect.

Undoubtedly, there are some factors that affect social change. These factors can be put in order as,

Developments in science and technology, urbanization, demographic changes, changes in family life, changes and developments in economic and political structure, natural environmental factors, education factor, social and individual values, ideology and conflicts among people.

It is possible to add the changes and developments that take place in the fields of media, communication and arts to these factors. Each of these factors may have a stronger or weaker effect on social change depending on the time involved, the social conditions and the content of social items (Özdemir, 2011).

While social change and transformation have an impact on all the institutions that make up the society, it reveals the necessity of bringing the solution proposals that will be set up to meet the new needs brought by new information and technologies to an optimum level. Unless the problems that arise due to change and transformation in the social structure are resolved, the society is dragged into the whirlpool of insolubility and the life of the society is threatened by adding new problems to existing problems. At this point, social entrepreneurship phenomenon can show its face to us as a structure that meets social needs of the society (Yılmaz, 2014).

Social entrepreneurship, in its simplest and plainest sense, focuses on a permanent and systematic social change and transformation from the social and cultural values of society in the name of solving social problems, beyond helping and donating to needy people.

While entrepreneurship in the classical sense requires *agents of change*, in other words, *entrepreneurs* (Thompson, 1999), in this regard, Dees (1998), defining social entrepreneurs, emphasized the need for social entrepreneurs' activities to be focused on social change, describing them as intermediaries of high responsibility. According to Bornstein (2007), social entrepreneurs are those who are constantly working to create positive social change and who have the necessary skills, creativity and determination to solve existing problems, they are, in other words, transformative forces. The concept of "transformative power" that Bornstein characterized has become a point of emphasis in the definition of many social entrepreneurs. This concept emphasizes the task of finding a solution to the social problems that social entrepreneurs undertake in society and in this way changing the society positively.

Dacin et al. (2010) stated that the main goal in traditional entrepreneurship is economic gain, while in social entrepreneurship the goal is to create social change and to provide the society with well-being. In this context, Mair and Marti (2006) emphasized that social entrepreneurship is the process of motivating and accelerating social change. Social entrepreneurship aims at a social development with the solution of social problems while trying to mobilize social change on the one hand, on the other hand, by carrying out the change in the positive direction (Mengü, 2016a). In this sense, as well as social entrepreneurs are people to lead the way in solving social problems, not only to criticize the system or the problems, but also to engage in initiatives to promote change, transformation and social development (Betil, 2010).

Combing through many problems in the fields of health, education, economics and social life and tries to solve problems with sustainable solutions made the social entrepreneurship different from other solution ways and showed its importance in the context of social change (Coşkun, 2015). Social entrepreneurs who dedicate themselves to reducing or solving social problems produce a number of change strategies (Bloom & Chatterji, 2009). At this point, sometimes while social transformation is being completed, and sometimes as a social remains at a limited effect (Mengü, 2016a).

Social change and transformation can take place through private companies, non-governmental organizations, local governments, charities (Prahalad, 2005) and entrepreneurs who are particularly involved in social problems. In the struggle with social problems, while the solutions put forward by actors such as central government, local government, voluntary organizations, social movements, non-governmental organizations, businesses focus on a limited change that deals with the problem party, the solution offered by the social entrepreneur aims not only for the disadvantaged problem party but also for a broader transformation of the boundaries rather than a limited change by including the problem generating system. As a matter of fact, Alvord et al. (2004), Martin and Osberg (2007), Zahra et al. (2008), Noruzi et al. (2010) pointed out that the solution of the social enterprise in the sense of influence represents a social transformation beyond a limited change (Mengü, 2016b).

Using the social vision, capital, entrepreneurship and leadership skills they have, social entrepreneurs can make a social change through a mechanism that can create social benefits for people with social needs (Thompson, Alvy, & Lees, 2000). In addition, social entrepreneurs are those who have the ability to act by sensing social change opportunities, even if the environmental conditions are negative. By this means, social entrepreneurs may react differently to changes and developments in the environment. The fact that many new social enterprises can be established in the times of economic crisis, especially due to the increase in social needs and expectations in undeveloped or developing countries is an example for this situation (Besler, 2010).

One of the main characteristics of social enterprises is to aim for a systematic change in the solution of social problems and to gain social support in the long term with system change instead of trying to correct similar events one by one and to spread the solution of social problems. In this context, social enterprises try to provide opportunities to the strengthening of individuals and communities by producing radical solutions to the social problems of disadvantaged groups such as women, infants, elderly people and people with disabilities. In this case, commercial activity is a tool rather than an aim for direct social change.

SOLUTIONS AND RECOMMENDATIONS

Social entrepreneurship has an undeniable influence in solving and reducing social problems, in social development and progress, in better conditions for future generations, and in ensuring equal opportunity in society. In this sense, the adoption of social policies by the state to support and encourage social entrepreneurs, who have important efforts and contributions to the solution or reduction of social problems, will be important and beneficial in terms of social prosperity.

It should not be forgotten that social entrepreneurship serves as catalyst for the solution of many important social and environmental problems by bringing dynamism to the economy, it is necessary to raise awareness within the society and awareness creation about the social enterprises which take this important task as a mission. Hereby, individuals should be encouraged to become independent individuals who can act by thinking about others, and the feelings of solidarity and cooperation should be promoted and mediated for the promotion of social entrepreneurships.

Although there are many studies in the literature on the concept of social entrepreneurship, the number of studies that theoretically address social entrepreneurship is relatively small. In the theoretical studies in question, as the dimensions of social entrepreneurship are examined, the sociological basis of the concept is brushed over with several dimensions and handled superficially. However, the number of studies approaching the concept from the sociological perspective is very few. In these studies, it is seen that usually the concepts of social value creation and social change are in the foreground. For this reason, in order to fill this gap in the literature and contribute to the field, it will be advantageous to make researches dealing with the concept of social entrepreneurship from a sociological perspective and examine the concepts such as social problems, social benefits, social needs, social awareness and social movement from a holistic point of view besides the concepts of social value and change in the future researches.

CONCLUSION

In addition to establishing many profit-making businesses through commercial enterprises in order to meet the economic needs of people, there is also a need for social enterprises whose main focal point is not profitability in order to meet social needs. The main purpose of these enterprises is to create social benefits by recognizing the social problems in the society and taking the sensitivities of the society into account. The basic mission of social entrepreneurs is to create social value, thus pioneering and initiating social change and transformation in society.

The close relationship of social entrepreneurship with the society, which aims to create solutions for social problems by creating social value by putting the social mission at the focal point and aims at realizing a social transformation in this way, attracted attention of sociology discipline as a requirement of the interdisciplinary nature of the concept, led to the necessity of looking at the concept from sociological point of view. The "social" word in the essence of the concept of social entrepreneurship is at a guiding position at the point of sociological perspective of the concept. The word 'social' is fundamental both to distinguish the concept from the concept of entrepreneurship in the classical sense and to explain the sociological dimensions of the concept. The elements that add sociological meaning to the concept of social entrepreneurship can be lined up as social problem, social benefit, social mission and vision, social capital, social value, social change and transformation.

The concept of social problem emerges first when the concept is examined from a sociological point of view. Being in the first place are poverty and unemployment, in addition to lack of basic services such as sheltering, education, health and etc., gender inequality, child and maternal deaths, reintegrating disabled people into the society and employing them, problems such as the spread of diseases of HIV / AIDS etc. although differs according to the level of development of the countries, they constitute the main problems of all countries of the world. Despite the fact that the state is the leading actor in solving social problems, in many countries the state is inadequate to solve these and similar problems with public resources. In a society where social problems cannot be solved or reduced, social welfare cannot be seen and this situation can threaten the future of society, as well as social unity and solidarity cannot be achieved. At this point, social entrepreneur shows his/her face as the person with a social purpose through the social awareness that takes action by becoming aware of social problems in society. Thus, social entrepreneurship is an important institution in the social structure as a mechanism to alleviate the burden of the state in solving or reducing social problems.

When we look at the concept of social entrepreneurship from a sociological perspective, the second concept that comes to mind is social benefit. It would not be wrong to express social benefit as 'social entrepreneurship' by activating the awareness of social problems in line with the principles of entrepreneurship. A social entrepreneur is someone who dreams and thinks of creating a social benefit out of profitability by exhibiting an altruistic, self-sacrificing and voluntary behavior after identifying social problems. Through social problem solving, social entrepreneurs try to be beneficial to those who are in need, and at second hand, to be beneficial to the society, and to engage in activities that social benefit.

In addition to social benefit, social mission and vision are other concepts which are discussed from the sociological perspective. What makes the social entrepreneur, who is aware of social problems and using entrepreneurship principles to create social benefits, unique, effective and meaningful is his/her mission which he/she uses in the direction of the relevant means. The most important mission of social entrepreneurship is to create social value. The change and development of the created mission needs to be achieved with a dynamic approach towards social problems. The vision of social entrepreneurs is to take on the role of an exchange agent by carrying out activities that will serve the community and create social benefits. Another element that a social entrepreneur needs in realizing the role of change agent is social capital. Social capital, which is a concept that makes great differences in reaching larger networks and resources as well as in the struggle to survive, plays an important role in reaching the mission and vision of the social entrepreneur.

When social entrepreneurship, which we have stated that the basic mission is to create social value, is approached from the sociological perspective, it can be said that the concept of social value is one of the most important and critical concepts for social entrepreneurship. Many definitions of social entrepreneurship in the literature suggest that the most basic meaning expressed by the social word in the concept is social value. Therefore, the main purpose of social entrepreneurship, which is based on the recognition of social problems on the basis of social problems, is to take on the role of an agent of change by creating social value, in other words to be a pioneer in social change and transformation.

The last concept we have dealt with from a sociological perspective is social change and transformation for the concept of social entrepreneurship in which social change is aimed. We can say that society in the modern world is never static and that social, political and cultural changes are often seen throughout society. Social entrepreneurship, as well, takes its place for social change and transformation in this change popularity. Along with being the pioneers in solving social problems, social entrepreneurs are not only those who criticize the system or the problems, but also those who are attempting to open the way for transformation and social development.

To sum up, social entrepreneur is the person who channeled all capital, knowledge, skills and experience into creating social value by providing social benefit and thus initiating and maintaining social change and transformation.

REFERENCES

Agafonow, A. (2014). Toward A Positive Theory of Social Entrepreneurship. On Maximizing Versus Satisficing Value Capture. *Journal of Business Ethics*, *125*(4), 709–713. doi:10.100710551-013-1948-z

Ağca, V., & Böyükaslan, H. D. (2016). Aile işletmelerinde iç girişimciliğin sosyal girişimciliğe etkisi: Afyonkarahisar'da bir araştırma. *Kastamonu Üniversitesi İktisadi ve İdari Bilimler Fakültesi Dergisi*, *13*, 200–220.

Aksan, G. (2016). Max Weber ve değerler sosyolojisi: Bir metodolojik ikilemin düşündürdükleri. *SEFAD*, *35*(35), 427–446. doi:10.21497efad.35126

Alvarez, S. A., & Barney, J. B. (2007). Discovery and creation: Alternative theories of entrepreneurial action. *Strategic Entrepreneurship Journal*, *1*(1–2), 11–26. doi:10.1002ej.4

Alvord, S. H., Brown, L. D., & Letts, C. W. (2004). Social entrepreneurship and societal transformation. *The Journal of Applied Behavioral Science*, *40*(3), 260–282. doi:10.1177/0021886304266847

Antoni, G. D. (2016). The emergence of social enterprises through the initiative of self-organized citizens: An analysis starting from Olson's approach to the logic of collective action. *International Review of Sociology*, *26*(1), 19–30. doi:10.1080/03906701.2016.1148335

Argüden, Y. (2005). Sosyal girişimcilik. In A. Bozgeyik (Ed.), *Girişimcilere yol haritası* (pp. 80–82). İstanbul: Hayat Yayınları.

Arslantaş, H. A. (2008). Sosyal değişme, kentleşme ve kentlileşmenin din üzerine etkileri. *İlahiyat Fakültesi Dergisi, 13*(2), 171-196.

Aslan, G., Araza, A., & Bulut, Ç. (2012). Sosyal girişimciliğin kavramsal çerçevesi. *Journal of Entrepreneurship and Development*, *7*(2), 69–88.

Austin, J., Stevenson, H., & Wei-Skillern, J. (2006). Social and commercial entrepreneurship: Same, different, or both? *Entrepreneurship Theory and Practice*, *30*(1), 1–22. doi:10.1111/j.1540-6520.2006.00107.x

Aytaç, Ö. (2002). *Sosyoloji/bir giriş denemesi*. Elazığ: Üniversite Kitabevi.

Aytaç, Ö. (2006). Girişimcilik: Sosyo-kültürel bir perspektif. *Dumlupınar Üniversitesi Sosyal Bilimler Dergisi*, *15*, 139–160.

Aytaç, Ö., & İlhan, S. (2007). Girişimcilik ve girişimcikültür: Sosyolojik bir perspektif. *Selçuk Üniversitesi Sosyal Bilimler Enstitüsü Dergisi*, *18*, 101–120.

Barendsen, L., & Gardner, H. (2004). Is the social entrepreneur a new type of leader? *Leader to Leader*, *34*(34), 43–50. doi:10.1002/ltl.100

Besler, S. (2010). *Sosyal girişimcilik*. İstanbul: Beta Yayınevi.

Betil, İ. (2010). Sivil toplum, sosyal sermaye, sosyal girişimcilik. *Journal of Entrepreneurship and Development*, *5*(1), 21–25.

Bhawe, N., Jain, T. K., & Gupta, V. K. (2006). *The entrepreneurship of the Good Samaritan: A development framework to understand social entrepreneurship using insights from qualitative study*. Retrieved 10.06.2017, from https://papers.ssrn.com/sol3/papers.cfm?abstract_id=902685

Bloom, N. P., & Chatterji, K. A. (2009). Scaling social entrepreneurship impact. *California Management Review*, *51*(3), 114–133. doi:10.2307/41166496

Bornstein, D. (2007). *How to change the world: Social entrepreneurs and the power of new ideas*. Oxford University Press.

Bornstein, D., & Davis, S. (2010). *Social entrepreneurship: What everyone needs to know*. New York: Oxford University Press, Inc.

Bozeman, B. (2007). *Public values and public interest: Counterbalancing economic individualism*. Washington, DC: Georgetown University Press.

Bridge, S., O'Neill, K., & Cromie, S. (1998). *Understanding enterprise, entrepreneurship and small firms*. London: Macmillan. doi:10.1007/978-1-349-26171-0

Bugg-Levine, A., & Emerson, J. (2011). Impact investing: Transforming how we make money while making a difference. *Innovations*, *6*(3), 9–18. doi:10.1162/INOV_a_00077

Certo, S. T., & Miller, T. (2008). Social entrepreneurship: Key issues and concepts. *Business Horizons*, *51*(4), 267–271. doi:10.1016/j.bushor.2008.02.009

Chell, E. (2007). Social enterprise and entrepreneurship: Towards a convergent theory of the entrepreneurial process. *International Small Business Journal*, *25*(5), 5–26. doi:10.1177/0266242607071779

Cho, A. H. (2006). Politics, values and social entrepreneurship: A critical appraisal. In J. Mair, J. Robinson, & K. Hockerts (Eds.), *Social entrepreneurship* (pp. 34–56). New York: Palgrave Macmillan. doi:10.1057/9780230625655_4

Cope, J., Jack, S., & Rose, M. B. (2007). Social capital and entrepreneurship. *International Small Business Journal*, *25*(3), 213–219. doi:10.1177/0266242607076523

Coşkun, E. (2015). *Gönüllü kuruluşların okul öncesi sosyal girişimcilik eğitimindeki rolü.* Yalova University Masters's Thesis.

Dacin, P. A., Dacin, M. T., & Matear, M. (2010). Social entrepreneurship: Why we don't need a new theory and how we move forward from here. *The Academy of Management Perspectives*, *24*(3), 37–57. doi:10.5465/AMP.2010.52842950

Dees, J. G. (1998). *The meaning of social entrepreneurship*. Retrieved 03.03.2017, from http://www.redalmarza.cl/ing/pdf/TheMeaningofsocialEntrepreneurship.pdf

Dees, J. G., Emerson, J., & Economy, P. (2001). *Enterprising nonprofits: A toolkit for social entrepreneurs*. New York: John Wiley and Sons, Inc.

Denizalp, H. (2009). *Toplumsal dönüşüm için sosyal girişimcilik rehberi*. Ankara: Sivil Toplum Geliştirme Merkezi.

Di Domenico, M., Haugh, H., & Tracey, P. (2010). Social bricolage: Theorizing social value creation in social enterprises. *Entrepreneurship Theory and Practice*, *34*(4), 681–703. doi:10.1111/j.1540-6520.2010.00370.x

Dönmezer, S. (1989). Atatürk inkılâpları ve sosyal değişme teorileri. *Atatürk Araştırma Merkezi Dergisi*, *5*(15), 523–537.

Emerson, J. (2003). The blended value proposition: Integrating social and financial returns. *California Management Review*, *45*(4), 35–51. doi:10.2307/41166187

Emerson, J., & Twersky, F. (1996). *New social entrepreneurs: The success, challenge, and lessons of non-profit enterprise creation*. San Francisco: Roberts Foundation.

Entrepreneur. (n.d.). Retrieved 01.03.2017, from https://www.merriam-webster.com/dictionary/entrepreneurship

Erkal, M. E. (2006). *Sosyoloji*. İstanbul: Der Yayınları.

Ersen, T. B., Kaya, D., & Meydanoğlu, Z. (2010). *Sosyal girişimler ve Türkiye: İhtiyaç analizi raporu*. TÜSEV Yayınları.

Estrin, S., Mickiewicz, T., & Stephan, U. (2013). Entrepreneurship, social capital, and institutions: Social and commercial entrepreneurship across nations. *Entrepreneurship Theory and Practice*, *37*(May), 479–504. doi:10.1111/etap.12019

Felício, J. A., Gonçalves, H. M., & Gonçalves, V. C. (2013). Social value and organizational performance in non-profit social organizations: Social entrepreneurship, leadership, and socioeconomic context effects. *Journal of Business Research*, *66*(10), 2139–2146. doi:10.1016/j.jbusres.2013.02.040

Fichter, J. (2001). *Sosyoloji nedir?* Ankara: Atilla Kitabevi.

Fowler, A. (2000). NGDOs as a moment in history: Beyond aid social entrepreneurship or civic innovation. *Third World Quarterly*, *21*(4), 637–654. doi:10.1080/713701063

Fukuyama, F. (1995). *Trust*. New York: Free Press Paperbacks.

Gibb, A. A. (1987). Enterprise culture - its meaning and implications for education and training. *Journal of European Industrial Training*, *11*(2), 2–38. doi:10.1108/eb043365

Glancey, K. S., & McQuaid, R. W. (2000). *Entrepreneurial economics*. New York: St. Martin's Press, Inc. doi:10.1057/9780333981245

Gonçalves, C. P., Carrara, K., & Schmittel, R. M. (2016). The phenomenon of social enterprises: Are we keeping watch on this cultural practice? *Voluntas*, *27*(4), 1585–1610. doi:10.100711266-015-9624-9

Görün, M., & Kara, M. (2010). Kentsel dönüşüm ve sosyal girişimcilik bağlamında Türkiye'de kentsel yaşam kalitesinin artırılması. *The Journal of American Science*, *8*(2), 140–164.

Hasan, S. (2005). Social capital and social entrepreneurship in Asia: Analysing the links. *Asia Pacific Journal Of Public Administration*, *27*(1), 1–17. doi:10.1080/23276665.2005.10779296

Hervieux, C., Gedajlovic, E., & Turcotte, M. F. B. (2010). The legitimization of social entrepreneurship. *Journal of Enterprising Communities: People and Places in the Global Economy*, *4*(1), 37–67. doi:10.1108/17506201011029500

Jamrozik, A., & Nocella, L. (1998). *The sociology of social problems: Theoretical perspectives and methods of intervention*. Cambridge University Press. doi:10.1017/CBO9780511819629

Koçak, O., & Kavi, E. (2014). Sosyal politika aktörü olarak sosyal girişimci belediyecilik. *Hak-İş Uluslararası Emek ve Toplum Dergisi*, *3*(6), 26–49.

Koe Hwee Nga, J., & Shamuganathan, G. (2010). The influence of personality traits and demographic factors on social entrepreneurship start up intentions. *Journal of Business Ethics*, *95*(2), 259–282. doi:10.100710551-009-0358-8

Kök, S. B., & Mert, E. (2016). *Girişimcilikte sosyal değer inşası: Sosyal girişimcilik*. Retrieved 06.07.2017, from https://www.avekon.org/papers/1514.pdf

Kongar, E. (1995). *Toplumsal değişme kuramları ve Türkiye gerçeği*. İstanbul.

Korosec, R., & Berman, E. (2006, May). Municipal support for social entrepreneurship. *Public Administration Review*, 446–460.

Kümbül Güler, B. (2008). Yoksullukla mücadelede sosyal girişimcilik: Ashoka üyelerinden örnek uygulamalar. *I. Ulusal Çalışma İlişkileri Kongresi Bildiriler Kitabı*, 816-838.

Kümbül Güler, B. (2010). *Sosyal Girişimcilik*. Ankara: Efil Yayınevi.

Kümbül Güler, B. (2011). Yoksullukla mücadelede sosyal girişimcilik: Ashoka üyelerinden sosyal yenilikçi örnek uygulamalar. *Sosyal Bilimler Enstitüsü Dergisi*, *13*(3), 79–111.

Light, P. (2005). *Searching for social entrepreneurship: Who might they be, where they might be found, what they do?* Paper presented at the Association for Research on Nonprofit and Voluntary Associations.

Light, P. C. (2008). *The search for social entrepreneurship*. Washington, DC: Brookings Institution Press.

Luthans, F., Luthans, K. W., & Luthans, B. C. (2004). Positive psychological capital: Beyond human and social capital. *Business Horizons*, *47*(1), 45–50. doi:10.1016/j.bushor.2003.11.007

Mair, J., & Marti, I. (2006). Social entrepreneurship research: A source of explanation, prediction and delight. *Journal of World Business*, *41*(1), 36–44. doi:10.1016/j.jwb.2005.09.002

Marshall, G. (2003). *Change, Social Change. In Oxford Dictionary Of Sociology*. Oxford University Press.

Martin, R. L., & Osberg, S. (2007, Spring). Social entrepreneurship: The case for definition. *Stanford Social Innovation Review*, 28–39.

Mengü, E. (2016a). *Sosyolojik perspektiften sosyal girişimcilik olgusu*. İstanbul University Master's Thesis.

Mengü, E. (2016b). *Yoksullukla mücadelede sosyal girişimcilik: Grameen mikrokredi modeli*. Yalova University Master's Thesis.

Miller, T. L., & Wesley, C. L. II. (2010). Assessing mission and resources for social change: An organizational identity perspective on social venture capitalists' decision criteria. *Entrepreneurship Theory and Practice*, *34*(4), 705–733. doi:10.1111/j.1540-6520.2010.00388.x

Monroe-White, T. (2014). Creating public value: An examination of technological social enterprise. In L. Pate & C. Wankel (Eds.), *Emerging research directions in social entrepreneurship* (pp. 85–109). Springer. doi:10.1007/978-94-007-7896-2_6

Mort, G. S., Weerawardena, J., & Carnegie, K. (2003). Social entrepreneurship: Towards conceptualisation. *International Journal of Nonprofit and Voluntary Sector Marketing*, *8*(1), 76–88. doi:10.1002/nvsm.202

Nicholls, A. (2006). *Social entrepreneurship: New models of sustainable social change*. Oxford, UK: Oxford University Press.

Özdemir, S. M. (2011). Toplumsal değişme ve küreselleşme bağlamında eğitim ve eğitim programları: Kavramsal bir çözümleme. *Ahi Evran Üniversitesi Eğitim Fakültesi Dergisi*, *12*(1), 85–110.

Özdevecioğlu, M., & Cingöz, A. (2009). Sosyal girişimcilik ve sosyal girişimciler: Teorik çerçeve. *Erciyes Üniversitesi İktisadi ve İdari Bilimler Fakültesi Dergisi*, *32*, 81–95.

Özensel, E. (2003). Sosyolojik bir olgu olarak değer. *Değerler Eğitimi Dergisi*, *1*(3), 217–239.

Özkalp, E. (2003). Kültür. In E. Özkalp (Ed.), *Davranış bilimlerine giriş*. Eskişehir: Anadolu Üniversitesi Yayınları.

Parsons, T. (1961). Some considerations on the theory of social change. *Rural Sociology*, *26*(3), 219–239.

Peredo, A. M., & McLean, M. (2006). Social entrepreneurship: A critical review of the concept. *Journal of World Business*, *41*(1), 56–65. doi:10.1016/j.jwb.2005.10.007

Perrini, F., & Vurro, C. (2006). Social entrepreneurship: Innovation and social change across theory and practice. In J. Mair, J. Robinson, & K. Hockerts (Eds.), *Social entrepreneurship* (pp. 57–85). Palgrave MacMillian. doi:10.1057/9780230625655_5

Prabhu, G. (1999). Social entrepreneurial leadership. *Career Development International*, *4*(3), 140–145. doi:10.1108/13620439910262796

Prahalad, C. K. (2005). *The Fortune at the Bottom of the Pyramid*. Wharton School Publishing.

Rennie, H. G. (2006). Social entrepreneurship and regional economic development: A conceptual framework. In J. Gatrell & N. Reid (Eds.), *Enterprising world* (pp. 257–270). Springer. doi:10.1007/1-4020-5226-X_21

Robinson, J. (2006). Navigating social and institutional barriers to markets: How social entrepreneurs identify and evaluate opportunities. In J. Mair, J. Robinson, & K. Hockerts (Eds.), *Social entrepreneurship* (pp. 95–120). New York: Palgrave MacMillan. doi:10.1057/9780230625655_7

Santos, F. M. (2009). *A positive theory of social entrepreneurship*. Retrieved 12.03.2017, from https://sites.insead.edu/facultyresearch/research/doc.cfm?did=41727

Santos, F. M. (2012). A positive theory of social entrepreneurship. *Journal of Business Ethics*, *111*(3), 335–351. doi:10.100710551-012-1413-4

Sastre-Castillo, M. A., Peris-Ortiz, M., & Danvila-Del Valle, I. (2015). What is different about the profile of the social entrepreneur? *Nonprofit Management & Leadership*, *25*(4), 349–369. doi:10.1002/nml.21138

Schuyler, G. (1998). *Social entrepreneurship: Profit as a means, not an end*. Retrieved 12.03.2017, from http://files.eric.ed.gov/fulltext/ED434219.pdf

Seyyar, A. (2005). *Sosyal güvenlik terimleri*. İstanbul: Papatya Yayınları.

Sharir, M., & Lerner, M. (2006). Gauging the success of social ventures initiated by individual social entrepreneurs. *Journal of World Business*, *41*(1), 6–20. doi:10.1016/j.jwb.2005.09.004

Sivathanu, B., & Bhise, P. (2013). *Challenges for social entrepreneurship, international journal of application or innovation in engineering and management*. Retrieved 16.05.2017, from http://www.ijaiem.org/RATMIG-2013/MGT%2025%20Challenges%20for%20Social%20Entrepreneurship.pdf

Smith, B. R., & Stevens, C. E. (2010). Different types of social entrepreneurship: The role of geography and embeddedness on the measurement and scaling of social value. *Entrepreneurship and Regional Development, 22*(6), 575–598. doi:10.1080/08985626.2010.488405

Smith-Hunter, A. E., & College, S. (2008). Toward multidimensional model of social entrepreneurship: Definitions, clarifications and theoretical perspectives. *Journal of Business & Economics Research, 6*(6), 93–112.

Social Impact. (n.d.). Retrieved 13.05.2017, from https://sosyaletkianalizi.ku.edu.tr/sayfa/tanimlar

Tan, W. L., Williams, J., & Tan, T. M. (2005). Defining the 'Social' in 'Social entrepreneurship': Altruism and entrepreneurship. *The International Entrepreneurship and Management Journal, 1*(3), 353–365. doi:10.100711365-005-2600-x

Thompson, J. J. (1999). The world of the entrepreneur - a new perspective. *Journal of Workplace Learning-Counselling Today, 11*(6), 209–224. doi:10.1108/13665629910284990

Thompson, J. L. (2002). The world of the social entrepreneur. *International Journal of Public Sector Management, 15*(5), 412–431. doi:10.1108/09513550210435746

Thompson, J. L., Alvy, G., & Lees, A. (2000). Social entrepreneurship: A new look at the people and the potential. *Management Decision, 38*(5), 328–338. doi:10.1108/00251740010340517

Thornton, P. H. (1999). The sociology of entrepreneurship. *Annual Review of Sociology, 25*(1), 19–46. doi:10.1146/annurev.soc.25.1.19

Trivedi, C., & Stokols, D. (2011). Social enterprises and corporate enterprises. *The Journal of Entrepreneurship, 20*(1), 1–32. doi:10.1177/097135571002000101

Value. (n.d.). Retrieved 10.03.2017, from https://www.merriam-webster.com/dictionary/value

Verheul, I., Wennekers, S., Audretsch, D., & Thurik, R. (2001). *An eclectic theory of entrepreneurship: Policies, institutions and culture.* Retrieved 10.03.2017 from, https://www.econstor.eu/bitstream/10419/85867/1/01030.pdf

Williams, D. A., & K'nife, K. A. K. (2012). The dark side of social entrepreneurship. *International Journal of Entrepreneurship, 16*, 63–75.

Yazıcı, M. (2014). Değerler ve toplumsal yapıda sosyal değerlerin yeri. *Fırat Üniversitesi Sosyal Bilimler Dergisi, 24*(1), 209–223.

Yılmaz, A. S. (2014). Bir sosyal değişim ajanı olarak girişimcilik eğitimi. *Journal of World of Turks, 6*(1), 297–310.

Young, R. (2006). For what it is worth: Social value and the future of social entrepreneurship. In A. Nichols (Ed.), *Social entrepreneurship: New models of sustainable social change* (pp. 56–73). Oxford University Press.

Yumuş, S. (2017). *Orhan Kemal'in romanlarında sosyal değerler.* Uludağ University, Master's Thesis.

Yunus, M. (2006). Social business entrepreneurs are the solution. In A. Nichols (Ed.), *Social entrepreneurship: New models of sustainable social change* (pp. 39–44). Oxford, UK: Oxford University Press.

Zahra, S., Rawhouser, H. N., Bhawe, N., Neubaum, D. O., & Hayton, J. C. (2008). Globalization of social entrepreneurship. *Strategic Entrepreneurship Journal*, *2*(2), 117–131. doi:10.1002ej.43

Zamantılı Nayır, D., & Karataş Gümüştaş, N. (2017). Belagat (retorik) ne sağlar? Sosyal girişimcilerin meşruiyet kazanma çabaları. *25. Ulusal Yönetim ve Organizasyon Bildiriler Kitabı,* 40-47.

KEY TERMS AND DEFINITIONS

Social Benefit: Refers to individuals' benefit from a positive social outcome of a planned and viable social enterprise, activity or movement, either materially or spiritually, in a way that enhances the welfare of the target group or the community.

Social Capital: Refers to the establishment, maintenance of social networks, and being in norms of behavior to maintain these networks.

Social Change: Refers to the changes that occur on the elements of the social system and its functioning or on the relative importance of these building elements and give rise to consequences for the execution in terms of the function of the system.

Social Mission: Refers to the reason for the existence of a social entrepreneur whose goal in the basis is to create a social value by solving social problems.

Social Problem: Refers to social situations, processes, regulations or attitudes that are perceived as undesirable and negatively, threatening social cohesion, laws, legislations, social institutions, economic welfare and the stability and future of individual freedoms.

Social Value: Refers to the reinforcing and encircling principles and beliefs that guide individuals in their lives, which direct their preferences, as well as the differentiation of societies and the unification of societies.

Social Vision: Refers to where the social entrepreneur sees his/her enterprise, where he/she locates his/her enterprise (Such as being a pioneer in social change and transformation by creating social value).

ENDNOTE

1 Marcus Garvey's motto from Monroe-White, 2014: 85.

Chapter 3
The Social Entrepreneur:
Personality Traits and Motivation Factors in Social Entrepreneurship

Beliz Ülgen
Istanbul Commerce University, Turkey

ABSTRACT

Although social entrepreneurs have some common characteristics with business or commercial entrepreneurs, undoubtedly they differ in many ways. In this chapter, social entrepreneurs are highlighted with their core personality traits and motivation factors that are different from the other entrepreneurs. In the beginning, the definitions of social entrepreneurs put forward by different authorities were presented. Immediately after these definitions, the three main typologies—social bricoleurs, social constructionists, social engineers—and their characteristics were examined. By its nature and purpose, a social enterprise needs some specific entrepreneurial traits and driving factors. In the last section of this chapter, these personality traits and motivation factors were discussed.

INTRODUCTION

Today, on the one hand scarcity of natural resources against the growing population, the dizzying speed of change, technological improvements and on the other hand financial, political and environmental crises cause to serious social problems such as poverty, unemployment, disability, epidemics or environmental pollution (Bornstein & Davis, 2010). The existence of social enterprises provides a meaningful value in reducing these mentioned problems.

When considering sustainability, there are different definitions and interpretations about social entreprises are included in the literature. Providing social benefits to society, managing social issues effectively are accepted as the most important aims of social entreprises in some literature (Weerawardena & Sullivan Mort, 2001) but in others, social entreprises are defined as sustainable ventures (Wolk, 2008) and their primary aim is to achieve sustainability by realizing both economic and social missions as like in profit organizations (Zhang & Swanson, 2014). According to Burkett (2010) financial sustainability and

DOI: 10.4018/978-1-5225-5687-9.ch003

social impact are two precursors of social entreprises' sustainability. Alter and Dawans (2006) associate the sustainability of social enterprises with the integration which places among leadership competence, financial capacity and work-oriented culture (Jamburia, 2013).

Although there are so many factors influence the success of social entrepreneurship, social entrepreneurs' personality traits and motivator factors may seen as antecedant factors. According to Bikse et al. (2015) social entrepreneurs have social vision, high sense of social responsibility, wide range of entrepreneurial skills and social competences. They diagnose and solve social problems not only at local area, but also they are in tendency to expand their activities globally (Bikse, Rivza, & Riemere, 2015).

Risk taking, innovativeness, self confidence and achievement orientation are some of similar personality traits of social entrepreneurs with business entrepreneurs. The nature and main theme of social enterprises require different personality traits such as empathy, compassion and altruism. In terms of motivation intrinsic rewards are more effective than extrinsic ones on the motivation of social entrepreneurs. Prosocial motivation, recognizing social opportunities, personal life experince and close support of the actors in social network can be defined as prominent motivating factors of social entrepreneurs.

BACKGROUND

Social entrepreneurs are different because their main aim is to establish a business which completely concentrates on social concerns, produce sustainable and effective benefits to society. Some of them try to help physically or mentally ill or disabled people, the others interest with environment protection, hunger and poverty, some of them provide education facilities to dropouts, produce medical and assistive devices for needs to ease their life. They place great importance to social values as well as financial ones and invest earnings to their own social mission instead of sharing with stakeholders (Boschee, 2006).

Some may have been influenced by a role model or guide behaviors or considerations in which they have close relationships in childhood, and may have decided to be social entrepreneurs by directing this role model.

Before becoming social entrepreneur, some of them may be working in different professions as designers, engineers, teachers, doctors or business people. They shift to social entrepreneurship because of family crises or problems in their immediate environment. On the other hand, some of them may have been affected by the behaviors or thoughts of a role model, with whom they had a close relationship during childhood. With the guidance of this role model, they may have decided to become a social entrepreneur. Alice Teppee Marlin, is one of these social entrepreneurs. At her young ages, her father and she regularly visited the Lower East Side of New York City where a large number of poor people live in difficult conditions. Whereby these visits, she had the opportunity to meet these people and their needs closely. Today she is founder of Social Accountability International (Bornstein & Davis, 2010).

Social Accountability International aims to enhance and advance the human rights and working conditions at work places in all over the world. SAI established SA8000 Standard which reflects labor provisions contained within the Universal Declaration of Human Rights and International Labour Organization (ILO) conventions and currently helps secure ethical working conditions for two million workers. Forced and Compulsory Labor, Freedom of Association and Right to Collective Bargaining, Child Labor, Discrimination, Health and Safety, Working Hours, Management System and Remuneration are the main elements of SA 8000 Standard. On the other hand, Social Accountability International helps companies in some processes such as building management systems for sustainable improvements, developing partnerships with external stakeholders, providing effective solutions to complex issues and encouraging a sense of ownership.

DEFINITIONS ABOUT SOCIAL ENTREPRENEUR

In the definition of Thake and Zadek (1997), social entrepreneurs have an enthusiasm to realize social justice. They aim to build a meaningful tie between their actions and the life quality of the people with whom they interest and desire to serve. They effort to create worthfile solutions related with society, organizations, economy and environment.

According to Dees (1998) social entrepreneurs are change agents in the social sector by:

1) adopting a mission to create and sustain social value; 2) recognizing and relentlessly pursuing new opportunities to serve that mission; 3) engaging in a process of continuous innovation, adaptation and learning; 4) acting boldly without being limited by resources currently in hand and; 5) exhibiting a heightened sense of accountability to the constituencies served and for the outcomes created (Lönnström, 2015; Fayolle & Matlay, 2010; Brooks, 2009).

Social entrepreneurs may seen as the reformers and revolutionaries of the society. They have an immense social vision which distinguish them from other entrepreneurs. They make a great effort to investigate all opportunities to meet all social needs and create valuable changes to improve the society. The extent of the area where they act is not so important. Their actions which point a certain social case in health, unemployment, education, peace and conflict resolution, environment, poverty, homelessness, women's equality (Praszkier & Nowak, 2011) or in any other societal dilemma may be limited only in local area or these actions may be taken for global advances (Dees, Emerson, & Economy, 2001). All activities of social entrepreneurs are directed to a specific social mission which carries a social value to each matters needed in society. On the one hand they try to achieve profit-oriented and social activities successfully, on the other hand they aim to expand the scope of these activities (Abu-Saifan, 2012).

Even though they have some common skills and personality traits, there are some differences between social entrepreneurs and business entrepreneurs. One of them is related with their purposes. Social entrepreneurs aim to spread social impact about any social problem which cannot be solved or realized by public or private institutions. On the other hand business entrepreneurs aim to increase their profit, share values and effort to retain existing customers and attract new ones. Social entrepreneurs mostly have struggle with uncertainties and constraints in financing their activities (Bornstein & Davis, 2010). According to Samer Abu-Saifan, the main objective of social entrepreneurs is to success their own social mission which includes all kind of innovative, reformative and social value based activities or changes (Bikse, Rivza, & Riemere, 2015) as they planned while business entrepreneurs' objective is to improve economic opportunities or financial gains (Abu-Saifan, 2012). However, from these explanations, it should not be excluded that social entrepreneurs do not care or pay attention to improve their financial earnings (Martin & Osberg, 2007). For creating new social benefits, they need to use these earnings.

TYPES OF SOCIAL ENTREPRENEURS

Three types of social entrepreneurs- *Social Bricoleur, Social Constructionist* and *Social Engineer-* were propounded by Hayak, Kirzner and Schumpeter (Zahra, Gedajlovic, Neubaum, & Shulman, 2009).

1. **Social Bricoleurs:** In 1962, anthropologist Claude Levi-Strauss used the term of bricologe which describes building or creating a new thing with whatever at hand (Martin & Osberg, 2007). After this definition at first Hayek then Baker and Nelson adopted the term of bricologe to entrepreneurial field. According to them, bricoleurs effort to create new alternatives by existing resources against to restrictions by government or some policies (Baker & Nelson, 2005).

Generally *Social Bricoleurs* concentrate on local based social concerns such as lack of education, health services or security of life. By their nature, social bricoleurs are motivated by solving local problems with available sources and opportunities in immediate environment. They need to diagnose and analyse any local social problem or need by considering environmental conditons and evaluating the situation from geographic or cultural aspects and to gather implicit knowledge. The most compeller issue for these entrepreneurs is to improve limited amount of local sources (Smith & Stevens, 2010).

Social Bricoleurs dedicate themselves to adress or discover social needs and they use their own qualifications-expertise and experience- to improve social wealth. They aim to create high level of utilitarian value in their local area. They perform all their activities far away from their egos and ambitions. Oswaldo Tell is a good example from Peru for this type of entrepreneurs. He is owner of North Peru Investment Company and also he founded the Center for Innovation and Business Development as a non-profit organization (Zahra, Gedajlovic, Neubaum, & Shulman, 2009). Another example is Bunker Roy who is an Indian social bricoleur. He founded Barefoot College in Rajasthan. The college aims to fulfill the education need of local community especially poor women (Williams & Gurtoo, 2016). In different regions from Africa to Himalayas, Roy educated women as solar engineers therefore they electrified their distant villages.

2. **Social Constructionists:** The other type *Social Constructionists* who aim to create new approches or solutions to large scaled social concerns. In contrast to *Social Bricoleurs*, they need to very extensive knowledge which has to be obtained from various sources instead of local knowledge. The large scope of social problem- it can affect regionally, nationally and even globally- leads *Social Constructionists* to establish sizable and integrated organizations (Lönnström, 2015). Their main advantage stem comes from their abilities and capacity to aware and manage a wide variety of opportunities, sources and create complex processes to develop social wealth (Zahra, Gedajlovic, Neubaum, & Shulman, 2009). Social Constructionists are more proactive than others to diagnose and identify the gaps and opportunities in the social market. Their solutions do not only appeal to local concerns but also can be applied in a wide range of contexts (Smith & Stevens, 2010). Jacqueline Novogratz is an American Social Constructionist and founder of Acumen Fund which is a non-profit organization. The fund aims to solve the global poverty problems by delivering goods and services to all destitute regions of the world.
3. **Social Engineers:** These type of entrepreneurs serve to realise extensive social aims. Social Engineers work as transformational agents in social entrepreneurial field. They mainly concentrate

on big scaled and complex issues which need mass solutions and support. On the other hand they have to use deep and comprehensive knowledge from various sources (Smith & Stevens, 2010).

When compared with the others, Social Engineers act as pioneers of innovation and of change related with any social concern. Their tendency is to destroy all existing institutions, systems, procedures or structures to build the new and more utilitarian or efficient ones. They have very deep and strong influence on society. Generally all reformist actions or fundamental social changes which are displayed by Social Entrepreneurs are interpreted as a threat by some other organizations or institutions. These actions can be taken towards addressing national, international or global problems or needs. They have an unbounded social vision and high level of capacity to bring together the mass amount of resources (Zahra, Gedajlovic, Neubaum, & Shulman, 2009). Muhammed Yunus is one of Social Engineers. He founded Grameen Bank in Bangladesh. The Bank aimed to provide micro credits without any security deposit to borrowers 97 percent of whom are women living below the poverty treshold. According to the system which was built by Muhammed Yunus, all borrowers are security deposits of each other and in this way they become naturally Grameen Bank's stockholder and they are involved in the Bank's management. All of them are responsible for well-being of themselves, peers or other applicants and lastly the well-being of Grameen Bank. The sucess model of Gramen Bank has spread all over the world and it has been applied in different countries. One of them is in the United States *The Good Faith Fund* and the other is the Amanah Ikhtiar in Malaysia (Müler, 2012; Bhawuk, Mrazek, & Munusamy, 2009).

Table 1 consists of the differences among these three typologies.

PERSONALITY OF SOCIAL ENTREPRENEUR

Social entrepreneurs share some same characteristics with business entrepreneurs such as entrepreneurial mind, risk taking, need for achievement or innovativeness. On the other hand the different nature of the social needs and problems differentiate socail entreprises' activities and priorities and definitely neccessiate different entrepreneurial characteristics. In this section, the prominent personality traits of social entrepreneurs are discussed.

Empathy

Empathy is an ability to perceive and understand the others' feeling or emotional states and to arrange one's own responses according to the perspective of the other person (Rogers, 1959; Davis, 1983a cited in Limbu, Jayachandran, Babin, & Peterson, 2016). In the Merriam-Webster Medical Dictionary empathy is defined as:

the action of understanding, being aware of, being sensitive to, and vicariously experiencing the feelings, thoughts, and experience of another of either the past or present without having the feelings, thoughts, and experience fully communicated in an objectively explicit manner (https://www.merriam-webster.com/dictionary/empathy).

Generally the following analogy is used to define empathy: mentally putting yourself in another person's shoes (Kemp, Bui, Krishen, Homer, & LaTour, 2017).

Table 1. A Typology of Social Entrepreneurship

Type	Social Bricoleurs	Social Contructionists	Social Engineers
What do they do?	Perceive and act upon opportunities to address a local social needs they are motivated and have the expertise and resources to address.	Build and operate alternative structures to provide goods and services addressing social needs that governments, agencies, and businesses cannot.	Creation of newer, more effective social systems designed to replace existing ones when they are ill-suited to address significant social needs.
Scale, Scope, Timing	Small scale, local in scope—often episodic in nature.	Small to large scale, local to international in scope, designed to be institutionalized to address an ongoing social need.	Very large scale that is national to international in scope and which seeks to build lasting structures that will challenge existing order.
Why Are They Necessary?	Knowledge about social needs and the abilities to address them are widely scattered. Many social needs are non-discernable or easily misunderstood from afar, requiring local agents to detect and address them.	Laws, regulation, political acceptability, inefficiencies and/or lack of will prevent existing governmental and business organizations from addressing many important social needs effectively.	Some social needs are not amenable to amelioration within existing social structures. Entrenched incumbents can thwart actions to address social needs that undermine their own interests and source of power.
Social Significance	Collectively, their actions help maintain social harmony in the face of social problems	They mend the social fabric where it is torn, address acute social needs within existing broader social structures, and help maintain social harmony.	They seek to rip apart existing social structures and replace them with new ones. They represent an important force for social change in the face of entrenched incumbents.
Effect on Social Equilibrium	Atomistic actions by local social entrepreneurs move us closer to a theoretical "social equilibrium."	Addressing gaps in the provision of socially significant goods and service creates new "social equilibriums."	Fractures existing social equilibrium and seks to replace it with a more socially efficient one,
Source of Discretion	Being on the spot with the skills to address local problems not on others' "radars." Local scope means they have limited resource requirements and are fairly autonomous. Small scale and local scope allows for quick response times.	They address needs left un-addressed and have limited/no competition. They may even be welcomed and be seen as a "release valve" preventing negative publicity/social problems that may adversely affect existing governmental and business organizations.	Popular support to the extent that existing social structures and incumbents are incapable of addressing mportant social needs.
Limits to Discretion	Not much aside from local laws and regulations. However, the limited resources and expertise they possess limit their ability to address other needs or expand geographically.	Need to acquire financial and human resources necessary to fulfill mission and institutionalize as a going concern. Funder demands oversight. Professional volunteers and employees are needed to operate organization.	Seen as fundamentally illegitimate by established parties that see them as a threat, which brings scrutiny and attempts to undermine the ability of the social engineers to bring about change. The perceived illegitimacy will inhibit the ability to raise financial and human resources from traditional sources. As a consequence, they may become captive of the parties that supply it with needed resources.

Source: Zahra, S. A., Gedajlovic, E., Neubaum, D. O., & Shulman, J. M. (2009). A typology of social entrepreneurs: Motives, search processes and ethical challenges. Journal of business venturing, 24(5), p.523.

Empathy involves three dimensions. *Affective empathy* means sharing or experiencing emotions of others. *Cognitive empathy* is to understand the others' needs by imagining himself or herself in the same situation with others (London & Morfopoulos, 2009). According to Gladstein (1983) while *cognitive empathy* is *intellectually taking the role or perspective of another person, affective empathy* is *responding with the same emotion to another person's emotion* (p. 468). Lastly, behavioral empathy refers the ability to control one's own emotions and behaviours for helping others (London & Morfopoulos, 2009).

Empathy necessitates understanding or knowing how others feel, but it doesn't neccessarily mean that people who have empathy will act prosocially. The have to care how others feel and be closely interested with others'welfare or other-based concerns. If these concerns become compatible or signify the equivalent importance with others' feelings, people can act prosocially (Jensen, 2016).

In the literature, there are various explanations about the traits, qualifications of social entrepreneurs. According to Drayton (2002), the considerable factor in nature of social entrepreneurs is *strong ethical fibre*. Some researchers argue that the values of social entrepreneurs include primarily sensitivity of social context and mostly depend on emotional connections with people and their behavior rely on helpfulness, altruism rather than egotism. Other researchers, namely, Mair and Noboa (2006) emphasize on empathy as a prominent trait of social entrepreneurs. They state that social entrepreneurs are so sensitive about perceiving and understanding the feelings of others or putting themselves in the place of others. The study of Bhawe, Jain and Gupta (2007) also supports this argument. The results indicates that social entrepreneurs can easily build the empathy between themselves and the people who are faced with social problems or have social needs and also empathy has an positive influence on social entrepreneurs ability to determine the opportunities in their environment (Ernst, 2012).

For social entrepreneurs, building a strong empathetic relationship with the people is a necessary entailment to start a social venture. Basically they concentrate on understanding, feeling the social concerns of people. They then aim to protect them by proactive and social oriented actions. The driving force of empathy takes great place in many of social entrepreneurships' stories (André & Pache, 2016). An example is *Teach for America* which is a non-profit organization aims to provide educational equity and exellence to all children (https://www.teachforamerica.org/about-us/our-mission). In the CEO Wendy Kopp's explanation of the story of *Teach for America*'s establishment, empathy is pointed out:

I found myself increasingly engrossed [our emphasis] by another issue: the failures of our public education system. The issue had first captured my attention as a college freshman. My roommate, who had attended public school in the South Bronx, was smart and creative. She was a brilliant poet. Still, she struggled under the academic demands of Princeton until she had time to gain the skills necessary to compensate for her weak preparation. [...] It's really not fair, I thought, that where you're born in our country plays a role in determining your educational prospects. [I made] an effort to figure out what could be done about this problem (Kopp 2003, pp. 4–5 cited in André & Pache, 2016).

Another example is about SAMU, French social health and social services that aims to reach out to children and young adults who are physically or socially distressed (Ticktin, 2011). Empathy was an important driving force for Xavier Emmanuelli who is founder of SAMU. He said that *After I saw these people, I realized that the world was unjust. I was really incensed* (Emmanuelli, 2012)

Compassion

The word *compassion* is derived from Latin word "compati" which means "to suffer with" (Strauss, C., Taylor, B. L., Gu, J., Kuyken, W., Baer, R., Jones, F., & Cavanagh, K., 2016). It is defined as *sympathetic pity and concern for the sufferings or misfortunes of others.* in Oxford English Dictionary (https://en.oxforddictionaries.com/definition/compassion). Some authors define compassion as other oriented emotion which shifts interest and attention from their own concerns to concerns of others (Nussbaum, 2001; Solomon, 1998; White, 1999). According to Lazarus, compassion is being moved by another's suffering and wanting to help (Lazarus, 1991). Compassion finds place in all religion but especially in Buddhism it's seen as a main doctrine which states emotional reponse with altruistic intention keeping others from suffering by caring ethical values. According to Dalai Lama, compassion is an emotion which should be felt with equal sincerity to both close others and strangers or others we do not know (Strauss, Taylor, Gu, Kuyken, Baer, Jones, & Cavanagh, 2016).

Compassion means that being aware of pain and have capacity to decrease or remove this pain with courtesy, patience, empathy and calmness. Self compassion refers one's self experience and compassion combines and enriches this with others' experiences (Feldman & Kuyken, 2011).

According to Lilius et al. (2011) compassion includes three interrelated phases.:

- **Noticing:** Indicates being sensitive to all happenings in the environment (from local to global level), perceiving or recognizing others' suffering cognitively.
- **Feeling:** Is an emphatic concern, emotional reponse to another's hurt, pain or suffering. The intense, deepness and contunity of feeling are not stable. Especially if a person has similar experiences with another's suffering, the feeling may be so intensive and it may take a long time. This is also related with seriousness degree or characteristics of the issue which cause to pain.
- **Responding:** The last phase is called *responding* which involves the enthusiasm to take an action conciously against to suffering and the reasons of suffering.

In addition to these three phases, Paul Gilbert emphasized two more concepts *distress tolerance* and *non-judgement. Distress tolerance* is defined as coping with troubles or difficulties instead of deferring or suppressing them. *Non-judgement* denotes avoiding condemning other people and tolerating their emotional reactions (Gilbert, 2017).

Miller et al. (2012) explain compassion as a fundamental encouraging factor for social entrepreneurs in creating new social ventures. Their model, which is developed to explain the prosocial motivator role of compensation on social entrepreneurship, includes *integrative thinking*, *prosocial cost benefit analysis* and *commitment* to others' suffering. *Integrative thinking* is concentrating on any social problem from different approaches and extensive point of views to realize collective gains. In *Prococial cost benefit analysis*, others' outcomes are valued more highly depending on compassion cause to increase perceived benefits of acting to facilitate others' pain. Commitment to decreasing or eliminating others' suffering is a hallmark characteristic of other-oriented people who have an ability in emotional connection, indigenize others' suffering or problems and have enthusiasm to solve these problem or decrease their suffering. Concisely, they feel wholehearted commitment to reform any social concern (Miller, Grimes, McMullen, & Vogus, 2012).

Altruism

The history of Altruism dates back to old times, from Aristotle to Freud. The word expresses self sacrifice in ancient Greek philosophy (Lähdesmäki & Takala, 2012). In 19th century August Comte derived Altruism from "alter" which means "other" or "care for others". In parellel with this, Green defined altruism as an willful action which is displayed for the welfare of others without expecting any benefits or in some cases the actor might suffer a loss (Suzuki & Miah, 2016). The general definition of Altruism is prioritizing others' interests before one's own. This definition is also admitted in different disciplines such as psychology, sociobiology, political science, economics, and management (Batson, Van Lange, Ahmad, & Lishner, 2003).

In definition of Kanungo and Mendonca (1996), altruism is seen as a kind of philantrophy-based behavior for others' benefit. Cialdini et al. (1997) emphasized two prime concepts "self" and "other" in Altruism. According to their opinion, the occurrence of "oneness" in Altruism depends on the concept of "other" which merges with the helper's sense of self (Singh & Krishnan, 2008). The other definition associates alturistic behavior with rewards. According to Macaulay and Berkowitz (1970), altruism means behaving for the benefit of another individual without any external reward expectation (Jeffries, Johnston, Nichols, Oliner, Tiryakian, & Weinstein, 2006). A similar definition was suggested by Ballinger and Rockmann (2010). In this definition altruism indicates a mutual relationship between helper and the person who is in trouble or has some needs. Helper aims to act to solve the trouble or meet the needs of others without caring own interests (Paraskevaidis & Andriotis, 2017).

In social psychology there are two core reasons to explain an altruistic behavior (Kanungo & Conger,1993):

- People help others because they expect that the others will help him or her in time. This is called as reciprocity norm.
- People help others because of their highly internalized social responsibility. They have a strong desire to help others without considering their own personal benefit. Their actions basically depend on moral values or moral obligations.

Altruism may be seen as prominent behavior in social entrepreneurship in comparison with business entrepreneurship. The main objective of a social entrepreneur is to provide an utility to society. This can be occured in two forms: a) providing utility only for society; b) providing utility both to society and herself/himself. Surely in form (a), the degree of altruism is higher than in form; (b) (Tan, Williams & Tan, 2005). Altruism is a natural characteristic of social entrepreneurs, for example, feeling responsibility or obligation to others' difficulties, helping others faithfully. Their actions are performed without any personal benefit expectancy and are based on unselfishness, self-sacrifice. The frame of their societal objectives- improving the quality conditions of others life or happiness – and the moral, spiritual and religious values are fundamental driving factors of social entrepreneurs' altruistic behaviors (London & Morfopoulos, 2009).

MOTIVATION FACTORS OF SOCIAL ENTREPRENEUR

When social entrepreneurs are compared with business entrepreneurs in terms of motivation factors, the most distinct difference is in the aims of both sides. For social entrepreneurs, altruism is a driving factor to achive their societal objectives rather than financial gain which are the main driving factors for business entrepreneurs (Boluk & Mottiar, 2014; Martin & Osberg, 2007; Ostrander, 2007).

Social entrepreneurs are motivated by improving social gains without expecting any personal benefit or economic gain. Their other motivation is to successfully complete their social missions. Additionally, rehabilitation of wrong or deficient social system, and changing current attitudes or approches, which cause to social issues, are conceived as motivating factors by social entrepreneurs (Sullivan Mort, Weerawardena, & Carnegie, 2003; London, 2010).

According to Santos,

Social entrepreneurship is not about exerting pressure or raising awareness but rather about developing and validating a sustainable solution to problems that often have a local expression but global impact (Santos, 2012).

While business entrepreneurs have hedonic and extrinsic motivations, social entrepreneurs act with intrinsic and eudemonic motivations. They consider others benefit more than their own benefit and they expect to realize the others' well-being without external reward or any financial gain (Braga, Proenca, & Ferreira, 2014). Helping society, concentration on non-monetary values, deep interest in social issues, personal fulfillment on social aims are suggested to be part of the defining characteristics of social entrepreneurs by Germak and Robinson (2014) (Rahdari & Moradi, 2016).

Creating a beneficial social value is the most important motivation factor for social entrepreneurs (Mair & Noboa, 2003). According to Nga and Shamuganathan (2010), social entrepreneurs' values, moral consciousness and high humanitarion sensitivity to social problems lead or motivate them to find effective solutions and improve social welfare. On the other hand, Austin *et al.* (2006) argue that social problem diagnosed by the social entrepreneur is the main driving force to initiate and sustain of their actions towards society (Ghalwash, Tolba, & Ismail, 2017).

Prosocial Motivation

Prosocial Motivation can be defined as a driving factor which appears with the interest in one's work (Kroll & Vogel, 2017). According to Grant *prosocial motivation is the desire to expend effort to benefit other people* (Grant, 2008). Prosocial motivation concentrates on others' benefit or welfare without neglecting self-interest (Bendell, 2017).

Social entrepreneurs concentrate on social concerns with a sense of empathy and sympathy. In sense of empathy, they share common life experiences with others and therefore they behave more alturistic to help others. On the other hand in sense of sympathy, social entrepreneurs' experiences are not similar with others' even they haven't any distressing experince. They act for others' benefit because of their feeling of pain or sense of compassion. These two senses both empathy and sympathy may be seen as prosocial motivation factors for social entrepreneurs (Powell & Baker 2013).

The concepts of "pleasure" and "pressure" are related with prosocial motivation. In Self Determination Theory, there are different types of motivation orginated from some specific reasons or goals. One of them is intrinsic motivation which means that being in any activity because of inner satisfaction or pleasure. The other one, extrinsic motivation concentrates on some outcomes or rewards for generating motivation (Lin, 2007). Pleasure based prosocial motivation is related with intrinsic motivation and refers to help others for pleasure or inner peace. On the other hand, pressure based prosocial motivation depends on extrinsic motivation and indicates to help others to fulfill any social responsibility or societal norm (Gebauer, Riketta, Broemer, & Maio, 2008).

According to Moon and Koh (2015), prosocial motivation has an effect on *the meaningfulness of social entrepreneurs' work, their pleasure with non-monetary values* and *entrepreneurial ability*:

- **Meaningfulness of the Work:** Prosocial motivation may improve the meaningfulness of their work which indicates a concord between the content of work and their own values, beliefs. Lönnström also emphasizes this situation. The excitative factor for social entrepreneurs is the harmony between their values and the values of societal issues that they aim to improve (Lönnström, 2015).
- **Pleasure with Non-Monetary Values:** Social entrepreneurs concentrate on social needs or social problems intensely. Making a significant contribution to society is the greatest motivation for themselves and while caring financial results, their primary goal is always to reduce social concerns.
- **Social Entrepreneurial Ability:** Their prosocial motivation and specific characteristics such as sensitivity and openness to social dynamics improve their self confidence on their ability to found social entreprise which creates significant social value.

Opportunities

Opportunity can be defined as a good chance for advancement or progress. The opportunity of social entrepreneurs occurs when they diagnose the social needs or social problems (Cajaiba-Santana, 2010).

Social entrepreneurs' opportunities which create social value such as providing medical care, struggling with unemployment, scarcity, climate change or helping to disabled people. Some problems or needs that can be interpreted as threats by others can be seen as an opportunity for social entrepreneurs. For example, while a wilderness and arid soil may be perceived as a threat by others, social entrepreneurs perceive this as an opportunity to build a playground for children or a park for the public weal. Social entrepreneurs aim to fulfill the implicit demand of any beneficiary in society. For example, some group of parents who have serious complaints about the local education system, they may not imagine or understand what kind of solutions should be created about this education based problem. This problem is so complex for social entrepreneurs because it's not so easy to persuade parents about an effective education systems with ideals and thoughts quite reverse of commerical entrepreneurs (Brooks, 2009).

Some specific personal life experiences highly influential on social entrepreneurs to create new opportunities. Any problem in their personal background such as race discrimination, poverty, ilness or having a disabled family member may be a driving force for themselves to perceive opportunities around them (Yitshaki & Kropp, 2016).

Social entrepreneurs are not interested in enhancing competitive advantage. They aim to create sustainable solutions for unmet social concerns and spread these solutions to out of their local area (Müller, 2012). Social entrepreneurs are in struggle for changing social problems to opportunities. From Table 2 it is indicated that social problems and opportunity relate over some social enterprises' examples.

Social Network

In establishing and sustaining their business, social entrepreneurs need to use their social network to procure or improve some resources, knowledge or skills as like business entrepreneurs. (Greve & Salaff, 2003). A social network can be defined as a network of social interactions and personal relationships. According to Zimmer (1990), the critical parts of social network are *density* refers the multeity and

Table 2. Examples of How Social Entrepreneurs Recognize and Solve Problems

Company	Problem	Opportunity Recognition	Solution
Job Factory, Switzerland	Youth unemployment	Own experiences: the social entrepreneur worked in a related field before	Engage at risk youth in internship at the Job Factory and offer accompanying coaching
Greemen Bank, Bangladesh	Lack to regular financial institutions. People trapped in the vicious cycle of owing debt to moneylenders and playing usurious interest rates.	Triggered by conversations with poor people. By experimenting with micro-credits provided by himself he saw that this was a successful inrevention for escaping poverty.	Provide microcredits to self-selected borrower groups of women without colleterals.
Atmosfair, Germany	Climate change caused through CO2 emissions	Developed from a research Project aiming to work out an approach for implementing voluntary CO2 compensation	Provide a variety of jobs in which mentally ill people can utilize their strengths. Work closely together with psychiatrists.
Pegasus, Germany	Difficulty for mentally ill persons to find a regular job.	An EU-sponsored Project to prepare mentally ill people for the job market failed because companies did not want to hire mentally ill people. The founder eventually established a company himself where people with mental disabilities can work.	Provide a variety of jobs in which mentally ill people can utilize their strenghts. Work closely together with psychiatrists.

Source: Müller, S. (2012). Business Models in Social Entrepreneurship. In Volkmann, C., Tokarski, K., and Ernst, K. (Eds.). Social entrepreneurship and social business. An Introduction and Discussion with Case Studies. Wiesbaden: Springer Gabler, p.113.

strength of ties in network; *reachability* states the existence of patways or set of connections among the network actors and *centrality* relates with prominence of any actor who stayed at the center of network (Rusinowska, Berghammer, De Swart, & Grabisch, 2011). It can be measured by the distance of this central actor from others and the number of other actors that can be reached by central actor (Zimmer, 1990). Generally, in the beginning part of their entriprises' story, entrepreneurs prefer to share their ideas, decisions or possibilities with the limited number of actors in their close social network. On the other hand as long as their business grows, the scope of their social network which they owned is also expanding (Greve & Salaff, 2003).

Social network is another important motivator or supportive source for social entrepreneurs. Some actors of their social network are friends, colleagues, professionals who work in the area of any social concern which is the target of social entrepreneurs' venture, members of their own family or relatives, the other social entrepreneurs seen as inspirers. Surely, these actors are positioned in close borders of social network but social entrepreneurs' aims are not limited by local societal problems or needs. They have an enthusiasm to expand their beneficial solutions from local area to many regions all over the world. Therefore they also need to be in international social networks (Ghalwash, Tolba, & Ismail, 2017).

According to results of a study, which was conducted by Omorede (2014) in South Africa, social network was found as a motivation factor for social entrepreneurs. The supportive relationship between social entrepreneurs and social networks' actors strengthen entrepreneurs both physiologically and psychologically. By virtue of this relationship, social entrepreneurs gather valuable information, gain innovative thoughts, provide financial support and improve their entrepreneurial skills to sustain their social venture (Omorede, 2014). In social network, the strong connection or communication especially between social entrepreneurs increases mutual trust therefore they can diagnose the social needs more easily, find more beneficial and creative solutions to social concerns (Nga & Shamuganathan, 2010).

CONCLUSION

Especially for the last ten years, the term of social entrepreneurship and social entrepreneurs gained a popularity in different fields from political, economic platforms to academic world (Sekliuckiene & Kisielius, 2015).

Social entrepreneurs dedicate themselves to create social value, behave altruistic against social problems and while they take into account the financial returns, they pay more attention to provide social benefit (Abu-Saifan, 2012). Depending on the complexity and scope of social problems and the amount of needed sources, social entrepreneurs can be classified in three typology. *Social Bricoleurs* concern small scaled and local-based social problems, *Social Constructionists* aim to meet more extensive social needs in a large scope from local to international arena. *Social Engineers* work as like as transformational entrepreneurs and they effort to make radical changes on available sytems or processes in very large scaled fields, international or global (Smith & Stevens, 2010).

The distinctive personality traits of social entrepreneurs have an direct impact on their intention to build up a social venture and sustain it. Aside from being sensitive to social concerns, they easily perceive and understand others' nuisances. They also feel compassion and this emotion leads them to take strong actions against all kind of social problems and to behave more altruistic. Social entrepreneurs are motivated by existent opportunities around their environment. They deeply concentrate on social problems and recognize each problem as an opportunity to help others or create a social value. Techological development, changes in public policy or public opinion, social and demographic changes are defined as sources of opportunities for social entrepreneurs (Brooks, 2009). Their social vision supports them to find out the opportunities from diverse sources (Nga & Shamuganathan, 2010). On the other hand, their personal experiences in their private life, the content and function of social network they owned, may seen as strong driving factors for social entrepreneurs.

In today's world where humane values such as compassion, helpfulness, empathy and altruism are often forgotten, social enterpreneurs with their sui generis motivations and personality traits, through their ventures, work towards protecting and spreading these humane values.

REFERENCES

Abu-Saifan, S. (2012). Social entrepreneurship: definition and boundaries. *Technology Innovation Management Review, 2*(2).

Alter, K., & Dawans, V. (2006). The Integrated Approach to Social Entrepreneurship - Building High Performance Organizations. *Social Enterprise Reporter, 204*, 1–4.

André, K., & Pache, A. C. (2016). From caring entrepreneur to caring enterprise: Addressing the ethical challenges of scaling up social enterprises. *Journal of Business Ethics, 133*(4), 659–675. doi:10.100710551-014-2445-8

Austin, J., Stevenson, H., & Wei-Skillern, J. (2006). Social and commercial entrepreneurship: Same, different, or both? *Entrepreneurship Theory and Practice, 30*(1), 1–22. doi:10.1111/j.1540-6520.2006.00107.x

Baker, T., & Nelson, R. (2005). Creating something from nothing: Resource construction through entrepreneurial bricolage. *Administrative Science Quarterly, 50*(3), 329–366. doi:10.2189/asqu.2005.50.3.329

Ballinger, G. A., & Rockmann, K. W. (2010). Chutes versus ladders: Anchoring events and a punctuated-equilibrium perspective on social exchange relationships. *Academy of Management Review*, *35*(3), 373–391. doi:10.5465/AMR.2010.51141732

Batson, C. D., Van Lange, P. A. M., Ahmad, N., & Lishner, D. A. (2003). Altruism and helping behavior. In M. A. Hogg & J. Cooper (Eds.), *Sage Handbook of Social Psychology* (pp. 279–295). London: Sage Publications.

Bendell, B. L. (2017). I don't want to be green: Prosocial motivation effects on firm environmental innovation rejection decisions. *Journal of Business Ethics*, *143*(2), 277–288. doi:10.100710551-015-2588-2

Bhawe, N., Gupta, V. K., & Jain, T. K. (2007). *The Entrepreneurship Of The Good Samaritan: A Qualitative Study To Understand How Opportunities Are Perceived In Social Entrepreneurship*. Paper presented at the Babson College Entrepreneurship Research Conference, Madrid, Spain.

Bhawuk, D. P., Mrazek, S., & Munusamy, V. P. (2009). *From Social Engineering to Community Transformation: Amul*. Grameen Bank and Mondragon as Exemplar Organizations.

Bikse, V., Rivza, B., & Riemere, I. (2015). The Social Entrepreneur as a Promoter of Social Advancement. *Procedia: Social and Behavioral Sciences*, *185*, 469–478. doi:10.1016/j.sbspro.2015.03.405

Boluk, K. A., & Mottiar, Z. (2014). Motivations of social entrepreneurs: Blurring the social contribution and profits dichotomy. *Social Enterprise Journal*, *10*(1), 53–68. doi:10.1108/SEJ-01-2013-0001

Bornstein, D., & Davis, S. (2010). *Social Entrepreneurship: What Everyone Needs to Know?* Oxford University Press.

Boschee, J. (2006). Social Entrepreneurship: The Promise and the Perils. In A. Nicholls (Ed.), Social Entrepreneurship: New Models of Sustainable Social Change. Oxford University Press.

Braga, J. C., Proenca, T., & Ferreira, M. R. (2014). Motivations for social entrepreneurship–Evidences from Portugal. *Tékhne (Instituto Politécnico do Cávado e do Ave)*, *12*, 11–21. doi:10.1016/j.tekhne.2015.01.002

Brooks, A. C. (2009). *Social entrepreneurship: A modern approach to social value creation*. Pearson Prentice Hall.

Burkett, I. (2010). *Sustainable Social Enterprise - What does it really mean?* Foresters Community Finance. Retrieved from http://cdn.socialtraders.com.au/app/uploads/2016/08/Sustainable-Social-Enterprise-Ingrid-Burkett.pdf

Cajaiba-Santana, G. (2010). Socially constructed opportunities in social entrepreneurship: a structuration model. In A. Fayolle & H. Matlay (Eds.), *Handbook of research on social entrepreneurship* (pp. 88–106). Cheltenham, UK: Edward Elgar. doi:10.4337/9781849804684.00010

Cialdini, R. B., Brown, S. L., Lewis, B. P., Luce, C., & Neuberg, S. L. (1997). Reinterpreting the empathy–altruism relationship: When one into one equals oneness. *Journal of Personality and Social Psychology*, *73*(3), 481–494. doi:10.1037/0022-3514.73.3.481 PMID:9294898

Davis, M. H. (1983a). Measuring individual differences in empathy: Evidence for a multidimensional approach. *Journal of Personality and Social Psychology*, *44*(1), 13–126. doi:10.1037/0022-3514.44.1.113

Dees, J. G. (1998). *The meaning of "Social Entrepreneurship"*. Stanford University; Draft report for the Kauffman Center for Entrepreneurial Leadership. Retrieved from https://csistg.gsb.stanford.edu/sites/csi.gsb.stanford.edu/files /TheMeaningofsocialEntrepreneurship.pdf

Dees, J. G., Emerson, J., & Economy, P. (2001). *Enterprising nonprofits: A toolkit for social entrepreneurs* (Vol. 186). John Wiley & Sons Inc.

Drayton, W. (2002). The citizen sector: Becoming as entrepreneurial and competitive as business. *California Management Review*, *44*(3), 120–132. doi:10.2307/41166136

Emmanuelli, X. (2012). *S'en fout la mort.* Paris: Editions Les Echappe's.

Ernst, K. (2012). Social Entrepreneurs and their Personality. In Social entrepreneurship and social business. An Introduction and Discussion with Case Studies. Springer Gabler. doi:10.1007/978-3-8349-7093-0_3

Fayolle, A., & Matlay, H. H. (2010). *Handbook of research on social entrepreneurship*. Edward Elgar. doi:10.4337/9781849804684

Feldman, C., & Kuyken, W. (2011). Compassion in the landscape of suffering. *Contemporary Buddhism*, *12*(01), 143–155. doi:10.1080/14639947.2011.564831

Gebauer, J. E., Riketta, M., Broemer, P., & Maio, G. R. (2008). Pleasure and pressure based prosocial motivation: Divergent relations to subjective well-being. *Journal of Research in Personality*, *42*(2), 399–420. doi:10.1016/j.jrp.2007.07.002

Germak, A. J., & Robinson, J. A. (2014). Exploring the motivation of nascent social entrepreneurs. *Journal of Social Entrepreneurship*, *5*(1), 5–21. doi:10.1080/19420676.2013.820781

Ghalwash, S., Tolba, A., & Ismail, A. (2017). What motivates social entrepreneurs to start social ventures? An exploratory study in the context of a developing economy. *Social Enterprise Journal*, *13*(3), 268–298. doi:10.1108/SEJ-05-2016-0014

Gilbert, P. (Ed.). (2017). *Compassion: Concepts, Research and Applications*. New York: Routledge Taylor & Francis.

Gladstein, G. A. (1983). Understanding empathy: Integrating counseling, developmental, and social psychology perspectives. *Journal of Counseling Psychology*, *30*(4), 467–482. doi:10.1037/0022-0167.30.4.467

Grant, A. M. (2008). Does intrinsic motivation fuel the prosocial fire? Motivational synergy in predicting persistence, performance, and productivity. *The Journal of Applied Psychology*, *93*(1), 48–58. doi:10.1037/0021-9010.93.1.48 PMID:18211134

Greve, A., & Salaff, J. W. (2003). Social networks and entrepreneurship. *Entrepreneurship Theory and Practice*, *28*(1), 1–22. doi:10.1111/1540-8520.00029

Jamburia, G. (2013). *Sustainability of Social Enterprises: A Case Study of Sweden*. Retrieved from http://www.diva-portal.org/smash/get/diva2:632746/FULLTEXT01.pdf

Jeffries, V., Johnston, B. V., Nichols, L. T., Oliner, S. P., Tiryakian, E., & Weinstein, J. (2006). Altruism and social solidarity: Envisioning a field of specialization. *The American Sociologist*, *37*(3), 67–83. doi:10.100712108-006-1023-7

Jensen, K. (2016). Prosociality. *Current Biology*, *26*(16), R748–R752. doi:10.1016/j.cub.2016.07.025 PMID:27554648

Kanungo, R. N., & Conger, J. A. (1993). Promoting altruism as a corporate goal. *The Academy of Management Executive*, *7*(3), 37–48.

Kanungo, R. N., & Mendonca, M. (1996). *Ethical dimensions of leadership* (Vol. 3). Sage.

Kemp, E., Bui, M., Krishen, A., Homer, P. M., & LaTour, M. S. (2017). Understanding the power of hope and empathy in healthcare marketing. *Journal of Consumer Marketing*, *34*(2), 85–95. doi:10.1108/JCM-04-2016-1765

Kopp, W. (2003). *One day, all children: The unlikely triumph of Teach for America and what I learnt along the way*. New York: Public Affairs.

Kroll, A., & Vogel, D. (2017). Changes in Prosocial Motivation over Time: A Cross-Sector Analysis of Effects on Volunteering and Work Behavior. *International Journal of Public Administration*, 1–13. doi:10.1080/01900692.2017.1347945

Lähdesmäki, M., & Takala, T. (2012). Altruism in business–an empirical study of philanthropy in the small business context. *Social Responsibility Journal*, *8*(3), 373–388. doi:10.1108/17471111211247947

Lazarus, R. S. (1991). *Emotion and adaptation*. Oxford, UK: Oxford University Press.

Lilius, J. M., Kanov, J., Dutton, J., Worline, M. C., & Maitlis, S. (2011). Compassion revealed: What we know about compassion at work (and where we need to know more). Academic Press.

Limbu, Y. B., Jayachandran, C., Babin, B. J., & Peterson, R. T. (2016). Empathy, nonverbal immediacy, and salesperson performance: The mediating role of adaptive selling behavior. *Journal of Business and Industrial Marketing*, *31*(5), 654–667. doi:10.1108/JBIM-03-2015-0048

Lin, H. F. (2007). Effects of extrinsic and intrinsic motivation on employee knowledge sharing intentions. *Journal of Information Science*, *33*(2), 135–149. doi:10.1177/0165551506068174

London, M. (2010). Understanding Social Advocacy: An Integrative Model of Motivation, Strategy, and Persistence in Support of Corporate Social Responsibility and Social Entrepreneurship. *Journal of Management Development*, *29*(3), 224–245. doi:10.1108/02621711011025768

London, M., & Morfopoulos, R. G. (2009). *Social entrepreneurship: How to start successful corporate social responsibility and community-based initiatives for advocacy and change*. New York: Routledge Taylor & Francis Group.

Lönnström, A. (2015). *The motivational values of social entrepreneurs* (Unpublished master's thesis). University of Jyväskylä School of Business and Economics, Finland.

Macaulay, J., & Berkowitz, L. (Eds.). (1970). *Altruism and helping behavior: Social psychological studies of some antecedents and consequences*. Academic Press.

Mair, J., & Noboa, E. (2006). Social entrepreneurship: How intentions to create a social venture are formed. In *Social entrepreneurship* (pp. 121–135). New York: Palgrave Macmillan. doi:10.1057/9780230625655_8

Martin, R. L., & Osberg, S. (2007). Social entrepreneurship: The case for definition. Stanford, CA: Stanford Social Innovation Review.

Merriam-Webster's Medical Dictionary. (n.d.). Retrieved from https://www.merriam-webster.com/dictionary /empathy

Miller, T. L., Grimes, M. G., McMullen, J. S., & Vogus, T. J. (2012). Venturing for others with heart and head: How compassion encourages social entrepreneurship. *Academy of Management Review*, *37*(4), 616–640. doi:10.5465/amr.2010.0456

Moon, C. W., & Koh, Y. S. (2015). Compassion, Pro-social Motivation and Social Entrepreneurship: An Empirical Investigation. *Proceedings of the Third Asia-Pacific Conference on Global Business, Economics, Finance and Banking*.

Müller, S. (2012). Business Models in Social Entrepreneurship. In C. Volkmann, K. Tokarski, & K. Ernst (Eds.), *Social entrepreneurship and social business. An Introduction and Discussion with Case Studies*. Wiesbaden: Springer Gabler. doi:10.1007/978-3-8349-7093-0_6

Nga, J. K. H., & Shamuganathan, G. (2010). The influence of personality traits and demographic factors on social entrepreneurship start up intentions. *Journal of Business Ethics*, *95*(2), 259–282. doi:10.100710551-009-0358-8

Nussbaum, M. (1996). Compassion: The basic social emotion. *Social Philosophy & Policy*, *13*(01), 27–58. doi:10.1017/S0265052500001515

Omorede, A. (2014). Exploration of motivational drivers towards social entrepreneurship. *Social Enterprise Journal*, *10*(3), 239–267. doi:10.1108/SEJ-03-2013-0014

Ostrander, S. A. (2007). The growth of donor control: Revisiting the social relations of philanthropy. *Nonprofit and Voluntary Sector Quarterly*, *36*(2), 356–372. doi:10.1177/0899764007300386

Paraskevaidis, P., & Andriotis, K. (2017). Altruism in tourism: Social exchange theory vs altruistic surplus phenomenon in host volunteering. *Annals of Tourism Research*, *62*, 26–37. doi:10.1016/j.annals.2016.11.002

Powell, E. E., & Baker, T. (2013). *How Can We Help? The Distinctive Impact of Empathy and Sympathy in the Emergence of Social Venture Missions*. Paper presented at the mini conference on social change, innovation, and entrepreneurial activity, Milan, Italy.

Praszkier, R., & Nowak, A. (2011). *Social entrepreneurship: Theory and practice*. Cambridge University Press. doi:10.1017/CBO9781139049467

Rahdari, A., Sepasi, S., & Moradi, M. (2016). Achieving sustainability through Schumpeterian social entrepreneurship: The role of social enterprises. *Journal of Cleaner Production*, *137*, 347–360. doi:10.1016/j.jclepro.2016.06.159

Rogers, C. R. (1959). A theory of therapy, personality, and interpersonal relationships as developed in the client-centered framework. In S. Koch (Ed.), *Psychology: A Study of a Science* (Vol. 3, pp. 184–256). New York: McGraw Hill.

Rusinowska, A., Berghammer, R., De Swart, H., & Grabisch, M. (2011). Social networks: Prestige, centrality, and influence. *Relational and Algebraic Methods in Computer Science*, 22-39.

Santos, F. M. (2012). A positive theory of social entrepreneurship. *Journal of Business Ethics, 111*(3), 335–351. doi:10.100710551-012-1413-4

Sekliuckiene, J., & Kisielius, E. (2015). Development of social entrepreneurship initiatives: A theoretical framework. *Procedia: Social and Behavioral Sciences, 213*, 1015–1019. doi:10.1016/j.sbspro.2015.11.519

Singh, N., & Krishnan, V. R. (2008). Self-sacrifice and transformational leadership: Mediating role of altruism. *Leadership and Organization Development Journal, 29*(3), 261–274. doi:10.1108/01437730810861317

Smith, B. R., & Stevens, C. E. (2010). Different types of social entrepreneurship: The role of geography and embeddedness on the measurement and scaling of social value. *Entrepreneurship and Regional Development*, *22*(6), 575–598. doi:10.1080/08985626.2010.488405

Solomon, R. C. (1998). The moral psychology of business: Care and compassion in the corporation. *Business Ethics Quarterly*, *8*(3), 515–533. doi:10.2307/3857435

Strauss, C., Taylor, B. L., Gu, J., Kuyken, W., Baer, R., Jones, F., & Cavanagh, K. (2016). What is compassion and how can we measure it? A review of definitions and measures. *Clinical Psychology Review*, *47*, 15–27. doi:10.1016/j.cpr.2016.05.004 PMID:27267346

Sullivan Mort, G., Weerawardena, J., & Carnegie, K. (2003). Social entrepreneurship: Towards conceptualisation. *International Journal of Nonprofit and Voluntary Sector Marketing*, *8*(1), 76–88. doi:10.1002/nvsm.202

Suzuki, Y., & Miah, M. D. (2016). Altruism, reciprocity and Islamic equity finance. *International Journal of Islamic and Middle Eastern Finance and Management*, *9*(2), 205–221. doi:10.1108/IMEFM-09-2014-0091

Tan, W. L., Williams, J., & Tan, T. M. (2005). Defining the 'social' in 'social entrepreneurship': Altruism and entrepreneurship. *The International Entrepreneurship and Management Journal*, *1*(3), 353–365. doi:10.100711365-005-2600-x

Thake, S., & Zadek, S. (1997). *Practical people, noble causes. How to support community based social entrepreneurs*. New Economic Foundation.

Ticktin, M. I. (2011). *Casualties of care: Immigration and the politics of humanitarianism in France*. Univ of California Press. doi:10.1525/california/9780520269040.001.0001

Weerawardena, J., & Sullivan-Mort, G. (2001). Learning, innovation and competitive advantage in not-for-profit aged care marketing: A conceptual model and research propositions. *Journal of Nonprofit & Public Sector Marketing*, *9*(3), 53–73. doi:10.1300/J054v09n03_04

White, J. (1999). Ethical comportment in organizations: A synthesis of the feminist ethic of care and the Buddhist ethic of compassion. *International Journal of Value-Based Management*, *12*(2), 109–128. doi:10.1023/A:1007779604630

Williams, C., & Gurtoo, A. (Eds.). (2016). *Routledge handbook of entrepreneurship in developing economies*. London: Routledge Taylor & Francis Group.

Wolk, A. M. (2008). *Advancing Social Entrepreneurship: Reccommendations for Policy Makers and Government Agencies*. Washington, DC: The Aspen Institute.

Yitshaki, R., & Kropp, F. (2016). Motivations and opportunity recognition of social entrepreneurs. *Journal of Small Business Management, 54*(2), 546–565. doi:10.1111/jsbm.12157

Zahra, S. A., Gedajlovic, E., Neubaum, D. O., & Shulman, J. M. (2009). A typology of social entrepreneurs: Motives, search processes and ethical challenges. *Journal of Business Venturing, 24*(5), 519–532. doi:10.1016/j.jbusvent.2008.04.007

Zhang, D. D., & Swanson, L. A. (2014). Linking social entrepreneurship and sustainability. *Journal of Social Entrepreneurship, 5*(2), 175–191. doi:10.1080/19420676.2014.880503

Zimmer, C. (1986). Entrepreneurship through social networks. In *The art and science of entrepreneurship*. Ballinger.

ADDITIONAL READING

Bacq, S., & Janssen, F. (2011). The multiple faces of social entrepreneurship: A review of definitional issues based on geographical and thematic criteria. *Entrepreneurship and Regional Development, 23*(5-6), 373–403. doi:10.1080/08985626.2011.577242

Barendsen, L., & Gardner, H. (2004). Is the social entrepreneur a new type of leader? *Leader to Leader, 2004*(34), 43–50. doi:10.1002/ltl.100

Batson, C. D., & Shaw, L. L. (1991). Evidence for altruism: Toward a pluralism of prosocial motives. *Psychological Inquiry, 2*(2), 107–122. doi:10.120715327965pli0202_1

Boehnke, K., Silbereisen, R. K., Eisenberg, N., Reykowski, J., & Palmonari, A. (1989). Developmental pattern of prosocial motivation: A cross-national study. *Journal of Cross-Cultural Psychology, 20*(3), 219–243. doi:10.1177/0022022189203001

Dacin, M. T., Dacin, P. A., & Tracey, P. (2011). Social entrepreneurship: A critique and future directions. *Organization Science, 22*(5), 1203–1213. doi:10.1287/orsc.1100.0620

Dacin, P. A., Dacin, M. T., & Matear, M. (2010). Social entrepreneurship: Why we don't need a new theory and how we move forward from here. *The Academy of Management Perspectives, 24*(3), 37–57. doi:10.5465/AMP.2010.52842950

Dey, P., & Lehner, O. (2017). Registering ideology in the creation of social entrepreneurs: Intermediary organizations, 'ideal subject' and the promise of enjoyment. *Journal of Business Ethics, 142*(4), 753–767. doi:10.100710551-016-3112-z

Dorado, S. (2006). Social entrepreneurial ventures: Different values so different process of creation, no? *Journal of Developmental Entrepreneurship, 11*(04), 319–343. doi:10.1142/S1084946706000453

Gabarret, I., Vedel, B., & Decaillon, J. (2017). A social affair: Identifying motivation of social entrepreneurs. *International Journal of Entrepreneurship and Small Business*, *31*(3), 399–415. doi:10.1504/IJESB.2017.084845

Greve, A., & Salaff, J. W. (2003). Social networks and entrepreneurship. *Entrepreneurship Theory and Practice*, *28*(1), 1–22. doi:10.1111/1540-8520.00029

Lounsbury, M., & Strang, D. 2009. Social entrepreneurship: Success stories and logic construction. In D. Hammack & S. Heydemann (Eds.), Globalization, philanthropy, and civil society: 71–94. Indianapolis: Indiana University Press.

McMullen, J. S., & Bergman, B. Jr. (2017). Social Entrepreneurship and The Development Paradox of Prosocial Motivation: A Cautionary Tale. *Strategic Entrepreneurship Journal*, *11*(3), 243–270. doi:10.1002ej.1263

Mody, M., Day, J., Sydnor, S., & Jaffe, W. (2016). Examining the motivations for social entrepreneurship using Max Weber's typology of rationality. *International Journal of Contemporary Hospitality Management*, *28*(6), 1094–1114. doi:10.1108/IJCHM-05-2014-0238

Mohiuddin, M., Parveen, R., Ibn Rahman, M., & Mazumder, M. N. H. (2013). Entrepreneurial Motivation and Social Enterprises: An Empirical Analysis on Founders of Social Ventures in Bangladesh. *Transnational Corporations Review*, *5*(2), 77–92. doi:10.1080/19186444.2013.11668680

Nicholls, A. (Ed.). (2008). *Social entrepreneurship: New models of sustainable social change*. USA: Oxford University Press.

Oncer, A. Z., & Yildiz, M. L. (2010). Creating sustainable value for society: Social entrepreneurship. *The Business Review, Cambridge*, *14*(2), 222–228.

Peredo, A. M., & McLean, M. (2006). Social entrepreneurship: A critical review of the concept. *Journal of World Business*, *41*(1), 56–65. doi:10.1016/j.jwb.2005.10.007

Prabhu, G. N. (1999). Social entrepreneurial leadership. *Career Development International*, *4*(3), 140–145. doi:10.1108/13620439910262796

Shaw, E., & Carter, S. (2007). Social entrepreneurship: Theoretical antecedents and empirical analysis of entrepreneurial processes and outcomes. *Journal of Small Business and Enterprise Development*, *14*(3), 418–434. doi:10.1108/14626000710773529

Short, J. C., Moss, T. W., & Lumpkin, G. T. (2009). Research in social entrepreneurship: Past contributions and future opportunities. *Strategic Entrepreneurship Journal*, *3*(2), 161–194. doi:10.1002ej.69

Smith, R., Bell, R., & Watts, H. (2014). Personality trait differences between traditional and social entrepreneurs. *Social Enterprise Journal*, *10*(3), 200–221. doi:10.1108/SEJ-08-2013-0033

Thompson, J. L. (2002). The world of the social entrepreneur. *International Journal of Public Sector Management*, *15*(5), 412–431. doi:10.1108/09513550210435746

Van Ryzin, G. G., Grossman, S., DiPadova-Stocks, L., & Bergrud, E. (2009). Portrait of the social entrepreneur: Statistical evidence from a US panel. *Voluntas*, *20*(2), 129–140. doi:10.100711266-009-9081-4

Vasakarla, V. (2008). A study on social entrepreneurship and the characteristics of social entrepreneurs. *ICFAI. Journal of Management Research*, *7*(4), 32–40.

Wallace, S. L. (1999). Social entrepreneurship: The role of social purpose enterprises in facilitating community economic development. *Journal of Developmental Entrepreneurship*, *4*(2), 153.

Yitshaki, R., & Kropp, F. (2011). Becoming a social entrepreneur: Understanding motivations using life story analysis. *International Journal of Business and Globalisation*, *7*(3), 319–331. doi:10.1504/IJBG.2011.042061

Zahra, S. A., Rawhouser, H. N., Bhawe, N., Neubaum, D. O., & Hayton, J. C. (2008). Globalization of social entrepreneurship opportunities. *Strategic Entrepreneurship Journal*, *2*(2), 117–131. doi:10.1002ej.43

KEY TERMS AND DEFINITIONS

Altruism: Altruism from "alter" which means "other" or "care for others." In parallel with this, altruism may be defined as an willful action which is displayed for the welfare of others without expecting any benefits or in some cases the actor might suffer a loss.

Compassion: Compassion means that being aware of pain and have capacity to decrease or remove this pain with courtesy, patience, empathy, and calmness.

Social Bricoleurs: They dedicate themselves to address or discover social needs and they use their own qualifications-expertise, experience- to improve social wealth. They aim to create high level of utilitarian value in their local area.

Social Constructionists: Social entrepreneurs who aim to create new approaches or solutions to large scaled social concerns.

Social Engineers: They mainly concentrate on big scaled and complex issues which need mass solutions and support.

Chapter 4
The Individual and Behavioral Factors of Social Entrepreneurs

Mine Afacan Fındıklı
Beykent University, Turkey

Uğur Yozgat
Istanbul Kültür University, Turkey

ABSTRACT

This chapter introduces the concept of social entrepreneurs and claims that some individual and behavioral factors contribute to social entrepreneurship. In this point of view, the purpose of this study is to highlight the leading individual and behavioral factors of the social entrepreneur. While exploring the theoretical framework, the theoretical foundations of social entrepreneurship and leading personality and behavioral characteristics have been investigated. The research is based on in-depth interviews with four participants to get a better understanding of the individual and behavioral factors of social entrepreneurs. As a result, the in-depth interviews showed that the social entrepreneurial potential encompass entrepreneurial motivations and psychological, social, managerial competencies. These dimensions contain self-motivation, self-efficacy, risk-taking, purposeful and success-oriented, strategic planning capacity, innovation capacity, social capital capacity, leadership capacity, resilience, resistance to uncertainty, conflict management capacity, and political maneuver capacity.

INTRODUCTION

Corporate Social entrepreneurs are those who can *hear the voice of the society* in which they live, identify the needs of the society appropriately and create meaningful values in the solution of social problems that concern the society (Thompson, 2002). Social entrepreneurs are defined as the producers of social value (Groot & Dankbaar, 2014). From this point of view, it seems that social entrepreneurs use their organizations - either for profit or non-profit - to provide social change and/or social value (Ferrel, Hirt, & Ferrel, 2016).

DOI: 10.4018/978-1-5225-5687-9.ch004

It is stated that the entrepreneurship, as a process, includes six main stages: 1) realization of an opportunity; 2) decision to initiate a venture; 3) assembling the resources; 4) actual launch an initiative; 5) building a successful business, and 6) harvesting the rewards (Curral, Santos, & Caetano, 2013). Considering this process definition, we could deduce that to create and sustain the social values, the successful social entrepreneurship may also start by realization of a need of the society and follow this process.

However, the only reason behind the success of social entrepreneurs is not only to be inclined to create social values by listening to *the voice of the society* but also to have the common qualities and values that successful entrepreneurs should bear.

Based on this point of view, the main purpose of this study was to highlight the individual and behavioral factors of the social entrepreneur. The result of the in-depth interview with four social entrepreneurs showed and confirmed that the entrepreneurial potential includes; entrepreneurial motivations and psychological, social, managerial competencies (ex: Curral, Santos, & Caetano, 2013). These dimensions contain; self-motivation, self- efficacy, visionary and strategic planning capacity, social innovation capacity, social capital capacity, leadership capacity, resilience, conflict management capacity and political maneuvers capacity.

THEORETICAL BACKGROUND

Social Entrepreneurship and the Concept of Social Entrepreneur

The common view of research conducted on entrepreneurship and its role in economic development is that entrepreneurship is the source of the structural change and the improvement in productivity in capitalist economies (Er, 2013), and the locomotive of economic growth. Considering the definitions for the concept; entrepreneurship is understood to embrace all the processes of exploration, identification, evaluation and utilization of opportunities (Sahasranamam & Sud, 2016).

In this framework, the entrepreneur is regarded as the person who organizes and manages the factors of production as well as the person who takes risk and makes innovations and develops the tried-and-tested technologies. The person who can hear the *voice of the society* by accurately predicting the needs of the society in which he lives, and creating meaningful values in solving social problems that are of interest to the society is called a social entrepreneur (Thompson, 2002). Within this perspective, it is understood that social entrepreneurship has the competence to perform innovations by considering opportunities to solve social problems. This concept, which is also called as social innovation, is recognized as *new ideas (products, services, and models) that simultaneously meet social needs (more effectively than alternatives) and create new social relationships or collaborations* (European Commission, 2010; Dro et al., 2011). Considering the four different types of social responsibility - economic, legal, moral and philanthropic (voluntary) - in Carroll's (1979) social responsibility pyramid, although voluntary responsibilities bear more meaning in recent times (Jackson & Jackson, 2014), it is argued that social entrepreneurship can be created in every sector. In the context of this information, when describing social entrepreneurship, it is not only one person that is in question. It is stated that this concept also applies to non-governmental organizations, public enterprises that fulfill voluntary social responsibilities, commercial enterprises that emphasize social responsibility projects, and to hybrid organizations as well (Light, 2006; Abdou, 2010; Groot & Dankbaar, 2014, Phipps & Prieto, 2015).

As a concept, it appears that social entrepreneurship was first voiced by Bowen in 1953, and entrepreneurs argue that they need to deal with social responsibility issues that overlap with the values of the society. It is understood that the concept of social entrepreneurship has been combining the world of profit-oriented business with the world of philanthropy for a social purpose since 2000s. Although social entrepreneurship, in this context, can be described as creating permanent solutions with entrepreneurship principles by determining social problems, it is seen that there is not yet a consensus on the definition of social entrepreneurship or social entrepreneur (Icerli & Sahin Karadal, 2014). It is also added that social entrepreneurship is not just about being beneficial to today's society, but it also includes a viewpoint of sustainability with the idea of leaving a livable world for future generations (Bornstein, 2007). Three principles have been emphasized in defining social entrepreneurship. The first of these principles is that social entrepreneurship is the process of creating value through the combination of new ways and resources; the second is that the intention is to discover opportunities for creating social value through social change or meeting needs; and the last one is that social entrepreneurship includes the provision of services and products as a process but also points to the creation of a new organization (Mair & Marti, 2006).

Social entrepreneurs can be described, under the light of this information, as change agents who seek, discover, and evaluate the opportunities to bring about positive social effects that will create social value or social change. These change agents may sometimes establish a profit-oriented business by using social issues in a creative way, while others may attempt to help individuals without a purpose of profit. Those in the third group can be profit-oriented or nonprofit, create economic value with their own programs, and create business and education opportunities for customer groups (Shaw & Carter, 2007).

Theoretical Foundations of Social Entrepreneurship

Although the concept of social entrepreneurship has had a few decades of history, it has been pointed out that social entrepreneurs have been undertaking their mission for centuries to realize the social transformation in an innovative way in areas such as education, health, environment and human rights (Sobhani & Gasnier, 2012). The fact that a social entrepreneur who aims to fulfill his mission of creating social value and being a change agent can continually capture new opportunities on the periphery depends heavily on following and learning what's going on around him/her and adapting his/her knowledge successfully (Jackson & Jackson, 2014). Considering that the process of social entrepreneurship is also *a process involving the innovative use and combination of resources to pursue opportunities to catalyze social change and/or address social needs* (Mair & Marti, 2006); it seems that the ability of social entrepreneurs to benefit from social networks has come to the forefront in ensuring the sustainability of resources (Jackson & Jackson, 2014).

In this context, it is seen that the first of the theoretical foundations of social entrepreneurs to be able to successfully realize the innovative transformation is the *Knowledge Spillover Theory*. The concept of Knowledge Spillover is defined as an involuntary or voluntary exchange of technological knowledge, and is expressed as the key to innovation activities (Lukach-Plasman, 2002). Since the social entrepreneur also creates a social innovation, s/he is the person who makes effective use of social networks to benefit from the knowledge spillover. During new business designs and creation of start-ups, the social entrepreneur accepts social change in the use of resources and information, and acquires new ideas and opportunities through the informal relationships s/he establishes (Kilic Kirilmaz, 2014).

Another theory behind the success of social entrepreneurship in achieving innovative transformation is claimed to be the *Theory of Planned Behavior* (Fishbein & Ajzen, 1975). It is thought that this theory, along with being a theory based on social psychology, may be useful for the social entrepreneur to exhibit behaviors that generate social value and to elucidate the three main factors influencing entrepreneurial intentions. These are; behavioral attitude, subjective norms (perceived social values and norms), and perceived behavioral control (Kim-Soon, Ahmad, & Ibrahim, 2016). Personal attitude refers to the degree of personal appreciation, positive or negative, which an individual has as an entrepreneur. Personal attitude includes not only emotional but also thought-based considerations based on judgment (Liñán & Chen, 2009). Subjective norms relate to the immediate surroundings that influence the individual's decision to become or not to become an entrepreneur, and they stand out as being influential on entrepreneurial intent. The dimension of perceived behavioral control is defined as the individual's perceived difficulty or simplicity of the process of becoming an entrepreneur, and it is pointed out that this is like the Social Cognitive Theory of Bandura (1997). According to the theory, the individual must positively assess his/her capacity to show a certain performance, and regulate his/her behaviors and believe in his/her competency (Kim-Soon, Ahmad, & Ibrahim, 2016).

Leading Personality and Behavioral Characteristics of Social Entrepreneurs

According to Vroom's (1964) expectation theory, a person's motivation is equal to the multiplication of the expectation for a specific behavior to lead to specific goal by the importance s/he assigns to that goal. For this reason, it is envisaged that the social entrepreneur will have both high motivation in fulfilling the goal important to him/her and the right behavior and the best choice that will help to achieve it. If the aim and expectation of the social entrepreneur is to increase social welfare and help untouched problems, s/he will prefer to develop social capital and to make effective use of social networks to achieve this aim. This ability helps him/her make different parties meet on the same table around a common idea and ideal (Zahra, Gedajlovic, Neubaum, & Shulman, 2008). Thus, s/he can create the necessary funds to reach his/her social goals. Starting from the definition:

social entrepreneurship is the whole process of the activities carried out to create new initiatives or to manage the existing enterprises in a more innovative way with the aim of increasing social welfare, and the processes of exploring, defining and exploiting opportunities (Zahra, Gedajlovic, Neubaum, & Shulman, 2009),

Social entrepreneurs act as the agents of change that create social innovations. This attitude and behavior are the indicators that s/he tends to have an innovative nature (Schumpeter, 1967) and to be competitive. Especially technical and industrial experiences are considered as the *sine qua non* (Hisrich & Peter, 1995). Showing ethical behavior in business processes is also a supporting element of being an agent of change. Starting from Carroll's social responsibility pyramid, it is envisaged that an unethical enterprise cannot be socially responsible, an enterprise that does not show social responsibility behavior will be far from ethical principles, and that the social entrepreneur will be firmly committed to ethical principles with the belief that s/he will be a role-model while exhibiting the social relations and the transformative power of social relations.

Having studied the concept of entrepreneurship in terms of behavior, Hisrich et al. (2005) pointed out that entrepreneurs have a strong tendency to take risks by taking initiatives after considering the risks of failure, and bringing social and economic resources together for implementation. The tendency to take risks by facing up to the failure is regarded as the indicator of an entrepreneur's tolerance to ambiguity, need for achievement, intrinsic control, desire for quick return and high self-confidence (Koh, 1996; Kim-Soon, Ahmad, & Ibrahim, 2016). Quite several studies confirm that entrepreneurial trends we talk about are related to personal characteristics (e.g. Crant, 1996; Phipps, 2012; Prieto, 2011; Zhang, Wang & Owen, 2015; Phipps & Prieto, 2015).

Additionally, since their social networks are broad and their social capital is strong, it is indicated that their attitudes and approaches are positive, their style is pragmatic, they behave according to circumstances, and they are committed to success-oriented behavior (Thompson, 1999; Thompson, 2002). The fact that social entrepreneurs who successfully exhibit these behaviors have political skills is also being discussed in a limited number of studies (Phipps & Prieto, 2015).

The fact that social entrepreneurs operate between public institutions and non-profit organizations and commercial enterprises representing the private sector, which are referred to as the third sector, is the basis for their flexibility in decision-making processes and for their taking pragmatic and rapid action (Cetindamar, 2010). It can be said that this is the way of preserving the dynamic balance in the arena in which they are to create social value and value. Kushner (2002) defines the five components that successful social initiatives make use of in social value creation as:

satisfaction of constituents, resource efficiency, operational efficiency, capacity to achieve targets, and adaptation to change (Knife, Haughton, & Dixon, 2014).

Again, it is suggested that most of the entrepreneurs put their initiatives into practice between 35-45 years of age (Nair & Pendey, 2006).

CURRENT STUDY

Although it might be claimed that due to similarity in terms of entrepreneurship the social entrepreneurs encompass commercial entrepreneurship's personality characteristics and behaviors, they differ from each other according to their paradigm about community's well being, in terms of ethical point of view and value creation.

As Santos (2012) mentioned:

social entrepreneurship is not specifically about creating market mechanisms or securing government subsidies or creating a social enterprise, it is about crafting effective and sustainable solutions using whatever combination of institutional means is deemed effective.

As it can be understood from this assumption, social entrepreneurship distinguishes from commercial entrepreneurship by focusing on value creation as opposed to value capture. Consequently, social entrepreneurs' actions have the effect of increasing society's aggregative utility. Unlike commercial entrepreneurs, the former are not concerned so much with the potential for value capture because they are motivated by the positive externalities their activities trigger and by the total utility of community (Agafonow, 2014).

Today, it is observed that social issues related with the society are handled by individual entrepreneurs because the state cannot provide adequate support. In the sector, which is called as the "non-profit sector", in areas that are neglected by the state and the private sector, social entrepreneurship activities provide important improvements in solving the problems about the humans and the environment. For this reason, it is observed that social entrepreneurship promises a good future, and its importance is increasing with each passing day (Koorsgaad, 2011). When the literature is reviewed, it is also observed that social entrepreneurship is intensely related with the entrepreneurship concept. It is mentioned by several authors that this concept has developed the general entrepreneurship concept (Ruvio & Shoham, 2011). Despite the interest in studies conducted on social entrepreneurship in Turkey, this field is relatively new and open to developments.

METHOD

The research is based on in-depth interviews allows the researchers to investigate the phenomenon in depth (Yin, 2009) This methodology was chosen to get a better understanding of the individual and behavioral factors of social entrepreneurs (Eisenhardt & Graebner, 2007). Interview questions were determined as a result of the review of literature based on value creation.

After gathering information about their childhood times, during in-depth interviews six main questions asked by researchers are given below:

1. It is known, as social entrepreneurs are innovators who undertake risks to create social values for well being of community. Who do you think is a social entrepreneur?
2. What are the prominent personalities and behavioral characteristics of social entrepreneurs?
3. It is stated that social entrepreneurs use social networks effectively to create social value. Do you think you have the ability to use effectively social networks? How do you define social value and in this purpose what do you do?
4. It is claimed that social entrepreneurs can demonstrate political behavior and direct the situation according to their own aims to create social value. Do you believe that you posses your political skills? Should it be?
5. It is important to ensure the adequacy and continuity of the resources that are used by the social entrepreneur. In that case, do you believe that you manage your resources effectively and efficiently? Such as human resources, information, financial resources… Could you tell us the role of strategic management and ethical values in this process?
6. Would you please define the work environments that may jeopardize the behavior of social entrepreneurship?

The data were collected through in-depth interviews. These interviews that lasted at least an hour conducted with four social entrepreneurs. Three participants were interviewed in Istanbul, and the other one (Tülin Akin) who lives in Aydın was interviewed through SKYPE.

Pattern matching and explanation buildings techniques were used for analyzing the collected data to explore whether the pattern of reported social entrepreneurship behaviors of four participants matches the theory of social entrepreneurship.

First, patterns arising from the data were jointly identified by the researchers then explanation building technique was used to identify contribution of the key components (Yin, 2009). Researchers capture logics by showing as much of the raw data as they can; text segments taken directly from interview transcripts are grouped into meaningful categories that constitute a pattern or set of behaviors associated with one or more logics. Once they have developed explanations about the categories and patterns of behavior that are meaningful to the researchers, the next challenge is to convince readers that the categories developed appropriately show sets of behaviors or practices that reflect the influence of guiding logic(s) (Reay & Jones, 2016).

The researchers are also interested in expanding the theory through qualitative methods to determine whether there exist common properties of personality and behaviors among the participants.

Study Participants

Brief information on social entrepreneur background of the participants is provided below. Since 1997, Ercan Tutal has voluntarily been producing alternative and innovative projects aimed at equal and full participation of disadvantaged people, individuals with special needs in the social life. Some of his projects have continued for more than a decade (ex. "Diving is Freedom", "the Alternative Camp project", "Music for All", "The Dreams Academy"). His mission is: *To create a barrier-free life for individuals with special needs.*

Serra Titiz has been working on sustainable development since 2003. She worked with youth, with women and vocational groups at large NGOs at managerial levels, has participated to international programs on NGOs and Civic Activism. Her work has always reflected social innovation. Serra Titiz is the founder and the managing director of a social enterprise: Mikado Sustainable Development Consulting, in Istanbul, Turkey. Her mission is: *To work for people together with people.*

Ibrahim Betil worked as manager in the greatest finance institutions of the country. Aside from senior-level duties, he has been known for his sensitivity and works on social issues since 1994. He is the founder of TEGV, TOG, Enka Schools, Teachers' Academy Foundation, Hrant Dink Foundation and Sen-De-Gel Association. He realizes projects together with national and international organizations by fighting against poverty, creating employment, and by producing projects for the development of the status of women and young people. His mission is: *To be volunteer not only to pass through the road but to change the road.*

Tülin Akin founded Tarimsalpazarlama.com in 2004. She received the first prize in e-export in the Stars of Export in 2007. She modeled Farmer Credit Cards with banks, founded the Farmers Club with Vodafone, and developed a special farmer's computer software with the support of Intel. She carried out various social responsibility projects to improve water awareness and prevent tractor accidents in rural areas. She was recognized with the Development of Agricultural Trade Award by the Agriculturists Foundation of Turkey in 2012, the Female Social Entrepreneur Award by Garanti - KAGIDER in 2013 and was nominated for Nobel by the UN in 2014. She is the founding partner of 'TABIT Agricultural Information and Communications Technologies' and 'Agricultural Marketing' companies. Her mission is *serving humans despite humans.*

Interview Process

In-person interviews lasted approximately one hour. All the interviews were conducted by two researchers, including 6 main open-ended questions and 18 sub-questions focusing on family life during their childhood, their personalities, their career history and their thoughts about the concept of social entrepreneurship and their social entrepreneurship behaviors sustained in their lives.

FINDINGS

As a result of the interview with the participants, the following information was obtained about the definition and characteristics of the social entrepreneur.

The Definitions of Social Entrepreneur

E.T.: Today, when a definition of a social entrepreneur is made, a person or institution that performs a charity or social responsibility project can be considered as a social enterprise; however, you must have an idea of your own to be a social entrepreneur, and this idea should be unique, in other words, it must not be an idea practiced before. For example, it is not possible for those who pursue the project "Dialogue in the Dark" in Turkey today to be called social entrepreneurs. Because it is Andres Heinnecke who brought it up. Heinnecke is the visionary and innovative person who established "Dialogue in the Dark" in Hamburg 20 years ago and could implement it in 50 countries throughout the world. Again, Victor Ananias who established the Wheat Association was a social entrepreneur. However, the other executives who started to work later in the Wheat Association were only part of the team despite their ten-year long endeavor. In this respect, it is the social entrepreneur who puts up an idea and makes up the organization; and those who later worked in the same team with him are the teammates and companions.

S.T.: Social entrepreneur is a person who has devoted his/her life to the solution of a social problem. S/he is the one who tries different ways to solve a problem. In my opinion, this is the most basic difference with an entrepreneur. An entrepreneur takes risks and creates difference; however, if the enterprise is not accepted and if there are no demands for it, s/he may have investments on some different fields or services. Social entrepreneur, on the other hand, devotes himself/herself to the solution of the problem to which s/he wants to find a solution and develops different methods for solution. For this reason, it is more sustainable. In some studies, I read that social entrepreneurs are more endurable and have longer lifespans especially during crises. Unlike Ercan, I believe that social entrepreneur does not consist of one single person. In my opinion, having a novel idea is not adequate to sustain and achieve success with it. I observed this in my two social enterprises. One of these was the Mikado and "Future is Brighter" Youth Platform. Nothing happens without a team.

I. B.: In my opinion, a social entrepreneurship does not occur with one single person. Social entrepreneur may be one single person, sometimes a group or even an organization. Being a social entrepreneur starts when the person worries about the problems of the society. The problems of the society are not limited with the country in which we live. This process starts with fleeing to the place where one is needed and with being able to notice the needs. I saw these needs and established the required structures, but one is not enough. Being a team is extremely important. Social entrepreneur establishes a sustainable enterprise for realizing a change and solving a problem. The enterprise must also be supported with an economic income. I established non-governmental organizations in various areas. However, I could not establish a network that would contribute economically to these non-governmental enterprises. All the non-governmental organizations I established sustain with donations. I provide the flow of funds through various organizations or individuals in the society. My purpose is not help other with donations. You only make begging seem attractive with donations. We use these aids to shape the life in the areas where we go to help and to teach new production methods.

T.A. supports both Ercan and Serra.

Naturally, there is only one person that developed new ideas and that undertakes the risk for the solution of a problem. This person is a social entrepreneur, but we are also a team. In this team, there are some members who are here just to work because the working conditions are humane, ethical and equalitarian. In such situations, these people are a part of the team but not social entrepreneurs. However, there are some friends among them that have adopted the social value like me, and they try to produce new projects. I think they are social entrepreneurs.

The participant's views support the definitions in academic studies. As it has been mentioned previously; it is expected that the social entrepreneur who aims to fulfill his mission to create a social value and to become an agent of change is able to continuously capture the new opportunities on the road and successfully put them into practice (Jackson & Jackson, 2014). As previously mentioned, three principles have been emphasized in defining social entrepreneurship. The first of these principles is that social entrepreneurship is the process of creating value through the combination of new ways and resources; the second is that the intention is to discover opportunities for creating social value through social change or meeting needs; and the last one is that social entrepreneurship includes the provision of services and products as a process but also points to the creation of a new organization (Mair & Marti, 2006).

The Efforts to Create Social Value

During our interview, although no direct questions were asked about the creation of social value, we have obtained some information from the statements of the participants.

E.T.: Social entrepreneurs are actually social revolutionists. All the projects they perform are revolutionary to create social value in the name of the country. The social value must be of an inclusive nature beyond the social value of a specific part of a society or a group. We make a difference in the lives of 1/3 of the population through the projects we realize. Due to the existence of several projects that we have carried out together with our business partners for more than 10 years, we now have a law regarding the disabled people. The 81 provincial municipalities of 81 provinces have Coordination Centers for the Disabled. Everyone in Turkey is now aware of the Disabled. Thanks to information technology, we announce our activities via our own software and our disabled friends work here. With the "Social Inclusion Band" we formed, young people are included and integrated in the society with the concert we organized.

He emphasizes that they are bravely carrying out the models that embrace the whole society in creating social values.

İ.B.: In order to define social value mentioned:

With the help of "Come! You, too! Association" development projects the lives of more than 200 thousand people from Senegal and Gambia changed within 3 years. We brought animal husbandry projects to this area with our philosophy "Do not give fish, but teach how to catch fish!". 2113 animals were distributed to families with the small cattle animal husbandry project. We ensured that local fishery was supported. 31 water wells were opened for 32 thousand 610 people. Poultry farms and 11 rice mills were established in 20 villages. Dealing with such issues made us create social values.

S.T. mentioned several projects for creation social value:

We support the formation of integrative working models and sustainable strategies to companies for contributing to the creation of a private sector that has a feeling of responsibility. We realize projects and trainings with many non-governmental organizations to develop the capacities of the NGOs in training active citizens for creating a sustainable and transparent civil society. In addition to these, we make the private sector, academic institutions and NGOs come together in various innovations projects with an innovative viewpoint. Our aim is to transfer a sustainable world to the next generations.

T.A. added,

We make the use of technology become widespread in agriculture with the "Smart Agriculture Projects". We cover the needs of people living in rural areas dealing with agriculture by using the opportunities of technology. We aim to increase their productivity and profitability, and depending on this, their life quality.

Considering these statements, it is possible to define "social value" as the activities on social change and transformation for ensuring that the society sustains its life in a healthy manner by including the human, nature and all other societies.

Behavioral Characteristics of a Social Entrepreneur

Another question of the interview was *Can you define the behavioral characteristics of yours as a social entrepreneur?*

E. T. stated,

Social entrepreneurship has dimensions of leadership, originality, innovation and creativity. The fact that the work done is sustainable is also of great importance. What I mean by sustainability is that the idea should be sustainable; and organizational growth is not a sign of sustainability. For this reason, sustainability is not to open branches all over the country. It is, to me, to talk to the local people in every city I visit, have conversations to raise awareness about the disabled life, and to make them sensitive to the environment. It is to transfer new ideas into the field where you want to create constant values and make them available.

The initiative you start should be sustainable. Social enterprise is such a methodological work that It should be perceived as a management of a conglomerate. Creation of social values requires not only a high degree of engagement but also strategic thinking. In this respect, you need to learn constantly to be a 'visionary', follow the agenda, find the real source of the problem, start with the real solution proposals, and analyze the conditions of the country for a successful strategic planning for the period you are in."

S. T.: I believe that social entrepreneur must have some leadership characteristics. I believe that a social entrepreneur must hold the team together, be the pioneer in forming the values, must be visionary, and stick to ethical values, and must have an innovative viewpoint. For this reason, in starting the social entrepreneurship my philosophy was "Working for people together with people". My aim was to become aware of the social needs, having worries in life as an individual, and making life become more livable. With this mission and with these values, me and my team mates proceed with success for more than ten years. A social entrepreneur is participative and becomes happy when s/he shares. Our system, which we grew by sharing and by creating social value, is expanding with this philosophy. For social value be sustainable, the strategic planning skill is necessary.

I. B.: I completely believe that the leadership capacity of a social entrepreneur must be in constant interaction with a visionary devotion and ethical values. As well as these behavioral skills, I also believe that a social entrepreneur should have better communication skills. I have always adopted the idea in my professional life that communication skills should be used, the decisions should be made in a mutual manner and the employees should be empowered. For this reason, a social entrepreneur must develop communication skills. Additionally, it is also necessary to have administrative and conceptual skills as well, because social enterprises are having the pioneering role of social transformation. Otherwise, they won't be able to respond to the needs of the society.

T. A.: I agree that there are certain properties a social entrepreneur should have. Meanwhile, the desire to give a hand to others, and the responsibility felt about the future generations stay behind these behaviors. I started the social enterprise with the philosophy of "serving humans despite humans". I believed that I would change the whole world. In this sense, the engagement, self- motivation and resilience for the creation of social value are important. However, when I look back, I cannot say that leadership characteristics are from my childhood. I was a very calm, quiet, and hardworking but I only showed my hardworking when I was asked. In later years, I improved myself with the thought, if I want to change my world I must lead people for this.

As mentioned before; when it is considered that the process of social entrepreneurship is:

a process involving the innovative use and combination of resources to pursue opportunities to catalyze social change and/or address social needs (Mair & Marti, 2006);

It is verified that the social entrepreneur needs to be visionary and have strategic management and leadership skills to maintain the sustainability of resources.

It is understood that the social entrepreneur uses these skills to support diversity, too.

E.T. added: As one of the important actors of Turkey's development policy, we try to serve about 8-10 million people in Turkey especially for a barrier-free life. We work for the barrier-free tourism and education policies in Turkey.

I. B. mentioned; I never put limits for myself in terms of region or society when I started social enterprises. Wherever I saw missing points, I went there believing that I could cause some benefits. Then I proceeded by knowing the value of human without considering the differences. If I set limits in a geographical area or with a certain society, there would be limitations in terms of religion, language, or race. Then I would become a man who helped only his own group. A social entrepreneur accepts social differences as a kind of social variety.

S. T.: The reasons for existence of our social enterprise is creating a sustainable transparent civil society, and a social innovation. Creating employment for young people without considering any differences. In this sense, the first institution that crosses the mind is our organization. To create a social value, we develop sustainable models with the help of stakeholders in the society especially in academic institutions and private sector. Our projects encompass all the society.

In addition, in successful maintenance of these projects, E.T.

It is another important feature that social entrepreneurs need to catch the trends of the period in this dynamic environment and relations. Information and communication technologies need to be adapted to all our services. Now that we are managing social benefit-creating processes with a social business sense, integrating the use of technology and establishment of our software teams, creation and printing of our films, photographs and planning of our websites have created a business model in which all our disabled friends are actively involved in business life.

T. A.: We must use technological infrastructure and resources that exist in our present time to sustain the social enterprises, to realize the projects with social stakeholders and to convince them. I usually give BATMAN as the example in such situations. BATMAN utilizes the technical equipment and technological infrastructure to establish goodness and trust in the society as the hero of the movie. He does not have special powers given to him like Superman or Spiderman. In this context, he reacts against the evil things around him by using the same technology used by the others. In this sense, social entrepreneur must follow technological changes in a close range and make use of the facilities provided by technology.

Academic literature emphasizes the ability of social entrepreneurs to benefit from social networks in the development of sustainable projects (Jackson & Jackson, 2014). In this frame, E. T. states;

In order to sustain the mechanisms that will ensure the continuity of the financial resources it is also necessary to create social networks. In an event or on an airplane trip, I assume every person around me as a social investor. The effective use of social networks on a target basis is essential for social entrepreneurs. However, it is not easy for a single person to announce himself as a social entrepreneur and to maintain his projects. For this reason, cooperation by social networks is needed in the creation and maintenance of the flow of financial funds and other resources. Besides, managing these relationships requires political skill. It is also a fact that the social entrepreneurs have encountered many restrictive obstacles. For this reason, it is imperative that social entrepreneurs exhibit dexterity on negotiations, conflict management and political maneuvers.

I. A.: As I mentioned before, communication has an important place in creating and developing social networks. In my viewpoint, this situation is a little bit different... As you know, I have been the senior manager in different institutions for many years. The people whom I made friends became my colleagues in social entrepreneurs in later years. The close relations I established in private sector and our keeping in contact led the way to cooperate in different projects today. However, when we mention political maneuvers, I care more about actions than words. I believe that every person sitting in front of me is more intelligent than me and has more perceptive skills. For this reason, I care about being transparent and proceeding with honesty. I present transparent information when I try to convince our stakeholders to participate in our projects. All my social enterprises are audited by independent auditors every year. I convince these auditing institutions, and I want them to audit me as a requirement of social responsibility projects. I use this transparency, I mean this accountability, as a political maneuver. I understand and interpret political maneuver in this way.

T. A.: At first, I was not skillful in presenting our projects in a way that would be understood by other. Then, I realized that each stakeholder had their own reason to be a part of a social benefit. It was also necessary to create a benefit for them. Sometimes a social project could be important for the reputation management or for the corporate social responsibility. Or sometimes the reason could be to increase togetherness and to empower the integrity of an organization by working in a project. For this reason, I saw that realizing our projects in a manner that would create values for each of us would establish cooperation with longer lifespans. I think this behavior which I developed may be considered as a political maneuver.

S. T:. As I mentioned before, we bring different social stakeholders together to realize social goals focused on development in a long term. Even so, it is not adequate for us to bring social stakeholders together to create funds. We always question how we may activate this togetherness to create new products. Encouraging people in this way and making them become volunteers for social change may in fact evoke political behaviors. Being able to manage crises, and being able to manage conflicts are important. I cannot claim that I can act in a complete political manner as a person myself. However, we can make projects become flexible, because we perform empathy when we are cooperating with different groups, and we can include different groups. Since problems, situation and the dynamic of groups change, we plant flexible changes or differences according to them. However, we never accept the aid of a group whose viewpoints we do not agree. Or we do not start a project with organizations which we notice that they have discriminative practices. For example, recently, an organization stated that it could support one of our projects only with the students of 7 universities in Turkey. We stated that it was impossible, and we explained that we planned to create value to all students over Turkey. They understood us eventually, and supported our project. I did not accept discrimination, and we ensured that they understood us and supported our project with our principles. I think this can be accepted as a political maneuver.

With these comments, they have supported the academic research on possession of broad social networks and political maneuvers (e.g.: Thompson, 1999; Thompson, 2002; Phipps & Prieto, 2015). It is also understood that exhibiting ethical behavior in business processes is one of the important dimensions of social entrepreneurs.

Personality Traits of a Social Entrepreneur

E. T.: To sustain an initiative successfully cannot be achieved only by being a good and moral person. But its role in safe and long-term business partnerships is undeniable. In addition, when we talk about ethical value, the first principle that comes to my mind is transparency. I inform all our friends in the team on every decision we make, and I want them to be informed about the process. In addition to being ethical, principled and well-intentioned, it is necessary to be transparent. A social entrepreneur is also resilient and self- motivated. The source of his/her internal motivation is his/her high awareness on the needs of the society. The social entrepreneur tries to help society by assuming the responsibility of being a citizen of the world without considering where the problem is.

S. T.: During my university education, I was the member of the NOGs of the university, which were only 2 in those times. Although it was expected that I would work in a company like P & G after I graduated from the university, I announced "I will become a social entrepreneur". My wish, from my early childhood years, was to be influential in increasing the social welfare. For this reason, my internal motivation was very high. Even if no one supported me, I believed in myself, I was hopeful, and I never recognized any obstacles. I used to work with devotion and patience. My sole problem was the youth and sustainability. What I needed was to improve myself. The way leading to this went through bringing social benefit to others, to young people. The place where my life became meaningful, where I realized myself, was this point. Today also I feel the same.

T. A.: Since my father was a primary school teacher, we lived in various towns and cities of Turkey with certain intervals. My parents were always role model for me. Especially my father said "You should make every place you travel become beautiful. A village teacher brings information as well as civilization to the place where s/he travels". I took him as a role model. I always wanted to help the society in which I lives in the context of its needs. In this respect, my sensitivity is high in terms of creating social awareness. In addition, I have the desire to start change to create social benefit. I have a dream of leaving more livable soil for future generations. I serve this goal of mine with my devotion. My internal motivation is always high. Of course, there are sometimes when I get tired and I pause. I do not personalize problems and I move on. I dream about the whole and do not care about small difficulties. I said, "I serve despite humans", when I internalize this philosophy, nothing can change my way. I believe that the thing I do has the power of transforming the world, and this is the source of my resistance. I was never extrovert, I was never the group leader. As my age furthered, when I realized that I had to socialize to realize my dreams, and I could do this by expanding my social networks, I received trainings. When you believe, everything is possible...

I. A.: In my opinion, we have an incorrect question that is asked to children by grown-ups in our society. This basic question is even valid for primary schools. This question is "What do you want to be when you grow up?" This question brings the perceptions of children to a different point. I always ask children "What do want to do?" not "What do you want to be?" "Being" is a statement of status in the society. I will be a banker, an academic, a manager... All right, you will become this or that, but what will you for the society and for yourself? On the other hand, the question "What do you want to do?" makes the individual give an answer that will make him/her become activated. For me "being" was not meaningful ever in my life.

Gaining a social status and earning money must be meaningful. However, spending the money I had for true purposes, doing meaningful jobs and sharing were always important for me. This is property coming from the high school years when I stayed at the school at weekends and went to visit other schools and paint their walls with my teachers or from my scout years. I have another sentence that is left from my scout years and that is my philosophy. This is "You will do something good everyday". For this reason, this is my life philosophy, and if everyone acts like this, the world will really change. A Social entrepreneur has a high sensitivity for the environment and society. S/he has a belief and an internal motivation for being able to change the world. S/he is resistant and hopeful in the face of difficulties. S/he believes that limits exist only in the brains of humans, and does not know any limits for his/her dreams. S/he acts instead of criticizing and works for change.

Within the context of these statements, it is observed that the prominent personality traits of a social entrepreneur are having a high internal motivation, being resistant, being hopeful about the future, having high awareness and sensitivity level, being helpful, hardworking, patient, and knowing no limits for change. It is understood that the most important internal motivation is their belief in providing a social benefit for the society and changing the world. *The happiness of working with people for people, the happiness of serving humans despite humans, the happiness of doing something good everyday* are their internal motivation sources.

Childhood Period of a Social Entrepreneur

When we wanted to have some information about their childhood, E.T.:

I think that this sensitivity comes from early ages and the social circle and the family have a direct impact on being sensitive about what is going around, which plays an important role in personal development. I do not know how much influence the family education status has on the development of a growing child, but my mother was a primary school graduate, we lost my father at a young age and my mother was the only anchor of the family. Because of this, I have always known that, since I was little, I have to work hard, be vigorous, stand up and be a leader. For this reason, I think that the circumstances having been experienced since early years of life are decisive in success of someone, in acquiring leadership qualities and in learning to stand up. If I had been a child raised by a prim family, I might have been someone leading an expected way of life, yet a successful, but not the person with today's identity.

I. B.: My father was a clerk in Marputçular. We were not a family with a big income. I entered the Robert College. I study 2 preparatory years and 3 secondary school years in the dormitory. I was always together with my teachers in this period. Especially one of our teachers was an important guide for me. We worked in the construction of a state school in Kavacık with my teachers in those years. I observed that there were many friends that had fewer things than me in Istanbul. With such weekend projects, my awareness and sensitivity on the problems of the society increased. In my university years, I participated in such projects. My family was the role model for me in terms of ethical values (being trustworthy, honest, just, working very hard, etc.). My teachers always guided me in this way.

S. T.: My father was also an entrepreneur. He also created his own brand through many difficulties. My mother had a very strong social side. I learnt to cope with difficulties from my father, and to improve my empathy skills from my mother. I grew up in a family that was authoritarian but did not impose their own thoughts. In brief, I grew up in an environment that was controlled but that was based on trust. My family was a role model for me, in developing my attitudes and behaviors. They did not give the freedom like "You may be whatever you want", but respected my choices because of our relation that was based on trust.

T. A.: My father was a primary school teacher and worked in villages. My mother was the daughter of a family that was a farmer in Kastamonu. I was born in Istanbul. I spent my childhood years in Kastamonu, Konya and Şanlıurfa because of my father duty. My father believed that he should bring civilization to every place he went. My father planted trees in the area that was near the Syrian border. That village became greener in those dry soils. After years, when I went to that village, I saw that that village was greener and more developed when compared with the other villages. I was impressed by this behavior. My family was the role model for me in serving the society and taught me that I had responsibilities. My mother was an entrepreneur, too. She worked in various jobs without hesitating. For this reason, I inherited entrepreneurship properties from my mother and social properties from my father. However, I was an introvert, quiet, calm person when I was a child. I did not have much conversation with others and had the syndrome for being in front of the blackboard in the classroom. I did not lead in games. In further years, I thought that these properties were necessary for me to be successful in job and I improved myself. If I would act on behalf of a farmer, I believed that I would represent them in the most accurate manner.

As a result of the interviews, it is observed that our participants had sensitivity and awareness on the society from early years of their lives. It is understood that leadership and entrepreneurship characteristics developed in our three participants since their childhood years. In this sense, they have an extrovert, social, and brave personality that does not hesitate to enter new environments. It is understood that, unlike the general consideration, our other participants developed themselves with trainings in socializing, establishing communications, expressing themselves, and representing others when they saw these missing points in them. In the light of this information, it is possible to claim that the most important properties in a Social entrepreneur are: (1) high social sensitivity and awareness; (2) the desire for taking initiative in creating a social change and having the courage for this. The communication skills that is required in sustaining a social enterprise and the administrative skills may be improved with trainings. The most important thing is showing devotion to social benefit, patience and endurance. The "mottos" our Social entrepreneurs stated in the interviews give us the signals for this.

The Most Negative Situation That Might Lower Down the Mood of a Social Entrepreneur

To find out the worst condition which could dampen the social entrepreneur, our question was, *What can the most important constraint that may undermine the attitudes and behaviors of social entrepreneurs be?*

E. T.: With such a personality, a social entrepreneur cannot be a classical employee within a certain period at a table. It is not possible for creativity to exist in such a working environment. Social entrepreneur is always in dynamism and can work 24/7, but if s/he is expected to achieve the desired attitudes and behaviors from a classical manager, s/he will want to escape from this environment. Social entrepreneurs will be in constant interaction and must be self-directed in a dynamic structure in a way that s/he will find place in social networks.

S. T.: Social entrepreneur constantly observes the needs and problems of the society and seeks ways to solve them. S/he lives with this. I planned my life only considering the goal for many years. Sometimes I travelled 3-4 times a week to make our voice heard by our stakeholders. I arrived first at our workplace and left the latest. I thought about our projects when I was on my way home. For this reason, while my peer comrades could become senior manager sin corporate institutions, I did not prefer that way. I did not want that the system would shape me with stereotypes behavior structures. Social entrepreneur is creative, bureaucracy does not allow this creativeness. Social entrepreneur does not work for annual targets of one single company with a high society conscious.

I. B.: I worked as a manager for many years in my business life. With the saying of our elderly, "I became. .....". However, this does not satisfy me fully. I have internalized the philosophy "Do something good everyday" coming from my scout years. I devoted myself to "do" rather than to "be", and became happy in this way, and for this reason, I chose to be Social entrepreneur because I liked to share goodness and happiness with other people. I had the happiness of not "owning" but of "sharing". I had the happiness of being the pioneer for social transformation in this geographical area. I had the happiness of touching their lives. The strict and formal business life did not give these to me. Creativity, dynamism and the integration around common values gives a person happiness and this is completely different from other happiness.

T. A.: Being the inspiration for other through our social enterprises, projects and seeing that the environment is changing give a person great happiness. In addition, announcing our projects through PR Agencies, through visual and written media to the society for 14 years and being the inspiration are very important. I imagine about changing not only this village of Aydın where I live, I also imagine of changing the whole world. For this reason, I think areas and relations limited with four walls would not be adequate for realizing myself.

Naturally, the needs of everybody and satisfaction styles vary according to the hierarchical order. Helping others is a way for realizing oneself for some people while having the government power is a need for some others. Some people devote themselves to find the treatment for a disease, while some others live only for themselves. Our participants who came to the forefront with the Social entrepreneur identities realized themselves, and when this is considered, it may be claimed that they stayed away from businesses that were not sincere and that were strict and working for annual targets of a business.

CONCLUSION

In this study, although it was aimed to define the personality and behavioral traits of social entrepreneurs, valuable information has also been obtained to clarify the concept of social entrepreneurship.

In the social enterprise model to which social entrepreneur has stepped for creating social benefit, in fact, with the inclusive business models over time, s/he also realizes significant amount of production for social benefit and creates employment. In addition to income-generating models, the boundaries of the social enterprise are expanding through technology-based investments, particularly through the software of firms that have formed a leading business partners in Turkey. Thus, by providing services to the private sector with the help of the non-profit social business model, a new lifestyle is presented for the masses for which social benefit is aimed.

Considering the definition of social entrepreneur, we distinguish a personality trait that creates value by taking risks and by seeing what it invisible to others, realizing innovation in a daring manner, independent and principled with a level of ability to take advantage of social networks and political skills significant in conflict-crises management as a trailblazer, visionary, inspirational and inclusive person. It is understood that s/he proceeds without a moment of hesitation with the awareness of what is going on around him/her and with internal motivation and durability. Furthermore, all of their initiatives are based on ethical values and on value creation for the well being of community. Although it might be claimed that due to similarity in terms of entrepreneurship the social entrepreneurs encompass commercial entrepreneurship's personality characteristics and behaviors, they differ from each other according to their paradigm about community's well being, in terms of ethical point of view and value creation. It is also noticed that social entrepreneurs encompass, satisfaction of constituents, resource efficiency, operational efficiency, capacity to achieve targets and adaptation to change to make broader a successful social value creation.

As stated in leadership theories, it is certain that the presence and support of followers in the leadership process is undeniable. It is obvious that there cannot be a single person behind the successful projects of a social entrepreneur, and that the mission undertaken with the aim of creating a social value is realized together with volunteering members with various abilities/skills in fields such as management, marketing, organizational design and effective fund management. But it is understood that the social entrepreneur identity is focused on a single person. The social entrepreneur alone gains this qualification as the producer of sustainable ideas.

When it comes to the fact that social entrepreneurship is inherently characterized by leadership-related qualities, it can be said that successful social entrepreneurs have realized their sound and sustainable projects with the help of their personality traits, values, attitudes and behaviors reflected in their values, and their management as well as communication skills.

As a result, the in-depth interview showed and confirmed that the entrepreneurial potential includes; entrepreneurial motivations and psychological, social, managerial competencies. These dimensions contain; self-motivation, self- efficacy, risk-taking, purposeful and success-oriented, visionary and strategic planning capacity, innovation capacity, social capital capacity, leadership capacity, resilience, resistance to uncertainty, conflict management capacity and political maneuvers capacity. As well as the cognitive properties of a social entrepreneur, personal properties and motivational properties are prominent properties. Based on these behaviors, there are the values that are transferred to the individuals from their families and relatives (being transparent, being just, responsibility, being ethical, honesty).

The sub-goal of this study is also, to encourage young people who find clues as to the existence of these traits in them to create social innovation and social values.

REFERENCES

Abdou, E., Fahmy, A., Greenwald, D. & Nelson, J. (2010). *Social Entrepreneurship in the Middle East - Toward Sustainable Development for the Next Generation.* Brookings Report.

Agafonow, A. (2014). Toward A Positive Theory of Social Entrepreneurship. On Maximizing Versus Satisficing Value Capture. *Journal of Business Ethics, 125*(4), 709–713. doi:10.100710551-013-1948-z

Bornstein, D. (2007). *How to Change the World: Social Entrepreneurs and the Power of New Ideas.* Oxford University Press.

Çetindamar, D., Tutal, E., Titiz, S., & Taluk, Ş. (2010). Sosyal Dönüşümün Ajanları: Social entrepreneurler. In *Social Entrepreneurship Conference.* Sakıp Sabancı Üniversitesi. Retrieved from http://www.sosyalinovasyonmerkezi.com.tr/yayin/2020100002.pdf

Çetinkaya Bozkurt, Ö., Kalkan, A., Koyuncu, O. & Alparslan, A. M. (2012). Türkiye'de Girişimciliğin Gelişimi: Girişimciler Üzerine Nitel Bir Araştırma. *Süleyman Demirel Üniversitesi Sosyal Bilimler Enstitüsü Dergisi, 15*, 229-247.

Curral, L., Santos, S., & Caetano, A. (2013). Theoretical foundation of the entrepreneurial potential. *Amity Business Journal, 2*(1), 1–11.

Eisenhardt, K., & Graebner, M. (2007). Theory building from cases: Opportunities and challenges. *Academy of Management Journal, 50*(1), 25–32. doi:10.5465/AMJ.2007.24160888

Ferrel, O. C., Hirt, G. A., & Ferrel, L. (2016). *Business: A Changing World* (5th ed.). McGraw- Hill Education.

Fishbein, M., & Ajzen, I. (1975). *Belief, Attitude, Intention and Behavior: An Introduction Theory and Research.* Reading, MA: Addison-Wesley.

Groot, A. & Dankbaar, B. (2014). Does Social Innovation Require Social Entrepreneurship? *Technology Innovation Management Review*, 14-26.

Hisrich, R. D., & Peters, M. P. (1995). *Entrepreneurship—Starting, Developing and Managing a New Enterprise.* Boston: Irwin.

İçerli, L., & Şahin Karadal, M. (2014). Sosyal entrepreneurlik. İstanbul: Beta Yayıncılık.

Jackson, W. T., & Jackson, M. J. (2014). Social Enterprises and Social Entrepreneurs: One Size Does Not Fit All. *Academy of Entrepreneurship Journal, 20*(2), 152–162.

Kılıç Kırılmaz, S. (2014). Sosyal Girişimcilik Boyutlarına Kuramsal Bir Bakış. *Journal of Economics and Management Research, 3*(2), 55–74.

Kim-Soon, N., Ahmad, A. R., & Ibrahim, N. N. (2016). Theory of Planned Behavior: Undergraduates' Entrepreneurial Motivation and Entrepreneurship Career Intention at a Public University. *Journal of Entrepreneurship: Research & Practice, 2016*, 1–14.

Knife, K., Haughton, A., & Dixon, E. (2014). Measuring Sustainability and Effectiveness of Social Value Creation by Social Sector Actors/ Social Enterprises, Within Developing Countries. *Academy of Entrepreneurship Journal, 20*(1), 1–23.

Light, P. C. (2006). Reshaping Social Entrepreneurship. *Stanford Social Innovation Review*, 47–51.

Lukach, R., & Plasmans, J. (2002). *Measuring Knowledge Spillovers Using Patent Citations: Evidence from the Belgian Firm's Data.* CESifo Working Paper, Nr.754.

Mair, J., & Marti, I. (2006). Social Entrepreneurship Research: A Source of Explanation, Prediction, and Delight. *Journal of World Business, 41*(1), 36–44. doi:10.1016/j.jwb.2005.09.002

Nair, K. R. G., & Pandey, A. (2006). Characteristics of Entrepreneurs: An Empirical Analysis. *The Journal of Entrepreneurship, 15*(1), 47–61. doi:10.1177/097135570501500104

Phipps, S. T. A., & Prieto, L. C. (2015). Politicking and Entrepreneurship: Determining The Critical Political Skill Dimensions for High Entrepreneurial Intentions. *Academy of Entrepreneurship Journal, 21*(2), 73–87.

Reay, T., & Jones, C. (2016). Qualitatively capturing institutional logics. *Strategic Organization, 14*(4), 441–454. doi:10.1177/1476127015589981

Sahasranamam, S., & Sud, M. (2016). Opportunity and Necessity Entrepreneurship: A Comparative Study of India and China. *Academy of Entrepreneurship Journal, 22*(1), 21–40.

Santos, F. M. (2012). A positive theory of social entrepreneurship. *Journal of Business Ethics, 111*(3), 335–351. doi:10.100710551-012-1413-4

Schumpeter, J. A. (1967). *The Theory of Economic Development.* New York: Oxford University Press.

Shaw, E., & Carter, S. (2007). Social Entrepreneurship: Theoretical Antecedents and Empirical Analysis of Entrepreneurial Processes and Outcomes. *Journal of Small Business and Enterprise Development, 14*(3), 418–434. doi:10.1108/14626000710773529

Sobhani, S., & Gasnier, A. (2012). Sosyal Girişimcilikten Kapsayıcı Piyasalara. In Büyüyen Kapsayıcı Piyasalar Türkiye'de Sosyal Girişimcilik Vakaları (pp. 1-7). İstanbul Bilgi Üniversitesi.

Thompson, J. L. (1988). The World of the Social Entrepreneur. *International Journal of Public Sector Management, 15*(5), 412–431. doi:10.1108/09513550210435746

Thompson, J. L. (1999). The World of the Entrepreneur- A New Perspective, *Journal of Workplace Learning-. Counseling Today, 11*(6), 209–215.

Yin, R. K. (2009). *Case Study Research Design and Methods* (4th ed.). Thousand Oaks, CA: Sage Publication Inc.

Zahra, A. M., Gedajlovic, E., Neubaum, D. O., & Shulman, J. M. (2009). A Typology of Social Entrepreneurship: Motives, Search Processes and Ethical Challenges. *Journal of Business Venturing, 24*(5), 519–532. doi:10.1016/j.jbusvent.2008.04.007

Zahra, S., Rawhouser, H., Bhaw, N., Neubaum, D., & Hayton, J. (2008). Globalisation of Social Entrepreneurship Opportunities. *Strategic Entrepreneurship Journal*, *2*(2), 117–131. doi:10.1002ej.43

ADDITIONAL READING

Adler, P. S., & Kwon, S.-W. (2002). Social Capital: Prospects for a New Concept. *Academy of Management Review*, *27*(1), 17–40.

Auerswald, P. (2009). Creating Social Value. *Stanford Social Innovation Review*, 51–55.

Bacq, S., & Janssen, F. (2011). The multiple faces of social entrepreneurship: A review of definitional issues based on geographical and thematic criteria. *Entrepreneurship and Regional Development*, *23*(5-6), 373–403. doi:10.1080/08985626.2011.577242

Bahadırlı, S., Demir, Y., Dikmener, G., Dinç, Y. E., Erhart, I., Gasnier, A., . . . Sönmez, O. (2012). Büyüyen Kapsayıcı Piyasalar - Türkiye'de Sosyal Girişimcilik Vakaları. İstanbul: İstanbul Bilgi Üniversitesi Yayınları, Publication No. 386.

Berzin, S. C. (2012). Where Is Social Work in the Social Entrepreneurship Movement? *Social Work*, *57*(2), 185–188. doi:10.1093wws004 PMID:23038880

Besler, S. (2010). *Sosyal Girişimcilik*. İstanbul: Beta.

Çetindamar, D. (2002). *Türkiye'de Girişimcilik*. İstanbul: TÜSİAD.

Corner, P., & Ho, D. M. (2010). How Opportunities Develop in Social Entrepreneurship. *Entrepreneurship Theory and Practice*, *34*(4), 635–659. doi:10.1111/j.1540-6520.2010.00382.x

Denizalp, H. (2007). Toplumsal Dönüşüm için Sosyal Girişimcilik Rehberi. 2nd Ed. Sivil Toplum Geliştirme Vakfı. Ankara: Fersa Matbaacılık.

Dess, J. G. (2001). The meaning of "social entrepreneurship". *Working paper*. Stanford, California: Stanford University.

Dess, J. G. (2007). Taking social entrepreneurship seriously. *Society*, *44*(3), 24–31. doi:10.1007/BF02819936

Girón, M. E., & Gardetti, M. Á. (2014). *Sustainable Luxury and Social Entrepreneurship: Stories from the Pioneers*. Sheffield, UK: Greenleaf Publishing.

Güler Kümbül, B. (2010). *Sosyal Girişimcilik*. Ankara: Efil Yayınevi.

Hu, J., Li, S.-J., Tsai, S. D.-H., & Liu, T. Y.-C. (2014). *Entrepreneurship in Asia: Social Enterprise, Network and Grassroots Case Studies*. New Jersey: World Scientific.

Mair, J., & Marti, I. (2006). Social Entrepreneurship Research: A Source of Explanation, Prediction, and Delight. *Journal of World Business*, *41*(1), 36–44. doi:10.1016/j.jwb.2005.09.002

Nicholls, A. (2006). *Social Entrepreneurship: New Models of Sustainable Social Change*. Oxford: Oxford University Press.

Nordic Council of Ministers. (2015). *Social Entrepreneurship and Social Innovation: Initiatives to Promote Social Entrepreneurship and Social Innovation in the Nordic Countries*. Copenhagen: Nordic Council of Ministers.

Peredo, A. M., & McLean, M. (2006). Social Entrepreneurship: A Critical Review of the Concept. *Journal of World Business*, *41*(1), 55–65. doi:10.1016/j.jwb.2005.10.007

Phipps, S. T. A. (2012). Contributors to an enterprising gender: Examining the influence of creativity on entrepreneurial intentions and the moderating role of political skill controlling for gender. *Academy of Entrepreneurship Journal*, *18*(1), 77–90.

Santos, F. M. (2012). A Positive Theory on Social Entrepreneurship. *Journal of Business Ethics*, *111*(3), 335–351. doi:10.100710551-012-1413-4

Seelos, C., & Mair, J. (2005). Social Entrepreneurship: Creating New Business Models to Serve the Poor. *Business Horizons*, *48*(3), 241–246. doi:10.1016/j.bushor.2004.11.006

Short, J. (2014). *Social Entrepreneurship and Research Methods* (1st ed.). Bingley, U.K.: Emerald Group Publishing Limited. doi:10.1108/S1479-838720149

Short, J. C., Moss, T. W., & Lumpkin, G. T. (2009). Research in social entrepreneurship: Past contributions and future opportunities. *Strategic Entrepreneurship Journal*, *3*(2), 161–194. doi:10.1002ej.69

Trexler, J. (2008). Social entrepreneurship as an algorithm: Is social enterprise sustainable? *Emergence*, *10*(3), 65–85.

Trivedi, C. (2010). Towards a Social Ecological Framework for Social Entrepreneurship. *The Journal of Entrepreneurship*, *19*(1), 63–80. doi:10.1177/097135570901900104

Weerawardena, J., & Mort, G. S. (2006). Investigating Social Entrepreneurship: A Multidimensional Model. *Journal of World Business*, *41*(1), 21–35. doi:10.1016/j.jwb.2005.09.001

Williams, D. A., & K'nife, K. A. K. (2012). The Dark Side of Social Entrepreneurship. *International Journal of Entrepreneurship*, *16*, 63–82.

KEY TERMS AND DEFINITIONS

Political Maneuvers: The political skills which provide the ability to understand others and use that knowledge to effectively influence situations. In related researches, it is known political skill has four key dimensions, namely social astuteness, interpersonal influence, networking ability, and apparent sincerity.

Resilience: The ability to manage stress and cope with difficult issues successfully through the process of adaptation to the demands of the task. Key components of resilience are stated as; problem-focused coping, emotion-focused coping, self-confidence, optimism, sense of purpose, support seeking.

Social Entrepreneurship: Change agents who seek, discover, and evaluate the opportunities to bring about positive social effects, and who reveal business solutions for social problems.

Social Value: The creation of benefits or reductions of costs for society—through efforts to address societal needs and problems—in ways that go beyond the private gains and general benefits of market activity.

Chapter 5
Social Innovation and Social Entrepreneurship

Muhsin F. Bayik
İstanbul Medipol University, Turkey

ABSTRACT

This chapter introduces social innovation, social entrepreneurship, corporate social responsibility, corporate social entrepreneurship, and new product development and argues that social entrepreneurs can utilize from the customer development process when working on a novel solution to create social and economic value. Social entrepreneurs can team up with companies for creating sustainable solutions for the society. Companies can integrate corporate social entrepreneurship into their strategies. City administrations can support social enterprises. The conclusion briefly describes possible weaknesses, limitations, and challenges for social innovation and social entrepreneurship.

INTRODUCTION

In non-industrialized countries, basic needs of millions of people are far from being met, since these people cannot afford products and services to satisfy their needs. The World Bank (2003) maintains that,

services to satisfy basic human needs, particularly those that contribute to health and education, are failing poor people in terms of access, quality, and affordability. The main reason for this failure appears to be the fact that public spending does not reach the poor and, if it does, service provision is often inefficient and of poor quality (Seelos & Mair, 2005).

Social development is *Development that meets the needs of the present without compromising the ability of future generations to meet their own needs* (Grimm, Fox, Baines, & Albertson, 2013). To put the definition into use, United Nations defined a set of Millennium Development Goals (MDGs) based on September 2000 General Assembly Resolution. MDGs are 8 goals for development and poverty eradication. Human rights, health, education and environmental issues are among the goals. Market efficiency, coupled with the resources and management expertise of large multinational companies,

DOI: 10.4018/978-1-5225-5687-9.ch005

are seen as crucial for achieving the goals. The European Commission (2002) also has requested more *direct corporate social responsibility (CSR) as a business contribution to sustainable development.* Social innovation is a multidisciplinary concept. It has an important role in reaching EU 2020 targets,

that aim to raise the activity rate among 20 to 64-year olds to 75%, to decrease the level of early school leavers to 10% and increase level of tertiary education, to reduce the risk of people falling into poverty and to cut carbon emissions to 80% of 1990s levels.

It is expected to offer solutions to society's critical challenges.

Social innovation is interdisciplinary and interconnected. It has a holistic understanding of social needs and by creating social values, it is in a better position to develop sustainable solutions to current societal challenges than free market solutions. Social innovation should be perceived as a collaborating agent between stakeholders, namely *state, private enterprise, free market, the charitable sector and individual citizens" that form the society* (Grimm, Fox, Baines, & Albertson, 2013).

The purpose of this chapter is to analyze social entrepreneurship, social innovation, and the relationship between these concepts.

SOCIAL INNOVATION

Social innovation has been defined by many researchers from different points of view. At present, there is no universally accepted single definition, and it is necessary to review some of the existing definitions to grasp the dimensions of the term.

Mulgan defined social innovations as *new ideas that work in meeting social goals* (Mulgan, 2007). Dawson and Daniel (2010) describe social innovation as *the process of collective idea generation, selection and implementation by people who participate collaboratively to meet social challenges.* Social goals may also serve other scientific, commercial, technical and organizational goals as well.

Social innovation is comprised of four fundamental elements: People, challenge, process and goal. The challenge is the starting point for problem solving or opportunity exploitation. The process is the way of tackling the challenge. The goal is to overcome the challenge to attain a better level of well-being (Dawson & Daniel, 2010).

Social Innovation is defined by the EU Commission as:

...Innovations that are both social in their ends and in their means. Social Innovations are new ideas (products, services and models) that simultaneously meet social needs (more effectively than alternatives) and create new social relationships or collaborations (EU-Commission, 2012a).

The European Business School (EBS) defined Social Innovations as ... *new solutions that address societal challenges in a way that is contextual, targeted, and promotes common welfare* (European Business School (EBS) 2012).

Social Innovation is defined as the *...introduction of new business models and market-based mechanisms that deliver sustainable economic, environmental and social prosperity* by INSEAD Social Innovation Centre (INSEAD, 2012).

Manzini defines social innovation as:

a process of change emerging from the creative re-combination of existing assets (from social capital to historical heritage, from traditional craftsmanship to accessible advanced technology) with the aim to achieve socially recognized goals in a new way (Manzini, 2014).

According to The International Handbook on Social Innovation, social innovation,

means fostering inclusion and wellbeing though improving social relations and empowerment processes: imagining and pursuing a world, a nation, a region, a locality, a community that would grant universal rights and be more socially inclusive (Moulaert, 2013).

The European Union defines social innovations as:

new ideas (products, services, and models) that simultaneously meet social needs (more effectively than alternatives) and create new social relationships or collaborations (Hubert, 2010).

The initial step for social innovation is to find a need which is not met and a solution on how it can be met. This can be tricky, because sometimes it can be a basic need like starvation, infectious diseases or people living on the street and it is easy to spot. In other times, needs may not be that obvious or easy to spot like discrimination or domestic violence, and that would need campaigners or groups to describe these.

The next step in innovation includes testing the promising idea to see if it works. After the reality check, some ideas may not survive. The solution might need to be revised or reshaped. Rather than theoretically testing the idea, taking it to a pilot study accelerates the evaluation process.

The third step in social innovation process is when the idea has passed the tests and it can be used in more places, and sometimes in slightly changed form. Scaling the idea needs strategy and vision, and the allocation of resources and benefiting from leverage, and identifying opponents' soft spots. The innovative entrepreneurs often need a habitat to find support. In that case, a formal approach for persuasion of potential backers may be necessary, including investment evaluation, influence estimation, and new tools to determine success like "social return on investment" or "blended value".

In the fourth step, innovations keep on evolving: learning from experience and adaption to new conditions converts the ideas into shapes which may be far from the anticipation of the pioneers. The journey may end up in an unexpected destination or unwanted use. In employment, in the business world and in the public sector, learning gets to be understood in a better way. Collaboration in open groups (utilized by U.K. National Health Service in the areas like cancer or primary care) or challenge-specific closed groups (used by some large cities to elaborate on transport road maps) have assisted to implant innovation and enhancement into traditional professions.

The social innovation exercise abides around the mile mark where science was over a century ago, when innovation or was dependent upon the eagerness and dynamism of focused individuals like Thomas Edison, who lived in their labs until the ultimate discovery moment. When the importance of science for economy and battles was understood, innovation was taken out of lofts or garages. Ideas were supported by public funds, R&D departments in large corporations and universities, and continuous testing of ideas became the standard. The fruits of that change are the new products coming to market each year.

Social innovation has way to go through such a transformation. It is being recognized that systematic approaches in return enable the expansion of efficient solutions and lower social costs. Key industries of the new century, namely health, education, childcare and eldercare, will have higher share of GDP than information technology and will need different approaches since they are part of the public policy and they depend upon co-creation by the user, patient or student (Mulgan, 2006).

SOCIAL ENTREPRENEURSHIP

Seelos and Mair define Social Entrepreneurship as *creating new models for the provision of products and services that cater directly to basic human needs that remain unsatisfied by current economic or social institutions*. Main objective is social value creation. Economic value creation comes into picture for the sustainability of the organization. It is the:

entrepreneurship that creates new models for the provision of products and services that cater directly to the social needs underlying sustainable development goals such as the MDGs (Seelos & Mair, 2005).

Social Entrepreneurship is defined as:

a dynamic process created and managed by an individual or team (the innovative social entrepreneur), which strives to exploit social innovation with an entrepreneurial mindset and a strong need for achievement, to create new social value in the market and community at large (Perrini & Vurro, 2006).

Social Entrepreneurship is seen as:

innovative approaches to solve social problems and at the same time creating economic value, where social entrepreneurs use their creative talent to develop solutions to social problems with the aim to use their businesses to make money and to make the world a better place to live (Mair, Robinson & Hockerts, 2006).

Social Entrepreneurship is defined to have three components:

identifying a segment in an unjust equilibrium lacking financial means or political influence, coming up with a social value proposition to change the status quo, progressing to a new steady state where the targeted group's potential is released (Martin & Osberg, 2007).

Waddock and Post view social entrepreneurs as "private sector citizens who play critical roles in bringing about catalytic changes in the public-sector agenda and the perception of certain social issues" (Waddock & Post, 1991). Roberts and King (1991) distinguished *entrepreneurial individuals who introduce and help to implement new ideas into practice, despite being outside of formal government positions*. (Roberts & King, 1991) Austin and colleagues (2006) portray social entrepreneurship as *innovative activities that create social value within or across government, business, or nonprofit sectors* (Austin, Leonard, Reficco, & Wei-Skillern, 2006). There exist differences between social and commercial entrepreneurship:

(1) Opportunity differences due to market failure; (2) mission differences resulting in differences in management, motivation, and tension between social and commercial activity; (3) different approaches in managing financial and human resources; and (4) performance measurement in social ventures that complicates accountability and stakeholder relations... social value creation is combining resources to exploit opportunities to solve social problems and contribute to human well-being (Short, Moss, & Lumpkin, 2009).

Dacin defines *the primary mission of the social entrepreneur* as *being one of creating social value by providing solutions to social problems*, argues that there are a great number of definitions for social entrepreneurship and it would be more beneficial to analyze as a context where other types of entrepreneurs may operate (Dacin, Dacin, & Tracey, 2011).

Social entrepreneurs are dedicated to fix basic problems which arise from both ends of the economic system. The focus is on accomplishing goals which will benefit the society rather than trying to make profit. The profit shows that the resources are well placed. The more profit means the more independent they will be from the changes in market conditions. (Gladwell, 2002).

Even though the research interest in social entrepreneurship is rising, the number of traditional enterprises driven by market and focusing on profit is the common business form. Social enterprises comprise between 2.9% to 4.6% of all the U.S. businesses depending on the definition, and a lot of venture capitalists currently hold the view that the effort needed does not justify the outcome. (Tiku, 2008). Social entrepreneurism has a long way to go to reach its potential in the society (Massetti, 2008).

The social entrepreneur needs to clearly lay out a persuasive social impact theory and workable business model to understand whether a bright idea can be turned into an opportunity worthy of serious commitment. Creating a workable business model needs coming up with an efficient operating model and developing achievable resource strategy. The model and the strategy should fit together, and the assumptions need to be realistic within the environment to be operated in. The final fit must be between the venture and dedication, skills and life stage of the entrepreneur involved in. When all the conditions are met, the success rate will be higher and a better estimate for social impact potential will be possible (Guclu, Dees, & Anderson, 2002).

Zahra et al. (2008) analyzed more than 20 social entrepreneurship definitions integrated them all into one inclusive definition:

Social entrepreneurship encompasses the activities and processes undertaken to discover, define, and exploit opportunities to enhance social wealth by creating new ventures or managing existing organizations in an innovative manner.

In this definition, social wealth covers areas of economic, societal, health, and environmental corners of human welfare. Three types of entrepreneurs were identified in their research: Social Bricoleur who deals with "small scale local social needs", Social Constructionist who covers a *broader social system by filling gaps to underserved clients introducing reforms and innovations* and Social Engineer who addresses *systemic problems by introducing revolutionary change*. The authors argue that social entrepreneurship should be evaluated in terms of total wealth which covers economic and social wealth. There are challenges in measuring social wealth, which comprises of tangible (e.g. number of people who used a service or amount of funds generated) and intangible outcomes like *happiness, wealth and general well-being* (Zahra, Rawhouser, Bhawe, Neubaum, & Hayton, 2008).

Groot and Dankbaar (2014) analyzed 20 social enterprises. The researchers argue that distinguishing social entrepreneurs from business entrepreneurs is not very useful, better is to consider "social" and "business" dimensions in all innovations. Some innovations may have a lower score on social compared to business or the opposite could be true where social score is higher than business score. Aspiring social entrepreneurs can learn from "normal" entrepreneurs. Politicians need to take into consideration that social innovation can also come from normal business entrepreneurship. Social impact of enterprises should be developed. Social innovation can come from many sources, so it does not require social entrepreneurship, but requires entrepreneurship.

CORPORATE SOCIAL RESPONSIBILITY

CSR is a concept whereby companies integrate social and environmental concerns in their business operations and in their interaction with their stakeholders on a voluntary basis (Commission of the European Communities, 2001). Companies are being involved in CSR projects at an increasing pace, but the results of a survey showed that most firms have not incorporated CSR into their structures in a significant manner. There is no prevailing model for that (Googins & Rochlin, 2006).

Sanzo et al. (2015) analyzed the business-nonprofit partnerships and evaluated the impact on the nonprofit's *development of innovations, capability building, and performance*. It was found that the collaboration model should be based not only on monetary partnerships but also include additional resources so that NGO can develop its capabilities to successfully complete the social mission. A positive correlation was detected between partnership success and the NGO's development of key capabilities and resources.

Corporate Social Entrepreneurship (CSE) is defined as:

the process of extending the firm's domain of competence and corresponding opportunity set through innovative leveraging of resources, both within and outside its direct control, aimed at the simultaneous creation of economic and social value (Austin, Leonard, Reficco, & Wei-Skillern, 2006).

CSE's target is to give a boost to CSE (Austin & Reficco, 2008). If a company wants to shift gears and move on from CSR to CSE, top management support is important. Social value in addition to economic value needs to be measured and performance indicators as well as incentive and rewards need to be aligned accordingly.

Corporate Social Intrapreneurs (CSI) are the change agents in the company. CSIs constantly promote for the incorporation of business and social values, focus on the reasoning and significance of the conversion, come up with innovative solutions to existing problems, illuminate and form synergies with coworkers' chores, coordinate efforts within or outside the company and always keep an eye on the costs.

CSE makes sure that creating social value is embedded within corporate values. CSE targets to change the purpose of the company:

from maximizing returns to investors to optimizing returns to stakeholders, who are significantly affected by the company actions and who in return impact the company.

Strategic cooperation which puts together complementary core competencies of different organizations can solve long standing issues for the society. Uniting distinct skills and resources bears strong co-generation of social and economic value (Austin, 2000).

Lai et al. (2015) analyzed the relationship organizational structure, organization strategy, R&D talent, R&D technology, uncertainty in environment, stakeholders in environment, corporate innovation capability, corporate sustainability and strategic corporate social responsibility (SCSR). It was found that *maintaining good organizational strategy, R&D technology, uncertainty in the environment and stakeholders in the environment ensure effective corporate innovation capability*. Additionally, corporate innovation capability positively influences corporate sustainability, and SCSR has a significant influence from corporate innovation capability to corporate sustainability.

THE CLUSTER OF CONCEPTS

A research finding emphasized the importance of civic engagement for social innovators. The stories told by philanthropists are important in getting new donors on board for new foundations. Philanthropy should not replace state for key services, but self-organized groups sometimes may provide efficient and low-cost solutions to social and environmental problems which appear to be unsolvable by government or large corporations (Maclean, Harvey, & Gordon, 2013).

Choi and Majumdar (2014) propose a model for social entrepreneurship as a cluster concept, since it involves multiple sub-concepts as *social value creation, social entrepreneur, social entrepreneurship organization, market orientation and social innovation*. A cluster is comprised of different concepts defined as sub-concepts (Gaut, 2000) and can exist in various level or combinations. Even if one or more items are missing from the total, it can still be referred to as the instance of the concept. Social entrepreneurship is illustrated in Figure 2. Since social value creation is the basic condition of social entrepreneurship, it is represented by a large circle covering the other four sub-concepts. Since social

Figure 1. Innovation, corporate sustainability and SCSR model
Source: Lai, Lin, & Wang, 2015

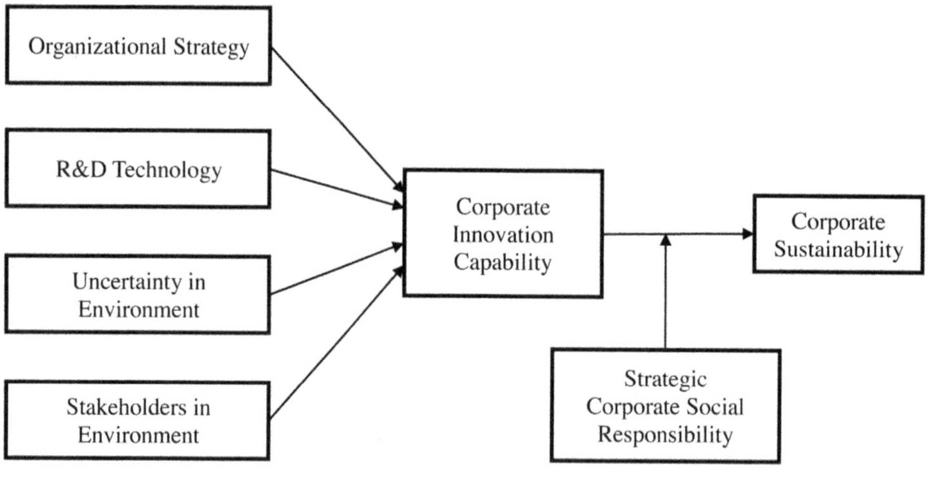

Figure 2. Social entrepreneurship as a cluster concept
Source: Short, Moss, & Lumpkin, 2009

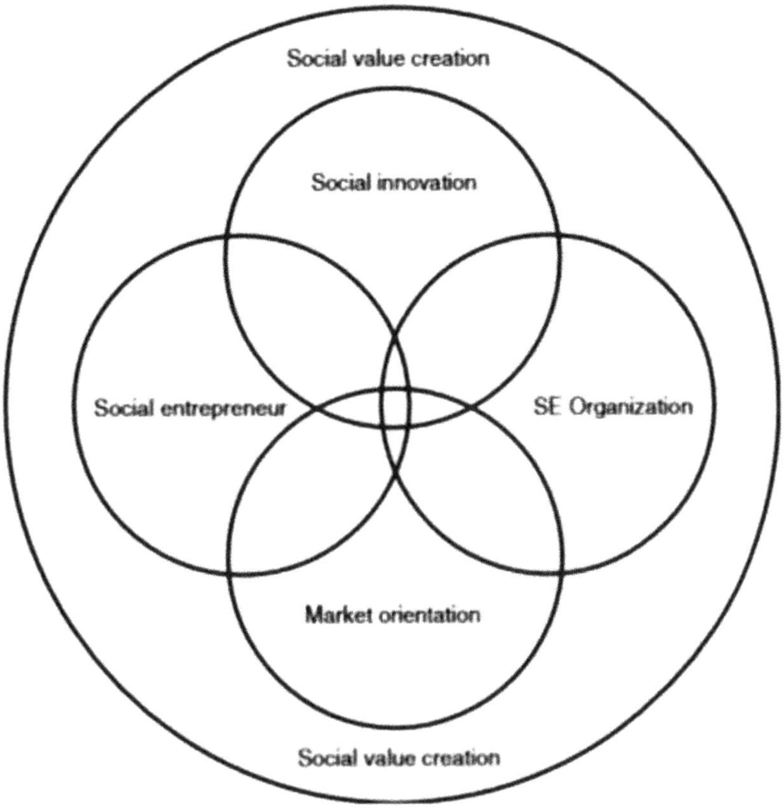

entrepreneurship organization, social innovation and market orientation are not prerequisites for social value creation, they can be present in increasing or decreasing amounts or in varying combinations (Gaut, 2000).

Previous research has mainly looked into commercial entrepreneurship where the focus was financial rather than social outcomes. The perception of the free market system has located the responsibility of protection and advancement of the public and social goods within the scope of the government. The red tape, political disagreements and rigid nature of the governments often led to inefficient social policies (Dees, 2007). Due to such results, social entrepreneurs take the stage to fill the gaps by favoring social returns in place of financial ones (Haughton, 2008).

Building a connection between social entrepreneurship and CSR could be an encouraging model for attaining MDGs. Up to the present time, CSR projects mainly focused on communities in developed countries, where realizing MDGs is not urgent.

By connecting with local entrepreneurs, companies may take part in projects which require distinctive, pertinent firm resources. By utilizing corporate funds rather than solely depending on philanthropic sources, entrepreneurs could benefit not only from financial resources but also industry knowledge, managerial expertise, and competences to implement social entrepreneurship projects (Seelos & Mair, 2005).

CSE is defined as:

the process of extending the firm's domain of competence and corresponding opportunity set through innovative leveraging of resources, both within and outside its direct control, aimed at the simultaneous creation of economic and social value (Austin, Leonard, Reficco, & Wei-Skillern, 2006).

The basic purpose of CSE is to speed up companies' structural conversion into strong developers of improvement in society.

Management acceptance and support will be crucial to adopt the importance of social innovation for all areas of the business. If social innovation would be considered as CSR 3.0, then it would stay within the CSR departments and not get the required attention it needs from company leaders. A big risk is that people would treat social innovation as a fad will go away in a couple of years. Academia can take front seat in moving the concept forward and make it here to stay. CSR managers are expected to be the change agents in leading the transformation in the company. This is a big shift from today, because many CSR departments are cars in current situation but are expected to be locomotives. CSR managers need to be the facilitators helping the company to discover the potential of social innovation for a sustainable future. Social innovation needs to be strongly connected to company innovation initiatives and finally become driver of it. It is important for the companies to have scale and diffusion in social innovation. Social innovation has to be scaled and to reach a lasting level to become really sustainable. Social innovation depends on the collaboration of all sectors. By focusing more on open innovation, knowledge sharing within and outside the company is important for success. The social entrepreneur can become the main strategic partner by creating social value shared among governments, companies and NGOs.

Social innovation is closer to the core business than the traditional thought and is a key of corporate sustainability for companies where triple bottom line needs are met. It is not a new version of CSR and has a great potential. The companies which adopt the strategy of corporate sustainability through social innovation will be most likely to lead the next decades (Osburg, 2013).

There is a rank of order for social and economic value creation (Dacin, Dacin, & Tracey, 2011) and social entrepreneurs meet both sets of conditions. A social value creation does not diminish or extinguish economic value, to the contrary, economical value is of utmost importance for the sustainability of social venture and social value. The focus can be on the social value created for the realization of social change, but the results are very tightly related to economic outcomes which will produce financial results for the social entrepreneur to accomplish the main mission (Dacin, Dacin, & Tracey, 2011).

Social entrepreneurship generally includes nonprofit organizations and persons with strong and deep ties to the community (Catford, 1998). Deficiency of private enterprise is generally a sign of community stagnation, and a hurdle for public sector efficiency (Boris & Steuerle, 1999). So, the presence of social entrepreneurship is strategically important for municipal governments (Bornstein, 2007).

There are many ways city administrators can support social entrepreneurs to develop new programs. Support functions include increasing awareness, assisting social entrepreneurs to get access to resources including direct support from the city funds, and coordinating efforts between social entrepreneurs and other related parties in program execution.

City administrations can gather data and supply data on major social issues and train social entrepreneurs in project development related issues like planning for facilities and applying to grants for resource development.

In a conducted survey, more than 50% of the city administrations in the research reported high levels of social entrepreneurship, and these works were majorly enhanced by city activities, including *infor-*

mation and community awareness building, coordination and support in program implementation, and assistance in resource acquisition (Korosec & Berman, 2006).

Information on city administration support for Social entrepreneurship is mostly nonexistent. Administrations involved in supporting social entrepreneurship may face legal questions regarding the allocation of public funds for certain faith or supporting an organization would appear as favoring one over others. Managers can learn from other organizations which have established guidelines, policies and criteria for support. Legal and ethical concerns are the initial steps towards establishing support process for local social entrepreneurship.

It is important to have managers who are innovative, practically oriented and have political skills which are important in reaching consensus between public and community leaders. New public-private partnerships also need to be developed in order to support and transform local communities with their in-house efforts and organizations (Korosec & Berman, 2006).

A DEVELOPMENT MODEL FOR SOCIAL ENTREPRENEURS

Linear model of innovation does not clearly reflect the actual steps taken in applied sciences. The model proposes a direct line where in actual life, some feedbacks change the course of the road and depending on the area, some processes may take place before the foreseen order in the model. The linear model does not consider the market factors and social demands (Mulgan, 2006). Recent perspectives consider the interactive nature of the innovation process, the importance of communication, and the edge provided by networks and clusters (Lubberink, Blok, van Ophem, & Omta, 2017).

In social organizations, new ideas start from an individual or group's problems and devotion. The new model is launched before ensuring the presence of financial resources and support from potential donors. Businesses do contribute to social sector by way of CSR projects, hence few have an impact on important issues like health, education, and welfare. Government bureaucracies may not serve as the best medium for social innovation.

Most of the social innovations fail. The reason behind failure could be the cost efficiency, solution not better than the other options, or side-effects hindering the benefit. Mulgan (2006) states that ideas fail due to lack of mechanisms in promotion, adaptation or scaling up, and defines three distinct characteristics of social innovations from technological ones. Firstly, social innovations are usually newer versions or hybrids of existing elements. Secondly, implementation involves cutting across various organizational, industrial or disciplinary boundaries. Finally, social innovations form new social relationships. Advances depend on the frequency and the quality of the connections and the grade of the connectors.

The traditional Product Development Diagram does not address the needs of the startups. (Bayik, 2017) Considering social enterprises, many of them are startups with an aim to solve unique social issues. In the model, there exist no customers. "First ship date" is underlined. The flow is linear, and it does not include the learning process of a small organization. There are no milestones in terms of sales, marketing and business development. Therefore, it can also be concluded that traditional product/service development diagram will not be solving the issues for social entrepreneurs.

In order to fix the problems in new product development, Blank (2013) suggests the model shown in figure 3.

In the Customer Discovery Process, one takes notes on *company vision, product assumptions, customers, conditions of the market, pricing, demand and competitors* (Blank, 2013). Potential customers must

Figure 3. The customer development model
Source: Blank, 2013

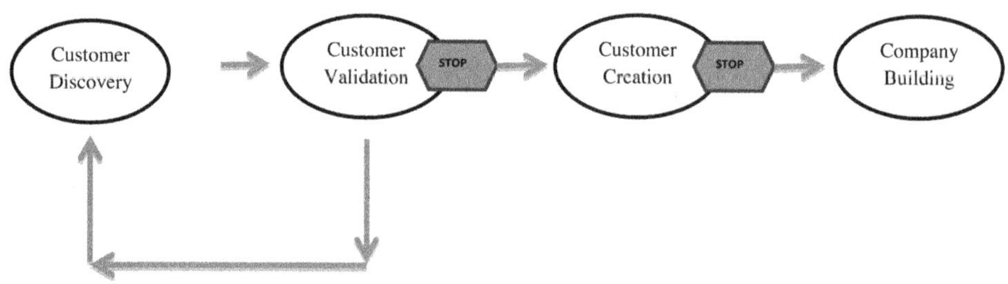

be listened to in order to test the assumptions. The aim is to understand the reference frame customers are doing business in, the problems they confront with, and their needs for the product. After the first contact with the customers, the product and the briefs need to be revised accordingly. The concept, which is revised, must be tested again by customers. The business model, which is comprised of presence of customers, a solution devised for, and a must-have product are also under scrutiny. After testing for pricing, distribution, and sales, one finds the potential buyers with a budget to purchase.

Documents for problem statement, revised product requirement, revised sales and revenue plan, and a business and product plan need to be prepared. Then it is time to go out to try to sell the product to a limited number of visionary customers.

If the customers are convinced to buy the product, one should proceed to Customer Validation. If not, one should go back to square one and try to learn more about the customers.

In Customer Validation Process, the first steps are sales preparation activities. They include:

forming a clear value proposition, preparing sales materials, creating a distribution channel plan, creating a sales road map, hiring a salesperson, agreeing upon product features and dates among product and Customer Development teams, and forming the advisory board.

Figure 4. Customer Discovery
Source: Blank, 2013

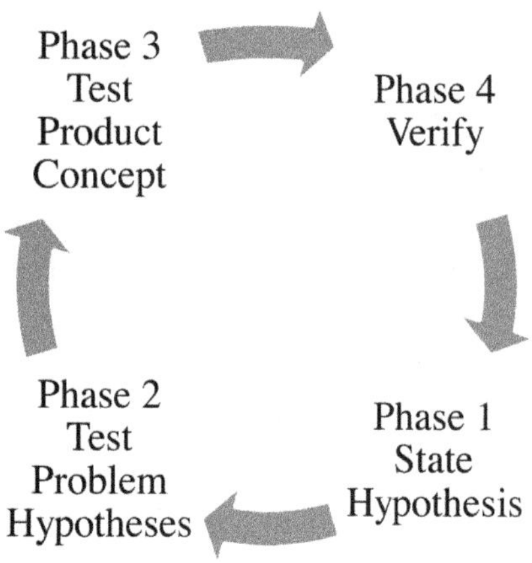

Figure 5. Customer Validation
Source: Blank, 2013

Then one tries to sell the product which is not finished or proven to customers. This can be either successful or not. The aim is to get all the sales road map questions answered. After some orders are placed, the company starts to work on the positioning of the product and the company. The initial positioning can be reviewed by industry experts and some analysts for feedback. Order quantity should be analyzed to see if it is going to be a financially sound business, which means it is solving the needs of the customers. The profitability of sales and channel must be analyzed. Knowledge should be acquired enough to scale the business. If all is positive, then the next step is Customer Creation.

Market type is selected and customer and sale targets are determined. Market size, total available share, and budget for product are estimated. The strategy is developed, aims, targets, milestones and Customer Creation budget are set. The messages for product positioning are formed. The launch of the product is realized, the audience, means of communication and message are chosen. Performance measures are adapted. Integrated marketing communication constituents focusing on demand creation are put to work.

At the Company Building stage, sales shift from "earlyvangelists" to mass market customers. Sales Staff will need to be increased and the sales budget will be changed accordingly. Executive management must be looked into with regards to scaling up. Customer Development team must be organized around business functions. Departments should form their mission in order to support corporate mission. Finally, the company builds fast response departments, with handy customer information and corporate information communication system.

In social entrepreneurship, the aim is to create social value in balance with economic value. Since economic value is inseparable from the social value while evaluating the success of the enterprise, and economic value is of major significance, then one can conclude that to found financially sound social enterprises, Blank (2013)'s Customer Development can be benefited from. There might be a need for adaptation depending on the area of the social enterprise, but the model seems to cover all corners in order to avoid ambiguity and to save time and funds for the social entrepreneurs.

Sustainability applications embrace liability and harmony in evaluations targeting advancement of stakeholder responsibility for triple bottom line performance (Sullivan Mort, Weerawardena, & Carnegie, 2003).

Figure 6. Customer Creation
Source: Blank, 2013

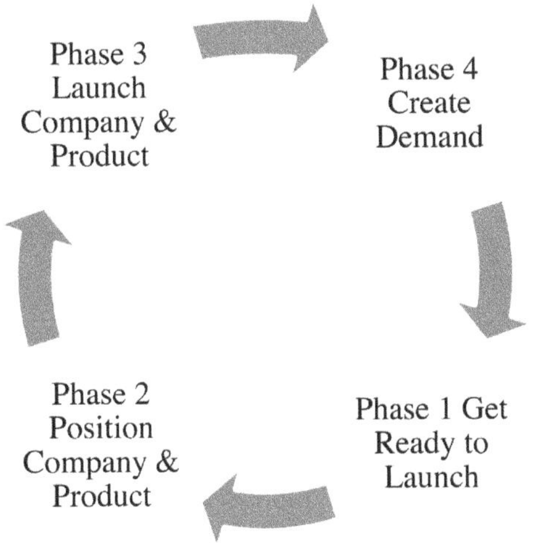

Figure 7. Company Building
Source: Blank, 2013

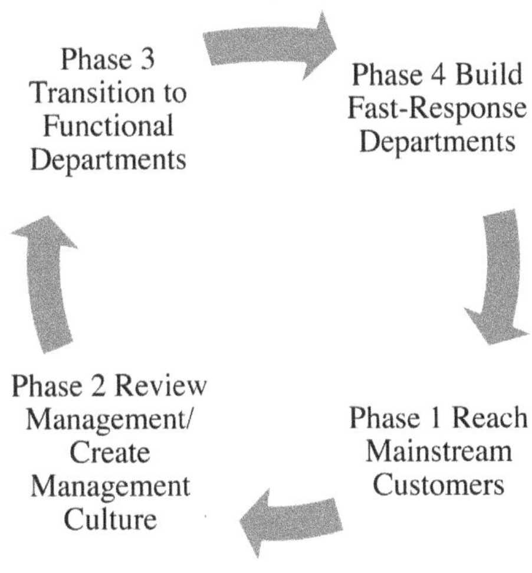

Social entrepreneurs view human life as mutually dependent with the living ecosystem. The steps to be taken need to be shaped by values and devotion to maintain and defend the long-term existence and rights of the community and environment. With such an approach, social entrepreneurs pursue to bring about continuing social value and to advance improvement of people by way of commitment for continuing and responsible innovations (Machan, 1999).

Local networks of entrepreneurs, investors, community, NGOs and governments in developing countries united towards a common goal has been reported to ease the generation of sustainable outcomes (Wheeler, McKague, Thomson, Davies, Medalye, & Prada, 2005). The closeness to the setting also supports such networks to develop their native capacities, to work together with resources and to pool knowledge in order to make the most of the long term affect in improving the quality of life and economic progress. Native capacities also advance applicable local solutions for actual problems enhancing trust and social capital. This generates a significant facet of competitive advantage for social entrepreneurs (Hart & London, 2005).

Innovative abilities are improved as people develop themselves by pairing and bartering intellectual and social capital (Littunen, 2000). This includes finding methods to enter "bottom of the pyramid markets" for social entrepreneurs. Such markets are overlooked by commercial entrepreneurs due to perceived high risk that doses not rationalize economic returns (Hart & London, 2005). Innovative processes and technologies are used by social entrepreneurs for the social and strategic fit of products and services to get into the underdeveloped and unfamiliar markets (Hart & Christensen, 2002). A more maintainable social and economic development is attained as such innovative initiatives slowly empower disadvantaged markets to involve in the activities of conventional markets.

The economic perspective supports the shareholder preeminence perspective where the duty of the entrepreneur is limited to the maximization of financial wealth. Social entrepreneur is inclined towards filling the gap where governments are unable to and corporations are not willing to due to commercial concerns (Haughton, 2008).

CONCLUSION

Social value creation is important for the society, but there is no one great model which includes all the major players in social innovation or social entrepreneurship yet. O'Riordan and Fairbrass (2013) describe 4 stages of CSR company behavior. At the bottom of the pyramid lie 'law abiders'. Those companies simply try to fulfill their base-line necessities of adhering to laws and regulations imposed upon them by their corresponding business environment. The second group of companies is labeled as 'parrots'. Initially they are like 'law abiders'. Adhering to standards, they do whatever they are required to do according to laws and regulations. These companies respond to social expectations as window dressers, so they take no substantial action. They keep a skeptical outlook regarding CSR. Third category is labeled as 'innovators'. In these companies, top management has undergone major change and they keep a long-term outcomes oriented approach for CSR. The fourth group is labeled as 'accountable companies' which practice all CSR behavior with triple bottom line impact for CSR business investments. The research was conducted in one industry only, so new industries need to be tested. Methods need to be found to apply the conceptualization into everyday practice. It also has to be sorted out on how to determine best business solution outcomes which most favorably align private and public interests.

Social entrepreneurs usually come up with innovative ideas in order to close the gap in the areas where state has not set as priority. The lack of state funding forces the social entrepreneur to come up with innovative ideas to solve the observed social problem. Since the resources are limited, the social entrepreneur must be thrifty on resource allocation. The first check point would be to start with the right set of problems to be solved. After making sure that the social entrepreneur is on the right track regarding issues to be solved, it is important to come with an innovative solution. Various industries borrow ideas from each other when it comes to problem solving. For profit businesses have been developing products or services for many years, so one could assume to follow the footsteps of such companies in new product or service development for social entrepreneurs. The industry has solved many issues in product development by analyzing the classical product development cycles and changing some of the processes in order to get better results in shorter time with less resource. Social entrepreneurs can adopt this approach for new product or service development, because they have much less to start with compared to for profit companies. The group of people who are thought to be underprivileged must be listened to. The social entrepreneur's vision can be true, but the starting point should be to listen to the very people who may be suffering from the lack of a certain resource or service. Only then the social entrepreneur would know the actual problems those people confront with, and their needs for a product or service. After the details are documented, the social entrepreneur should go back and double check the briefs with the "potential customers". This is the Customer Discovery phase in Blank's (2013) methodology. The potential customer is someone referred to as the user or beneficiary after the service is going to be offered, and since this is going to be a social enterprise, it does not necessarily mean the purchase of the services.

The social entrepreneur needs to form a clear value proposition, prepare sales materials, create a distribution channel plan, create a sales road map, hire a salesperson, agree upon product features and dates among product and Customer Development teams and form the Advisory Board. One should try to sell the unfinished or unproven product to customers. The feedback from the market will be used to work on the product and scaling the business.

Target market is selected and customer and sale numbers are determined. Market size, and budget for product is determined. The strategy is developed, aims, targets, milestones and Customer Creation budget are set. The messages for product positioning are formed. The launch of the product is realized.

At the Company Building stage, sales shift from "earlyvangelists" to mass market customers. The number of sales staff will be increased and sales budget will be increased accordingly. Customer Development team needs to be organized around business functions.

Adopting the business perspective in new product development strategy will bring efficient processes for social entrepreneurs. Fine tuning the social enterprise idea without making a large investment will leave the social entrepreneur with more capital to experiment with in order to discover the right product for the right audience. The down side of Customer Development process is that since it is a new method being used in for profit startups, there are not many examples for not-for-profit enterprises. The guidelines are not clearly written down, and the challenges along the way wait to be confronted. The more the social entrepreneurs adopt Customer Development, the clearer the path will become for future social entrepreneurs. More experience will bring in guidelines and practices for benchmarking. More study is needed on social value creation to shed light for future social entrepreneurs.

CSE focuses on creation of economic and social value simultaneously while leveraging resources within and outside company's direct control. CSE enables the extending of competence within the company and opportunities coming with innovative leveraging of resources. While many companies are being involved in CSR, for most companies, it is not a part of the company structure and there is no blue print for embedding CSR into the company. Since CSE is the upgrade level for CSR practitioners, companies which have not adopted CSE strategies yet need to look into what they can do to start with CSE at the first place. Rather than using the corporate energy first to start CSR and then to convert to CSE, companies can save time and resources by starting from CSE practices. Top management support will be crucial at CSE adoption phase. Social value in addition to economic value needs to be measured. Performance indicators, incentives and rewards should be revised in order to motivate people to be involved in social value creation in addition to economic value creation. Corporate Social Intrapreneurs (CSIs) should be acquired or bred within to be the change agents in the company. CSIs will promote for the blending of business and social values, will come up with innovative solutions to enduring problems, form synergies within the workforce, coordinate efforts within and outside the company and keep an eye on the budget. One can tell if a company has created economic value by analyzing the balance sheet and other financial tables. There are strict guidelines and procedures, so annual reports describe the company to a certain extent. Companies can be compared to each other, or a company can be evaluated on the past quarters or years. For social value creation there is no universal measurement yet, and the companies do not disclose everything they do on a social value report. When one reads about the social value creation projects of a company, one cannot deduce if a certain project was a priority or it could have been postponed and another more important project could have been undertaken. There is no social value measurement tool yet, and this can lead to the subjective evaluation of the efforts of a company for social value creation.

A CSI and a social entrepreneur can work on the same project towards a common goal. Existing models emphasize work groups within the company, but considering the environment for social value creation could be beneficial for both parties. By connecting with local social entrepreneurs, companies can be aware of social issues in the vicinity and can contribute to local projects with the workforce and various sources which will give birth to additional social value on top their own CSE projects. Strategic cooperation of different parties can get together complimentary core competencies and can solve some issues for the society which could not have been solved otherwise.

The municipal support for social entrepreneurship projects can be beneficial in two ways. The first method is to support the social entrepreneurs in their causes by supplying them with information, increase awareness about their projects, provide access to resources, and coordinate efforts between social entrepreneurs and other related parties in implementation. The social entrepreneur is not in competition with city administration, to the contrary, acts as a complimentary power for overlooked issues. Therefore, the support of city administration of social entrepreneurs is a good strategy for getting the work done with highly motivated people and without increasing the head count on the payroll. The second method to assist social entrepreneurs can be by introducing social entrepreneurs and companies which have adopted CSE strategy to work on city projects related to creating social value. The city can also supply the parties with city funds or help them apply for available grants. The city can train individuals on project development including planning. The support of the city for such collaboration can bring more transparency to public spending on social issues, and the society can have a larger percentage of support having observed the burden is shared with private companies. City administrators and CSIs can learn from other organizations which have guidelines and policies. In overcoming the legal issues, the corporate legal team can help the people involved in the project. The development of the political skills of the managers will be crucial in building public-private partnerships. City administrations publish the work accomplished each year. They announce the social projects supported by the city. What gets unnoticed is a project which is not supported by the city. The impact of a social project cannot be measured efficiently, so it is not easy to make a comparison among the projects which were supported. The urgency of the social issues is also important. The more urgent issues are expected to have priority, but urgency of the waiting list of the issues is not being reported. There is a need for the city administration to come up with an urgency based issue listing.

Social entrepreneurship education needs to be integrated into entrepreneurship education. Business schools need to make necessary adjustments in the entrepreneurship programs for learning requirements of social entrepreneurs. The steps can be perceived as initial, and upon making field surveys, other approaches can be further developed. Social entrepreneurship issues, cases, and analysis can be weaved into traditional courses. Social entrepreneurs can be invited to classrooms or they can be visited at their facilities or at the field. Students can also develop teaching cases from the very social enterprise they had visited. They can prepare social enterprise business plans to the issues they come across. Students can work on small scale social enterprise consulting projects. For the students who want to acquire greater amount knowledge and experience, social enterprise internships can be organized (Tracey & Phillips, 2007).

In many cases, personal and corporate aims of the entrepreneur are not separable (London, 2008). The education curriculum needs to cover the required bases to grow the desire to create a more sustainable world (Johnson, 2005).

Social entrepreneurs are expected to come up with innovative ideas, so the education must include social innovation. Political skills are important in getting city administration support, so social entrepreneurs should also be trained on how to establish conduct with public authorities and how to develop projects with the city. CSE is an important issue and all the college graduates are potential members of the CSE teams. To create social value within the company, there is a need for intrapreneurs, so the social entrepreneurship education must cover intrapreneurship issues in case the students will need it in the future.

Social value creation education is going to become more important in the future. Either by starting their own enterprises, or cooperating with companies, or working for companies which want to create social value in addition to economic value, individuals will need to have skills to create social value. Entrepreneurship courses are still electives for students who want to start their own businesses, but at the background, businesses are changing to embrace social value creation. The need of the students, who are the future workforce, is to get educated on how to create social value, but currently social value creation education has not been prioritized by the academic world.

Social entrepreneurs, normal entrepreneurs with social dimensions, corporations embracing strategic corporate social responsibility, and city administrations all want to create social impact on societal problems of various sizes. The common point of all these groups is the target segment. In marketing terms, they try to serve the same target market. Since the resources are scarce, and a cooperation between the players would create a bigger social impact, then social business models should be revised accordingly. Besides developing measures for social wealth and social impact, the factors which affect the growth of those should also be studied.

Social entrepreneurs should be more business minded than social-only outcome aimed enterprises, so that the social businesses will keep running independently and will be able to contribute to underserved groups or causes. Corporations should develop methods to include social dimensions in their projects, since SCSR contributes to the sustainability of the corporation. From a sustainability point of view, social businesses and corporations seem to be converging to a certain extent on a continuum, where one is adopting the business mind and the other adopting the social mind. Regarding new product or service development, social businesses borrow the established methods from corporations to come up with faster and more focused solutions to societal problems. NGOs are not immune from the changes in the society and business environment. An NGO should learn how to develop its organization and staff while cooperating with a corporation. For the social projects, the support of a corporation helps them to achieve their target, so it is important to be able to partner with the right corporation. To serve and to be served by a corporation for a social cause might need an NGO to walk the extra mile, so they need to be ready for organizational development to accomplish the task.

City administrators are going to be not only the supporters of social enterprises, corporations with SCSR focus and NGOs, but also coordinators of such groups. Related legislation might need to be revised to enable more cooperation between such diverse groups, and the social projects of the city waiting for the right time and partner can be finally undertaken by a such consortium. The city will be able to contribute to the sustainability of the corporations and to the growth of social businesses and NGOs.

Social wealth creation is a result of the common work of all the partners in the field, and the size of the social impact will be determined by the level of cooperation of such partners.

FUTURE RESEARCH DIRECTIONS

The stage of social entrepreneurship and social innovation research can be considered at their infancy period. There are certain areas which will need more attention in the future.

The creativity of city administration leaders to develop various tools to support up and coming social entrepreneurs need to be analyzed (Korosec & Berman, 2006).

More research is necessary for municipal funding guidelines for social entrepreneurship, as well as contractual and legal concerns in supporting entrepreneurship (Korosec & Berman, 2006).

Social innovation has a cross-cutting nature. Its boundaries sometimes can be more inclusive, and the related sectors can change. New scales need to be developed regarding measures of spending on social innovation and indicators of its level of activity (EU Commission, 2012b).

Social wealth meaning and dimensions should be analyzed by future studies. Social entrepreneurship antecedents need further analysis with a focus on individual, societal and organizational factors (Zahra, Rawhouser, Bhawe, Neubaum, & Hayton, 2008).

Future research can focus on SCSR factors which affect corporate sustainability (Lai, Lin, & Wang, 2015).

REFERENCES

Alvord, S. H., Brown, L. D., & Letts, C. W. (2004). Social entrepreneurship and societal transformation: An exploratory study. *The Journal of Applied Behavioral Science*, *40*(3), 260–282. doi:10.1177/0021886304266847

Austin, J. E. (2000). *The collaboration challenge: How nonprofits and businesses succeed through strategic alliances* (Vol. 109). John Wiley & Sons.

Austin, J. E., Leonard, H., Reficco, E., & Wei-Skillern, J. (2006). Social entrepreneurship: it's for corporations too. *Social entrepreneurship: New models of sustainable social change*, 169-180.

Austin, J. E., & Reficco, E. (2008). Corporate social entrepreneurship. *Int'l J. Not-for-Profit L., 11*, 86.

Barendsen, L., & Gardner, H. (2004). Is the social entrepreneur a new type of leader? *Leader to Leader, 2004*(34), 43–50. doi:10.1002/ltl.100

Bayik, M. (2017). Innovative Processes in New Product and Service Development. In *Global Business Strategies in Crisis* (pp. 215–229). Springer International Publishing. doi:10.1007/978-3-319-44591-5_15

Bekkers, V. J. J. M., Tummers, L. G., & Voorberg, W. H. (2013). *From public innovation to social innovation in the public sector: A literature review of relevant drivers and barriers*. Rotterdam: Erasmus University Rotterdam.

Blank, S. (2013). *The four steps to the epiphany: successful strategies for products that win*. BookBaby.

Boris, E. T., & Steuerle, C. E. (1999). *Nonprofits and Government: Collaboration and Conflict*. Washington, DC: Urban Institute Press.

Bornstein, D. (2007). *How to change the world: Social entrepreneurs and the power of new ideas*. Oxford University Press.

Brooks, A. C. (2009). *Social entrepreneurship: A modern approach to social value creation*. Pearson Prentice Hall.

Catford, J. (1998). Social entrepreneurs are vital for health promotion—but they need supportive environments too. *Health Promotion International, 13*(2), 95–97. doi:10.1093/heapro/13.2.95

Chauvin, B., Hermand, D., & Mullet, E. (2007). Risk perception and personality facets. *Risk Analysis, 27*(1), 171–185. doi:10.1111/j.1539-6924.2006.00867.x PMID:17362408

Chell, E., Nicolopoulou, K., & Karataş-Özkan, M. (2010). *Social entrepreneurship and enterprise: International and innovation perspectives*. Academic Press.

Choi, N., & Majumdar, S. (2014). Social entrepreneurship as an essentially contested concept: Opening a new avenue for systematic future research. *Journal of Business Venturing, 29*(3), 363–376. doi:10.1016/j.jbusvent.2013.05.001

Commission of the European Communities. (2001). Promoting a European Framework for Corporate Social Responsibilities. COM (2001) 366 final, Brussels.

Cools, E., & Van Den Broeck, H. (2008). Cognitive styles and managerial behaviour: A qualitative study. *Education + Training, 50*(2), 103–114. doi:10.1108/00400910810862092

Corner, P. D., & Ho, M. (2010). How opportunities develop in social entrepreneurship. *Entrepreneurship Theory and Practice, 34*(4), 635–659. doi:10.1111/j.1540-6520.2010.00382.x

Crant, J. M. (1996). The proactive personality scale as a predictor of entrepreneurial intentions. *Journal of Small Business Management, 34*(3), 42.

Dacin, M. T., Dacin, P. A., & Tracey, P. (2011). Social entrepreneurship: A critique and future directions. *Organization Science, 22*(5), 1203–1213. doi:10.1287/orsc.1100.0620

Davis, S. M. (2002). *Social entrepreneurship: Towards an entrepreneurial culture for social and economic development*. Academic Press.

Dawson, P., & Daniel, L. (2010). Understanding social innovation: A provisional framework. *International Journal of Technology Management, 51*(1), 9–21. doi:10.1504/IJTM.2010.033125

Dees, J. G. (2007). Taking social entrepreneurship seriously. *Society, 44*(3), 24–31. doi:10.1007/BF02819936

EU-Commission. (2012a). *Social innovation*. Retrieved September 14, 2017, from http://ec.europa.eu/enterprise/policies/ Innovation/policy/social-Innovation/index_en.htm

EU-Commission. (2012b). *Strengthening social innovation in Europe – a journey to affective assessment and metrics*. Retrieved September 14, 2017, from http://ec.europa.eu/enterprise/policies/Innovation/files/social- Innovation/strengthening-social-Innovation_en.pdf

European Business School (EBS). (2012). Retrieved September 14, 2017, from http://www.ebs.edu/socialinnovation.html

European Commission. (2002). *Corporate social responsibility: A business contribution to sustainable development*. Luxembourg: Office for Official Publications of the European Communities.

Gardner, C. A., Acharya, T., & Yach, D. (2007). Technological and social innovation: A unifying new paradigm for global health. *Health Affairs, 26*(4), 1052–1061. doi:10.1377/hlthaff.26.4.1052 PMID:17630448

Gaut, B. (2000). Art as a cluster concept. In N. Carroll (Ed.), *Theories of art today* (pp. 25–44). Madison, WI: University of Wisconsin Press.

Gladwell, M. (2002). *The Tipping Point: How Little Things Can Make a Big Difference*. Boston: Little, Brown and Company.

Googins, B. K., & Rochlin, S. A. (2006). *Corporate Citizenship: Top to Bottom*. Academic Press.

Grimm, R., Fox, C., Baines, S., & Albertson, K. (2013). Social innovation, an answer to contemporary societal challenges? Locating the concept in theory and practice. *Innovation (Abingdon), 26*(4), 436–455. doi:10.1080/13511610.2013.848163

Groot, A., & Dankbaar, B. (2014). Does Social Innovation Require Social Entrepreneurship? *Technology Innovation Management Review, 4*(12).

Guclu, A., Dees, J. G., & Anderson, B. B. (2002). The process of social entrepreneurship: Creating opportunities worthy of serious pursuit. *Center for the Advancement of Social Entrepreneurship, 1*, 1-15.

Hart, S. L., & Christensen, C. M. (2002). The great leap: Driving innovation from the base of the pyramid. *MIT Sloan Management Review, 44*(1), 51.

Hart, S. L., & London, T. (2005). Developing native capability. *Stanford Social Innovation Review, 3*(2), 28–33.

Haughton, C. (2008). The edge of reason. *Director, 61*(7), 70–74.

Hemingway, C. A. (2005). Personal values as a catalyst for corporate social entrepreneurship. *Journal of Business Ethics*, *60*(3), 233–249. doi:10.100710551-005-0132-5

Holme, R., & Watts, P. (1999). *Corporate social responsibility*. Geneva: World Business Council for Sustainable Development.

Hubert, A. (2010). *Empowering people, driving change: Social innovation in the European Union*. Bureau of European Policy Advisors (BEPA). Retrieved September 14, 2017, from http://ec. europa. eu/bepa/pdf/publications_pdf/social_innovation. pdf

INSEAD. (2012). *What is "social innovation"?* Retrieved September 14, 2017, from http://www.insead.edu/facultyresearch/centres/isic/ home/about_us.cfm

Johnson, B. (2005). Overcoming "doom and gloom": Empowering students in courses on social problems, injustice, and inequality. *Teaching Sociology*, *33*(1), 44–58. doi:10.1177/0092055X0503300104

Korosec, R. L., & Berman, E. M. (2006). Municipal support for social entrepreneurship. *Public Administration Review*, *66*(3), 448–462. doi:10.1111/j.1540-6210.2006.00601.x

Lai, W. H., Lin, C. C., & Wang, T. C. (2015). Exploring the interoperability of innovation capability and corporate sustainability. *Journal of Business Research*, *68*(4), 867–871. doi:10.1016/j.jbusres.2014.11.043

Lepoutre, J., Justo, R., Terjesen, S., & Bosma, N. (2013). Designing a global standardized methodology for measuring social entrepreneurship activity: The Global Entrepreneurship Monitor social entrepreneurship study. *Small Business Economics*, *40*(3), 693–714. doi:10.100711187-011-9398-4

Lettice, F., & Parekh, M. (2010). The social innovation process: Themes, challenges and implications for practice. *International Journal of Technology Management*, *51*(1), 139–158. doi:10.1504/IJTM.2010.033133

Littunen, H. (2000). Entrepreneurship and the characteristics of the entrepreneurial personality. *International Journal of Entrepreneurial Behaviour & Research*, *6*(6), 295–310. doi:10.1108/13552550010362741

Llewellyn, D. J., & Wilson, K. M. (2003). The controversial role of personality traits in entrepreneurial psychology. *Education + Training*, *45*(6), 341–345. doi:10.1108/00400910310495996

London, M. (2008). Leadership and Advocacy: Dual roles for corporate social responsibility and social entrepreneurship. *Organizational Dynamics*, *37*(4), 313–326. doi:10.1016/j.orgdyn.2008.07.003

Lubberink, R., Blok, V., van Ophem, J., & Omta, O. (2017). A Framework for Responsible Innovation in the Business Context: Lessons from Responsible-, Social-and Sustainable Innovation. In *Responsible Innovation 3* (pp. 181–207). Cham: Springer. doi:10.1007/978-3-319-64834-7_11

Machan, T. R. (1999). Entrepreneurship and ethics. *International Journal of Social Economics*, *26*(5), 596–609. doi:10.1108/03068299910216103

Maclean, M., Harvey, C., & Gordon, J. (2013). Social innovation, social entrepreneurship and the practice of contemporary entrepreneurial philanthropy. *International Small Business Journal*, *31*(7), 747–763. doi:10.1177/0266242612443376

Mair, J., Robinson, J., & Hockerts, K. (Eds.). (2006). *Social entrepreneurship*. New York: Palgrave Macmillan. doi:10.1057/9780230625655

Manzini, E. (2014). Making things happen: Social innovation and design. *Design Issues*, *30*(1), 57–66. doi:10.1162/DESI_a_00248

Martin, R. L., & Osberg, S. (2007). Social entrepreneurship: The case for definition. Stanford, CA: Stanford Social Innovation Review.

Massetti, B. L. (2008). The social entrepreneurship matrix as a" tipping point" for economic change. *Emergence*, *10*(3), 1.

McCrae, R. R., & Costa, P. T. (1986). Personality, coping, and coping effectiveness in an adult sample. *Journal of Personality*, *54*(2), 385–404. doi:10.1111/j.1467-6494.1986.tb00401.x

Moulaert, F. (Ed.). (2013). *The international handbook on social innovation: collective action, social learning and transdisciplinary research.* Edward Elgar Publishing. doi:10.4337/9781849809993

Mulgan, G. (2006). The process of social innovation. *Innovations*, *1*(2), 145–162. doi:10.1162/itgg.2006.1.2.145

Mulgan, G. (2007). In and Out of Sync: The Change of Growing Social Innovations. *Nesta*, *2007*, 21–25.

Mulgan, G., Tucker, S., Ali, R., & Sanders, B. (2007). *Social innovation: what it is, why it matters and how it can be accelerated.* Academic Press.

Nga, J. K. H., & Shamuganathan, G. (2010). The influence of personality traits and demographic factors on social entrepreneurship start up intentions. *Journal of Business Ethics*, *95*(2), 259–282. doi:10.100710551-009-0358-8

O'Riordan, L., & Fairbrass, J. (2014). Managing CSR stakeholder engagement: A new conceptual framework. *Journal of Business Ethics*, *125*(1), 121–145. doi:10.100710551-013-1913-x

Osburg, T. (2013). Social innovation to drive corporate sustainability. In *Social Innovation* (pp. 13–22). Springer Berlin Heidelberg. doi:10.1007/978-3-642-36540-9_2

Perrini, F., & Vurro, C. (2006). Social entrepreneurship: Innovation and social change across theory and practice. In Social entrepreneurship (pp. 57-85). Palgrave Macmillan UK.

Rexhepi, G., Kurtishi, S., & Bexheti, G. (2013). Corporate social responsibility (CSR) and innovation–the drivers of business growth? *Procedia: Social and Behavioral Sciences*, *75*, 532–541. doi:10.1016/j.sbspro.2013.04.058

Roberts, D., & Woods, C. (2005). Changing the world on a shoestring: The concept of social entrepreneurship. *University of Auckland Business Review*, *7*(1), 45–51.

Roberts, N. C., & King, P. J. (1991). Policy entrepreneurs: Their activity structure and function in the policy process. *Journal of Public Administration: Research and Theory*, *1*(2), 147–175.

Rüede, D., & Lurtz, K. (2012). *Mapping the various meanings of social innovation: Towards a differentiated understanding of an emerging concept.* Academic Press.

Sanzo, M. J., Álvarez, L. I., Rey, M., & García, N. (2015). Business–nonprofit partnerships: A new form of collaboration in a corporate responsibility and social innovation context. *Service Business*, *9*(4), 611–636. doi:10.100711628-014-0242-1

Seelos, C., & Mair, J. (2005). Social entrepreneurship: Creating new business models to serve the poor. *Business Horizons*, *48*(3), 241–246. doi:10.1016/j.bushor.2004.11.006

Shaw, E., & de Bruin, A. (2013). Reconsidering capitalism: The promise of social innovation and social entrepreneurship? *International Small Business Journal*, *31*(7), 737–746. doi:10.1177/0266242613497494

Short, J. C., Moss, T. W., & Lumpkin, G. T. (2009). Research in social entrepreneurship: Past contributions and future opportunities. *Strategic Entrepreneurship Journal*, *3*(2), 161–194. doi:10.1002ej.69

Sullivan Mort, G., Weerawardena, J., & Carnegie, K. (2003). Social entrepreneurship: Towards conceptualisation. *International Journal of Nonprofit and Voluntary Sector Marketing*, *8*(1), 76–88. doi:10.1002/nvsm.202

Tan, W. L., Williams, J., & Tan, T. M. (2005). Defining the 'social' in 'social entrepreneurship': Altruism and entrepreneurship. *The International Entrepreneurship and Management Journal*, *1*(3), 353–365. doi:10.100711365-005-2600-x

The World Bank. (2003). *World development report 2004: Making services work for poor people.* Washington, DC: Oxford University Press.

Tiku, N. (2008). Do-Gooder finance: How a new crop of investors is helping social entrepreneurs. *INC. Magazine*.

Tracey, P., & Phillips, N. (2007). The distinctive challenge of educating social entrepreneurs: A postscript and rejoinder to the special issue on entrepreneurship education. *Academy of Management Learning & Education*, *6*(2), 264–271. doi:10.5465/AMLE.2007.25223465

Waddock, S. A., & Post, J. E. (1991). Social entrepreneurs and catalytic change. *Public Administration Review*, *51*(5), 393–401. doi:10.2307/976408

Weerawardena, J., & Mort, G. S. (2006). Investigating social entrepreneurship: A multidimensional model. *Journal of World Business*, *41*(1), 21–35. doi:10.1016/j.jwb.2005.09.001

Wheeler, D., McKague, K., Thomson, J., Davies, R., Medalye, J., & Prada, M. (2005). Creating sustainable local enterprise networks. *MIT Sloan Management Review*, *47*(1), 33.

Wood, S. (2012). Prone to progress: Using personality to identify supporters of innovative social entrepreneurship. *Journal of Public Policy & Marketing*, *31*(1), 129–141. doi:10.1509/jppm.11.060

Zahra, S. A., Rawhouser, H. N., Bhawe, N., Neubaum, D. O., & Hayton, J. C. (2008). Globalization of social entrepreneurship opportunities. *Strategic Entrepreneurship Journal*, *2*(2), 117–131. doi:10.1002ej.43

ADDITIONAL READING

Banks, K. (Ed.). (2016). *Social entrepreneurship and innovation: International case studies and practice.* Kogan Page Publishers.

Elkington, J., & Hartigan, P. (2008). *The power of unreasonable people: How social entrepreneurs create markets that change the world.* Harvard Business Press.

Goldsmith, S. (2010). *The power of social innovation: How civic entrepreneurs ignite community networks for good.* John Wiley & Sons.

Murray, R., Caulier-Grice, J., & Mulgan, G. (2010). *The open book of social innovation.* London: National endowment for science, technology and the art.

Nicholls, A., & Murdock, A. (2012). The nature of social innovation. In Social innovation (pp. 1-30). Palgrave Macmillan UK. doi:10.1057/9780230367098_1

Yunus, M., Moingeon, B., & Lehmann-Ortega, L. (2010). Building social business models: Lessons from the Grameen experience. *Long Range Planning*, *43*(2), 308–325. doi:10.1016/j.lrp.2009.12.005

KEY TERMS AND DEFINITIONS

Corporate Social Entrepreneurship: The process of extending the firm's domain of competence and corresponding opportunity set through innovative leveraging of resources, both within and outside its direct control, aimed at the simultaneous creation of economic and social value.

Corporate Social Responsibility: A concept whereby companies integrate social and environmental concerns in their business operations and in their interaction with their stakeholders on a voluntary basis.

Social Entrepreneurship: Encompasses the activities and processes undertaken to discover, define, and exploit opportunities in order to enhance social wealth by creating new ventures or managing existing organizations in an innovative manner.

Social Innovation: New ideas that work in meeting social goals.

Chapter 6
Lean Approach to Social Entrepreneurship

Adnan Veysel Ertemel
Istanbul Commerce University, Turkey

ABSTRACT

This chapter proposes an alternate view to social entrepreneurship emphasizing that for-profit and non-profit entrepreneurship are in essence indifferent. It then discusses the latest trends in commercial entrepreneurship world together with implications on social entrepreneurship. In doing so, the lean startup phenomenon and closely related concepts, namely customer development philosophy, business model innovation, value proposition design, and jobs-to-be-done theory are explored with implications on social entrepreneurship.

INTRODUCTION AND BACKGROUND

Social entrepreneurship is gradually getting more and more attention from both scholars and practitioners. Brock, Steinder, and Kim (2008) have identified thirteen different definitions of social entrepreneurship.

DEFINING SOCIAL ENTREPRENEURSHIP

One of the notable definitions define social entrepreneurship as one that creates innovative solutions to immediate social problems and mobilizes the ideas, capacities, resources, and social arrangements required for sustainable social transformations (Alvord, Brown, & Letts, 2004).

In years, another related term called social enterprise has emerged. Social enterprise sees social venture as a for-profit entity that pursues a social mission. Dees (1994) first defined social enterprise as a private organization dedicated to solving social problems and providing socially important goods. Social enterprises combine innovation, entrepreneurship and social purpose and seek to be financially sustainable by generating revenue from trading. Social entrepreneurship is about applying the best of for-profit entrepreneurship to the pursuit of a social mission, or purpose. Thus, social entrepreneurship is a means to making nonprofit organizations less bureaucratic (Dees, 1998).

DOI: 10.4018/978-1-5225-5687-9.ch006

Complying this point of view, this study adopts Robinson's (2006) definition of social entrepreneurship which is defined as:

a process that includes: the identification of a specific social problem and a specific solution, the evaluation of the social impact, the business model and the sustainability of the venture; and the creation of a social mission-oriented for-profit or a business-oriented nonprofit entity that pursues economic, social, and environmental outcomes.

Having introduced this new school of thought, Dees further suggest that social entrepreneurship is at one end of the scale representing non-profit (purely philanthropic) entrepreneurship, whereas for-profit (purely commercial) entrepreneurship is at the other end. In between is the hybrid model compromising the two extremes.

Social Enterprise Spectrum

Depending on these three categories (purely philanthropic, hybrid, purely commercial) there are different benefits and returns for stakeholders who commit resources to a social enterprise:

- **Purely Philanthropic Social Enterprise**: The general motive of purely philanthropic enterprises is that they are mission-driven. Their methods and aims entail the appeal to good will and the creation of social values. Beneficiaries do pay nothing for the offering. The capital required to build a philanthropic enterprise is commonly raised by donations and grants. The workforce consists of volunteers. Suppliers make donations.
- **Hybrid Social Enterprise:** Enterprises in this domain have mixed motives. Their methods and aims embrace a balance of social mission and market orientation in order to create both social and economic value. Beneficiaries (customers) do pay subsidized rates for the goods or services or there is a mix of full payers and those who pay nothing. Financial funds are raised at below market capital rates. Their workforce is paid below market wages and/or there is a mix of volunteers and fully paid staff. Suppliers typically offer special discounts and/or there is a mix of in-kind contributions and full prices.
- **Purely Commercial Social Enterprise:** Purely commercial enterprises are those characterized as completely market-driven. Their methods and aims are appeal to self-interest, including the creation of economic values. Customers pay fair market prices. Investors provide capital at market rates. The workforce receives market salaries and suppliers charge full market prices.

Based on the social enterprise spectrum, Alter (2007) further differentiates hybrid social enterprises into four distinct categories, namely, non-profit enterprises with income-generating activities, social enterprises, socially responsible businesses and enterprises practicing social responsibility. To the left side of the spectrum among the hybrids are those non-profit enterprises with income-generating activities and social enterprises whose business activities generate profits to fund their social mission and report back to their stakeholders. To the right side of the hybrid spectrum there are for-profit enterprises, socially responsible businesses and enterprises practicing social responsibility which create social value but are mainly driven by profits and are accountable to shareholders.

Figure 1. Social Enterprise Spectrum, adopted from Alter (2007)

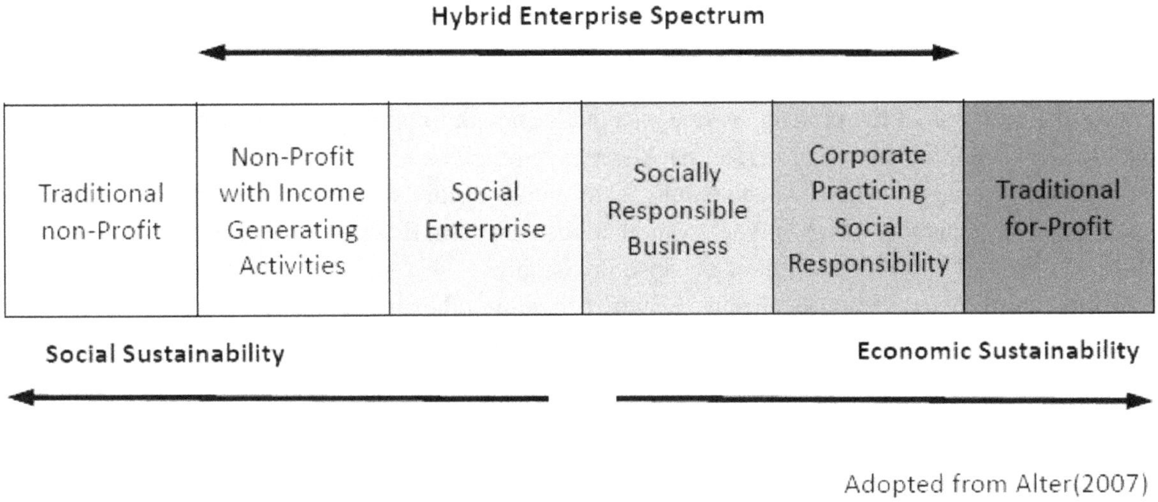

Depending on these categories there are different benefits for different stakeholders.

In recent years, there is even an alternative view that sees social entrepreneurship and commercial entrepreneurship phenomenon as indifferent saying either phenomenon should be viewed with the aim of stakeholders' ultimate benefit in mind. That benefit, looking from Marketing 3.0 perspective is not making profit but rather having a meaningful purpose (Kotler, 2010).

Nevertheless, it can be acknowledged, in any case, that social entrepreneurship should not be treated in isolation from commercial, for-profit entrepreneurship.

INTRODUCING THE LEAN APPROACH

Be it for-proft or non-profit, opportunity recognition and pursuing a viable business model is at the heart of entrepreneurship.

For-profit entrepreneurship requires that entrepreneurs are passionate about existing opportunities (Venkataraman, 1997; Shane & Venkataraman, 2000; Alvarez & Barney, 2007). Likewise, social entrepreneurship also requires being passionate about opportunities (Murphy & Coombes, 2008; Zahra, Rawhouser, Bhawe, Neubaum, & Hayton, 2008).

We live in a fast-changing world in which the speed of adaptation is higher than ever. This new era of entrepreneurship is full of new opportunities most of which are yet to be discovered. Brand new business models are yet to be found which will cause many existing models to be disrupted. With so many uncertainties, Donald Rumsfeld's somewhat philosophical quote is quite true – "we face with a lot of unknown unknowns" in the modern world. The most proper way of conducting entrepreneurial endeavor, thus, is using a discovery minded approach. "Lean Startup" phenomenon (Ries, 2011), which has roots in Silicon Valley, is the ideal methodology to be adopted for this mindset. Borrowing from the Toyota's lean production philosophy, lean startup movement aims at minimizing the waste in terms of effort, money and time during entrepreneurial journey by embracing making mistakes. Lean startup has widely influenced entrepreneurship ecosystem globally. It even has effects on new product development methodologies. Clearly, the approach has powerful implications to social entrepreneurship. The main idea in lean approach is to make cheap and fast experiments on riskiest assumptions of the business early in the process. In this approach, the entrepreneur develops Minimum Viable Products (MVPs) – a minimalistic version of the product/service idea that's enough to make potential customers experience the idea and get feedback – and iterate quickly between various alternatives. The MVPs can even be fake products because the most valuable thing is the entrepreneurs' time. If an MVP doesn't get enough traction, the entrepreneur has to "pivot" to another business idea. Pivoting here means making a radical change in strategy (not tactic) without a change in vision.

Lean startup phenomenon is closely related with some other recently introduced concepts. On a more philosophical level, the complementary concept is Blank's (2005) customer (rather than product) development approach. Blank argues that understanding the essential needs, pain points, gain expectations of a few carefully selected potential customers is crucial to the success of a new startup. Starting from time zero onwards, entrepreneurs should constantly be in contact with their potential customers and be willing to be flexible enough major changes on product as required.

Lean Startup Principles

There has been a silent revolution at the heart of the entrepreneurial ecosystem, Silicon Valley in the last decade. Up until recent years, investors used to expect well-crafted and long business plans that are full of untested hypothesis about the entrepreneurial venture. However, leading thinkers like Steve Blank and Eric Ries realized that although a plan for a disruptive startup looks great on paper, when the product is ready on the shelves or available for download, customers didn't buy or responded in unexpected ways. Validating Mike Tyson's famous quote saying 'everyone has a plan until they get punched in the face', a significant percentage of well-crafted business plans turn out to be useless when they get in contact with the customers for the first time.

Blank states that a lean approach has the following distinct characteristics (Blank, 2013);

- **It Favors Experimentation Over Elaborate Planning:** A perfect plan without validation is completely useless according to the lean philosophy. Therefore, every hypothesis needs to be validated with experiments.
- **It Prioritizes Customer Feedback Over Intuition:** Experimental approach is all about getting feedback and potential insight from customers.
- **It Emphasizes Iterative Design Over Traditional Big Design Up Front Development:** Since lean philosophy seeks to explore 'unknown unknowns', there is a high probability that each experiment will lead to a completely different path. Hence, iterative design is best approach to adopt.

Many large-scale enterprises including General Electric and Intuit have adopted the lean startup approach across their internal operations to gain competitive advantage. To exemplify the case, well known as the number one tax automation software company, Intuit, used to make a single change to its software in hundred days. After adopting lean approach, Intuit now runs hundreds of simultaneous experiments during the tax season.

Driving Forces for the Lean Approach

Lean approach is becoming popular worldwide. Because, rapidly developing technology enabled there are more than two billion mobile users worldwide which also includes poor people in under-developed countries. Additionally, cost of technology-enabled devices is decreasing dramatically. This not only results in ownership of mobile – even smart phones - by the poor but it also causes a new phenomenon, that brings about Internet of things (IoT) to be widespread worldwide. IoT is about low-cost tiny smart devices with sensors, microchips and Internet connectivity. Sensors, especially, are ideal for monitoring usage of products. Now low-cost sensors can be paired with mobile devices to get live data. Thanks to these developments, measurement of field data is much easier for projects in social entrepreneurship.

Lean Startup Methodology

Characterizing the new venture creation process as '*a chaotic organization involving constant search for a viable business model*', Blank and Ries acknowledge that a high rate of hypothesis invalidation is expected in startups. They suggest following a lean (startup) approach, which is borrowed from Toyota's lean manufacturing system aimed at minimizing waste. Just like lean manufacturing, lean startup approach minimizes the time and effort required in each attempt to search for a viable business model. This is achieved by quickly iterating through a process called Build-Measure-Learn loop.

Build-Measure-Learn-Loop

The loop is about building a product (or service) very quickly, measuring whether the idea worked and gather learning about customers. The involved steps in the process is detailed below;

1. **Identify Hypothesis:** Adopting the *jobs-to-be-done* mentality identify exactly what is the ideal target group, what are their pains and what solution they need. In this first step, in order to save time and energy not pursuing the wrong business, the entrepreneur should first pick up leap of faith assumptions. If invalidated entrepreneurs should be flexible enough to pivot to a radically different route.
2. **Conduct Customer Discovery:** Following *customer development* approach, the entrepreneur should '*get out of the building*' and try to figure out what the target group actually needs or wants. In this phase, the entrepreneur tries to achieve 'customer-problem fit' – verification that customers really have the stated problems.
3. **Define Value Proposition:** Based on the insight from customer development interviews, identify what solution will cure the pains or fulfill gain expectations. If the value proposition is validated in steps 4 and 5, 'problem-solution fit' will be achieved.
4. **Build a Minimum Viable Product:** According to the developed hypothesis and the value proposition, develop a minimalistic product that has just enough number of features needed to test the hypothesis.
5. **Conduct Experiment and Measure the Results:** Define clear and actionable metrics and conduct the experiment to test MVP and get results.
6. **Learn About the Target Group:** Use the collected data to refine the model for the product. According to the results, either persevere with the idea or pivot to a radically different idea.

Figure 2. Build Measure Learn Loop

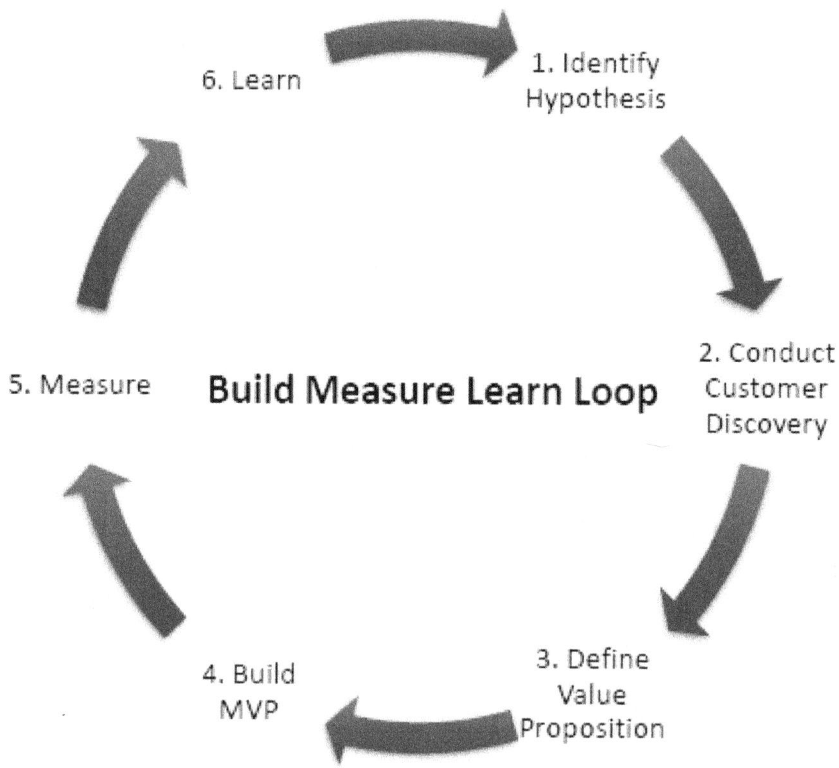

The crucial thing here is to iterate this cycle as quickly as the team can. Building something is time-consuming most of the time. Lean approach suggests using a different mindset here, to get the quickest results, building a Minimum Viable Product (MVP) instead of a full-fledged product is preferred. Minimum viable product is the one with minimalistic features, even a fake ore half working prototype that's just enough to have few customers experience it and gather feedback. Using static pages with links to other static pages (i.e. clickable pdf resembling a working site) or concierge (manual) MVPs where founders manually deliver service to few customers are some examples to experiments that can be quickly tested.

Having gathered feedback and learned about the customers, the venture either perseveres (sticks) with the idea or pivots to a radically different idea. Pivoting here means making a radical change in strategy without a change in vision (Ries, 2011). Pivoting in lean startup is just like the case of pivoting in basketball, the founder should keep one leg steady (stay tuned with customer needs as learned in previous iteration) while he can step the other leg to anywhere.

Optimal Learning Loop

The related dynamics involved in the customer learning process can be depicted with figure 3.

The dynamics are namely; speed, learning and focus. The entrepreneur has to be good at all three throughout the process. Lean approach is about speeding up the learning process. If this couldn't be achieved the chances are that entrepreneurs will run out of resources before they can find product-market

Figure 3. Optimal Learning Loop in Lean Approach

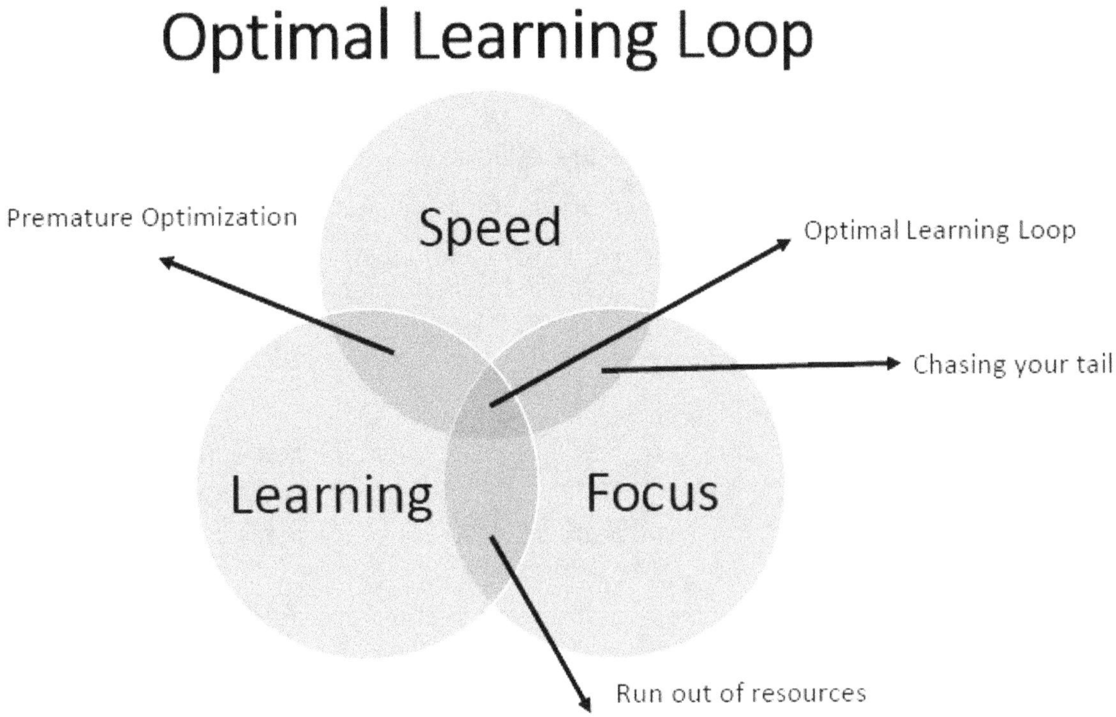

fit. If focus, that is, clear long-term vision is lacking it's probable that entrepreneurs fall into premature optimization trap. If learning is omitted the entrepreneurs might well be detaching themselves from the customer realities and chasing their own tail.

LEAN STARTUP AND INTERRELATED CONCEPTS

Built upon the fail fast fail cheap mantra, lean approach has radically transformed the Silicon Valley in particular and commercial entrepreneurial ecosystem in general over the past decade. This revolution even has effects on traditional product development practices.

Lean startup revolution has several complementary concepts all of which are introduced in the last decade. On a theoretical level, Jobs-to-be-Done theory (Christiensen, 2007; Ulwick, 2005) lays out the foundation of the lean approach. The theory states that whatever customers buy or use, in essence, they hire that product or service till they fulfill the job to be done in their mind.

Osterwalder's Business Model Innovation and Value Proposition Design concepts are used as a tool in the lean approach. The idea behind this concept is the fact that business planning is outdated and in today's fast changing world with quickly evolving business environments, being flexible to make major changes to business models and observe results are more prominent. Jobs-to-be-Done theory can be utilized in Value proposition design to come up with ideal value proposition that perfectly address the pain points or gain expectations in potential customers mind.

Figure 4. Lean appraoch and related concepts

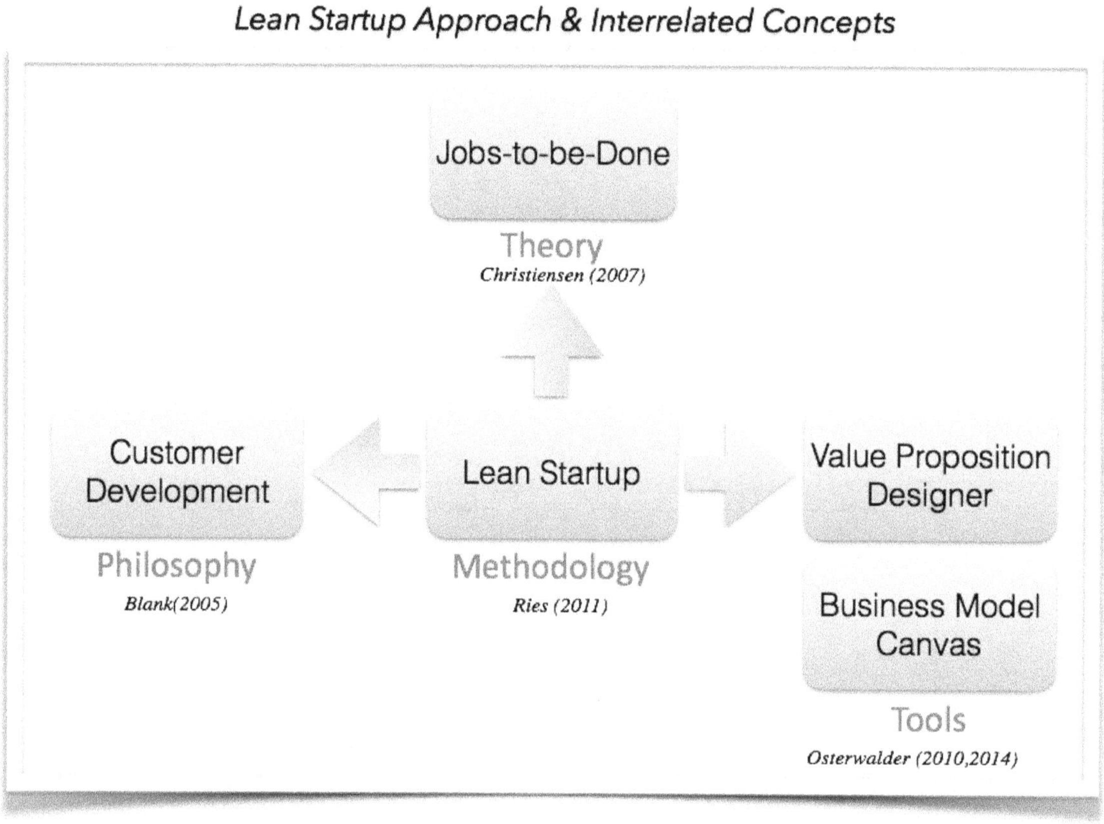

Customer development is the philosophy side of the big picture emphasizing the crucial importance of the customer contact and customer validation starting from time zero onwards in the entrepreneurial journey.

JOBS-TO-B-DONE THEORY

Jobs to be done theory was developed independently by several authors including Christensen (2007), Ulwick (2005), and Nitterhouse (1997). It describes the things customer are trying to get done in their work or life that causes them to buy a product or service in the first place. A customer job can be the tasks they are trying to perform or complete, the problems they are trying to solve or the needs they are trying to satisfy. These jobs are universal and independent of any solution or technology. As an illustration to the phenomenon, we can give Henry Ford's famous quote, *If I had asked people what they wanted, they would have said faster horses,* as an example. He didn't think the "job" as a "faster horse" but as *getting Point A to Point B as quickly as possible*. This mode of thinking is crucial in jobs-to-be-done theory.

Thought in this way, entrepreneurs can find clever shortcuts to get the job at hand done. As Theodore Levitt said *people do not want a quarter-inch drill, they want a quarter inch hole.* This notion is so crucial but often neglected. Instead of trying to improve existing products like creating a better screwdriver with quarter-inch drill, entrepreneurs can innovate at dramatically improved rate by instead trying to find better ways to create a quarter-inch hole to get the job done.

As a good illustration of the point, a website (www.shoulditakemyumbrealla.com) helps individuals decide what to do in a potentially rainy day by just asking zip code and affirms the user that she should take her umbrella or not. This jobs-to-be-done oriented solution is contrary to the process that involves checking the temperature, humidity level and the like parameters.

Job Types

Fundamentally, a "job" is an unmet want or need. But it has many requirements – not just functional but also emotional and social ones. This suggests that context and circumstances are equally important.

- **Functional Jobs**: Functional jobs imply the tasks that needs to be performed functionally to solve the specific problem.
- **Social Jobs**: Social jobs imply the end-users' need for looking good or gain social power or social status. These describe how the end-users want to be perceived by others like looking cool or be perceived by competent.
- **Emotional/Personal Jobs**: Emotional jobs involve the end-users' seeking of an emotional state for the sake of feeling emotionally good. For example, the user might want to feel good, have peace of mind or feel secure by using a product.
- **Supporting Jobs**: The job in question might be a sub-set of a bigger job and link to that job as a supporting job. There are different types of supporting jobs;
    - **Buyer of Value:** Jobs related to buying a value such as comparing offers, deciding a product to buy or taking delivery of a product
    - **Co-Creator of Value:** Jobs related to co-creating value such as writing product reviews or participating to design phase of a product
    - **Transferrer of Value:** Jobs related to the ends of a value proposition like cancelling subscription or reselling a product.

Jobs to Be Done Applied to Social Sector

An Indian initiative – ChoutuKool is a perfect example to the jobs-to-be-done theory applied for social impact. For Indian population living in rural areas, having a refrigerator at home is a luxury. According to the United Nations Commission on Sustainable Development, one third of all food is lost to spoilage in India. Founders of an innovative business, Godrej closely analyzed the "jobs" in the mind of a typical Indian family and came up with the idea that what's needed is not exactly a refrigerator. Rather, it's something that people can store their essentials for 1 up to 2 days. Something that's rather lightweight so that they can also carry from one place to another. After this finding, the business developed a brand new type of product, ChoutuKool (meaning "little cool" in Hindi) that includes a thermoelectric chip instead of a heavy compressor. The resulting product is portable taking up to 45 liters of food. It works both with battery or electricity. Most importantly its price is less than half price of the cheapest refrigerator.

In just two years more than hundred thousand ChotuKools were sold in Indian market. This case illustrates that, specific needs of the particular user segment, in other words, the job at hand plays a crucial role in determining the right product configuration.

Figure 5. ChotuKool at work

CUSTOMER DEVELOPMENT PHILOSOPHY

Blank argues that business model is a great way to organize thinking. But what's written first in the canvas is just a series of assumptions. To validate or invalidate those assumptions, 'getting out of the building' mentality is essential. This mentality consists of quickly designing experiments, run tests and gather data about the key assumptions about the business. Only this way the assumptions stated in business model canvas becomes facts.

Constructing the hypothesis. Learn whether other people have the same problem or need that the entrepreneur thinks they have.

Phases of Customer Development Process

Figure 6 illustrates the phases of the customer development process.

Customer Discovery

Customer discovery phase involves testing the problem in the field. Using this approach, the entrepreneur's understanding of the customer problem or the need is tested. The point is to verify that problem hypothesized actually exists on the field by the target group. Verification of the problem against customers in the field means achieving customer-problem fit).

Figure 6. Customer Development Process (Blank, 2005)

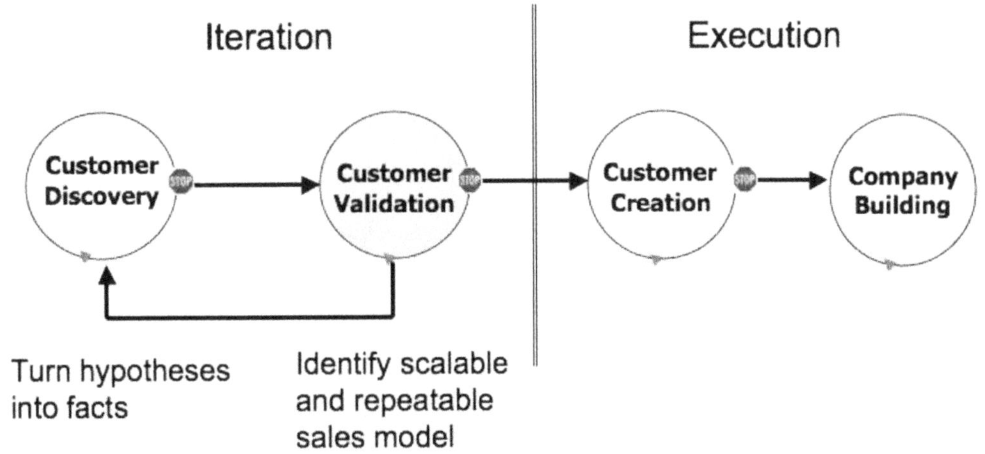

Customer Validation

Customer validation is about contacting with and understanding customers for figuring out how to build a prototype. In this phase, entrepreneur needs to test his solution against the pain points and gain expectations to find problem-solution fit. The pain should ideally be felt so deeply that customers should be impatient to wait for a full product. If this is not achieved, the entrepreneur should always be open to pivot to another idea. This iterative process should be repeated over and over in search for the ideal configuration where a perfect product-market fit is achieved. Product-market fit indicates that all the building blocks in the business model is ideal in acquiring, capturing and delivering value to the customers.

This step is inclusive of testing positioning; testing various ways to sell the product to actual customers and see which benefit resonated well with the audience. In product market fit, entrepreneur should make trials and errors to find out which acquisition channel worked better than all the alternatives.

The remaining two blocks of customer development process is no longer about search for a business model, but rather execution of the found model. Creating demand and scale to build a functional organization oriented towards constant and rapid execution.

Customer Creation

Customer creation is the end of search phase and the start of execution phase. In order to start the execution mode, the business has to make sure that it has found the optimum business model (knows its market, customers, exact product/service features, sales channel, pricing etc.) in search of the ideal business configuration. In this phase, end-user demand is build and driven to the sales channel to scale the business.

Company Building

Company building phase aims at transitioning the organization from a startup to a company focused on executing a validated model. Company building phase is more about managing the life cycle of existing products and the launch of follow-on products. These functions are typically the job of the product management and engineering teams. It results in a linear process where the entrepreneur has to make a plan and refine it into detail.

BUSINESS MODEL CANVAS

Business model canvas, as a tool to use in lean approach, is developed by Osterwalder (2010). Osterwalder defines business modelling as the rationale for how an organization creates, delivers and captures value. In doing so, business model is a canvas with 9 building blocks describing different aspects of the business.

The building blocks comprising the canvas are as follows:

1. **Customer Segments:** The very specific set of target groups with similar characteristics. For social ventures, the target segments should be selected from those who will receive the greatest impact from the business.
2. **Value Proposition:** Describes the unique benefit the target segments will receive by using the product and service. The value proposition should position the business against alternatives. For example, value proposition for Volvo automobile company is a single word: Safety. For social ventures, impact value potentially to sector or problem as a whole should be mentioned.

Figure 7. Business model canvas (Osterwalder, 2010)

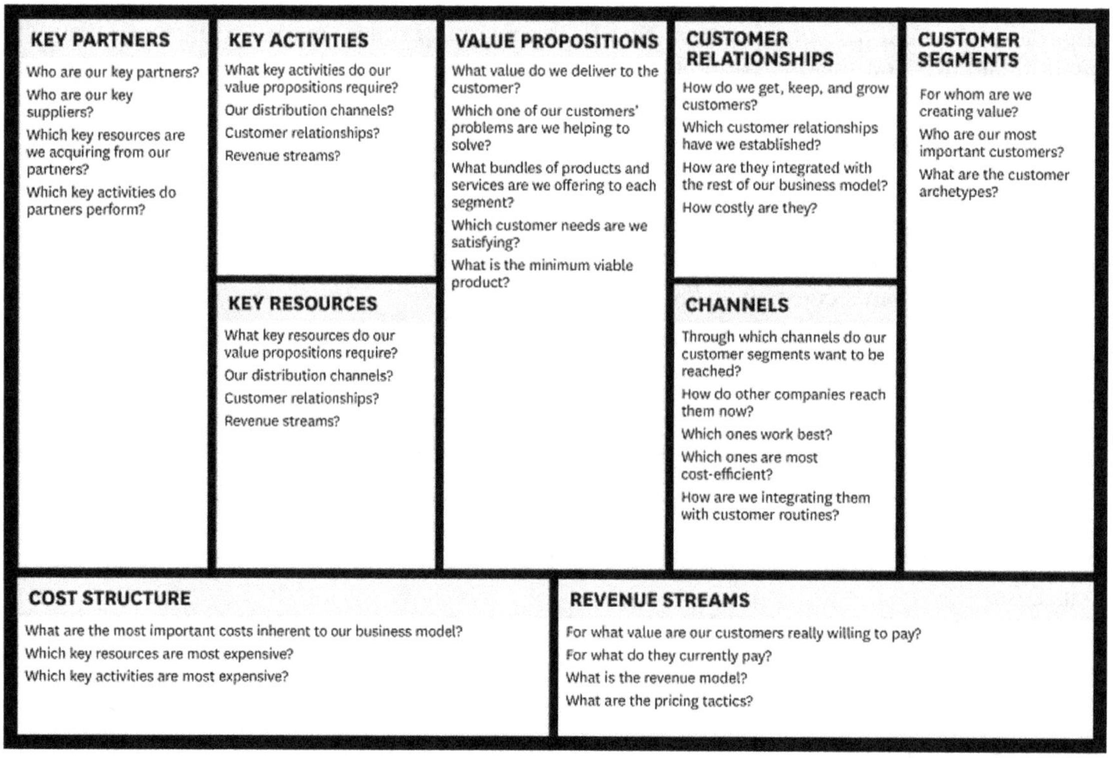

3. **Channels:** Describes how the value proposition will be delivered to target groups through sales, distribution and communication activities.
4. **Customer Relationships:** Describes how to acquire, keep and retain customers through different customer relationship management activities. For social ventures, building relationship based on trust and dignity is particularly important.
5. **Key Partnerships:** Describes the partnerships the business works with to deliver the value to the target groups. For social, this building block includes all the partnering organizations, possibly government and NGOs and other social enterprises trying to solve for the same cause. Moreover, it might also be helpful to identify and write possible opponents who might resist against the idea.
6. **Key Activities:** The key processes the business is going to do to deliver the promised value. For social ventures, it should be ensured that all activities performed across the value chain with the partners are aligned to have the intended impact.
7. **Key Resources:** Describes the key assets to deliver the promised offering. Social ventures can think of the resources as "inputs" – the resources to create impact and business value – in theory of change.
8. **Revenue Streams:** The revenue the business makes by delivering the promised value. For social ventures to have self-efficacy be sustainable, this building block should is equally important.
9. **Cost Structure:** Describes both fixed and variable cost structure of the entrepreneurial business.

The key notion in business modelling is that, as opposed wasting time and energy developing a lengthy business plan full of untested assumptions, a short and to-the-point business model can easily describe all aspects of the business and new iterations on those hypothesis could be done with the least effort. Using the customer development philosophy, entrepreneurs should "get out of the building" and validate or invalidate their hypothesis quickly to iterate on the business model.

In the end, business model aims at describing how a business model creates, captures and delivers value. These dimensions can be detailed as;

- **Value Creation (Value Proposition, Customer Segments):** Describes how the business create solutions that solve specific problems or create benefits of target segments. The focus here is trying to address and unmet need of a viable target segment. Understanding the mentality outlined in jobs-to-be-done theory is vital to value creation activities.
- **Value Delivery (Key Partnerships, Key Activities, Key Resources):** Describes which processes or partnership activities the business undertake to deliver the value to target segments. Possible innovation in value chain or distribution systems might make the products or services more accessible to the society.
- **Value Capture (Cost Structure, Revenue Streams):** Describes how the business generate revenue and become financially sustainable. The social entrepreneur should take into account philanthropic support, market capital and the like dimensions. Given this, coupling cost structure with revenue streams, the value capture part should prove sustainability of the business. While ensuring sustainability of the business, making the product or service more affordable is also a crucial aim of the social entrepreneur.

Incorporating Impact to Business Model Canvas

For social ventures, business impact is an additional concern that must be placed on top of the whole canvas. The perfect alignment of the impact and business model is the ideal case in social entrepreneurship. Gelobter (2015) designed a variation of business model canvas, named "The Lean Change Canvas" for use in social entrepreneurship. As shown in Figure 8, the questions to be answered is slightly changed accompanying building blocks to accommodate for social ventures.

VALUE PROPOSITION DESIGN

Osterwalder's Business model canvas aims at depicting the ideal business configuration in full detail. However, the majority of entrepreneurs' time should be spent on thoroughly understanding the exact customer persona, their pain points and gain expectations in their minds. This is exactly what jobs-to-be-done theory concentrates on. Thus, having witnessed the necessity of a further investigation of first two building blocks of business model canvas, namely - customer segments and value proposition, Osterwalder authored a new model in his latter book; Value Proposition Designer (Osterwalder, 2014).

Figure 8. The Lean Change Canvas (Gelobter, 2015)

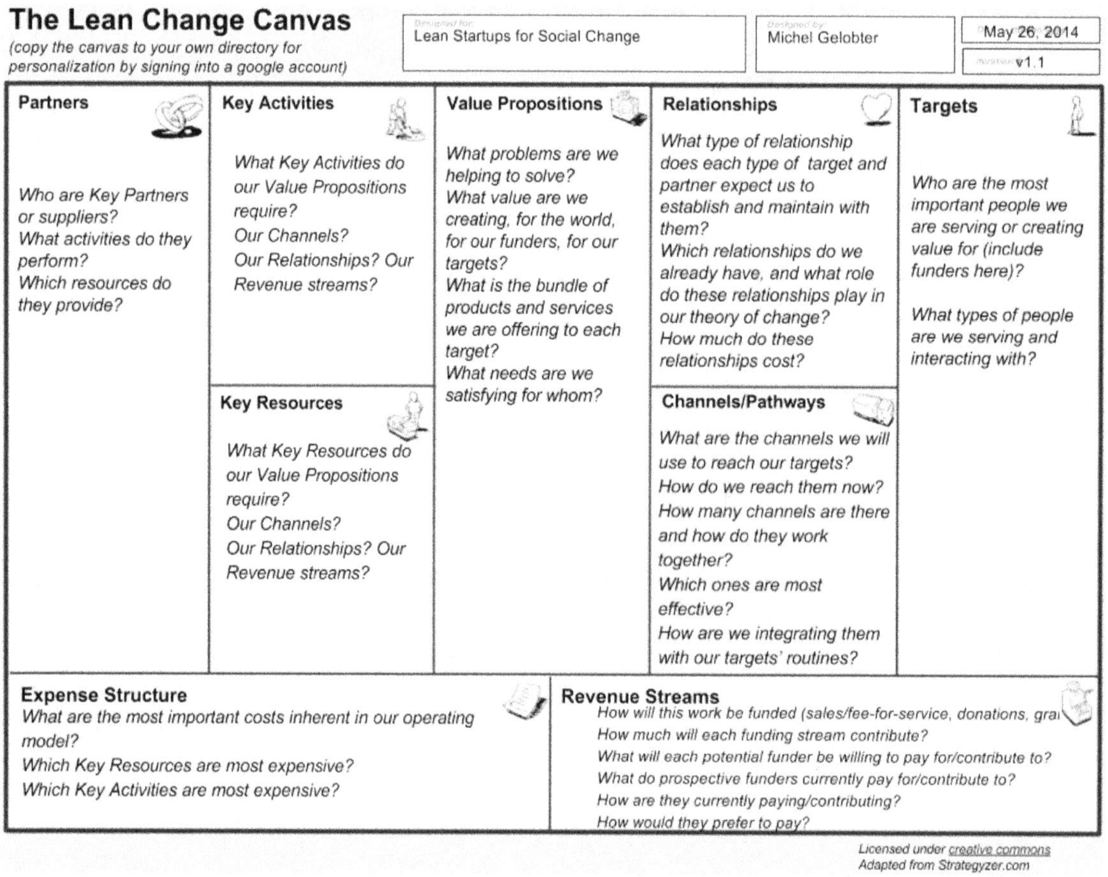

Osterwalder, proposes a map called *Value Proposition Map* (also known as Value Proposition Canvas) to help the entrepreneur find *problem-solution fit* in market. Product market fit implies that offered products fit exactly to the needs of the specific customers in the form of pain relievers and gain creators. In other words, it means there is evidence that customers really care about certain jobs (to be done), pains and gains.

The model argues that a products and services in a value proposition should be stated as gain creators or pain relievers. Gain creators show how the products create customer gains. Pain relievers show how the products alleviate customer pains.

Customer Jobs describe what the customers are trying to get done in their lives, as stated in jobs-to-be-done theory. Pains describe bad outcomes, risks and obstacles related to customer jobs. Gains describe the outcomes customers want to achieve.

The idea is to write down all possible customer jobs, pains and gains and then analyze which one is a priority in the mind of customers and which solution is a perfect cure to that need by designing and testing different experiments with lean approach.

Relating Other Concepts to Lean Methodology

Lean startup, Jobs to be done theory, customer development philosophy, value proposition design and business model canvas tools are all part of the same notion that adopts a customer-needs-first approach. Complementing each other in different aspects, these concepts adopt a validation based, agile and iterative path to entrepreneurial endeavor. Each concept and its relation to the big picture is given below;

Figure 9. Value Proposition Map (Osterwalder, 2014)

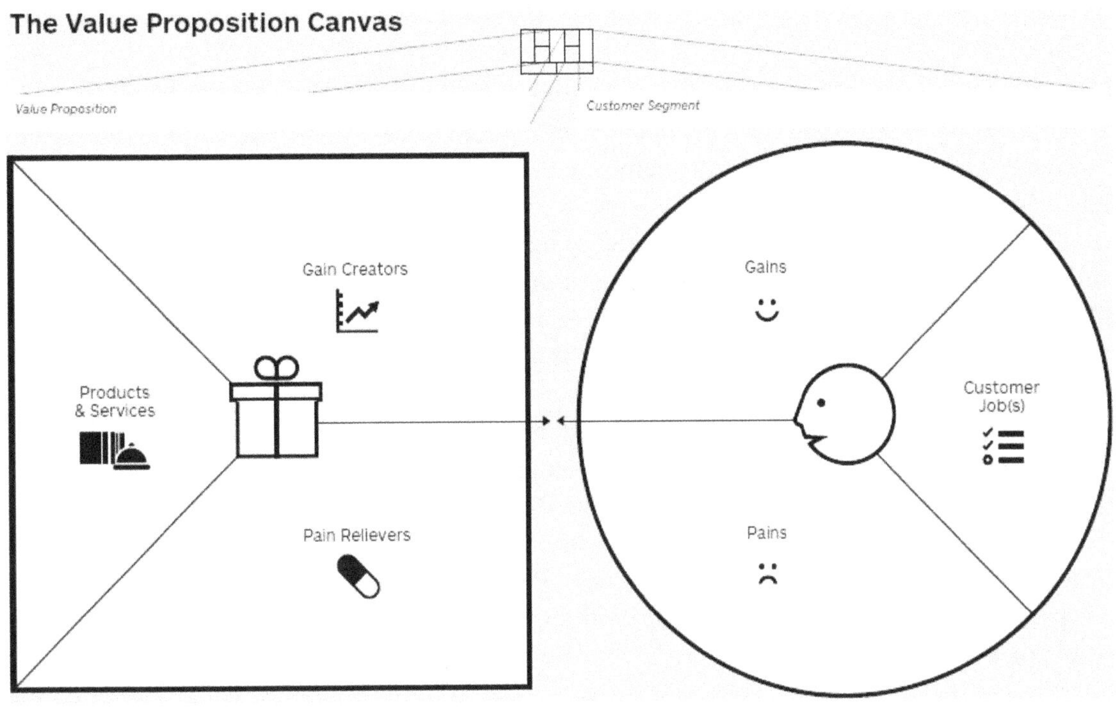

Jobs to be done theory addresses the underlying needs, in other words, jobs, to be done in the mind of users. Value proposition designer is a tool to analyze and depict the "jobs" together with the pain relivers and gain creators in a structured manner. Business model canvas zooms out from the point in the previous step and takes a whole snapshot of the business at large including cost strucuture, partnerships, revenue streams, customer relationships and distribution channels.

On a philosophical level, customer development mindset advises that entrepreneurial journey should start with validating that really customers have the stated problems. Afterwards, whether or not the proposed solution proves to be a cure for the problem should be tested. Only after taking these steps and validating at small scale should the entrepreneur start executing the plan at large.

In the end, all of the concepts mentioned above complement each other in helping the entrepreneur adopting the lean approach that favors experimental and iterative manner. After all, lean startup constitutes the methodology partf of the notion by advising how to conduct lean experiments for validation or invalidating of the idea with fast build-measure-learn cycles.

LEAN APPROACH IN PRACTICE

Lean startup approach calls for agile mindset that incorporates fast and cheap experiments along the entrepreneurial journey. Pivoting, experiment design and Minimum viable products (MVPs) deserve special attention in this approach. This section discusses each concept in detail.

Pivot Types

1. **Zoom-in / Zoom-out Pivot** Zoom-in pivot happens when the entrepreneur choose to zoom to only one feature and discard all remaning features from the product.

Flickr story is a typical example to zoom-in pivoting. Initially the entrepreneurs developed a massive multiplayer online (MMO) game. As the founders introduced a new feature, photo upload and achieved interestingly high engagement rates, the company decided to zoom-in pivot and focus only to photo uploading and discard everything else.

Zoom-out pivot is needed when the product or market scope is bigger than initially expected. For example, in its initial days, Youtube founders positioned the platform for just dating purposes. After a while, they questioned themselves and said there is no restriction for anyone to upload a video for any purpose. Hence, they made a zoom-out pivot for the platform.

2. **Platform Pivot:** Platform pivot means transitioning an application into a platform or, based on the market response transitioning a platform back to an application or app.
3. **Business Model Pivot:** This pivot is used when there is a need for a radical shift in business model. For example, a business operating in B2C (business to consumer) mode might find it more viable to switch to B2B (business to business) model. Business model pivot also includes change in sales channel, way of developing relationships with customers or switch from low cost leadership strategy to product differentiation strategy etc.

4. **Customer Segment Pivot:** Although the product solves real problems of a specific customer segment, sometimes a completely different customer segment might be more profitable hence making it meaningful to pivot customer segments.
5. **Need Pivot:** This happens when satisfying the current need is insufficient for the entrepreneur to pursue for being profitable or the entrepreneurs have discovered a much more promising need that's currently unmet in competitive landscape.
6. **Value Pivot:** Value pivot happens when the model for monetizing delivered value is changed. For instance, instead of setting a one-time fee for the product, the entrepreneurs might decide to switch to subscription based model. Customers might perceive this model cheaper but entrepreneurs might find this model more profitable in the long run.
7. **Channel Pivot:** Channel pivot means using a more efficient channel strategy for delivering the value to the customers.
8. **Technology Pivot:** Technology pivot happens when the product is delivered on a different technological platform (androis vs. iOS, Microsoft vs. Linux etc.).
9. **Growth Model Pivot:** When scaling up the startup, there are different growth models entrepreneurs can choose from. Growth model pivot happens when a different growth strategy is chosen. For instance, Dropbox used to rely on paid growth strategy in its initial days. As they discovered that cost of acquiring a new customer using this strategy is relatively high, they tried viral growth strategy by asking existing users to invite their friends and get extra storage as a reward. This strategy worked and Dropbox uses the same growth strategy up to now.

Minimum Viable Product (MVP)

Minimum viable product (MVP) is the minimum version of the entrepreneurial idea, the one that contains only the key features to be tested. Ries defines it as 'minimum set of features needed to get feedback and learn from early adopters of the venture idea. The trick here is two folds; avoid building something that no-one wants and maximize the amount of learning that can be achieved.

Deconstructing MVP

To further deconstruct MVP philosophy (Geldro, 2013);

- **Minimum:** Refers to the least amount of effort (and time) required to offer value to customers,
- **Viable:** It should be as complete a product or service as possible. Sometimes multiple features should be bundled together to get a sense of how customers will interact with the full thing rather than just one element,
- **Product:** There should be some element of 'transaction' or 'currency' exchanged between the venture and the customer to help test whether they will be really committed to buying or using the product as opposed to the case of an interview where potential customers indicate they are interested or not.

In lean startup approach, the idea is to start building MVP even in the very start of ideation phase and continue to build more functional MVPs as the venture progresses. In the very beginning even seemingly real fake products using prototyping tools can be used to gather feedback from potential users.

TYPES OF MINIMUM VIABLE PRODUCTS

Landing Page

Landing page is a method where a single web page describes the value proposition with a clear and compelling marketing message. Sometimes embedded with a short explainer video, landing page aims at tracking conversion rates based on actionable (vs. vanity) metrics by using a call-to-action (CTA). These metrics could be either a click-to-buy button, sign-up or leaving email address for being one of early users. The opposite of actionable metrics are vanity metrics that must be avoided by entrepreneurs. Vanity metrics include number of visits to the landing page or average time spent on site, those that might be good at making the entrepreneur feel good but they are not meaningful and actionable metrics.

Brochure / Flier

Even though the solution is not ready yet, testing different needs and different value propositions can be done by making different brochures for different variations of the idea. Coupled with a call to action like urging the customers to send designated SMS to a number or entering a URL is ideal to gather feedback on which variation worked well and which didn't.

Demo Video

The idea can be showcased using an explainer video. When used with a clear call to action, this method is very effective for gathering quantitative feedback from potential customers. Having difficulty to cut through the clutter in highly competitive cloud sharing solutions, Dropbox founder shoot a video explaining the unique experience Dropbox delivers.

Imposter MVP

This method involves taking an existing product and add one or more new features. This way is much easier than building a product from scratch.

Concierge MVP

In concierge MVP, the steps or services are performed manually that may later be automated. In a social business venture that is based on responding to inquiries or giving alert messages automatically by short messages (SMS) or directing the phone callers to respective services by Interactive Voice Response (IVR) those steps can initially be performed manually having few real people behind.

MVP vs. Pilot Programs

In social entrepreneurship practices, it's common to see pilot phase of the Project where the donators give relatively smaller funds to test whether the idea is working.

MVP is quite different from pilot programs. Pilot programs are undertaken when the things are quite well-developed but the donators want to test it on a small population before scaling up. On the contrary, minimum viable products are designed to test certain hypothesis to help the team move forward quickly based on what works. Pilot programs are typically undertaken once throughout the project whereas multiple MVPs are designed and conducted regularly throughout the project.

Experimental Mindset

Ries argues that a startup can be described as a series of experiments about the entrepreneurial venture.

The idea behind lean approach is to design scientific experiments that are just enough to validate or invalidate the critical hypothesis of the venture. The experiments don't just happen in laboratories. Thanks to advancing technology and new analytical tools, companies are using data-driven approach to decide virtually anything about the business they are in. Companies like Google, Facebook, and Dropbox use this phenomenon popularized as: *the market knows and decides on anything*. By making two different versions of an offering and testing which one leads to more conversion, *known as A/B testing*, a data-driven company can make sure which variation is preferred by the market. The experiment subject can be whether the color of the call-to-action button should be red or blue. Or it could be trial of different headlines featuring completely different benefits a solution. Facebook constantly makes different A/B tests at various levels. It's quite common that a Facebook user in a control group unknowingly sees a different version of the same screen whereas other users see the normal screen. As another example to A/B testing, Google discovered that human beings can differentiate 41 different shades of blue. As a search engine showing mainly blue-colored links, the company tried and tested each one of the tones to see which one leads to more conversions, in this case clicks. This experiment helped Google increase their annual turnover by 200 million dollars (Hern, 2014).

This approach is quite different from traditional research methods like surveys. People might indicate they love and want to use a product. But when the real product is ready, many of those people don't actually but or use the product. The unique benefit of experimental approach over traditional survey based methods is that; experiments are a way from moving beyond what people say to what they actually behave.

LEAN EXPERIMENT TYPES

Pick-Up Test

In this test, various different versions of a product are placed on a table. Which version is picked-up is observed. The test doesn't stop there, one or more features are added or dropped and the result is observed again. The product variations could be a box containing the value proposition with a clear message using tangible benefits

Click-Through Test

If the product has digital dimension (at least showcased in a digital page), click-through rate of each version is observed with A/B test.

Smoke Test

This method involves using a fake buy button that allows people to demonstrate their intent to buy. Since people only try to buy products which are perceived as real value-add, this test is a very useful method to see the potential of the idea.

Crowdfunding

Setting up a crowdfunding campaign and asking potential users to contribute is a good way to see if people really care enough to finance the project.

Lean Principles Applied to Social Entrepreneurship

In lean approach, Blank argues that testing in the building, that is, testing without touching the field and getting real feedback from real people, is nonsense. Therefore, the most crucial step in lean approach is 'getting out of the building' (GooB).

For social ventures, there is even an additional step involved – *Getting out of the way*: giving the product and going away. After a while, when the team comes back they observe whether the product was actually used or used for intended purpose. Alternative way to do this is by asking another observer (teacher, parent, and neighbor) report whether the product was used as desired. Another alternative is by embedding a meter or sensor to the product. An education software given to disadvantaged people in a tablet, for example, can be tracked to see how many hours did the pupils stay connected to the program. As an example to autonomous sensor feedback, newly installed toilets in an underdeveloped region could have low-cost sensors embedded inside to track the number of uses.

Lean mindset calls for a quite different approach than the traditional social entrepreneurship approach. Table 1 summarizes the main differences of the two approaches in various dimensions.

Unlike the commercial ventures, when it comes to social entrepreneurship, social ventures should consider an additional element; impact factor on top of the other factors in non-profit sector. Theory of change is the mainly used model to cater for peculiarities of the social ventures. Theory of change quite simply is a theory of how and why an initiative works (Weiss, 1995) According to the theory of change, the process for achieving social impact involves mapping the linkages between input, process, output, expected outcomes and ultimately the impact. The process begins with identifying desired outcomes,

Table 1. Comparison of lean versus traditional social entrepreneurship

Lean Social Entrepreneurship	Traditional Social Entrepreneurship
Business Model	Strategic Plan / Business Plan
Hypothesis Driven	Implementation Driven
Talk to people and understand what they need and build incrementally based on feedback	Comply with donor specifications. Plan in detail before implementation
Failure is expected	Failure is exception
Move quickly	Move at a measured pace

using a backwards planning approach continues with mapping the intermediate outcomes and activities, or interventions, required to deliver long term changes.

Regarding impact creation and management, there are four main stages involved; estimating impact, planning impact, monitoring impact and evaluating impact (So, 2006).

Lean startup methodology is especially related with second and third stages of this process namely; impact planning and impact monitoring stages. By designing rapid experiments and constantly measuring feedback the entrepreneurs try to learn from the customers in the field as fast as they could.

Lean approach requires a radical shift in the mindset. For instance, getting in contact should not be viewed as for compliance or auditing, but instead as a chance to learn from and get insights from the field.

The main principles for lean for social mindset are as follows;

- **Customer-First Approach:** Social ventures might lack the focus of customers. In lean approach, however is touching real pain points of the actual users in the field is crucial. All other concerns including should follow this principle
- **Low-Cost Technology:** Increasingly widespread low-cost technologies like sensors, mobile technology etc. for data collection should be used to achieve efficiency.
- **Fast Feedback Loops:** Iterative process and collection of feedback from users in a continuous and rapid manner is vital to lean approach

Build-Measure-Learn Loop for Social Projects

Based on the typical build-measure-learn loop of the lean startup methodology, the social venture owners should follow a similar but a slightly different version of the same process. Listed below are the nuances for the social sector.

Build the Impact Hypothesis

In hypothesis development, the pain points are more than inconveniences or annoyances, but rather potentially life-saving factors.

Choose Experiment Method

- **Technology**: In the case of social sector, the technology to be used should be low-cost and accessible to even disadvantaged people like sending SMS message in an efficient manner
- **Survey**: Even when survey method is chosen, survey design and questions should not look alike that of typical social impact projects. It should involve asking a few short un-disturbing questions but asking them more frequently in the feedback loop.

A Working Case of Lean Approach Applied to Social Entrepreneurship

The Coalition for Humane Immigrant Rights of Los Angeles (CHIRLA) organization is a best practice case study of the lean approach applied in social sector (Murray, 2015). The organization serves immigrant people in Los Angeles facing barriers related to discrimination, language, poverty etc. Seeking new ways to meet the needs of its community, the organization successfully used lean approach to find and validate more than a dozen financially sustainable product offerings in just a few hours.

The team in the organization initially developed and listed more than twenty ideas that have potential social impact and that are financially viable. The ideas included prepaid debit cards, English classes, health insurance products etc. Afterwards, the team conducted market research for similar products offered from similar organizations. In building phase, the team picked half of the ideas and developed fliers of not-yet-developed products. The fliers included a call-to-action like sign-up link so that the team could be able to measure how much demand each idea generates.

In the next phase, the team made customer discovery and testing by conducting a survey that focuses on the new product ideas. As a result of the process, the organization decided to drop many of ideas due to insufficient demand and persevered with the remaining ideas. The customer discovery process even brought about unintended consequences. A new product idea on 1-day intensive training for passing driver's license exam for non-english speaking immigrants was proposed as a side effect of this process. Adopting the lean approach, the organization achieved high demand, demonstrated impact and financial sustainability.

CONCLUSION AND RECOMMENDATIONS FOR ADOPTING LEAN FOR SOCIAL STARTUPS

Lean startup approach has radically transformed the commercial entrepreneurial ecosystem over the past decade. Contrary to this approach, in social sector, entreprenurship involves undertaking large-scale projects with little or no tolerance to change. Those projects are characterized with slow change processes as opposed to rapid testing, multi-year planning as opposed to incremental iterative development and vanity metrics as opposed to actionable metrics.

Donation mechanisms in social sectors dictate making projections of how the budged will be spend. As a result, social entrepreneurs become reluctant to change initial plans even though they find new insights and learnings along the way.

These complexities make it difficult to adopt lean mindset in social entrepreneurship. With these difficulties in mind, adopting lean approach in social sector requires considerable effort. Below are some recommendations applying lean approach to peculiarities of the social sector;

- **Special Funds for Lean Prototyping and Experimentation:** New kind of funds should encourage smaller and cheaper experiments for rapid prototyping and experimentation in social sector. Such funds should be released in small batches and experiments' length should not exceed several months.
- **Organize Lean Contests and Hackhathons**: Lean mindset should be encouraged with lean contests and hackathons.. Providing seed grants encourages smaller players to make innovative new experiments on new project ideas. Emphasize should be on speed and flexibility.
- **Teaching Lean Approach for Social Change with Fellowship Programs:** This approach helps existing leaders become equipped with the lean toolkit for social change.
- **Encourage Experimentation in Granting Programs:** Entrepreneurs should be encouraged to make rapid experiments by making some changes in existing grants. Some guidelines for change are as follows;

- Asking social entrepreneurs to write down what type of experiments they are planning.
- Signalling in the guidelines that the grant giver is open to experimentation proposals for testing new project ideas.
- Being open to giving smaller prototype grants
- Differentiating the grant proposal outline from the traditional linear activity model. This involves laying out the initial hypothesis, defining experimentation method to validate or invalidate the hypothesis. Typically, the teams should generate and record learnings on a weekly basis.

If lean approach is to be adopted successfully, everyone should be prepared for high rate of failures. Experimenting in communities call for trust, full transparency and careful design. All in all, the key executives or leaders of all stakeholders should buy in and internalize the lean mindset. It should be also noted that rapid testing just couldn't solve some problems in social sector.

Power of Lean for Social Sectors

The process by which nonprofit organizations develop and launch new products and programs can stretch for months or even years. The lean process, in contrast, enables teams to build and test a new approach in a matter of weeks or even days. If that approach is not effective, teams can pivot away quickly. If the approach needs improvement, they can undertake new iterations rapidly. And if the approach shows promise, they can cite data to prove its effectiveness so that funders can invest in it with confidence.

Limitations of Lean for Social Entrepreneurship

Traditional funding processes for nonprofits discourage rapid experimentation by reinforcing risk aversion and an adherence to top-down planning

There are limitations to applying lean in the social sector. It cannot replace longitudinal research. Lean works best as a tool for testing and improving discrete programs and processes. It cannot serve as a master strategy, and it cannot answer fundamental questions about the theory of change

REFERENCES

Alter, S. K. (2007). Social Enterprise Typology. *Virtue Ventures*. Retrieved from http://www.4lenses.org/setypology/print

Alvarez, S. A., & Barney, J. B. (2007). Discovery and creation: Alternative theories of entrepreneurial action. *Strategic Entrepreneurship Journal*, *1*(1-2), 11–26. doi:10.1002ej.4

Alvord, S., Brown, L., & Letts, C. (2004). Social Entrepreneurship and Societal Transformation: An Exploratory Study. *The Journal of Applied Behavioral Science*, *40*(3), 260–283. doi:10.1177/0021886304266847

Berstell, G., & Nitterhouse, D. (1997). Looking'outside the box'. *Marketing Research*, *9*(2), 4.

Blank, S. (2005). *The Four Steps to the Epiphany: Successful Strategies for Products that Win*. Cafepress.com.

Blank, S. (2013). Why the lean start-up changes everything. *Harvard Business Review, 91*(5), 63–72.

Brock, D. D., Steinder, S. D., & Kim, M. (2008). Social entrepreneurship education: Is it achieving the desired aims? *USABE 2008 Proceedings*.

Christensen, C. M., Anthony, S. D., Berstell, G., & Nitterhouse, D. (2007). Finding the right job for your product. *MIT Sloan Management Review*, *48*(3), 38.

Dees, J. G. (1994). *Social enterprise: Private initiatives for the common good*. Harvard Business School.

Dees, J. G. (1998). *The meaning of social entrepreneurship*. Retrieved from www.slideshare.net/rvangeldro/building-mvp

Gelobter, M. (2015). *Lean startups for social change: the revolutionary path to big impact*. Berrett-Koehler Publishers.

Hern, A. (n.d.). *Why Google has 200m reasons to put engineers over designers*. Retrieved from https://www.theguardian.com/technology/2014/feb/05/why-google-engineers-designers

Kotler, P., Kartajaya, H., & Setiawan, I. (2010). *Marketing 3.0: From products to customers to the human spirit*. John Wiley & Sons. doi:10.1002/9781118257883

Mair, J., Robinson, J., & Hockerts, K. (Eds.). (2006). *Social entrepreneurship*. New York: Palgrave Macmillan. doi:10.1057/9780230625655

Murphy, P. J., & Coombes, S. M. (2009). A model of social entrepreneurial discovery. *Journal of Business Ethics*, *87*(3), 325–336. doi:10.100710551-008-9921-y

Murray, P., & Ma, S. (2015). *The Promise of Lean Experimentation*. Academic Press.

Osterwalder, A., & Pigneur, Y. (2010). *Business model generation: a handbook for visionaries, game changers, and challengers*. John Wiley & Sons.

Osterwalder, A., Pigneur, Y., Bernarda, G., & Smith, A. (2014). *Value proposition design: How to create products and services customers want*. John Wiley & Sons.

Ries, E. (2011). *The lean startup: How today's entrepreneurs use continuous innovation to create radically successful businesses*. Crown Business.

So, I., & Caponyala, A. (2006). How Impact Investors Actually Measure Impact. *Stanford Social Innovation Review*. Retrieved from https://ssir.org/articles/entry/how_impact_investors_actually_measure_impact

Ulwick, A. W. (2005). *What customers want: Using outcome-driven innovation to create breakthrough products and services* (Vol. 71408673). New York: McGraw-Hill.

United Nations. (n.d.). *Division for Sustainable Development*. Retrieved from https://sustainabledevelopment.un.org/memberstates/india

Venkataraman, S. (1997). The distinctive domain of entrepreneurship research. *Advances in Entrepreneurship, Firm, Emergence, and Growth*, *3*(1), 119–138.

Venkataraman, S., & Shane, S. (2000). The promise of entrepreneurship as a field of research. *Academy of Management Review*, *25*(1), 217–226.

Weiss, C. H. (1995). Nothing as Practical as Good Theory: Exploring Theory-based Evaluation for Comprehensive Community Initiatives for Children and Families. In *New Approaches to Evaluating Community Initiatives: Concepts, Methods, and Contexts*. Washington, DC: Aspen Institute.

Zahra, S. A., Rawhouser, H. N., Bhawe, N., Neubaum, D. O., & Hayton, J. C. (2008). Globalization of social entrepreneurship opportunities. *Strategic Entrepreneurship Journal*, *2*(2), 117–131. doi:10.1002ej.43

Chapter 7
Creating Competitive Advantage With Social Entrepreneurship

Murat Yalcintas
Istanbul Commerce University, Turkey

ABSTRACT

This chapter probes ways of creating competitive advantage with social entrepreneurship by determining the instruments that social enterprises can apply to achieve competitive advantage. The chapter first develops the concepts of social entrepreneurship and competitive advantage within their common framework by examining the relevant literature. Then, it proposes shared value, social intrapreneurship, strategic partnership, differentiation, and recruiting talents as instruments for social entrepreneurs to achieve competitive advantage and mentions various cases as examples. The chapter concludes by proposing a measurement framework that focuses on the interaction between business and social results.

INTRODUCTION

What is the purpose of an entrepreneurial activity? For decades the applicable view was that the enterprises belonged to their shareholders and the purpose of an enterprise was to maximize shareholder wealth. Today this view is no longer uniformly accepted. Many believe that shareholders do not own enterprises, enterprises are legal entities owning themselves. A shareholder is an important stakeholder of an enterprise, but only one of many. Furthermore, the enterprises are to be run to the best interests of, not only the shareholders but a broader range of constituents, customers, suppliers, employees etc. society as a whole (Chandler, 2015). Increasingly more companies have started responding to the interests of all stakeholders and generating the most value for the society.

If an enterprise continues to exist and to make profit for a long term, it most probably means that the enterprise was able to create value, economic value and social value. Economic value is created when the enterprise makes profit. Social value is the net social and environmental benefits and values generated by the enterprise to the society. As these definitions indicate, both terms are connected; for example, employee wages are related both to economic value (cost of production) and social value (income distribution).

DOI: 10.4018/978-1-5225-5687-9.ch007

In this chapter, we define social enterprise as an organization with the core purpose of creating social value, an organization who applies business principles to solving social problems. It can be a nonprofit or for-profit organization whilst the primary motive is social change respectively well-being (Volkmann, Tokarski, & Ernst, 2012). Social entrepreneurs are change-makers in the society, they are agents of social and economic progress. The innovative approach of social entrepreneurs brings a positive change to the society and most of the times to the economy as well, especially in the underdeveloped areas.

Social entrepreneurship, already a big topic for decades, received increased attention after 2006 due to Muhammad Yunus winning the Nobel Peace Prize with the Grameen Bank microcredit model. The rising economic inequality throughout the world and crisis in environment, health and financial systems contributed to the concept of sustainable organizations dealing with social problems. In this sense, social enterprises target social needs unmet by government or by conventional business and where traditional nonprofit organizations did not live up to expectations.

Social enterprises target unfulfilled social needs by creating social value with sustainable solutions. A sustainable solution requires creating both economic and social value. Social entrepreneurship, can be carried out by nonprofit or for-profit enterprises. For nonprofits the benefit is only needed for the sustainability of the operations. In the second case, the profit is sought but the central core of the enterprise is social commitment. For both cases, the sustainability relies on its ability to develop a competitive advantage. To achieve and maintain competitive advantage i.e. to achieve sustainable competitive advantage, enterprises should generate more value, both economic and social, than competitors.

This chapter explores ways of creating competitive advantage with social entrepreneurship. As the relevant literature suggests, social enterprises possess some peculiar characteristics which do not exist in conventional business. Those characteristics can be exploited by the social enterprise as unique resources to devise strategies that lead to achieve competitive advantage. Or a social enterprise may also reach competitive advantage by positioning itself within its industry. The chapter develops the concepts of social entrepreneurship and competitive advantage within their common framework and determines the instruments that social entrepreneurs can utilize to build competitive advantage; namely shared value, social intrapreneurship, strategic partnership, differentiation and recruiting talents. Each instrument is theoretically elaborated and illustrated with field examples. This chapter will help both practitioners and academicians to understand how to achieve competitive advantage in social enterprises.

BACKGROUND

Social enterprises have emerged as significant organizational players in market economies. More market driven than traditional nonprofit ventures, and with the capacity to be financially self-sustaining, the term "social enterprise" has been coined by government and other stakeholders to denote socially-driven businesses (Di Domenico, Tracey, & Haugh, 2010). Social enterprises, a hybrid model of business organization, finance social purpose through commercial activity ensuring that the social outcome and economic performance are integral. Since they usually emerge in communities with limited access to resources, they are obliged to find innovative ways of achieving competitive advantage.

SOCIAL ENTREPRENEURSHIP AS A HYBRID MODEL

In the broadest sense, social entrepreneurship is a process by which people form institutions to advance solutions to social problems such as environmental destruction, corruption, poverty, illiteracy etc. It is about ordinary people doing extraordinary things. To manage inequalities in the society, social entrepreneurs set up mechanisms by developing innovative business models to improve society's capacity to handle problems. An "idealized" definition of social entrepreneurship can be stated as follows (Dees, 1998);

Social entrepreneurs play the role of change agents in the social sector, by:

- *Adopting a mission to create and sustain social value (not just private value),*
- *Recognizing and relentlessly pursuing new opportunities to serve that mission,*
- *Engaging in a process of continuous innovation, adaptation, and learning,*
- *Acting boldly without being limited by resources currently in hand, and*
- *Exhibiting a heightened sense of accountability to the constituencies served and for the outcomes created.*

The purpose of a social entrepreneur is to generate a social impact usually by addressing a need that is being overlooked by other institutions. Since social entrepreneurship is commonly referred as *entrepreneurial activity with an embedded social purpose*, as any other entrepreneurial activity, social enterprises also need to make profits to be sustainable and viable in the long term. Although Thompson (2002) argues that the *main world of the social entrepreneur is the voluntary (nonprofit) sector* social entrepreneurship occurs not only in nonprofit sector but also in profit-seeking firms that have some commitment to doing good (Thompson,, 2002). Compared to for-profit organizations aiming to increase the profit for their shareholders, these social enterprises try to generate profit to develop and grow their businesses.

The social entrepreneur's revenue model might be complex and funded by different sources. The Schwab Foundation for Social Entrepreneurs distinguishes between three different types of social enterprises based on their financial model (Müller, 2012):

- **Leveraged Nonprofit:** The entrepreneur drives an innovation that addresses a market or government failure. Private and public organizations are engaged to help drive and multiply the innovation. The venture continuously depends on outside philanthropic money. The general motive of this category of enterprises is that they are mission-driven. Their methods and aims entail the appeal to good-will and the creation of social values. Beneficiaries (customers) do pay nothing for their product or service offers. The capital required to build a philanthropic enterprise is commonly raised by donations and grants. The workforce consists of volunteers. Suppliers make in-kind donations.
- **Hybrid Nonprofit:** The entrepreneur also follows a non-profit approach. However, the organization includes some degree of cost-recovery by selling goods and services. Other sources of funding can include public and philanthropic money, grants, loans, or equity. Beneficiaries (customers) do pay subsidized rates for the goods or services or there is a mix of full payers and those who pay nothing. Financial funds are raised at below market capital rates.

- **Social Business:** The venture generates turnover and profits and is thus self-sustaining. Financial surpluses are reinvested in the venture and used to grow the solutions. Maximizing profits and wealth accumulation is not a priority. These enterprises are completely market-driven and can be seen as purely commercial (Volkmann, Tokarski, & Ernst, 2012).

Even though there are social entrepreneurs using donations, state, or philanthropy money as (part of) their income, they usually prefer earned income strategies to reduce dependency of outside funding. This is also a major difference to traditional non-profits that often use donations, philanthropy money, or state money as a major source of income.

Following the above revenue model, there are similar kinds of entrepreneurial organizations with related purposes (Dess & Anderson, 2003). For-profit social enterprises are entrepreneurial organizations that are legally incorporated as for-profit entities and they are explicitly designed to serve a social purpose while making a profit. Nonprofit enterprises are commercial enterprises within their nonprofit structure and they are legally prevented from distributing economic surplus. A socially responsible business' primary goal is profit and it tries to achieve commercial success in ways that respect ethical values, people, communities, and the environment. There are also purely profit oriented enterprises which are engaged in the social sector simply in search of profits.

The borderline between for-profit and nonprofit companies is fuzzy. Although the difference is in the company mission, - the mission of the for-profit company is to create value and economical return for the shareholders and the mission of the nonprofit company is to solve social problems - the demands of customers, employees and investors are forcing business not to focus only on profits. The people are becoming more and more sensitive to social issues. That is why, as the companies respond to technological changes, they also started to respond social changes to recognize and seize new opportunities. The concept of social enterprise challenges the idea that people become entrepreneur exclusively to make money. Social entrepreneurs go into business to make a difference. In "Creating a World without Poverty" Nobel Peace Prize winner Muhammed Yunus contends that by reducing humans to one dimensional profit seekers economic theory has produced a narrow interpretation of capitalism which has failed to capture the essence of a human being. It has blinded people to other uses of business (Bornstein & Davis, 2010).

For-profit companies can also create value for the society by donating what they can. But social entrepreneurship is one step ahead, it is about creating sustainability and being a change-maker. It is a hybrid model between for-profit and nonprofit ends, it can be anything. The company with such a mission may donate all the profit 100% or only 2%, or it can give away one pair of shoe for every shoe it sells or it can operate on social areas such as environment, poverty alleviation or job creation. The social entrepreneurship includes nonprofit organizations that use business models to achieve their missions, as well as for-profit organizations whose primary purpose is social. These organizations aim to simultaneously produce profits while achieving their social and environmental objectives. Social entrepreneurs pursue double or triple bottom line goals where performance is measured in terms of social impact, financial performance and environmental impact.

There are companies such as Nika, a bottled water company in USA, which donates 100% of its profits to projects providing access to drinking water all over the world, or TOMS which helps a person in need for every product purchased. There are other entrepreneurs providing bare necessities such as solar power, hearing aids, cataract surgeries, foot-powered water pumps etc. directly to the slums, poor villages and under developed areas. For the second kind of enterprises, it is very difficult to develop viable business models.

COMPETITIVE ADVANTAGE

The success of an organization depends upon its resourcefulness in gaining and maintaining competitive advantage. Competitive advantage is simply what an organization does better than its competitors. When an organization can do something that its competitors cannot do, or owns something that competitors desire but do not have, that can represent a competitive advantage. For the for-profit commercial organizations, maintaining a competitive advantage means enjoying higher profit ratios than competitors, thus it is highly desirable.

The basic purpose of an organization is value creation. For the commercial organizations the desired created value is the financial profit, for the social organizations it is the social value. Social value can be defined as the search for social progress by removing barriers to inclusion, offering help for the temporarily weak or those lacking a voice, and reducing the undesirable side effects of economic activity (Rueda-Armengot, Estelles-Miguel, Gato, Guillem, & Peris-Ortiz, 2017).

Barney (1991) defined the competitive advantage as:

the ability of a business to derive greater profits in a competitive industry based on a value-creating strategy not simultaneously implemented by any current or future competitor.

This competitive advantage is sustainable when the advantage resists erosion by competitors who are unable to duplicate the benefits of the strategy (Barney, Firm Resources and Sustained Competitive Advantage, 1991). A social enterprise may think that, not being in a competitive industry, it has no competitors or at least it doesn't have to compete with any other organization to fulfill its mission. But the truth is that social organizations compete for a much smaller pool of resources than commercial organizations. And when they are nonprofit social organizations, they compete for the same volunteers and the same grants. Thus, we can define sustainable competitive advantage in nonprofit organizations as a superior market position that captures the provision of superior customer and social value and/or the achievement of lower costs, which resists imitation and which results in a market share dominance and industry leadership position (Weerawardena & Mort, Learning, Innovation and Competitive Advantage in Not-for-Profit Aged Care Marketing: A Conceptual Model and Research Propositions, 2001). In other words, competitive advantage for a nonprofit organization is its ability to gain a superior market position in the market it serves through the creation of superior social value to its multiple stakeholders.

There are two main approaches on how organizations can achieve and maintain competitive advantage; the industrial organization (I/O) view and the resource based view (RBV) (David, 2013). The industrial organization approach to competitive advantage advocates that external (industry) are more important than internal factors for achieving competitive advantage. The resource based approach contends that internal resources are more important than external factors for achieving competitive advantage.

INDUSTRIAL ORGANIZATION VIEW

The advocates of I/O view, such as Michael Porter, claim that organizational performance is primarily determined by industry forces. A primary example of this view, his widely acclaimed five-forces model focuses on analyzing external forces as basis for achieving competitive advantage (Porter, 1980). According to the model competitive advantage is determined by positioning in an industry. From this perspective, to achieve competitive advantage companies should enter in attractive industries and understand fully the key factors in that industry such as entry barriers, scale economies, technological advances, product differentiation, the level of competition etc. Understanding these factors, companies should position themselves accordingly within that industry. For this positioning, Michael Porter brought up the idea of value chain.

Since companies achieve competitive advantage by delivering superior value to its customers, it is important to discern value creating activities in the organization from the ones which do not. Thus, Porter (1985) introduced the value-chain framework suggesting that a company's activities can be divided into two main group; primary activities and support activities. Primary activities are practices which are related to the flow of the product to customer whereas the support activities merely support them. Value chain approach argues that organizations should endeavor to maximize the value they create in every single activity in their operation. An organization creating more value than its competitors through its value chain would achieve competitive advantage.

Competitive advantage cannot be understood by looking at a firm as a whole. It stems from the many discrete activities a firm performs in designing, producing, marketing, delivering, and supporting its product. Each of these activities can contribute to a firm's relative cost position and create a basis for differentiation. A cost advantage, for example, may stem from such disparate sources as a low-cost physical distribution system, a highly efficient assembly process or superior sales force utilization. Differentiation can stem from similarly diverse factors, including the procurement of high quality raw materials, a responsive order entry system, or a superior product design. A systematic way of examining all the activities a firm performs and how they interact is necessary for analyzing the sources of competitive advantage...The value chain disaggregates a firm into its strategically relevant activities in order to understand the behavior of costs and the existing and potential sources of differentiation. A firm gains competitive advantage by performing these strategically important activities more cheaply or better than its competitors.

RESOURCE BASED VIEW (RBV)

The proponents of the resource based view argue that organizational performance will primarily be determined by internal resources of an organization. These resources can be physical, human or organizational. Physical resources include all plant, equipment, buildings, materials, machines etc. The employees with their trainings, abilities, skills etc. can be grouped under human resources. Organizational resources are the intangible assets such as organizational structure, processes, know-how, company culture, trademarks, reputation and so on. According to this view, the organization may exploit opportunities and neutralize threats with the help of its resources.

According to resource based view, the organization's internal resources should be considered first in devising strategies that lead to competitive advantage. The company should develop, strengthen and exploit its unique resources. Furthermore, it is advantageous if the devised strategy based on these unique resources cannot be currently implemented by any competitor. If the competition cannot duplicate that particular strategy, then the organization can achieve sustainable competitive advantage.

Jay Barney, one of the most prominent advocates of the RBV, argued that sustained competitive advantage derives from the resources and capabilities a firm controls that are valuable, rare, imperfectly imitable, and not substitutable (Barney, Firm Resources and Sustained Competitive Advantage, 1991). A resource is valuable if it enables a firm to conceive strategies that improve its effectiveness and efficiency. If a particular valuable resource is possessed by large number of firms then each of these firms have the capability of exploiting this resource in the same way, thereby implementing a common strategy doesn't give any firm competitive advantage. That is why that particular resource should be rare in order to create competitive advantage. However, valuable and rare resources can be sources of sustained competitive advantage if the competition that do not possess these resources cannot obtain them. Thus, these resources must be imperfectly imitable in order to lead to sustainable competitive advantage. The last requirement is that there must be no equivalent valuable resource that is either not rare or imitable. Because if there is an equivalent available resource the competition can implement the same strategy in a different way using a similar resource. Barney concludes by reminding that firms cannot expect to "purchase" sustained competitive advantages on open markets but they must find them in the rare, imperfectly imitable and non-substitutable resources already controlled by the firm.

INSTRUMENTS FOR COMPETITIVE ADVANTAGE

Competitive advantage is a feature which allows an organization to outperform its competitors by offering clients better value and deriving greater profits. The triple bottom line framework evaluates the performance of an organization in three different dimensions; financial, social and environmental. Within this framework, a competitive advantage allows an organization either to create a higher financial profit or a greater social value or a better environmental conservation.

Social entrepreneurs can use different approaches to develop competitive advantage. Porter and Kramer (2011) formulized their approach based on industrial organization view by introducing the concept of shared value. Shared value concept includes reconceiving products and markets, improving company value chain, and upgrading the social and physical infrastructure at the company's locations. Resource based view also offers similar tools to social entrepreneurs for competitive advantage; namely use of social intrapreneurship, strategic partnership, differentiation and recruiting talents. The extent to which social entrepreneurs are able to use these unique competency-based factors determines the level of competitiveness of the social enterprise.

SHARED VALUE

Michael Porter and Mark Kramer introduced the concept of shared value which involves creating economic value in a way that also creates value for society by addressing its needs and challenges (Porter & Kramer, 2011). The authors had addressed the issue first in 2002 in a Harvard Business Review (HBR) article by discussing how corporate philanthropy could create social and economic value, introducing their ideas about using social programs to enhance the firm's competitive context (Porter & Kramer, 2002). Later in 2006, with a broader analysis, the concept of integrating corporate social responsibility (CSR) into core business strategy was proposed (Porter & Kramer, 2006). In 2011, in another HBR article Porter and Kramer (2011) defined shared value as:

policies and operating practices that enhance the competitiveness of a company while simultaneously advancing the economic and social conditions in the communities in which it operates

and argued that the purpose of the corporation must be redefined as creating shared value, not just profit. This redefinition of the mission of the for-profit companies brings all the enterprises under the umbrella of social entrepreneurship because according to the authors creating shared value is a self-interested behavior to create economic value by creating societal value.

For-profit companies have traditionally excluded social and environmental considerations from their strategies, since they are considered to raise costs and reduce profits. Solving social problems are ceded to governments and to NGOs. Corporate responsibility programs—a reaction to external pressure—are to improve firms' reputations and treated as necessary expenses. But the competitiveness of a company and the health of the communities around it are closely linked. A business needs a successful community, not only to create demand for its products but also to provide critical public assets and a supportive environment. A weak community can affect negatively the value chain of a company operating in it.

Companies can create economic value by creating societal value. According to Porter and Kramer (2011) there are three distinct ways to do this: by reconceiving products and markets, redefining productivity in the value chain, and building supportive industry clusters at the company's locations. These three ways are interrelated and mutually reinforcing and they are an integral part of profit maximization.

The starting point for creating shared value by reconceiving products is to identify all the societal needs, benefits, and harms that could be embodied in the firm's products. With this approach product differentiation and market repositioning according to societal needs become important factors for gaining competitive advantage.

In advanced economies, demand for products and services that meet societal needs is rapidly growing. Healthier foods, environment-friendly consumer products and cause-sensitive goods and services are gaining more and more popularity. People are willing to consume and to pay a premium for goods and services with a societal value. The increasing market share of ecological produces is a good example of this trend. Another example is Levi Strauss, the company that invented blue jeans more than 140 years ago. Levis' Well thread initiative recycles old material into new clothing, while Waste Less, Levi Strauss's new line launched last spring, reuses about eight 12- to 20-ounce plastic bottles per garment. In 2013 alone, the collection used 7.9 million recycled bottles to make products such as Levi's 511 Slim Fit Jeans and Trucker jackets.

Furthermore, in developing countries markets are underserved and there are huge populations which cannot be served by classical products. The need can only be fulfilled by innovative approaches. Microfinancing introduced first in Bangladesh by Dr. Muhammad Yunus proves that even classical financing methods can be redesigned according to market conditions. In Bangladesh, 78% of the people live underneath the poverty line of 2 USD per day. Since poor people have no collaterals they are lacking access to conventional financial services. Muhammad Yunus built up a financial institution that provides micro credits to poor women in Bangladesh without collaterals. Instead of a collateral, borrower-group of five women is jointly responsible for the loan. If one member cannot pay back the weekly installment the peers in the group must recompense. Thus, the group serves as a social collateral. The scheme had a tremendous success; in 2009 the number of active borrowers was 6.43 million (Müller, 2012). The initiative of Muhammad Yunus spread across the globe.

Societal problems can create economic costs in a company's value chain. Improvements in the value chain activities such as use of scarce resources (water, energy etc.) or human resource management can create both economic and social values and provide a competitive advantage to the social enterprise. A good principle of value chain improvement for social entrepreneurship is co-creation as in the case of Agua Par La Vida (Müller, 2012). Agua Par La Vida is an organization which provides access to safe drinking water in rural Nicaragua. Agua Par La Vida provides the material and the villagers build the system that delivers homes safe drinking water. The building of the water system only starts when all the families in the community commits themselves to participate in the construction of the system. So, the value chain improvement through co-creation permits the organization to bootstrap scarce resources and the beneficiaries take ownership of the project and are able to maintain and repair the system. It means a more competitive value chain with cheaper and highly committed workforce.

A more competitive value chain can also be achieved by having the operations in the locations with the lowest labor and logistics costs. For example, Madecasse is a company that produces high-end chocolate in Madagascar. Madagascar is a poor agricultural island in Africa where fifty percent of its population lives below the poverty line. Africa produces 85 percent of the world's cocoa, and Madagascar is widely recognized as having the best cocoa in the world. However, less than 1 percent of the world's chocolate is produced in Africa.

Medacasee was founded by two social entrepreneurs McCollum and Brett Beach who served together in Madagascar with the Peace Corps. They loved the nation and they stayed in the island even after their duty ended. Since its launch in 2006, Madecasse has worked with cacao farmers in northern Madagascar to grow, ferment, and dry their cocoa beans in a manner that greatly enhances their flavor and, thereby, their value for making chocolate. This value-added process has doubled the income of the farmers with whom Madecasse works. Madecasse provides equipment and technical training to the farmers. It also buys the cured beans they produce and uses them to make chocolate through a partnership with an in-country chocolate factory. Cocoa farmers in Madagascar are accustomed to selling their beans immediately, as a commodity for export, because of their subsistence-based economic lives. Madecasse offers them incentive to undertake the value-added process by paying them in advance at double the amount they would receive from cocoa importers (Jill & Lyons, 2016). The chocolate produced by Madecasse is a rival to the finest chocolates made in Europe. Three team members located in the United States are responsible for the marketing, promotion, and distribution of the Madagascar-made chocolate in the United States and Europe. Madecasse generates social change in Madagascar, as the value of chocolate is five times that of cocoa beans, and also makes financial profits achieving a double-bottom line.

In every stage of its value chain a social enterprise can create societal value. The procurement phase can include purchases from disadvantaged suppliers or environmentally friendly products as in the Madecasse case. For human resources disadvantaged individuals can be employed with training and development opportunities. In the production environment friendly practices provide the most common examples. As target customers, social enterprises can choose serving the disadvantaged markets such as the microfinancing model of Dr. Yunus' Grameen Bank in Bangladesh.

Porter and Kramer (2011) asserts that without supporting clusters productivity suffers because:

the success of every company is affected by the supporting companies and infrastructure around it. Productivity and innovation are strongly influenced by "clusters," or geographic concentrations of firms, related businesses, suppliers, service providers, and logistical infrastructure in a particular field such as IT in Silicon Valley, cut flowers in Kenya, and diamond cutting in Surat, India.

Furthermore, deficiencies in the framework conditions surrounding the cluster such as poor public education, poor transportation infrastructure or poverty create internal costs for companies. Companies can improve their competitiveness and create shared value by building clusters to improve company productivity while ameliorating the framework conditions surrounding the cluster. The company should focus first on the cluster weakness which constitutes the biggest constraint to its competitiveness. Such a regional infrastructure enhancement action usually requires the collaboration of many actors such as NGO's, government agencies and private sector.

A good example of improving competitiveness by strengthening local suppliers and local infrastructure is Coca-Cola's Coletivo initiative in Brazil (Porter, Hills, Pfitzer, Patscheke, & Hawkins, 2011). The project aimed to increase the employability of low income youth while strengthening Coca Cola's retail distribution channels and brand strength to increase local product sales. The Coletivo initiative, in partnership with local NGOs, trains local youth for two months in retailing, business development, and entrepreneurship while also pairing youth with a local retailer to get their first job experience and recommend ideas for improvement. Since launching the initiative in 2009, Coca-Cola has trained thousands of youth in retailing, business operations, and basic entrepreneurship concepts. In 2012 the company was operating 135 Coletivos across Brazil, each with an average of 500 students with a total budget of several millions of dollars. This cluster improvement project has profitable double line; social returns are youth job placement and youth self-esteem and financial returns are company sales and brand image.

SOCIAL INTRAPRENEURSHIP

Taking into consideration the definitions of Churchill for entrepreneurship:

The concept of entrepreneurship is seen as the process of uncovering and developing an opportunity to create value through innovation and seizing that opportunity without regard to either resources (human and capital) or the location of the entrepreneur – in a new or existing company...

and Istocescu for intrapreneurship:

Intrapreneurship represent the initiation and implementation of innovative systems and practices within an organization, by some of its staff under the supervision of a manager who takes the role of an intrapreneur, in order to improve the economical performance of the organization, by using a part of its resources, namely those that previously have not been used in an appropriate manner. Intrapreneurship improves the economical and financial performance of the company, by applying a more efficient use of the resources and by using a suitable motivational system for its employees (Maier & Zonovia Pop, 2011),

we can argue that a for-profit company can establish within its existing system social enterprises. Such a "social intrapreneurship" can be an important source of competitive advantage.

Bornstein and Davis (2010) gives a very good example of a for-profit firm achieving competitive advantage by social intrapreneurship;

One of the leading examples of social entrepreneurship in the United States is ShoreBank Corporation, the nation's first community development and environmentally conscious bank holding company. Head-

quartered on Chicago's South Side, today ShoreBank is a $2.4 billion company with for-profit banks and social-purpose affiliates in five states, as well as global consulting and financial arms. It began by lending money to local businesspeople on the South Side of Chicago who rehabilitated the neighborhood's housing stock. If ShoreBank had set up shop in a middle-class community, we would simply call it a bank – a good bank, to be sure. But its founders intentionally opened in a poor area of Chicago that was reeling from the flight of the middle class, where banking services had become all but nonexistent. ShoreBank developed a business model attuned to the needs of this under-bank community and, in process, helped transform it. The bank sought to maximize the social impact of its lending, while maintaining a healthy profit margin. Had ShoreBank sought to maximize profits, it would have done what many other banks did at the same time: abandon the inner cities. Instead, it became the only bank to support the landmark Community Reinvestment Act, which aimed to halt the redlining of poor neighborhoods. Moreover, two of ShoreBank's founders Ron Grzywinski and Mary Houghton, took several trips to Bangladesh to share their banking experiences with officials of the Grameen Bank and BRAC. Through ShoreBank's affiliated nonprofit arm, Yunus and a senior BRAC manager traveled to the United States in exchanges that led to the establishment of microfinance programs in several U.S. states and attracted the attention of key policy makers, notably Bill and Hillary Clinton, then governor and first lady of Arkansas, who carried their support for microfinance into the White House.

Sesame Workshop is a nonprofit educational organization which is best known for its flagship series "Sesame Street". The organization has the mission to help kids grow smarter, stronger, and kinder by combining a curriculum that addresses children's critical developmental needs with the sophisticated use of media and a large dose of fun. The organization was founded in 1968 with the aim of using television as a tool to help children learn and it pioneered the concept of teaching kids through television. Sesame Workshop has grown into a worldwide educational phenomenon, reaching millions of children in more than 150 countries. The organization operates in a highly competitive context increasingly dominated by large, for-profit children's media companies. To continue to deliver on its mission in this context, Sesame Workshop has sought to engage in social entrepreneurship by supporting its educational programs with revenue-generating activities, which include global product licensing, book publishing, domestic and foreign distribution of local-language television programs, coproduction, and overseas syndication of its portfolio of educational programs (Austin, Stevenson, & Wei-Skillern, 2006). Sesame Workshop being a nonprofit educational organization has charitable, tax-exempt status. According to their 2016 audited consolidated financial statements, %29 of their revenue is from corporate, foundation and government support, %30 is from product licensing and %41 from distribution fees and royalties. This consolidated revenue is generated by 4 nonprofit and 3 for-profit subsidiaries (Sesame Workshop, 2017). The creation of these subsidiaries is a fine example of intrapreneurship as a competency leading to competitive advantage.

STRATEGIC PARTNERSHIP

Another method of achieving competitive advantage for social entrepreneurs is to form strategic alliances with commercial for-profit firms or nonprofit organizations. Such an alliance would provide the social entrepreneur with the capabilities necessary to perform a sustainable operation. Partnerships for both for-profit and social ventures serve as a conduit to assist organizations in acquiring necessary resources.

Through partnerships social enterprises can gain human resources and funding, as well as additional outlets. As a result, they are able to serve more people and better achieve their value creation goals.

Strategic collaboration with nonprofit organizations may help social enterprises ensure profitability without sacrificing social performance. When pursuing social impact, there are often complementary activities that would contribute to a social enterprise's success but cannot be done profitably. In these cases, it helps to have a nonprofit partner or to be operating in a hybrid organization that includes a nonprofit affiliate.

For example, Dr. Yunus of Bangladesh has formed Grameen Danone with participation of Danone France to market inexpensive yogurt products to Bangladeshi villagers, particularly children. With this partnership Grameen addressed to malnutrition problem of poor village children where Danone presented itself as a good corporate citizen, fortified its brand name and gained exposure to a large new market.

Another example can be the partnership of Root Capital which is an agricultural impact investor that grows rural prosperity in poor, environmentally vulnerable places in Africa, Asia, and Latin America by providing capital, delivering financial training, and strengthening market connections for small and growing agricultural businesses. Since 1999, Root Capital has disbursed more than $1 billion in credit to 632 businesses, representing over 1.2 million smallholder farmers. Root Capital's lending, as a nonprofit social investment fund, is directed towards businesses that are too big for microfinance, but generally unable to secure credit from conventional commercial banks. Root Capital has formed a partnership with Starbucks and Green Mountain Coffee Roasters to source coffee from farming cooperatives in the developing world. Root Capital has provided capital, training and brokering market connections so that farmers could develop quality products and market them.

Also, the cases Fabricacion Modular Valenciana (FMV) and Modular Logistica Valenciana (MLV), two partner companies of Ford in Spain, illustrated how cooperation between for-profit and nonprofit organizations may form synergy of competitiveness. FMV and MLV were founded in 2000 as a result of cooperation between Ford and the ONCE (Spanish National Foundation for the Blinds) Foundation. The company started as a special employment center with 49 employees in an area of 3.000m2 inside the Ford factory and provided logistic services, pre-assembly, and assembly of automotive components. It has grown to become the largest Ford logistics operator in the region. Some 95% of its employees are disabled; 70% are physically disabled, 8% are mentally handicapped and the remainder have sensory disabilities (Rueda-Armengot, Estelles-Miguel, Gato, Guillem, & Peris-Ortiz, 2017). This is an excellent example of the complete integration of people with disabilities in a competitive industrial workplace. They won the Ford award for diversity in 2013.

The case of CitySoft is a good example of strategic cooperation between a social enterprise and a non-profit organization. CitySoft, a web development and management firm committed to hiring predominantly lower-income urban adults, realized that existing training programs were not effectively preparing urban adults for success in high tech careers. Thus, CitySoft spun-off a nonprofit called CitySkills to partner with training organizations and employers to create the necessary infrastructure and "labor pipelines" for recruiting, training, and placing inner-city residents in upwardly mobile information technology jobs (Dess & Anderson, 2003).

In addition, social enterprises don't mobilize resources in such a way as to set up competitive barriers, but they rather use resources in cooperative fashion, and often share them with other organizations (Dacin, Dacin, & Matear, 2010). Social enterprises often work collaboratively with other nonprofit organizations, business, and government to attain the resources critical for the organization. For example, Aravind Eye Clinic has a global outreach program to teach people its techniques. Another example is the creation of

September 11th Fund as response to the destruction of the World Trade Center on 9/11/2001. Two non-profit social enterprises, the New York Community Trust and the United Way of New York City, came together to establish the fund. The fund collected USD 534 million from more than two million donors and provided cash assistance, counseling and other services to the families of those affected in the 9/11 attacks. The distribution of assets was completed in 2004 and the fund was dissolved.

DIFFERENENTIATION

The most powerful differentiation tool of a social enterprise is its cause based products as long as they are scarce and hard to duplicate. Consumers want more cause based products and they are even willing to pay a premium for it. If a social enterprise can develop a reputation for its social performance and deliver goods or services whose cost and quality are deemed on par with competitors, some customers may value the social commitment and prefer these products. Nonprofit social enterprises tend also to follow differentiation as a primary focus of their competitive strategy (Weerawardena & Mort, 2012). That is, they tend to differentiate in terms of their cause, which is critically important in markets cluttered with closely competitive causes, providing a substantial variety of choices to potential donors.

A viable model for business to serve underdeveloped areas by differentiation is developed by Aravind Eye Hospitals chain in India. In this cross-subsidization model better-off customers pay more for the same service than poor people, who pay little or nothing. Aravind had a major impact in eradicating cataract related blindness in India. The first Aravind Eye Hospital was founded in 1976 as a modest 20-bed hospital in a home. In this hospital, six beds were reserved for people who could not afford to pay while the remaining were for paying patients. As of 2012, Aravind had treated nearly 32 million patients and performed 4 million surgeries, the majority of them being cheap or free, making it the world's largest and most productive eye-care service group. Aravind also established an outreach program wherein doctors reach out to remote villages to conduct eye camps sponsored by various organizations. As this case proves, a successful business model based on solving a social problem by product differentiation can become a very powerful competency for a social enterprise in achieving and sustaining competitive advantage.

There are multiple case studies showing that innovation-based competitive strategies substantially contribute to the achievement of social value in nonprofit social enterprises. Innovation-based strategies are found out to be uniquely characterized by a primary focus on differentiation, with innovations directed at product, process, and system change levels (Weerawardena & Mort, 2012). Social value creating innovations are usually non-technical innovations, instead they rather involve new forms of social institutions, social relationships, and forms of business practices. Institute for One World Health is a fine example of a nonprofit social enterprise differentiating through both technical and non-technical innovation;

One World Health is the first non-profit pharmaceutical company created in the United States. Founded as a medical research organization by pharmaceutical scientist Victoria G. Hale in 2000, it aims to address the developing world's need for affordable medicines to treat infectious diseases that otherwise would be overlooked due to the absence of a viable market. One World Health seeks to challenge the assumption that pharmaceutical research and development is too expensive to create new medicines for the world's poor. Through partnership and collaboration with pharmaceutical scientists, non-profit hospitals in the United States and abroad, biotechnology industries, companies, universities and or-

ganizations, drug research is brought from the lab into the clinic and on to regulatory approval and manufacturing for patients in the developing world. An experienced team of pharmaceutical scientists is assembled to identify the most promising drug and vaccine candidates to be developed into medicines. They then partner with companies and non-profit hospitals and organizations in the developing world to conduct medical research on new cures, and manufacture and distribute medicines to populations at risk (OECD, 2010).

From another perspective, Prahalad (2012) identifies the least developed markets as the source of radical innovations and gives as example:

a 2000-dollar car (Tata Nano); 50-dollar cataract surgery (Aravind Eye Care System); less than USD 0.01 per minute of cell phone time (Airtel); a modern, well-appointed 20-dollar hotel room (Ginger); and a supercomputer (Eka) that costs less than USD 40 million to develop (Prahalad, 2012).

He argues that in order to operate profitably in such markets, the organizations have to transcend technology and product perspectives of innovation and focus on total delivery of value.

Another source of competitive advantage through differentiation is brand loyalty. Companies try to maintain customer loyalty through their branding. People tend to be loyal to brands which inspire them and where they can identify themselves with the mission and core values of the company. Social enterprises should develop a brand reputation that signals serious commitment to both social impact and business discipline. It is found that positive social beliefs held by consumers are associated not only with greater purchase likelihood but also with longer-term loyalty and advocacy behaviors. More importantly, it is proved that a brand that positions itself on social impact, integrating its social strategy with its core business strategy, is more likely than brands that merely engaging in corporate social responsibility to reap a range of benefits in the consumer domain (Du, Bhattacharya, & Sen, 2007).

Furthermore, trust in a brand is important and is a key factor in the development of brand loyalty (Lau & Lee, 1999). Literature review reveals two dimensions of trust; perceived credibility and benevolence of the target (Doney & Cannon, 1997). Perceived credibility is how much the partner's statement can be relied on. Benevolence is the extent to which the partner is genuinely interested in the other's welfare and motivated to seek joint gain. A social enterprise which contributes to society's wellbeing has strong core values and is benevolent. Thus, we can argue that social enterprises are likely to have more brand loyalty than commercial enterprises.

RECRUITING TALENTS

Strategic human resource management is a means of gaining competitive advantage through an organization's most important assets: its people (Orlando, 2000). Human resources which have experience, knowledge and skills provide value to the organization and contribute to sustainable competitive advantage if these resources create value, remain hard to imitate, and are rare (Barney & Wright, 1998). Talent is rare, valuable, and hard to substitute. Organizations that attract and retain better talent outperform those which do not.

Social enterprises, usually having limited financial resources, are rarely able to pay market rates for their human resources (Oster, 1995) and they often rely upon volunteers to fill their ranks. The nature of social enterprises induces an expectation that the employees work for the cause rather than for the financial benefits and it is impossible especially for nonprofit social enterprises to compete with commercial enterprises in providing monetary benefits to the employees. Although social enterprises face more constraints than commercial enterprises in attracting talent, they nevertheless possess some advantages. Social enterprises can develop a larger network of strong supporters who identify themselves with the mission and core values of the enterprise and leverage resources outside their organizational boundaries.

The case of Ducks Unlimited which is the world's largest and most effective private waterfowl and wetlands conservation organization is a clear example of how a social enterprise can manage a wide diversity of human resources to gain competitive advantage. Ducks Unlimited was founded by a small group of sportsmen with the mission of habitat conservation when North America's drought-plagued waterfowl populations had plunged to unprecedented lows in 1937. More than 80 years, Ducks Unlimited conserves, restores, and manages wetlands and associated habitats for North America's waterfowl. It is nonprofit grassroots, volunteer-based organization. As of January 1, 2017, Ducks Unlimited Inc. had 620,853 adult members and 45,357 youth members. In 2016 the volunteers hosted 3,900 grassroot events, such as member and sponsor banquets, shooting and fishing tournaments, and golf outings, raising USD 221.7 million. The total area influenced and conserved in North America is 157,660,148 acres (Ducks Unlimited, 2017).

Another source of competitive advantage for social enterprises is the nonpecuniary motivation and diversity of its employees. Cultural diversity in an organization improves the quality of thought, performance and decision making (Nemeth, 1992). An organization with a diversity of perspectives has more resources to draw on and is more creative and innovative (Orlando, 2000). The value acquirable from a large number of dissimilar individuals working together is rather high, and in most cases a given organization's mix is rare and impossible to imitate. Furthermore, since the employees and the other stakeholders share the same core values, the organization's ability to communicate with its environment is highly improved.

Employees of social enterprises are attracted and motivated mostly by inherent factors such as a belief in the organization's mission and core values or an opportunity to actualize their individual values. Value and goal conformance positively affect employee performance, tenure, and career success. (Bhati & Manimala, 2011). This can be considered as a competency for a social enterprise because there are numerous studies proving that a match between the employee values and the organizational values is an antecedent for employee commitment and job satisfaction (O'Reilly, Chatman, & Caldwell, 1991).

Commitment of Mirakle Couriers employees is the key to the company's success. Mirakle Couriers is a national award-winning courier agency in Mumbai, India that employs low-income deaf adults. Dhruv Lakra founded Mirakle Couriers after his MBA in social entrepreneurship at Oxford. The enterprise currently employs 4 managers and 64 deaf employees. In 2010 the enterprise won the Indian national award for the empowerment of people with disabilities. The award was given by the president of India, for the company's efforts to empower the deaf through meaningful employment.

FUTURE RESEARCH DIRECTIONS

Social entrepreneurs try to achieve sustainable social goals using business practices. They pursue double or triple bottom line goals, i.e. creation of social, financial and environmental value. However, managing a social mission and at the same time achieving financial sustainability is not an easy task. To improve profitability and to scale operations, social enterprises may sometimes compromise their focus on social outcomes and try to improve profitability. Social impact assessment is regarded as a tool to support social enterprises to achieve financial results without compromising their mission (Mair & Sharma, 2012). With such an assessment the organization can understand what approaches work, what results are achieved and what are the opportunities and threats. Assessment also promotes accountability and transparency, and facilitates the communication of the social enterprise with its stakeholders.

This chapter aspires to develop a theory to explain the conditions under which social enterprises can achieve their dual mission and how they can be most effective and efficient. The achievement of the dual mission requires the measurement of financial outcomes and the social impact. Enterprises can easily track their economic data and link financial benefits to their management strategies. But they lack the data and the framework to link their social value creation to their business success; i.e. the link between the two components of their dual mission. Measurement approaches that link social and business results are necessary to develop viable management strategies for social enterprises.

Instruments ensuring a link between creation of social value and achievement of economic results are theoretically discussed in this chapter. To put these concepts in practice empirical research is required. Future studies should present some empirical evidence to support the validity of these instruments and define the boundaries of a measurement framework that focuses on the interaction between business and social results similar to Balanced Scorecard (BSC) system.

BSC is a strategic management system that measures the strategic performance of an enterprise. It links different performance criteria; whether the enterprise stays focused on its key strategy elements such as mission, vision and core values, and whether the operational objectives such as financial results and performance goals are met. Ultimately a similar performance measurement system can be devised for social enterprises to assess whether the dual or triple bottom line goals are met.

CONCLUSION

Over the last decades nonprofit organizations and commercial organizations started to recognize opportunities in each other's areas. Nonprofits appreciate managerial and financial competences that ensure viability and growth of an organization and commercials value the ingenuity and the value creation of the social sector. Entrepreneurs realize that social value creation may as well generate financial profits and are less and less interested in managing organizations that focus solely in creating financial value. Similarly, people motivated by social concerns, people who wanted to "make a difference" consider being a businessperson, a social entrepreneur, as an alternative to volunteering in a nonprofit.

In addition, social entrepreneurship proves to be the best method to access large markets in developing and industrialized countries that are underserved by traditional business (Bornstein & Davis, 2010). In 2004 C. K. Prahalad introduced the term "Bottom of the Pyramid" (BOP) in his influential book called "The Fortune at the Bottom of the Pyramid" (Prahalad, 2004). BOP describes a market of over four billion people who live on less than USD 2/day with a purchasing power parity of USD 5 trillion (Prahalad, 2012). Challenges of these markets such as conserving the environment, developing innovative products, conserving brand loyalty, motivating staff, forming distribution channels and maintaining affordable pricing can only be met by social enterprises.

The defining characteristic of a social enterprise is the pursuit of double mission; financial sustainability and social value creation. To create social value the social enterprise follows strategies that generate revenue from commercial activities and cannot rely solely on donations and grants as traditional nonprofits do. The pursuit of financial sustainability and social objectives requires the generation of sufficient revenue to invest in business activities while following social objectives. This challenge requires social enterprises to build and maintain competitive advantage without sacrificing social aspirations. Although a trade-off may exist between economic and social objectives, there are circumstances in which social mission enhances financial performance. Certain instruments may ensure a close link between creation of social value and successful achievement of economic results. These instruments help to use the social objective as a strategic resource and create favorable conditions for the generation of economic value. Within this context, shared value, social intrapreneurship, strategic partnership, differentiation and recruiting talents can be depicted as instruments for social entrepreneurs to achieve the double mission.

Shared value is a self-interested behavior that generates economic value by creating social value. Reconceiving products and markets, redefining productivity in the value chain, and building supportive industry clusters at the company's locations are the three interrelated and mutually reinforcing instruments of shared value (Porter & Kramer, 2011). Social entrepreneurs can reconceive their products and markets to deliver more economic, social or environmental benefits. They can also improve the efficiency and productivity of their internal operations by redefining productivity in their value chain. The improvement of the company's external environment by developing local clusters also enhances the productivity. These three distinct strategies can become an integral part of profit maximization and significant factors for gaining competitive advantage.

The main advantage of intrapreneurship is the usage of resources and infrastructure of the existing organization for innovation purposes (Schmitz & Scheuerle, 2012). Social intrapreneurship, i.e. social entrepreneurship in entrenched organizations, usually defines individuals working within an established organization and developing practical solutions to social problems. These individuals can use and leverage existing resources to create a competitive advantage for the social enterprise.

Generating social impact requires many resources. Cooperating with other organizations is an effective and efficient way of creating synergy and using complementary resources. RBV approach assumes that resources provide the basis for an organization's strategy and by acquiring valuable resources an organization can achieve competitive advantage. Social enterprises, especially in early stages, often have a low resource base. That is why cooperating with other organizations and using their resources can be an important instrument of competitive advantage for social enterprises.

The principal challenge of social entrepreneurs is to translate problems into opportunities and this challenge can usually be met by differentiation. A social enterprise differentiates mostly by its cause based products and its social performance. Consumers value cause based products and services, and they are mostly ready to pay a premium for them. Another form of differentiation for social enterprises is by innovation. These innovations are usually non-technical, and they often involve new forms of business practices, and they may become a very powerful instrument for creating social and sometimes financial value. Another instrument of competitive advantage through differentiation is brand loyalty. Stakeholder brand loyalty in social enterprises will result in greater purchase likelihood, longer-term loyalty and advocacy behaviors.

Human resources of a social enterprise are one of its most important assets and its vanguard. The workforce of a social enterprise includes paid workers and volunteers. In most of the cases volunteers form a decisive part of the workforce and they are indispensable for the continued existence of the social enterprise (Blank, 2012). Social enterprises regard them as a rare and must wanted resource; volunteers freely decide to support the social enterprise without expecting any financial interest. Regular employees also are usually paid less than market rates and work for the cause rather than financial benefits (Oster, 1995). Consequently, social enterprises can develop a larger network of workforce that is highly inspired, motivated, loyal and low cost. These human resources qualities are very difficult to attain for commercial enterprises and they constitute a strong competency for social enterprises.

This chapter analyses these instruments and provides insights into social entrepreneurship theory and practice with theoretical concepts and examples of successful implementations. It shows how a social enterprise, a commercial organization with an embedded social purpose, can use its social mission in order to improve its competitiveness. Social entrepreneurs need to develop skills to acquire and maintain these instruments as well as to improve their organizational capabilities. In most social enterprises strategies are formulated more by social and ethical values rather than economic considerations (Doherty, Haugh, & Lyon, 2014). The chapter informs us that social entrepreneurs can develop strategies to create social impact and turn at the same time their social mission into a resource that improves the financial well-being of their enterprise.

REFERENCES

Austin, J., Stevenson, H., & Wei-Skillern, J. (2006, January). Social and Commercial Entrepreneurship: Same, Different, or Both? *Entrepreneurship Theory and Practice*, *30*(1), 1–22. doi:10.1111/j.1540-6520.2006.00107.x

Barney, J. (1991, March). Firm Resources and Sustained Competitive Advantage. *Journal of Management*, *17*(1), 99–120. doi:10.1177/014920639101700108

Barney, J., & Wright, P. M. (1998). On becoming a strategic partner: The role of human resources in gaining competitive advantage. *Human Resource Management*, *37*(1), 31–46. doi:10.1002/(SICI)1099-050X(199821)37:1<31::AID-HRM43.0.CO;2-W

Bhati, A., & Manimala, M. J. (2011). *Talent Acquisition and Retention in Social Enterprises: Innovations in HR Strategies*. Bangalore: Indian Institute of Management.

Blank, C. (2012). Human Resource Management and Volunteer Motivation. In C. K. Volkmann, K. O. Tokarski, & K. Ernst (Eds.), *Social Entrepreneurship and Social Business* (pp. 66–82). Wiesbaden: Springer Gabler. doi:10.1007/978-3-8349-7093-0_4

Bornstein, D., & Davis, S. (2010). Social Entrepreneurship. New York: Oxford.

Chandler, D. (2015). *Corporate Social Responsibility, A Strategic Perspective*. New York: Business Expert Press.

Dacin, P., Dacin, T., & Matear, M. (2010, August). Social Entrepreneurship: Why We Don't Need a New Theory and How We Move Forward From Here. *The Academy of Management Perspectives*, *24*(3), 37–57. doi:10.5465/AMP.2010.52842950

David, F. (2013). *Strategic Management* (14th ed.). Pearson.

Dees, G. (1998). *The Meaning of "Social Entrepreneurship"*. The Kauffman Center for Entrepreneurial Leadership.

Dess, G., & Anderson, B. B. (2003). For-Profit Social Ventures. In M. Kourilsky & W. Walstad (Eds.), Social Entrepreneurship. Senate Hall Academic Publishing.

Di Domenico, M. L., Tracey, P., & Haugh, H. (2010, July). Social bricolage: Theorizing social value creation in social enterprises. *Entrepreneurship Theory and Practice*, *34*(4), 681–703. doi:10.1111/j.1540-6520.2010.00370.x

Doherty, B., Haugh, H., & Lyon, F. (2014, January). Social Enterprises as Hybrid Organizations: A Review and Research Agenda, 16. *International Journal of Management Reviews*, *16*(4), 417–436. doi:10.1111/ijmr.12028

Doney, P. M., & Cannon, J. P. (1997). Trust in buyer-seller relationships. *Journal of Marketing*, *61*(2), 35–51. doi:10.2307/1251829

Du, S., Bhattacharya, C., & Sen, S. (2007). Reaping relational rewards from corporate social responsibility: The role of competitive positioning. *International Journal of Research in Marketing*, *24*(3), 224–241. doi:10.1016/j.ijresmar.2007.01.001

Ducks Unlimited. (2017, February). *Fact Sheet.* Retrieved from ducs.org: http://www.ducks.org/media/_global/_documents/stateFactSheets/NationalFactSheet.pdf

Jill, K., & Lyons, T. (2016). *Understanding Social Entrepreneurship*. New York: Routledge.

Lau, G. T., & Lee, S. H. (1999). Consumer's Trust in a Brand and the Link to Brand Loyalty. *Journal of Market Focused Management*, *4*(4), 341–370. doi:10.1023/A:1009886520142

Maier, V., & Zonovia Pop, C. (2011, December). Entrepreneurship versus Intrapreneurship. *Review of International Comparative Management*, *12*(5), 971–976.

Mair, J., & Sharma, S. (2012). Performance Measurement and Social Entrepreneurship. In C. K. Volkmann, K. O. Tokarski, & K. Ernst (Eds.), *Social Entrepreneurship and Social Business* (pp. 175–189). Wiesbaden: Springer Gabler. doi:10.1007/978-3-8349-7093-0_9

Müller, S. (2012). Business Models in Social Entrepreneurship. In C. Volkmann, K. O. Tokarski, & K. Ernst (Eds.), *Social Entrepreneurship and Social Business* (pp. 105–131). Wiesbaden: Springer Gabler. doi:10.1007/978-3-8349-7093-0_6

Nemeth, C. J. (1992). Minority dissent as a stimulant to group performance. In S. Worchel, W. Wood, & J. A. Simpson (Eds.), *Group process and productivity* (pp. 95–111). Newbury Park, CA: Sage.

O'Reilly, C., Chatman, J., & Caldwell, D. (1991). People and organizational culture: A profile comparison approach to assessing person-organization fit. *Academy of Management Journal*, *34*(3), 487–516. doi:10.2307/256404

OECD. (2010). Social Entrepreneurship and Social Innovation. In *SMEs* (pp. 185–215). Entrepreneurship and Innovation.

Orlando, R. (2000). Racial Diversity, Business Strategy, and Firm Performance: A Resource-Based View. *Academy of Management Journal*, *43*(2), 164–177. doi:10.2307/1556374

Oster, S. M. (1995). *Strategic management for nonprofit organizations: Theory and cases*. New York: Oxford University Press.

Porter, M. (1980). Competitive strategy: Techniques for analyzing industries and competition. New York.

Porter, M. (1985). *Competitive Advantage: Creating and Sustaining Superior Performance*. New York: Free Press.

Porter, M., Hills, G., Pfitzer, M., Patscheke, S., & Hawkins, E. (2011). *Measuring Shared Value: How to Unlock Value by Linking Social and Business Results*. FSG.

Porter, M., & Kramer, M. (2002, December). The Competitive Advantage of Corporate Philanthropy. *Harvard Business Review*, 56-68.

Porter, M., & Kramer, M. (2006, December). Strategy and Society: The Link between Competitive Advantage and Corporate Social Responsibility. *Harvard Business Review*, 78-92.

Porter, M., & Kramer, M. (2011, January-February). Creating Shared Value. *Harvard Business Review*, 62-77.

Prahalad, C. K. (2004). *The fortune at the bottom of the pyramid: Eradicating poverty with profits*. Philadelphia: Wharton Business Publishing.

Prahalad, C. K. (2012). Bottom of the Pyramid as a Source of Breakthrough Innovations. *Journal of Product Innovation Management*, *29*(1), 6–12. doi:10.1111/j.1540-5885.2011.00874.x

Rueda-Armengot, C., Estelles-Miguel, S., Gato, M., Guillem, J., & Peris-Ortiz, M. (2017). Social Entrepreneurship in the Automotive Industry: A Win-Win Experience. In M. Peris-Ortiz, F. Teulon, & D. Bonet-Fernandez (Eds.), Social Entrepreneurship in Non-Profit and Profit Sectors (pp. 99-104). Springer. doi:10.1007/978-3-319-50850-4_8

Schmitz, B., & Scheuerle, T. (2012, February). Article. *ACRN Journal of Entrepreneurship Perspectives*, *1*(1), 13–36.

Sesameworkshop. (2017). *Financials*. Retrieved from http://www.sesameworkshop.org/about-us/financials/

Thompson, J. (2002). The World of the Social Entrepreneur. *International Journal of Public Sector Management*, *15*(5), 412–431. doi:10.1108/09513550210435746

Volkmann, C., Tokarski, K. O., & Ernst, K. (2012). Background, Characteristics and Context of Social Entrepreneurship. In C. Volkmann, K. O. Tokarski, & K. Ernst (Eds.), *Social Entrepreneurship and Social Business* (pp. 4–30). Wiesbaden: Springer Gabler. doi:10.1007/978-3-8349-7093-0_1

Weerawardena, J., & Mort, G. S. (2001). Learning, Innovation and Competitive Advantage in Not-for-Profit Aged Care Marketing: A Conceptual Model and Research Propositions. *Journal of Nonprofit & Public Sector Marketing*, *9*(3), 53–73. doi:10.1300/J054v09n03_04

Weerawardena, J., & Mort, G. S. (2012, Spring). Competitive Strategy in Socially Entrepreneurial Nonprofit Organizations: Innovation and Differentiation. *Journal of Public Policy & Marketing*, *31*(1), 91–101. doi:10.1509/jppm.11.034

Chapter 8
Human Resources Management in Social Entrepreneurship

Burcu Kümbül Güler
Dokuz Eylul University, Turkey

ABSTRACT

With the rise of social entrepreneurship, social enterprises have gained popularity as socially innovative organizations which try to balance their economic and social missions. In the competitive environment of social economy, good management and investment in human resources have become requirements of social enterprises for their survival. Among the management practices, human resources management acts as a tool for gaining competitive advantage and it builds mutual trust between the staff and the organization. Emphasizing the significance and challenges of human resources management, this chapter explains human resources main practices—recruitment, career management, training, and compensation and performance management—in social entrepreneurship.

INTRODUCTION

Social entrepreneurship definitions are various in the literature and the conceptualization of the construct includes many dimensions such as social mission, continuous innovation, use of resources, credibility, accountability, sustainability, creating social value, opportunity recognition, commitment to collective purpose, etc. (Waddock & Post, 1991; Leadbeater, 1997; Dees, 1998; Sullivan Mort, Weerawardena, & Carnegie, 2003). As can be derived from these dimensions, in social entrepreneurship social needs are tried to be met by achieving sustainability (Mair & Marti, 2004) which leads us to accept social entrepreneurship as the interaction of social mission and economic goals.

Social entrepreneurship can be regarded as a response to unmet individual and societal needs (Haugh, 2007) while encompassing creating of social enterprises (Haugh, 2005). Unlike traditional for-profit sector, social enterprises in the realm of social entrepreneurship has emerged as mission-driven organizations which have emerged in reaction to social, economic and/or environmental problems. The relationship between social entrepreneurship and social enterprise can be found in some of the definitions in the field. For instance, social entrepreneurship is seen as,

DOI: 10.4018/978-1-5225-5687-9.ch008

the entrepreneurship leading to the establishment of new social enterprise, and the continued innovation in existing ones (Sullivan Mort, Weerawardena, & Carnegie, 2003).

Global Entrepreneurship Monitor (2006) also regards social entrepreneurship as *any attempt at new social enterprise activity or new enterprise creation* (Harding, 2007). Thus, it is highly probable that social entrepreneurship leads to the creation or the development of a social enterprise; however a social enterprise is not necessarily or permanently engaged in a social entrepreneurship process (Brouard & Larivet, 2010). Although the relationship is uni-directional, there is an inevitable connection between these concepts and in this chapter, human resources management (HRM) will be discussed on both social entrepreneurship level and on social enterprise level.

As the organizations of the process of social entrepreneurship, social enterprises are located *at the crossroads of market, public policies and civil society* (Nyssens, 2006). There are some factors which enable the growth of these enterprises recently. One contributing factor is the former donor-dependent organizations' seeking of more commercial sources of revenue -like earned income- due to the change in philanthropic giving. In addition, market opportunities for new entrants emerged because of the change in public service delivery. Also, new forms of capitalism have directed attention and resources towards the market potential of social enterprises. Consequently, with the rise of social enterprises' blending social and economic values, boundaries between for-profit, non-profit and public sectors have been blurring (Doherty, Haugh & Lyon, 2014). Within this context, as social enterprises develop in number and also in quality, management of these organizations has become an important issue. First, establishment and foundation of these organizations, and then their legitimacy and sustainability require good managerial knowledge and practice (Borzaga & Solari, 2001).

Within the management issues of all organizations including for-profit, public and non-profit social enterprises, human resources management constitutes a very important area. Leaders of all three sectors have been aware of the importance of human resources in capacity building and organizational effectiveness. Regarding HRM resemblance in non-profit and for-profit sectors, there are two strands of research opposed to each other. One strand of research claims that there is an increasing institutional isomorphism between the sectors. According to this view, social enterprises are converging in their human resources (HR) practices with public and for-profit organizations. Thus, social enterprises borrow good HRM practices from other sectors. On the other hand, second strand of research believes that social enterprises are unique in nature. Therefore, they have different challenging areas than public and for-profit counterparts. These areas include legislation and regulation, production and service quality, finance, and talent acquisition, retain and development in terms of HRM (Baluch, 2012; Borzaga & Solari, 2001).

In line with the difference in HRM approach, social enterprises are also regarded as different entities from for profit organizations because of their explicit social orientation and indirect profit-oriented. Although they explicitly deal with social issues, they generally have difficulty in resource management and economic value creation which are main requirements of organizational sustainability (Austin, Gutierrez, Ogliastri, & Reficco, 2006). Moreover, economic demands on social enterprises make them less competitive when compared with for-profit organizations in providing adequate compensation and incentives for their employees (Bhati & Manimala, 2011; von Eckardstein & Brandl, 2004). However, mission statements of social enterprises are recognized as influential tools that intrinsically motivate employees towards meeting organization's purpose. A distinctive characteristic of social enterprises is the "pursuit of social mission" which explains the fact that these organizations' focus of attention is on realization of non-economic values rather than maximization of profit (von Eckardstein & Brandl, 2004). In other words, social enterprises differ from private organizations in terms of being value-driven and employees of social enterprises feel committed and identify themselves with organization's values. Even as the non-profit sector faces fiscal uncertainty, short staffing, and retention problems, the vast majority of non-profit workers are motivated by the chance to do something worthwhile in an environment dedicated to the mission above everything else (Light, 2002).

The aim of this chapter is twofold. First, the need and challenges for human resources management in social entrepreneurship will be discussed on theoretical basis. Second, human resources main practices –recruitment, career management, training, compensation and performance management- in social entrepreneurship will be explored.

NEED FOR HUMAN RESOURCES MANAGEMENT IN SOCIAL ENTERPRISES

With the rise of social entrepreneurship, social purpose organizations have evolved into sustainable, performance-driven social enterprises (Nicholls, 2008a; Nicholls & Cho, 2006). These social enterprises are playing a significant role in revitalizing the local community. By providing self-help, employing jobless or untrained people, empowering the disadvantaged, developing local jobs, businesses, and human resources they contribute both to the human resources and economic well-being of the local area (Desa, 2007; Woolley, 2014). In a sense, they act like change agent in transformation of the society. While social enterprises are transforming the social economy by providing recruitment through organizations such as "Work Integrated Social Enterprises (WISEs)" (Spear, 2002; Spear & Bidet, 2005), they also benefit from human resources management practices in order to attract and retain talented, mission oriented and socially responsible workforce.

HRM process in social enterprises requires special attention since workforce of social enterprises is composed of both paid employees and volunteers (Blank, 2012). Although there is a contradiction about the causal relationship between motivation behind volunteer work and non-profit employment, Lee and Wilkins' (2011) study indicates a positive relation between volunteering and non-profit employment and there are vast amount of people both volunteering and working on full time basis at social entrepreneurship.

Social entrepreneurship requires recruiting and developing staff with business skills to achieve sustainability while inspiring them to develop special passion for their work to reach social mission (Weerawardena & Mort, 2006). That is why, the number of both paid employees and volunteers, their expertise and experience are significant factors affecting the success of social enterprises (Cooper, 1993). Because of the harsh competitiveness in the social market, human resources appear to be one of the requirements of social enterprises. External competitive environment and internal challenges of management compel social entrepreneurs to re-evaluate HRM policies and to integrate HR practices with their mission in a strategic manner (Weerawardena & Mort, 2006; Khatun & Hasan, 2016). Within this context, HRM can be regarded as a tool for gaining competitive advantage for social enterprises (Borzaga & Solari, 2001). As Akingbola (2006) states, the need for professional delivery of services and accountability requirements of the new funding environment makes the employees of social enterprises the most critical stakeholder. Since the growth and scaling up needs adequate and appropriate human resources, social enterprises are required to put the necessary skill-set in place, through either recruitment of new employees or replacing the ones who are not capable (Kickul & Lyons, 2012).

CHALLENGES OF MIXED WORKFORCE

Social enterprises benefit from two different workforce types –full-time employees and part-time volunteers- but how they arrange their staffing depends on the organization's strategy. Some of them rely heavily and successfully on part-time volunteers, and volunteers can be assigned to major leadership positions. On the other hand, other organizations work with professional employees on full time basis and use volunteers only in limited roles – as board members, fundraisers, and advisors (Dees, Emerson, & Economy, 2002).

According to the famous "Social Enterprise Spectrum" offered by Dees (1998), workforce is considered as one of the key stakeholders of the social enterprises. If the organization is purely philanthropic like charities, their workforce is mostly composed of volunteers. If the enterprise is on the other edge of the spectrum and if it is purely commercial then workforce is compensated at the market level. If the organization has a hybrid nature, then workforce is composed of both volunteers and paid employees and being compensated below market rate. Therefore, voluntary sector in which social enterprises operate has a unique people management style where there is "employee mix" which means that large numbers of professional and unpaid volunteers work together towards achieving the organization's goals.

This employee mix consists of employees with different academic backgrounds, experience, dedication and motivation. Therefore, a rational and orderly use of human resources is an obligation for social enterprises (Austin, Gutierrez, Ogliastri, & Reficco, 2006). Accordingly, HRM of social enterprises is generally composed of two dimensions: management of volunteers and also paid employees who are working with contracts (Cunningham, 1999; Parente, Lopes & Marcos, 2014; Van Vuuren, de Jong, & Seydel, 2008). Thus, HRM should modify itself according to the needs of these different types of workforce and with strategic HRM thinking, social enterprises should decide about the appropriate combination of these groups (von Eckardstein & Brandl, 2004).

A mixed employee force is a complex context to work in, for paid workers, volunteers, and management alike. One of the difficulties of such a mixed employee force is paid employees' perception of threat from volunteers to their own position in the organization. Volunteers' invaluable experience, credentials and emotional commitment may be perceived as threat by paid employees (McCurley & Lynch, 1996). Reaction from the volunteers to this kind of employee perception is a potential stress source and creates a strain between professionalism and voluntarism. Such a competitive atmosphere between paid and unpaid workers may demoralize volunteers. When they realize that their contribution to the organization is not as welcomed as they may have hoped for and their dedication to the organization is not respected, they may feel less motivated to exert themselves for the organization (Van Vuuren, de Jong, & Seydel, 2008).

There are many differences between paid employees and volunteers. First of all, paid employees of social enterprises are the ones who work with formal work contract and they generally work on full time basis. However, volunteers of social enterprises work without a work contract -generally they form psychological contract- and they typically work part time. The formal contract for paid employees includes an expectation of the length of commitment and the nature of expected tasks and roles. The psychological contract includes feelings about what volunteers give to the non-profit, and what they get in return, and it is abstract and beyond the formal contract (Blank, 2012). Other important distinction is motivation. Whereas volunteer work satisfies a need to help others (Burke, 2012) which is an intrinsic motivation; the motivation of paid staff might be more extrinsic based on instrumental goals such as pay and status. For this reason, paid employee motivation deals more with organizational issues such as job performance, absenteeism, tenure, and productivity. Since volunteers are not paid, they are emotionally committed to the organization and they are motivated with intrinsic rewards –such as autonomy, participation to the decision-making process, meaningful work, etc. In this regard, HRM's task is to adjust a fit between the needs of the social enterprises and motives of the volunteers. As this fit increases, more satisfaction and more commitment will be achieved. To understand the needs of the volunteers, it is important to realize the functions served by volunteering. Some of the volunteers are driven by their values -like humanitarism, while the others seek to learn more about the world by which they can gain an understanding of the world. While some develop themselves psychologically through volunteering, some have a career mission and wish to acquire career-related experience. Some individuals strengthen their social relationships in volunteer work, and some reduce their negative feelings, such as guilt. To serve to needs of the volunteers, social enterprises establish "volunteer programs" which provides structures for the recruitment of volunteers, the individual check and positioning within the social enterprise, the assignment of tasks, duties and positions as well as for the necessary trainings (Blank, 2012).

In order to increase the motivation of volunteers and to make them more included to the cause of the organization, social enterprises are suggested to put some activities into practice. These are; asking volunteers' advice and ideas about events and projects, keeping them informed about the activities, inviting them to some occasions and meetings, getting to know more about them, being flexible and embracing them while paying attention to their diverse characteristics (i.e. gender, culture, language and age, etc.), being aware of their changing needs, and following up with them to show the benefit of their participation (Burke, 2012). It is crucial to take the advantage from a leadership style that fosters trust building, cooperation, teamwork, competition, personal development, success, value creation, fun and commitment among the volunteers. Beyond traditional management, through "management-by-partnership", better results can be obtained than by a merely formal supervision (Blank, 2012).

In essence, other than extrinsic motivators, both paid staff and volunteers of the social enterprises can be motivated through fulfilment of some needs and desires such as autonomy, participation in decision making, balance between efficiency and social mission, attention to beneficiaries and societal issues, owning the enterprise economically as well as psychologically and good leadership (Borzaga & Solari, 2001).

HUMAN RESOURCES MANAGEMENT PRACTICES IN SOCIAL ENTERPRISES

Human resources management (HRM) is defined as:

the design of formal systems in an organization to ensure the effective use of employees' knowledge, skills, abilities, and other characteristics to accomplish organizational goals (Pynes, 2013).

Considered as one of the intangible organizational capital, human resources bring together the value of knowledge, abilities, and capabilities of individuals. Management of human resources provides the development of this knowledge and experience, while improving the productivity and effectiveness of the organization (Austin, Gutierrez, Ogliastri, & Reficco, 2006).

The discipline of HR has been studied within economic and business research areas with a focus on especially for-profit enterprises with a strategic lens. Expenditure for personnel and its influence on organizational performance are among the reasons of the development of this management practice (von Eckardstein & Brandl, 2004). In addition, with good practices of HRM, both private and social organizations have enduring relationship with their employees. This trust based relationship will have a positive impact on high performance and therefore the organization can create social and economic value (Austin, Gutierrez, Ogliastri, & Reficco, 2006). Moreover, through HRM based proper training and professional development, organizations can achieve talent development in order to meet tomorrow's challenges. As mentioned before, growing competitiveness in the non-profit sector leads social enterprises to invest in their human resources since they are regarded as an important and indispensable resource for adapting to the changing environment (Baluch, 2012).

HRM includes the practices of human resources such as; recruitment and selection, performance appraisal, compensation and reward management, training and development. As in the case for commercial enterprises, HRM is among basic skills that are needed for social entrepreneurship. Like financial systems, governance, and accounting, human resources department should function well enough in a healthy and sustainable social enterprise (Chahine, 2016). Human resources departments of social enterprises need to take a proactive role and a have a strategic mind set to meet the changing demands of their environment (Lynn, 2003). As stated earlier, economic, social concerns and demands are important challenge areas for social entrepreneurs. In order to overcome the tension between these two goals, there is a high expectancy from HRM practices of the enterprise (Ohana & Meyer, 2010). Thus, within intense competition and with limited access to funding opportunities and resources, like their business counterparts, social enterprises also think strategically and benefit from HRM in order to improve organizational efficiency and reduce costs (von Eckardstein & Brandl, 2004). For instance, in order to have an advantageous position among governing bodies with successful funding and grant applications, adequate recruitment techniques of HRM are helpful (Cunningham, 1999). There are other smart HRM practices that social enterprises benefit from, such as *development of local population as a source of future workers* and *formation of teams of volunteers*. Some of these practices and their contribution to social and economic value generation can be observed from Table 1 which is adopted from Austin et al. (2006).

Table 1. HRM practices contributing to social and economic value generation in social enterprises

HRM Practice	Social Value Generation	Economic Value Generation
Personnel development policies oriented to retention of human resources	Adequate compensation and improved quality of life for workers. This generates social benefits for them and their families.	Worker retention policies generate long-term relationships with the company, capitalizing investment in these policies.
Performance evaluation processes that emphasize goal completion and achievement of results	Effectiveness in the achievement of social goals improves organization's relations with actors.	Effectiveness in achievement of goals optimizes social investments and creates possibilities for the generation of new projects for the organization.
Development of the local population as a source of future workers	Community development favours residents and the enterprise's workers. This generates employability.	Creates better sources for recruitment of qualified personnel lead to growth in the effectiveness of HR. This improves company product and service offerings.
Formation of teams of volunteers	Organizational capacities to generate social impacts are multiplied.	HR costs are reduced. Image of the organization in the community is strengthened.
Participative mechanisms in management	Promotes development of workers and empowers them.	Leader-centred management risk is reduced and thus sustainability of organization is increased.

Source: Austin (2006).

Although there are some benefits, some obstacles also arise when HRM is introduced to social enterprises. First area of concern is *cultural barriers to managerialism* which asserts the idea that adopting private sector techniques bears a potential danger for social enterprises. For instance, there is a hesitation whether it alienates or not if volunteers are treated with formal management techniques, since they devote their time and energy for altruistic reasons. In addition, participative nature of these voluntary organizations can constitute a barrier for the development of top-down management-led initiatives where there is limited employee involvement in decision making. Second are of concerns is "funding constraints" for social enterprises. Since the cost of human resources represents nearly the highest proportion of expenditure, the management of social enterprises expose to the difficulty of justifying the costs of introducing HRM policies. Compensation scheme, training and development of staff are negatively affected from these income restraints. Third area of concern is "organizational size" which reflects the fact that many social organizations are small and medium sized. Being small in size may act as a barrier for complicated HRM practices to realize (Cunningham, 1999).

There are also other HR challenges for young and talented employees to be reluctant to stay at social enterprises. For instance, undefined career paths, unclear performance management and expectations, lack of benefits, poor funding opportunities that do not support decent employment and limited training (Burke, 2012) are among the shortcomings of today's demanding environment. In addition, due to the limited funding opportunities from public sector in times of austerity, social enterprises need to cut employment costs. Cost reduction results in increasing job insecurity, short-term contractual work, growing job demands and work intensification, pay reductions for the social sector employees. During the times of worsening employment conditions, employees of social enterprises are expected to increase their contributions, while employers are cutting the inducements used to bring about these contributions such as decreased benefits and job security. This imbalanced, underinvestment type of employment relationship creates a negative attitude towards HRM strategies of the organization and may result in negative behaviours like higher turnover, absence and lower commitment (Baluch, 2017).

In order to determine what type of HRM used in different social enterprises, Ridder and McCandless (2010) identify four types of HRM in social enterprises. They assume that architecture of HRM in social enterprises changes according to two dimensions: "organization's strategic orientation" and "human resource base". Organization's strategic orientation includes values, mission, and goals of the social enterprise. Human resource base is influenced from needs and motivations of employees. Differentiating the two dimensions with low and high focus, the authors suggest four types of HRM: 1) Administrative HRM; 2) Motivational HRM; 3) Strategic HRM; and 4) Values-driven HRM. Figure 1 shows the combination of these dimensions, including four cells of HRM types, each having low and high focus.

As seen in Figure 1, when there is a low focus on both the strategic orientation and HR base, "administrative HRM" emerges. If social enterprises do not have future perspectives and are not willing to invest in their employees, they have an "Administrative HRM". "Motivational HRM" occurs when there is low strategic focus and high human resource emphasis. These social enterprises focus on social mission and satisfying diverse needs of their employees. These highly motivated workers who show stronger nonmonetary orientation and commitment to the mission of the organization are one of the main strengths of social enterprises. Therefore, motivating them is an important starting point for developing HRM strategies. "Strategic HRM" is characterized by a low focus on the HR base and a high emphasis on the strategic orientation. These social enterprises with "strategic HRM" orientation are more prone to respond to market demands such as funding pressures and constraints. However, this orientation can have a negative effect on the motivation, satisfaction, and commitment of the intrinsically motivated

Figure 1. An analytical framework of human resource management in non-profit organizations
Source: Ridder & McCandless (2010)

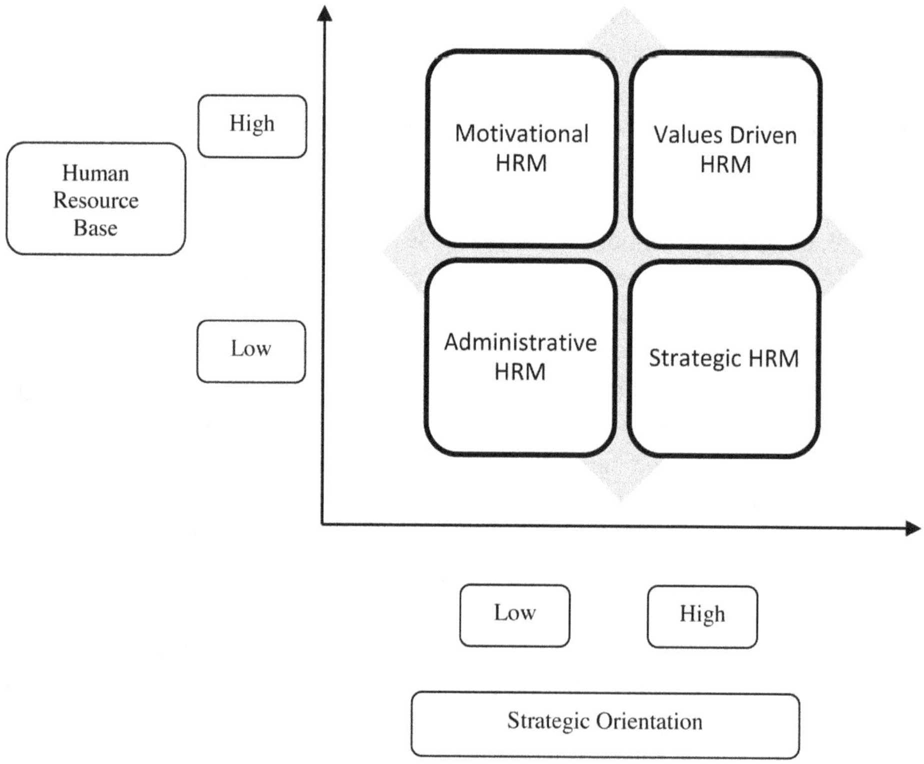

employees. If there is high focus on both dimensions of strategic orientation and HR base, "values-driven HRM" occurs. These social enterprises have commitment both to the social mission and also to employee development. Moreover, with "values-driven HRM", social enterprises invest in their employees and retain a focus on their human resources in strategic decision-making processes as a means to accomplish their mission and goals (Ridder & McCandless, 2010).

Consequently, the dilemma of social enterprises in terms of social mission and profit orientation results in dramatic changes in the operating environment of HR. There occurs a need for a strategic focus to make balance between adapting to change and the pressure to do more social good. Within this context, having a values-driven HRM with proper use of HR practices has become more significant than ever (Akingbola, 2006). The new operating environment of social enterprises requires adequate HR practices like recruitment, career management, training, compensation and also performance management which are reviewed below.

Recruitment

Recruitment is the process of attracting qualified candidates to apply for vacant positions within an organization. When decision is made about who will be selected for the position, this is the final stage of recruitment, which is called as "selection". Both recruitment and selection are required mechanisms for effective planning of human resources need of the organizations (Pynes, 2013). Difference between private and social organizations is also seen in the recruitment practice. Due to the combined nature of social and economic values, employees of social enterprises are expected to fulfil business requirements and sustainability while considering achieving social mission, ethics, equity, and accountability (Bhati & Manimala, 2011). Mixed workforce employed within these organizations serve for these two social and economic missions, by ensuring two abilities which are social work and administrative management (Austin, Gutierrez, Ogliastri, & Reficco, 2006). That is why; social enterprises' way of employment which combines volunteers and paid employees is perceived by some scholars as an innovative employment structure (i.e. Defourny & Borzaga, 2001).

Human resources retention is a major strategic issue for social enterprises where talent and commitment to a social mission are hardly found permanent employee characteristics (Ohana & Meyer, 2010). In a study of Indian social enterprises depending on a survey of 100 founders, major challenges of human resources are found as: recruiting qualified staff (70%), clearly defining roles and responsibilities (39%), distributing decision-making authority beyond the founding team (34%), establishing HR policies and procedures (26%), training employees in new skills (25%), retaining employees (24%), managing lower-level employees (23%), keeping up morale among employees (20%) (Understanding Human Resource Challenges in the Indian Social Enterprise Sector, 2012). These findings notify that, recruitment is a special area of human resources especially for attracting and retaining qualified staff in social enterprises. Successful recruitment should start with the understanding that human capital of social enterprises should not be considered as a financial expense. Rather, the workforce should be considered as a valuable asset that contributes to the organization. Therefore, aiding the organization to reach its mission and helping it to maintain the competitive advantage, workforce of the social enterprises requires investment through HRM practices.

The strategies used for recruitment of staff can be considered both for professional employees and also for volunteers. For staff selection, interview technique can be used in order to get to know the applicant personally. This technique also is an opportunity for the applicant to reach the necessary information which influences his/her decision to accept the job offer. Moreover, knowledge, behaviour and personality tests are also suitable to use, especially in the pre-selection stage if there are many applicants. Especially for the recruitment of managerial positions and board members, assessment centre technique is recommended. Although relatively time-consuming, in this technique applicants are required to accomplish different tasks such as presentations, discussions, etc. Afterwards, the observers rate the applicants' performance. Observing the applicants while they display their behaviour as role play under simulated working conditions provides a detailed prognosis for future suitability of the proven candidate (von Eckardstein & Brandl, 2004).

In essence, professional employees generally go through a formal recruitment process and selected for a position after careful deliberation. In terms of recruitment techniques used by social enterprises, Ban et al. (2003) found that the most viable options are newspaper ads word of mouth and professional associations. These are used more in medium to large social enterprises than small organizations. Newspaper ads and word of mouth techniques are used because of their low cost. Word of mouth is sometimes used with employee referral process and one creative strategy is to pay for the person who referred a successful hire. Job search engine sites are also very popular for recruitment over Internet. Bridgestar (www.bridgestar.org), Commongood Careers (www.cgcareers.org), Idealist (www.idealist.org), Cadip (www.cadip.org), Social Enterprise Alliance Job Board (https://socialenterprise.us/resources/jobs) and Work for Good (https://www.workforgood.org) are some examples of these job search sites where social enterprises can announce their hiring and volunteer needs.

For the volunteers, on the other hand, selection procedures are considered as less important because if the person is willing to donate his/her labour to the social mission of the organization, it is very hard to reject his offer. Thus, volunteers are often recruited directly and without formal selection procedures and they tend to fill a "try-out" position. The problem is the process of becoming committed to the social enterprise's mission becomes longer for volunteers than for professionals. However, from a strategic HRM perspective, if the volunteers are considered as source of performance contributors to the competitive social enterprises, then selection techniques should also be applied in the recruitment process (Cnaan & Cascio, 1998; von Eckardstein & Brandl, 2004). Volunteer recruitment can be achieved via university career centres where university students can be reached who are eager to volunteer. Moreover, even for professional employment social enterprises can work with alumni associations of universities. For instance, Wharton School has been giving service to the graduates to connect with employers of social enterprises (MBA Career Resources). The Tamer Center for Social Enterprise with the collaboration of Columbia Business School's career center works for providing resources and networks to the students who want to pursue their careers in social enterprises. Developing relationships with organizations, organizing career panels, and publicizing job announcements are among the services given at the center (https://www8.gsb.columbia.edu/socialenterprise/careers).

In addition, there are some corporate volunteering programs that encourage already employed staff of private companies to involve themselves in social enterprises (Hobbs, 2011). Corporate volunteering is a kind of volunteering for employees who are motivated to give their time, effort, expertise, knowledge and money in order to benefit individuals or groups outside the organization they work for. These employees do not receive additional compensation for the volunteer work they do. Corporate volunteering activities provide benefits to four parties: employees, companies, social enterprises and the community. Beyond donations and sponsorships, with corporate volunteering, employees of private companies have the opportunity to be involved in the social environment by actualizing meaningful work. An example is Disney's corporate volunteering program in which company employees have given over 495,000 hours to assist non-profits' professionalization in several areas such as education/literacy, hunger/homeless, healthcare, child/family care services, entertainment, community restoration, and the natural environment (Chang, 2013; Herzig, 2006). Within the framework of corporate volunteering, there are also employee secondment programmes where an employee is loaned to work or volunteers for community. This is a programme providing benefits not only to the outside community, but also to the employees of the private enterprise. For instance, a retail company Marks and Spencer's employees are seconded to work for community organizations and this partnership between the two organizations can be imitated by social enterprises for recruiting employees who want to volunteer. The tripartite benefits of secondment are summarized in Table 2.

Board member recruitment is another important issue within recruitment process. In order to reduce the first stage initial effort, some newly founded social enterprises build their boards out of their close network, such as family members and friends. However, this is considered as a disadvantage as the enterprise grows if board members do not possess the relevant skills, representation, network and reputation to provide strategic guidance. For this reason, in order to search for capable board members, social enterprises are advised to benefit from the following recruitment techniques: 1) soliciting recommendations from investors, foundations and other social enterprises; 2) searching through intermediary platforms; 3) research, identify and reach out to people with expertise in or passion for the cause; 4) attending networking events. Moreover, when selecting board members, social enterprises are also recommended

Table 2. Tripartite benefits of secondment

Benefits for the Employee	Benefits for the Receving Organization	Benefits for the Company
•Learning alternative business methods •Meeting the challenge of developing and achieving in a new environment •Developing new and existing skills •Improving the company's knowledge of the local community •Making contributions to local community •Acquiring a new perception of the business	•Acquiring professional expertise and skills for which the organization amy not have had the necessary funds otherwise •Acquring management skills which bring a fresh,, creative approach to problem solving •Gaining experience from a large organization resulting in a more business-like approach	•Enhanced capabilities of the returning secondee •Opportunity to invest practical help in the community •Increased knowledge of the local community •Enhanced company image and profile as the secondee becomes the company's "ambassador"

Source: Created by the author depending on Rogovsky (2000)

to take into account these qualifications: complimentary personality with the team of the enterprise and being in alignment with social and economic objectives of the social enterprise (Achleitner, Heinecke, Mayer, Noble, & Schöning, 2012).

For the recruitment source of employees, in a study of 71 Indian social enterprises and 59 individuals working in the social enterprise sector, commercial sector is found to be an important source for hiring mid and senior manager. Besides, the study also found that hiring and developing local talent to manage local operations makes better sense than recruiting professionals from outside (Vaidyanathan, Chatterjee, Murthy, & Naswa, 2014). However, it is questionable whether to use an outsider or a full-time permanent professional. If the social enterprise prefers outsiders based on temporary contract instead of employing regular full-time or part-time staff, the result may be high level of employee turnover leading to retention problems and loss of organizational memory (Akingbola, 2006). On the other hand, permanent employees are able to develop experience, skill and qualification within the integration process in social enterprises. They eventually develop good organizational citizenship behaviour when they are allowed to engage in the activities. Their positive contributions are vital for the organization and they should be appreciated by the leaders of social enterprises. Instead of just being concerned with financial issues, social entrepreneurs should also give value to the workforce by appropriate use of HRM techniques (Ohana & Meyer, 2010).

As mentioned earlier, social enterprises have been forced to become more business-like in the competitive environment. However, with the development of the commercial side due to the market forces, social enterprises are criticized for becoming less distinguishable from private organizations. The dependence on profits creates an isomorphism problem which further leads the organization to become highly professionalized and they tend to become an imitator of business world (Ohana & Meyer, 2010). The commercialization may negatively impact the job satisfaction of the workforce because they tend to think that espoused values are inconsistent with those in use and that their organization is not working on their social mission to sustain public good any more (Akingbola, 2006). In addition, low rates of compensation, difficulty in motivation of volunteers, inexplicit job descriptions, lack of development and career opportunity within a small organization, low level of resources for rewarding employees are difficult practices of HRM in social entrepreneurship for both acquisition and retention of talented employees (Bhati & Manimala, 2011). These are all challenges of HRM that social entrepreneurs should be aware of during the recruitment process of their workforce.

Career Management

Among HR functions, career management is also an important mechanism in order to retain successful employees. Within career management, career development programs are used to provide employees with advancement opportunities within the organization so that they will not have to look elsewhere. For the survival of the social enterprise, it is vital to prepare employees to meet future organizational needs with adequate career development (Pynes, 2013). Once employees have acquired a position in a social enterprise and tend to commit for the mission of the organization, it is natural for them to look for wider responsibilities within the organization (Ban, Drahnak-Faller, & Towers, 2003). Especially new generation employees (millennials and/or Generation Y) who are seeking personal satisfaction, interesting work, and flexibility more than financial gain can be motivated by actualization of their career aspirations within the organization. Besides, this new generation employees are prone to career mobility where they can find learning and development opportunities. Thus, it can be a great success for the social enterprise if HR department can implement a successful career management and can provide career options for these intrinsically motivated employees. Taking the time and spending resources to develop employees is a kind of signal that they are valued by the enterprise. However, compared with larger and more professional social enterprises, in many small social enterprises, there are limited options to move up within the organization (Ban, Drahnak-Faller, & Towers, 2003; Lyons & Kuron, 2014; Pynes, 2013).

According to Driver's (1980) career concepts model, there are four different career types: 1) Steady-state career which involves life-time commitment to an occupation; 2) linear career which continues throughout life as the individual moves up an occupational ladder; 3) spiral career which evolve through a series of different positions and; 4) transitory careers which entail a continuous change. Among these careers, linear career is considered to be suitable for private sector and spiral career is regarded as a typical path for non-profit professionals. People who pursue a spiral career seek creativity, interpersonal relationship, and self-development and these can be provided by social enterprises. Considering the differences between private and social sectors, career management within social enterprises should pay attention the appropriateness of reward systems. Since the spiral career pattern requires availability of challenge, flexible and meaningful work, and decision making, the employees of social enterprises should not be treated as their for-profit counterparts (Onyx & Maclean, 1996; Ban, Drahnak-Faller, & Towers, 2003).

Training

In terms of HRM, recruitment which is the ability of social enterprises to reach the skills and knowledge in the labour market is very important. Besides that, designing and implementing orientation programs and training activities to meet the needs of staff, making them to acquire supervisory skills is a crucial and valuable HRM practice (Royce, 2007). By training, social enterprises establish a learning environment in which the skills needed to adapt to change are provided (Baluch, 2012). Training is embedded in the process of realizing values and missions that social entrepreneurs set out to achieve. For this reason, it has a positive impact on the performance of social enterprises (Akingbola, 2006). Like their business counterparts, social enterprises organise the training of their staff, including both paid and unpaid volunteers. While devising programmes for the improvement of skills, they can either devote part of their resources for improvement and they might sponsor the development of specific graduate and post-graduate programmes, especially for volunteer gaining (Borzaga & Solari, 2001). In essence, training in social enterprises is considered as an important contributing factor for volunteers' tenure, productivity, and retention within the organization (Cnaan & Cascio, 1998).

As the first introductory step of training, orientation is important for the retention of volunteers. Main reason of orientation is simply sharing knowledge about the organization, its mission and purpose. It is a very influential and welcoming HRM practice within training which integrates volunteers to the organizational culture and operational practices of the social enterprise. Orientation is also beneficial for the management of the enterprise because various clues gathered during this process can help in deciding whether the individual will be a good fit in the organization. In order to have a successful orientation program, HRM should emphasize: 1) cause orientation; 2) system orientation; and 3) social orientation. First, cause orientation helps volunteers comprehend the mission, vision and purpose of the organization. It helps the volunteer to grow commitment emotionally to the organization and its mission. Second, system orientation is the managerial or procedural information the volunteer will need while working with the organization. Third, social orientation supports volunteers in their understanding of the organizational culture. It includes learning the names of supervisors, meeting other volunteer and paid staff members and it creates a welcome feeling. If all three aspects of orientation are achieved, volunteers will more likely to receive the emotional and informational support needed to be successful in their assignments (Edwards, 2012).

Social enterprises are more inclined to provide training than the other organizations in the for-profit sector and likely to integrate training to their strategy. Akingbola (2006) specifies the reasons why training is vital in social enterprises: 1) the link between employees' intrinsic motivation and the mission; 2) non-profit executives' positive attitude towards training; 3) skills needed to adapt to change emphasize the importance of training and learning in non-profits; 4) non-profits require diverse skill sets and a range of technical skills.

There are some doubts about which staff should need more training and when they need. Volunteers of social enterprises generally are not qualified in the given sector of the organization. Therefore they need specific, adequate and appropriate training at the beginning of their career in order not to be assigned to simple tasks which in the long run might deteriorate their intrinsic motivation towards organization's social mission (von Eckardstein & Brandl, 2004). Moreover, compared with "being charitable" in 1950s and also "being militant" in 1960s and 1970s, today's voluntary workers are found to work with more productive objectives and activities fulfilling specific needs (Defourny & Borzaga, 2001). This change in volunteers' perspectives requires training more than ever. In addition, training investments for full-time employees might be considered more economical and strategic than volunteer training (von Eckardstein & Brandl, 2004) since full-timers are considered to be in a long-term and reciprocal relationship with the organization. Especially for the executives of the social enterprises some programs can be designed to enhance the leadership skills within non-profit sector. Related with career development practices, training opportunities, on-the-job learning and even attending conferences are regarded as beneficial for leadership development. Because of the fast changing and demanding environment, social enterprises' training needs should be updated to keep up with the changes in the sector. Specific training needs for social enterprises can be leadership, governance, community building skills, finance, fundraising, grant/project writing, marketing, volunteer administration, planning, relationship building with grant givers and other enterprises, utilizing community resources, assessing and managing risk, communication, program evaluation and finally social impact measurement as a recent need. The most suitable option for training is half-day or day-long seminars and certificate programs more than traditional undergraduate level courses (Austin, Regan, Samples, Schwartz, & Carnochan, 2011; Burke, 2012; Dolan, 2002). However, academic institutions and universities have been offering new graduate level courses and programs to attract the executives of social enterprises. In addition, organizations such as Social Enterprise Alliance have been creating webinars on several managerial issues at low rate for their member social enterprises (https://socialenterprise.us/2017-community-programs/social-finance-webinar-series).

In social enterprises, training of human resources can be achieved by organizational learning. Building bridges between individual employees' knowledge and collective organizational knowledge increase organizational learning. There are three mechanisms to be successful at organizational learning: effective communication and coordination, documenting institutional memory, performance measurement. First, to achieve organizational learning, social enterprises can develop effective communication and coordination mechanisms both within the organization and with the external actors. Another mechanism that is used in social enterprises is to document institutional memory. Since large numbers of people work in some organizations and also if the enterprise is too large, then using audits to document ongoing practices is a way of creating organizational learning. Performance measurement, which will be reviewed below is also another mechanism to build a learning environment. By evaluating individual performance in the achievement of strategic goals, the organization can make corrections and subsequently improve the productivity (Austin, Gutierrez, Ogliastri, & Reficco, 2006).

Compensation

Designing, implementing and maintaining compensation systems are significant procedures of HRM. Enterprises' decisions about salaries, incentives and benefits are crucial in attracting, retaining, and motivating employees. Decisions about pay levels and structures influence the ability of the organization to be competitive to attract competent applicants and to retain the talented and productive employees (Pynes, 2013). Because compensation is a kind of motivating factor and motivators can be classified as "intrinsic" and "extrinsic". Both rewards are important sources of motivation for employees in private and social enterprises. Intrinsic rewards include the job itself, such as having challenging job tasks, gaining new skills, developing job knowledge, and increased responsibility. On the other hand, extrinsic rewards are part of the job situation that is provided by others. Extrinsic rewards are composed of salary and benefits or status that the individual gets from the position s/he holds (Pynes, 2013). For instance, maintaining a salary structure including incentives and bonuses is one way of compensation that increases motivation (Robinson & Klein, 2007). Besides, profit sharing which is considered among strategic HRM practices (Delery & Doty, 1996) is found to be a motivating factor for the staff of social enterprises. These practices indicate the importance of compensation in retaining of staff in social enterprises. It is argued that, even though employees are attracted by the mission of the social enterprises at first, if the compensation is not satisfactory enough, they may have an intention to leave (Brown, Yoshioka & Munoz, 2004).

However, there is also evidence that intrinsic rewards are important for the employees working in social organizations, generally more than the ones employed in for profit organizations (Light, 2002). Since these employees tend to perceive their work as an opportunity to serve for the common good, help the needy people or contribute to the realization of social mission, they are attracted to the social enterprise because of social values which are intrinsic in nature (Akingbola, 2006). Empirical studies also suggest that non-profit employees have a stronger nonmonetary gain orientation than the public or for-profit employees. For instance, one study found that working unpaid overtime is much more exercised by non-profit employees (Almond & Kendall, 2000) and this behaviour is considered as high level of commitment to the organization (Ridder & McCandless, 2010). This is also because of the nature of social enterprises where there is an expectation on employees to work for the social cause, not the salary (Brown, Yoshioka & Munoz, 2004).

There are contradictory views about the wage levels of different sectors. While some research indicates that pay level of non-profit sector are higher or equal, other studies show higher wage level in for-profit sector than non-profit. There are two possible explanations for this difference in wage levels. One depends on the donative labour hypothesis which states that low wage pay in non-profit sector is because of the nature of the goods or service provided. In this sector, with lower wages, more intrinsically motivated employees could be recruited. The second explanation of wage differential is about the different characteristics of social enterprises, employees, or jobs. According to this explanation, non-profit jobs are located in more low-pay industries, rather than the non-profit nature of the organization (Ridder & McCandless, 2010). In either case, generally, non-profit organizations are not able to compete with their for-profit counterparts in compensation management and pay lower than the other sectors (Akingbola, 2006; Brown, Yoshioka, & Munoz, 2004).

Compensation of social enterprises is subject to a greater variety of influences than public and/or private sector. In terms of equity principles, social enterprises must compare themselves with organizations that provide similar services and are similarly situated in terms of size and structure, revenue sources, benefits and position titles and benchmark equivalents. Moreover, they should also be careful about external and internal equity and employee equity (Pynes, 2013).

Performance Management

Performance management encompass:

all the activities, systems and processes that are deployed to enable and support employees to contribute the maximum of their knowledge, skills and abilities to the organization (Akingbola, 2015).

In order to make performance management legitimate and to achieve sustainable organizational performance, integration of performance appraisal into the organizational strategy should be realized by the organizations (Walk & Kennedy, 2017). Performance management in social enterprises is of both individual and organizational importance and it will be reviewed here on two levels: 1) Performance appraisal of the workforce and; 2) Performance measurement of the enterprise.

Before that, it should be mentioned that there are two opposing perspectives about performance management in the social enterprises. One view mentions about the advantages, while the other expresses the disadvantages of performance management. It is considered as advantageous and especially important for maintaining efficiency at social enterprises. For organizational development, performance management provides an evaluation about which achievements have been realized and what should be done for further social impact. In other words, performance measurement is both a feedback and a road map to support management action for organizational success. It can also be complemented with training. After the evaluation of performance, inadequate competency can be eliminated through the training of employees (Hobbs, 2011). On the other hand, performance evaluation and implementing pay for performance plans may be disadvantageous since they have potential damaging effects on intrinsic motivation of the staff (Ridder & McCandless, 2010). As Walk and Kennedy (2017) investigated, the language used in the performance management process is mirroring the one that is used in for-profit enterprises. The scholars are warning social enterprises for becoming more business-like which eventually might be damaging for their social value creation image. In addition, after performance appraisal, social entrepreneurs should be careful about over-engineering of job roles and responsibilities which might result in decreased autonomy and lessening proactive employee behaviour (Walk & Kennedy, 2017).

Performance Appraisal Of The Workforce

Performance appraisal has been defined as *the process through which managers ensure that employees' activities and outputs contribute to the organization's goals* (Noe, Hollenbeck, Gerhart, & Wright, 2016). It is an attempt to sustain the fit between HR practices aiming to increase individual performance with the objective of maximizing organizational outcomes (Walk & Kennedy, 2017). It should be emphasized that performance appraisal is interrelated with the other HR practices in order to achieve competitive advantage. Retention and motivation of the employees, learning by training, rewarding by compensation management are all possible through performance appraisal execution (Akingbola, 2015).

There is a wide range of reasons for management of organizations to use performance appraisal. Keeping focus on the social mission, objective assessment of achievements, identifying training and development needs, career management and succession planning, improving the individual/team and corporate performance, enabling the manager to recognize employee's achievements, allocating financial rewards and promotion, providing motivation for a psychologically healthier work life, determining the continuation or discontinuation of employment (Akingbola, 2015; Brown & Redman, 2017; Walk & Kennedy, 2017) are seen as important contributions of performance appraisals on the organizational level. On the individual level, there are also some benefits. With the feedback gathered after performance appraisal, employees are able to understand the influence of their behaviours on the outcomes, their self-esteem increases, and they identify their strengths and mitigate their weaknesses. In effect, if performance appraisal systems are well-designed and executed adequately and fairly, then they positively affect employees, managers, and organizations towards achieving the social mission of the organization (Walk & Kennedy, 2017).

In terms of both attracting and retaining volunteers, performance management has a crucial role in human resources development. Experienced social enterprises deal with monitoring and performance appraisal systems by generating leaders among volunteers and integrating these volunteer leaders to organization's strategic planning activities. Thus, volunteers feel more involved and accepted by the organization. This kind of volunteer management creates a culture for performance and efficiency within the organization (Austin, Gutierrez, Ogliastri, & Reficco, 2006).

Performance Measurement of the Enterprise

Performance measurement within social enterprises is an accepted practice of organizational life and majority of the organizations measure their social impact (Millar & Hall, 2013). However, performance measurement is a difficult process for many organizations because of the vagueness of organizational metrics to define and measure effectiveness. Compared with for-profit organizations, it is more challenging to appraise the performance level of the social enterprises. Intangible social goals, lack of financial measures such as profitability and shareholder return constitute a problem for performance management (Kaplan, 2001). However, for sustainability reasons, social enterprises also have financial concerns and they can and should make profits in order to be paid as salaries or used as reinvestment for social purposes (Baruch & Ramalho, 2006). Moreover, as the sector moves towards sustainability and funding bodies demand detailed reporting (Royce, 2007) social enterprises are more confronted with pressure to evaluate their performance in order to show competency, achieve legitimacy within the area that they work in and gain funding from government, agencies and donors (Baluch, 2012; Kaplan, 2001). Market-based approach of social entrepreneurship urges the organizations to involve in social impact and social performance measurement. Moreover, social enterprises serve to multiple stakeholders to whom they are accountable and should prove their effectiveness to these stakeholders in social mission (Baluch, 2012).

In social entrepreneurship, Nicholls (2010) proposes three key performance contexts which are 1) sociality; 2) innovation; and 3) market orientation. These contexts and related factors in the process of performance measurement in social entrepreneurship are provided on Table 3. First, sociality is about organization's social mission and making a social impact. Social entrepreneurs are aware of value of control metrics being used to show social impact and they also report these achievements to key stakeholders. Control metrics relate to the sociality of the organization and focus on assessing and justifying its performance. Second, innovation is an evidence of an important link between planning metrics and strategic innovation around mission objectives in social entrepreneurship. As social entrepreneurs, the people who relentlessly try to find new and better models of change to enhance the effectiveness of their mission objectives, planning metrics for innovation allows them to create a model better than today. And lastly, in terms of market orientation, accountability metrics are used to bring stakeholders into the strategic assessment and planning of the social mission. These metrics provide stakeholders with a means of making a judgement on the fit between how the organization should act and how it does act for the time being. Social entrepreneurship uses accountability metrics to legitimize, to innovate, and to embed beneficiaries into the mission (Nicholls, 2010).

In line with the statements of Nicholls (2010), within the sociality context of social entrepreneurship, it is very important for the social enterprises to be judged on the basis of the progress they make in the attainment of their social missions. Especially, in the competition for survival, achieving the goals and aims of the organization are vital signs for performance. Stakeholder satisfaction, which should be regularly measured, is also essential for the success of social enterprises. After defining the stakeholders

Table 3. Performance measurement in social entrepreneurship

Epistemology	Category of Metric	Social Entrepreneurship Context	Strategic Focus
What is being measured?	Control	Sociality	Social return on investment
Why measure?	Planning	Innovation	Mission objectives
Measure for whom?	Accountability	Market orientation	Stakeholders

Source: Nicholls (2010)

and understanding their criteria for organization's performance, satisfaction surveys can be implemented. The performance of social enterprise is based on the integration of inputs, process and outcomes, and it is determined by social mission achieved and also economic cost of the mission (Austin, Gutierrez, Ogliastri, & Reficco, 2006). As a conclusion, double or triple "bottom line" which combines environmental and social aims with economic viability (Millar & Hall, 2013) has been a crucial factor for performance management. Since social enterprises are under increasing pressure to indicate their performance more than ever in today's demanding social economy, performance of social enterprises needs to be measured.

CONCLUSION

The concept of social entrepreneurship has been growing fast and interest from either academics or practitioners to the field continues to develop. Social entrepreneurship is about finding sustainable and innovative solutions to social problems. Derived from the concept of social entrepreneurship, social enterprises are accepted as the organizations which adopt some form of commercial activity while pursuing social goals. Thus, there is a difference between private sector organizations and social enterprises in that, for social enterprises achieving social change -such as reducing poverty, empowerment of the disadvantaged, community development- is prior than private wealth creation (Doherty, Haugh, & Lyon, 2014).

In recent years, however, "doing good" and achieving social change is not a sufficient attractive characteristic for the success of social enterprises. In order to achieve both sustainability and effectiveness, these social organizations are needed to strive for good management practices (Cunningham, 1999). Despite the organizational and mission differences, just like their for-profit counterparts they also need to survive within the market pressure by aligning the organization with adequate HRM practices. Increasing competition, globalisation and continuous change in the social market have become challenging for the sustainability of social enterprises. In this realm, social entrepreneurs want to manage their organizations with professional management techniques borrowed from private organizations. Thus, economic considerations and profit-making start to dominate the social enterprises, while social mission seeking becomes deteriorated. This choice paves the way for HRM to cope with the growing tension between the economic and social orientation of the organization (Ohana & Meyer, 2010). In order to survive in the harsh environment, attracting and retaining the talent, providing them with the necessary tools and training and moreover creating a meaningful work for them have become crucial for these enterprises. Therefore, as suggested by Ridder and McCandless (2010) values-driven HRM approach should be adopted. Since competing in terms of efficiency is very difficult for social enterprises, the nature of this HRM approach will enable them to show their respect and concern for the welfare of their workforce which in the long run have a positive impact on the social and economic organizational outcomes.

Highlighting the vitality of HRM within social enterprises, this chapter tries to introduce HR practices. Recruitment, career management, training, compensation and performance management as main HR practices are evaluated with a social enterprise perspective. It should be mentioned that applying these HR practices, social enterprises may succeed in creating a good working environment, attract and retain the best people which constitute the most important asset for today's organizations. If social entrepreneurs develop good HRM systems within their organizations, they will eventually take the advantage of emotionally committed, competent and motivated workforce.

REFERENCES

Achleitner, A. K., Heinecke, A., Mayer, J., Noble, A., & Schöning, M. (2012). *The governance of social enterprises: Managing your organization for success.* Schwab Foundation for Social Entrepreneurship. Retrieved from http://www3.weforum.org/docs/WEF_Governance_Social_Enterprises_2106_light.pdf

Akingbola, K. (2006). Strategy and HRM in nonprofit organizations: Evidence from Canada. *International Journal of Human Resource Management, 17*(10), 1707–1725. doi:10.1080/09585190600964350

Akingbola, K. (2015). *Managing human resources for nonprofits.* New York, NY: Routledge.

Almond, S., & Kendall, J. (2000). Taking the employees' perspective seriously: An initial United Kingdom cross-sectoral comparison. *Nonprofit and Voluntary Sector Quarterly, 29*(2), 205–231. doi:10.1177/0899764000292001

Austin, J., Gutierrez, R., Ogliastri, E., & Reficco, E. (2006). *Effective management of social enterprises: Lessons from businesses and civil society organizations in Iberoamerica.* Harvard University, David Rockefeller Center for Latin American Studies.

Austin, M. J., Regan, K., Samples, M. W., Schwartz, S. L., & Carnochan, S. (2011). Building managerial and organizational capacity in non-profit human service organizations through a leadership development program. *Administration in Social Work, 35*(3), 258–281. doi:10.1080/03643107.2011.575339

Baluch, A. M. (2012). *Human resource management in nonprofit organizations.* New York: Routledge.

Baluch, A. M. (2017). Employee perceptions of HRM and well-being in nonprofit organizations: Unpacking the unintended. *International Journal of Human Resource Management, 28*(14), 1912–1937. doi:10.1080/09585192.2015.1136672

Ban, C., Drahnak-Faller, A., & Towers, M. (2003). Human resource challenges in human service and community development organizations: Recruitment and retention of professional staff. *Review of Public Personnel Administration, 23*(2), 133–153. doi:10.1177/0734371X03023002004

Baruch, Y., & Ramalho, N. (2006). Communalities and distinctions in the measurement of organizational performance and effectiveness across for-profits and nonprofit sectors. *Nonprofit and Voluntary Sector Quarterly, 35*(1), 39–65. doi:10.1177/0899764005282468

Bhati, A., & Manimala, M. J. (2011). Talent acquisition and retention in social enterprises. *Journal of Security and Sustainability Issues, 1*(1), 39–52. doi:10.9770/jssi.2011.1.1(4)

Blank, C. (2012). Human Resource Management and Volunteer Motivation. In K. Volkmann, K. O. Tokarski, & K. Ernst (Eds.), *Social Entrepreneurship and Social Business* (pp. 65–82). Wiesbaden: Springer Gabler. doi:10.1007/978-3-8349-7093-0_4

Borzaga, C., & Solari, L. (2001). Management challenges for social enterprises. In C. Borzaga & J. Defourny (Eds.), *The Emergence of Social Enterprise* (pp. 333–349). London: Routledge.

Brouard, F., & Larivet, S. (2010). Essay of clarifications and definitions of the related concepts of social enterprise, social entrepreneur and social entrepreneurship. In A. Fayolle & H. Matlay (Eds.), *Handbook of research on social entrepreneurship* (pp. 29–56). Cheltenham: Edward Elgar. doi:10.4337/9781849804684.00008

Brown, M., & Redman, T. (2017). Performance Appraisal. In A.Wilkinson, T. Redman, & T. Dundon (Eds.), Contemporary human resource management: Text and cases (pp. 189-210). Pearson Education.

Brown, W., Yoshioka, C. F., & Munoz, P. (2004). Organizational Mission as a Core Dimension in Employee Retention. *Journal of Park and Recreation Administration, 22*(2), 28–43.

Burke, R. J. (2012). Human resource management in the nonprofit sector: setting the stage. In R. J. Burke & C. L. Cooper (Eds.), *Human resource management in the nonprofit sector: passion, purpose and professionalism* (pp. 3–50). Edward Elgar Publishing. doi:10.4337/9780857937308.00007

Chahine, T. (2016). *Introduction to Social Entrepreneurship.* Boca Raton, FL: CRC Press. doi:10.1201/b19475

Chang, Y. K. (2013). *How and why employees engage in corporate volunteering* (Doctoral dissertation). Available from ProQuest Dissertations and Theses. Available from ProQuest Dissertations and Theses database. (UMI No.1428359955)

Cnaan, R. A., & Cascio, T. A. (1998). Performance and commitment: Issues in management of volunteers in human service organizations. *Journal of Social Service Research, 24*(3-4), 1–37. doi:10.1300/J079v24n03_01

Cooper, A. C. (1993). Predicting new firm performance. *Journal of Business Venturing, 8*(3), 241–253. doi:10.1016/0883-9026(93)90030-9

Cunningham, I. (1999). Human resource management in the voluntary sector: Challenges and opportunities. *Public Money & Management, 19*(2), 19–25. doi:10.1111/1467-9302.00161

Dees, J. G. (1998). Enterprising nonprofits. *Harvard Business Review, 76*, 54–69. PMID:10176919

Dees, J. G., Emerson, J., & Economy, P. (2002). *Enterprising nonprofits: A toolkit for social entrepreneurs* (Vol. 186). John Wiley & Sons.

Defourny, J., & Borzaga, C. (2001). From third sector to social enterprise. In C. Borzaga & J. Defourny (Eds.), *The Emergence of Social Enterprise* (pp. 1–28). London: Routledge.

Delery, J. E., & Doty, D. H. (1996). Modes of theorizing in strategic human resource management: Tests of universalistic, contingency and configurational performance predictions. *Academy of Management Journal, 39*(4), 802–835. doi:10.2307/256713

Desa, G. (2007). Social entrepreneurship: snapshots of a research field in emergence. In K. Hockerts, J. Mair, & J. Robinson (Eds.), *Values and opportunities in social entrepreneurship* (pp. 6–28). New York: Palgrave Macmillan.

Doherty, B., Haugh, H., & Lyon, F. (2014). Social enterprises as hybrid organizations: A review and research agenda. *International Journal of Management Reviews, 16*(4), 417–436. doi:10.1111/ijmr.12028

Dolan, D. A. (2002). Training needs of administrators in the nonprofit sector: What are they and how should we address them? *Nonprofit Management & Leadership*, *12*(3), 277–292. doi:10.1002/nml.12305

Edwards, H. C. (2012). Orientation: Welcoming New Volunteers into the Organization. In T. D. Connors (Ed.), *The Volunteer Management Handbook: Leadership Strategies for Success* (2nd ed.; pp. 227–235). John Wiley & Sons. doi:10.1002/9781118386194.ch9

Harding, R. (2007). *GEM UK 2006*. London: London Business School.

Herzig, C. (2006). Corporate volunteering in Germany: Survey and empirical evidence. *International Journal of Business Environment*, *1*(1), 51–69. doi:10.1504/IJBE.2006.010128

Hobbs, S. (2011). The Latest Approach to Volunteer Recruitment: Competency - Competence Pathways and Volunteer Resource Management Systems. In T. D. Connors (Ed.), *The Volunteer Management Handbook: Leadership Strategies for Success* (2nd ed.; pp. 205–225). John Wiley & Sons. doi:10.1002/9781118386194.ch8

Kaplan, R. S. (2001). Strategic performance measurement and management in nonprofit organizations. *Nonprofit Management & Leadership*, *11*(3), 353–370. doi:10.1002/nml.11308

Khatun, F., & Hasan, M. (2016). Human Resource Management in Social Enterprises: A Study on BRAC. *European Journal of Economics Law and Politics*, *3*(2), 37–57.

Kickul, J., & Lyons, T. S. (2012). *Understanding Social Entrepreneurship: The Relentless Pursuit of Mission in an Ever Changing World*. New York, NY: Routledge.

Leadbeater, C. (1997). *The rise of the social entrepreneur*. London: Demos.

Lee, Y. J., & Wilkins, V. M. (2011). More similarities or more differences? Comparing public and nonprofit managers' job motivations. *Public Administration Review*, *71*(1), 45–56. doi:10.1111/j.1540-6210.2010.02305.x

Light, P. C. (2002). The content of their character: The state of the nonprofit workforce. *The Nonprofit Quarterly*, *9*(3), 6–16.

Lynn, D. B. (2003). Symposium: Human resource management in nonprofit organizations. *Review of Public Personnel Administration*, *23*(2), 91–96. doi:10.1177/0734371X03023002001

Lyons, S., & Kuron, L. (2014). Generational differences in the workplace: A review of the evidence and directions for future research. *Journal of Organizational Behavior*, *35*(S1), 139–157. doi:10.1002/job.1913

Mair, J., & Marti, I. (2004). *Social Entrepreneurship: What Are We Talking about? A Framework for Future Research*. Barcelona: IESE, University of Navarra.

Millar, R., & Hall, K. (2013). Social return on investment (SROI) and performance measurement: The opportunities and barriers for social enterprises in health and social care. *Public Management Review*, *15*(6), 923–941. doi:10.1080/14719037.2012.698857

Nicholls, A. (2010). The functions of performance measurement in social entrepreneurship: control, planning and accountability. In K. Hockerts, J. Mair, & J. Robinson (Eds.), *Values and opportunities in social entrepreneurship* (pp. 241–272). New York: Palgrave. doi:10.1057/9780230298026_13

Nicholls, A., & Cho, A. H. (2006). Social entrepreneurship: The structuration of a field. In A. Nicholls (Ed.), *Social entrepreneurship: New models of sustainable social change* (pp. 99–118). Oxford, UK: Oxford University Press.

Noe, R. A., Hollenbeck, J. R., Gerhart, B., & Wright, P. M. (2016). *Fundamentals of human resource management* (6th ed.). Boston, MA: McGraw-Hill/Irwin.

Nyssens, M. (2006). *Social Enterprise at the Crossroads of Market, Public Policies and Civil Society*. London: Routledge.

Ohana, M., & Meyer, M. (2010). Should I stay or should I go now? Investigating the intention to quit of the permanent staff in social enterprises. *European Management Journal*, *28*(6), 441–454. doi:10.1016/j.emj.2010.06.007

Onyx, J., & Maclean, M. (1996). Careers in the third sector. *Nonprofit Management & Leadership*, *6*(4), 331–345. doi:10.1002/nml.4130060404

Parente, C., Lopes, A., & Marcos, V. (2014). Social Entrepreneurship Profiles: Lessons from Organizational and Management Dynamics. *Journal of Social Entrepreneurship*, *5*(1), 22–41. doi:10.1080/19420676.2013.820782

Pynes, J. E. (2013). *Human resources management for public and nonprofit organizations: A strategic approach* (3rd ed.). San Francisco, CA: Jossey Bass.

Ridder, H.-G., & McCandless, A. (2010). Influences on the architecture of human resource management in nonprofit organizations: An analytical framework. *Nonprofit and Voluntary Sector Quarterly*, *39*(1), 124–141. doi:10.1177/0899764008328182

Robinson, A., & Klein, K. (2007). *Selling Social Change (Without Selling Out): Earned Income Strategies for Nonprofits*. San Francisco, CA: Jossey-Bass.

Rogovsky, N. (2000). *Corporate community involvement programmes: Partnerships for jobs and development*. International Institute for Labour Studies.

Royce, M. (2007). Using human resource management tools to support social enterprise: Emerging themes from the sector. *Social Enterprise Journal*, *3*(1), 10–19. doi:10.1108/17508610780000718

Spear, R. (2002). *National Profiles of Work Integration Social Enterprises*. EMES European Research Network.

Spear, R., & Bidet, E. (2005). Social enterprise for work integration in 12 European countries: A descriptive analysis. *Annals of Public and Cooperative Economics*, *76*(2), 195–231. doi:10.1111/j.1370-4788.2005.00276.x

Sullivan Mort, G., Weerawardena, J., & Carnegie, K. (2003). Social entrepreneurship: Towards conceptualization. *International Journal of Nonprofit and Voluntary Sector Marketing*, *8*(1), 76–88. doi:10.1002/nvsm.202

Understanding Human Resource Challenges in the Indian Social Enterprise Sector. (2012). Retrieved from http://intellecap.com/sites/default/files/publications/intel lecap_hr_report_web_0.pdf

Vaidyanathan, M. M., Chatterjee, S., Murthy, M. S. S., & Naswa, M. T. (2014). *Talent Infusion in Social Enterprise*. Retrieved from http://niiticonsulting.com/pdf/talent%20infusion%20paper%201.pdf

Van Vuuren, M., de Jong, M. D., & Seydel, E. R. (2008). Commitment with or without a stick of paid work: Comparison of paid and unpaid workers in a nonprofit organization. *European Journal of Work and Organizational Psychology*, *17*(3), 315–326. doi:10.1080/13594320701693175

von Eckardstein, D., & Brandl, J. (2004). Human resource management in nonprofit organizations. In A. Zimmer & E. Priller (Eds.), *Future of civil society: Making Central European nonprofitorganizations work* (pp. 297–314). Wiesbaden: VS Verlag fur Sozialwissenschaften. doi:10.1007/978-3-322-80980-3_17

Waddock, S. A., & Post, J. E. (1991). Social entrepreneurs and catalytic change. *Public Administration Review*, *51*(5), 393–407. doi:10.2307/976408

Walk, M., & Kennedy, T. (2017In press). Making Nonprofits more Effective: Performance Management and Performance Appraisals. In J. K. A. Word & J. E. Sowa (Eds.), *The Nonprofit Human Resource Management Handbook: From Theory to Practice*. New York, NY: Routledge.

Weerawardena, J., & Mort, G. S. (2006). Investigating social entrepreneurship: A multidimensional model. *Journal of World Business*, *41*(1), 21–35. doi:10.1016/j.jwb.2005.09.001

Woolley, J. L. (2014). Opportunities for Social Value Creation Across Supply Chain Interactions. In L. Pate & C. Wankel (Eds.), *Emerging Research Directions in Social Entrepreneurship* (pp. 51–66). Springer. doi:10.1007/978-94-007-7896-2_4

ADDITIONAL READING

Akingbola, K. (2006). Strategy and HRM in nonprofit organizations: Evidence from Canada. *International Journal of Human Resource Management*, *17*(10), 1707–1725. doi:10.1080/09585190600964350

Akingbola, K. (2015). *Managing human resources for nonprofits*. New York, NY: Routledge.

Austin, M. J., Regan, K., Samples, M. W., Schwartz, S. L., & Carnochan, S. (2011). Building managerial and organizational capacity in non-profit human service organizations through a leadership development program. *Administration in Social Work*, *35*(3), 258–281. doi:10.1080/03643107.2011.575339

Baluch, A. M. (2017). Employee perceptions of HRM and well-being in nonprofit organizations: Unpacking the unintended. *International Journal of Human Resource Management*, *28*(14), 1912–1937. doi:10.1080/09585192.2015.1136672

Ban, C., Drahnak-Faller, A., & Towers, M. (2003). Human resource challenges in human service and community development organizations: Recruitment and retention of professional staff. *Review of Public Personnel Administration*, *23*(2), 133–153. doi:10.1177/0734371X03023002004

Borzaga, C., & Defourny, J. (Eds.). (2001). *The Emergence of Social Enterprise*. London: Routledge.

Burke, R. J., & Cooper, C. L. (Eds.). (2012). *Human resource management in the nonprofit sector: passion, purpose and professionalism*. Edward Elgar Publishing. doi:10.4337/9780857937308

Guo, C., Brown, W. A., Ashcraft, R. F., Yoshioka, C. F., & Dong, H. K. D. (2011). Strategic human resources management in nonprofit organizations. *Review of Public Personnel Administration, 31*(3), 248–269. doi:10.1177/0734371X11402878

Khatun, F., & Hasan, M. (2016). Human Resource Management in Social Enterprises: A Study on BRAC. *European Journal of Economics Law and Politics, 3*(2), 37–57.

Kickul, J., & Lyons, T. S. (2012). *Understanding Social Entrepreneurship: The Relentless Pursuit of Mission in an Ever Changing World*. New York, NY: Routledge.

Lynn, D. B. (2003). Symposium: Human resource management in nonprofit organizations. *Review of Public Personnel Administration, 23*(2), 91–96. doi:10.1177/0734371X03023002001

Ohana, M., & Meyer, M. (2010). Should I stay or should I go now? Investigating the intention to quit of the permanent staff in social enterprises. *European Management Journal, 28*(6), 441–454. doi:10.1016/j.emj.2010.06.007

Pynes, J. E. (2013). *Human resources management for public and nonprofit organizations: A strategic approach* (3rd ed.). San Francisco, CA: Jossey Bass.

Ridder, H.-G., & McCandless, A. (2010). Influences on the architecture of human resource management in nonprofit organizations: An analytical framework. *Nonprofit and Voluntary Sector Quarterly, 39*(1), 124–141. doi:10.1177/0899764008328182

Royce, M. (2007). Using human resource management tools to support social enterprise: Emerging themes from the sector. *Social Enterprise Journal, 3*(1), 10–19. doi:10.1108/17508610780000718

Van Vuuren, M., de Jong, M. D., & Seydel, E. R. (2008). Commitment with or without a stick of paid work: Comparison of paid and unpaid workers in a nonprofit organization. *European Journal of Work and Organizational Psychology, 17*(3), 315–326. doi:10.1080/13594320701693175

Volkmann, K., Tokarski, K. O., & Ernst, K. (Eds.). (2012). *Social Entrepreneurship and Social Business*. Wiesbaden: Springer Gabler. doi:10.1007/978-3-8349-7093-0

KEY TERMS AND DEFINITIONS

Career Management: A practice of human resources management that prepare employees to meet future organizational needs with adequate career development.

Compensation Management: A practice of human resources management including strategic decisions about pay levels, pay structures, and incentive pay systems which influence the ability of an organization to compete in the marketplace to attract the most qualified and competent applicants and retain its most talented and productive employees.

Human Resources Management: A discipline of formal systems design in organizations in order to ensure the effective use of employees' knowledge, skills, abilities, and other characteristics to accomplish organizational goals.

Performance Management: Practice of human resources management including all the activities, systems and processes that are deployed to enable and support employees to contribute the maximum of their knowledge, skills and abilities to the organization.

Recruitment: A practice of human resources management which includes the process of attracting qualified candidates to apply for vacant positions within an organization.

Social Enterprise: Organizations that are driven by a social mission and seeking business solutions to social problems with an explicit aim to benefit the community.

Training: A practice of human resources management encompassing design and implementation of orientation programs and training activities to meet the needs of staff for making them to acquire necessary skills.

Volunteer: Person who gives service without any income expectation on voluntary basis, for a variety of reasons such as learning new skills, self-development, enhancing self-esteem, preparing for a career, expressing personal values and community commitment.

Chapter 9
The Social Expat-Preneur:
Examining a Growing International Career Model Supporting Global Social Entrepreneurship

Charles M. Vance
Loyola Marymount University, USA

Rebecca Bergin
Loyola Marymount University, USA

ABSTRACT

Social entrepreneurship extends beyond home country borders as individuals seek to find meaning and share passion with the world. The globalization of corporations and individuals has resulted in a surge in expatriate social entrepreneurs. These individuals have broken down barriers to pursue a passion and increase social awareness around the globe. This chapter describes an international career model of five different forms of expatriate social entrepreneurs or "social expat-preneurs" within the broader international career construct of self-initiated expatriates—(1) pre-departure, (2) transitioned, (3) retired senior, (4) avocation-driven, and (5) social expat-intrapreneur—with vivid examples of each form. This chapter also outlines benefits to host countries and examines the importance of further research.

INTRODUCTION

Organizations of all sizes are recognizing and exploiting opportunities for expansion abroad, facilitated by our overall global general trend of increasing international collaborations, global mobility, advancements in telecommunications, and growing variety and attractiveness of government-promoted incentives that encourage foreign direct investment, (Collings, 2014). Parallel with this international expansion is an increasing recognition among organizations and their many stakeholders of the imperative of corporate governance at home and abroad that is in line with principles of sustainability, or the triple bottom line (Stenzel, 2010; Norman & MacDonald, 2004; Gupta & Vegelin, 2016).

DOI: 10.4018/978-1-5225-5687-9.ch009

With their eye on their financial bottom line, international corporations in their foreign locations are increasingly developing their own social responsibility initiatives as well as partnering with both the private and nonprofit sectors to also address social and environmental needs (Gonzalez-Perez & Leonard, 2013). Within this global sustainability movement, social entrepreneurship is increasingly seen as a major driver in identifying opportunities to solve or mitigate pressing social and environmental needs, and in developing new social entrepreneurial ventures of many varieties to implement plans for addressing those needs (Stenn, 2017). And these social entrepreneurship efforts are being instigated by entrepreneurs found in nonprofit, public, and private sectors. According to Konda, Starc, and Rodica (2015),

It is not surprising that social entrepreneurship is becoming increasingly important. Social entrepreneurship is a process, a logic of action, which can take place in different organisational contexts: a charity, a commercial organisation, a government organisation, a community organisation, or through a new venture.

The above continued international business and attendant social entrepreneurship expansion provide an increasing array of attractive opportunities for individuals who wish to work in foreign environments and thereby develop valuable global competencies (Vance, 2005). Research suggests that despite their active international expansion abroad, organizations generally fall short in helping their employees develop these valuable competencies. With this realization, individuals increasingly are assuming greater responsibility for advancing their global competence development and international careers (Inkson & Arthur, 2001). This shift from a traditional company-directed effort to a more individualized focus in employee career and professional development has received growing attention in recent literature related to self-initiated expatriates (SIEs) who travel abroad on their own initiative (McNulty & Vance, 2017). Or while they are already working abroad, many individuals self-initiate into new working arrangements in their effort to support themselves as well as ultimately build global career capital (Doherty, Richardson, & Thorn, 2013; McNulty & Vance, 2017). Here we distinguish SIEs from migrants who depart from or even flee their home country primarily motivated by economic and/or socio-political necessity (Haug, 2008). We also here distinguish SIEs from those typically of a younger age who are motivated to travel abroad more by curiosity and the compelling attraction of adventure than by professional career advancement considerations (Inkson & Myers, 2003).

SIEs are rather entrepreneurial in nature and tend to be undaunted by occupational and organizational constraints, desiring to have maximum influence on their own international career progression and direction rather than to be dependent upon organizations, and vulnerable to capricious decision-making and politics (Andresen, Al Ariss & Walther, 2012). Although many SIEs secure employment with local organizations based in the host country or with local operations of multinational organizations, a growing number become involved in new venture operations or begin their own new ventures, whether profit or nonprofit (McNulty & Vance, 2017).

In this chapter, we first will examine SIEs who become expatriate entrepreneurs or "expat-preneurs" in their new host country environments. We then will identify a segment of expat-preneurs who have significant engagement in social entrepreneurial activities. Based on our review of the literature and our own professional experience, we then will begin to classify these "social expat-preneurs" into various distinct career categories. This social expat-preneur career conceptual framework development is an important early step in improving our understanding, and for guiding future field research about significant players behind the growing number of initiatives in social entrepreneurship who are greatly fomenting and supporting the global sustainability movement.

SIEs AS EXPAT-PRENEURS

A primary motive of SIEs for going abroad is to gain cross-cultural competencies that ultimately will facilitate their personal growth and professional career development (Vaiman, Haslberger & Vance, 2015; Vance & McNulty, 2014). SIEs recognize that as organizations strive to compete in an increasingly integrated and global marketplace, they are placing a greater premium on global leadership competence in guiding their talent pool recruitment (Brookfield Global Relocation Services, 2016). Leading international firms understand that individuals who identify with multiple nationalities or have significant international experience are more effective problem solvers and demonstrate more creativity than their peers who have remained in a domestic context (Maddux, Galinsky & Tadmor, 2010). With their significant and meaningful international experience, SIEs therefore recognize that they are well positioned in their future career advancement to take advantage of this increased appetite for global leadership talent.

With their view of themselves as being largely in control of the pace and direction of their careers, SIEs have a decidedly entrepreneurial mindset. They perceive, plan, and execute their careers. In taking initiative to advance their international career development, SIEs normally choose between two primary paths: (1) move under their own initiative to a new country and seek job opportunities with local firms or international firms in the local environment (Vance, 2005); or (2) as a former company-assigned expatriate, remain in the host country to seek new employment, either in another traditional company-assigned expatriate position or a in new business opportunity. One recent field study determined that greater than 40% of former company-assigned expatriates elected to leave their firm upon the completion of their assignment and pursue new professional employment prospects in the same host country (McNulty, De Cieri, & Hutchings, 2013).

As previously mentioned, SIEs may obtain work opportunities in a foreign country with established organizations, such as larger multinational corporations (MNCs) and locally-based firms, as well as local organizations of all sizes in the public and nonprofit sectors. Field research by Vance & McNulty (2014) on careers of current expatriates—broadly defined as all those "ex patria" (out of their home country) and employed in a different country for an extended amount of time—noted that most of the SIEs were employed by small local companies, and they frequently were involved in entrepreneurial roles and activities associated with new business development, including establishing new business ventures with local host country partners. Often when unable to obtain local employment with established organizations, these SIEs begin to pursue self-employment and new venture partnership opportunities to legally and financially support their international experience abroad in their chosen host country.

Here we distinguish these SIE entrepreneurs or expat-preneurs from self-employed migrants, who tend to be low-skilled and leave their home country due to economic and socio-political crises (Haug, 2008). These migrant "necessity entrepreneurs" frequently resort to entrepreneurial activities because discrimination from local citizens or their lack of marketable skills or both prevent them from obtaining traditional employment in the new host country. In comparison, expat-preneurs generally have higher-level, marketable professional skills that are sought after in the local host country. These expat-preneurs also often fit the description of "opportunity entrepreneurs" —those who recognize and pursue an attractive opportunity in the local marketplace, whether they identified the opportunity before leaving their home country or after arrival, or recognized the opportunity while they were completing a traditional MNC-assigned expatriate assignment in the host country (Borozan & Pfeifer, 2014). Although this distinction between SIE entrepreneurs and self-employed migrants is controversial (for example, see Andresen, Bergdolt, Margenfeld, & Dickmann, 2014), particularly among highly-skilled migrants who are very entrepreneurial by nature (e.g., "immigrant entrepreneurs," Saxenian, 2002; Kloosterman & Rath, 2001), our conceptualization of expat-preneurs makes a major distinction from self-employed migrants based on McNulty and Brewster's (2017) characterization of migrants (including immigrant entrepreneurs) as exiting their home country on a permanent basis, and many with the conscious goal of attaining citizenship in the new country (Zolin & Schlosser 2013; Al Ariss & Syed 2011; Al Ariss & Ozbilgin 2010; Castles & Miller 2009), being motivated primarily by the push of perceived socio-political and economic necessity (Saxenian 2002; Khosa & Kalitanyi, 2015). From this general perspective, migrants do not perceive their new environment as a "host country" that is providing a temporary home and location for employment, but rather view the host country as becoming their new home country. SIEs on the other hand, including expat-preneurs, generally perceive their new working and living environment as temporary or at least indefinite, and do not immediately consider the host country as their new permanent home.

Expat-preneurs demonstrate classic behavioral traits and characteristics of entrepreneurs who pursue independent work, with their strong entrepreneurial intent, internal locus of control, high self-efficacy, flexibility, proactive personality, and inclination to forge ahead despite the presence of uncertainty and risk (Yan 2010; Prabhu, McGuire, Drost & Kwong 2012). However, unlike other SIEs who travel abroad by their own agency and resourcefulness and eventually obtain work in the host country with an MNC or locally-based organization (Suutari & Brewster 2000), expat-preneurs early begin to engage in discovering local host country opportunities and initiating their own independent business developments efforts, or by engaging in new venture development activities with local partners that address local environment demand and business needs (Zahra & George 2002).

According to Vance et al. (2016), expat-preneurs are increasing their involvement in host country new venture opportunities, whether these opportunities were anticipated before moving abroad (classified as "pre-departure expat-preneurs"), or after moving to the foreign location (termed "transitioned expat-preneurs") when they recognize new venture opportunities and begin to pursue them and engage in entrepreneurial activity for self-employment. Unlike migrant necessity entrepreneurs who typically have little economic choice and are constrained into entrepreneurial employment for self-support, expat-preneurs as "opportunity entrepreneurs" generally have more options and greater flexibility to allow new venture exploration. Their typically higher and more marketable skills are used in observing the local environment, and in recognizing, pursuing, and exploiting local opportunities while also potentially making greater local economic contributions (Block & Wagner 2010; Deli 2011; Borozan & Pfeifer 2014). As previously mentioned, unlike permanent displacement-oriented migrants, these expat-preneurs typically intend to return to their home countries at some future time (Zolin & Schlosser, 2013; Castles & Miller, 2009). Many even anticipate eventually expanding their business development interests between their original home country and the new host country, a counterpart to the traditional brain gain and brain drain characterizations more recently referred to as "brain circulation" (Tung, 2008).

As mentioned previously, whereas some expat-preneurs decide to move abroad with no premeditation and eventually find employment with host country firms that recognize and value their expertise to support new entrepreneurial initiatives for company growth, both at home and abroad, others move abroad with a preconceived entrepreneurial motive. The premeditated approach of these pre-departure expat-preneurs, either through a traditional expatriate assignment or on their own, allows them to plan for and then pursue their predetermined, specific new venture idea in a host country. Using their own financial resources and personal connections to establish a new venture, many pre-departure expat-preneurs are motivated by the opportunity to introduce new products or services into fertile, untapped markets. On the other hand, post-departure transitioned expat-preneurs begin to pursue a new expat-preneur career path in the host country merely by chance and without pre-departure anticipation, or they do so because of exigency related to unanticipated professional or personal circumstances (Vance, McNulty, Paik, & D'Mello, 2016). Many post-departure expat-preneurs are SIEs who originally traveled to the foreign country with the plan to obtain local employment either with an MNC or a local employer. Even after obtaining employment with a local firm, these entrepreneurial SIEs often eventually cast off on their own, alone or with a local partner, to create new ventures. As previously mentioned, they also can be professionals who complete their expatriate assignment or leave their international positions at MNCs in midstream, and shift to roles as entrepreneurs in their adopted host country.

Whether their recognition to develop an entrepreneurial career abroad occurs before they leave their home country, during their foreign stay, or upon the completion of a traditional MNC expatriate assignment may depend upon various factors, such as the SIE's personality (Baron, Tang & Hmieleski 2011), degree of social and capital resources available (Davidsson & Honig 2003), their aptitude for opportunity recognition in the local host country (Baron 2006), and their appetite for and tendency toward risk taking (Hayward, Forster, Sarasvathy & Fredrickson 2010). A particularly notable factor is that personal life circumstances and social relationships often drive the decision by expat-preneurs to remain in the host country for the longer term, such as with a marriage to a local citizen who desires not to leave the expat-preneur's initially-perceived temporary host country environment (see Vance & McNulty, 2014). This expatriate therefore may unexpectedly become an "accidental entrepreneur" (Lewin, 1998), and seek some form of new venture self-employment to provide financial support for legally and economically remaining in the host country, especially if he or she is treated as an outsider and not able to break into the local business labor market to obtain suitable employment.

Vance et al (2017) describe the experience of one former American expatriate who had worked for a U.S.-based MNC in South Korea, during which time he had married a local Korean woman who preferred to remain in her home country. At the termination of his expatriate assignment and facing repatriation to his company headquarters in New Jersey, this expatriate decided to follow his wife's wishes, leaving his American firm and remaining in South Korea to obtain local employment. However, perceiving that he had few local professional connections and feeling like an outsider with great difficulty in being hired, he eventually chose to take advantage of his considerable experience and professional communication skills to launch his own consulting firm, where he now coaches local Korean executives in their personal English communications and in optimizing their organizational communications efforts. Thus, such strong personal ties in the local host country environment may contribute social and human capital resources available to the expat-preneur, as well as provide a strong incentive to engage in new venture opportunity recognition.

SOCIAL EXPAT-PRENEURS

Although globalization has brought many benefits, millions still struggle with poverty, disease, pollution, and other social challenges. The ever-growing globalization trend has forced many to rethink the way we address social and environmental problems around the world, and efforts aimed at improvement have come from the private (i.e., for-profit), public, and nonprofit sectors alike. Bornstein and Davis (2010) describe social entrepreneurship as a process by which individual leaders, through their own agency, build or transform institutions to advance solutions to social problems, such as poverty, illness, illiteracy, environmental degradation, human rights abuses, and corruption. These individuals are social entrepreneurs, and their agendas can be both focused within a domestic context as well as transnational. Often the drive to bring about change leads these social entrepreneurs to make an impact on individuals, communities, and environments in international locations. These expatriate social entrepreneurs or "social expat-preneurs" who venture abroad to apply their social entrepreneurial energies and implement their visions are active and high-achieving citizens of the global sustainability movement who shape the world through an endeavor that balances the quest for profit or financial viability with social and environmental betterment (Munoz, 2010). Thus, the convergence of globalization and increased commitment toward corporate social responsibility and sustainability (whether intrinsically or extrinsically motivated) has contributed to the growth of this particular class of SIEs and expat-preneurs, individuals going abroad of their own accord and eventually starting social entrepreneurship ventures.

The concept of corporate social responsibility ("CSR"), or the idea that businesses should be responsible for their impact on society, has become widely accepted (Barkemeyer & Glavas, 2016). Although the concept of social entrepreneurship is in line with CSR, a key difference is that social entrepreneurs begin their efforts with a desire to make a social impact, while CSR is a general concept that is not limited to businesses that began with a social focus. Rather it may also include a business that has recently implemented a CSR function to reverse actual or perceived harm committed by the company itself.

A social expat-preneur differs from a traditional expat-preneur in terms of purpose. Traditional entrepreneurs (expatriates or not) derive their mission from the general desire to create something that solves an existing problem, and in most cases the innovation is focused on financial profitability. For social entrepreneurs, the heart of their mission is to bring needed change to society. Although social entrepreneurs are often identified within the nonprofit sector, even entrepreneurs leading for-profit organizations can center their innovative efforts and newly directed energies upon social good and environmental protection (Choi & Gray, 2010). Such private sector social entrepreneurs use a business venture as the vehicle in which change is brought about. In a recent field study of private-sector expat-preneurs in Europe by Vance et al. (2017), many of the interviewees cited social reasons as a core contributor to their decision to start a business abroad. These social expat-preneurs felt a drive to improve the quality of life in their chosen location, and they made positive social impact an important priority of their business mission.

Social expat-preneurs come from a variety of backgrounds and international contexts, yet all are committed to the greater good and sustainability of our global society. Building upon social entrepreneur typology construction work as provided by Zahra, Gedajlovic, Neubaum and Shulman (2009), and based on our review of the literature and our own personal experiences abroad, we have identified five different yet often interrelated categories of social expat-preneurs: (1) pre-departure; (2) transitioned; (3) retired senior; (4) avocation-driven; and (5) social expat-intrapreneur (see Figure 1). We now will examine each of these categories in more detail, with one or more graphic illustrations for each category.

Figure 1. Categories of social expat-preneurs

1. **Pre-Departure**: Has identified a social entrepreneurial venture before leaving the home country.
2. **Transitioned**: Worked as a traditional expatriate in the host country before terminating the assignment and becoming engaged in a new social venture.
3. **Retired Senior**: Retired from previous professional career and has become engaged in social entrepreneurship either on a full or part-time basis in the host country.
4. **Avocation-Driven**: An expatriate with current regular employment (e.g., in the for-profit sector) who is engaged in a new social entrepreneurial venture development and ongoing activities on the side.
5. **Social Expat-Intrapreneur**: A volunteer or regular employee within a nonprofit organization involved in addressing environmental and social challenges, and who exercises entrepreneurial orientation and initiative to bring innovation and improvements, and to pursue new ventures opportunities from within larger structure of the organization.

Pre-Departure

As with other pre-departure expat-preneurs, pre-departure social expat-preneurs intend to have a positive impact and make a difference in an international context before moving abroad. This category is commonly comprised of young idealistic people venturing abroad during or immediately following university studies or high school graduation. These individuals may go abroad on their own or through the sponsorship of any of a multitude of international humanitarian and service volunteer organizations. Pearl S. Buck, the Pulitzer Prize winner and author of *The Good Earth,* spent her early years in China as the daughter of very entrepreneurial American missionaries who spent much of their time building social and educational support systems. Buck also later served as a missionary in China as well, marrying a missionary who focused his social entrepreneurial service on agricultural economics.

Pre-departure social expat-preneurs also may be found in the private sector, venturing abroad with a strong focus in their work on social entrepreneurial objectives. For example, Alice Johnston grew up in Texas and attended Syracuse University in the mid 1980's. Seeking to create a new beginning, she decided to move to Italy to put down roots. After starting and running several businesses in Italy, Johnston settled on the island of Sardinia. As Italy was facing a huge recession in the late 2000's, she witnessed her beautiful island being destroyed. Real estate developers had abandoned projects underway when the real estate boom died. This situation Sardinia covered in half-finished projects and with a workforce facing no work demand. Searching for a sustainable income for the island, Johnston noticed the local proliferation of oak trees. As a child in Texas, she remembered using acorns to create flour for baking. She knew the acorn nut had value. Upon further research, Johnston realized that the acorn cap also held value for its use in leather tanneries. She recognized an opportunity to help get the Sardinian population back to work while at the same time protecting the oak trees and environmental sustainability of her island home. With the assistance of a successful Kickstarter campaign, Johnston founded the Sardinian Acorn Action. Her creativity, vision and passion for change created sustainable, environmental friendly work in her community.

Transitioned

The transitioned social expat-preneur typically is someone located in a foreign environment and engaged in some form of employment without a social entrepreneurial focus, such as a person on assignment with a MNC. At some point this individual decided to change from the past forms of work and focus more or even completely in social entrepreneurship ventures. For example, Charles McJilton had an earlier career in the U.S. military, working in various parts of Asia, including Japan. At some point, Charles decided to leave this military service career, and after considerable self-reflection, including spending a significant amount of time living among the homeless in Japan, decided to form a special food supply nonprofit venture, Second Harvest Japan, to serve those individuals in the larger Tokyo area who somehow were missed by Japan's existing social safety net.

Kiersten Pilar Miller is another example of a transitioned social expat-preneur, but this time remaining within her original private sector context. She moved to Rome on assignment with the Home Box Office (HBO) series "Rome." She fell in love with the city and wanted to remain in Rome following the assignment. During this time, her daughter was born. She soon realized how few resources there were for expatriate mothers like herself. Miller opened The Milk Bar in Rome in 2009 as a store, serving as a meeting place and information point for helpful guidance about pregnancy, breastfeeding, and motherhood. But she didn't stop there. As her customers began telling her heartbreaking stories of their experiences giving birth in hospitals abroad, she was inspired to expand her business to address the local social need of bringing education services to the birthing process, and setting worldwide standards for the quality of care during childbirth. The aim of her new online education entity, Bellies Abroad, is to provide expatriates with the very best information, and to direct them to quality medical care at fair prices and with a support system to match. The business further expanded when Ms. Pilar Miller brought on a co-founder, Swedish Expat-preneur Jennie Sili. Bellies Abroad gives parents and parents-to-be the confidence and information they need to have the birth and parenthood experiences they are looking for, instead of what is easiest for hospital staff and what is most lucrative for medical professionals. As of publication, Bellies Abroad had recently been honored to be accepted into the Fellowship of the Laudato Si Challenge, a social entrepreneurship challenge inspired by Pope Francis.

Retired Senior

We are currently witnessing a growing global phenomenon of baby-boomer retirement. In the U.S., those of 55 years and older, who comprised 26.5 percent of the civilian non-institutional population in 1990, is estimated to become 39.4 percent in 2050. The percentage of those 65 years and older also is expected to increase, with the percentage of those under 25 years expected to decrease. In fact, the 65-years-and-older civilian non-institutional population is expected to steadily grow, increasing its representation in the population from 15.5 percent in 2005 to 25.3 percent in 2050 (Toosi, 2012; 2006). This trend continues beyond the U.S.: by 2050, in all major regions of the world other than Africa, it is anticipated that nearly one-quarter or more of the population will be 60 years or over. The current potential support ratio (PSR), defined as the number of people aged between 20 and 64 for every person 65 years or older, varies among countries. Asian countries have PSRs of 8.0 (although Japan at 2.1 has the lowest PSR in the world), while Europe's PSR is 3.5. But by 2050, seven Asian countries and 25 European countries are projected to have PSRs below 2.0 (United Nations, 2015).

Particularly in wealthier Western countries, this growing global "silver tsunami" trend is generating an increasing number of individuals with relatively good health, longevity, education, and financial independence. Many of these individuals have the personal interest, disposition, and financial resources, even more than previous generations, to support their meaningful part-time or even temporary full-time work as volunteers with NGOs and nonprofit organizations dedicated to addressing social and environmental needs (Myers, Inkson & Pringle, 2017; Einolf, 2009). Thus, we are witnessing an increase of individuals from this older category interested in serving as volunteers abroad to support nonprofit organizations in social charitable and environmental causes in less-developed economies (Lasker, 2016). In these new foreign environments, these senior citizens of the world have the potential to exercise their entrepreneurial tendencies to bring helpful innovations to the existing NGO and other nonprofit organizations where they serve, as well as recognize social entrepreneurship opportunities and develop new social entrepreneurship ventures of their own.

A significant cause of this movement of older individuals from wealthier to less-developed countries, particularly among retirees, is the more favorable economic environment presented by the lower cost of living in these foreign countries (Hayes, 2014). The displacement of these retired individuals, with extra time on their hands and a dispositions toward altruism and giving back to the global community, places them in a positions to volunteer and serve locally, and in many cases exercise their entrepreneurial tendencies to become at least part-time social entrepreneurs. Joseph O'Haver is an example of this retired senior form of social expat-preneur. Educated in Arizona and spending a large portion of his career in social work in Arizona before starting his own consulting company in Florida, Joe made and befriended a professional acquaintance from Nicaragua, who eventually convinced Joe and his wife Beverly, upon their retirement, to move down to the attractive country community of Granada in Nicaragua, about 50 kilometers from the capital city of Managua. Lower cost of living was somewhat of a consideration in their decision to move to Nicaragua, but a greater attraction was the opportunity to add adventure into their retirement with an opportunity to live outside of the U.S. While there Joe has recognized the need for added educational opportunities for young people in his area to promote their future career and life opportunity success, and on a part-time basis, approximately three half-days per week, he has established a regular no-cost English language instruction program for local young people. He and Beverly also have expanded their volunteerism into working with an arts/music school based in Granada, serving children who otherwise would not be exposed to those aspects in their education.

Avocation-Driven

Some professionals serving abroad on traditional expatriate assignments, particularly in less-developed countries, are often exposed to social and environmental challenges that are much more apparent to them than to locals who have become very accustomed to the conditions in their own home country. Although many of these traditional expatriates focus only upon their relatively sheltered life within the support structure of their multinational corporation, others desire to get involved in community projects to help address local needs. They engage in this meaningful activity through volunteering their time and skilled services for local charities, fundraising, or even starting new ventures on the side that address these social or environmental needs. In some cases, these social entrepreneurs who provide their service as a part-time side avocation decide to leave their traditional expatriate assignment and become full-time social entrepreneurs in the local environment, totally dedicating their efforts to building their social entrepreneurial ventures (Fraser, 2013).

Avocation-driven expat-preneurs also may venture abroad with the sole purpose of starting a social venture. After learning of the poverty, sickness, and fear that is the reality in the lives of many children in Uganda, Jeami Duncan traveled as a self-initiated expatriate from her home in California to the Gulu region of northern Uganda in search of a way to help. After immersing herself in the culture, she learned that one of the community's greatest needs was access to education. Jeami founded Mercy's Village International, with a mission to ensure that underprivileged children have access to a quality education, regardless of ethnicity, socioeconomic background, or circumstances. Mercy's Village International opened their first school in 2009 with 65 students, and has grown to 6 classrooms with 215 students. Now in more of a flexpatriate work and lifestyle arrangement (Mayerhofer, Müller & Schmidt, 2010), Jeami oversees of her work in Uganda on a part-time basis, with regular trips to Uganda from her job and home in California.

Social Expat-Intrapreneur

Some often overlooked yet very important entrepreneurs in the for-profit sector are "intrapreneurs," recognized leaders or even revolutionaries in their organization who identify and persuade the large corporation to pursue a new opportunity or direction of strategic importance to the organization (Park, Kim & Krishna, 2014). And with large NGOs and charitable organizations there are social intrapreneurs who develop and lead new ventures from within the larger framework of the organization. These special internal social entrepreneurs have existed since the beginning of these nonprofit organizations, providing support and innovative ideas to enhance their growth and impact.

There likely will be a significant increase of social expat-intrapreneurs as the ranks of global volunteerism continues to grow, as was mentioned before. These individuals, from within the support structures of large NGOs and other nonprofit organizations, will exercise their entrepreneurial orientations in finding new opportunities for innovation and improvement to better meet current environmental and social service objectives, and to expand the organization's reach to other target challenges of social entrepreneurship.

A powerful example of such social expat-intrapreneurs is Mother Teresa, who also at a very early age was a pre-departure social entrepreneur who desired to travel abroad to serve the needs of the poor, sick, and needy. From within the huge global structure of the Roman Catholic Church she eventually moved to India, and in 1950, after recognizing a clear need in Calcutta, with the Vatican's blessing established a new venture that would become the Missionaries of Charity. By 1997 the initial 13-member Calcutta group had grown to more than 4,000 sisters who managed charity centers, orphanages, and AIDS hospices worldwide, caring for the poor, blind, homeless, refugees, disabled, aged dying, alcoholics, and victims of epidemics, floods, and famine (Spink, 1997).

Other social expat-intrapreneurs may be found working in more traditional foreign assignments with multinational firms. These multinational organizations, at least partly due to high local institutional pressures and public relations initiatives to measure and demonstrate CSR activities and impact, are encouraging their employees, including their expatriates, to identify opportunities and create ventures within the multinational corporate umbrella to assist with sustainability and CSR efforts (Pedersen & Gwozdz, 2014).

Employment within the CSR function of a multinational corporation may interest those individuals interested in social entrepreneurship as a way to gain knowledge and training under corporate support before venturing out to start their own business. By implementing policies that allow for training and support of CSR-focused employees, it may be possible for MNCs to retain these talented individuals to help within the company when the next social challenge arises.

DISCUSSION

McHenry and Welch (2017) point out that the internationalization of corporations is perhaps led by the internationalization of individuals—individual knowledge acquisition and motivation of the key leader or leaders are fundamental to the future internationalization of the corporation. In a similar fashion, the global expansion of needed social entrepreneurship contributing to improved global sustainability is likely greatly dependent upon the development of international career orientations of individual entrepreneurs dedicated to addressing pressing social and environmental needs abroad, as well as in the domestic context.

In this chapter, we have examined and distinguished different career types or roles of individual expatriate social entrepreneurs who are contributing to the growing tapestry of social service and environmental improvement efforts toward global sustainability. We have identified and described five distinct types of social expat-preneurs who work and operate under different conditions and circumstances: (1) pre-departure; (2) transitioned; (3) retired senior; (4) avocation-driven; and (5) social expat-intrapreneur. Our findings are consistent with the individual motive research of Bernardo and Santos (2015), who found that the pursuit of a social venture assisted with satisfying many personal needs, such as a hobby (or side hustle) for those with stable employment, retirees using free time for social purposes, and a new career path for the unemployed or dissatisfied with current employment. These results correspond respectively to the social expat-preneur career types in our model of avocation-driven, retired senior, and transitioned social expat-preneurs. Although having different conditions and characteristics, as other SIEs and expat-preneurs, social expat-preneurs tend to have higher professional and marketable skills than most migrants (Vance, Larrieu, Bergin, Mercado, Richmond, Walden, & Reeser, 2017). But unlike the more self-serving other SIEs, social expat-preneurs demonstrate a strong sense of passion for making a difference in the world. Regardless of category, all social expat-prenuers share a common desire to improve global social issues. An increase in social expatriate entrepreneurship is likely to equate to an increase in programming aimed at solving global social issues.

This conceptual framework of social expat-preneur careers represents an important early step in improving our understanding of individual career characteristics of those expatriates engaged in efforts to better our world. This improved understanding can help guide future needed descriptive and prescriptive field research about the lives and careers of these active individual participants at the front of the growing number of initiatives in social entrepreneurship and global sustainability, and of particular need within developing countries.

We certainly don't mean to imply that social entrepreneurship is only needed in developing countries, and that they merely serve as charitable targets for the social entrepreneurial efforts of the wealthy developed countries of the West which themselves have no need of healing. On the contrary, social entrepreneurial efforts are needed and opportunities exist everywhere. But for various reasons, and under differing pre-departure and post-departure circumstances, individuals continue to and increasingly find themselves abroad and recognize opportunities to develop initiatives and new ventures to address social and environmental needs. We also do not mean to suggest here that local host country citizens are not well suited to be effective social entrepreneurs. In fact, their knowledge of the local environment is essential to the successful planning and implementation of social entrepreneurial efforts. Nevertheless, it is possible that expatriates, who have not yet learned what is "not possible" in the new host country environment, may be able to recognize opportunities and means for achieving social and environmental improvements that may be overlooked by local individuals.

In fact, it has long been accepted that a country's economic vibrancy and health are closely associated with the strength and success of its entrepreneurial sector (Aquino 2005; Floyd & McManus 2005). Understanding this connection, many countries purposely encourage and facilitate educational initiatives, financial inducements, and networking opportunities that support entrepreneurial activity (Lee, Sohn & Ju 2011; Kara, Chu & Benzing 2010; Heilbrunn & Kushnirovich 2008). In addition, when compared with local host country entrepreneurs, there is growing evidence that immigrant entrepreneurs (i.e., expat-preneurs) have a disproportionately positive impact on a country's entrepreneurial success and growth, and increasingly involving international new ventures (Kerr & Kerr 2016; Zolin & Schlosser 2013). Vinogradov and Jørgensen (2017), for example, noted that immigrant entrepreneurs were significantly more successful than local host country entrepreneurs in recognizing opportunities in international business development. In a similar fashion, social expat-preneurs may have a distinct advantage over their local counterparts in recognizing social entrepreneurial venture opportunities, including those involving engagement with foreign partners and already-developed and tested resources and approaches.

As is the case with immigrant entrepreneurs who have received less attention than their local host country counterparts in the international entrepreneurship literature (Vance & McNulty 2014; Vissak & Zhang 2014), more research is needed to better understand the individual interests, characteristics, needs, and challenges of social expat-preneurs to better support their growth and involvement on the global stage. With more conceptual development and field research, an improved understanding may lead to more informed choices as individuals navigate their careers throughout their unfolding life space. In addition, greater and improved understanding of the social expat-preneur phenomenon may promote effective support systems and national policy that further facilitate social and environmental improvement efforts surrounding sustainability goals.

REFERENCES

Al Ariss, A., & Ozbilgin, M. (2010). Understanding self-initiated expatriates: Career experiences of Lebanese self-initiated expatriates in France. *Thunderbird International Business Review*, *52*(4), 275–285. doi:10.1002/tie.20355

Al Ariss, A., & Syed, J. (2011). Capital mobilization of skilled migrants: A relational perspective. *British Journal of Management*, *22*(2), 286–304. doi:10.1111/j.1467-8551.2010.00734.x

Andresen, M., Al Ariss, A., & Walther, M. (2012). *Self-Initiated Expatriation: Individual, Organizational, and National Perspectives*. New York: Routledge.

Andresen, M., Bergdolt, F., Margenfeld, J., & Dickmann, M. (2014). Addressing international mobility confusion: Developing definitions and differentiations for self-initiated and assigned expatriates as well as migrants. *International Journal of Human Resource Management, 25*(16), 2295–2318. doi:10.1080/09585192.2013.877058

Aquino, N. (2005). Entrepreneurship is main driver of growth. *Business World, 29*(1), 1.

Barkemeyer, R., & Glavas, A. (2016). Corporate Social Responsibility in Developing Country Multinationals: Identifying Company and Country-Level Influences. *Business Ethics Quarterly, 26*(3), 347–378. doi:10.1017/beq.2016.42

Baron, R. (2006). Opportunity recognition as pattern recognition: How entrepreneurs 'connect the dots' to identify new business opportunities. *The Academy of Management Perspectives, 20*(1), 104–119. doi:10.5465/AMP.2006.19873412

Baron, R. A., Tang, J., & Hmieleski, K. M. (2011). The downside of being 'up': Entrepreneurs' dispositional positive affect and firm performance. *Strategic Entrepreneurship Journal, 5*(2), 101–119. doi:10.1002ej.109

Bernardino, S. & Santos, J. (2015). Antecedents of a new social venture in Portugal: The influence of education and professional background. *Tehkne – Review of Applied Management Studies, 13*(2), 122-134.

Block, J. H., & Wagner, M. (2010). Necessity and Opportunity Entrepreneurs in Germany: Characteristics and Earnings Differentials. *Schmalenbach Business Review, 62*(2), 154–174. doi:10.1007/BF03396803

Bornstein, D., & Davis, S. (2010). *Social entrepreneurship: What everyone needs to know*. New York: Oxford University Press.

Borozan, D., & Pfeifer, S. (2014). Exploring entrepreneurs' motivation: Comparison of Croatia, European post-socialist and developed countries. *The Journal of Entrepreneurship, 23*(2), 263–287. doi:10.1177/0971355714535305

Brookfield Global Relocation Services. (2016). *Global mobility trends survey — Breakthrough to the future of global talent mobility.* Retrieved from http://globalmobilitytrends.bgrs.com/#/role-of-mobility

Castles, S., & Miller, M. J. (2009). *The Age of Migration: International Population Movements in the Modern World* (4th ed.). Basingstoke, UK: Palgrave MacMillan. Retrieved from http://www.jcer.net/index.php/jcer/article/view/188

Choi, D. Y., & Gray, E. (2010). *Values-centered entrepreneurs and their companies*. Routledge.

Collings, D. (2014). Integrating global mobility and global talent management: Exploring the challenges and strategic opportunities. *Journal of World Business, 49*(2), 253–261. doi:10.1016/j.jwb.2013.11.009

Davidsson, P., & Honig, B. L. (2003). The role of social and human capital among nascent entrepreneurs. *Journal of Business Venturing, 18*(3), 301–331. doi:10.1016/S0883-9026(02)00097-6

Deli, F. (2011). Opportunity and necessity entrepreneurship: Local unemployment and the small firm effect. *Journal of Management Policy and Practice, 12*(4), 38–57.

Doherty, N., Richardson, J., & Thorn, K. (2013). Self-initiated expatriation and self-initiated expatriates: Clarification of the research stream. *Career Development International*, *18*(1), 97–112. doi:10.1108/13620431311305971

Einolf, C. J. (2009). Will the boomers volunteer during retirement? Comparing the baby boom, silent, and long civic cohorts. *Nonprofit and Voluntary Sector Quarterly*, *2*(38), 181–199. doi:10.1177/0899764008315182

Floyd, D., & McManus, J. (2005). The role of SME's in improving the competitive position of the European Union. *European Business Review*, *17*(2), 144–150. doi:10.1108/09555340510588011

Fraser, I. (2013). *Expats—Heroes of Social Enterprise and Innovation.* Retrieved from https://www.angloinfo.com/blogs/global/angloinfo-world-expat-life/expats-the-heroes-of-social-enterprise-and-innovation/

Gonzalez-Perez, M., & Leonard, L. (2013). *International Business, Sustainability and Corporate Social Responsibility*. Bingley, UK: Emerald Group Publishing Limited. doi:10.1108/S2051-5030(2013)11

Gupta, J., & Vegelin, C. (2016). Sustainable development goals and inclusive development. *International Environmental Agreement: Politics, Law and Economics*, *16*(3), 433–448. doi:10.100710784-016-9323-z

Haug, S. (2008). Migration networks and migration decision-making. *Journal of Ethnic and Migration Studies*, *34*(4), 585–605. doi:10.1080/13691830801961605

Hayes, M. (2014). We Gained a Lot Over What We Would Have Had: The Geographic Arbitrage of North American Lifestyle Migrants to Cuenca, Ecuador. *Journal of Ethnic and Migration Studies*, *40*(12), 1953–1971. doi:10.1080/1369183X.2014.880335

Hayward, M. L. A., Forster, W. R., Sarasvathy, S. D., & Fredrickson, B. L. (2010). Beyond hubris: How highly confident entrepreneurs rebound to venture again. *Journal of Business Venturing*, *25*(6), 569–578. doi:10.1016/j.jbusvent.2009.03.002

Heilbrunn, S., & Kushnirovich, N. (2008). The impact of policy on immigrant entrepreneurship and businesses practice in Israel. *International Journal of Public Sector Management*, *21*(7), 693–703. doi:10.1108/09513550810904514

Inkson, K., & Arthur, M. (2001). How to be a successful career capitalist. *Organizational Dynamics*, *30*(1), 48–61. doi:10.1016/S0090-2616(01)00040-7

Inkson, K., & Myers, B. (2003). The big "OE": Self-directed travel and career development. *Career Development International*, *8*(4), 170–181. doi:10.1108/13620430310482553

Kara, O., Chu, H., & Benzing, C. (2010). Determinants of entrepreneur's success in a developing country. *Journal of Business and Entrepreneurship*, *22*(2), 1–15.

Kerr, S., & Kerr, W. (2016). *Immigrant Entrepreneurship.* National Bureau of Economic Research Working paper 22385.

Khosa, R. M., & Kalitanyi, V. (2015). Migration reasons, traits and entrepreneurial motivation of African immigrant entrepreneurs: Towards an entrepreneurial migration progression. *Journal of Enterprising Communities: People and Places in the Global Economy*, *9*(2), 132–155. doi:10.1108/JEC-07-2014-0011

Kloosterman, R., & Rath, J. (2001). Immigrant entrepreneurs in advanced economies: Mixed embeddedness further explored. *Journal of Ethnic and Migration Studies*, *27*(2), 189–202. doi:10.1080/13691830020041561

Konda, I., Starc, J., & Rodica, B. (2015). Social challenges are opportunities for sustainable development: Tracing impacts of social entrepreneurship through innovations and value creation. *Economic Themes*, *53*(2), 215–233. doi:10.1515/ethemes-2015-0012

Lasker, J. N. (2016). *Hoping to help; The promises and pitfalls of global health volunteering*. New York: Cornell University Press.

Lee, J., Sohn, S., & Ju, Y. (2011). How Effective Is Government Support for Korean Women Entrepreneurs in Small and Medium Enterprises? *Journal of Small Business Management*, *49*(4), 599–616. doi:10.1111/j.1540-627X.2011.00338.x

Lewin, D. (1998). The accidental entrepreneur. *Computers in Physics*, *12*(6), 518–519. doi:10.1063/1.168753

Maddux, W., Galinsky, A., & Tadmor, C. (2010). Be a better manager: Live abroad. *Harvard Business Review*. Retrieved from https://hbr.org/2010/09/be-a-better-manager-live-abroad

Mayerhofer, H., Müller, B., & Schmidt, A. (2010). Implications of flexpatriates' lifestyles on HRM practices. *Management Review*, *21*(2), 155–173.

McHenry, J., & Welch, D. (2017). Entrepreneurs and Internationalization: A study of Western immigrants in an emerging market. *International Business Review*.

McNulty, Y., & Brewster, C. (2017). Theorising the meaning(s) of 'expatriate': Establishing boundary conditions for business expatriates. *International Journal of Human Resource Management*, *28*(1), 27–61. doi:10.1080/09585192.2016.1243567

McNulty, Y., De Cieri, H., & Hutchings, K. (2013). Expatriate return on investment in the Asia Pacific: An empirical study of individual ROI versus corporate ROI. *Journal of World Business*, *48*(2), 209–221. doi:10.1016/j.jwb.2012.07.005

McNulty, Y., & Vance, C. M. (2017). Dynamic global careers: A new conceptualization of expatriate career paths. *Personnel Review*, *46*(2), 205–221. doi:10.1108/PR-06-2015-0175

Munoz, J. (2010). *International Social Entrepreneurship: Pathways to Personal and Corporate Impact*. Business Expert Press. doi:10.4128/9781606491072

Myers, B., Inkson, K., & Pringle, J. (2017). Self-initiated expatriation (SIE) by older women: An exploratory study. *Journal of Global Mobility: The Home of Expatriate Management Research*, *5*(2), 158–173. doi:10.1108/JGM-10-2016-0050

Norman, W., & MacDonald, C. (2004). Getting to the bottom of "triple bottom line". *Business Ethics Quarterly*, *14*(2), 243–262. doi:10.5840/beq200414211

Park, S. H., Kim, J. N., & Krishna, A. (2014). Bottom-up building of an innovative organization: Motivating employee intrapreneurship and scouting and their strategic value. *Management Communication Quarterly*, *28*(4), 531–560. doi:10.1177/0893318914541667

Pedersen, E., & Gwozdz, W. (2014). From Resistance to Opportunity-Seeking: Strategic Responses to Institutional Pressures for Corporate Social Responsibility in the Nordic Fashion Industry. *Journal of Business Ethics*, *119*(2), 245–264. doi:10.100710551-013-1630-5

Prabhu, V. P., McGuire, S. J., Drost, E. A., & Kwong, K. K. (2012). Proactive personality and entrepreneurial intent: Is entrepreneurial self-efficacy a mediator or moderator. *International Journal of Entrepreneurial Behaviour & Research*, *18*(5), 559–586. doi:10.1108/13552551211253937

Saxenian, A. L. (2002). *Local and Global Networks of immigrant professionals in Silicon Valley*. Public Policy Institute of California.

Spink, K. (1997). *Mother Teresa: A Complete Authorized Biography*. New York: HarperCollins.

Stenn, T. (2017). *Social Entrepreneurship as Sustainable Development: Introducing the Sustainability Lens*. Springer. doi:10.1007/978-3-319-48060-2

Stenzel, P. L. (2010). Sustainability, the triple bottom line, and the global reporting initiative. *Global Edge Business Review, 4*(6), 1-2.

Suutari, V., & Brewster, C. (2000). Making their own way: International experience through self-initiated foreign assignments. *Journal of World Business*, *35*(4), 417–436. doi:10.1016/S1090-9516(00)00046-8

Tung, R. L. (2008). Brain circulation, diaspora, and international competitiveness. *European Management Journal*, *26*(5), 298–304. doi:10.1016/j.emj.2008.03.005

United Nations. (2015). *World Population Prospects: The 2015 Revision, Volume I: Comprehensive Tables*. Retrieved from https://esa.un.org/unpd/wpp/publications/

Vaiman, V., Haslberger, A., & Vance, C. M. (2015). Recognizing the important role of self-initiated expatriates in effective global talent management. *Human Resource Management Review*, *25*(3), 280–286. doi:10.1016/j.hrmr.2015.04.004

Vance, C. M. (2005). The personal quest for building global competence: A taxonomy of self-initiating career path strategies for gaining business experience abroad. *Journal of World Business*, *40*(4), 374–385. doi:10.1016/j.jwb.2005.08.005

Vance, C. M., Larrieu, R. J., Bergin, R., Mercado, J., Richmond, J., Walden, M., & Reeser, C. (2017). A Field Exploration of the "Expat-preneur" Phenomenon. *Global Business and Organizational Excellence*, *36*(6), 34–43. doi:10.1002/joe.21812

Vance, C. M., & McNulty, Y. (2014). Why and how women and men acquire expatriate career development experience: A study of American expatriates in Europe. *International Studies of Management & Organization*, *44*(2), 34–54. doi:10.2753/IMO0020-8825440202

Vance, C. M., McNulty, Y., Paik, Y., & D'Mello, J. (2016). The expat-preneur: Conceptualizing a growing international career phenomenon. *Journal of Global Mobility*, *4*(21), 202–224. doi:10.1108/JGM-11-2015-0055

Vinogradov, E., & Jørgensen, J. (2017). Differences in international opportunity identification between native and immigrant entrepreneurs. *Journal of International Entrepreneurship, 15*(2), 207–228. doi:10.100710843-016-0197-5

Vissak, T., & Zhang, X. (2014). Chinese immigrant entrepreneurs' involvement in internationalization and innovation: Three Canadian cases. *Journal of International Entrepreneurship, 12*(2), 183–201. doi:10.100710843-014-0128-2

Yan, Y. X. (2010). The Chinese Path to Individualization. *The British Journal of Sociology, 61*(3), 489–512. doi:10.1111/j.1468-4446.2010.01323.x PMID:20840429

Zahra, S. A., Gedajlovic, E., Neubaum, D. O., & Shulman, J. M. (2009). A typology of social entrepreneurs: Motives, search processes and ethical challenges. *Journal of Business Venturing, 24*(5), 519–532. doi:10.1016/j.jbusvent.2008.04.007

Zahra, S. A., & George, G. (2002). Absorptive capacity: A review, reconceptualization, and extension. *Academy of Management Review, 27*(2), 185–203.

Zolin, R., & Schlosser, F. (2013). Characteristics of immigrant entrepreneurs and their involvement in international new ventures. *Thunderbird International Business Review, 55*(3), 271–284. doi:10.1002/tie.21543

ADDITIONAL READING

Altman, Y., & Baruch, Y. (2012). Global self-initiated corporate expatriate careers: A new era in international assignments? *Personnel Review, 41*(2), 233–255. doi:10.1108/00483481211200051

Andresen, M., & Biemann, T. (2013). A taxonomy of internationally mobile managers. *International Journal of Human Resource Management, 24*(3), 533–557. doi:10.1080/09585192.2012.697476

Arp, F. (2014). Emerging giants, aspiring multinationals, and foreign executives: Leapfrogging, capability building, and competing with developed country multinationals. *Human Resource Management, 53*(6), 851–876. doi:10.1002/hrm.21610

Arp, F., Hutchings, K., & Smith, W. (2013). Foreign executives in local organisations: An exploration of differences to other types of expatriates. *Journal of Global Mobility, 1*(3), 312–335. doi:10.1108/JGM-01-2013-0006

Arthur, M. B., Inkson, K., & Pringle, J. K. (1999). *The new careers: Individual action & economic change*. Thousand Oaks, CA: Sage Publications.

Baruch, Y. (2004). Transforming careers: From linear to multidirectional career paths - organizational and individual perspectives. *Career Development International, 9*(1), 58–73. doi:10.1108/13620430410518147

Baruch, Y. (2006). Career development in organisations and beyond: Balancing traditional and contemporary viewpoints. *Human Resource Management Review, 16*(2), 125–138. doi:10.1016/j.hrmr.2006.03.002

Baruch, Y., Dickmann, M., Altman, Y., & Bournois, F. (2013). Exploring international work: Types and dimensions of global careers. *International Journal of Human Resource Management, 24*(12), 2369–2393. doi:10.1080/09585192.2013.781435

Bird, A. (2001). International assignments and careers as repositories of knowledge. In M. E. Mendenhall, T. M. Kuhlmann, & G. K. Stahl (Eds.), *Developing global business leaders: Policies, processes, and innovations* (pp. 19–36). Westport, CT: Quorum Books.

Black, J. S., Gregersen, H. B., Mendenhall, M. E., & Stroh, L. K. (1999). *Globalizing people through international assignments*. Massachusetts: Addison-Wesley.

Black, J. S., Morrison, A., & Gregersen, H. B. (1999). *Global explorers: The next generation of leaders*. New York: Routledge.

Bohannon, L. F. (2001). Going global. *Career World, 29*(6), 28–30.

Cappellen, T., & Janssens, M. (2005). Career paths of global managers: Towards future research. *Journal of World Business, 40*(4), 348–360. doi:10.1016/j.jwb.2005.08.003

Cappellen, T., & Janssens, M. (2010). The career reality of global managers: An examination of career triggers. *International Journal of Human Resource Management, 21*(11), 1884–1910. doi:10.1080/09585192.2010.505090

Cappellen, T., & Janssens, M. (2010). Enacting global careers: Organizational career scripts and the global economy as co-existing career referents. *Journal of Organizational Behavior, 31*(5), 687–706. doi:10.1002/job.706

Cerdin, J., & Bird, A. (2008). Careers in a global context. In M. Harris (Ed.), *Handbook of research in international human resource management* (pp. 207–227). New York, NY: Lawrence Erlbaum Associates.

Cerdin, J., & Pargneux, M. (2010). Career anchors: A comparison between organization-assigned and self-initiated expatriates. *Thunderbird International Business Review, 52*(4), 287–299. doi:10.1002/tie.20350

Cerdin, J., & Selmer, J. (2014). Who is a self-initiated expatriate? Towards conceptual clarity of a common notion. *International Journal of Human Resource Management, 25*(9), 1281–1301. doi:10.1080/09585192.2013.863793

Eby, L. T., Butts, M., & Lockwood, A. (2003). Predictors of success in the era of the boundaryless career. *Journal of Organizational Behavior, 24*(6), 689–708. doi:10.1002/job.214

Emanoil, P. (1999). Study abroad expands cultural view, life skills, and academic experience. *Human Ecology Forum, 27*(3): 10-14.

Inkson, K., Arthur, M. B., Pringle, P., & Barry, S. (1997). Expatriate assignment versus overseas experience: Contrasting models of international human resource development. *Journal of World Business, 32*(4), 351–368. doi:10.1016/S1090-9516(97)90017-1

McNulty, Y. (2014). Modern expatriation through the lens of global careers, psychological contracts, and individual return on investment. *Global Business and Organizational Excellence, 33*(2), 27–43.

Suutari, V. (2003). Global managers: Career orientation, career tracks, life-style implications and career commitment. *Journal of Managerial Psychology, 18*(3), 185–207. doi:10.1108/02683940310465225

Taylor, S., Napier, N.K., & Mayrhofer, W. (2002). Women in global business: Introduction.

Taylor, S., Napier, N. K., & Mayrhofer, W. (2002, January). Women in global business: Introduction. *International Journal of Human Resource Management, 13*(5), 739–742. doi:10.1080/09585190210125886

Tharenou, P. (2003). The initial development of receptivity to working abroad: Self-initiated

Tharenou, P. (2003, December). international work opportunities in young graduate employees. *Journal of Occupational and Organizational Psychology, 76*(4), 489–515. doi:10.1348/096317903322591604

Thomas, D. C., & Inkson, K. (2004). *Cultural intelligence: People skills for global business managers.* San Francisco: Berrett-Koehler.

Thompson, M. A. (2000). *The Global Resume and CV Guide.* New York: John Wiley & Sons.

Yan, A., Zhu, G., & Hall, D. T. (2002). International assignments for career building: A model of agency relationships and psychological contracts. *Academy of Management Review, 27*(3), 373–391.

KEY TERMS AND DEFINITIONS

Corporate Social Responsibility (CSR): An organization's commitment to contribute to the welfare of its employees, the surrounding physical environment, and the larger local and global community where the business operates.

Expat-Preneur: An expatriate who engages in entrepreneurial activity.

Expatriate: Anyone living and working in a foreign location and away from the home country.

Intrapreneur: An individual who engages in entrepreneurial and innovative activity within an existing organization.

Sustainability: An objective to make decisions that do not compromise the financial, social, and environmental health affecting future generations.

Social Entrepreneurship: The recognition of opportunities and corresponding development of new initiatives and ventures that address social and environmental needs.

Self-Initiated Expatriate: An individual who relocates to a foreign country for the purpose of gaining international work experience and building international career capital.

Chapter 10
Performance Measurement in Social Enterprises:
Social Impact Analysis

Ayla Zehra Öncer
Marmara University, Turkey

ABSTRACT

This chapter begins with the notion of performance management and then focuses on the concept of social impact in order to deeply examine the measurement of performance in social enterprises. The chapter argues the importance of measuring social impact which is the crucial process in social investment and discusses which measurement method to choose. It then introduces the classification of methods in various forms based on the related literature. The chapter continues by explaining the most frequently used social impact measurement methods including cost effectiveness and cost benefit analyses, social accounting and auditing, SROI, balanced scorecard, SIMPLE, benefit-cost ratio, BACO ratio, expected return metric, cost per impact, and blended value. Finally, the conclusion focuses on the overall perspective of the subject, critical areas to pay attention to, and limitations.

INTRODUCTION

The grasp of the concept of sustainability has led the social dimension of the subject to be expanded and become more and more practical especially in recent years. This brought along corporate business executives to discuss their social performances and to think about how they can create value in this field. Parallel to these developments, there has been a huge increase in the number of nonprofit social enterprises. These initiatives have created a new business area by focusing on market-oriented businesses that create social value. Social enterprises have become a pioneer in creating social value in a wide variety of areas and with very different activities. The most important issue to be addressed at this point is the way value is created as well as the measurement of the social value created, in other words the social impact. The necessity of determining the social performances of both corporate and nonprofit social enterprises has led to the development of methodologies, tools and practices for measuring social

DOI: 10.4018/978-1-5225-5687-9.ch010

impact. The measurement of social impact provides evidence of the value created by social enterprises with an output-oriented perspective.

This chapter will explain the concept of performance measurement and social impact which is the indicator of performance in social enterprises. Then the measurement of social impact and the importance of this measurement will be mentioned. Since there are various measurement methods available for social enterprises, how to choose the appropriate measurement method will be explained in following section. After explaining the approaches that can be used for the selection, the diverse classifications in the literature will be mentioned and the most frequently used methods of social impact measurement will be explained.

PERFORMANCE MEASUREMENT

Performance measurement has emerged as a vital issue for profit-oriented businesses and various performance measurement systems have been developed throughout history. The development of performance measurement systems can be summarized within four phases. Until the late 1950s, it was particularly focused on production, cost and efficiency. Between the 1950s and the 1960s, financial performance outcomes have gained importance for other departments as well as production (Bititci, Garengo, Dörfler, & Nudurupati, 2011). From the 1960s until the late 1980s, performance measurement systems involved some other non-financial indicators like business strategy, quality, flexibility and customer satisfaction (Kaplan, 1984; Simons, 1995). In the fourth and the last phase, with the development of the stakeholder theory, it has come to the point that the performance should be measured by considering company's internal and external environment in other words all stakeholders related (Bititci, Garengo, Dörfler, & Nudurupati, 2011; Freeman, 1984). This approach has caused to examine performance measurement in a multidimensional perspective and has emerged ecological and social dimensions to the measurement systems beside financial dimension. However, performance measurement is usually based on the achievement of the goal and does not consider social or environmental issues. The efficiency is often represented by the achievement of defined and measurable organizational goals. Achieving such organizational goals can be explored using traditional performance measurement systems. But involvement of the influence of social and environmental dimensions makes it difficult to identify, measure and evaluate such effects. Measuring performances through the inclusion of economic, environmental and social dimensions involve challenges in it, but it also makes it even more difficult to address such measures in the context of social enterprises. First, the development of an extensive and reliable performance measurement system is expensive and in social enterprises, managers have limited resources and time restrictions to collect and analyze data to feed the measurement system. Secondly, a performance measurement system for a social enterprise should include various performance indicators that cover multiple goals in terms of economic, environmental and social performance. Finally, due to the content-based nature of a particular set of measures that reflect the sensitivity of specific groups, there is slight empirical evidence that performance measurement systems have any effect on actual business practices (Bull, 2007; Paton, 2003).

PERFORMANCE IN SOCIAL ENTERPRISES: SOCIAL IMPACT

The mission of creating economic value should not be the sovereign mission of social entrepreneurs, and it is not (Dees, 1998; Peredo & McLean, 2006; Perrini 2006), they prioritize direct social impacts against the economic mission like creating profit and market share (Ormiston & Seymour, 2011). Social impact is related with identifying and evaluating the value of activities. It is crucial to understand what social impact means, why it matters and whether it can be measured.

In general terms, the social impact can be defined as *the change that occurs as a result of an activity* or *the consequences of an action/activity/project/program result on different people*. The impact can be perceived as positive or negative; can be obtained with or without planning and it can occur in short or long term (Tüsev, 2013). It is used for the impact of a corporation on society on the economic, environmental and social dimensions. The term is often replaced by terms such as social value creation (Emerson, Wachowicz, & Chun, 2000) and social return (Clark, Rosenzweig, Long, & Olsen, 2004). Below are definitions of the term social impact according to various authors:

Social impact is any of the great variety of changes in physiological states and subjective feelings, motives and emotions, cognitions and beliefs, values and behaviour that occur in an individual, human, or animal, as a result of the real, implied, or imagined presence or actions of other individuals (Latané, 1981). It can be defined as the total impact that a non-profit organization has on all of its stakeholders (Dillenburg, Greene, & Erekson, 2003).

Social value is created when resources, inputs, processes, or policies are combined to generate improvements in the lives of individuals or society as a whole (Emerson, Wachowicz, & Chun, 2000). It is the portion of the total outcome that happened as a result of the activity of an organisation, above and beyond what would have happened anyway (Clark, Rosenzweig, Long, & Olsen, 2004). Social impact is the consequences to human populations of any public or private actions that alter the ways in which people live, work, play, relate to one another, organise to meet their needs and generally act as a member of society (Burdge & Vanclay, 1996). It refers to impacts (or effects, or consequences) that are likely to be experienced by an equally broad range of social groups as a result of some course of action (Freudenburg, 1986). Social impacts are the wider societal concerns that reflect and respect the complex interdependency between business practice and society (Gentile, 2002).

As understood from the above definitions, social impact refers to the change that the corporation has created on all stakeholders, especially society. Therefore, measuring the size of this change, in other words, measuring the social impact arises as a very important issue. Measuring social impact refers to the process of defining, monitoring and implementing measures to reveal benefits for beneficiaries and communities through the demonstration of social impacts (McLoughlin, Kaminski, Sodagar, Khan, Harris, Arnaudo, & Mc Brearty, 2009). In other words, it is the process of ensuring evidence that the corporations' actions provide a real and concrete benefit to community or the stakeholders.

THE IMPORTANCE OF MEASURING SOCIAL IMPACT

It has become a necessity to measure the value created by social enterprises as they have started to carry out different activities and operate in wide range of fields around the world. The existence of social enterprises is emerged from a social need or due to a higher value for the beneficiaries. The measurement of social impact requires the provision of these benefits through evidence of social implications and the measurement of social contributions in a systematic, effective and appropriate manner (McLoughlin, Kaminski, Sodagar, Khan, Harris, Arnaudo, & Mc Brearty, 2009). Social enterprises should use social value evaluating and measurement methods to improve their performance, to create influence on their stakeholders, to meet community needs. Social impact analysis is based on the desire to uncover the value that cannot be calculated by traditional cost benefit analysis techniques.

There has been an increase in social and environmental reporting since the 1990s; the first Global Reporting Initiative (GRI), the Kyoto Principle, the carbon footprint calculations, the Dow Jones Sustainability Index and so on. Different approaches have emerged in the light of these developments in the form of new measurement methods and indicators, and standardization of the processes to understand the value created. Measuring performance has become so crucial because of the growing difficulty to raise funds from investors and donors and the increasing competition in this area. As social entrepreneurship become widespread all over the world it is imperative to measure the effects they create.

As already mentioned, since social enterprises operate in many different fields and deal with a wide variety of social issues the impact they create can be complex and ambiguous (Paton, 2003). As a consequence of this complexity and ambiguity there are a number of different measures to assess the performance of social enterprises. It will be extremely useful to give consistency to the measurement of social enterprise (Bull, 2007; Ryan & Lyne, 2008).

The volunteers and people working in social enterprises and community organizations can clearly be able to see the value and benefits created by their organizations' work. But there are benefits to measure the social impact in more detail. Performance measurement will provide a way for social enterprises to compare their performance with other organizations and a way to measure economic and social performance against desired objectives (Zahra, Gedajlovic, Neubaum, & Schulman, 2009). The feedback will help the organisation to learn and improve. They have to cope with increased funding pressures. (Kotler & Andreasen, 1996). It will also help investors and donors to assess the performance of social enterprises and decide their investments.

Social enterprises are obliged to prove that the money they have obtained has been spent effectively and that the necessary benefits have been achieved (Bouckaert & Vandenhove, 1998). It will bring accountability to social entrepreneurship, allowing for a way to show the community or environmental benefits. It seeks to identify and quantify this impact. Brand management activities are also being applied regarding how non-profits differentiate themselves from others. However, just because a social issue is unpopular does not mean it is not worthy to spend money and time for it (Polonsky & Landreth, 2005). Therefore, performance measurement is also extremely important in terms of why the money is spent and what is achieved as a result. It suggests ways for social entrepreneurs to evaluate possible opportunities and decide the ones to go after (Young, 2003). As a result, social impact measurement helps the development of social enterprise in general, improves investors' confidence and provides social satisfaction.

WHICH MEASUREMENT METHOD TO CHOOSE

There is no single tool or method that can be applied by all companies to be used to measure the impact of social entrepreneurship. Depending on their activities, their objectives and the dimensions of the impacts they are measuring, companies will choose different methods for their needs. There is a wide range of measurements from qualitative assessments focusing on describing impacts to assessments of concrete impacts that focus on social return on investment (Short, Moss, & Lumpkin, 2009). In other words, social impact measurement varies from qualitative, self-developed measures to multidimensional quantitative measures.

With examining current performance measurement techniques, it is possible to mention three basic categories that meet different needs. There are the ones that focus on internal evaluation of the social enterprise and are attached to operations and managerial decision making. There are criterions focus specifically on measuring social value creation and social impact. And last, there are measures which have been created for impact investors who invest in ventures expecting both financial return and a social return on investment (Simon & Barmeier, 2011).

When the performance measurement is examined in depth, it is not possible to talk about the existence of a measurement tool that can be used universally, for all companies, and covers all social impacts. The involvement of social enterprises in many different sectors, serving different purposes, and especially the different expectations of different stakeholder groups, makes the measurement and choice of measurement tool even more challenging (Arena, Azzone, & Bengo, 2015). At this point it will be accurate to consider two theories that can contribute to the social enterprises paradigm; the Contingency Theory and the Multiple-constituency Theory.

The Contingency Theory emerged in the 1960s and explained how the system approach could be used, accepting the rationale for handling organizations. The theory has developed a more flexible approach to the assumptions and rigid principles of classical theories. It sees the organization as a system and studies the association with the internal and external environment. The main purpose of the classical and neo-classical period is to improve the institutional performance. In this context, classical and neo-classical theorists tried to determine the most efficient organizational structures and management styles with different characteristics in order to increase productivity. The Contingency Theory rejects the concept of universal "most accurate, most efficient, the best" management principles, strategies or organizational structures in all circumstances and conditions, because all concepts of organization depend on the conditions. The structure of the organization, the management strategy and management style will vary according to the conditions. Companies should determine the most accurate and most efficient ones for themselves with undertaking the internal and external analysis. This is because internal and external environmental conditions such as the size of each organization, the technology it uses, the organizational culture, suppliers, the sector in which it is located and etc. are different from each other. The theory tries to understand the characteristics of these situations and to develop the organizational structure and management style appropriate to the situation. The essence of the approach focuses on the variables that affect the organization and what their effects are. Instead of generalizing organizations, the theory examines each company by reducing them to situations they are in. This point of view guides us in measuring the performance of social enterprises. As mentioned above, it is not possible to accept a single instrument of measurement to determine the performance of social enterprises that are highly diverse in management styles, strategies, and operate in diverse areas. Each social enterprise should choose a measurement tool that will meet its needs at the highest level, taking into account the internal and external environmental variables.

Another approach that can be taken into account in measuring the performance of social enterprises is the multiple-constituency theory (Kanter & Brinkerhoff, 1981; Herman & Renz, 1997; Connolly, Conlon, & Deutsch, 1980; Pfeffer & Salancik, 1978). The theory provides criterions for assessing effectiveness from the preferences of multiple constituencies for the outcomes of organizational performance. In other words, the effectiveness of an organization emerges from a collective structure consisting of a combination of different stakeholder perspectives (Zammuto, 1984). Various actors related an organization require different kinds of effectiveness measures for different kinds of decisions, so no single effectiveness indicator will be sufficient for all the constituencies (Kanter & Brinkerhoff, 1981). For instance, while managers may be more interested in structural measures, customers prefer output-oriented measures. In summary, the multiple-constituency theory tells us that a standard measurement instrument is not permissible and that we have to choose between different measurement tools.

Based on the fact that social enterprises operate in complex and multi-dimensional environments, it is appropriate to examine social impact measurement tools with a stakeholder-based approach by adapting the theories summarized above. Each stakeholder interacting with social enterprises has its own needs and expectations. Therefore, in order to be able to measure the social impact, social enterprise managers must first identify the stakeholder groups and then select the appropriate measurement tool as needed. So, it will be right to follow a process such as defining the stakeholders, examining their interactions with the social enterprise, identifying their needs, selecting the most suitable measuring instrument to meet the needs, evaluating and providing feedback.

The most critical steps involved in this process can be described as defining stakeholders and identifying their needs. The primary stakeholder groups for social enterprises can be listed as investors, managers, employees, beneficiaries and donors and each of these stakeholders may need different types of information. For instance, donors need to know if money they donate is being used appropriately, while employees are concerned with the business opportunities offered to them and managers need to understand whether the organization is capable to achieve its goals. It will therefore be useful to select a measurement tool that will provide the knowledge to meet the expectations of each stakeholder. In this case, SROI or cost benefit analysis can be used to meet the demand of donors, while social accounting and auditing can be used for employees' requests and BSC for managers' expectations on internal evaluation (Costa & Pesci, 2016).

In addition to meet the expectations of the stakeholders', social impact measurement also depends on the capacity of organization and focus of the measurement. For instance, if the organization is small in size with limited resources in time, a simpler measurement tool (Cost-Effectiveness Analysis) will be chosen, and it will be appropriate to select a method that requires a certain level of knowledge (Social Return on Investment or Social Accounting and Auditing) if it is big enough and have that capacity. Similarly, the focus of measurement is also affects the selection of the method. For a social enterprise focused on measuring economic impact, SROI would suffice, while SIMPLE would be more appropriate for an organization which prefers to measure the impact on environment, economy and society.

THE CLASSIFICATION OF METHODS

In literature, there are about thirty different social impact measurement methods in different sources. In these sources, different classifications are made such as; qualitative (the balanced scorecard, the triple bottom line, etc.) and quantitative (social return on investment, blended value, etc.), classical (cost-effectiveness analysis, cost-benefit analysis, etc.) and non-classical (Robin Hood Foundation, Acumen Fund, etc.), internal (social accounting and auditing, etc.) and external (Baco Ratio, etc.). In this section, a summary of the most frequent classifications is explained.

First of all, Schaltegger et al. (2000) compared the two approaches to define environmental management accounting (EMA) -monetary internal environmental accounting and corporate internal environmental accounting- in their working paper. And then suggest a classification to integrate both perspectives by explaining EMA including five dimensions as:

1. **Units of Measurement**
   Monetary: Includes the environmentally differentiated conventional management accounting systems and deals with the environmentally driven impacts on a company expressed in monetary terms.
   Physical: Focuses on company's ecological impact on the natural environment in terms of physical units.
2. **Time Perspective**: The classification of methods whether it focuses in short or long term;
   Long-Term Focus: Qualifies the fact that ecological problems are often long-lasting.
   Short-Term Focus: Qualifies the fact that management generally has a short-term perspective for the satisfaction of stakeholders.
3. **Time Frame**: The classification of methods depending on whether it is p*ast-orientated* and focuses on the past or f*uture-orientated* and focuses on the future while making sense of the data.
4. **Information Production**: The classification according to the production of information;
   Routinely Generated Information: Expresses general accounting systems that routinely produce information for management.
   Ad Hoc Information: Specific accounting methods that produce information on a needs basis for particular decisions.
5. **Scope**: The classification of methods according to serve the information needs of *internal* or *external* company stakeholders.

As seen in the categorization, time perspective, time frame and scope dimensions are particularly related with the classification of social impact methods.

Then another classification is made by Clark et al. (2004) including five dimensions as follows:

1. **Functional Category**: The broadest classification of the methods;
   Process: Methods used to pursue the efficiency and effectiveness of outputs or indicators that management uses to track operational processes.
   Impact: Methods that relate outputs and outcomes, and attempt to prove incremental outcomes relative to the next best alternative.
   Monetization: Methods used to monetize outcomes or impact by translating them into a dollar value.
2. **Impact Value Chain:** The classification of the methods according to the types of data required in the analysis;
   Inputs: The resources necessary for the operation of the organization.
   Outputs: Indicators involved in the organization processes that may be directly measured by the management.
   Outcomes: Specific changes in attitudes, behaviors, skills and knowledge that result from organizational activities.
   Impact: The difference between the outcome for the social interest of the presence and absence of the organization.
   Goal Alignment: The process of assessing whether outcomes or impacts met desired goals and defining the ways of improvement of operations.
3. **Assessment Purposes in Investment Process**

Screening: Methods help the investor who wants to invest for social reasons to screen the enterprises by examining certain qualities.
Partnership Formation: Methods useful to clarify and arrange the investors' expectations and to build trust.
Management Operation: Methods useful for tracking daily activities, and provides data for management decision making and/or investor oversight.
Scaling: Methods help to clarify key input/activity relationships that direct outputs and outcomes, and explain what needs to be scaled.
External Reporting: Methods useful for reporting to stakeholders outside of the enterprise which need performance reports.
Exit: Methods provide information beneficial to exit decisions.
Retrospective Evaluation: Methods useful for backward-looking social impact evaluation.

4. **Applicability to Life-cycle Stages**: The classification of methods according to the life-cycle stage of the enterprise whether it is a *start-up*, in *expansion* or in *maturity*.
5. **Time Breakdown**: Classification that estimates the time required to implement the method;
Management: Time spent by management to fulfil the method.
Staff: Time spent by other non-management employees.
Third-Party Consultant: Time spent by a hired third-party consultant for advice or data collection.
Investor: Time spent by investors or funders to implement the method.

After examining the studies of Schaltegger et al. (2000) and Clark et al. (2004), Maas and Liket (2011) distinguished another six dimensions of social impact measurement methods:

1. **Purposes**: The classification of methods depending on what the user wants to measure;
Screening: Methods help the assessment and performance of investment opportunities concerning particular goals of investors.
Monitoring: Methods used to help management for operational decision making.
Reporting: Methods help to communicate with the external stakeholders regularly.
Evaluation: Methods used to assess impact or achievements for organizational learning.
2. **Time Frame:** The classification of methods through three different time perspectives;
Prospective: Methods intend to measure impacts that are expected.
Ongoing: Methods used to evaluate continuing processes.
Retrospective: Methods used to assess the past activities performance.
3. **Orientation:** The classification of methods according to the focus on inputs or outputs;

Methods help to assess differences in *input* or *output* as a result of social activity.

4. **Length of Time Frame**: The classification of methods whether it focuses in short or long term;
Short Term: Methods used to measure short-term effects to prove progress.
Long Term: Methods used to measure some significant impacts which do not occur until the long term.
5. **Perspective**: The classification of methods used to determine the extent of an impact based on its beneficiaries;

Methods used to assess impact on individuals (*Micro*), impact on organizations (*Meso*) and impact on society (*Macro*).

6. **Approach**: The classification of methods according to the focus on the approach to produce social impact.
   Process Methods: Methods help to track the efficiency and cost effectiveness of continuing operational processes
   Impact Methods: Methods used to measure operational outputs and their impacts.
   Monetarization: Methods help to measure social and environmental indicators and exchange them into a monetary value.

And lastly, we can mention the classification of Rinaldo (2010) who identified four variables as below:

1. **Motivation**: The classification of the methods according to the focus on the reason of the evaluation;

The basic drives of the measurement can be; assessing *effectiveness*, assessing *efficiency*, *taking stock of a situation, and communicating* with stakeholders, providing *quality mark* and the *requirements of funders.*

2. **Readiness**: Expresses whether the vision and main social purpose of the enterprise is defined or undefined, so the classification can be specified in the form of *clarified aim* and *unclarified aim.*
3. **Capacity**: Classification of the methods in accordance with the ienterprise's capacity;

Whether it is *small* with limited resources in time, money and staff and entirely new to social impact measurement, or want to conduct an impact measurement but as a *medium* enterprise need more staff and time or need to involve service users or beneficiaries into the evaluation process to overcome the time pressure, or as a *large* enterprise it can be confident on using some methods require a certain level of knowledge and specified techniques.

4. **Impact Type**: The classification of the methods depending on the type of the impact that enterprise want to evaluate; which can be distinguished as *environmental, economic, holistic* (multi-dimensional) and *volunteering impact.*

As mentioned above, the measurement of social impact has been classified in different categories where some of them have similarities and some of them are totally distinct. The primary reason for these classifications is to make a better evaluation of the multiple measurement methods. In the light of the theories mentioned in the previous section, social enterprises should examine the classifications and select the most viable and suitable measurement method for their organizations that best meets the stakeholder expectations at the highest level.

SOCIAL IMPACT MEASUREMENT METHODS

The literature aiming the measurement of the performance of social enterprises is in its early stages and therefore there are numerous methodologies, approaches, tools to measure the social impact of these initiatives. This section will cover the most commonly used social impact measurement methods in social enterprises.

Cost-Effectiveness Analysis

Cost-effectiveness analysis (CEA) is the most commonly used method of economic evaluation when the priorities of social services are determined. It is an economic tool that has been conducted since the 1990s for performance measurement and represents the economic analysis of social enterprise activity. The method is the economic expression of the costs of programs, which the benefits cannot be expressed in terms of money. It is the examination of the cost and the outcomes of the alternative means of accomplishing an objective, in order to select the one with the highest effectiveness relative to its cost. In other words, it is a comparison of the costs of existing possibilities to achieve a given objective. So, the lowest total cost is selected, taking into account all the direct and indirect costs of each possibility. CEA is a ratio obtained by proportioning the costs incurred when carrying out a social enterprise activity to a non-monetary output or benefit (Tuan, 2008).

CEA refers to the relationship between social service outputs (benefits) and inputs (costs) that can be used to perform these services (Mitton & Donaldson, 2004). The cost is represented by money, while the output assessed by measurable units such as the lifetime gained, life saved, the number of patient days reduced (Currie & Manns, 2002; Russell, 1996). In CEA, costs are expressed in terms of money, and the results are often expressed as cost per unit of effectiveness for each alternative (e.g. cost per child cured of polio). In this method, the social program with the lowest cost per unit of effectiveness (high efficiency and least cost) is preferred. In CEA, output is measured by natural units (Drummond, Aguġar-Ibanez, & Nġxon, 2006). For example, in the treatment of chronic heart failure, where lifesaving is the promise, the most appropriate outcome measure is the years of life acquired. It is used especially when the benefit created by an activity is not possible to be expressed in monetary terms (Tuan, 2008). For instance, the impact would be the number of children cured from polio and divides it by the cost of the vaccination. So, CEA is more useful when measuring the effectiveness of certain activities on an individual basis. Yet the measures of cost-effectiveness are individual, they can only express one impact area at a time. So, the cost effectiveness analysis addresses an approach to measure the potential benefit of certain activities (Chmelik, Musteen, & Ahsan, 2016).

There are two main purposes of using CEA; first is to combine the outcomes with costs to ensure that the social program alternatives within the same field are ranked according to the activity results, and the second is to avoid the uncertainties regarding the evaluation of the different aspects of the social program benefits by considering the benefits to costs ratio without making them into common units (Tuan, 2008). CEA is widely used when a need for a project arises, but where there is uncertainty about what is the best way to intervene. And also, specifically in health care, for example, where it is difficult to value an outcome but where the results can be counted and compared.

The key criticism related with CEA is in the use of a ratio measure. The prediction of costs and effectiveness may result in incorrect outcomes due to the use of a ratio measure, so it would be beneficial to use sensitivity analysis to test the distribution of the cost effectiveness ratio relative to the normal distribution.

Cost-Benefit Analysis

Cost-benefit analysis (CBA) is examining the ratio between total social costs and total social benefits (Black, Hashimzade, & Myles, 2009). Since the 1990s, traditional CBA has been extended to include impacts on society. It is a more demanding approach to analyse costs and outcomes as it requires outcomes to be monetized and a comprehensive measurement of costs. The CBA thus assures a full account of the net benefits provided to the society and the various stakeholders. It is an economic assessment technique that measures the costs and social benefits of alternatives in monetary basis. It is used to estimate whether the cost of an alternative is worth the benefits. In other words, it allows assessing whether the return of investments has exceeded the cost of the investment (Robinson, 1993). The purpose of the CBA is to help decide whether a project is worthwhile and to compare program alternatives to choose the best one (Tuan, 2008). According to Culyer (2005), CBA is defined as the method of comparing costs (based on monetary terms) and benefits of various alternative action plans. It is an analysis method that requires the calculation of present values using the societal discount rate. This systematic comparison of costs is based on the following considerations as; deciding which project maximizes the difference between social benefits and costs; and deciding on the size of the social benefits derived from projects with varying costs.

CBA is an economic analysis in which the costs and social impacts of an investment are evaluated in accordance to these two measures: (a) Net present value: the total value of all costs, revenues, and social impacts, discounted to reflect the same accounting period which is formulized as;

$PresentValue = FutureValue \,/\, \left(1+i\right)^n$ where i is the discount rate and n is the time period (Saruhan & Öncer, 2004). Costs and benefits will occur over time and in general, future costs and benefits have a lower weight than the same unit or benefit cost occurring now. Therefore, it is necessary to calculate and compare the present value of the future benefits and costs. (b) Benefit-cost ratio: the discounted value of revenues divided by discounted value of costs, which is formulized as;

$PV(B)/PV(C) > 1$, where PV stands for the present value for benefits and costs. The decision maker should choose the project with the highest benefit-cost ratio. Briefly CBA allows the social enterprise to assess how efficiently a project is running with the comparison against other alternatives.

However, it may not always be possible to express benefits in monetary terms. Therefore, two different approaches have been developed in the literature to measure the expected utility from a project (Kernick, 2002; Folland, Goodman, & Stano, 2006). The first approach is human capital in which the expected benefit is measured using the present value of the individual's future income. But due to the human capital approach is causing a distinction between high income and low income, employees and non-workers (elderly, children, etc.), the willingness-to-pay approach has been developed (Kernick, 2002; Phillips, 2005). This approach is about assessing how much people will pay to maintain or to improve the current situation (Gafni, 1998). In other words, the willingness-to-pay approach is a method for measuring individuals' valuation of a project by asking how much they are willing to pay to have the project introduced (Gafni, 2001).

Social Accounting and Auditing

One of the pioneers in the development of social accounting and auditing is John Pearce, who was also a social enterprise thinker and activist. He defined social accounting as a framework which allows an organization to build on existing documentation and reporting and develop a process whereby it can account for its social performance, report on that performance and draw up an action plan to improve on that performance, and through which it can understand its impact on the community and be accountable to its key stakeholders (Pearce, 2003). It is an example of an internal performance measurement technique and a well-established framework for monitoring, evaluation accountability to stakeholders and a process which helps the organization to assess its performance of social, environmental and economic objectives (Nicholls, 2009, Stevenson, Taylor, Lyon, & Rigby, 2010). This performance measurement technique focuses evaluating the progress towards mission objectives through core activities. The method is usually qualitative in approach and makes an assessment of internal performance using descriptive metrics - such as target audience characteristics or stakeholder attributes - and some financial data. It conducts impact measurement through accounting for specific descriptive outcomes of strategic action. These metrics look at individual or community level changes or developments are highly non-comparative and individualistic which can be specified as a weakness of the technique. The main problem with qualitative metrics, which have an organizational focus and usually discuss on what the organization does, is to identify the appropriate measurement focus (Nicholls, 2009).

The terms "social audit" and "social accounting" refer to component parts of the process; however, they are usually used instead of each other confusingly for the whole process. Internal data are first collected and analyzed -social accounting-, then results are audited independently -social audit-, and finally results are disseminated -reporting- (Gibbon & Dey, 2011).

It is possible to study the process in 3 basic steps. The first one is *planning*, which includes addressing what, why, and how the social enterprise works for. It involves the clarification of the vision, mission, values, objectives and the stakeholders of the organization. Planning forms the foundation of the process. The second step is *accounting* which includes determining the content of the process by establishing social accounting systems that collect relevant information for a certain period of time, allowing to report the performance of the social enterprise in accordance with its values and objectives. The social accounting systems provide both quantitative and qualitative data for management. All collected information will be compiled, analyzed and evaluated by management. The last step is *reporting and auditing* where all qualitative and quantitative data are brought together and interpreted. This report is then audited by an impartial people and verified that the information has been collected and interpreted correctly, thus it is revealed that the organization activities in the accounting period are reflected fairly and honestly. At the end of the process a social report is prepared and shared with the public. The social report clearly demonstrates what the organization has achieved as a result of its activities, how it has accomplished it, how much it has cost, and the perspectives of the different stakeholders (Zappalà & Lyons, 2009).

Social accounting and auditing uses eight principles to support its process, to ensure validation is effective and to provide constant improvement which are; clarifying purpose (why the organization undertake the social accounting process), defining scope (determining values, objectives and stakeholders), engaging stakeholders (including the views of the interacting stakeholders), materiality (determining what to include in the social accounts), benchmarking (making comparisons of performance and impact), transparency (indicating the findings are accurate and fair), verification (verifying the social accounts impartially), and embedding (assuring the process embedded in its life cycle and practices). The use of these principles provides a platform for sustaining, validating and continually improving the effective social accounts of the organization (Social Audit Network, 2011).

Social Return on Investment

Another framework devised which focuses on quantifying social value is Social return on investment (SROI). In profit-oriented business enterprises Return on investment (ROI) is the valid performance measurement. ROI compares investment gains to investment costs. Over time, the researchers have tried to measure the value created by social enterprises. Similarly to ROI, social return on investment compares the ratio between the net benefits of a project and the investment required to gain that benefit. (Nicholls, 2009; Luke, Barraket, & Eversole, 2013; Rotheroe & Richards, 2007). SROI was first developed by the Roberts Enterprise Development Fund (a non-profit philanthropic social venture founded in 1997 in San Francisco, CA) (REDF, 2000; Emerson, 1999; 2003) in the late 1990's, culminated methodology tools in 2000. The purpose of REDF's SROI was to indicate the collective social value with the total investments made by each social enterprise in its portfolio. Even though REDF has no longer implemented the SROI methodology since 2000, the method influenced many of the approaches and was improved by the New Economics Foundation (NEF, 2007; Nicholls, 2004). This improved approach has made the SROI more comprehensive by including several other methods.

Main idea of SROI is based on cost-benefit analysis (Emerson, Wachowicz, & Chun, 2000), combining both quantitative and qualitative approaches and monetizing values to social and environmental results (NEF, 2007), but SROI differentiates from cost-benefit analysis, because it is designed as a practical management tool for both small and large organizations rather than from a macro perspective. Both methods use financial proxies to measure costs and benefits of an investment or a project (Nicholls, 2009; Gibbon & Dey, 2011). The SROI analysis involves some calculations to identify the social return on investment (Nicholls, 2009); the first one calculates the full Blended Value of a project that combines its financial value and a monetized value of its social impact, the second one determines the financial investment in the project and the third one establishes the blended return on investment which combines the enterprise and social returns. In summary, the SROI analysis examines social value in relation to the created benefits and its costs (Rotheroe & Richards, 2007), which enables a ratio of benefits to costs to be calculated, for instance a ratio of 2:1 indicates that an investment of 1$ delivers 2$ of social value. SROI is simply about value, rather than money, where money is only a common unit to express value.

The NEF's SROI approach focuses on four areas; the first one is centralizing the stakeholders' objectives in the measurement process as stakeholder engagement, the second is focusing on the areas which stakeholders identify as important, the third is defining the impact map to clarify how the impact would be enabled and the last one is calculating the return on investment ratio. As briefly mentioned when SROI analysis process is examined in detail, it is seen that several important stages should be emphasized (Nicholls, 2004; 2009; Cabinet Office, 2009). Primarily the organization should define its boundaries to establish its stakeholders, to decide how to involve stakeholders, to determine the key social objectives and to identify the materiality of outcomes. Secondly, it should define the cause and effect chain from inputs to outputs to outcomes by developing an impact map where, inputs are the total costs of the project, outputs are the quantitative effects (number of people trained, number of jobs created, etc.), outcomes are the direct and indirect changes in target stakeholders and their societies (increased drug use, better levels of education, etc.). In third stage, the organization should identify appropriate indicators to capture the elements within the impact map and monetized values for them should be determined to calculate the impact. This stage involves developing outcome indicators which show whether the outcome has occurred, and by how much, evidencing outcomes by finding data to show whether outcomes have happened and then valuing them. The data can be collected by one-to-one interviews, record keeping, focus groups, workshops and questionnaires. And valuation process is referred to as monetization where financial proxies are used to estimate the social value of non-traded goods to different stakeholders. For instance, for the project of decreasing the use of drugs on young people, the level of drug use can be the indicator and the average amount spent by young people on drugs can be the proxy. Fourthly, the impact should be established by eliminating the aspects of change that would have happened anyway or are a result of other factors with the help of the collected and monetized evidence on outcomes in the previous stage. This stage involves the calculation of deadweight, attribution and calculating the impact. Deadweight is calculated as a percentage expressing the amount of outcome that would have happened even if the activity had not taken place. Comparison groups or benchmarks on the same group of people that have been affected from the intervention required for this calculation. Attribution is an assessment of how much of the outcome is contributed by other organizations or people. It is also calculated as a percentage and refers the part of deadweight that outcome can be attributed to other people or organizations. The last thing to do in this stage is calculating the impact. Impacts are the changes discounted by a deadweight analysis, which is the extent to which outcomes will be achieved without the interventions of the social enterprise. It is calculated by multiplying the quantity of the outcome by financial proxy for a total value, subtracting the deadweight or attribution from this total (repeated for each outcome) and adding up the total to reach the overall impact of the outcomes included. The fifth stage, involves the calculation of SROI. At this stage, the present value of the social impact determined for each estimated year is calculated and summed up to arrive the discounted total benefit, then this discounted value of total benefit divided by the total investment (total inputs) which gives the ratio of e.g. 2:1. In sixth and last stage, a report should be prepared for organization itself and for stakeholders to share findings and process should be embedded in organization.

It would also be appropriate to follow these principles for an effective social return on investment analysis as; involving stakeholders, understanding what changes, valuing the things that matter, including only what is material, avoiding over-claiming, being transparent and verifying the results (REDF, 2000).

There are both strengths and weaknesses in every performance measurement method. SROI have strengths in enabling a comparative analysis between different enterprises that can lead to a competitive advantage on gathering support from investors (Ryan & Lyne, 2008). It is a consistent and clear approach to understand and report the changes caused by an organization. It also has an ability to manage risk, to identify opportunity and to raise the finance required to achieve organizations' mission (NEF, 2009). On the other hand, SROI should not be the sole indicator of social performance as it is one of many measurement methods available, just like the return on investment (ROI) would not be the only method used for financial decision making (Lingane & Olsen, 2004).

Balanced Scorecard

The efficient use of investment capital is no longer the sole determinant for competitive advantages, but intangible factors such as intellectual capital, knowledge creation or excellence in customer orientation become more important (Figge, Hahn, Schaltegger, & Wagner, 2002). Kaplan and Norton introduced the Balanced Scorecard (BSC) based on a Notion that financial indicators alone were insufficient to measure performance (Kaplan & Norton, 1992). BSC intends to balance financial and non-financial, short-term and long-term and both qualitative and quantitative success measures with internal analysis of an organization to evaluate the efficiency (Kaplan & Norton, 1992; 1996). Similarly, the social balanced scorecard (SBSC) is an internal analysis tool used by social enterprises to monitor and examine both qualitative and quantitative data.

According to Kaplan and Norton (2001), social enterprises have difficulty in defining their strategy. The scorecards they use mostly have a focus on increasing operational efficiency. In BSC financial perspective (success) is the primary objective, which doesn't suit for social enterprises. In a private sector, customers both pay for a good or service and receive it however, in social initiatives; donors provide the financial resources, whereas other beneficiaries do receive it. So, they modify the architecture of BSC by placing customers or constituents at the top of their Balanced Scorecards by developing objectives for both groups and identifying the internal processes. Compared to the original BSC, the customer definition is expanded in social balanced scorecard. In addition to this structural modification social enterprises should determine a long-term and over-arching objective at the top of their scorecard by considering three different high-level perspectives as; a. *cost incurred* which emphasizes importance of operational efficiency, b. *value created* which identifies the benefits provided by the enterprise to its beneficiaries, c. *legitimizing support* which emphasizes the importance of meeting the objectives of the initiative's funding source. Then the internal processes and learning and growth objectives should be defined to achieve the top objective.

After Kaplan and Norton, Somers (2005) developed the Social Enterprise Balanced Scorecard (SEBC) with some changes on the original BSC. The SEBC includes an expanded financial perspective with a focus on sustainability involving environmental and social performance, social goals above the financial perspective and finally a broadened customer perspective with a distinction between the stakeholder groups who provide financial resources and who benefit from the services.

Lastly, Bull (2007) suggested adapting the BSC into social enterprises since it has not a characteristic focus on profit. Bull's BSC involves five perspectives as; return: the multi-bottom line, a learning organization, the stakeholder environment, internal activities and visioning. The multi-bottom line was renamed from financial in the original BSC where the perspective of profit maximization and market exploitation is replaced with an approach to strategies that provide social or environmental benefits. So, this section focuses on social, environmental and financial sustainability and accountability. A learning organization section was renamed from learning and growth with a focus on ability to change and improve by measuring knowledge and learning opportunities such as culture, creativity, participative decision making, team working and leadership. The stakeholder environment was renamed from the customer section which involves customers, beneficiaries, funders, communities and society as a whole and focuses on the relations with these stakeholders. The internal activities section has a focus on business practices, internal structure, communications, and quality and management systems of the enterprise. The visioning is the final section with a concern on engaging with initiative's mission and business plans, and how these are communicated to the various stakeholder parties.

Social IMPact Measurement for Local Economies

The Social IMPact measurement for Local Economies, so called SIMPLE methodology, was created to develop capabilities to systematically measure impacts of social enterprises by McLoughlin et al. (2009) as a holistic and flexible approach to the concept. The SIMPLE model offers a five-step approach to impact measurement called scope it, map it, track it, tell it and embed it. These five steps ensure conceptualizing the impact problem (SCOPE IT), identifying and prioritizing impacts for measurement (MAP IT), developing appropriate impact measures (TRACK IT), reporting impacts (TELL IT) and embedding the results in management decision-making (EMBED IT). It is a robust strategic tool which helps organization both identifying impacts for measurement, determining impact measures and implementing them into strategic decision-making. The method is designed to evaluate impact in a holistic way and to continuously view it, to provide constant improvement and integrate it into decision-making processes. The SIMPLE methodology meets the need for a model which fills the gap between social impact evaluation and overall strategic decision-making process by embedding the social impact considerations into social enterprise management and involves internal and external aspects of social impact.

The five stages of the model specifically developed to prevent the impact measurement difficulty and make it accessible for training and management purposes. The first three stages focus on measuring the impact, while the last two stages focus on integrating these measurements into reporting and decision-making process. The Scope It stage of the SIMPLE methodology is the first level which helps to understand the impact problem and impact drivers. This stage clarifies what impact means in an organization and why they are measuring impact by identifying four key impact drivers as; mission and objectives, stakeholder drivers, external drivers (the SE impact context) and internal drivers (the organizational context and management decision making). In the Map It stage organization identifies the linkages between outputs, outcomes and impacts of the social enterprise, which means the specific impacts for measurement. This level reclassifies impact categories by adding the economic level to the traditional triple bottom line (financial, social and environmental) to be able to measure the impacts that financial measures fail to capture. The third stage is Track It where the key impact indicators assigned to outcomes to allow generating ongoing quantitative data to represent the impacts. The stage consists of four steps as; determining the outcomes and impact that will be measured, designing indicators that to collect pertinent impact data, developing a data collection strategy and implement this strategy. Tell It is the fourth stage that focuses on reporting the collected evidence in a rational way by presenting the improvement over time for all stakeholders. The final stage is Embed It, which all the processes are integrated into the organization and where the data collection and reporting becomes as a norm. It can be stated that the SIMPLE methodology is a strategic method to measure the social impact in a multi-dimensional approach.

Robin Hood Foundation Benefit-Cost Ratio

The Robin Hood Foundation is a non-profit founded in New York City targeting poverty. The organization fights against poverty by providing grants to over 200 non-profit initiatives in several areas as; early childhood and youth, education, jobs and economic security, relief and survival. They developed a benefit-cost ratio with the purpose of transforming the outcomes of the 200+ diverse programs into a monetized value that constantly measures progress towards eliminating poverty. The ratio assigns a dollar figure to the amount of philanthropic good that a grant does per dollar of cost and used to compare the impact of one grant against other. For the calculation, they take a program's total dollar value benefit and divide it by the amount of funding (cost) which allows comparing the impact of many different programs on a same scale (www.robinhood.org). With this measurement, the foundation decides which programs will be funded and how much money will be spent on each program and it provides a better understanding of the impacts of the grants (Tuan, 2008). The method has strength in a way to compare different programs and especially their economic impacts but also has a weakness when the objective of the program is nonmonetary such as better education or better health services.

Acumen Fund's BACO Ratio

Acumen Fund is a non-profit venture fund founded to invest in and to provide loans to both for-profit and non-profit institutions in areas as; bringing agriculture, education, health, water, housing and energy to the poor (Acumen Fund, 2017). Acumen wanted to measure the social impact created by investments' and compare it with other charitable projects available for the social subject that address the same issue. They wanted to inform investors that their capital will be used in the most effective way by explaining how much social output will be provided compared to the best available charitable option for every dollar spent. Therefore, they developed the BACO ratio (Best Available Charitable Option) to evaluate the social impact and cost-effectiveness of each investment. The aim of the analysis is to demonstrate whether the social investment will perform better than a reasonable alternative with a quantified indicator which refers to the net cost per social impact unit. In other words, Acumen Fund was able to quantify the social impact with BACO ratio and compare each investment with a real or hypothetical charitable alternative. The BACO ratio is calculated for each investment alternative and is reassessed on an annual basis after the investment.

Acumen Fund follows a process for various scenarios that change the projection of financial leverage and social impact to achieve the most realistic prediction of cost effectiveness. So, the BACO ratio is calculated according to three assuming financial scenarios as; full return on investment (principal plus interest), return of only the principle and complete loss. In addition, the social impact estimations are also analyzed with three scenarios as; initial projections generated from the original investment plan, conservative projections developed by Acumen Fund based on moderate growth plans, and revised projections that are updated on a real-time basis using actual impact data. This approach enables to estimate the most appropriate BACO ratio (Acumen Fund, 2007).

The Hewlett Foundation's Expected Return Metric

The William and Flora Hewlett Foundation is one of the largest philanthropic institutions in the United States which was founded in 1966 to support programs on education, environment, global development and population, performing arts, and effective philanthropy. Foundation developed the Expected Return (ER) methodology to evaluate potential investments in a systematic and quantitative process, to assess the impact of the grants and so, to make better judgements on funding. Expected return is a quantitative method to evaluate and compare potential investments for similar purposes. It is the systematization process of existing information to simplify decision-making (William and Flora Hewlett Foundation, 2008) by predicting the potential benefits, success probabilities and costs of a particular grant. The calculation provides to think about potential benefits and investment risk (Person, Strong, Furgeson, & Berk, 2009).

The method answers the following questions to transform the existing knowledge into a consistent and measurable form: a. What's the goal? (Defining the target/the ultimate outcome, the topical and geographic scope of potential investments and the measurement metric); b. How much good can it do? (Estimating benefits in a perfect world measures different outcomes of potential investments under ideal conditions); c. Is it a good bet? (Estimating likelihood of success expresses the inevitable risk by taking into account three components as; strategic accuracy, grantee success and external conditions); d. How much difference will we make? (Estimating the philanthropy's contribution which describes its share of impact by combining financial contribution and degree of influence); e. What's the price tag? (Estimating cost by taking into account program cost and overhead cost) (William and Flora Hewlett Foundation, 2008). The method seeks for an answer to the questions summarized above and so the ER calculation depends on four measures as; benefits in the perfect world, likelihood of success, philanthropy's contribution, and the costs of the strategy, and the equation is as follows:

Expected Return = (Benefit in the Perfect World x Likelihood of Success x Philanthropy's Contribution) / Cost

As a result, ER calculation aims to systematically evaluate investments by quantifying the objectives, benefits, risks and costs of potential philanthropic investments and is used to determine the most effective strategies to achieve particular goals.

Cost Per Impact

The Center for High Impact Philanthropy (CHIP) is a university-based center as collaboration between the School of Social Policy and Practice and the Wharton School of University of Pennsylvania, focuses on philanthropy for social impact. They developed the Cost per Impact method to help investors around the globe on their investment decisions. Cost per impact is of great importance for the concept of high impact philanthropy. It defines the success of a particular objective by associating it with the costs required to achieve it and guides the investor to decide. Therefore, it aims to provide a starting point for evaluating an opportunity and answers how much does change cost.

Cost per impact calculation involves three steps. In the first step *cost* is calculated. The data required to calculate the cost is generally gained from nonprofits organizations as their own cost estimates. All direct costs incurred by the nonprofit organization are included and the costs covered by other partners were not. The second step involves the evaluation of *results*. The empirical results gathered from past implementations of the nonprofits and/or third-party evaluations of the programs and a primary impact that the program produces is used to provide simplicity. The third and the last calculation is the *ratio* where the costs divided by the results, to produce the cost per impact metric and eventually to link the costs to the identified impact (CHIP, 2017).

Blended Value

The Blended Value concept was first introduced by Emerson (2003) based on the basic idea that the world is neither economic nor social, but both. According to Emerson, in order to understand the concept of Blended Value, some traditional beliefs need to be left behind. Firstly, economic value and social value created in the organization should not be thought apart from each other. Often these two conceptual frameworks are treated separately in value proposition. However, they need to be recognized as a combination and evaluated together. Secondly, the transformative nature of the investment and the dynamic interaction between social and economic components must be well understood. Because, in fact, every economic value measured contains social value and economic value within every social value. All organizations operate with interaction in economic, social, and environmental areas. These fields cannot be considered independent of each other. In addition, there is a social value function in all profit-oriented business enterprises, and a function of creating economic value in all nonprofit organizations. Thus, all returns generated create a blended value consisting economic, social, and environmental aspects and it has to be realized that value is a result of the blending of these three elements. In summary, in order to increase social and financial value, these three elements have to be integrated and evaluated as a whole in Blended Value.

This combination of value is also valid for returns. So, the concept of Blended Return on Investment (ROI) is valid for returns. Blended ROI is the tool that evaluates the returns obtained by the application of social capital and new frameworks to evaluate the interaction between value elements have to be created.

Table 1. Summary of social impact measurement methods

Measurement Method	Definition	Significant Literature
Cost-Effective Analysis (CEA)	The method is the economic expression of the costs of programs, which the benefits cannot be expressed in terms of money. It is a comparison of the costs of existing possibilities to achieve a given objective.	Russell (1996), Currie and Manns (2002); Mitton and Donaldson (2004); Drummond et al. (2006);Tuan (2008)
Cost-Benefit Analysis (CBA)	It is an economic assessment technique that measures the costs and social benefits of alternatives in monetary basis that allows assessing whether the return of investments has exceeded the cost of the investment and requires the calculation of present values using the societal discount rate.	Robinson (1993); Tuan (2008); Black et al. (2009)
Social Accounting and Auditing	It is a well-established internal performance measurement method to monitor, evaluate and provide accountability to stakeholders and a process which helps to assess performance of social, environmental and economic objectives of organization.	Pearce (2003); Nicholls (2009), Stevenson et al. (2010); Gibbon and Dey (2011); Social Audit Network (2011)
Social Return on Investment (SROI)	The analysis examines social value in relation to the created benefits and its costs involving calculations to identify the social return on investment as; the full Blended Value of a project that combines its financial value and a monetized value of its social impact, the financial investment and the blended return on investment which combines the enterprise and social returns.	Roberts Enterprise Development Fund (2000); NEF (2007); Rotheroe and Richards (2007); Nicholls (2009)
Balanced Scorecard (BSC)	It is an internal analysis tool intends to monitor and examine financial and non-financial, short-term and long-term and both qualitative and quantitative success measures including perspectives of different stakeholders to evaluate the efficiency.	Kaplan and Norton (2001); Somers (2005); Bull (2007)
SIMPLE Methodology	The model offers a holistic and flexible five-step approach to impact measurement called scope it, map it, track it, tell it and embed it, which helps identifying impacts for measurement, determining impact measures and implementing them into strategic decision making.	McLoughlin et al. (2009)
Robin Hood Foundation Benefit-Cost Ratio	The Ratio allows comparing the impact of many different programs on a same scale by transforming the outcomes of the programs into a monetized value that constantly measures progress.	Robin Hood Foundation (2017)
Acumen Fund's BACO Ratio	The ratio quantifies the social impact and cost-effectiveness of each investment and compares it with other charitable projects available for the social subject that address the same issue.	Acumen Fund (2017)
The Hewlett Foundation's Expected Return Metric	The calculation aims to evaluate investments by quantifying the objectives, benefits, risks and costs of potential philanthropic investments and is used to determine the most effective strategies to achieve particular goals.	William and Flora Hewlett Foundation (2008)
Cost Per Impact	It defines the success of a particular objective by associating it with the costs required to achieve it and guides the investor to decide and aims to provide a starting point for evaluating an opportunity and answers how much does change cost.	CHIP (2017)
Blended Value	According to this method all returns generated create a blended value consisting economic, social, and environmental aspects value is a result of the blending of these elements and they have to be integrated and evaluated as a whole.	Emerson (2003)

In addition, there is a need for the Social Management Information System (Social MIS) infrastructure to keep track of the Blended Value. In other words, a system that defines, tracks and evaluates the value mix combination including socio-financial ratios. As these approaches and systems evolve, we will also increase our competence to understand, track and evaluate the value creation process.

CONCLUSION

In summary, literature on the measurement of the social impact created by social enterprises is still developing and not accurate. The proposed methods for the topic are predominantly based on considering both social and economic performance. Social entrepreneurs can test their own spending decisions by measuring their activities and their social impact, as well as informing investors about the issue. The crucial point here is to understand what the social impact means to various stakeholders and to adopt a method that will meet the expectations. It should be emphasized at this point that there is no method that can be called the most accurate or the most successful. Each method has its own strengths and weaknesses. It is therefore not possible to mention one valid method to meet the needs of all social enterprises. It is also very important which information to use as well as the decision on which method to choose. In order to obtain accurate and valid results, it is absolutely necessary to use right and quality data in measurement process.

In general, when looking at the overall approaches, it seems that each of them has the basic principles of making stakeholder expectations a focal point, requiring transparency in all activities, adopting change and development and so on. In the case of social initiatives, this perspective can not be considered otherwise. With the appropriate measurement methods in which the right information is used, social enterprises will be able to reveal their own successes, meet stakeholder expectations, and ensure that the initiative and its activities are sustainable.

In addition to the methodologies summarized above, there are around 30 different measurement tools in the literature. However, they have not been addressed since they are not used as frequently as the methods mentioned in this chapter.

REFERENCES

Acumen Fund. (2017). Retrieved from http://acumen.org/sectors/

Acumen Fund Metrics Team. (2007). Acumen Fund Concepts: The Best Available Charitable Option. New York: Author.

Arena, M., Azzone, G., & Bengo, I. (2015). Performance measurement for social enterprises. *Voluntas*, *26*(2), 649–672. doi:10.100711266-013-9436-8

Bititci, U., Garengo, P., Dörfler, V., & Nudurupati, S. (2011). Performance measurement: Challenges for tomorrow. *International Journal of Management Reviews*, *14*(3), 305–327. doi:10.1111/j.1468-2370.2011.00318.x

Black, J., Hashimzade, N., & Myles, G. (2009). *Dictionary of Economics*. Oxford University Press. doi:10.1093/acref/9780199237043.001.0001

Bouckaert, L., & Vandenhove, J. (1998). Business ethics and the management of non-profit organizations. *Journal of Business Ethics*, *17*(9/10), 1073–1081. doi:10.1023/A:1006071416514

Bull, M. (2007). Balance: The development of a social enterprise business performance analysis tool. *Social Enterprise Journal*, *3*(1), 49–66. doi:10.1108/17508610780000721

Burdge, R. J., & Vanclay, F. (1996). Social impact assessment: A contribution to the state of the art series. *Environmental and Social Impact Assessment*, *14*(1), 59–86. doi:10.1080/07349165.1996.9725886

Cabinet Office, Office of the Third Sector. (2009). *A guide to Social Return on Investment*. Society Media.

Center for Global Development Official Website. (n.d.). Retrieved from https://www.cgdev.org

Chmelik, E., Musteen, M., & Ahsan, M. (2016). Measures of Performance in the Context of International Social Ventures: An Exploratory Study. *Journal of Social Entrepreneurship*, *7*(1), 74–100. doi:10.1080/19420676.2014.997781

Clark, C., Rosenzweig, W., Long, D., & Olsen, S. (2004). *Double bottom line project report: Assessing social impact in double bottom line ventures*. New York: Rockefeller Foundation.

Connolly, T., Conlon, E. M., & Deutsch, S. J. (1980). Organizational effectiveness: A multiple constituency approach. *Academy of Management Review*, *5*, 211–218.

Costa, E., & Pesci, C. (2016). Social impact measurement: Why do stakeholders matter? *Sustainability Accounting. Management and Policy Journal*, *7*(1), 99–124.

Culyer, J. A. (2005). *Dictionary of Health Economics*. Edward Elgar Publishings.

Currie, G., & Manns, B. (2002). *Evidence-Based Health Economics: From Effectiveness to Efficiency in Systematic Review* (C. Donaldson, M. Mugford, L. Vale, B. M. J. Books, & B. M. A. House, Eds.). London: Tavistock Square.

Dees, G. (1998). Enterprising nonprofits. *Harvard Business Review*, *76*(1), 55–66. PMID:10176919

Dillenburg, S., Greene, T., & Erekson, O. H. (2003). Approaching socially responsible investment with a comprehensive ratings scheme: Total social impact. *Journal of Business Ethics*, *43*(3), 167–178. doi:10.1023/A:1022987127960

Drummond, M. F., Aguġar-Ibanez, R., & Nġxon, J. (2006). Economic Evaluation. *Singapore Medical Journal*, *47*(6), 456–462. PMID:16752012

Emerson, J. (2003). The blended value proposition: Integrating social and financial returns. *California Management Review*, *45*(4), 35–51. doi:10.2307/41166187

Emerson, J., Wachowicz, J., & Chun, S. (2000). *Social return on investment: Exploring aspects of value creation in the non-profit sector*. San Francisco: The Roberts Foundation.

Figge, F., Hahn, T., Schaltegger, S., & Wagner, M. (2002). The sustainability balanced scorecard: Linking sustainability management to business strategy. *Business Strategy and the Environment*, *11*(5), 269–284. doi:10.1002/bse.339

Folland, S., Goodman, A. C., & Stano, M. (2006). *The Economics of Health and Health Care*. New York: Pearson Prentice Hall.

Freeman, R. E. (1984). *Strategic management: A stakeholder approach*. Marshfield, MA: Pitman.

Freudenburg, W. R. (1986). Social impact assessment. *Annual Review of Sociology*, *12*(1), 451–478. doi:10.1146/annurev.so.12.080186.002315

Gafni, A. (1998). Willingness to Pay. *PharmacoEconomics*, *14*(5), 465–470. doi:10.2165/00019053-199814050-00001 PMID:10344912

Gafni, A. (2001). Willingness to Pay (WTP): The New-Old Kid on the Economic Evaluation Block. *Canadian Journal of Nursing Research*, *33*(1), 59–64. PMID:11928155

Gentile, M. C. (2002). *Social Impact Management: A Definition*. Discussion Paper. The Aspen Institute.

Gibbon, J., & Dey, C. (2011). Developments in Social Impact Measurement in the Third Sector: Scaling Up or Dumbing Down? *Social and Environmental Accountability Journal*, *31*(1), 63–72. doi:10.1080/0969160X.2011.556399

Herman, R. D., & Renz, D. O. (1997). Multiple constituencies and the social construction of non-profit organization effectiveness. *Nonprofit and Voluntary Sector Quarterly*, *26*(2), 185–206. doi:10.1177/0899764097262006

Kanter, R. M., & Brinkerhoff, D. (1981). Organizational performance: Recent developments in measurement. *Annual Review of Sociology*, *7*(1), 321–349. doi:10.1146/annurev.so.07.080181.001541

Kaplan, R., & Norton, D. (1992). The Balanced Scorecard. *Harvard Business Review*, *70*, 71–79. PMID:10119714

Kaplan, R., & Norton, D. (1996). *The Balanced Scorecard: Translating strategy into action*. Boston, MA: Harvard Business School Press.

Kaplan, R., & Norton, D. (2001). Transforming the balanced scorecard from performance measurement to strategic management: Part 1. *Accounting Horizons*, *15*(1), 87–104. doi:10.2308/acch.2001.15.1.87

Kaplan, R. S. (1984). The evolution of management accounting. *The Accounting Review*, *59*, 390–418.

Kernick, D. (2002). *Getting Health Economics into Practise* (D. Kernick, Ed.). Radclife Medical Press.

Kotler, P., & Andreasen, A. (1996). *Strategic Marketing for Nonprofit Organizations* (5th ed.). Upper Saddle River, NJ: Prentice Hall.

Latané, B. (1981). The psychology of social impact. *The American Psychologist*, *36*(4), 343–356. doi:10.1037/0003-066X.36.4.343

Lingane, A., & Olsen, S. (2004). Guidelines for social return on investment. *California Management Review*, *46*(3), 116–135. doi:10.2307/41166224

Luke, B., Barraket, J. and Eversole, R. (2013). Measurement as legitimacy versus legitimacy of measures, Performance evaluation of social enterprise. *Qualitative Research in Accounting & Management*, *10*(3- 4), 234-258.

Maas, K., & Liket, K. (2011). Social impact measurement: classification of methods. In *Environmental management accounting and supply chain management* (pp. 171–202). Springer, Netherlands. doi:10.1007/978-94-007-1390-1_8

McLoughlin, J., Kaminski, J., Sodagar, B., Khan, S., Harris, R., Arnaudo, G., & Mc Brearty, S. (2009). A strategic approach to social impact measurement of social enterprises: The SIMPLE methodology. *Social Enterprise Journal*, *5*(2), 154–178. doi:10.1108/17508610910981734

Mitton, C., & Donaldson, C. (2004). *Priority Setting Toolkit: A Guide to The Use of Economics in Healthcare Decision Making*. London: BMJ Publishing Group.

New Economics Foundation. (2009). *Proving and Improving: A Quality and Impact Toolkit for Social Enterprise*. Retrieved from http://www.proveandimprove.org/new/

New Economics Foundation (NEF). (2007). *Measuring real value: A DIY guide to social return on investment*. London: New Economics Foundation. Retrieved from http://www.neweconomics.org/

Nicholls, A. (2009). We do good things, don't we?: Blended value accounting in social entrepreneurship. *Accounting, Organizations and Society*, *34*(6-7), 755–769. doi:10.1016/j.aos.2009.04.008

Nicholls, J. (2004). *Social return on investment: Valuing what matters*. London: New Economics Foundation.

Ormiston, J., & Seymour, R. (2011). Understanding Value Creation in Social Entrepreneurship: The Importance of Aligning Mission, Strategy and Impact Measurement. *Journal of Social Entrepreneurship*, *2*(2), 125–150. doi:10.1080/19420676.2011.606331

Paton, R. (2003). *Managing and measuring social enterprises*. Thousand Oaks, CA: Sage.

Pearce, J. (2003). *Proving and Improving. Improve It – Social Auditing to Win Business Conference*. London: Unted Kingdom.

Peredo, A. M., & McLean, M. (2006). Social entrepreneurship: A critical review of the concept. *Journal of World Business*, *41*(1), 56–65. doi:10.1016/j.jwb.2005.10.007

Perrini, F. (2006). Social entrepreneurship domain: setting boundaries. In F. Perrini (Ed.), *The new social entrepreneurship* (pp. 1–25). Cheltenham, UK: Edward Elgar.

Person, A. E., Strong, D. A., Furgeson, J., & Berk, J. A. (2009). *Maximizing the Value of Philanthropic Efforts through Planned Partnerships between the U.S. Government and Private Foundations*. Mathematica Policy Research Inc.

Pfeffer, J., & Salancik, G. R. (1978). *The External Control of Organizations*. New York: Harper & Row.

Phillips, C. J. (2005). *Health Economics: An Introduction for Health Professionals*. Blackwell Publishing Ltd. doi:10.1002/9780470755228

Polonsky, M. J., & Landreth, S. (2005). Should we evaluate the social impact of nonprofit organizations? *American Marketing Association Marketing and Public Policy Conference*, Washington, DC.

Rinaldo, H. (2010). *Getting Started in Social Impact Measurement: A guide to choosing how to measure social impact*. Norwich, CT: The Guild.

Roberts Enterprise Development Fund-REDF. (2000). *SROI methodology*. San Francisco: Author.

Robin Hood Foundation Official Website. (n.d.). Retrieved from https://www.robinhood.org

Robinson, R. (1993). Economic Evaluation and Health Care: Cost-Benefit Analysis. *BMJ (Clinical Research Ed.)*, *307*(6909), 924–926. doi:10.1136/bmj.307.6909.924 PMID:8241859

Rotheroe, N., & Richards, A. (2007). Social Return on Investment and social enterprise: Transparent accountability for sustainable development. *Social Enterprise Journal*, *3*(1), 31–48. doi:10.1108/17508610780000720

Russell, L. B., Gold, M. R., & Siegel, J. E. (1996). The Role of Cost Effectiveness Analysis in Health and Medicine. *Journal of the American Medical Association*, *276*(14), 1172–1177. doi:10.1001/jama.1996.03540140060028 PMID:8827972

Ryan, P. W., & Lyne, I. (2008). Social enterprise and the measurement of social value: Methodological issues with the calculation and application of the social return on investment. *Education, Knowledge & Economy*, *2*(3), 223–237. doi:10.1080/17496890802426253

Saruhan, Ş. C., & Öncer, A. Z. (2004). Değer Hedefli İşletmecilik. Nihad Sayar Eğitim Vakfı Yayını, 529(762).

Schaltegger, S., Hahn, T., & Burritt, R. (2000). *Environmental Management Accounting – Overview and Main Approaches Working paper*. Centre for Sustainability Management.

Short, J., Moss, T., & Lumpkin, G. (2009). Research in social entrepreneurship: Past contributions and future opportunities. *Strategic Entrepreneurship Journal*, *3*(2), 161–194. doi:10.1002ej.69

Simon, J., & Barmeier, J. (2010). *More than money: Impact investing for development*. Retrieved from https://www.cgdev.org/publication/more-money-impact-investing-development

Simons, R. (1995). *Levels of control—how managers use innovative control systems to drive strategic renewal*. Boston, MA: Harvard Business School Press.

Social Audit Network. (n.d.). *What is Social Accounting and Audit*. Retrieved from http://www.socialauditnetwork.org.uk/getting-started/what-is-social-accounting-and-audit/

Somers, A. B. (2005). Shaping the balanced scorecard for use in UK social enterprises. *Social Enterprise Journal*, *1*(1), 43–57. doi:10.1108/17508610580000706

Stevenson, N., Taylor, M., Lyon, F., & Rigby, M. (2010). *Joining the dots: Social impact measurement experiences and future directions for the Third Sector organizations in the East of England Report*. Centre for Enterprise and Economic Development Research, Third Sector Research Centre at Middlesex University with Malin Arvidson, Third Sector Research Centre at Southampton University.

The Center for High Impact Philanthropy (CHIP). (n.d.). *Cost Per Impact Pathways*. Retrieved from http://live-pennimpact.pantheon.io/wpcontent/uploads/2016/2015/03/CHIP_CostPerImpact_Pathways.pdf

Tuan, M. (2008). *Measuring and/or Estimating Social Value Creation: Insights into Eight Integrated Cost Approaches*. Working Paper. Bill & Melinda Gates Foundation Impact Planning and Improvement.

Türkiye Üçüncü Sektör Vakfı Yayını. (2013). *Sosyal Etki Analizi: Sosyal Girişimler ve STK'lar için Yöntemler*. İstanbul: Seminer Notları.

William and Flora Hewlett Foundation. (2008). *Making Every Dollar Count: How expected return can transform philanthropy*. Author.

Young, D. (2003). *New trends in the US non-profit sector: Towards market integration? In The Non-Profit Sector in a Changing Economy* (pp. 61–77). Paris, France: OECD.

Zahra, S., Gedajlovic, E., Neubaum, D., & Schulman, J. (2009). A typology of social entrepreneurs: Motives, search processes and ethical challenges. *Journal of Business Venturing*, *24*(5), 519–532. doi:10.1016/j.jbusvent.2008.04.007

Zammuto, R. F. (1984). A comparison of multiple constituency models of organizational effectiveness. *Academy of Management Review*, *9*(4), 606–661.

Zappalà, G., & Lyons, M. (2009). Recent approaches to measuring social impact in the Third sector: An overview. The Centre for Social Impact Background Paper, No:6.

ADDITIONAL READING

Alvord, S., Brown, L., & Letts, C. (2004). Social entrepreneurship and societal transformation: An exploratory study. *The Journal of Applied Behavioral Science*, *40*(3), 260–283. doi:10.1177/0021886304266847

Amit, R., & Zott, C. (2001). Value creation in e-business. *Strategic Management Journal*, *22*(6-7), 493–520. doi:10.1002mj.187

Arvidson, M., & Lyon, F. (2014). Social impact measurement and non-profit organizations: Compliance, resistance, and promotion. *Voluntas*, *25*(4), 869–886. doi:10.100711266-013-9373-6

Auerswald, P. (2009). Creating social value. *Stanford Social Innovation Review*, *7*(2), 51–55.

Boschee, J. (1995). Social entrepreneurship. *Across the Board*, *32*(3), 20–25.

Boyne, G. (2002). Public and private management: What's the difference? *Journal of Management Studies*, *39*(1), 97–121. doi:10.1111/1467-6486.00284

Clark, C., & Brennan, L. (2012). Entrepreneurship with social value: A conceptual model for performance measurement. *Academy of Entrepreneurship Journal*, *18*(1), 13.

Coffey, P. (2006). Social impact measurement: methodology assessment, initiation report for the SIMPLE project, SEL/University of Brighton, Brighton.

Dentchev, N. A. (2004). Corporate social performance as a business strategy. *Journal of Business Ethics*, *55*(4), 395–410. doi:10.100710551-004-1348-5

Eccles, R. G. (1991). The performance measurement manifesto. *Harvard Business Review*, *69*(1), 131–137. PMID:10109469

Foster, W., & Bradach, J. (2005). Should nonprofits seeks profits? *Harvard Business Review*, *1*(February-March), 92–100. PMID:15724577

Fowler, A. (2000). NGDOs as a moment in history: Beyond aid to social entrepreneurship or civic innovation? *Third World Quarterly*, *21*(4), 637–654. doi:10.1080/713701063

Ittner, C. D., & Larcker, D. F. (1998). Innovations in performance measurement: Trends and research implications. *Journal of Management Accounting Research*, *10*, 205–238.

Lepak, D. P., Smith, K. G., & Taylor, M. S. (2007). Value creation and value capture: A multilevel perspective. *Academy of Management Review*, *32*(1), 180–194. doi:10.5465/AMR.2007.23464011

Mair, J., & Martı, I. (2006). Social entrepreneurship research: A source of, explanation, prediction, and delight. *Journal of World Business*, *41*(1), 36–44. doi:10.1016/j.jwb.2005.09.002

Nicholls, J. (2007). *Why measuring and communicating social value can help social enterprise become more competitive*. United Kingdom: Cabinet Office Office of Third Sector.

Ormiston, J., & Seymour, R. (2011). Understanding value creation in social entrepreneurship: The importance of aligning mission, strategy and impact measurement. *Journal of Social Entrepreneurship*, *2*(2), 125–150. doi:10.1080/19420676.2011.606331

Pearce, J., & Doh, J. P. (2005). The high impact of collaborative social initiatives. *MIT Sloan Management Review*, *46*, 329–339.

Rahaman, A., Lawrence, S., & Roper, J. (2004). Social and environmental reporting at the VRA: Institutionalised legitimacy or legitimation crisis? *Critical Perspectives on Accounting*, *15*(1), 35–56. doi:10.1016/S1045-2354(03)00005-4

Russell, S. (2013). *Journey to Impact A practitioner perspective on measuring social impact*. United Kingdom: HouseMark and Midland Heart.

Sawhill, J., & Williamson, D. (2001). Measuring what matters in nonprofits. *The McKinsey Quarterly*, *2*, 98–107.

Speckbacher, G. (2003). The economics of performance management in nonprofit organizations. *Nonprofit Management & Leadership*, *13*(3), 267–281. doi:10.1002/nml.15

Weerawardena, J., & Mort, G. S. (2006). Investigating social entrepreneurship: A multidimensional model. *Journal of World Business*, *41*(1), 21–35. doi:10.1016/j.jwb.2005.09.001

Young, R. (2006). For what it is worth: social value and the future of social entrepreneurship. In A. Nicholls (Ed.), *Social entrepreneurship: new models of sustainable social change* (pp. 56–73). Oxford: Oxford University Press.

Zadek, S. (1998). Balancing performance, ethics, and accountability. *Journal of Business Ethics*, *17*(13), 1421–1441. doi:10.1023/A:1006095614267

KEY TERMS AND DEFINITIONS

Performance Measurement: The process of collecting, analyzing and reporting data regularly and systematically to track the resources used by a corporation, its products and services, and the outcomes obtained.

Social Impact: A significant and positive change that arises from an action, activity, project or program on a social challenge which affects all relevant stakeholders.

Social Impact Measurement: The study of determining the extent of the success of a nonprofit organization and the impact created on relevant stakeholders towards a social problem.

Chapter 11
Utilizing Social Networks in Social Entrepreneurship

Nuray Atsan
Akdeniz University, Turkey

ABSTRACT

This chapter focuses on the linkage between social networks and social entrepreneurship and argues that social networks are crucial in social entrepreneurship and social entrepreneurs rely on different compositions of social networks in different stages of the entrepreneurial process. Drawing from network approach in entrepreneurship, this chapter continues by exploring the theoretical framework including conceptualizations of social entrepreneurship and social networks. It then introduces evolution of social networks in comply with organizational growth process. As a result, the chapter discusses utilizing social networks in social entrepreneurship. The conclusion reflects on possible characteristics of network usage and composition through the life cycle of social enterprises.

INTRODUCTION

In today's world, social entrepreneurship has become a global phenomenon by gaining increased attention both managerial and scholarly all over the world (Mair & Marti, 2006; Zeyen, Beckman, Mueller, Dees, Khanin, Krueger, Murphy, Santos, Scarlata, Walske, & Zachakaris, 2012). Social entrepreneurship has become an important approach in addressing social problems. Due to the inadequacy of traditional approaches in addressing society's problems, social entrepreneurship is seen as an alternative way to mobilize resources, increase efficiency through innovative partnerships, increase levels of performance and responsibility, and achieve a sustainable social impact. Nevertheless, there is still a lack of a clear understanding and a comprehensive picture of social entrepreneurship phenomenon (Weerawarden & Mort, 2006; Martin & Osberg, 2007). In order to become a structured field of study, social entrepreneurship's key concepts, constructs and its linkage with related concepts need to be defined and clarified.

Particularly, network dynamics of social enterprises has been lacking. Social entrepreneurship research has not yet studied social networks in much depth. Except for a few studies (Busch, 2013; 2014; Dufays & Huybrechts, 2014), a relationship is not established between social networking approach and

DOI: 10.4018/978-1-5225-5687-9.ch011

social entrepreneurship. However, in the establishment and enhancement of social enterprises, it can be observed that social entrepreneurs are in constant connection with their social networking ties from the perception of venture opportunities, to the foundations of resources and the sustainability of the enterprise. In order for social entrepreneurs to be successful in personal and organizational sense, the leverage role of social networks is emphasized in achieving better results with less effort (Busch, 2014). While various studies show that social networks are important and underline the need for new studies in explaining social entrepreneurship (Haugh, 2005; Certo & Miller, 2008; Dufays & Huybrechts, 2014), studies at conceptual and empirical levels are still insufficient (Busch, 2014). Particular to the research at social networks in social entrepreneurship, the impact which social networks have on the different growth stages of social entrepreneurial initiatives is not yet fully understood.

Based on the use of social network theory in the conventional entrepreneurship literature, this study aims to bring the social network perspective that is missing in the literature to the forefront. For this reason, this study will focus on the network dynamics of social entrepreneurs and on the change of networks throughout the life cycle of social enterprises. By integrating social network concepts into social entrepreneurship, it can be possible to draw a comprehensive picture to explain the development and performance of social enterprises.

As in any study, it is important to state the definition which this study is based on. Since this study looks at social entrepreneurship from a network perspective, Thompson et al.'s (2000) definition,

individuals who are motivated by the opportunity to adopt an innovative approach and creative use of resources and contacts to satisfy needs which the state welfare and private (author's adding) system cannot or will not meet...

is taken as the base. On the other hand, network dynamics can be studied in the literature in terms of structure, content, and governance (Hoang & Antoncic, 2003; Jack, Moult, Anderson, & Dodd, 2010; Busch, 2014). In this study, while describing the network at different stages of the social enterprise, in particular, different characteristics of networks in terms of structure, content, and governance have been tried to be addressed.

In the remainder of this article, first we review research in entrepreneurship and social entrepreneurship literature and provide a linkage for its relationship with networks and network theory. Then we examine the evolution of networks through the business life cycle of a social enterprise. Before conclusion, we provide some ideas for future research in the domain of linkage of social entrepreneurship and network approach.

THEORETICAL FRAMEWORK AND RELATED CONCEPTS

Entrepreneurship and Social Networks

The "social networking approach to entrepreneurship", which was addressed by Aldrich and Zimmer (1986) who argued in the literature that entrepreneurs' behavior is embedded in their social relations, has become one of the most widely used theoretical perspectives in the scientific debate on the establishment and growth of businesses (Osgaard & Birley, 1996; Brüderl & Preisendörfer, 1998). Social networks are generally defined as individuals, organizations, and groups of relations between these actors (Brass,

Butterfield, & Skaggs, 1998). According to Heidt (2006), networks are the network of resources or social relationships surrounding individuals, groups, and organizations and the qualities of the connections in these networks (cited in Ozer, 2016). Entrepreneurship networks are defined as social networks that entrepreneurs can use to create and sustain an enterprise and that involve information and exchange relations (Witt, Schroeter, & Merz, 2008). The related literature assumes that entrepreneurs benefit from social network resources and try to mobilize these resources throughout the life cycle of their businesses. Numerous empirical studies have revealed the importance of social networks in establishing and growing new businesses (Brüderl & Preisendörfer, 1998; Jenssen & Koenig, 2002; Peltier & Naidu, 2012). In most cases, social networks play an inspirational role during the idea (opportunity) creation phase and also help in the evaluation of the idea. Leyden et al. (2013) reported that social networks constitutes a mechanism for the entrepreneur to create and exploit entrepreneurial opportunities. Besides, social networks provide access to information, advices and suggestions in the resource acquisition phase. Moreover, sharing of explicit and implicit knowledge and experiences can help the entrepreneur in overcoming difficulties in the acquisition of obligatory resources (Anderson & Jack, 2002).

The relation of social network theory to entrepreneurial organizations has traditionally been established in two ways (Anderson & Jack, 2002). The first of these focuses on the content of entrepreneurial relationships. This factor claims that entrepreneurial enterprises can access critical resources that they do not inherently possess through entrepreneurs' social networks (Osgaard & Birley, 1996). The second is interested in the structure revealed by the direct or indirect ties between actors. The main claim here is that within a network structure, the differentiating positions of the actors will have a strong impact on the flow of resources and hence on the outputs of the venture (Hoang & Antoncic, 2003).

The process of implementing a business idea or product/service and establishing an enterprise requires a number of resources. These resources are usually technical advice and opinions on whether information, business idea or product will work, experience, physical assets, initial capital and financial resources, know-how, reputation and legitimacy (Birley, 1985; Burton, Sørensen, & Beckman, 2002; Witt, Schroeter, & Merz, 2008). In addition, they require complementary resources to produce and deliver their products and services. Establishing communication and networking skills of entrepreneurial candidates are critical in providing these resources. The criticality of resources for the business and their availability in the market increase the likelihood that the entrepreneur will apply his/her networks. The less a resource is on the market, the more the need to resort to social networks to access that resource (Witt, Schroeter, & Merz, 2008). In fact, if we consider entrepreneurs as people who organize and coordinate resources, it can be understood that social networks are directly related to entrepreneurial ideas. The organization and coordination of resources require social activity and social interaction. Establishing a new business means activating existing social relations while creating new ones. In other words, entrepreneurship is a matter of relationship; it inherently has networking and sustaining activity (Brüderl & Preisendörfer, 1998). In this regard, it is claimed that the personal networks of an entrepreneur are strategically the most valuable sources of a company (Johannisson, 2000).

Social networks are structures based on strong or weak ties that make it possible to reach more people than can be reached and that are made of relationships between actors (Granovetter, 1973). Strong ties include close relationships (i.e. family members and close friends) with high emotional intensity that includes deep and continuous connections (Ozer, 2016). Weak ties that Uzzi (1996) defined as "relationships at arm's length" are irregular and rare connections without long-term social relationships among individuals. There are various approaches as to which of the strong and weak ties in network structures are beneficial to actors. According to Granovetter (1973), the weak ties that the individual has provided him with more benefits than the strong ties. Granovetter (1973) argues that the weak ties of a person can get them to the social communities that they have no access otherwise and provide them with the information that cannot be obtained at first hand when compared to strong ties. Weak ties are less reliable but more convenient in terms of access to new information. However, researchers such as Coleman (1990) and Uzzi (1996) argue that network structures consisting of strong ties provide more benefits to the individual compared to weak ties. This is because, in a network connected by strong ties, information can be accessed more easily, more transfer of resources can be performed, cooperation can be made in problem-solving, and there is more trust among actors (Uzzi, 1996; Podolny, 2001).

Personal networks represent "collaborative" relationships which individuals build in businesses, with other businesses and with other people. Networking is a social process that occurs over time. Network structures contain ties in the social structure that transmit information, create opportunities, and provide access to resources. In the general sense, a tie establishes a connection among actors that directs the flow of goods, services, and information, and provides interaction among individuals. A network structure occurs when many actors interact. The position of an actor in the network structure affects their status, impact and rights and obligations. For example, in a study that examined the role of social entrepreneurs as catalysts in collaborative projects, it was revealed that social entrepreneurs' structural position in the network influence the scale of the project that they can coordinate (cited in Dufay & Huybrechts, 2014). Similarly, the position of a person in a network structure has an influence that makes it easier or harder for that person to access knowledge and resources (Özer, 2016). Having the opportunity to establish strong or weak ties that may be necessary depending on the nature of the work being performed or having a central position that will make it easier to manage resources that can be obtained from the network means being advantageous in using resources and catching opportunities compared to other people. On the other hand, according to Burt (1995), the structural holes expressed by the absence of any connection among individuals within a social network structure will provide competitive advantage for those who fill this gap. Again, according to Burt (1995), people who make connections among different individuals by taking advantage of the structural holes will have more advantages as they will use the information and resources on both sides and will have advantages such as timely access to information and controlling information flow. Accordingly, the less dense the ties in an entrepreneur's social network, the more benefits they will be creating by linking these ties.

On the other hand, the relationship of social networks with the success and performance of entrepreneurial firms is also frequently addressed. It can be argued that social networks play an important role in entrepreneurial performance and in the growth of entrepreneurial enterprises (Aldrich & Zimmer, 1986). A well-established topic in the literature is that trustworthy strong work, family and social networks are the key factor in the development of entrepreneurship enhancing business performance, credibility and career satisfaction (McMillan, 1983; Ostgaard & Birley, 1996; Burton, Sørensen, & Beckman, 2002; Davidsson & Honig, 2003). Social relationships and social ties are important channels for gaining access to information. Compared with the information obtained through formal channels, the information obtained through network ties are often more useful and reliable. As mentioned earlier, weak ties are particularly claimed to present more precious information (Granovetter, 1973). Therefore, having a wide network of very weak ties is an element that increases the success of the business. On the other hand, network connections provide access to customers and suppliers. The greater the number of customers is, the greater the likelihood that the business will be successful. Likewise, networking can also allow a new business to expand its financial capital structure. Initial capital is usually obtained from relatives and acquaintances in personal networks rather than from institutional mechanisms; this is especially beneficial for establishing initiatives in the early stages and surviving in the first years. Aside from these functions, family networks provide free workforce and emotional support. Employees from the family reduce the effort of the new entrepreneur to control employees. Emotional support from the spouses is important in ensuring emotional balance (Brüderl & Preisendörfer, 1998). It must also be underlined that the greatest power of social networks in being successful is to find resources less expensive than they could be obtained on markets and secure resources that would not be available on market at all e.g. reputation and customer's contacts (Witt, 2004). In a nutshell, social networks can enhance the success of businesses through the creation of organizational assets in the form of human, market, financial and technological capital (Peltier & Naidu, 2012).

Social Entrepreneurship and Social Networks

Social networks may play a vital role in the entrepreneur process. In most cases, social networks play an inspirational role during the idea (opportunity) creation phase and also help in the evaluation of the idea. Social networks provide access to information, advices and suggestions in the resource acquisition phase. Moreover, sharing of explicit and implicit knowledge and experiences can help the entrepreneur in overcoming difficulties in the acquisition of obligatory resources (Anderson & Jack, 2002).

When it comes to social entrepreneurship, the role of networks in the entrepreneurial process is becoming even more vital. Austin et al. (2006) and Dufays and Huybrechts (2014) argue that building and mobilizing a supportive social network is crucial in social entrepreneurship due to the lack of resources of the enterprises. In their empirical study examining the success factors in social entrepreneurship, Sharir and Lerner (2006) have shown that social networks are the most important factor affecting the long-term viability of social enterprises. Similarly, in their studies evaluating different social initiative cases, Alvord et al. (2004) have revealed that the success of social enterprises is to cultivate relationships with a variety of local partners.

Granovetter (2005) argues that social networks influence the economy in three main ways. Firstly, social networks influence the flow and quality of information. For example, networks are used to receive support in decision-making and problem-solving (Hoang & Antoncic, 2003; Brady & Haugh, 2008). Secondly, they constitute an important source of rewarding and punishing. Thirdly, social networks lead to the emergence of trust which in turn can affect the operational behavior of these actors. For example, Uzzi and Lancester (2003) have shown in their study that the sense of trust particularly created by strong networks facilitates the transfer of novel and private knowledge. Brady and Haugh (2008) indicate that a dense social network has the potential to link the actor to resources which can be turned to additional resources such as economic and political advantage. On the other hand, networking is important in developing the trust and credibility required, especially locally, to encourage the community to support the activities. One of the findings of Shaw and Carter's (2007) study is that founders, key staff and volunteers' involvement in local networks are necessary for building credibility for their social enterprise. Social networks are an economic facilitator in creating prosperity due to low transaction costs, cooperation and business opportunities (Fukuyama, 1996). As a result of these three main effects, social networks will facilitate the access to resources, organizational efficiency and legitimacy obtained after tough challenges in the context of social entrepreneurship (Dufays Huybrechts, 2014).

Social entrepreneurs require different resources to establish their initiatives, to apply innovative solutions and to ensure the continuity of their initiatives. Besides the workforce resources such as employees and volunteers, financial resources are especially important for the sustainability of the enterprise. These resources manifest themselves from the cooperation with the private sector to the funds received from the state, from the donations received from citizens to the funding and entrepreneurial activities known as business philanthropy (cited in Kümbül Güler, 2008). In order for the social entrepreneur and his/her venture to create sustainable social benefits with broad effects, they should mobilize the resources outside the organization's boundaries. Social enterprises are by nature constrained by resource limitations. For this reason, in order to increase the capacity of the organization with limited resources, social entrepreneurs focus on building a large relationship and outsourcing network, developing the skills to efficiently manage various relationships within this network, and seeking creative arrangements to deal with environmental obstacles (Besler, 2010). For example, in their qualitative work carried out with Israeli social initiatives, Sharir and Lerner (2006) have shown that increasing interaction with the ecosystem is necessary since it helps social entrepreneurs to obtain resources and get political support.

According to Leadbeater's (1997) theory on social entrepreneurship, social entrepreneurship starts when an individual uses his or her own social network to mobilize others towards a social goal. Society is the most important resource for creating value for social entrepreneurs. Voluntary human resources that will devote their time and capital are necessary for the establishment and sustainability of social initiatives. To obtain the resources with a critical importance for their venture, social entrepreneurs need to work in partnership and cooperation with other social enterprises, non-profit organizations, business circles, and governments (Besler, 2010). For example, in their empirical study, Shaw and Carter (2007) have revealed the importance of social networks to provide access to market and customer information, identify opportunities, learn funding sources and provide local support for activities. They have also found the role of networks in identifying local contexts and helping to identify unmet social needs. What is more, in order to ensure the continuity of the initiative after it has started operating, an important strategy is to co-operate and/or form partnerships with other non-governmental organizations, public institutions and private enterprises (Haugh, 2007). In this respect, the diversity of social entrepreneurs' relations and the management of these relationships is vital for the continuation of their activities. Moreover, the expectation that these relationships to be established with the stakeholders around will be long-lasting is one of the characteristics of social enterprises (Leadbeater, 1997, Shaw & Carter, 2007). By nature, social entrepreneurs who are successful to create a greater social value rely on colloborative approaches and work with diverse stakeholders to build up and conduct their ventures (Alvord, Brown, & Letts, 2004; Austin, Stevenson, & Wei-Skillern, 2006).

EVOLUTION OF SOCIAL ENTERPRISE NETWORKS THROUGH BUSINESS LIFE CYCLE

Social enterprises, just like any other business, are growing and evolving organisms which move through a series stages of changes. Each stage has a unique context which influences the source needs and challenges of the initiative. Ventures need to address these source needs and challenges in order to grow and sustain their operations (Busch, 2013). Furthermore, it is emphasized that these life stages of initiatives have, rather than linear and incremental, dynamic and repetitive features depending on the differentiated resource needs created by changes in the market and opportunities (Busch, 2013).

Social Networks are dynamic as well (Johannisson, 1996; Greeve & Salaff, 2003) and entrepreneurs might rely on different compositions of social networks in different stages of the entrepreneurial process due to differing resource needs and resource acquisition challenges (Klyver & Hindle, 2007). When it is evaluated in terms of the evolution of the enterprises, the influence of social networks can be seen from the stage of recognition of opportunities to the stage of growth. For this reason, many researchers emphasize that social networks are evolutionary and organic constructs (Jack, Moult, Anderson, & Dodd, 2010; Peltier & Naidu, 2012). Brady and Haugh (2008) also stated that network usage varies according to the development stages of the enterprise. Similarly, Hite and Hesterly (2001) stated that in addition to the composition and quality of network connections in the success of initiatives, the ability to use these connections according to the needs of the different developmental stages of the enterprise is also important. Therefore, since organizations are faced with different resource requirements, demands and challenges at different stages of development, social networks need to be addressed in a dynamic perspective. Organizations' ability to meet these changing demands by harmonizing/organizing their social networks has a significant impact on their organizational performance (Hite & Hesterly, 2001).

Dynamics of networks along the business life cycle have generally been studied using the two-stage (Peltier & Naidu, 2012) and three-stage model (Greve & Salaff, 2003; Jack, Moult, Anderson, & Dodd, 2008). In his study, Busch (2013) suggested a four-stage life cycle model consisting of 'opportunity recognition', 'emergence', 'growth' and 'sustained growth'. Our study adopted a three-stage business life cycle model, namely 'opportunity recognition', 'start-up' and 'growth'. The growth stage is considered to be the last stage as it is considered to be the stage where sustainability is achieved. In this three-stage model, the *opportunity recognition* represents the prestart-up period before the firm starts operation where the social entrepreneur perceives the existence of a social need, *start-up* represents the early period after the firm starts operation and the *growth* stage represents subsequent take-off and growth.

Social Networks in Opportunity Recognition Stage

In social entrepreneurship, creating social change is the main goal. In which context and for whom social change will be created is about the perception of opportunities. The process of social entrepreneurship begins with the recognition and evaluation of social opportunities, especially in the local context. The basic criterion for perceiving opportunities is whether it can meet a social need. As mentioned in the previous sections, the social problems that the private and public sectors leave unsolved create opportunities for social entrepreneurs (Shaw & Carter, 2007).

Social entrepreneurs evaluate social opportunities according to the accessibility to resources necessary to utilize these opportunities (Weerawardana & Mort, 2006). Austin et al. (2006) believe that the emergence of social entrepreneurship depends on perceived support for access to resources. Access to resources in social entrepreneurship is a more challenging and difficult process than it is in commercial entrepreneurship. This is because compared to classical entrepreneurs, resources of social entrepreneurs are limited. Social entrepreneurs can benefit from their social capital to reach resources. Social capital is formed by social networks built with stakeholders. Many researchers have also shown in their studies that entrepreneurs' social networks are important for opportunity recognition and exploitation (Davidsson & Honig, 2003; Klyver & Hindle, 2003; Dufays & Huybrechts, 2014). Birley (1985) and Butler and Hansen (1991) found that social networks are important in the 'pre-start-up' phase to help the entrepreneur decide whether to go ahead with the business or not, and if so in which specific field. The socio-cognitive framework that De Koning and Muzyka (1999) put forth about the recognition of opportunities shows that in order to recognize opportunities, entrepreneurs use the cognitive mechanisms of information gathering, thinking through articulating, and resource assessing through active interaction with an extensive network of people. This network includes the entrepreneur's inner circle (the set of people with whom an entrepreneur has long-term, stable relationships, they are not partners in the venture), ''action sets'' (people recruited by the entrepreneur to provide necessary resources for the opportunity), partnerships (start-up team members), and a network of weak ties (a network used to gather general information that could lead to identifying an opportunity or to answering a general question).

Potential social entrepreneurs are likely to act only after they have identified a viable social opportunity through reflection and further incubation of an idea (Weerawardena & Mort, 2006). Monllor and Attaran (2008) posits that social entrepreneurs follow a "creativity model of opportunity recognition" through a reflective process of incubation, insight, and evaluation (Figure 1).

The preparation stage of this model sees a social entrepreneur's exposure to entrepreneurial opportunities as well as their upbringing, educational infrastructure, and experience as a tool in defining opportunities. Exposure to social entrepreneurship is closely related with the flow and processing of information. The differences in information influence the birth of opportunities (Shane, 2000). Access to information is possible through social networks. If we look from the reverse angle, social networks influence the flow and control of information (Dufays & Huybrechts, 2014). For this reason, researchers emphasize that the process of entrepreneurship is under the influence of environment, family, partners, customers and other stakeholders and networks as well as entrepreneurs themselves (Brüderl & Preisendörfer, 1998; Hoang & Antoncic, 2003). In recognizing new opportunities, diverse networks, especially those with structural holes and weak ties, provide as much benefit as diverse information from social networks (Klyver & Hindle, 2003; Dufays & Huybrechts, 2014; Özdemir, 2010). Nevertheless, social entrepreneurs often rely on local communities that have a local need or problem to improve their social value proposals. For a social problem to be transformed into an opportunity for social enterprise, local community members and other stakeholders must be aware of this problem and must have common values and interests to address it. In other words, there should be a consensus that something must be done to change the situation. Social entrepreneurs and their initiatives co-ordinate the voluntary public support for this social mission (Zeyen, Beckman, Mueller, Dees, Khanin, Krueger, Murphy, Santos, Scarlata, Walske, & Zachakaris, 2012). Therefore, at this stage, social entrepreneurs are often deeply-embedded in the local community/context. Being embedded in the local context provide the legitimacy that social initiatives need especially in their first stages (Busch, 2013).

The last stage of Monllor and Attaran's model involves the examination of the resources needed by the initiative, the process of organizing them and the creation of the support system. This is the stage

Figure 1. Creativity model of opportunity recognition
Source: Monllor and Attaran (2008)

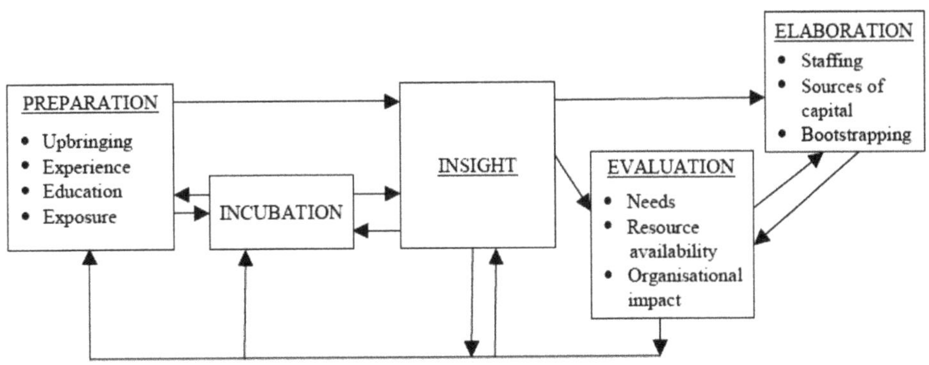

in which social networks are put into effect for the implementation of the initiative. At this stage, to formulate the social value proposition, social entrepreneurs need to benefit from different stakeholders and reconcile the values and ideas of potential funders, customers, and the community. As an example, Kümbül Güler (2008) states that business partnerships to be established with appropriate companies provide funding for the items that would normally be difficult for the organization to pay for; in other words, it will cause decreasing transaction costs for the organization. It has been shown that more centrally positioned actors have more leverage in shaping strategy and influencing stakeholders (Austin, Stevenson, & Wei-Skillern, 2006; Busch, 2014).

Social Networks in Startup Stage (Emergence)

Social entrepreneur actually creates an enterprise to exploit an opportunity (Haugh, 2005). In startup stage, social enterprises are focused on refining their model and operations. At this stage, there is still uncertainty and at the same time legitimacy, recognition, market knowledge, experience is often low (Hite & Hesterly, 2001). In addition, to successfully exploit the identified opportunity, an entrepreneur will need to garner and deploy various resources to ensure survival. They need to access information, initial capital and to motivate by encouragement (Butler & Hansen, 1991).

The establishment of social enterprises and the sustainability of their activities require financial resources just like in profit-oriented organizations. The financial resources of a social enterprise usually come from membership/user fees, foundation grants, individual contributions and government payments. Investment options are limited. In terms of human resources, social enterprises rely on a great deal of voluntary help and effort. Social entrepreneurs often recruit people who primarily contribute resources (e.g. volunteer time or funding) based on the shared mission (Beckman & Zeyen, 2014). Depending on the constraints of financial resources, social entrepreneurs are not able to pay market rates or offer incentives such as stock options (Wie-Skillern, Austin, Leonard, & Stevenson, 2007). Therefore, the most important tools that social entrepreneurs use to inspire their stakeholders are shared vision and pride (Busch, 2013).

The constraints of financial resources of social enterprises and the fact that their resources come from outside the enterprise make it necessary for them to rely on external partners to access resources and to develop multi-stakeholder relationships at the start-up stage. This potentially leads to a multiplexity of a social venture's ties. Especially large-scale solutions require inputs from different stakeholders. At this stage, the interpersonal ties of the social entrepreneur are the basic mechanisms used to access all kinds of sources. For example, due to being embedded in the local context, state institutions such as municipalities play an important role in the early stages of social enterprise as they help increase access to resources, support in implementation and awareness.

A major problem with the startup stage is getting funding. At this stage when social entrepreneurs start a new venture and are searching for external finance, entrepreneurs rely more heavily on personal and *dense* networks (Hite & Hesterly, 2001), often including a high proportion of family members. This concept subsequently falls under the Granovetter's (2005) idea of "strong" ties, which reflect interactions with the closest environment of the entrepreneur. An example of strong ties would be a sibling or parent helping out for free in some aspects of the startup activities (Davidsson & Honig, 2003). *Strong* ties, such as those often involved in family membership, may provide emotional and psychological support when deciding whether to start a new venture and startup operations as well (Greve & Salaff, 2003; Klyver & Hindle, 2007). These ties provide secure and consistent access to resources. Such active encouragement and support by friends or family is one of the strongest indicators of initiating an entrepreneurial discovery process in Davidsson and Honig's (2003) Swedish study. Their further analysis shows this is especially important in the early stages, while formal contacts become more important as the venture progresses.

Social Networks in Growth Stage

Once operations are stable, social enterprises are considered to be in the growth stage since their focus is now primarily on growth. In fact, the pressures of the funders, the demand for the products and services of the enterprise, the driving force of the entrepreneur's social mission and efforts to spread social influence can lead social enterprises to a rapid transition to the growth stage (Austin, Stevenson, & Wei-Skillern, 2006). Growth is the lifeblood of social enterprises. These organizations are built upon the energy and enthusiasm of people. To attract these people and motivate them, they need to be given new challenges, new opportunities. To provide a stream of new opportunities, an organization has constantly to develop and grow (Leadbeater, 1997). However, as the unbrilled growth can be a drain on the organization's talent and resources, organization may need to plan for a long-term growth strategy in earlier stages (Austin, Stevenson, & Wei-Skillern, 2006).

The process of organizational growth in social sector where human and financial capital is scarce poses tremendous challenges, Perhaps the most pressing challenges when it gets mature are how to secure its permanence and an orderly management succession (Leadbeatter, 1997). Even the businesses that overcome the obstacles in front of the growth and reach a certain size can rarely provide on their own a social effect which they desire (Wie-Skillern, Austin, Leonard, & Stevenson, 2007).

The reliance on networks is not constrained to the opportunity recognition and startup stages. At the growth stage, the impact of social networks continues on the life cycle of social enterprises. In this stage, there is a need to create the conditions for sustainability in the marketplace. The need for sustainability brings along the need for a broader range of resources that necessitates access to a diverse range of strong/trusted contacts (Volans, 2009). Social enterprises aim to achieve financial sustainability by combining financial, physical and human resources (Haugh, 2005). Entrepreneurs continue to rely on networks for business information, advice and problem solving, with some contacts providing multiple resources (Johannisson, Alexanderson, Nowicki, & Senneseth, 1994).

At this stage, the dominant discussion in the literature is about the reinforcement of the tendency of entrepreneurs to work based on diverse social networks involving structural holes and numerous weak ties (Hite & Hesterly, 2001). However, at this stage, social networks are embedded in the business context as they were never before (Klyver & Hindle, 2007). In other words, it can be said that along with growth, inter-organizational connections developed by social enterprises that provide resource and information exchange relations between firms replace interpersonal networks of entrepreneurs.

The lack of options for social enterprises to merge with or be purchased by other businesses makes it necessary for them to create unique ways in order to cope with growth. One of these ways is to develop strategic partnerships/alliances with larger companies that might anchor the social initiative (Volans, 2009). Thus, operational difficulties such as inadequate distribution channels and beneficiaries' purchasing skills which adversely affect scalability and expansion of social impact can be overcome. (Busch, 2013). Another way is to establish a closer relationship with the state and the policy-makers (Leadbeatter, 1997). The aspects of social entrepreneurship that change the current system require a strong involvement of significant parts of the public administration (state, municipalities, political parties etc.) and a broad impact can only be achieved through the support of legislation (Busch, 2013). Social enterprise has a nature based on context and adaptation of the operational model to different cultural and institutional contexts requires innovative and harmonized solutions in terms of legal procedure and local norms (Busch, 2013). Creating enabling ecosystems is vital in order to reach critical mass and to contextualize solutions while enhancing and sustaining scale and scope of solutions and impact (Volans 2009; Beckman & Zeyen, 2014).

The literature on social entrepreneurship shows that entrepreneurs who have been able to enhance the impact area of their enterprises apply an approach that can integrate local embeddedness with global growth. Social franchising and licensing are other approaches that entrepreneurs use. With the establishment of independent, self-governing branches, social franchising / licensing system both ensures that the social enterprise protects its micro-business model and provides rules connected forms of coordination (processes, systems, monitoring) that increase the effectiveness and scalability of the solution (Beckman & Zeyen, 2014).

Briefly, at this stage, social entrepreneurs not only try to expand their domains and networks but also try to make the enterprise's role and business models sustainable in the ecosystem and in the broader institutional context. In this regard, inter-organizational networks become the main network format for social entrepreneurs and businesses.

FUTURE RESEARCH DIRECTIONS

Future studies in the examination of how and why social enterprises' networks evolve should consider the charateristics of social entrepreneur and the entreprises as well. For example, entrepreneurs may differ in their individual propensity and capability to form network connections (cited in Hite, & Hesterly, 2001). Entrepreneurs may also differ in terms of their career experiences and pool of connections. On the other hand, due to the nature of specific industries, resource needs of the enterprises may vary which will affect the network utilization. Moreover, the evaluation of social network utilization in terms of the organization and structural attributes may provide a richer understanding. Especially important is research that examines the relationship between social networks and performance measures at various stages of the organizational and entrepreneurial life cycle (Peltier & Naidu, 2012). Thus, future research should consider both individual and firm characteristics.

Having examined the impacts of social networks on social entrepreneurship at conceptual level, this study can be improved with empirical studies to be carried out in local and international contexts. Along with the evolution of social enterprises in particular, there is a growing need for longitudinal studies in literature which will allow us to monitor the changes in the content and structure of social networks.

CONCLUSION

Through innovative applications of social problems, social entrepreneurship creates social impact and change in areas where the state and the private sector have difficulties in delivering services. Social entrepreneurs have a social role embedded in social context. The problems for which that they find solutions usually develop within the local context. In order to implement the solutions developed to solve these problems, they use their relations based on the context. Social entrepreneurs continue their activities in a multi-dimensional network including the community members (customers) that they serve, the labor force (and volunteers) and income providers (donors, funders, investors, local organizations and the state) who provide the service) that should be based on trust (Kümbül Güler, 2010). Moreover, social enterprises are often dependent on resources outside of their organizations (board members, donors, partners, volunteers) and accessing to and securing these resources is possible when the social entrepreneur and all the employees of the enterprise manage and cultivate the social networks of the organization (Austin, Stevenson, & Wei-Skillern, 2006). Therefore, the success of social enterprises arises along with the success in network management.

Growth is a natural process in social enterprises just like it is in profit-oriented organizations. Since the reason for the existence of social entrepreneurs is to create social change, scaling seems unavoidable as social change can only occur when a large number of people alter their behavior (Beckman & Zeyen, 2014). Parallel to the growth trends of social enterprises, their network usage, and composition also change. Johannisson (1996) argues that the need for networking and the structure and degree of networking activity may vary dependent on the stage of life cycle. The empirical study of Klyver and Hindle (2007) also indicates that the importance of the structural diversity in social networks has changed throughout the entrepreneurial process. When evaluated in terms of the evolution of businesses, the varying influence of social networks can be seen from the recognition of opportunities stage to the growth stage.

The process of social entrepreneurship begins with the recognition and evaluation of social opportunities, especially in the local context. Both diverse information from social networks and diverse networks with structural gaps and weak ties are beneficial in the perception of opportunities. On the other hand, it is clear that to improve their social value propositions, social entrepreneurs often rely on local communities that have a local need or problem, their opinions, and their material and spiritual support.

Limited resources of social enterprises and the fact that their resources are outside the enterprise require them to rely on external stakeholders and to develop multi-stakeholder relationships during the establishment stage of their enterprises in order to access resources. Especially large-scale solutions will require inputs from different stakeholders. At this stage, the interpersonal ties of the social entrepreneur are the basic mechanism used to access all sorts of sources.

At the growth stage, the social entrepreneur both tries to expand the domain and networks and to make the role of the enterprise sustainable in the ecosystem and in the broader institutional context. To this end, the tendency of social entrepreneurs to use an approach that can integrate local embeddedness with global growth comes to the forefront. Social initiative has a nature based on context and adaptation of the operational model to different cultural and institutional contexts requires innovative and harmonized solutions in terms of legal procedure and local norms. Strategic alliances with large companies, proactive engagement with policy-makers, social franchising and licensing are often used as growth mechanisms.

In conclusion, no matter at what stage their initiatives are, social entrepreneurs must be knowledgeable, vigilant and determined about developing and using suitable networks.

REFERENCES

Aldrich, H., & Zimmer, C. (1986). Entrepreneurship through social networks. In D. Sexton & R. W. Smilor (Eds.), *Art and Science of Entrepreneurship* (pp. 3–23). New York, NY: Ballinger Publishing Company.

Alvord, S. H., Brown, L. D., & Letts, C. W. (2004). Social entrepreneurship & societal transformation: An exploratory study. *The Journal of Applied Behavioral Science*, *40*(3), 260–282. doi:10.1177/0021886304266847

Anderson, A. R., & Jack, S. L. (2002). The articulation of entrepreneurial social capital: Content and process. *Entrepreneurship and Regional Development*, *14*(3), 193–210. doi:10.1080/08985620110112079

Arenius, P., & Clercq, D. (2005). A network-based approach on opportunity recognition. *Small Business Economics*, *24*(3), 249–265. doi:10.100711187-005-1988-6

Austin, J., Stevenson, H., & Wei-Skillern, J. (2006). Social and commercial entrepreneurship: Same, different, or both? *Entrepreneurship Theory and Practice*, *30*(1), 1–22. doi:10.1111/j.1540-6520.2006.00107.x

Beckmann, M., & Zeyen, A. (2014). Franchising as a Strategy for Combining Small and Large Group Advantages (Logics) in Social Entrepreneurship: A Hayekian Perspective. *Nonprofit and Voluntary Sector Quarterly*, *43*(3), 502–522. doi:10.1177/0899764012470758

Besler, S. (2010). Sosyal Girişimcilik. In S. Besler (Ed.), *Sosyal Girişimcilik* (pp. 3–28). İstanbul: Beta Yayınları.

Birley, S. (1985). The role of networks in the entrepreneurial process. *Journal of Business Venturing*, *1*(1), 107–117. doi:10.1016/0883-9026(85)90010-2

Brady, A., & Haugh, H. (2008). Social Entrepreneurship & Networks. *Journal of Finance and Management in Public Services*, *6*(3), 29–44.

Brass, D. C., Butterfield, K. D., & Skaggs, B. C. (1998). Relationships and unethical behavior: A social network perspective. *Academy of Management Review*, *23*(1), 14–31.

Bruderl, J., & Preisendorfer, P. (1998). Network support and the success of newly founded businesses. *Small Business Economics*, *10*(3), 213–225. doi:10.1023/A:1007997102930

Burt, R. S. (1995). *Structural Holes: The Social Structural of Competition*. Harvard University Press.

Burton, M. D., Sørensen, J. B., & Beckman, C. M. (2002). *Coming from good stock: Career histories and new venture formation*. Retrieved July 2017 from Cornell University, ILR School site: http://digitalcommons.ilr.cornell.edu/articles/250/

Busch, C. (2013). Social *entrepreneurs as network orchestrators –how and why do social entrepreneurs build up and leverage social networks to perform* (Unpublished doctoral dissertation). The London School of Economics and Political Science.

Busch, C. (2014). Substantiating Social Entrepreneurship Research: Exploring the Potential of Integrating Social Capital and Networks Approaches. *International Journal of Entrepreneurial Venturing*, *6*(1), 69–84. doi:10.1504/IJEV.2014.059401

Butler, J., & Hansen, G. S. (1991). Network evolution, entrepreneurial success, and regional development. *Entrepreneurship and Regional Development*, *3*(1), 1–16. doi:10.1080/08985629100000001

Certo, S. T., & Miller, T. L. (2008). Social Entrepreneurship: Key Issues and Concepts. *Business Horizons*, *51*(4), 267–271. doi:10.1016/j.bushor.2008.02.009

Chen, S. (2011). The study on organizational development for social enterprises in Taiwan. *African Journal of Business Management*, *5*(29), 11614–11629.

Coleman, J. S. (1990). *Foundations of social theory*. Cambridge, MA: Harvard University Press.

Davidsson, P., & Honig, B. (2003). The role of social and human capital among nascent entrepreneurs. *Journal of Business Venturing*, *18*(3), 301–331. doi:10.1016/S0883-9026(02)00097-6

De Koning, A. J., & Muzyka, D. F. (1999). *Conceptualising Opportunity Recognition as a Socio-Cognitive Process*. SSE/EFI Working Paper Series, No:13.

Dufays, F., & Huybrechts, B. (2014). Connecting the Dots for Social Value: A Review on Social Networks and Social Entrepreneurship. *Journal of Social Entrepreneurship*, *5*(2), 214–237. doi:10.1080/19420676.2014.918052

Fukuyama, F. (1996). *Trust: The Social Virtues and the Creation of Prosperity*. Touchstone Books.

Granovetter, M. (1973). The Strength of Weak Ties. *American Journal of Sociology*, *78*(6), 1360–1379. doi:10.1086/225469

Granovetter, M. (2005). The Impact of Social Structure on Economic Outcomes. *The Journal of Economic Perspectives*, *19*(1), 33–50. doi:10.1257/0895330053147958

Greve, A., & Salaff, J. W. (2003). Social networks and entrepreneurship. *Entrepreneurship Theory and Practice*, *28*(4), 1–22. doi:10.1111/1540-8520.00029

Haugh, H. (2005). A research agenda for social entrepreneurship. *Social Enterprise Journal*, *1*(1), 1–12. doi:10.1108/17508610580000703

Haugh, H. (2007). Community-Led Social Venture Creation. *Entrepreneurship Theory and Practice*, *31*(2), 161–182. doi:10.1111/j.1540-6520.2007.00168.x

Hite, J., & Hesterly, W. (2001). The evolution of firm networks: From emergence to early growth of the firm. *Strategic Management Journal*, *22*(3), 275–286. doi:10.1002mj.156

Hoang, H., & Antoncic, B. (2003). Network-based Research in Entrepreneurship: A Critical Review. *Journal of Business Venturing*, *18*(2), 165–187. doi:10.1016/S0883-9026(02)00081-2

Jack, S., Moult, S., Anderson, A. R., & Dodd, S. (2010). An entrepreneurial network evolving: Patterns of change. *International Small Business Journal*, *28*(4), 315–337. doi:10.1177/0266242610363525

Jenssen, J. I., & Koenig, H. F. (2002). The effect of social networks on resource access and business start-ups. *European Planning Studies*, *10*(8), 1039–1046. doi:10.1080/0965431022000031301

Johannisson, B. (1996). The Dynamics of Entrepreneurial Networks. In P. Reynolds, S. Birley, J. Butler, W. Bygrave, P. Davidson, W. Gartner, & P. McDougal (Eds.), *Frontiers of Entrepreneurship Research* (pp. 253–267). Wellesley, MA: Babson College.

Johannisson, B. (2000). Networking and entrepreneurial growth. In D. L. Sexton & H. Landström (Eds.), *The Blackwell Handbook of Entrepreneurship* (pp. 368–386). Oxford, UK: Blackwell Publishers.

Johannisson, B., Alexanderson, O., Nowicki, K., & Senneseth, K. (1994). Beyond anarchy and organization: Entrepreneurs in contextual networks. *Entrepreneurship and Regional Development*, *6*(4), 329–356. doi:10.1080/08985629400000020

Klyver, K., & Hindle, K. (2007). The role of social networks at different stages of business formation. *Small Enterprise Research, 15*(1), 22–38. doi:10.1080/13215906.2007.11005830

Kümbül-Güler, B. (2008). *Sosyal Girişimciliği Etkileyen Faktörlerin Analizi* (Unpublished doctoral dissertation). Dokuz Eylül University, SBE, İzmir.

Kümbül-Güler, B. (2010). Bireysel ve Çevresel Özelliklerin Şekillendirdiği Sosyal Girişimci Davranış. In S. Besler (Ed.), *Sosyal Girişimcilik* (pp. 161–199). İstanbul: Beta Yayınları.

Larson, A., & Starr, J. A. (1993). A network model of organization formation. *Entrepreneurship Theory and Practice, 17*(2), 5–16. doi:10.1177/104225879301700201

Leadbeater, C. (1997). *The rise of the social entrepreneur*. London: DEMOS. Retrieved July 2017 from http://www.demos.co.uk/publications/socialentrepreneur

Lehner, O. M., & Kaniskas, J. (2012). Opportunity Recognition in Social Entrepreneurship: A Thematic Meta Analysis. *The Journal of Entrepreneurship, 21*(1), 25–58. doi:10.1177/097135571102100102

Leyden, D. P., Link, A. N., & Siegel, D. S. (2013). *A theoretical analysis of the role of social Networks in entrepreneurship*. The University of North Carolina, Department of Economics Working Paper Series, 13-22. Retrieved July 2017 from http://bryan.uncg.edu/assets/research/econwp/2013/13-22.pdf

Mair, J., & Marti, I. (2006). Social Entrepreneurship Research: A Source of Explanation, Prediction, and Delight. *Journal of World Business, 41*(1), 36–44. doi:10.1016/j.jwb.2005.09.002

Martin, R. L., & Osberg, S. (2007, Spring). Social Entrepreneurship: The Case for Definition. *Stanford Social Innovation Review*. Retrieved July 2017 from www.ssireview.org

McMillan, I. C. (1983). The politics of new venture management. *Harvard Business Review, 61*(6), 8–16.

Monllor, J., & Attaran, S. (2008). Opportunity recognition of social entrepreneurs: An application of the creativity model. *International Journal of Entrepreneurship and Small Business, 6*(1), 54–67. doi:10.1504/IJESB.2008.017389

Ostgaard, T. A., & Birley, S. (1995). New Venture Growth and Personal Networks. *Journal of Business Research, 36*(1), 37–50. doi:10.1016/0148-2963(95)00161-1

Özdemir, A. A. (2010). Sosyal Girişimcilik Niyeti ve Girişimcilik-Davranış İlişkisi. In S. Besler (Ed.), *Sosyal Girişimcilik* (pp. 139–160). İstanbul: Beta Yayınları.

Özer, F. (2016). *The change in social capital based on closed and strong relations: The structural evolution of İslamic social capital in Turkish organizational life* (Unpublished PhD. Dissertation). Marmara University, Social Sciences Institute, İstanbul.

Ozgen, E., & Baron, R. (2007). Social sources of information in opportunity recognition: Effects of mentors, industry networks, and professional forums. *Journal of Business Venturing, 22*(2), 174–192. doi:10.1016/j.jbusvent.2005.12.001

Peltier, W., & Naidu, G. M. (2012). Social networks across the SME organizational lifecycle. *Journal of Small Business and Enterprise Development, 19*(1), 56–73. doi:10.1108/14626001211196406

Podolny, J. M. (2001). Networks as the Pipes and Prisms of the Market. *American Journal of Sociology*, *107*(1), 33–60. doi:10.1086/323038

Shane, S. (2000). Prior knowledge and the discovery of entrepreneurial opportunities. *Organization Science*, *11*(4), 448–469. doi:10.1287/orsc.11.4.448.14602

Sharir, M., & Lerner, M. (2006). Gauging the success of social ventures initiated by individual social entrepreneurs. *Journal of World Business*, *41*(1), 6–20. doi:10.1016/j.jwb.2005.09.004

Shaw, E., & Carter, S. (2007). Social entrepreneurship: Theoretical antecedents and empirical analysis of entrepreneurial processes and outcomes. *Journal of Small Business and Enterprise Development*, *14*(3), 418–434. doi:10.1108/14626000710773529

Shepherd, D., & DeTienne, D. (2005). Prior knowledge, potential financial reward, and opportunity identification. *Entrepreneurship Theory and Practice*, *29*(1), 91–112. doi:10.1111/j.1540-6520.2005.00071.x

Thompson, J., Alvy, G., & Lees, A. (2000). Social Entrepreneurship - A New Look at the People and the Potential. *Management Decision*, *38*(5), 328–338. doi:10.1108/00251740010340517

Uzzi, B. (1996). The Sources and Consequences of Embeddedness for the Economic Performance of Organizations: The Network Effect. *American Sociological Review*, *61*(4), 674–698. doi:10.2307/2096399

Uzzi, B., & Lancaster, R. (2003). Relational Embeddedness and Learning: The Case of Bank Loan Managers and Their Clients. *Management Science*, *49*(4), 383–399. doi:10.1287/mnsc.49.4.383.14427

Weerawardena, J., & Mort, G. S. (2006). Investigating social entrepreneurship: A multidimensional model. *Journal of World Business*, *41*(1), 21–35. doi:10.1016/j.jwb.2005.09.001

Wie-Skillern, J., Austin, J. E., Leonard, H., & Stevenson, H. (2007). *Entrepreneurship in the Social Sector*. Sage Publications.

Witt, P. (2004). Entrepreneurs' networks and the success of start-ups. *Entrepreneurship and Regional Development*, *16*(5), 391–412. doi:10.1080/0898562042000188423

Witt, P., Schroeter, A., & Merz, C. (2008). Entrepreneurial resource acquisition via personal networks: An empirical study of German start-ups. *Service Industries Journal*, *28*(7), 37–41. doi:10.1080/02642060701846846

Young, D. R. (2001, December). *Social Enterprise in the United States: Alternate Identities and Forms*. Paper presented at the EMES Conference, Trento, Italy.

Zeyen, A., Beckman, M., Mueller, S., Dees, J. G., Khanin, D., Krueger, N., ... Zachakaris, A. (2012). Social Entrepreneurship and Broader Theories: Shedding New Light on the 'Bigger Picture'. *Journal of Social Entrepreneurship*, 1–20.

Zhang, J. (2010). The problems of using social networks in entrepreneurial resource acquisition. *International Small Business Journal*, *28*(4), 338–361. doi:10.1177/0266242610363524

ADDITIONAL READING

Ardichvili, A., Cardozo, R., & Ray, S. (2003). A Theory of entrepreneurial opportunity identification and development. *Journal of Business Venturing*, *18*(1), 105–123. doi:10.1016/S0883-9026(01)00068-4

Badelt, C. (1997). Entrepreneurship Theories of the Non-Profit Sector. *Voluntas*, *8*(2), 162–178. doi:10.1007/BF02354193

Bauer, C. M., Guzmán, C., & Santos, F. J. (2012). Social Capital as a Distinctive Feature of Social Economy Firms. *The International Entrepreneurship and Management Journal*, *8*(4), 437–448. doi:10.100711365-012-0230-7

Casson, M., & Della Giusta, M. (2007). Entrepreneurship and social capital: Analyzing the impact of social networks on entrepreneurial activity from a rational action perspective. *International Small Business Journal*, *25*(3), 220–242. doi:10.1177/0266242607076524

Chell, E. (2007). Social Enterprise and Entrepreneurship: Towards a Convergent Theory of the Entrepreneurial Process. *International Small Business Journal*, *25*(1), 5–26. doi:10.1177/0266242607071779

Datta, A., & Jessup, L. (2009). Expanding Opportunities in a Shrinking World: A Conceptual Model Explicating the Role of Social Networks and Internet-based Virtual Environments in Social Entrepreneurship. *International Journal of Virtual Communities and Social Networking*, *1*(4), 33–49. doi:10.4018/jvcsn.2009092203

Dees, J. G. (1998). Enterprising nonprofits. *Harvard Business Review*, *76*, 54–67. PMID:10176919

Dees, J. G. (2001). The meaning of "social entrepreneurship", Center for the Advancement of Social Entrepreneurship, Fuqua School of Business, Duke University, Durham, NC. Retrieved July 2017 from http://www.fuqua.duke.edu/centers/case/documents/dees_SE.pdf

Dubini, P., & Aldrich, H. E. (1991). Personal and Extended Networks Are Central to the Entrepreneurial Process. *Journal of Business Venturing*, *6*(5), 305–313. doi:10.1016/0883-9026(91)90021-5

Evald, M. R., Klyver, K., & Svendsen, S. G. (2006). The changing importance of the strength of ties throughout the entrepreneurial process. *Journal of Enterprising Culture*, *14*(1), 1–26. doi:10.1142/S0218495806000027

Gulati, R. (1998). Alliances and networks. *Strategic Management Journal*, *19*(4), 293–317. doi:10.1002/(SICI)1097-0266(199804)19:4<293::AID-SMJ9823.0.CO;2-M

Hansen, E. L. (1995). Entrepreneurial networks and new organizational growth. *Entrepreneurship Theory and Practice*, *19*(4), 7–19. doi:10.1177/104225879501900402

Hite, J. M. (2005). Evolutionary processes and paths of relationally embedded network ties in emerging entrepreneurial firms. *Entrepreneurship Theory and Practice*, *29*(1), 113–144. doi:10.1111/j.1540-6520.2005.00072.x

Hockerts, K. (2006). Entrepreneurial Opportunity in Social Purpose Business Ventures. Social Entrepreneurship. (pp. 142-154). Derleyen J. Mair, J. Robinson ve K. Hockerts. New York: Palgrave MacMillan.

Johannisson, B. (1987). Anarchists and organizers: Entrepreneurs in a network perspective. *International Studies of Management & Organization*, *27*(1), 49–63. doi:10.1080/00208825.1987.11656445

Kapucu, N. (2008). Effective Nonprofit Governance and Social Capital: A Network Analysis Perspective. *A.Ü. Siyasal Bilgiler Fakültesi Dergisi*, *63*(2), 65–89.

Kilduff, M., & Tsai, W. (2003). *Social networks and organizations*. London, UK: Sage. doi:10.4135/9781849209915

Korsgaard, S. (2011). Opportunity Formation in Social Entrepreneurship. *Journal of Enterprising Communities: People and Places in the Global Economy*, *5*(4), 265–285. doi:10.1108/17506201111177316

Larson, A., & Starr, J. A. (1993). A Network Model of Organization Formation. *Entrepreneurship Theory and Practice*, *17*(2), 5–15. doi:10.1177/104225879301700201

Lehner, O. M., & Kaniskas, J. (2012). Opportunity Recognition in Social Entrepreneurship: A Thematic Meta Analysis. *The Journal of Entrepreneurship*, *21*(1), 25–58. doi:10.1177/097135571102100102

Meyskens, M., Robb-Post, C., Stamp, J. A., Carsrud, A. L., & Reynolds, P. D. (2010). Social ventures from a resource-based perspective: An exploratory study assessing global ashoka fellows. *Entrepreneurship Theory and Practice*, *34*(4), 661–680. doi:10.1111/j.1540-6520.2010.00389.x

Mort, G. S., Weerawadena, J., & Carnegie, K. (2003). Social Entrepreneurship: Towards conceptualisation. *International Journal of Nonprofit and Voluntary Sector Marketing*, *8*(1), 76–88. doi:10.1002/nvsm.202

Peredo, A. M., & McLean, M. (2006). Social entrepreneurship: A critical review of the concept. *Journal of World Business*, *41*(1), 56–65. doi:10.1016/j.jwb.2005.10.007

Powell, W. W., & Smith-Doerr, L. (1994). Networks and economic life. In N. J. Smelser & R. Swedberg (Eds.), *The Handbook of Economic Sociology* (pp. 368–402). Princeton, NJ: Princeton University Press.

Prabhu, G. N. (1999). Social entrepreneurship leadership. *Career Development International*, *4*(3), 140–145. doi:10.1108/13620439910262796

Short, J. C., Moss, T. W., & Lumpkin, G. T. (2009). Research on social entrepreneurship: Past contributions and future opportunities. *Strategic Entrepreneurship Journal*, *3*(2), 161–194. doi:10.1002ej.69

Singh, R. P. (2000). *Entrepreneurial opportunity recognition through social networks*. London: Garland Publiching, Inc.

Thompson, J., & Doherty, B. (2006). The Diverse World of Social Enterprise: A Collection of Social Enterprise Stories. *International Journal of Social Economics*, *33*(5/6), 361–375. doi:10.1108/03068290610660643

Thompson, J. L. (2002). The world of social entrepreneur. *International Journal of Public Sector Management*, *15*(5), 412–431. doi:10.1108/09513550210435746

Ucbasaran, D., Wright, M., & Westhead, P. (2003). A Longitudinal Study of Habitual Entrepreneur: Starters and Acquirers. *Entrepreneurship and Regional Development*, *15*(3), 207–228. doi:10.1080/08985620210145009

Uzzi, B. (1997). Social structure and competition in interfirm networks: The paradox of embeddedness. *Administrative Science Quarterly*, *42*(1), 35–67. doi:10.2307/2393808

Uzzi, B. (1999). Embeddedness in the making of financial capital: How social relations and networks benefit firms seeking financing. *American Sociological Review*, *64*(4), 481–505. doi:10.2307/2657252

Zahra, S. A., Gedajlovic, E., Neubaum, D., & Shulman, J. (2009). Atypology of social entrepreneurs: Motives, search processes and ethical challenges. *Journal of Business Venturing*, *24*(5), 519–532. doi:10.1016/j.jbusvent.2008.04.007

KEY TERMS AND DEFINITIONS

Entrepreneurial Networks: Social networks that entrepreneurs can use to create and sustain an enterprise and that involve information and exchange relations.

Social Network: Network of resources or social relationships surrounding individuals, groups, and organizations and the qualities of the connections in these networks.

Strong Ties: Close relationships with high emotional intensity that includes deep and continuous connections. For example, family members and close friends.

Weak Ties: Relationships at arm's length that are irregular and rare connections without long-term social relationships among individuals. For example, school alumni friends.

Chapter 12
Social Entrepreneurship for Sustainable Economic Growth

Ebru Beyza Bayarçelik
İstanbul Gelişim University, Turkey

Fulya Taşel
Maltepe University, Turkey

ABSTRACT

The purpose of this study is to explore the link between social entrepreneurship and economic growth. For nations' economic development there are several influencing factors that can be listed. Entrepreneurship has been an interest to academics and practitioners for a few decades and accepted as one of the important factors that are playing an essential role in advancing economic development. Social entrepreneurship (SE) is a new area of entrepreneurship, which focuses on creating social value initially for individuals. Thus, it is possible to say that social entrepreneurship should improve the wellbeing of individuals by generating social value. Hence, satisfying social needs embraces both social and economic aspects, which will also affect economic wellbeing in a positive manner. The argument of this research is social entrepreneurship is an important catalyzer of economic wellbeing and economic growth.

INTRODUCTION

21th century still has very big social problems that governments and individuals have to deal with. Regarding to those problems, although world leaders are set "Millennium Development Goals" through by the United Nations, sustainable development could not been achieved, so problems are neither reduced in quantity nor the violence of the problems. This situation makes it necessary to bring new, different, extraordinary and pragmatic perspectives to these problems. Today, public, private sector, civil society and multilateral agencies are involved to provide timely and effective interventions to social problems. Therefore, Social entrepreneurship activities which are thought to provide a new point of view for social problems, especially those of civil society origin. And also there is big the expectation that social entrepreneurship can come down to the heart of the problem, act locally, and transform the system completely through continuous development and improvement. As a matter of fact, while social entrepreneurship is

DOI: 10.4018/978-1-5225-5687-9.ch012

constantly expanding its field of application on a global scale, it is becoming more and more catalytic in many countries' economies (Güler, 2011).

Rapid economic growth and radical transformation of social, economic and cultural life, often as a result of technological change, has led also to increased inequalities both within and between countries across the globe. Thus also causes systematic retreat of government from the provision of public goods in the face of new political ideologies in both developed and developing countries that direct people's self-efficacy. As a result of this transformation while the 'supply side' of resources available for public goods starts to lessen contrary more social and environmental value 'demand side' of resources are rapidly increase (Nicholls, 2004) (Shown Table 1.1). For last thirty years, social entrepreneurial activities are become more important and surfaced as global issues as part of these social and environmental demand and supply side developments (Nicholls, 2006; Mair & Marti, 2006).

Entrepreneurship has been an interest to academics and practitioners for a few decades. The term 'entrepreneur' has been used by Cantillon in 1755, to describe an individual with foresight and ingenuity who, within the parameters of economic markets, are willing to embrace uncertainty and engage proactively in pursuits of profit (Küçük, 2005). The modern concept of entrepreneurship in which much of the academic research is grounded was articulated by Schumpeter (1934), who saw an entrepreneur as visionary and innovator, making new combination of resources in an effort that could lead to "creative destruction " of existing combinations as a new product, process or market that replaces the old one (Eren & Kocapınar, 2009).

For new century entrepreneurship, for both new and established companies, is a major source of wealth and job creation, economic and technological growth, and social transformation (Zahra, 2016). Risk taking and innovation is a basic characteristic of entrepreneurs who introduced new technologies that help to emerge new industries, creating new jobs and changing and developing social and economic conditions of nations (Baumol, 2010; Phillips, Lee, Ghobadian, O'Regan, & James, 2015; McMullen & Warnick, 2016, Pathak & Muralidharan, 2017). On the other hand one of the important impact of entrepreneurship is improving the quality of life by stimulating innovation which is accepted as a means of creating momentum for growth in developed, emerging and less developed economies (Zahra, 2016).

Demographic shifts, liberalization of national economies and attendant markets, institutional and state failures have occurred to developed more social consciousness within businesses, providing new formation of social ventures (Zahra, 2008). As a consequence of these changes "social entrepreneurship" concept

Table 1.1 Drivers behind the growth of social entrepreneurship

Supply Side	Demand Side
Increase in global per capita wealth/ improved social mobility	Rising crises in environment and health
Extended productive lifetime	Rising economic inequality
Increase in number of democratic governments	Government inefficiencies in public service delivery
Increased power of multinational corporations	Retreat of government in face of free market ideology
Better education levels	More developed role for NGOs
Improved communications	Resource competition

Source: Adapted from (Nicholls, 2006), "Social Entrepreneurship New Models Of Sustainable Social Change "

starts to discuss and investigate by both practitioners and scholars in management, strategic management, and entrepreneurship (Mair & Martí, 2006; Marshall, 2011;Pol & Ville, 2009; Sullivan, Weerawardena, & Carnegie, 2002; Zahra, Gedajlovic, Neubaum, Shulman, 2009). Although this concept is not new, there is not enough study about social entrepreneurship as a theoretical concept that differentiates from other concepts like social economy, corporate social responsibility, social change and social innovation. This concept is inherently complex and it is difficult to map where its conceptual boundaries are and partly because not much literature is available in the field (Trivedi, 2011).

According to Nicholls (2006) social entrepreneurship is "innovative and effective activities that focus on resolving social market failures and creating opportunities to add social value systematically by using a range of organizational formats to maximize social impact and bring about change". For the purposes of this chapter, social entrepreneurship is defined as the process by which effective, innovative, and sustainable solutions are pioneered to meet social and environmental challenges. The basic difference between traditional and social entrepreneurship is traditional entrepreneurship primarily concerned with discovering and exploiting business opportunities, social entrepreneurship is about channeling entrepreneurial activity towards solving social problems and improving the quality of life and enhancing human development (Marshall, 2011). Although some researchers refer to social entrepreneurship as nonprofit enterprises in search of alternative funding strategies and management schemes to create social value. The other researchers consider social entrepreneurship, the socially responsible practice of commercial businesses (Pathak & Muralidharan, 2017).

Entrepreneurship has an important influence on balancing economic purposes and social well- being. The main duty of social entrepreneurship in addition to new venture creation with a social purpose, is to meet social and societal needs that have not yet been addressed by the state or the commercial sector (Alvord, Brown, & Letts, 2004; Thompson, 2002). Unlike the commercial and capitalistic economy, which is narrowly concerned with meeting strictly financial objectives, social entrepreneurship promotes a logic of unity that favors social cohesion and welfare.

LITERATURE REVIEW

The concept of Entrepreneurship, increased importance from industrial society to information society, is one of the most interesting topics of business and economics literature. While the literature on social entrepreneurship is relatively new, the main concepts of this chapter have an established history. The foundations of entrepreneurship literature emerged in the 1700s (by Cantillon), the concept of a social entrepreneurship starts to investigate in the 1990s (Luke & Chue, 2013).

A Historical Perspective of Entrepreneurship

In the historical perspective, the word "entrepreneur" is coming from French roots '*entreprendre*', literary translated means "between-taker" or "go-between" (Hisrich, Peters, & Shepher, 2010). Richard Cantillon (1680-1734), an Irish international banker and author, was the first to acknowledge the term 'entrepreneur' as economic meaning in the literature. According to him, society is divided into two main classes: the risk-taking entrepreneurs and the non-entrepreneurial consumers and worker. Cantillon illustrate the entrepreneur as:

someone who exercises business judgment in the face of uncertainty, who engages in arbitrage and bears risk, and who is seen as an equilibrating function within the economic system (Lynskey & Yonekura, 2002).

Jean-Baptiste Say (1767-1832) another French economist, advanced the idea of entrepreneur in the early 1800s. According to Say entrepreneur shifts economic resources out of the area of lower productivity and into the area of higher productivity and greater yield (Praszkier & Nowak, 2012).

Early definitions and researches of entrepreneurship are assumed an entrepreneur as who responded to an *exogenous* influence that impacted upon the market. In spite of this assumption, Joseph A. Schumpeter (1883-1950) identified the entrepreneur as a dynamic, proactive influence and the principal *endogenous* cause of change in the economic system. He was studied long-term economic development and structural changes in capitalist societies. According to author, the entrepreneur is the figure in a society who discovers, often in an existing knowledge pool, ideas untried in commercial reality and introduces them into economic life (Lynskey & Yonekura, 2002). So as for Schumpeter, entrepreneurs can be the owners or operates a company, thus they are innovator and leader who transforms inventions and ideas into economically viable entities responsible for introducing changes in at least one of the following ways: 1) the introduction of a new product or a new quality of product; 2) the introduction of a new production method; 3) the opening of a new market; 4) the acquisition of a new source of raw materials; or 5) the reorganization of a sector of activity (Schumpeter, 1934). On the other hand contemporary study of Drucker (1985) stress the role of an entrepreneur as someone who *always searches for change, responds to it, and exploits it as an opportunity.*

The entrepreneurial process is defined as *how, by whom and with what effects opportunities to create new goods and services are discovered, evaluated and exploited* (Shane & Venkataraman, 2000). Therefore, entrepreneurship can be an important way to restore a better balance between economic purposes and social well- being (Fayolle & Matlay, 2010).

Definition of Social Entrepreneurship

Social entrepreneurship is defined as better accommodation a social dimension within the traditional economic behavior, to take into consideration social problems, countries' and communities' contexts and situations (Fayolle & Matlay, 2010). This concept has arisen as a universal phenomenon to bridge the gap between the demands for fulfilment of social and environmental needs, and the corresponding supply of resources (Nicholls, 2006). SE is emerged as a reaction to failure of market, state or/and both in meeting social needs (Singh, Majumdar, & Saini, 2017). Social entrepreneurship have their origins to classical entrepreneurship features which are opportunity identification (Zahra & Covin, 1995; Shane, 2003), innovation (Burgelman, 1983; Drucker, 1985; Schumpeter, 1934; Sharma & Chrisman, 1999; Antoncic & Hisrich, 2003) and risk taking (Stevenson & Jarillo, 1990; Dess & Lumpkin, 1996; Coulter, 2001, Antoncic & Hisrich, 2003), as key dimensions that come together to provide social values by *combining resources in new ways* for *stimulating social change or meeting social needs* (Ruvio & Shoham, 2010). Social enterprises are the products of social entrepreneurship (Dees, 1998; Triverdi & Stokols, 2011; Luke & Chu, 2013). So as they can occur within or across the nonprofit, business or government sectors (Austin, Stevenson, & Wei-Skillern, 2006) but differ from traditional non-profit organizations especially because of their business-like approach to social issues. Emerging norms within the social enterprise sector include revenue generation, market, client and commercial focus, and at times self-funding operations (Luke & Chu, 2013).

Although social entrepreneurship is interested and studied by academic scholars and business practitioner for last three decade, there is no consensus on the conceptualization and definition of social entrepreneurship. This is because the concept is inherently complex and it is difficult to map where its conceptual boundaries are and partly because not much literature is available in the field (Zahra, 2009; Short, Moss, & Lumpkin, 2009; Nicolopoulou, 2014). Most of the scholarly research on SE has been tried to find out identification of what it is and what it does and does not have in common with commercial entrepreneurial activity (Dees 1994; Short, Moss, & Lumpkin, 2009; Trivedi & Stock, 2008; Trivedi, 2010; Nicolopoulou, 2014). Besides, some scholars argue that social entrepreneurship is multidimensionality of the concept of entrepreneurship and social (Mair & Martí, 2006; Nicholls, 2006; Peredo & McLean, 2006). Entrepreneurship directs to starting a business and to value creation for the entrepreneurs or society. Innovation is used to take advantage of new opportunities. A social dimension refers to social mission and social value creation that are characteristics to distinguish social entrepreneurship and economic entrepreneurship (Brinckerhoff, 2001; Tan, Williams, &Tan, 2005; Bollingtoft & Ulhoi, 2005).

The term 'social enterpreneur' is first used by Banks (1972) who stressed on *managerial skills could be deployed to address social problems, as well as business challenges*. After Banks researches, social entrepreneurship studies concentrate on the management of non-profit organizations and public institutions. In 1973, Etzioni draw attention on the necessary innovations and reforms for society could not activate alone by neither the state nor the market alone. Unless the source would be 'a third alternative' that could combine the efficiency of the entrepreneurial market place with the welfare orientation of the state. Another important contribution on social entrepreneur concept came from Chamberlain (1977). He generalized socially motivated business executives who should more responsible for themselves and their corporations to constructive issues to social problems by applying more humanitarian policies and rules (Nicholls, 2006).

Social entrepreneur is the main actor in making significant and diverse contributions to their communities and societies, offering creative solutions to complex and persistent social problems (Zahra, Gedajlovic, Neubaum, & Shulman, 2009). There are many emerging definition on social entrepreneurs. The most widely cited definition of social entrepreneurship was offered by Greg Dees who is often referred to as the father of social entrepreneurship education, in 1998. Dees says that social entrepreneurs play the role of change agents in the social sector by:

- Adopting a mission to create and sustain social value (not just private value)
- Recognizing and relentlessly pursuing new opportunities to serve that mission
- Engaging in a process of continuous innovation, adaptation, and learning
- Acting boldly without being limited by resources currently at hand,
- Exhibiting a heightened sense of accountability to the constituencies served and for the outcomes created (Praszkie & Nowak, 2012).

Brouard and Larivet (2010) analyzed 28 different definitions of social entrepreneur that associated with their traits and their actions, cited in the literature between 1999-2008 years. They defined social entrepreneur according to the intersection of findings as;

Social entrepreneurs as any individuals who with their entrepreneurial spirit and personality will act as change agents and leaders to tackle social problems by recognizing new opportunities and finding innovative solutions, and are more concerned with creating social value than financial value.

So, social entrepreneur is someone who designs and implements an intervention, product, or service that improves the well-being of marginalized individuals and populations (Chahine, 2016). Social entrepreneurs may work in different sectors, such as private, public, and community sectors, but they all bring in the original spirit, vision, method, and knowledge of economic entrepreneurship, while, at the same time, inspiring this into the public and social sphere (Squazzoni, 2009). The Skoll Foundation (2005) noted that *unlike business entrepreneurs who are motivated by profits, social entrepreneurs are motivated to improve society*. Creativity, innovation, and resourcefulness are the characteristics of entrepreneurship most significant to social entrepreneur (Praszkie & Nowak, 2012).

Social entrepreneurs have always existed in the history like Florence Nightingale, Gandhi, Martin Luther King Jr. But in the past they were called visionaries, humanitarians, philanthropists, reformers, saints, or simply great leaders. Attention was paid to their courage, compassion, and vision but rarely to the practical aspects of their accomplishments (Bornstein & Davis, 2010). Fazle Abed and Mohammad Yunus are the pioneers of social entreprnuers from Bangledes, India. Yunus, an economics professor who had established the Grameen Bank, a for-profit, antipoverty bank whose majority shareholders were the women villagers it served. Abed, founded BRAC, a nonprofit organization involved in rural education, health care, microfinance, and social and economic development (Bornstein & Davis, 2010).

Most research on theory development in the area of social entrepreneurship has been guided by management theories and terminology and have tried to differentiate social entrepreneurship from corporate entrepreneurship (Triverdi & Stokols, 2011). Zahra and his colleagues (2009) define social entrepreneurship as:

encompasses the activities and processes undertaken to discover, define, and exploit opportunities in order to enhance social wealth by creating new ventures or managing existing organizations in an innovative manner.

On the other hand, Martin and Osberg (2007) describe social entrepreneurship in 3 items;

1. Identification a stable yet unjust equilibrium which the excludes, marginalizes or causes suffering to a group which lacks the means to transform the equilibrium;
2. Identification of an opportunity and developing a new social value proposition to challenge the equilibrium, and
3. Forging a new, stable equilibrium to alleviate the suffering of the targeted group through imitation and creation of a stable ecosystem around the new equilibrium to ensure a better future for the group and society

For Mair and Marti (2006a), social entrepreneurship is:

...a process of creating value by combining resources in new ways...intended primarily to explore and exploit opportunities to create social value by stimulating social change or meeting social needs.

Thus, social entrepreneurship refers to innovative activity with a social objective in either the for-profit sector, such as in social-purpose commercial ventures or in corporate social entrepreneurship or in the nonprofit sector, or across sectors, such as hybrid structural forms, which mix for-profit and nonprofit approaches. When summed the all definitions of social entrepreneurship; create social value, rather than personal and shareholder wealth, and that the activity is characterized by innovation, or the creation of something new rather than simply the replication of existing enterprises or practices are the most important difference from the other types of entrepreneurship (Austin, Stevenson, & Wei-Skillern, 2006).

Then when examine the difference between social and business entrepreneurship, the establishment purpose, or what the enterprise is trying to maximize and the mission statement is the main difference. While economic opportunity is at the heart of a business, socio-environmental problems are at the core of a social enterprise. Business entrepreneurs look for an opportunity to create and satisfy new needs (and wants), whereas social entrepreneurs focus on serving basic and long-standing socio-environmental needs (Trivedi & Stokols, 2011). Therefore, social entrepreneurship has been developing all private, public and non-profit sectors. SE's core competence is strategic focus on social impact and an innovative approach to achieve its mission, reflect the combination of social mission and entrepreneurial creativity, so this combination makes SE distinct from other public, private or civil sector activity (Nicholls, 2006).

In new decade, society's expectation from government and from business has been rapidly changing. The government is trying to liaison to reduce the tension between business and society. Companies use corporate social responsibility, (CSR) which is *companies integrate social and environmental concerns into business operations and in their interaction with their stakeholders on voluntary basis* (European Commission, 2002), is not sufficient for new social needs and wants. Nowadays companies can meet expectation of CSR and enhance their corporate reputation with collaboration with social entrepreneurs. Business companies can integrate social and business goals in many different methods. Social entrepreneurs can conceptualize, innovate and implement CSR projects of the companies, and companies can support them to achieve the social mission (Singh, Majumdar, & Saini, 2017). There are many good examples from companies. A social entrepreneur Ramana Babu Killi who is founder of Green basis in India, successfully defined and implemented major CSR projects in agriculture and dairy sectors, for a Central Public Sector Enterprise, Goa Shipyard Limited in India. The main idea of this project is to develop livelihood opportunities, so it will increase agricultural and milk productivity. These projects benefited small and marginal farmers, women farmers, landless agricultural labors, unemployed tribal youth and micro-entrepreneurs (Singh, Majumdar, & Saini, 2017). Istanbul Social enterprise (ISE) is another social entrepreneur enterprise that is established with the aim of creating sustainable social values and uses the power of marketplace to unlock particularly 'for-profit' private investment capital to address societal challenges in Turkey. ISE is also successfully developed projects, name of "Dialogue in The Dark" And "Dialogue in The Silences" association with Turkcell one of the biggest GSM company in Turkey. The aim of these projects are to raise awareness about the contribution to society by people with disability and elderly people, leading to an inclusive behavior and to improve the social economic condition of handicapped people, especially blind, visually and hearing impaired people.

The Effect of Social Entrepreneurship on Economic Growth

Economic growth is one of the most important subjects that almost all of the countries are trying to achieve to maintain their sustainable development. The consequences of a few percent changes in the growth rate of a nation can have huge consequences for the well-being and living standards of its citizens. Economic development is not just about growth of aggregate output, but also about the fundamental transformation of an economy, ranging from its sectoral structure, to its demographic and geographic makeup and to its entire social and institutional fabric (Acemoglu, 2012).

Generally, economic wealth and standards of living are strongly dependent on the resources that a country can generate such as the level of national income. The notion of welfare usually refers to the material aspects of well-being, such as access to economic resources. However, it can refer to less tangible conditions such as contentment, happiness, an absence of threat, and confidence in the future. At the conceptual level, the performance of well-being is always two-fold: quality of life can be perceived by objective and subjective measurements. The objective measure of quality of life is about fulfilling the societal and cultural demands for material wealth, social status, and physical well-being. On the other hand, there are subjective analyses that can be used for measuring quality of life. For example individual satisfaction can be used for subjective measurements for quality of life such as feeling good and being satisfied with things in general (Koponen, 2012).

Many scholars are interested in the key question that which factors are affecting economic growth. There are numerous researches, which has been studied since late 1950s such as Solow (1956) and Swan (1956), which they suggest that capital, labor and productivity explain the rates of growth in each economy. While the neoclassical tradition identified investment in physical capital as the driving force of economic performance (Solow, 1956), Arrow (1962) supported the idea that technological progress was endogenous to "learning by doing" in the capital-goods industry. Later on Romer (1986) extended that approach by introducing R&D that produces innovation, and Lucas (1988) introduced human capital as another important input (Wu, Zhuo, & Wu, 2017). The endogenous growth theory (Romer, 1986; 1990; Lucas, 1988) emphasizes the accumulation of knowledge, and hence the creation of knowledge capital. The concept of social capital adds a social component to those factors shaping economic growth and prosperity (Audretsch, Keilbach, & Lehmann, 2006).

One of the most important scholars who have a significant contribution to the field of entrepreneurship literature is Schumpeter (1934). He highlighted the important role of entrepreneurs and their impact on the business cycle. He linked growth to a theory of business cycles and considered innovation a force sustaining long-term economic growth (Wu, Zhuo, & Wu, 2017).

Entrepreneurship has often been cited as the engine of economic growth (Neck, Brush, & Allen, 2009). Initially, only economics scholars studied entrepreneurship, seeking relationships with economic growth and addressing entrepreneurship from a purely economic point of view (Rey-Marti, & Ribeirio-Soriano, & Palacios-Marques, 2016). One of the most famous French economists, J. B. Say stated that the entrepreneur shifts economic resources out of the area of lower productivity and into the area of higher productivity and greater yield (Praszkier & Nowak, 2012). But recently, psychology, sociology, and anthropology developed contributions in the study of entrepreneurship from a social point of view (Rey-Marti, & Ribeirio-Soriano, & Palacios-Marques, 2016).

In many countries, government policies to address social and economic challenges are complemented by activities within the social economy. Social economy activities attempt to meet unsatisfied social and societal needs and contribute to finding solutions to problems such as unemployment, exclusion, inequality, lack of access to welfare services, and intergenerational poverty. Though the social economy has received wider attention recently due to the lasting impact of the global economic crisis, its contribution to more inclusive economic development has long been recognized.

Economics is a science about human needs' fulfillment. The rising of home economics assumption that people in fulfilling their needs tend to try improving their life better based on what their rationality say. These assumptions then, lead to the assumption of self-interest and the opportunity which mean that economics is the study of human fulfilling their needs by making choices and conducting transactions with others (Wiguna & Manzilati, 2014).

It is very important to understand that the success of a nation's economic growth is crucial to better meet the needs of the individual. The process of development is related with the need to satisfy basic contributions to the quality of life. On the other side social entrepreneurship improves the quality of life and enhancing human capital, which is also an important determinant for economic growth of a country. Furthermore welfare and productivity are related as improvements in fulfillment of basic needs such as goods and services, education, health and nutrition, which enhance well-being. And also fulfillment of basic needs can also be seen as an investment in human capital, and can stimulate productivity and economic growth (Perlo-Freeman & Webber, 2009). But sometimes the economic, social and political institutions (such as markets, companies, charities and bureaucracies) that are designed to provide the basic needs for the individuals in society may have difficulties of meeting the basic needs of individuals (especially the ones for health and education) in a society in terms of access, quality and affordability (Mair, 2010; Seelos & Mair, 2005). The main reason for this failure is mainly because of that public spending does not reach the poor and, if it does, service provision is often inefficient and of poor quality. Because of this reason corporations are trying to take the responsibility for meeting social and environmental challenges more proactively so as to achieve a more sustainable pattern of development (Seelos & Mair, 2005). Social enterprises are vital for economic growth and make a major contribution in local economies through job creation, improving quality of life for the local people, enabling many social services and increasing income levels (Jilenga, 2017).

Entrepreneurship is related to the economic aspect that is economic growth, but economic growth contains the improving of human's life quality aspect. This means, there is social aspect in growth that has not been raised yet (Wiguna & Manzilati, 2014). There is an important link between the concepts of social entrepreneurship and economic benefit. And also entrepreneurship can be an important way to restore a better balance between economic purposes and social well-being. In fact entrepreneurship can be a great source of economic well-being (Fayolle & Matlay, 2010). The main purpose of the social entrepreneurship is creating value by combining resources in a new way and as a result of this process try to exploit opportunities to create social value by stimulating social change or social needs. Hence satisfying social needs embraces both social and economic aspects (Mair & Marti, 2006; Wiguna & Manzilati, 2014; Rey-Marti, & Ribeirio-Soriano, & Palacios-Marques, 2016).

Figure 1 shows the main actors of social entrepreneurship and points out the relation between social entrepreneurs and social capital and the benefits to the national level business system and also the effects on economic value, growth and country's well-being. The main role of social entrepreneurs is to balance social interests with market mechanisms by the power and ability to combine social and economic factors for broader scale and more purposive issues of value co-creation. Integration of social practices with business practices plays an important role for creating patterns to develop the business system of a region or country. Social entrepreneurs becomes as main catalysts and accelerators. They are necessary for innovations and development of society (Koponen, 2012).

Social entrepreneurship refers to a process of catering to locally existing basic needs that are not addressed by traditional organizations. Depending on the need addressed, the process usually involves the provision of goods or services and/or the creation of missing institutions or the reshaping of inadequate ones. However, the main objective is to change or modify the social and/or economic arrangements that create the situation of failure to satisfy basic needs (Mair, 2010). Canadian Center for Social Entrepreneurship (CCSE) defined social entrepreneur as:

Figure 1. Conceptual framework for enhancement of social entrepreneurship role in quality of life management (Koponen, 2012)

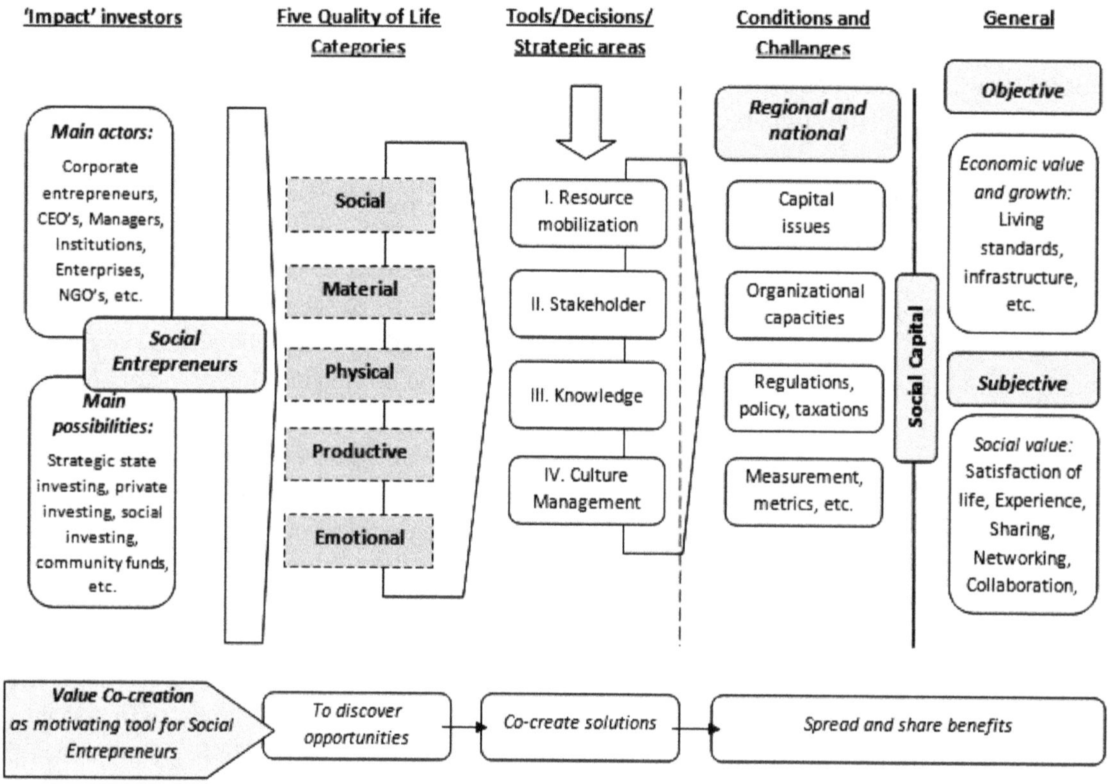

Social entrepreneurs are leaders in the field of social change, and can be found in the private, public and not- for- profit sectors. These social innovators combine an entrepreneurial spirit with a concern for the "social" bottom line, as well as the economic one, recognizing that strong, vibrant communities are a critical factor in sustaining economic growth and development. (CCSE, 2001).

Studying traditional entrepreneurship, sees the creation of social wealth as a byproduct of economic value created by entrepreneurs. But for social entrepreneurship the primary objective is creating social value while economic value creation is often a byproduct that allows the organization to achieve sustainability and self-sufficiency (Seelos & Mair, 2005). And it can be said that social entrepreneurship is different from the other types of entrepreneurship because of the higher priority given to promoting social value and development and also the effort of capturing economic value. It is possible to say that social entrepreneurship is an important topic that combines both economic and social value together. Previous studies about the entrepreneurship and the effects on economic development have received a great attention in literature but the link between social entrepreneurship and the economic effects is still very rare (Mair & Marti, 2006). Social entrepreneurship as a form of organizing has caught attention because it builds on the promises of achieving economic prosperity along with social benefits. Social ventures are built on the basis of efficiency and effectiveness, the optimization of resource allocation and utilization, along with a focus on creating opportunities for growth and economic sustainability (Ratiu,

Cherry, & Nielson, 2014). The most prevalent goal of traditional ventures is to create economic value. In contrast, social ventures are distinguished by having the objective of social value creation. Social value is the improvement of social welfare, or meeting the needs of society that are underserved by government and economic organizations. Figure 2 illustrates the economic and social value creation. Left side shows the traditional view of value creation The right side of the figure illustrates the relationship between social value and economic value. Economic profit and buyers' surplus remain the same. Social value can be thought of as the value of a product or service beyond its economic value (Woolley, 2014).

Social entrepreneurship is exposed by local, social, economic and political arrangements, so the social entrepreneurship reveal itself differently in different economic and social contexts. According to Jackson and Deeg, (2008) research, they identify the contexts where social entrepreneurship takes place conform to three main types:

1. The liberal economy, in which the market mechanism is considered the best way to shape and maintain economic and social justice.
2. The cooperative economy, in which the state plays an important role in redistributing wealth, and markets are conditioned by regulative interventions.
3. The informal economy, in which neither the state nor the market can create wealth and maintain social justice but instead affiliation to social groups determines the local creation and distribution of wealth and justice (a good example is India, but many countries of Latin America and Asia also conform to this type) (Fayolle & Matlay, 2010).

In wealthy economies, social entrepreneurs trying to renewing old institutions as they do building new ones. But on the other hand in poor and weak economies, social entrepreneurs are more often focused and enhanced on basic needs such as drinking water, providing primary health care and education, delivering electricity, and promoting improved sanitation and nutrition, that people in developed economies already possessed (Borstein, 2010).

In Europe, social entrepreneurship is almost always launched by means of a joint initiative, common ownership and democratic management structure. In 1990 SE was first seen in the third sector in Europe. An Italian journal, which is named Impresa Sociale, is the first example of social enterprise. It

Figure 2. Economic and social value creation (Woolley, 2014)

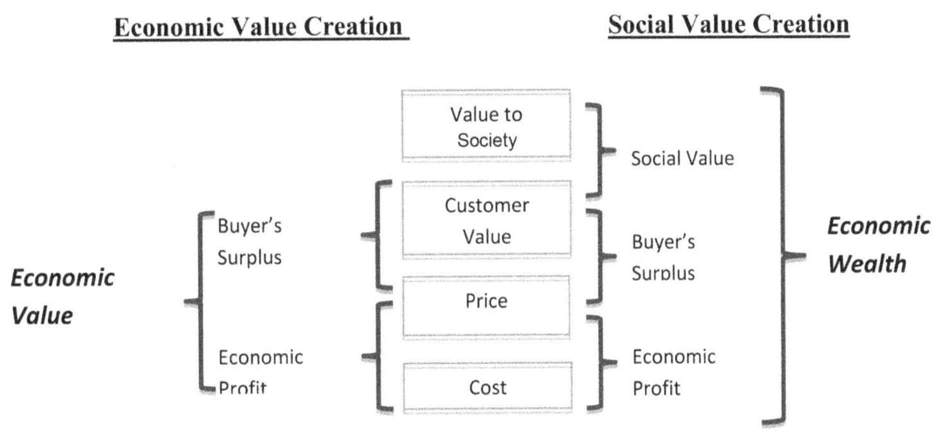

started to study new entrepreneurial initiatives that main idea is response to social needs that had been inadequately met, or not met at all, by public services (Borzaga & Santuari, 2001). By the same times, European researcher's attention the existence of similar moves, in various other EU countries in 1996 (Fayolle & Matlay, 2010). The European Commission formed EMES to study *the emergence of social enterprise in Europe*. EMES defined SE as *the sector located between the private and the public sector, which operates in accordance with the social mission and requires entrepreneurial spirit* (European Commission, 2010).

In the United States, the concepts of social enterprise also arise similar timing with Europe in the early 1990s. Harvard Business School in 1996 started 'Social Enterprise Initiative' that is the milestones of SE basis in US. After HB school, US leading universities like Columbia, Berkeley, Duke, Yale, New York and different nonprofit foundations have set up training and support programs for social enterprises as well as social entrepreneurs (Fayolle & Matlay, 2010). Conversely to European perspective of SE, the quest for market resources by US non- profit organizations led the latter to adopt commercial practices inspired by the business world. They emphasize the whole business community and its various interactions with social entrepreneurship. In US, Private foundations that most of these are authorized by large family fortunes which often originating in business activities, play major role in social entrepreneurial activities (Fayolle & Matlay, 2010). Beside these it is very difficult to find statistical data related with the social entrepreneurship. Thomson Reuters Foundation, Deutsche Bank, UnLtd and the Global Social Entrepreneurship Network conduct the world's first experts' poll to 45 of the world's biggest economies as ranked by the World Bank to find out which countries are creating the best environment for social entrepreneurs. Depending on the 2016 survey results United States is in the first place Canada is in the second and United Kingdom is in the third place (Thomson Reuuters Foundation, 2016).

Each society functions with a set of economic and political rules created and enforced by the state and the citizens collectively. Economic institutions shape economic incentives such as the incentives to become educated, to save and invest, to innovate and adopt new technologies and so on. It is the political process that determines what economic institutions people lives under, and it is the political institutions that determine how this process works. As institutions influence behavior and incentives in real life, they forge the success or failure of nations. Individual talent matters at every level of society, but even that needs an institutional framework to transform it into a positive force (Acemoglu & Robinson, 2013).

The role of government and public policies play in fostering entrepreneurial activity is evident in the work on entrepreneurship. According to Wu et al. (2017) government policies that shape the institutional environment in which entrepreneurial activities are take place. Government policies and institutional environments fundamentally influence the allocation of entrepreneurial efforts and reduce constraints on entrepreneurship. Moreover, the relationship between government policy and entrepreneurial activity varies across countries and regions (Wu, Zhuo, & Wu, 2017). Some researches indicate the importance of cross-country differences in the performance of economic and technological development and innovation are shaped by institutions and institutional arrangements. This has implications for technical change and innovation outcomes, but also entrepreneurial outcomes. (Rao-Nicholson, & Vorley, & Khan, 2017).

In general there are two main approaches about social entrepreneurship. The first one is defining social entrepreneurship as an innovative social venture. The second approach is a narrow one and defining social entrepreneurship, as the use of economic activities to approach social needs by generating earned income. Referring to the second approach, connecting directly the social needs with economic activities is an innovation and, thus, the use of economic activities to approach social needs represents a social innovation of the traditional (economic) entrepreneurial activities (Lisetchi & Brancu, 2014).

Social innovation, defined as *innovative activities and services that are motivated by the goal of meeting a social need* on the other side social entrepreneurs focus on bringing about improved social outcomes for a particular community or group of stakeholders (Phillips, Lee, Ghobadian, O'Regan, & James, 2015).

There is an important connection between innovation and entrepreneurship. Innovation is an inseparable part of entrepreneurship. Schumpeter mostly sees an entrepreneur as an innovator whose role in economic development establishes a relationship between entrepreneurship and innovation. Schumpeter is considered as one of the first scholars who have developed ideas and theories in the field of entrepreneurship. Schumpeter envisioned entrepreneurship as an engine of growth. One of his revolutionary statements is that *Not only with regard to the economy, but also socially the entrepreneur must be on top of the pyramid of society*. Schumpeter states that, while profit motive is the central engine of entrepreneurship, entrepreneurship is socially productive, when in the process of pursuing self-interest, the entrepreneurs boost social wealth by creating new jobs, markets, technologies, institutional forms, and industries (Rahdari, Sepasi & Moradi, 2016).

Harding (2004) point out the important relation between social entrepreneurship and employment opportunities. Harding emphasizes the previous studies results, which could have important implications and suggests that social entrepreneurs are effective at job creation. All types of socially oriented organization create more jobs on average than mainstream entrepreneurial enterprises (Harding, 2004). Therefore it is possible to say that outcome of entrepreneurship is job and wealth creation. Hence job creation leads to economic growth, which in turn contributes to the overall wealth of individuals and society (Rey-Marti, & Ribeirio-Soriano, & Palacios-Marques, 2016; Neck, Brush, & Allen, 2009; Jilenga, 2017).

Social entrepreneurship can supply a positive force not only to spur economic development directly but also, and especially, to provide fertile ground for such growth to take root and to ensure its sustainability. Social entrepreneurs contribute fertilizer in the form of social capabilities and address inequalities across different dimensions (social, economic and political) that can be a source of unbalanced progress making social and economic development vulnerable (Mair, 2010).

FUTURE RESEARCH DIRECTIONS

Entrepreneurship is the one of the most important engine for economic growth. Although there are many studies about social entrepreneurship, which are investigating the relations with social economy, social innovation, social value creation, differences between profit business, there is not any research that investigating the relation between social entrepreneurship and economic growth. It is apparent that economy related issues and concepts such as employment, welfare, income, gender, human capital and income distribution should be analyzed for further research.

Future studies may contribute toward investigating other issues that have been uncovered during this review process, most importantly toward developing a clearer understanding of how social entrepreneurship differ from commercial entrepreneurship that indirect effects of economic growth (Phillips, 2015).

Definitions of social entrepreneurship should be involve both economic and social outcomes. Future researchers should clarify the meaning and dimensions of these economic and social outcomes of SE concept. On the other hand most of the studies are conceptual in social entrepreneurship so as for future studies, quantitative analysis should be include on studies of social entrepreneurship and sustainable economic growth.

CONCLUSION

In today's environment there are several different issues that nations should handle with, such as economical issues, social issues, environmental issues etc. Nations are trying to achieve sustainable development goals to sustain their economic well-being but sometimes it's very difficult to achieve, and sometimes they cannot even reach their targets for a certain period of time. On the other hand increasing inequalities between individuals, higher rates of unemployment, economic crises etc. generate social problems. Therefore it is very important to find new solutions methods with different perspectives.

Social entrepreneurship is a new concept that generates new opportunities for the individuals by socially innovative and effective activities and tries to find better solutions to eliminate the social market failures. The main duty of social entrepreneurship in addition to new venture creation with a social purpose is to meet social and societal needs that have not yet been addressed by the state or the commercial sector.

The basic difference between traditional and social entrepreneurship is, traditional entrepreneurship primarily concerned with discovering and exploiting business opportunities, social entrepreneurship is about channeling entrepreneurial activity towards solving social problems and improving the quality of life and enhancing human development. Quality of life is about fulfilling the societal and cultural demands for material wealth, social status, and physical well-being.

Economics is a science about human needs' fulfillment. Individuals' increased well-being is a important indicator and is necessary for a nation to achieve economic development. As a result it is very important to understand that the success of a nation's economic growth is crucial to better meet the needs of the individual. There is an important link between the concepts of social entrepreneurship and economic well-being. And also entrepreneurship can be an important way to restore a better balance between economic purposes and social well-being. The main argument of this research is social entrepreneurship is an important catalyzer of well-being of individuals which should be the primary objective of nations who are trying to achieve sustainable development.

REFERENCES

Acemoglu, D. (2012). Introduction to economic growth. *Journal of Economic Theory*, *147*(2), 545–550. doi:10.1016/j.jet.2012.01.023

Acemoglu, D., & Robinson, J. A. (2013). *Why Nations Fail: The Origins of Power, Prosperity, and Poverty*. Profile Books.

Alvord, S. H., Brown, L. D., & Letts, C. W. (2004). Social entrepreneurship & societal transformation: An exploratory study. *The Journal of Applied Behavioral Science*, *40*(3), 260–282. doi:10.1177/0021886304266847

Antoncic, B., & Hisrich, R. D. (2003). Clarifying The Intrapreneurship Concept. *Journal of Small Business and Enterprise Development*, *10*(:1), 7–24. doi:10.1108/14626000310461187

Audretsch, D. B., Keilbach, M. C., & Lehmann, E. E. (2006). *Entrepreneurship and Economic Growth*. Oxford University Press. doi:10.1093/acprof:oso/9780195183511.001.0001

Austin, Stevenson, & Wei-Skillern. (2006). Social and commercial entrepreneurship: The same, different or both? *Entrepreneurship Theory and Practice, 30*(1), 1-2.

Baumol, W. J. (2010). *The Microtheory of Innovative Entrepreneurship*. Princeton, NJ: Princeton University Press. doi:10.2307/j.ctt21668j9

Bollingtoft, A., & Ulhoi, J. P. (2005). The networked business incubator—leveraging entrepreneurial agency? *Journal of Business Venturing, 20*(2), 265–290. doi:10.1016/j.jbusvent.2003.12.005

Bornstein, D., & Davis, S. (2010). *Social Entrepreneurship What Everyone Needs To Know*. New York: Oxford University Press, Inc.

Borzaga, C., & Santuari, A. (2001). Italy: from traditional co- operatives to innovative social enterprises. In C. Borzaga & J. Defourny (Eds.), *The Emergence of Social Enterprise* (pp. 166–181). London: Routledge.

Brinkerhoff, P. (2001). Why you need to be more entrepreneurial — an how to get started. *Nonprofit World, 19*(6), 12–15.

Brouard, F., & Larivet, S. (2010), Essay of clarifcations and defnitions of the related concepts of social enterprise, social entrepreneur and social entrepreneurship. Handbook Of Research On Social Entrepreneurship.

Burgelman, R. A. (1983). Corporate entrepreneurship and strategic management: Insights from a process study. *Management Science, 29*(12), 1349–1364. doi:10.1287/mnsc.29.12.1349

CCSE. (2001). *Social entrepreneurship*. Discussion Paper No 1. Canadian Center for Social Entrepreneurship (CCSE).

Chahine, T. (2016). *Introduction to Social Entrepreneurship*. Taylor & Francis Group.

Chell, E. (2007). Social enterprise and entrepreneurship. *International Small Business Journal, 25*(1), 5–26. doi:10.1177/0266242607071779

Dees, J. G. (1998). Enterprising nonprofits: What do you do when traditional sources of funding fall short? *Harvard Business Review, 76*(1), 55–67. PMID:10176919

Dess, G. G., & Lumpkin, G. T. (2005). The Role of Entrepreneurial Orientation in Stimulating Effective Corporate Entrepreneurship. *The Academy of Management Executive, 19*(1), 147–156.

Drucker, P. F. (1985). *Innovation and entrepreneurship*. New York: Harper Business.

Eren, E., & Kocapınar, E. B. (2009). Is Intelectual Capital Antecedent Of Enterpreneurship Orientation. *Journal of Global Srategic Management, 3*(2), 121–135. doi:10.20460/JGSM.2009318465

European Commission. (2010). *Europe 2020. A Strategy for Smart, Sustainable and Inclusive growth*. Retrieved from http://eurlex.europa.eu/LexUriServ/LexUriServ.do?uri=COM:2010:2020:FIN:EN:PDF

Fayolle, A., & Matlay, H. (2010). *Handbook of Research on Social Entrepreneurship*. Edward Elgar Publishing Limited. doi:10.4337/9781849804684

Flaminio Squazzoni, F. (2009). Social Entrepreneurship and Economic Development in Silicon Valley, A Case Study on The Joint Venture: Silicon Valley Network. *Nonprofit and Voluntary Sector Quarterly, 38*(5), 869–888. doi:10.1177/0899764008326198

Harding, R. (2004). Social Enterprise: The New Economic Engine? *Business Strategy Review, 15*(4), 39–43. doi:10.1111/j.0955-6419.2004.00338.x

Hisrich, R. D., & Peters, M. P. (2010). *Entrepreneurship* (8th ed.). New York: McGraw-Hill.

Jackson, G., & Deeg, R. (2008). From comparing capitalisms to the politics of institutional change. *Review of International Political Economy, 15*(4), 680–709. doi:10.1080/09692290802260704

Jilenga, M. T. (2017). Social Enterprise and Economic Growth: A Theoretical Approach and Policy Recommendations. *International Journal of Academic Research in Accounting Finance and Management Sciences, 7*(1), 41–49.

Koponen, D. (2012). Conceptual Framework for quality of life management: Social entrepreneurship perspective. *Economics and Management, 17*(4), 1372–1377. doi:10.5755/j01.em.17.4.3002

Küçük, O. (2005). *Girişimcilik ve Küçük İşletme Yönetimi*. Ankara: Seçkin Press.

Lisetchi, M., & Brancu, L. (2014). The entrepreneurship concept as a subject of social innovation. *Procedia: Social and Behavioral Sciences, 124*, 87–92. doi:10.1016/j.sbspro.2014.02.463

Luke, B., & Chu, B. (2013). Social enterprise versus social entrepreneurship: An examination of the 'why' and 'how' in pursuing social change. *International Small Business Journal, 31*(7), 764–778. doi:10.1177/0266242612462598

Lynskey, J., & Yonekura, S. (2002). *Entrepreneurship And Organization: The Role Of The Entrepreneur In Organizational Innovation*. Oxford University Press.

Maclean, M., Harvey, C., & Gordon, C. (2012). Social innovation, social entrepreneurship and the practice of contemporary entrepreneurial philanthropy. *International Small Business Journal, 3*(7), 747–763.

Mair, J. (2010). Social entrepreneurship: taking stock and looking ahead. In Handbook of Research on Social Entrepreneurship (pp. 15-28). Edward Elgar Publications. doi:10.4337/9781849804684.00007

Mair, J., & Martí, I. (2006a). Social entrepreneurship research: A source of explanation, prediction, and delight. *Journal of World Business, 41*(1), 36–44. doi:10.1016/j.jwb.2005.09.002

Marshall, R. S. (2011). Conceptualizing the international for-profit social entrepreneur. *Journal of Business Ethics, 98*(2), 183–198. doi:10.100710551-010-0545-7

Martin, R. J., & Osberg, S. (2007). Social Entrepreneurship: The Case for a Definition [Spring.]. *Stanford Social Innovation Review*, 29–39.

McConnell, C. (2002). *Economics Principles, Problems, and Policies*. New York: McGraw-Hill Iriwn.

McMullen, J. S., & Warnick, B. (2016). The downside of blended value and hybrid organizing. *Journal of Management Studies, 53*, 630–662. doi:10.1111/joms.12150

Minniti, M. (2008). The role of government policy on entrepreneurial activity: Productive, unproductive, or destructive? *Entrepreneurship Theory and Practice*, 1042–2587.

Neck, H., Brush, C., & Allen, E. (2009). The landscape of social entrepreneurship. *Business Horizons*, *52*(1), 13–19. doi:10.1016/j.bushor.2008.09.002

Nicholls, A. (2006). *Social entrepreneurship: New models of sustainable change*. New York: Oxford University Press.

OECD. (2014). *Job Creation and Local Economic Development*. Paris: OECD Publishing.

Pathak, S., & Muralidharan, E. (2017). Economic Inequality and Social Entrepreneurship. *Business & Society*, 1–41.

Peredo, A. M., & McLean, M. (2006). Social entrepreneurship: A critical review of the concept. *Journal of World Business*, *41*(1), 56–65. doi:10.1016/j.jwb.2005.10.007

Perlo-Freemon, S., & Webber, D. J. (2009). Basic Needs, Government Debt and Economic Growth. *World Economy*, *32*(6), 965–994. doi:10.1111/j.1467-9701.2009.01181.x

Phillips, W., Lee, H., Ghobadian, A., O'Regan, N., & James, P. (2015). Social Innovation and Social Entrepreneurship: A Systematic Review. *Group & Organization Management*, *40*(3), 428–461. doi:10.1177/1059601114560063

Pol, E., & Ville, S. (2009). Social innovation: Buzz word or enduring term? *Journal of Socio-Economics*, *38*(6), 878–885. doi:10.1016/j.socec.2009.02.011

Praszkier, R., & Nowak, A. (2012). *Social Entrepreneurship Theory and practice*. Cambridge University Press.

Rahdari, A., Sepasi, S., & Moradi, M. (2016). Achieving sustainability through Schumpeterian social entrepreneurship: The role of social enterprises. *Journal of Cleaner Production*, *137*, 347–360. doi:10.1016/j.jclepro.2016.06.159

Rao-Nicholson, R., Vorley, T., & Khan, Z. (2017, August). Social innovation in emerging economies: A national systems of innovation based approach. *Technological Forecasting and Social Change*, *121*, 228–237. doi:10.1016/j.techfore.2017.03.013

Ratiu, C., Cherry, B., & Nielson, T. R. (2014). Humility in Social Entrepreneurship: A Virtuous Circle. In Emerging Research Directions in Social Entrepreneurship (pp. 11-33). Springer. doi:10.1007/978-94-007-7896-2_2

Rey-Marti, A., Ribeirio-Soriano, D., & Palacios-Marques, D. (2016). A bibliometric analysis of social entrepreneurship. *Journal of Business Research*, *69*(5), 1651–1655. doi:10.1016/j.jbusres.2015.10.033

Ruvio, A. A., & Shoham, A. (2010). A multilevel study of nascent social ventures. *International Small Business Journal*, *29*(5), 562–579. doi:10.1177/0266242610369741

Schumpeter, J. A. (1934). *The theory of Economic Development*. Cambridge, MA: Harvard University Press.

Seelos, C., & Mair, J. (2005). Social entrepreneursjip: Creating new business models to serve the poor. *Business Horizons*, *48*(3), 241–246. doi:10.1016/j.bushor.2004.11.006

Shane, S. (2003). *A General Theory of Entrepreneurship: The Individual–Opportunity Nexus*. Northampton, MA: Edward Elgar. doi:10.4337/9781781007990

Sharma, P., & Chrisman, J. J. (1999). Towards a reconciliation of the definitional issues in the field of corporate entrepreneurship. *Entrepreneurship Theory and Practice*, *23*(3), 11–27. doi:10.1177/104225879902300302

Short, J., Moss, T., & Lumpkin, G. (2009). Research in Social Entrepreneurship: Past Contributions and Future Opportunities. *Strategic Entrepreneurship Journal*, *3*(2), 161–194. doi:10.1002ej.69

Singh, A., Majumdar, S., & Saini, G. S. (2017). Corporate Social Responsibility and Social Entrepreneurship: An Indian Context. *Journal of Entrepreneurship and Innovation in Emerging Economies*, *3*(1), 71–76. doi:10.1177/2393957516684451

Squazzoni, F. (2009). Social Entrepreneurship and Economic Development in Silicon Valley: A Case Study on The Joint Venture: Silicon Valley Network. *Nonprofit and Voluntary Sector Quarterly*, *38*(5), 869–883. doi:10.1177/0899764008326198

Stevenson, H. H., & Jarillo, C. J. (1990). A Paradigm of Entrepreneurship: Entrepreneurial Management. *Strategic Management Journal*, *11*(5), 17–27.

Sullivan, M. G., Weerawardena, J., & Carnegie, K. (2002). Social entrepreneurship: Towards conceptualization. *International Journal of Nonprofit and Voluntary Sector Marketing*, *8*(1), 76–88. doi:10.1002/nvsm.202

Tan, W.-L., Williams, J., & Tan, T.-M. (2005). Defining the 'social' in 'social entrepreneurship': Altruism and entrepreneurship. *The International Entrepreneurship and Management Journal*, *1*(3), 353–365. doi:10.100711365-005-2600-x

Thompson, J. L. (2002). The world of the social entrepreneur. *International Journal of Public Sector Management*, *15*(5), 412–431. doi:10.1108/09513550210435746

Thomson Reuters Foundation. (2016). Retrieved from http://poll2016.trust.org/

Triverdi, C., & Stokols, D. (2011). Social Enterprises and Corporate Enterprises: Fundamental Differences and Defining Features. *The Journal of Entrepreneurship*, *20*(1), 1–32. doi:10.1177/097135571002000101

Wiguna, A. B., & Manzilati, A. (2014). Social Entrepreneurship and Socio-entrepreneurship: A Study with Economic and Social Perspective. *Procedia: Social and Behavioral Sciences*, *115*, 12–18. doi:10.1016/j.sbspro.2014.02.411

Woolley, J. L. (2014). Opportunities for Social Value Creation Across Supply Chain Interactions. In Emerging Research Directions in Social Entrepreneurship (pp. 51-67). Springer. doi:10.1007/978-94-007-7896-2_4

Wu, J., Zhuo, S., & Wu, Z. (2017). National innovation system, social entrepreneurship, and rural economic growth in China. *Technological Forecasting and Social Change*, *121*, 38–250. doi:10.1016/j.techfore.2016.10.014

Zahra, S., Rawhouser, H. N., Bhawe, N., Neubaum, D. O., & Hayton, J. C. (2008). Globalization of social entrepreneurship. *Strategic Entrepreneurship Journal*, *2*(2), 117–131. doi:10.1002ej.43

Zahra, S. A., & Covin, J. G. (1995). Contextual influences on the corporate entrepreneurship–performance relationship: a longitudinal analysis. Journal Business Venturing, 10, 43–58.

Zahra, S. A., Gedajlovic, E., Neubaum, D. O., & Shulman, J. M. (2009). A typology of social entrepreneurs: Motives, search processes and ethical challenges. *Journal of Business Venturing*, *24*(5), 519–532. doi:10.1016/j.jbusvent.2008.04.007

ADDITIONAL READING

Dacin, P. A., Dacin, M. T., & Matear, M. (2010). Social Entrepreneurship: Why We Don't Need a New Theory and How We Move Forward From Here. *The Academy of Management Perspectives*, *24*(3), 37–57. doi:10.5465/AMP.2010.52842950

Dobele, L., & Pietere, A. (2015). Competitiveness of Social Entrepreneurship in Latvia. *Regional Formation and Development Studies*, *3*(17), 40–50.

Estrin, S., Mickiewicz, T., & Stephan, U. (2016). Human capital in social and commercial entrepreneurship. *Journal of Business Venturing*, *31*(4), 449–467. doi:10.1016/j.jbusvent.2016.05.003

Lisetchi, M., & Brancu, L. (2014). The entrepreneurship concept as a subject of social innovation. *Procedia: Social and Behavioral Sciences*, *124*, 87–92. doi:10.1016/j.sbspro.2014.02.463

Matei, L., & Matei, A. (2012). The social enterprise and the social entrepreneurship instruments of local development. A comparative study for Romania. *Procedia: Social and Behavioral Sciences*, *62*, 1066–1071. doi:10.1016/j.sbspro.2012.09.182

Mirabella, R., & Young, D. R. (2012). The Development of Education for Social Entrepreneurship and Nonprofit Management Diverging or Converging Paths? *Nonprofit Management & Leadership,Vol.*, *23*(1), 43–57. doi:10.1002/nml.21049

Nicolopoulou, K. (2014). Social Entrepreneurship between Cross-Currents: Toward a Framework for Theoretical Restructuring of the Field. *Journal of Small Business Management*, *52*(4), 678–702. doi:10.1111/jsbm.12130

Qureshi, I., Kistruck, G. M., & Bhatt, B. (2016). The Enabling and Constraining Effects of Social Ties in the Process of Institutional Entrepreneurship. *Organization Studies*, *37*(3), 425–447. doi:10.1177/0170840615613372

Satgar, V. (2016). Reviews: Economic sociology. *International Socialist Review*, *31*(2), 158–175.

Schaltegger, S., & Wagner, S. (2011). Sustainable Entrepreneurship and Sustainability Innovation: Categories and Interactions. *Business Strategy and the Environment*, *20*(4), 222–237. doi:10.1002/bse.682

Surie, G., & Groen, A. (2017). The importance of social entrepreneurship in national systems of innovation — An introduction. *Technological Forecasting and Social Change*, *121*, 181–183. doi:10.1016/j.techfore.2017.05.010

Tukamushaba, E. K., Orobia, L., & George, B. P. (2011). Development of a conceptual model to understand international social entrepreneurship and its application in the Ugandan context. *Journal of International Entrepreneurship, Vol*, *9*(4), 282–298. doi:10.100710843-011-0079-9

KEY TERMS AND DEFINITIONS

Economic Growth: Economic growth is the increase in the real output of the country in a specific period of time.

Economy: Economics is a discipline of studying how people perform economic activities and how they try to satisfy their wants and needs from scarce resources.

Entrepreneur: They are the change agent in both non-profit and profit companies. They take competitive advantage by taking risks, finding new market opportunity and making innovation for continues improvement.

Social Entrepreneurship: Social entrepreneurship is a process that manage by social entrepreneurs whose aim to create a social value to society and community by discovering, clarifying, and taking advantage of opportunities to improve social wealth by making innovation either existing or establishing new venture.

Social Innovation: One side of social innovation is to enhance the quality and quantity of life while the other side is to produce innovative and new solutions to social problems that promote citizens welfare and environmental sustainability.

Chapter 13
Social Entrepreneurial Leadership for a Better World

Müge Leyla Yıldız
Marmara University, Turkey

ABSTRACT

This chapter introduces the concept of entrepreneurial leadership and argues that it offers potential contributions to economic and social wealth. A theoretical framework of social entrepreneurial leadership and the characteristics of social entrepreneurial leaders is then posited. The similarities between social entrepreneurialism and other leadership styles such as ethical, transformative, authentic, sustainable, and servant leadership are explored. The conclusion reflects on the various understandings of social entrepreneurial leadership and how social entrepreneurial leaders can be characterized as the primary actors for a better world.

INTRODUCTION

Since the 1980s, an entrepreneurial revolution has spawned due to the internet, new materials and products, financial and social networks, and paradigmatic changes in politics, economics, and societies (Fernald, Solomon, & Tarabishy, 2005). Entrepreneurship could be the answer to many problems faced by societies. It can be described also as a driver of economic development (Austin, Stevenson, & Wei-Skillern, 2006). During the last ten years, the world economy has developed rapidly by fostering entrepreneurial activity. According to the Global Entrepreneurship Index (2017), the total early stage entrepreneurial activity rate is almost 40 percent of the adult population aged 18 to 64 years around the world. In other words, two- fifths of the economically active population around the world are in the process of starting or have started already a business. Over the next five years, they are estimated to hire approximately 2–5 employees. One of the reasons they may choose to remain small is so that they can manage complexity easily. In addition, sophisticated technology and communications may enable entrepreneurs, particularly in developed economies, to operate on their own, perhaps as part of a broader value network (Herrington & Kew, 2017a). If entrepreneurs receive adequate assistance, new ventures could add billions to the global economy.

DOI: 10.4018/978-1-5225-5687-9.ch013

One of the contributions entrepreneurs and entrepreneurial firms make is to define market economies and expand the world economy. They are the most important drivers of the economy. Furthermore, they play a crucial role in technological change and productivity growth through innovating. They are changing the prevailing market structures (Kuratko & Hodgetts, 2004). Colleges and universities around the world are offering more courses related to entrepreneurship and innovation (Mair & Marti, 2006; Zahra, Gedajlovic, Neubaum, & Shulman, 2009). As said by Drucker (1985), entrepreneurship is not relevant to genes, it is a discipline, and it can be taught. Thus, it can be encouraged by education (Kuratko, 2005).

The entrepreneurial activities of firms affect the quality of human and social life. They have led to a flourishing concern in society about corporate social performance (Mahoney & Roberts, 2015) and numerous academic and practitioner research endeavors. The literature suggests a causal relationship between corporate social performance and traditional financial measures of a firm's success (Zhao & Murrell, 2016; Kiser, Leipziger, & Shubert, 2014; Makni, Francour, & Bellavance, 2009; Griffin & Mahon, 1997). Multidimensional constructs of corporate social performance can be configured in terms of economic responsibilities to investors and consumers, ethical responsibilities to society, and legal responsibilities to the government and the community (Carroll, 1979; Mahoney & Roberts, 2015). Increasingly, corporations are expected to take responsibility for meeting social and environmental challenges more proactively so that corporate social responsibility has become synonymous with sustainability (Seelos & Mair, 2005) in some quarters.

After corporate scandals such as Enron and Worldcom, social enterprises, and their social missions, have gained increased attention and popularity from researchers, business managers as well as customers, workers, and other stakeholders (Yıldız, 2016). The mission of social enterprises is to:

create and pursue opportunities relentlessly, without regard to alienable resources currently controlled, with a view to both creating wealth that may be reinvested in the business to assure its sustainability, and social value (Chell, 2007).

Social value can be defined as societies' needed goods and services provided by organizations. For example, promoting community awareness or development or providing more accessible and fairer education systems creates social value.

Today, businesses are not the only players searching for profitable solutions to social problems (Porter & Kramer, 2011). A whole generation of social entrepreneurs is pioneering new business models to serve societal needs (Seelos & Mair, 2005). In recent years, there has been a broadening of the definition of social entrepreneurship and social entrepreneurs. According to Ashoka, as the largest international network of social entrepreneurs, these individuals identify and explore the most crucial social problems and create innovative solutions to address them. Both social entrepreneurship and social activism are creating social value and raising awareness about social issues with their activities. However, social activism denotes action for influencing mostly governments without providing income (Martin & Osberg, 2007). Non-profit social organizations aim also to solve societal issues through creating social value. Many non-profit organizations have social missions also, but having a social mission does not mean that they are successful enterprises or sustainable ventures (Castro-Salazar, 2013). However, social entrepreneurs create sustained social outcomes through direct action; these are hybrid ventures, known also as third sector organizations, a combination of a profit based business organization with the social mission of a non-profit organization.

By embracing sustainability, social entrepreneurs are determined to drive social change by serving the needs of ever greater numbers of underprivileged people who have hitherto been neglected wholly or partially by the traditional commercial and governmental entities (Nga & Shamuganathan, 2010). It can be said that social entrepreneurial leaders transform perceptions of creating value not for their social enterprises only but also commercial businesses. From a business perspective, Porter and Kramer (2011) suggested that social entrepreneurship should be measured by its ability to create shared value, not just social benefit. For example, India Unilever created a new direct to home distribution system run by underprivileged female entrepreneurs. This initiative, called Project Shakti, creates shared value: it is not the female entrepreneurs only who benefit by gaining an income source but also society by securing hygiene products to protect against the spread of diseases.

Every social sector leader is not well suited to entrepreneurship (Dees, 1998). Further, not every business leader is an entrepreneur. A social entrepreneur can be a very sophisticated and multifaceted person who is definetly a leader. (Dees, 1998-2001; Prabhu, 1999; Borins, 2000; Casto-Salazar, 2013). *Social entrepreneurs are entrepreneurial leaders of social value creation-oriented organizations with profit used for the benefit of society, not for their own interest all around the world.* Social entrepreneurial leaders have been defined by Prabhu (1999) as:

persons who create and manage innovative entrepreneurial organizations or ventures whose primary mission is the social change and development of their client group.

Social entrepreneurial leadership behavior can be different from for-profit or not-for-profit leaders, so Prabhu (1999) discussed proposing to build on mainstream leadership literature. The characteristics and behaviours of social entrepreneurs can be similar leaders and entrepreneurs' infinite qualities highlighted in leadership and business literature. There is currently insufficient research into social entrepreneurial leaders (Prabhu, 1999) or leadership types of social entrepreneurs. To address this gap, this chapter is structured around three questions. First, how can the concepts of entrepreneurial leadership be explained? Second, which characteristics and behaviors do social entrepreneurial leaders possess? In other words, which leadership's characteristics and behaviors have social entrepreneurs? Social entrepreneurs can be defined as non-profit entrepreneurial leaders; however, all social entrepreneurs do not have the same leadership style. Therefore third, are there any similarities or differences between social entrepreneurial leadership and other leadership styles? in the extant literature suggests that social entrepreneur have some characteristics similar to that of leadership styles. Every social entrepreneur is a social entrepreneurial leader with a unique leadership style. In this chapter, similarities of and differences between social entrepreneurs' features and behaviors and other leadership styles are discussed through propositions. Propositions might be helpful for the directions of the future researches.

ENTREPRENEURIAL LEADERSHIP

"Entrepreneur" is a word that derives from the French language. It is a combination of "Entre" meaning in between and "Preneur" meaning to undertake. In French, it refers to someone who undertakes a significant activity to create value (Dees, 1998). In business contexts, it means designing, running a business, and taking financial risk in order to accrue profit. According to Schumpeter, a robust definition of entrepreneurship should include innovation such as new products, new processes of production, and new organizational forms. In the economics literature, an entrepreneur is considered as one of the main production factors during the establishment of an enterprise. According, again, to Schumpeter, businesses start to enter the process of extinction when their innovative activities disappear (McCraw, 2007). Adam Smith, in his book of "Wealth of Nations", defends the concept that the economic wealth level will increase due to the invisible hands of entrepreneurs.

Researchers, inventors, and scientists are the people creating innovation, but those who will mesh these innovations together with demand are entrepreneurs. Today, defining every individual who sets up a business with the hope for profit as entrepreneur is wrong (Saruhan & Yildiz, 2017). Being an entrepreneur is associated with starting a business, but this is a weak definition of a term with a much more significant meaning. Firstly, entrepreneurship can be defined as *a societal mechanism that converts technical information into products and services.* Second, entrepreneurship is a mechanism that enables the discovery and mitigation of temporal and spatial economic inefficiencies (Kirzner, 1997). Finally, Schumpeter's (1934) point of view that, *entrepreneurially-based innovation drives change in products and services* (Vecchio, 2003). Dacin et al. (2010) compared three types of entrepreneurs - conventional, institutional, and cultural entrepreneurs with social entrepreneurs. Conventional entrepreneurs refer to innovative people who work for for-profit organizations. Institutional entrepreneurs aim at institutional reform and development in their profit based organizations; they may be transformational leaders. Cultural entrepreneurs are individuals who pursue cultural enlightenment with for-profit or non-profit organizations such as museums and art festivals. There are overlaps between these types of entrepreneur and social entrepreneurs.

The extant entrepreneurship literature devotes considerable discussion to the role entrepreneurs play within their businesses and as opinion leaders in their markets and the general economy (Fernald, Solomon, & Tarabishy, 2005). Entrepreneurs seek opportunities, investigating, achieving set goals, taking risks, and innovating (Lepnurm & Bergh, 1995). The current literature often describes entrepreneurs as innovators, paradigm shifters, and visionaries in order to create more value. They should develop their leadership qualities to increase the performance of their businesses (Fernald, Solomon, & Tarabishy, 2005). Social perception, impression management, persuasion, social influence, and social adaptability are social skills of entrepreneurs, which are relevant potentially to their success (Baron & Markman, 2000). Entrepreneurs and leaders have some characteristics such as vision, which comprises the idealized goals to be achieved in the future. Vision is a key component in the leadership style of all leaders; however, some researchers suggested that entrepreneurs have not a vision at least a formal and explicit vision. Most of the researches in the literature emphasized the importance of vision in the entrepreneurial context (Ruvio, Rosenblatt, & Hertz-Lazarowitz, 2010; Cogliser & Brigham, 2004; Gupta, MacMillan, & Surie, 2004).

Although entrepreneurs' traits and leaders' traits are similar, there are some differences between managing an enterprise and leading it. Management is a function, which has to be in every organization regardless of whether or not it is profit based. By its simplest definition, leadership is the skill of affecting a group of people for the achievement of a goal. The source of this effect can be both formal and informal since the top management assigns some managerial power to people. Organizations need powerful leaders and strong management to ensure organizational effectiveness (Robbins, 2005). Each manager does not have to be a leader but if they are, it can be good for the organization's performance. While the manager is serving the vision of the organization, the leader tries to realize her/his own vision.

Leadership is a process rather than a position in organizations. Leadership is an art and truly enlightened leaders lead from the heart (Palestini, 2009).

Leadership research has been ongoing for decades by not only people employed specifically as researchers but also leaders, managers, and even emperors. The prior leadership research and theory has analyzed leader traits and their behaviors; the contingency theories have tried to explain both leader and situational variables. The trait approach known as the Great Man approach identified the characteristics of leaders and the differences between leaders and non-leaders. Effective leaders' characteristics include charisma and intelligence. Whereas the behavioral approach to leadership categorized leaders' behaviors, the contingency approach to leadership aimed at a more comprehensive picture of leadership. Contemporary perspectives on leadership reframe it as a dynamic process with different variables (Hopkins & O'Neil, 2015). Leadership theories imply that a leader displays the same style to all subordinates. For example, the leader-member exchange (LMX) theory considers both parties and defines the quality of the relationships between leaders and followers. It derives from the vertical dyad linkage theory and argues that leaders develop relationships with different qualities and this situation affects individual and organizational outcomes (Martin, Gregory, Karl, Olga, & McNamara, 2005). Mardanov (2008) suggests that the positive attitude of leaders toward their members improves employee attitudes toward work, leaders, and the organization.

Although entrepreneurship is a relatively new field of management research, leadership has been studied since around 500 BC. Entrepreneurial leadership is a new concept and not the same as leadership; it is a new kind of leadership style. Amidst the prevailing and persistent global uncertainties, entrepreneurial leaders shape social and economic opportunities. They enact new profit models for reducing uncertainty (Gupta, MacMillan, & Surie, 2004). Entrepreneurial leaders are cognitively ambidextrous, enshrining a new worldview incorporating social, environmental and economic responsibility and sustainability, and self and social awareness to guide action (Greenberg, McKone-Sweet, & Wilson, 2011). Ambidexterity literally means the ability to use both hands with equal ease. Cognitive ambidexterity is one of the features of ambidextrous leadership (Yıldız, 2016). Rosing et al. (2011) defined ambidextrous leaders as possessing the ability to support their followers through both explorative and exploitative behaviors, flexibly switching between those behaviors.

Entrepreneurial leadership generally involves three stages: idea generation is in the early stages of a venture, idea structuring, and idea promotion (Cogliser & Brigham, 2004). The entrepreneurial leader is also the hearth of the entrepreneurial team. He/she is essential to select and motivate the team members who achieve the vision to create strategic value (Chen, 2007; Gupta, MacMillan & Surie, 2004). One of the most valued abilities of entrepreneurial leaders is the ability to attract qualified entrepreneurial team members.

By definition, entrepreneurial leadership is a:

form of leadership distinctive from other types of leadership which enables entrepreneurs and leaders to cope with highly turbulent and competitive environments (Gupta, MacMillan, & Surie, 2004; Bagheri & Pihie, 2011).

In essence, it seeks to demonstrate a new style of evolving leadership, which offers a break from the past and movement into the future.

SOCIAL ENTREPRENEURIAL LEADERS

With a focus on income, it is important to distinguish between social entrepreneurs and commercial entrepreneurs. Seelos and Mair (2005) focus on the entrepreneur's motivation to capture value in order to distinguish between the two types of entrepreneurship. Business enterprises create social value also for their stakeholders but it is not their main vision. In order to create social value efficiently, organizations must manage their social performance as carefully and deliberately as they manage their financial performance.

Social entrepreneurs and business entrepreneurs are different from each other in important ways. The social entrepreneur's main purpose is to make the world a better place (Dees, Emerson & Economy, 2001). In addition, social entrepreneurs have to face different challenges in justifying their existence (Dees, Emerson & Economy, 2002) and they differ from commercial entrepreneurs due to the way social missions interact with performance systems (Austin, Stevenson, & Wei-Skiller, 2006). There is a broad array of social entrepreneurial attributes, for example confidence, practical compassion, commitment, determination, discernment, empathy, enthusiasm, honesty, humility, initiative, integrity, risk-taking, optimism, proactivity, wisdom, sensitivity, and sincerity (Castro-Salazar, 2013). The characteristics of successful social entrepreneurial leaders can be similar to those of successful commercial entrepreneurs (Castro-Salazar, 2013; Bornstein & Davis, 2010; Light, 2008). A social entrepreneur's primary focus is to foster social change (Seelos & Mair, 2005; Weerawardena & Sullivan Mort, 2006), prioritizing social rather than financial goals (Thompson, Kiefer, & York, 2011). Unlike a commercial entrepreneur who often recruits and retains talent, social entrepreneurs are rarely able to pay market rates for key hires. Many professionals in many sectors, from lawyers to managers, work with lower compensation (Austin, Stevenson, & Wei-Skiller, 2006). Most employees are volunteers, even in top positions such as CEOs and board members. According to Dees (1998), social entrepreneurs and their passion or missions are not a new concept; however, the hybrid organizations created by them are new solutions and represent the most effective methods found by these individuals for serving their social missions.

While society might wish for more entrepreneurial behavior in all sectors, they have a need for different leadership types and styles. Although every social sector leader is not well suited to being entrepreneurial (Dees, 1998), social enterprises' leaders have entrepreneurial features. However, social entrepreneurial leaders are not lone actors; they are a part of the team.

A summary of the social entrepreneurial leaders literature presented in Table 1 suggests definitions and descriptions of social entrepreneurial leaders and facilitates the development of a heuristic leadership style.

Masseti (2008) provides a sample of the ways social entrepreneurs have been defined in the literature by Drayton (2002), Sullivan Mort, Weerawardena and Carnegie (2003), Roberts and Woods (2005), Hartigan (2006) and Korosec and Berman (2006) as well as the characteristics that have been attributed to their success. Some of these characteristics are a powerful, new, system change idea or passion, creativity (see things differently), strong ethical fiber, innovativeness, risk-taking propensity, opportunity-orientation, entrepreneurial personality, team player, collaborative leader, and a genuine, long-term, focused commitment to their communities.

Although not all social entrepreneurs will possess the characteristics seen in Table 1 to the same degree, that array of definitions is useful and important because it presents the social entrepreneurial leader phenomenon multi-subjectively, according to different authors, and thus provides a starting point in order to profile social entrepreneurs. Social entrepreneurs share certain characteristics with their for-

Table 1. Definitions of social entrepreneurial leaders

	Source	Definition
1	Waddock and Post (1991)	Individuals who bring about changes in the perception of social issues. . ..lay critical roles in bringing about "catalytic changes" in the public sector agenda and the perception of certain social issues. (p. 393)
2	Dees (1998)	They play the role of change agents in the social sector, by: • Adopting a mission to create and sustain social value (not just private value), • Recognizing and relentlessly pursuing new opportunities to serve that mission, • Engaging in a process of continuous innovation, adaptation, and learning, • Acting boldly without being limited by resources currently in hand, • Exhibiting a heightened sense of accountability to the constituencies served and for the outcomes created.
3	Prabhu (1999)	Persons who create or manage innovative entrepreneurial organizations or ventures and whose primary mission is the social change and development of their client group. (p. 140)
4	Thompson, Alvy and Lees (2000)	People who realize where there is an opportunity to satisfy some unmet need that the state welfare system will not or cannot meet, and who gather together the necessary resources (generally people, often volunteers, money and premises) and use these to "make a difference." (p. 328)
5	Borins (2000)	Leaders that innovate in public sector organizations.
6	Dees (2001)	[They] are one species in the genus entrepreneur. They are entrepreneurs with a social mission. (p.3)
7	Brinkerhoff (2002)	Individuals constantly looking for new ways to serve their constituencies and add value to existing services
8	Drayton (2002)	[They] have the same core temperament as their industry-creating, business entrepreneur peers. . . . A major change agent, one whose core values center on identifying, addressing and solving societal problems. [He/she is an] entrepreneur without a powerful, new, system change idea. They have four other necessary ingredients: creativity, widespread impact, entrepreneurial quality, and strong ethical fiber. (p.124)
9	Thompson (2002)	Individuals with the qualities and behaviors we associate with the business entrepreneur but who operate in the community and are more concerned with caring and helping than making money. (p. 413)
10	Boschee and McClurg (2003)	[He/she] is any person, in any sector, who uses earned income strategies to pursue a social objective, and a social entrepreneur differs from a traditional entrepreneur in two important ways: Traditional entrepreneurs frequently act in a socially responsible manner. . ..Secondly, traditional entrepreneurs are ultimately measured by financial results. (p. 3)
11	Sullivan Mort et al. (2003)	The virtuousness of their mission to create better social value; • Unity of purpose and action in the face of complexity; • An ability to recognize opportunities to create better social value for their clients; and • Their propensity for risk-taking, pro-activeness and innovativeness in decision making (p. 82).
12	Tan, Williams, and Tan (2005)	Legal person engaged in the process of entrepreneurship that involves a segment of society with the altruistic objective that benefits accrue to that segment of society. (p. 360)
13	Hartigan (2006)	Whose work is aimed at progressive social transformation. . .. business to drive transformational change. While profits are generated, the main aim is not to maximize financial returns for shareholders but to grow the social venture and reach more people in need effectively. Wealth accumulation is not a priority—revenues beyond costs are reinvested in the enterprise in order to fund expansion. (p. 45)
14	Korosec and Berman (2006)	[They] are defined as individuals that take the initiative to identify and address important social problems in their communities. (p.448–449) Individuals that develop new programs, services, and solutions to specific problems and those that address the needs of special populations. (p. 449)
15	Light (2006)	An individual, group, network, organization, or alliance of organizations that seeks sustainable, large-scale change through pattern-breaking ideas in what or how governments, nonprofits, and businesses do to address significant social problems. (p.50)
16	Sharir and Lerner (2006)	[He/she] is acting as a change agent to create and sustain social value without being limited to resources currently in hand. (p. 3)
17	Shaw and Carter (2007)	Individuals who establish enterprises primarily to meet social objectives rather than generate personal financial profit. (p.419)
18	Jones et al. (2008)	[They] are deeply enmeshed within their social context (p.6).
19	Zahra et al. (2009)	They share a passion for pursuing social issues, major differences exist among them in how they discover social needs (i.e., search (processes), pursue social opportunities, and impact the broader social system (p.523).
20	Pless (2012)	They work at multiple levels: pooling (sharing similar resources) and trading (complementary) resources within and between sectors (government, for profit and not for profit). (p.319).
21	Germak and Robinson (2014)	They are restless, mission-driven individuals that strive to change the world, their cities, and their communities by implementing sustainable business ventures designed to create social impact. (p.5)
22	Skoll Foundation (2017)	[The individual] aims for value in the form of transformational change that will benefit disadvantaged communities and ultimately society at large. Social entrepreneurs pioneer innovative and systemic approaches for meeting the needs of the marginalized, the disadvantaged and the disenfranchised—populations that lack the financial means or political clout to achieve lasting benefit on their own. (p.1)

profit counterparts such as risk-taking, proactiveness, and independence (Zahra, Gedajlovic, Neubaum, & Shulman, 2009). They are predictable because they combine a social purpose with a for-profit organizational structure (Dees & Anderson, 2002). The most cited characteristics of social entrepreneurial leaders in the literature are vision, innovativeness, proactiveness, strategic initiatives and risk-taking (Chen, 2007; Gupta, MacMillan, & Surie, 2004; Kuratko, 2007; Bagheri & Pihie, 2011).

The definitions of social entrepreneurs highlighted their social activities related directly to *innovation* and maximization of total wealth, which means both social and economic wealth (Zahra, Gedajlovic, Neubaum, & Shulman, 2009). Entrepreneurial *innovativeness* is an important ability of entrepreneurial leaders. In addition, Leadbeater (1997) suggested that social entrepreneurs are entrepreneurial, innovative, and transformatory. They run enterprises and create new products/services, new ways of solving problems; therefore, they are innovators. They transform institutions, environments, and society; thus, they are change agents. They are aiming to change the world by putting it on a trajectory toward sustainability.

All entrepreneurs have found innovative ways to turn their vision into a reality. All leaders have a *vision* but social entrepreneurial leaders are imbued with a strong impulse of a vision to make the world a better place (Dees, Emerson and Economy, 2001) through creating and maintaining social value by changing underlying social and economic structures.

They are proactive, strategic thinkers who are driven by their passion to implement innovative new ideas to solve social problems. They seek also opportunities while behaving ethically in terms of the processes, which they follow and the activities they undertake. These characteristics require new leadership skills combinations. Austin et al. (2000) applied entrepreneurs' PCDO (people, context, deal, opportunity) framework developed by Sahlman (1996) to social entrepreneurs. According to Figure 1 presents a revised social entrepreneurship framework, social value proposition is an integrating variable, surrounded by an opportunity circle (top-center) and people and capital circles (bottom-center). The contextual forces, which are tax, regulatory, socio-cultural, political, demographic, macroeconomic and regulatory, shape the other variables, which are managed by entrepreneurs (Austin, Stevenson, & Wei-Skillern, 2006).

Social entrepreneurs have passion to solve social causes but most of them do not have a formal business education. However, business procedures need to be configured and implemented in order to earn money (Heinecke, Klobhofer & Krzeminska, 2014). According to Schwab foundation research, they have faced some leadership challenges such as building a management team, delegation and succession, balancing and integrating, personal and professional development. Yet, they strive to create new business models to serve their social mission.

Herrington and Kew (2017) examined, in detail, the characteristics of social entrepreneurs in the world. They found that males are generally more likely to be social entrepreneurs than women are; however, in developing economies including Malaysia, Lebanon, Israel, and Argentina female entrepreneurs are more likely to start a social venture than men are. The results suggest that people aged 25–34 and 35–44 have the highest propensities to be involved in social entrepreneurial activity around the world. In addition, people with higher levels of education are more likely to engage in social entrepreneurial activity.

Entrepreneurs identify a needs gap or opportunity, injecting vision, motivating others to build networks, securing the resources, taking risks, and introducing necessary control systems (Thompson, 2001). Zahra et al. (2009) identified three types of social entrepreneurs: Social Bricoleur, Social Constructionist, and Social Engineer. Social Bricoleurs discover and address small-scale local social needs. Social Constructionists pursue reforms and innovations and see opportunities by filling gaps in provision to underserved

Figure 1. Social Entrepreneurship Framework
Note: SVP = social value proposition Source: Austin et al., (2006)

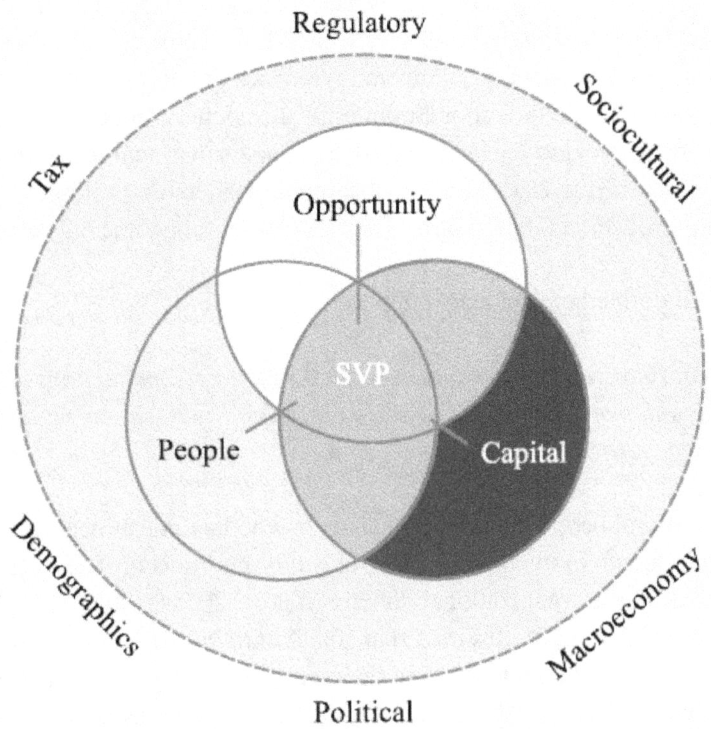

people. Social Engineers change the existing social structures by recognizing systemic problems (Zahra, Gedajlovic, Neubaum, & Shulman, 2009). Additionally, they might often need to work with other non-profit organizations, businesses and governments to attain critical resources for the organization (Austin, 2000). They have diverse network relations with funders, volunteers, managers, and other non-profit organizations who become their alliances easily, and other partners.

The definitions of social entrepreneurs highlighted their vision, motivation to achieve, entreprenurial innovativeness and leadership. *Social entrepreneurs can be defined as non-profit entrepreneurial leaders;* however, all social entrepreneurs may not have the same leadership style. Although there are lots of research on social entrepreneurship and social entrepreneurs' heroic characteristics, only a few studies have discussed the social entrepreneurs' leadership style.

SOCIAL ENTREPRENEURIAL LEADERS AND THEIR LEADERSHIP STYLES

Clearly, social entrepreneurs provide innovative or exceptional leadership in social enterprises (Dees, 1998; Prabhu, 1998; Weerawardena & Sullivan Mort, 2006). Dees (1998) describe social entrepreneurs as "one special breed of leaders." Social entrepreneurs seem to be rather similar in their leadership style. Which leadership theories or style can explain the characteristics and behaviors of social entrepreneurial leaders?

The Social Entrepreneur as an Ethical Leader

There is no template for social entrepreneurs; however, they can be ethical models in the private, public and non-profit sectors (Ţigu, Iorgulescu, Răvar, & Lile, 2015). Some characteristics of social entrepreneurs are a willingness to self-correct, to share credit, to work quietly and with a strong ethical impetus (Bornstein, 2007). Leadership style with a strong ethical impetus can be classified in different ways: ethical leadership (Brown, Trevino & Harrison, 2005), transformational leadership (Bass, 1985; 1998; Bass & Avolio, 1993), authentic leadership or sustainable leadership (Yildiz, 2016). Social entrepreneurs can be an example of servant leadership? They are not moral people only but also creative leaders (Prabhu, 1999).

Brown et al. (2005) defined ethical leadership as:

the demonstration of normatively appropriate conduct through personal actions and interpersonal relationships, and the promotion of such conduct to followers through two-way communication, reinforcement and decision making (p. 120).

Ethical leaders are moral people and moral managers who become ethical role models and institute clear ethical codes of conduct in the organization for guiding followers. They behave ethically in their personal lives as well as in the organizational domain (Yildiz, 2016).

Although some researchers have observed that social entrepreneurs might possess certain egoistic behaviors in common with their counterparts in the commercial sphere (Zahra, Gedajlovic, Neubaum, & Shulman, 2009; Davis, 2002), social entrepreneurs' behaviors are based often on ethical motives and moral responsibility and there can be an "expression of altruism" (Mair & Marti, 2006). According to Zahra et al. (2009), egoism is especially relevant because of the passion of social entrepreneurs to create social value and lead to social enterprise. Social entrepreneurial leaders ensure the profit is well used for the benefit of society, not for their own interest and they are committed fully to the success of their enterprise. Therefore, given these findings, the author proposes the following:

Proposition One: Social entrepreneurs have similar characteristics to ethical leaders.

The Social Entrepreneur as a Transformational Leader

In the 1980s, two basic leadership approaches were suggested: transformational leadership and transactional leadership. James McGregor Burns (1978) was the first to use this distinction. Based on Burns' (1978) work, transformational leadership (Bass, 1985; Bass & Avelio, 1993) focuses on how the leader affects followers. Bass (1985) developed the Multifactor Leadership Questionnaire based on this approach (Alimo-Metcalfe & Alban-Metcalfe, 2001). Transformational leaders inspire followers with their vision and stimulate them to challenge themselves and their way of thinking, while uniting them around a common vision and core values. Transformational leadership contains four components: charisma or idealized influence (attributed or behavioral), inspirational motivation, intellectual stimulation, and individualized consideration (Bass, 1985, 1998; Bass & Avolio, 1993; Bass & Steidlmeier, 1999). Such leaders work hard to ensure effectiveness and productivity (Weihrich, Cannice & Kootz, 2010).

According to Bass (1999), idealized influence and inspirational leadership are displayed when the leader envisions a desirable future, articulates how it can be reached, sets an example to be followed, sets high standards of performance, and shows determination and confidence. Followers want to identify with such leadership (Bass, 1999). Intellectual stimulation is displayed and the leader helps followers to become more innovative and creative. Individualized consideration is displayed when leaders pay attention to the developmental needs of followers and support and coach the development of their followers. The leaders delegate assignments as opportunities for growth (Burns, 1978; Bass, 1985-1995-1999; Bass & Avolio, 1995; Bass & Steidlmeier, 1999; Bass & Riggio, 2006). Most entrepreneurs generally tend to be transformational leaders.

The entrepreneurial leadership process, including social entrepreneurial leadership, involves the creation or transformation of organizations. They are not only developing new ideas or even social movements (Robinson 2006) but also change organizations from vision to value creating process. According to Martin and Osberg (2007), the social entrepreneur aims for large-scale transformational benefit. Litzy et al. (2010) argued also that both transformational leaders and social entrepreneurs inspire their followers, and support the creativity and contributions of their followers. Social entrepreneurs transform society while transformational leaders mostly change organizations. Transformational leaders have also some ethical impulse in common with social entrepreneurs. The findings suggest the following:

Proposition Two: Social entrepreneurs have similar characteristics to transformational leaders.

The Social Entrepreneur as an Authentic Leader

Authentic leadership has its origins in Greek philosophy in terms of concepts of individual values and ethical choices (Avolio & Gardner, 2005). Authentic leadership was first popularized by George's (2013) book entitled Authentic Leadership: Rediscovering the Secrets to Creating Lasting Value. He defined the characteristics of authentic leaders as acting from the heart (mission), establishing strong values, trusting relationships, self-discipline, and passion with purpose. Building on his work, Walumbwa et al. (2008) defined authentic leadership as:

a pattern of leader behavior that draws upon and promotes both positive psychological capacities and a positive ethical climate, to foster greater self-awareness, an internalized moral perspective, balanced processing of information and relational transparency on the part of leaders working with followers, fostering positive self-development (p.94).

The most important three characteristics of authentic leaders are a focus on self-awareness, an emphasis on the true self, and a grounding in moral leadership (Avolio & Gardner, 2005; Hopkins & O'Neil, 2015). Bass (1998) described transformational leaders as being hopeful, optimistic, self-aware, and moral. Although authentic leaders have these characteristics also, all authentic leaders will not necessarily be transformational leaders. What sets apart authentic leaders is their values, beliefs and proclivities for acting as role models for their followers (Avolio & Gardner, 2005).

Authentic leaders can be defined also as,

those who are deeply aware of how they think and behave and are perceived by others as being aware of their own and others' values/moral perspectives, knowledge, and strengths; aware of the context in which they operate; and who are confident, hopeful, optimistic, resilient, and of high moral character (Avolio, Luthans, & Walumbwa, 2004, as cited in Avolio & Gardner, 2005).

Authentic leaders' internalized moral perspective and relational transparency with their followers could be linked with social entrepreneurial leaders. Authentic leaders may be particularly relevant to the social welfare characteristic of social entrepreneurship research (Walumbwa, Avolio, Gardner, Wernsing, & Peterson, 2008; Short, Moss & Lumpkin, 2009). Thus, based on the previous research, the author concludes the following:

Proposition Three: Social entrepreneurs have similar characteristics to authentic leaders.

The Social Entrepreneur as a Sustainable Leader

Sustainability requires organizations and leaders to think in terms of long-term profit and long-term organizational survival. Sustainability is an idea that involves ethical cultures. The sustainability view in business is rooted in the perception that organizations are part of nature. As such, they should create sustainable value and combine their business performance with a concern for both society and the environment (McCann & Sweet, 2014). Sustainable leadership is not just a humanistic and managerial approach that facilitates positive organizational outcomes such as reducing unwanted turnover and innovations. Sustainable leadership is a way of thinking that is holistic, humanistic and ecological (Hargreaves & Fink, 2011). Lambert (2011) proposed that *sustainable leadership should be vigilant, constantly 'scanning' the environment to check for deterioration in the conditions in which the institution operates* (p.136).

Sustainable leadership can be defined as that which is *concerned with creating current and future profits for an organization while improving the lives of all concerned* (McCann & Holt 2011). According to Slankis (2006) sustainable leaders exhibit social and environmental consciousness, business credibility, adaptability, patience, translational skills, broad system thinking, change orientation, energy and passion, mentoring and development, and persuasiveness. Sustainable leaders consider long-term visions in all business decisions.

Sustainability consists of at least environmental, economic, and social pillars (Weerawardena & Sullivan Mort, 2001). Avery and Bergsteiner (2011) emphasized, there is no one "right" way within the overall sustainable leadership paradigm (p.5). Creating sustainable social value is one of the important characteristics of social entrepreneurs. They promote change, empower their followers, are socially just, recognize human resources talent and take care of them, create a better future in both economic and social terms. Social entrepreneurs create sustainable social, economic, and environmental values. The findings suggest the following:

Proposition Four: Social entrepreneurs have similar characteristics to sustainable (sustainability-oriented) leaders.

The Social Entrepreneur as a Servant Leader

Servant and leader are two opposite concepts; however, the notion of servant leaders is considered as a leadership paradigm for the 21st century. Greanleaf (1977) proposed this concept after reading Herman Hesse's Journey to the East. In that book, the character Leo was a servant of the group, and together, that group including Leo, were on a journey. One day he disappears and the group is totally lost and they cannot continue on their journey.

The servant leader is servant first. It begins with the natural feeling that one wants to serve. Then conscious choice brings one to aspire to lead. The best test is: do those served grow as persons: do they, while being served, become healthier, wiser, freer, more autonomous, more likely themselves to become servants? (Greenleaf, 1977;2002).

Servant leaders help subordinates to reach their maximum potential. Servant leaders:

want their subordinates to improve for their own good, and view the development of followers as an end, in and of itself, not merely a means to reach the leader's or organization's goals (Ehrhart, 2004).

They serve their followers first, even when self-sacrifice is required.

Linen et al. (2010) identified nine dimensions in order to characterize and understand servant leadership: emotional healing, creating value for the community, conceptual skills, empowering, helping subordinates grow and succeed, putting subordinates first, behaving ethically, long-term relationships, and servanthood. Spear (2010) proposed ten characteristics of servant leadership including listening, empathy, awareness, persuasion, conceptualization, foresight, stewardship, commitment to the growth of people, and building community. Based on this identification, servant leader knows each follower like transformational leaders, and behave ethically like ethical leaders.

Considering that the social entrepreneurs do not want to manage the organization by themselves, in other words that they do not want to be heroes (Seanor & Meaton, 2007), we can define them as servant leaders. Instead of aspiring to be heroes, or be referred to as heroes, they want to make their visions into realities. They, being aware of prevailing social problems, generate new solutions by ethical impulses in order to change the world they see. In doing so, they are using a business model as an intermediary for social and economic wealth. Social entrepreneurial leaders are bringing a completely different approach to entrepreneurship. The findings suggest the following:

Proposition Five: Social entrepreneurs have similar characteristics to servant leaders.

FUTURE RESEARCH

Taking into consideration the early stage of the field, there is still much scope to analyze and explore social entrepreneurial leadership. Indeed, there are wide varieties of research questions, which require further attention. What are the motivational constructs of social entrepreneurial leaders? What are the most effective ways for a social entrepreneur to manage volunteers/employers? How can entrepreneurs communicate to different stakeholders? What motivates social entrepreneurs to engage in social enterprise instead of following more stable or predictable career pathways? What are the reason/motives which explain why social entrepreneurial leaders start social enterprises? Is it just a desire to help something else? Are they creating a business or a world to live in for themselves and others?

Short et al. (2009) suggested a number of theoretical ideas that may be relevant to the study of social entrepreneurship. Mair and Marti (2006) suggest future directions in the areas of structuration theory, institutional entrepreneurship, social capital, and social movements about social entrepreneurial leadership.

In this chapter, social entrepreneurial leadership has been defined, discussed, and explored theoretically vis-à-vis other leadership styles which have been delineated in the literature. Future studies should present empirical evidence to define the behaviors of social entrepreneurial leaders and his/her relations with followers and other shareholders. Because the literature on social entrepreneurship is usually case-based and conceptual, there is certainly much potential for empirical investigations using an array of qualitative, quantitative, and mixed methodologies in order to understand the behaviors of social entrepreneurial leaders and their motivations for instigating and maintaining social enterprises.

CONCLUSION

Today, humanity's awareness of and concern for prevailing social problems is higher than it has ever been, not least because of the advent and diffusion of information and communication technologies. In the era of the internet and ubiquitous communications, Y and Z generations have grown up exposed to a very different consciousness and level of social awareness compared to their forebears. This social awareness has enabled values such as freedom, ethics, responsibility, sustainability, as well as the rights of humans, employees, women, and the disenfranchised to gain more importance.

People realize the nature and extent of income inequalities at various spatial scales, and the proliferation of corruption and injustices in the world economy resulting in deleterious economic, social, and environmental consequences. In addition, they are less fearful and reluctant to voice their dissatisfaction and needs on these issues. Not all environmental, social, and economic problems can be addressed feasibly by businesses and the government. Some individuals, called social entrepreneurs, are identifying and implementing sustainable solutions in order to improve economic and social wealth. These social entrepreneurs have created a new business model that militates against the financial impediments faced commonly by non-profit organizations. In other words, they are adapting their social visions and fostering social change through the merging and co-evolution of social values and business models. If entrepreneurialism is a new form of leadership, then social entrepreneurs represent a paradigm shift, creating social transformation by generating social value.

The nature of social entrepreneurship makes it a fascinating research area to be approached from different disciplinary perspectives (Mair & Marti, 2006). The extant research has characterized the many features of social entrepreneurs (as summarized in Table 1) and tried to understand "how" entrepreneurs act (Dees, 1998). Indeed, as illuminated in this chapter, social entrepreneurial leaders can be defined as ethical, transformational, authentic, sustainable, and servant leaders. Social entrepreneurial leaders have special leadership skills and behaviors.

Like servant leadership, both ethical and authentic leadership resonate with social entrepreneurs. It is not surprising that there are some similarities with, and differences between, the ethical, authentic, and transformational theories of leadership. For example while ethical leaders emphasize ethical standards and moral management more than transformational leaders, authentic leaders emphasize authenticity and self-awareness (Brown & Trevino, 2006). As discussed in the literature, it would right to define the social entrepreneur as ethical, transformational, authentic, sustainable, and servant leaders. Nevertheless, social entrepreneurial leaders have unique leadership styles.

However, it would be inappropriate to overly generalize and assume social entrepreneurs are overwhelmingly homogeneous. They can and do span very different ages, social positions, gender, and countries. Blake Mycoskie was only 35 when he founded TOMS, and William Foote was only 31 when he started Root Capital (www.rootcapital.org). Similarly, model and activist Lauren Bush was only 22 when she started FEED (www.feedprojects.com). They are changing the world into a healthier, more compassionate, more ethical, fairer and more equal place in many ways.

Since the competitive environment is changing rapidly and the boundaries between profit and non-profit sectors are similarly dynamic, social entrepreneurship and their leaders or leadership styles become more interesting to research. Followers are supporting social entrepreneurial leaders with admiration and getting inspired by them. Victor Ananias, founder of the Wheat Association and Blake Mycoskie, founder of TOMS, among many others, are leaders who should be studied and understood more. In order to realize sustainable development objectives, society needs entrepreneurial leaders who are far more social. Society needs social entrepreneurs to help find new ways to realize social improvements in the next century (Dees, 1998).

REFERENCES

Ashoka Organization Website. (n.d.). Retrieved June 10, 2017, from https://www.ashoka.org/

Austin, J., Stevenson, H., & Wei-Skillern, J. (2006). Social and Commercial Entrepreneurship: Same, Different, or Both? *Entrepreneurship Theory and Practice*, *30*(1), 1–22. doi:10.1111/j.1540-6520.2006.00107.x

Austin, J. E. (2000). *The collaboration challenge: How nonprofits and business succeed through strategic alliances*. San Francisco: Jossey-Bass Publishers.

Avery, G. C., & Bergsteiner, H. (2011). Sustainable leadership practices for enhancing business resilience and performance. *Strategy and Leadership*, *39*(3), 5–15. doi:10.1108/10878571111128766

Avolio, B. J., & Gardner, W. L. (2005). Authentic leadership development: Getting to the root of positive forms of leadership. *The Leadership Quarterly*, *16*(3), 315–338. doi:10.1016/j.leaqua.2005.03.001

Bagheri, A., & Pihie, Z. A. L. (2011). On Becoming an Entrepreneurial Leader: A Focus on the Impacts of University Entrepreneurship Programs. *American Journal of Applied Sciences*, *8*(9), 884–892. doi:10.3844/ajassp.2011.884.892

Bass, B. M. (1985). *Leadership and performance beyond expectations*. New York: The Free Press.

Bass, B. M. (1995). Transformational leadership. *Journal of Management Inquiry*, *4*(3), 293–298. doi:10.1177/105649269543010

Bass, B. M. (1999). Two decades of research and development in transformational leadership. *European Journal of Work and Organizational Psychology*, *8*(1), 9–32. doi:10.1080/135943299398410

Bass, B. M., & Avolio, B. J. (1995). *MLQ: Multifactor Leadership Questionnaire* (2nd ed.). Mind Garden.

Bass, B. M., & Riggio, R. E. (2006). *Transformational Leadership* (2nd ed.). Lawrence Erlbaum Associates, Inc.

Bornstein, D. (2007). *How to Change the World: Social Entrepreneurs and the Power of New Ideas, Updated Edition*. Oxford University Press.

Brown, M. E., & Treviño, L. K. (2006). Ethical leadership: A review and future directions. *The Leadership Quarterly*, *17*(6), 595–616. doi:10.1016/j.leaqua.2006.10.004

Brown, M. E., Treviño, L. K., & Harrison, D. A. (2005). Ethical leadership: A social learning perspective for construct development and testing. *Organizational Behavior and Human Decision Processes*, *97*(2), 117–134. doi:10.1016/j.obhdp.2005.03.002

Brown, M. E., Treviño, L. K., & Harrison, D. A. (2005). Ethical leadership: A social learning perspective for construct development and testing. *Organizational Behavior and Human Decision Processes*, *97*(2), 117–134.

Carroll, A. (1979). A Three-Dimensional Conceptual Model of Corporate Social Performance. *Academy of Management Review*, *4*, 497–505.

Chell, E. (2007). Social Enterprise and Entrepreneurship: Towards a Convergent Theory of the Entrepreneurial Process. *International Small Business Journal*, *25*(1), 5–23. doi:10.1177/0266242607071779

Chen, M. (2007). Entrepreneurial Leadership and New Ventures: Creativity in Entrepreneurial Teams. *Creativity and Innovation Management*, *16*(3), 239–249. doi:10.1111/j.1467-8691.2007.00439.x

Cogliser, C. C., & Brigham, K. H. (2004). The intersection of leadership and entrepreneurship: Mutual lessons to be learned. *The Leadership Quarterly*, *15*(6), 771–799. doi:10.1016/j.leaqua.2004.09.004

Dacin, M. T., Dacin, P. A., & Tracey, P. (2011). Social Entrepreneurship: A Critique and Future Directions. *Organization Science*, *22*(5), 1203–1213. doi:10.1287/orsc.1100.0620

Dacin, P. A., Dacin, M. T., & Matear, M. (2010). Social Entrepreneurship: Why We Don't Need a New Theory and How We Move Forward From Here. *The Academy of Management Perspectives*, *24*(3), 37–57. doi:10.5465/AMP.2010.52842950

Dees, J. G. (1998). Enterprising Non-profits. *Harvard Business Review, 76*, 55–67.

Dees, J. G., Emerson, J., & Economy, P. (2001). *Enterprising Nonprofits: A Toolkit for Social Entrepreneurs*. Wiley.

Dienesch, R. M., & Liden, R. C. (1986). Leader-Member Exchange Model of Leadership: A Critique and Further Development. *Academy of Management Review*, *11*(3), 618–634.

Drayton, W. (2002). The Citizen Sector: Becoming as Entrepreneurial and Competitive as Business. *California Management Review*, *44*(3), 120–132. doi:10.2307/41166136

Felício, J. A., Gonçalves, H. M., & Gonçalves, V. C. (2013). Social value and organizational performance in non-profit social organizations: Social entrepreneurship, leadership, and socioeconomic context effects. *Journal of Business Research*, *66*(10), 2139–2146. doi:10.1016/j.jbusres.2013.02.040

Fernald, L. W., Solomon, G. T., & Tarabishy, A. (2005). A New Paradigm: Entrepreneurial Leadership, Southern. *Business Review (Federal Reserve Bank of Philadelphia)*, 1–11.

Germak, A. J., & Robinson, J. A. (2014). Exploring the Motivation of Nascent Social Entrepreneurs. *Journal of Social Entrepreneurship*, *5*(1), 5–21. doi:10.1080/19420676.2013.820781

Greenberg, D., McKone-Sweet, K., & Wilson, H. J. (2011). *The New Entrepreneurial Leader*. Berrett-Koehler Pub.

Greenleaf, R. K. (1977). *Servant Leadership*. New York: Paulist Press.

Griffin, J. J., & Mahon, J. F. (1997). The Corporate Social Performance and Corporate Financial Performance Debate: Twenty-Five Years of Incomparable Research. *Business & Society*, *36*(1), 5–31. doi:10.1177/000765039703600102

Gupta, V., MacMillan, I. C., & Surie, G. (2004). Entrepreneurial leadership: Developing and measuring a cross-cultural construct. *Journal of Business Venturing*, *19*(2), 241–260. doi:10.1016/S0883-9026(03)00040-5

Hargreaves, A., & Fink, D. (2005). *Sustainable Leadership*. Jossey-Bass.

Hartigan, P. (2006). It's about people, not profits. *Business Strategy Review*, *17*(4), 42–45. doi:10.1111/j.0955-6419.2006.00433.x

Heinecke, A., Kloibhofer, M., & Krzeminska, A. (2014). *Leadership in Social Enterprise How to Manage Yourself and the Team, Schwab Foundation For Social Entrepreneurship*. Economic World Forum. Retrieved June 10, 2017, from http://www.schwabfound.org

Herrington, M., & Kew, P. (2017). *GEM Report on Social Entrepreneurship*. Retrieved June 10, 2017, from http://www.gemconsortium.org/

Herrington, M., & Kew, P. (2017a). *GEM Global Report 2016/17*. Retrieved June 10, 2017, from http://www.gemconsortium.org/

Hopkins, M. M., & O'Neil, D. A. (2015). Authentic leadership: Application to women leaders. *Frontiers in Psychology*, *6*, 959. doi:10.3389/fpsyg.2015.00959 PMID:26236254

Jones, R., Latham, J., & Betta, M. (2008). Narrative construction of the social entrepreneurial identity. *International Journal of Entrepreneurial Behaviour & Research*, *14*(5), 330–345. doi:10.1108/13552550810897687

Kieser, C., Leipziger, D., & Shubert, J. (2014). *Creating Social Value: A Guide for Leaders and Change Makers*. Greenleaf.

Kuratko, D. F. (2005). The Emergence of Entrepreneurship Education: Development, Trends, and Challenges. *Entrepreneurship: Theory and Practice, 29*(5), 577 - 598.

Kuratko, D. F. (2007). Entrepreneurial Leadership in the 21st Century. *Journal of Leadership & Organizational Studies*, *13*(4), 1–11. doi:10.1177/10717919070130040201

Kuratko, D. F., & Hodgetts, R. M. (2004). *Entrepreneurship: Theory, Process, Practice*. Thomson South Western.

Leadbeater, C. (1997). *The rise of the social entrepreneur*. London: DEMOS. Retrieved July 2017 from http://www.demos.co.uk/publications/socialentrepreneur

Liden, R. C., Wayne, S. J., Zhao, H., & Henderson, D. (2008). Servant Leadership: Development of a Multidimensional Measure and Multi-Level Assessment. *The Leadership Quarterly*, *19*(2), 161–177. doi:10.1016/j.leaqua.2008.01.006

Mahoney, L.S., & Roberts, R.W. (2015). Corporate Social Performance. *Research on Professional Responsibility and Ethics in Accounting*, 73--99.

Mair, J., & Marti, I. (2006). Social entrepreneurship research: A source of explanation, prediction, and delight. *Journal of World Business*, *41*(1), 36–44. doi:10.1016/j.jwb.2005.09.002

Makni, R., Francoeur, C., & Bellavance, F. (2009). Causality between Corporate Social Performance and Financial Performance: Evidence from Canadian Firms. *Journal of Business Ethics*, *89*(3), 409–422. doi:10.100710551-008-0007-7

Martin, R., Gregory, T., Karl, C., Olga, E., & McNamara, R. (2005). The role of leader-member exchanges in mediating the relationship between locus of control and work reactions. *Journal of Occupational and Organizational Psychology*, *78*(1), 141–147. doi:10.1348/096317904X23763

Martin, R. L., & Osberg, S. (2007, Spring). Social Entrepreneurship: The Case for Definition. *Stanford Social Innovation Review*, 29–39.

Massetti, B. L. (2008). The Social Entrepreneurship Matrix as a "Tipping Point"" for Economic Change. *Emergence*, 1–8.

McCann, J., & Sweet, M. (2014). The Perceptions of Ethical and Sustainable Leadership. *Journal of Business Ethics*, *121*(3), 373–383. doi:10.100710551-013-1704-4

McCraw, T. K. (2007). Prophet of innovation, Josep Schumpeter and creative destruction. The Belknap Press of Harvard University Press.

Nga, J. K., & Shamuganathan, G. (2010). The influence of personality traits and demographic factors on social entrepreneurship start up intentions. *Journal of Business Ethics*, *95*(2), 259–282. doi:10.100710551-009-0358-8

Pless, N. M. (2012). Social entrepreneurship in theory and practice: An introduction. *Journal of Business Ethics*, *111*(3), 317–320. doi:10.100710551-012-1533-x

Porter, M., & Kramer, M. R. (2011, January). Creating Share Value. *Harvard Business Review*, 201–229.

Prabhu, G. N. (1999). Social entrepreneurial leadership. *Career Development International*, *4*(3), 140–145. doi:10.1108/13620439910262796

Predo, A. M., & McLean, M. (2006). Social entrepreneurship: A critical review of the concept. *Journal of World Business*, *41*(1), 56–65. doi:10.1016/j.jwb.2005.10.007

Rosing, K., Frese, M., & Bausch, A. (2011). Explaining the heterogeneity of the leadership-innovation relationship: Ambidextrous leadership. *The Leadership Quarterly*, *22*(5), 956–974. doi:10.1016/j.leaqua.2011.07.014

Ruvio, A., Rosenblatt, Z., & Hertz-Lazarowitz, R. (2010). Entrepreneurial leadership vision in nonprofit vs. for-profit organizations. *The Leadership Quarterly*, *21*(1), 144–158. doi:10.1016/j.leaqua.2009.10.011

Saruhan, S. C., & Yıldız, M. L. (2016). *Contemporary Management Science*. Istanbul: Beta.

Schott, T., Rogoff, E., & Herrington, M. (2017). *GEM 2016/2017 Report on Senior Entrepreneurship*. Retrieved June 10, 2017, from http://www.gemconsortium.org/

Seanor, P., & Meaton, J. (2007). Making sense of social enterprise. *Social Enterprise Journal*, *3*(1), 90–100. doi:10.1108/17508610780000724

Seelos, C., & Mair, J. (2005). Social entrepreneurship: Creating New Business Models to Serve the Poor. *Business Horizons*, *48*(3), 241–246. doi:10.1016/j.bushor.2004.11.006

Shaw, E., & Carter, S. (2007). Social entrepreneurship: Theoretical antecedents and empirical analysis of entrepreneurial processes and outcomes. *Journal of Small Business and Enterprise Development*, *14*(3), 418–434. doi:10.1108/14626000710773529

Shaw, E., Shaw, J., & Wilson, M. (2002). Unsung entrepreneurs: Entrepreneurship for social gain. Durham, UK: University of Durham Business School – –The Barclays Centre for Entrepreneurship.

Short, J. C., Moss, T. W., & Lumpkin, G. T. (2009). Research In Social Entrepreneurship: Past Contributions and Future Opportunities. *Strategic Entrepreneurship Journal*, *3*(2), 161–194. doi:10.1002ej.69

Skoll Foundation. (2009). *What is social entrepreneur?* Retrieved June 10, 2017, from http://skoll.org/

Spears, L. C. (2010). Character and Servant Leadership: Ten Characteristics of Effective, Caring Leaders. *The Journal of Virtues & Leadership*, *1*(1), 25–30.

Sullivan Mort, G., Weerawardena, J., & Carnegie, K. (2003). Social Entrepreneurship: Toward Conceptualization. *International Journal of Nonprofit and Voluntary Sector Marketing*, *8*(1), 76–88. doi:10.1002/nvsm.202

Tan, W., Williams, J., & Tan, T. (2005). Defining the 'Social' in 'Social Entrepreneurship': Altruism and Entrepreneurship. *The International Entrepreneurship and Management Journal*, *1*(3), 353–365. doi:10.100711365-005-2600-x

Teasdale, S., McKay, S., Phillimore, J., & Teasdale, N. (2011). Exploring gender and social entrepreneurship: Women's leadership, employment and participation in the third sector and social enterprises. *Voluntary Sector Review*, *2*(1), 57–76. doi:10.1332/204080511X560620

Terjesen, S., Lepoutre, J., Justo, R., & Bosma, N. (2009). *Global Entrepreneurship Monitor Report on Social Entrepreneurship Executive Summary*. Retrieved June 10, 2017, from http://www.gemconsortium.org/

(2013). The many faces of social entrepreneurial leadership. InNormore, H., & Erbe, N. (Eds.), *Collective Efficacy: Interdisciplinary Perspectives on International Leadership*. Emerald Group Publishing Limited.

Thompson, J., Alvy, G., & Lees, A. (2000). Social entrepreneurship – –a new look at the people and the potential. *Management Decision*, *38*(5), 328–338. doi:10.1108/00251740010340517

Thompson, J. L. (2002). The world of the social entrepreneur. *International Journal of Public Sector Management*, *15*(5), 412–431. doi:10.1108/09513550210435746

Thompson, N., Kiefer, K., & York, J. G. (2011). Distinctions not Dichotomies: Exploring Social, Sustainable, and Environmental Entrepreneurship. In G. T. Lumpkin & J. A. Katz (Eds.), *Advances in Entrepreneurship, Firm Emergence and Growth: Exploring Social, Sustainable, and Environmental Entrepreneurship* (Vol. 13). Bingley, UK: Emerald Group Publishing Limited. doi:10.1108/S1074-7540(2011)0000013012

Ţigu, G., Iorgulescu, M.-C., Răvar, A. S., & Lile, R. (2015). A Pilot Profile of the Social Entrepreneur in the Constantly Changing Romanian Economy. *Amfiteatru Economic*, *17*(38), 25–43.

Van der Spek, T., Schreven, A. M., & Van der Velden, F. (2014). *Leadership in Social Business*. Context, International Cooperation.

Vecchio, R. P. (2003). Entrepreneurship and leadership: Common trends and common threads. *Human Resource Management Review*, *13*(2), 303–327. doi:10.1016/S1053-4822(03)00019-6

Walumbwa, F. O., Avolio, B. J., Gardner, W. L., Wernsing, T. S., & Peterson, S. J. (2008). Authentic leadership: Development and validation of a theory-based measure. *Journal of Management*, *34*(1), 89–126. doi:10.1177/0149206307308913

Weerawardena, J., & Sullivan Mort, G. (2001). Learning, innovation and competitive advantage in not-for-profit aged care marketing: A conceptual model and research propositions. *Journal of Nonprofit & Public Sector Marketing*, *9*(3), 53–73. doi:10.1300/J054v09n03_04

Weerawardena, J., & Sullivan Mort, G. (2006). Investigating Social Entrepreneurship: A Multidimensional Model. *Journal of World Business*, *41*(1), 21–35. doi:10.1016/j.jwb.2005.09.001

Yıldız, M. L. (2016). Ethical Leadership: To Be or Not To Be A Moral Person. In M.L. Yıldız (Ed.), Leadership Studies (2nd ed.). Beta.

Zahra, S. A., Gedajlovic, E., Neubaum, D. O., & Shulman, J. M. (2009). A typology of social entrepreneurs: Motives, search processes and ethical challenges. *Journal of Business Venturing*, *24*(5), 519–532. doi:10.1016/j.jbusvent.2008.04.007

Zhao, X., & Murrell, A. J. (2016). Revisiting the Corporate Social Performance-Financial Performance Link: A Replication of Waddock and Graves, Strategic Management Journal. *Special Issue: Replication in Strategic Management*, *37*(11), 2378–2388.

ADDITIONAL READING

Alvord, S. H., Brown, D. L., & Letts, C. W. (2004). Social entrepreneurship and societal transformation: An exploratory study. *The Journal of Applied Behavioral Science*, *40*(3), 260–282. doi:10.1177/0021886304266847

Avolio, B. J., Gardner, W. L., Walumbwa, F. O., Luthans, F., & May, D. R. (2004). Unlocking the mask: A look at the process by which authentic leaders impact follower attitudes and behaviors. *The Leadership Quarterly*, *15*(6), 801–823. doi:10.1016/j.leaqua.2004.09.003

Bass, B. M. (2000). The future of leadership in learning organizations. *Journal of Leadership & Organizational Studies*, *7*(3), 18–40. doi:10.1177/107179190000700302

Bass, B. M., & Steidlmeier, P. (1999). Ethics, character, and authentic transformational leadership behavior. *The Leadership Quarterly*, *10*(2), 181–21. doi:10.1016/S1048-9843(99)00016-8

Brown, M. E., & Trevino, L. K. (2014). Do Role Models Matter? *An Investigation of Role Modeling as an Antecedent of Perceived Ethical Leadership*, *122*, 587–598.

Crews, D. E. (2010). Strategies for Implementing Sustainability: Five Leadership Challenges. *S.A.M. Advanced Management Journal*, 15–21.

Hill, T. L., Kothari, T. H., & Shea, M. (2010). Patterns of Meaning in the Social Entrepreneurship Literature: A Research Platform. *Journal of Social Entrepreneurship*, *1*(1), 5–31. doi:10.1080/19420670903442079

Hoch, J. E., Bommer, W. H., Dulebohn, J. H., & Wu, D. (2016). Do Ethical, Authentic, and Servant Leadership Explain Variance Above and Beyond Transformational Leadership? A Meta-Analysis. *Journal of Management*, 1–29.

Kantabutra, S., & Avery, G. C. (2011). Sustainable leadership at Siam Cement Group. *The Journal of Business Strategy*, *32*(4), 32–41. doi:10.1108/02756661111150954

Kociatkiewicz, J., & Kostera, M. (2012). The Good Manager: An Archetypical Quest for Morally Sustainable Leadership. *Organization Studies*, *33*(7), 861–878. doi:10.1177/0170840612445124

Maak, T., & Stoetter, N. (2012). Social Entrepreneurs as Responsible Leaders: 'Fundación Paraguaya' and the Case of Martin Burt. *Journal of Business Ethics*, *111*(3), 413–430. doi:10.100710551-012-1417-0

MacMillan, I. C. (1983). The politics of new venture management. *Harvard Business Review*, *61*(6), 8–16.

Mair, J., Robinson, J., & Hockerts, K. (2004). *(edsEds). Social Entrepreneurship*. Basingstoke, UK: Palgrave Macmillan.

Mayer, D. M., Kuenzi, M., Greenbaum, R., Bardes, M., & Salvador, R. (2009). How low does ethical leadership flow? Test of a trickle-down model. *Organizational Behavior and Human Decision Processes*, *108*(1), 1–13. doi:10.1016/j.obhdp.2008.04.002

McCann, J., & Sweet, M. (2014). The Perceptions of Ethical and Sustainable Leadership. *Journal of Business Ethics*, *121*(3), 373–383. doi:10.100710551-013-1704-4

Murphy, P. J., & Coombes, S. M. (2009). A Model of Social Entrepreneurial Discovery. *The Journal of Business*, *87*, 325–336.

Neider, L. L., & Schriesheim, C. A. (2011). The Authentic Leadership Inventory (ALI): Development and empirical tests. *The Leadership Quarterly*, *22*(6), 1146–1164. doi:10.1016/j.leaqua.2011.09.008

Neubert, M. J., Carlson, D. S., Kacmar, K. M., Roberts, J. A., & Chonko, L. B. (2009). The virtuous influence of ethical leadership behavior: Evidence from the field. *Journal of Business Ethics*, *90*(2), 157–170. doi:10.100710551-009-0037-9

Northouse, S. G. (2010). *Leadership, theory and practice*. Thousand Oaks, CA: Sage.

Price, T. L. (2003). The ethics of authentic transformational leadership. *The Leadership Quarterly*, *14*(1), 67–81. doi:10.1016/S1048-9843(02)00187-X

Riggio, R. E., Zhu, W., Reina, C., & Maroosis, J. A. (2010). Virtue-based measurement of ethical leadership: The Leadership Virtues Questionnaire. *Consulting Psychology Journal: Practice and Research*, *62*(4), 235–250. doi:10.1037/a0022286

Stone, A. G., Russell, R., & Patterson, K. (2003). Transformational versus servant leadership: A difference in leader focus. *Leadership and Organization Development Journal*, *25*(4), 349–364. doi:10.1108/01437730410538671

Svensson, G., & Wood, G. (2007). Sustainable leadership ethics: A continuous and iterative process. *Leadership and Organization Development Journal*, *28*(3), 251–268. doi:10.1108/01437730710739666

Wallace, B. (2005). Exploring the meaning(s) of sustainability for community based social entrepreneurs. *Social Enterprise Journal*, *1*(1), 78–89. doi:10.1108/17508610580000708

Wallace, S. L. (1999). Social entrepreneurship: The role of social purpose enterprises in facilitating community economic development. *Journal of Developmental Entrepreneurship*, *4*(2), 153–174.

Zahra, S. A., Ireland, R. D., Gutierrez, I., & Hitt, M. A. (2000). Introduction to Special Topic Forum Privatization and Entrepreneurial Transformation: Emerging Issues and a Future Research Agenda. *Academy of Management Review*, *25*(3), 509–524.

Zahra, S. A., Rawhouser, H. N., Bhawe, N., Neubaum, D. O., & Hayton, J. C. (2008). Globalization of social entrepreneurship opportunities. *Strategic Entrepreneurship Journal*, *2*(2), 117–131. doi:10.1002ej.43

Zeyen, A., Beckman, M., Mueller, S., Dees, J. G., Khanin, D., Krueger, N., ... Zachakaris, A. (2012). Social Entrepreneurship and Broader Theories: Shedding New Light on the 'Bigger Picture'. *Journal of Social Entrepreneurship*, 1–20.

KEY TERMS AND DEFINITIONS

Authentic Leadership: A pattern of leader behavior that draws upon and promotes both positive psychological capacities and a positive ethical climate, to foster greater self-awareness, an internalized moral perspective, balanced processing of information and relational transparency on the part of leaders working with followers, fostering positive self-development.

Entrepreneurial Leadership: It is a form of leadership distinctive from other types of leadership which enables entrepreneurs and leaders to cope with highly turbulent and competitive environments.

Ethical Leadership: The demonstration of normatively appropriate conduct through personal actions and interpersonal relationships, and the promotion of such conduct to followers through two-way communication, reinforcement and decision making.

Servant leaders: Leaders who help subordinates to reach their maximum potential. Servant leaders "want their subordinates to improve for their own good, and view the development of followers as an end, in and of itself, not merely a means to reach the leader's or organization's goals.

Social Entrepreneurial Leader: They are proactive, strategic thinkers who are driven by their passion to implement innovative new ideas to solve social problems. They seek also opportunities while behaving ethically in terms of the processes, which they follow and the activities they undertake.

Sustainable Leaders: Leaders concerned with creating current and future profits for an organization while improving the lives of all concerned. They exhibit social and environmental consciousness, business credibility, adaptability, patience, translational skills, broad system thinking, change orientation, energy and passion, mentoring and development, and persuasiveness.

Transformational Leaders: They inspire followers with their vision and stimulate them to challenge themselves and their way of thinking, while uniting them around a common vision and core values. Transformational leadership contains four components: charisma or idealized influence (attributed or behavioral), inspirational motivation, intellectual stimulation, and individualized consideration.

Chapter 14
Towards Cooperative With Competitive Alliance:
Insights Into Performance Value in Social Entrepreneurship

Miftachul Huda
Universiti Teknologi Malaysia, Malaysia

Sari Laelatul Qodriah
Universitas Muhammadiyah Cirebon, Indonesia

Budi Rismayadi
Universitas Buana Perjuangan, Indonesia

Aprilia Hananto
Universitas Buana Perjuangan, Indonesia

Endah Nurhawaeny Kardiyati
Universitas Muhammadiyah Cirebon, Indonesia

Aminuddin Ruskam
Universiti Teknologi Malaysia, Malaysia

Badlihisham Mohd Nasir
Universiti Teknologi Malaysia, Malaysia

ABSTRACT

The advantage of competitive atmosphere in business has a significant role in helping to enhance productivity. It is necessary to empower competitive awareness with cooperative engagement to give clear understanding for core guideline and insightful view on promoting social entrepreneurship. This chapter attempts to explore the initiated engagement between cooperative and competitive concern paid attention in the particular way among the firms along with increasing popularity to achieve certain objectives like growing the business with entrepreneurship. The finding reveals that attracting growing amounts of cooperative and competitive alliance should be strengthened to gain the feedback and insights into

DOI: 10.4018/978-1-5225-5687-9.ch014

performance value in social entrepreneurship where this is eventually integrated with the entrepreneurship in a way that underlies the value to run the potential business. This chapter is supposed to contribute significant insights into exploring the key role of strategies to give the beneficial feedback to perform continuous improvement in social entrepreneurship.

INTRODUCTION

The advantage of competitive awareness in the business has a significant role to help enhance the productivity (Chen, Kuo-Hsien & Tsai, 2007), where this is eventually integrated with the entrepreneurship in the way which underlies the value to run the potential business (Cardy, & Selvarajan, 2006). In order to concern the aims consolidated with engaging the beliefs in the variety of organizations, attempts to boost the attractive initiation to grow in both talent and attention with enhancing effectivity should be transformed to achieve the certain objectives. This includes motivating the sense to growing the business with entrepreneurship in terms of social and commercial basis. At this point of view, social entrepreneurship here refers to the techniques used by the companies to start-up their production process widely set out to develop by addressing social, cultural, and environmental issues in order to solve the solutions (Fish & Wood, 2017). With this regard, the extent of certainty on the activities and initiative program about what exactly social entrepreneurship would be contributed refers to enhance the competitive and cooperative basis. It aims to assure the practical result to be achieved through the program initiative associated with combining innovation and creativity integrated into creating the critical thinking way between social and environmental challenges (Perron, Côté & Duffy, 2006). Through incorporating the material resource as the entire opportunity in addressing the values with the sorts of social entrepreneurship, focusing on transforming systems and practices would result in the potential strength of performance to run the entrepreneurship.

However, although many has been employed about the significant essence of entrepreneurship (Bornstein & Davis, 2010; Cho, 2006; Choi & Majumdar, 2014; Dacin, Dacin & Matear, 2010; Smith & Stevens, 2010), there has been lack of scholarly attention to elaborate in the practical way in both cooperative and competitive alliance, which may become an insightful point of view to the potential performance in order to run the entrepreneurship. Thus, this chapter aims to explore the particular way about the cooperative and competitive alliance to achieve the feedback and insights into performance value in social entrepreneurship. The three core objectives will be dealing with developing the systematic approach to identifying cooperative with competitive alliance on strengthening an actual performance in action to encompass the great deal of social entrepreneurship. This initiative needs to elucidate the set of literature about the theories of the significant essence of the creative thinking with competitive alliance for envisioning the direction in social entrepreneurship. Moreover, this chapter aims to explore the key themes and concepts that underpin performing powerful decisions as an ability to empower the performance value in social entrepreneurship.

LITERATURE REVIEW

Strategic Initiation Between Cooperative and Competitive Alliance

The initiative of combining the strategic alliances between cooperative and competitive initiation has a significant role to give insights on achieving the goal. In terms of getting cooperated with others, the need to have a key assurance in gaining advantage among the human behavior subsequence should enlarge the potential substance increasingly to the productivity. In order to achieve competitive advantages, attempts to combine the potential assets which firms have for instance may cooperate with addressing the capabilities to run the business within their work plan. With this regard, the initiative of setting the cooperative policy should be taken into consideration as an essential part of making strategic integrity amidst the firms. Through providing the strategic alliance, addressing the learning process in the business world needs to enhance alliance management with resource-sharing to create the value of competitive advantage in creating new business area (Haeussler, Patzelt, & Zahra, 2012). In the era of competitive business world, this initiative needs to enhance the potential value to create opportunities in opening the collaboration with other firms. For instance, one company in providing instant food may need to have collaboration with other part of food supply of ingredient. This might create the opportunities with enhancing the competitive advantage where this is usually enlarged to have a connection into the social entrepreneurship.

In addition, the potential value of competitive advantage should enhance the techniques used by the companies to start-up their production process widely set out to develop in addressing social, cultural, and environmental issues in order to provide the solutions (Fish & Wood, 2017). This combination is entirely a point of view in creating the business value in the sense that determines the innovative initiation of big data in looking at the market to transmitting into the product with most demand (Huda et al., 2016). The systematic approach to identifying cooperative and competitive alliance on strengthening an actual performance in action to encompass the great deal of social entrepreneurship needs to start enhancing the creative thinking. Moreover, the competitive alliance for envisioning the direction in social entrepreneurship can manage the entire process of empowering the performance value in performing ability with powerful decisions in social entrepreneurship. As an important attainment in strategic alliance, getting competitive advantage should be taken in serious attempt with an integrative approach to the formation in managing the opportunity amidst the contemporary conflict. This is because firms' outstanding attempt needs to get to linkage on the exchange initiative to be shared to develop in distributing good services together with capabilities and resources (Nag, Russo, & Vurr, 2014). Through strategic alliance in enabling the potential value into the performance with some entrepreneurship value, these two features can make the achievement of competitive advantages to enhance entrepreneurial initiative integrated into the innovative inquiry in possessing the required resources in acknowledging the competitive and dynamic markets.

In addition, enhancing the cooperative arrangement assigned with getting relationship into the competitive advantage should coordinate with deliberating the opportunity to deliver the resources with capabilities through the initiation to start working with partners. Moreover, enhancing the line needs to take into consideration to develop inter-organizational relationships among the firms to maintain the strategic alliances. With the attempts in creating the new competitive advantages for the firms as the way engaged into additional resources, the capabilities as the function to direct strategic alliances in order to get logical and timely response can be engaged into performing unprecedented numbers between firms with intense and rapid changes to contribute into the economic activity. In this view, being formed into such technology within the globalization, especially large global competitors, should establish multiple strategic alliances. Attempts to provide the special attention to generate the advanced technologies to the market strategy can also be initiated into the competitive advantage to develop social entrepreneurship within the digital approach (Haeussler, Patzelt, & Zahra, 2012). Cooperative behavior in general which can direct the strategic alliance is required to get actively involvement in the problem solving to the solution among the partners. Creating the value combined with alliance management to support the cooperation and coordination to lead to the success in obtaining the social entrepreneurship has to get involved with the conflict management skills practice. Being trustworthy among the partners to consolidate the resources in gaining the several factors of activities in the cooperative organizational behavior could be designed in the achievement of competitive advantages. With such capabilities in identifying an appropriate alliance, the persuasion among the partners in the market could foster the alliance structure through the decision-making process of being more attention in alliance formation.

Towards Performance on Cooperative and Competitive Alliance

The performance way refers to enhance the initiative of considering the cooperative engagement associated with competitive alliance. This engagement needs to be involved to meet the relational risk as an attempt in selecting the compliance partnership in developing the alliances in providing the strategic initiation with resources. These can be viewed through distribution channels of the certain products in the sense to manufacture the capability with intellectual property associated with knowledge expertise. Moreover, the capital equipment with project funding can be engaged to the cooperation collaborating the synergy among the partnerships along with creating the committed trust to achieve the goal and create the benefits. This refers to enhance the overall objective in diminishing the total risk in order to ensure in behaving the competitive advantages. Distributing the competitive advantage with collaborative initiation advantage has to be developed through a cooperative strategy in the sense which can manage the firm's market place success (Shi, Sun, & Prescott, 2012). Competitive advantages integrated with the technological capabilities firms should significantly give insights in influencing the customer value through the functional and educational experience. Attempts to ensure a competitive advantage would provide an important dimension in the global economy associated with the rapid technological changes. In this view, the factors challenging firms of competitive advantage in maintaining the strategic competitiveness needs to constantly upgrade current competitive advantages in order to grow the formation of alliances. While developing new ones to enhance the strategic alliance to boost the competitiveness, linkage networks in the different forms of creating the sustainability initiated with competitive advantage refer to gain competitive advantages in the sense which could provide the hypotheses to foster the strong focus on the creation of value compared to competition reducing and uncertainty reducing alliances (Smith & Stevens, 2010). It tends to be formed as an attempt in responding the competitors' actions coped with the strategic alliance and competition in different form of alliances.

In addition, the level of strategic alliance to obtain the complementary business needs to especially respond to enlarge the competition with the probability of entering into alliances firms. It points out strategic alliance designed to reduce uncertainty in creating the competitive advantages contemplated through the complementary alliances in possessing those developed advantages to be more complementary in the corporate-level of strategies. Attempts to enhance the initiation to embark the strategies to develop collaborate awareness would be used to the knowledge management for the firms to gain maximum value from this knowledge. As a result, crucial knowledge firms in the initiative to properly distribute and organize the formation and use of alliances has an entire effort to successfully commercialize inventions gained to those involved with the firms. Through cooperating with other organizations, the revenues may help transform cross-border alliances to better use their competitive advantages through selecting the integration initiation to enhance their knowledge and resources (Walter, Kellermanns, & Lechner, 2012). It is necessary to embark the firms in order to take advantages of opportunities to the full range of telecommunications and information system manufacture. In this view, attempts to choose in surfacing the rapidly changing global economy needs to characterize the components in seeking to move among the company from group deriving broadly focused in relationships between the two components which can play a key role. Associated with existing market-based relationship, the participants' role playing in concentrating trust in network should get involved into the performance evaluation with profit-sharing and risk management. In particular, being more complex, the network to transmit cooperative strategy is particularly effective in manufacturing the design formed by firms in the sense which enhances the strategic alliances. These have to fulfil the close relationships clustered together into joint venture, equity strategic alliance, and no equity strategic alliance in contributing the section of strategic alliance to enlarge the potential value of competitiveness (Das & Teng, 2000).

In line with exploring the initiative of firms to have such kind of form to share legally independent firm through collaborative capabilities, utilizing the resources appropriately into the strategic alliance needs to particularly maintain competitive advantages in the market which can be enhanced these processes through this experiential learning. Attempts to deliberately manage the importance of these constructs in this section to accumulate knowledge about alliances become new alliancing opportunities. Together with underlining the capable initiation for alliance management, the path of building capabilities on the components including individual skills in the way to manage alliances should be considered in particular approach into social contemptibility in undertaking these efforts to put firms on influencing their products. Through approaching the form of building experiences and proactivity in managing the procurement of partner firms with the long-term relationship to transfer tacit knowledge, it is necessary to point out attempts to behave the learned experiences with attempting to codify tacit knowledge to underlie the way to work together among the partners within joint venture (Uddin & Akhter, 2011). Such attempts in taking place in working with underlining expertise and experience among the partners would be pivotal views in fostering the sustainable competitive advantage in the sense which leads to participate in the operations management. Through this initiation, managing the tacit knowledge being as an entire part of important source in enabling the competitive advantage could be explicated amongst many firms in working together within the particular joint venture endeavour in the sense which generally represents optimal form of alliances to participate the competitive market. As a result, sharing the resources with creating competitive advantages needs to coordinate joint ventures coming from any different firm which may potentially access to manufacture the marketing strategy through sharing and combining resources with capabilities of firms to underlie the way to prepare new markets, using technical information and reciprocal flows of intelligence data.

Performance Value for Social Entrepreneurship

Considered as an innovative approach to point out the social value in creating the activity across the non-profit, Business Company and government sectors, social entrepreneurship refers to enhance the approach for activity with social objectivity together with social-purpose commercial ventures (Felício, Gonçalves, & da Conceição Gonçalves, 2013). In order to achieve the benefit from the social entrepreneurship, applying the business expertise would be consolidated with typically referring to the market based skills including the competitive and talents which can be trained to create the value to underlie the entrepreneurship in running the business (Ridley-Duff & Bull, 2015). With this regard, both non-profit sector and organizations should go beyond developing innovative approaches to earn income (Stam, Arzlanian & Elfring, 2014). It indicates that the underlying process driven across creating social value in personal and social aspect is eventually shared with the activity characterized by an innovative procedure context (Huda et al., 2017b). This regards the potential value to create the new innovation concisely associating with the replication of existing enterprises applied across creating social value to enhance the outcome for the public good.

In terms of maintaining the sustainable systems in the way to manage the new ventures with an innovative manner, the approach to enhance the way undertaken to discover, define and exploit opportunities to determine such activities and processes aims to achieve the social enterprise objectivity. By highlighting the consolidated approach, an innovative strength to enhance social wealth needs to consider in particular as the means employed in creating enhanced potential for managing the wealth-resources (Kroeger & Weber, 2014). With regard to emphasizing the innovation, the social entrepreneurship could achieve the goal of alleviating the social problem in the community (Phillips, Lee, Ghobadian, O'Regan, & James, 2015). It indicates that social entrepreneurship could be acted as change agents where they capture innovation in a methodical process in trying to build the initiative in social equilibrium (Phillips, Lee, Ghobadian, O'Regan, & James, 2015). In order to meet the essential characteristics as an attempt to solve the challenges like inaccuracy to the business measurement and lack of confidence in terms of attempting the entrepreneurship growth, accessing the competitive acknowledgement could undertake the innovative activities in addressing the ability to recognize the opportunities to use in creating the value for instance in transmitting the counseling service through mobile application (Huda et al., 2017g). At this point of view, the basis of inquiry of the resources to assure the initiatives taken into account being committed in achieving their purpose to better understand the innovation in the context of social enterprises will allow social entrepreneurship by exploring the critical factors raising the presence of social entrepreneurship. Such this process of social enterprise needs to assure the endurance in achieving the trends of market demands in the way which in the industrial level the potential assurance should cover the best approach with social enterprise to gain the sustainable competitive advantage through their innovations.

In addition, possessing such better understanding of the exploration in social entrepreneurship with the competitive advantage will have a point of view in contributing innovative success as an attempt to underlying the sustainable competitive strength to achieve the advantage. This view has to do with behavioral substance with entrepreneurship awareness (Ebbers, 2014). The essence of competitive strength to allow the competitors to maintain the stability for accessing geographic location should be engaged into highly skilled labor to have good skills in managing the natural resources with including high-grade or low-cost and high entry barriers and power source, etc (Kickul & Lyons, 2016). Such this distinctive feature could describe the attribute in accessing the digital technology to be considered to enhance the competitive strength to gain the competitors with possessing the competencies in digital age (Huda et al., 2017c). This can be gained by offering clients better and greater value in the way which would be eventually advertising the products and services with lower prices and also with higher quality interest's consumers. Attempts to recognize these unique products and services would become an insightful view towards the target markets. The value inquiry through understanding competitive strength would be more effective to help producing the advantage gained through increasing the customer expectations with choices.

METHODOLOGY

The stage of this study is the literature analysis gathered from the critical review in exploring the empowerment of competitive strength engaged in building entrepreneurship. Each phase employs the approach and method in reviewing the recent works on ethical engagement to gain the competitive strength underlying to grow the entrepreneurship performance. This investigation will be conducted using keywords of competitive strength, cooperative engagement and social entrepreneurship from peer-reviewed journals and books. Then, the key element into interpretations, conceptualizations, and modelling was examined to deal with a profound discussion into the conceptual level assigned to transform technical requirements.

ANALYSIS AND DISCUSSION

Competitive Strength as the Potential Value in Social Entrepreneurship

With regard to the challenges of inaccuracy to the business measurement and lack of confidence in terms of attempting the entrepreneurship growth, accessing the competitive acknowledgement could be undertaken through pointing out the innovative activities in addressing the ability to recognize the opportunities to use in creating the value. In order to achieve this, the one which needs to consider is knowledge understanding of being supportive as an essential process of developmental steps to build the connections with competitive awareness to strengthen the learning in promoting social entrepreneurship. It underlined the initial attempts as the core foundation with a deep impact to give the good feedback to enable them in facing challenges and solve problems more efficiently (Anshari, Almunawar, Shahrill, Wicaksono, & Huda, 2017; Felício, Gonçalves, & da Conceição Gonçalves, 2013). As a result, the need to empower competitive and cooperative engagement should be considered as a core guideline to give clear understanding and insightful view on the importance of promoting social entrepreneurship. This could contribute to the significant insights towards different aspects of exploring the role of cultural identities about the key strategies to give the beneficial feedback as the key role to perform continuous improvement in social entrepreneurship. With elevating an individual to open opportunities for the establishment to transform continuously for the better achievement in the business growth, this initiative aims to explore the systematic approach to be developed in identifying both cooperative with competitive alliance in order to strengthen an actual performance in action to encompass the great deal of social entrepreneurship. The initiative to elucidate the set of literature about the theories of the significant essence of the creative thinking with competitive alliance for envisioning the direction in social entrepreneurship needs to engage with exploring the key themes and concepts that underpin performing powerful decisions as an ability to empower the performance value in social entrepreneurship.

In addition, cooperative arrangement should be taken in serious consent with gaining strategic alliances where the firms can get benefit in improving effective alliances set up through the competitive performance. As the strategic position to share resources, there should optimize domestic and global markets in order to grow the extent of profitability engines (Fish & Wood, 2017). In this view, attempts to the interfirm collaborations with ubiquitous phenomenon in forming the extent of strategic alliances need to continue strategic alliances in ensuring their growth initiation combined with popularity enhancement. It refers to the corporate social responsibility with competitive arrangement (Kim & Qian, 2015). Since dramatically increasing about emerging business firm's at the global average in recent years, the necessity to embark the strategic alliances should cooperate with addressing major essence towards competition occurrence increasingly into sets of allied companies in the sense that should address alliance on cooperative and competitive in engaging the rivals (Kim, 2017). Towards the individual firms to point out the potential value to produce the optional view of strategic integrity, the popular choice to consolidate with many alliances has to take a note in pointing out the presence of potential synergies in the sense which give insights into succeeding the alliance itself (Phillips, Lee, Ghobadian, O'Regan, & James, 2015). Moreover, the flexibility with enhancing the levels of risk management, for instance, would potentially make a significant point of view to generate the strategic alliances associated with the growth of preferred alternative. With growing both domestic and international alliances, bringing worldwide collaborations along with the high support from united technologies, such as the aerospace industry, is entirely engaged into obtaining critically important success to the firms. Notwithstanding, both are success in bringing the innovation with something new to possess the market area with addressing the trend through cooperation and integration of knowledge understanding of the marketplace.

In terms of knowledge flows generated into the firms, it becomes the way to elaborate strategic alliances. Facilitating knowledge integration refers to serving in giving solution on the difficulty condition through integrating knowledge towards strategic enhancement. It is sure that alliances with characterizing collaborative arrangement associated with mutual interdependence could fit the indication to take the influence from the market trends. With this regard, attempts to enhance mutual interdependence together with strengthening vulnerable risk could point out management in leading to shared control arranged into the collaboration approach. Both cooperation and competition arranged with creating chance amidst additional complexity for firms need to face the risk of vulnerable with the mutual interdependence. Through effective management of alliances, the initiative to take advantage should be admitted to the necessary task cooperated with strategic alliances. With the potential chance to enhance the performance towards the firm's challenging risk for instance, managing the difficulty situation through various reasons has to do with the way to set up strategic alliances in obtaining the competitive advantage consistently by enhancing the firm's performance. It is necessary to embark the commitment to arise strategic alliances transmitted into developing resources, knowledge and subsequent skills. These should be enlarged with pointing out an important issue to be solved with cooperative enhancement. The particular side to compete successfully with important option is needed to obtain in taking over challenging issues to be consolidated with difficult competitive environment. In the practical view increasingly to manage alliance initiative to be success, affecting partner expectations could be measured in providing the insightful view which firms' performances can take advantage to improve along with their support team (Shi, Sun, & Prescott, 2012). Towards the stream of decisions managers can highlight in ensuring timely schedule to control the alliances influences, attempts to make the structural integrity into organization stability should provide an entire ability to do the things which can lead to succeed for the firms and their labor. In particular, the alliance management with superior practice is key role to give insights in driving the rule to achieve competitive advantage taken for the firms. It indicates the management of effective alliance could deal with strengthening the initiative to take benefit in raising their firms from the challenging issues which may happen at any time.

Valuable Insights of Competitive Advantage for Strategic Partnership Alliance

In the attempts to obtain the extent of competitive advantage, the need to focus on content and process simultaneously arranged to the firms will enlarge the initiative for strategic alliances. Moreover, attempts to primarily concentrate on the content issue integrated into alliance formation through theoretical and empirical explanations should emphasize the way of particular governance structured into forming certain alliances with focusing on the firms towards their risk management transmitted to the performance indicator. The particular design approaching for social network enhancement refers to the knowledge understanding to be aware of alternative forms (Maseleno et al., 2018; Mortati & Cruickshank, 2012). In particular, it can initially achieve in outlining the entire task to manage the way of alliances to be formed. With a particular attention to the knowledge in attempting effectively to manage alliances, it is required with the way to form the alliance process in successfully managing entire processes the designed in concentrating on the dynamic aspects of collaborative arrangements (Bengtsson, Eriksson & Wincent, 2010; Huda et al., 2018b). With a significant attribution signed into the effective alliance management, it is important to note in encountering an under-investigated phenomenon within the domestic context in the sense which needs to emphasize alliance management oriented with cooperative ventures under the international level. Through getting more critical in enhancing the knowledge understanding to possess the superior firm performance, the effective alliances management should direct positively with regard to the related initiation in contributing to the managerial practices through reducing the failures of alliance (Solitander & Tidström, 2010). As a result, the duty in improving the investments in relation-specific assets at this point of view refers to emphasize in committing alliance to give insight into the firms 'performance.

In line with cooperating the entire task to get an insightful key performance, strategic partnership alliance has to be generated with enlarging the competitive advantage in the sense which gives anticipated alliance outcomes assigned to take advantage into the corporation and firms. In this view, the focus initially needs to further examine the main component of alliance to get the advantage of the additional benefits primarily in creating value for the primary business-level strategies. Towards the key role to direct in the right path to consult with the effective alliances and corporate social responsibility (CSR) for instance, the capacity earned from tangible or intangible assets has to be reflected into the sense of alliances initiative (Seitanidi & Crane, 2009). In gaining the value with a synergy reflected in providing the partners through generating the alternative side of organizational configurations, the strategy generated through alliances could be an initiation integrated to contribute in creating the value involving the effective risk management, market entries of efficient cost and also the knowledge understanding among the partners on the strategic alliance. Among those strategic alliances, it can be managed to create the particular essence in assisting the firms through several sources in minimizing transaction costs where this scale relates to the strategic alliances. Moreover, the partnership alliance coped with certain environments refers to entirely control the reposition with reducing the dependence on resources outside of their and themselves in dynamic markets. As a result, the allocation patterns towards alliance investments could have such influential insights into the firm's resource thus, consequently creating the market initiated among the companies to form the positions in seeking to effectively respond to challenges such as competitive environment and hygienic cleaning service. At this point of view, the right partners in developing the suitable alliance to direct through creating value from alliances are consolidated with requiring the companies in selecting the relationship and the design to be adapted fitting to the need appropriately.

Furthermore, trough managing the alliances in taking the beneficial value in assuring the process with a powerful enabler, the value creation in the recent analyses would give an entire initiative to deliver the economic companies to run well within their work plan (Bouncken, Pesch, & Gudergan, 2015; Park, Srivastava & Gnyawali, 2014). In terms of creating potential value, the key part of the firm's strategies in both new and old trends needs to maintain in considering alliances with an overview of top executives on effective management as a source of competitive advantage. With this regard, the strategic alliance should do with contributing to the knowledge about strategic alliances assigned with the effective alliance management. Through drawing primarily from the alliances' benefits, the management of critical effective alliance needs to be realized in helping to reduce opportunistic behavior among the partners. Moreover, the additional value could be achieved to create such kind of unintended outcomes among the partners. Among those, there can be viewed such as transaction cost economics (TCE) (David & Han, 2004), in which this attainment should do with the management initiative of social network. At this point of view, the resource-based view in strengthening the alliances is considered to give insights with considerable attention to deal with influencing formation of strategic alliance. Towards the theoretical rational factors derived from alliance formation, the strategic alliances viewed as intermediate governance structures should be configured into commitment and stability. In this view, using the transaction cost theory is explicated referring to alliance transaction costs aligned with the several characteristics concerned to direct entirely with more efficient markets. It indicates attempts to organize the successful alliances in the sense that ability to control the firm's alliance coordination costs should coordinate communication patterns integrated into decision networks and decomposing tasks among partners incurred in coordinating actions through organizing the firm's boundary.

Networking Strategic Actions for Alliance Formation and Value

The point of view in obtaining the networking initiation has to be involved with the firm's strategic actions. Attempts to embed the social context affected by considering direct and indirect ties with network actors may concisely enhance the relationships between inter-organizational and intra-organizational side in the sense which can give insights into the alliance formation. Social network should be engaged with social venture (Meyskens, Carsrud & Cardozo, 2010). With the value in generating the firm's social context, the initiation of emerging the strategic action to generate networking initiation for alliance formation could become an outstanding value to consistently tie into the company (Thomaz & Swaminathan, 2015; Ridley-Duff & Bull, 2015). Moreover, the collection of potential value with a point of view in generating tangible and intangible assets should be sustained to assure the resource heterogeneity with competitive advantage. In this regard, getting source of heterogeneous resource-based perspective could be enhanced to deliver the firm's preferential access through addressing its idiosyncratic resources. It is necessary to point out the product of the firm's scale referring to tacit and knowledge-basis especially to locate the optimal resource configuration. In particular, the formation of resource-based alliance can be indicated to develop the extent of firm in bonding the alliances with the value of possible combinations used to the value-creating resources. Through collecting the resources, it is important to note that attempts to maximize the potency which can behave are entirely engaged into creating independently towards generating the networking strategic actions.

In addition, both alliance formation and implementation here should refer to the resource stocks accumulated across the process of trying to maximize the value of the firm's link connection among others. With this regard, strategic choices signed to optimize both technological and competitive environments could cover the commitment between partners to have chance in the learning process and working together with the attempts to try in creating the potential value of maximizing an alliance's available resources (Huda, Sabani, Shahrill, Jasmi, Basiron, & Mustari, 2017a). As a result of enhancing the initiative in looking at the opportunities, recognizing with the certainty to recognize strategic alliance in maintaining competitive advantages through diminishing the critical view of enhancement to impose the abilities with theoretical arguments should gather the formation subsequently consolidated to use the firm resources in exploiting the resource-based approach. Referring to the live interaction with moral engagement in gaining the key role to hold considerable promise for exploring the role of strategic alliances (Huda, Siregar, Ramlan, Rahman, Mat Teh, Said, Jamsari, Yacub, Dacholfany, & Ninsiana, 2017b), this initiative can be engaged to provide an important base for understanding the effective management of alliances. In particular, this approach with a critical focus of exploring the resource-based view of alliances should do with carrying out all assets, capabilities, processes, information and knowledge to assure the process itself controlled by the firm. In this analysis, the use of the particular resource(s) is entirely a point of view to gather working together that enhance organizational efficiency and effectiveness. Referring to deal with the several characteristics of these configurations including commitment and stability, it would enable to appropriately select the way recognized to use aligning with intermediate structures for strategic alliances.

In considering the strategic initiation concerned with negotiating alliance stability enhancement, attempts to take a note in monitoring the partnership performance relatively to carry out the contractual commitments include those contingent contracts. In the attempts to dealing with considering being more efficient, markets place with the hierarchies approach towards the organizing the firm's boundary-spanning activities refer to perform successful alliances in resulting the product of alliances in minimizing the firm's transaction costs. In this view, between the sum of its transaction and production costs refers to the firm's ability in directing the control alliance coordinated with decomposing tasks among partners (Warner & Sullivan, 2017). It indicates the way of coordinating actions through integrated networks and their associated communication patterns could provide an important basis to see decision with the resource-based approach. Moreover, it is required to hold a considerable promise to deal with gaining the recognizance of exploring the role of strategic alliances. With this regard, attempts to maintain the competitive advantages in understanding the effective management of alliances become an outstanding element in delivering the processes of information and knowledge controlled by the firm. In order to enable such resource(s) in focusing on this approach with a critical view, enhancing the capabilities of efficiency and effectiveness for the organizational work needs to explore the resource-based view of alliances referring to all assets in the sense which selects the use of strategies. This initiative should point out the alliance formation to strengthening the strategic initiation for the firm resources.

Enhancing Productivity Through Strategic Alliances and Competitive Awareness

To maintain the awareness of competitive with strategic alliance, it is important to consider taking benefit through receiving the increasing emphasis to enhance the alignment in creating the multiple initiations. With the traditional explanations of alliance formation, the emerging trend of competitive enhancement refers to the strategic initiation in accessing to concisely develop the supportive encouragement which is important to take the primary benefits of alliances. With regard to behaving the available resources in the development of new resources through the alliance, the lack of ethical view can be viewed through the alliances examined as a means to make such exploitation into the firm's resource basis (Schweitzer, 2014). As such, the firm performance with addressing the resource-based view should give the priority in generating the significance of competitive advantages in leading to the positive insights to develop in creating the inimitable value among the customers. Since the way of enhancing the competitive advantage, attempts to possess the resources among the firms should behave the increasing complexity of markets place. It should point out the pivotal view in generating the acceleration amidst the rapid globalization is committed to compete effectively in making it significant for firms to have all of the resources necessary to fit in many markets. With regard to some settings, the view to assist in helping to see the formation of management about enhancing the productivity among the firms might be a pivotal rule needed for competitive markets especially to the fast-cycle firms related to acting independently towards the resources parity (Choi & Majumdar, 2014). Moreover, the entire initiation in possessing competitive awareness attempts to provide access to information of the markets on alliances into technology resources. The initiative to take advantage through generating the resource-based alliances may get access to Information and technology (IT) management with referring to the special access to the primary reason for alliances.

In addition, considered as the resources to access to the way to share the risks and development of economies with the complementary resources in the scale of the primary firms, the market place might enable to have entire initiative for learning with its dynamic benefits to provide additional motivation to form alliances. In this view, to achieve this initiation goal, the need to have experimental basis configured into the learning process has to be taken into consideration in generating knowledge understanding which is unique to the target of forming the alliance (Haeussler, & Higgins, 2014). Attempts to assist at consolidating the learning set up through competence behavior for instance transmitted into the alliances firms would provide their own resource to overcome the limitations through extending competitive advantages in the application of their core competencies to be achieved in an appropriate way. Moreover, the extent of this contribution may enhance the initiative performance among alliances to boost the members' competencies from such kind of core rigidities in the sense which can dispute in constraining the competitive ability among the firm. Building the resource which is valuable to encounter the firms from the challenging task such as providing the ingredient for the food product should corporate with looking at the resource bundle. The extent of this alliance is valuable to give such kind of integration in terms of technological resources in addressing to take note for another firm's complementary resources. It can be viewed such as the access in maximizing the specific markets held by one partner with the pooling of resources in producing the beneficial substance among the alliance partners. In particular, the complementary knowledge for engaging the partners to carry out important resources could potentially bring financial, physical, technological, and managerial substance assigned into an alliance (Seitanidi

& Crane, 2009). Firms with their network of relationships to bring social capital with other firms might enhance the competitive performance tied into the capability of alliance management.

In addition, attempts to determine the alliance management with involving every partner about the role of the ability to enhance the alliance among the firms' managers should bring along with the clarity of direction needed to properly support the alliance. Moreover, these discussions should give insights into the firm's operating integrity armed into the beneficial value of alliance's goals in the way to understand the activities the procedural stage. This would be initially enlarged into the virtual interaction basis (Huda, Maseleno, Jasmi, Mustari, & Basiron, 2017c). Towards task efficiency coordinated with innovations process, operational managers to pursue in reaching primarily to concentrate to work together with contributing collectively to find ways to balance their interests should enlarge the source of competitive advantage in the sense which transmit the successful attainment among the managers at all levels. With this regard, it is important to note the way to effectively manage the tension between cooperation and competition needs to consolidate those of their counterparts in partner firms within the learning process (Brouthers, Nakos, & Dimitratos, 2015). In order to provide the basis for procedural stage of cooperation, understanding of managing this initiative is required to enhance the norm of reciprocity in recognizing the basis of stable relationships. Through comprehending the norm of reciprocity, the alliance partner's solving initiation could provide effective alliance management in bordering the exploitation way for instance towards the norm calls explicated among the parties to assist their partners rather than harm those in the sense which such acts might take advantage to them. About the reciprocity norm in the attempts to respond through engaging the focal firm's cooperative behavior, it is the necessity to suggest such parties commit to enlarge prevention towards kind to those damaging their interests. As a result, the alliance with reciprocity norm would also gain partners' commitment to go through the process associated between experience and knowledge in exploring new opportunities on coordinating resources to anticipate problems.

Strengthening Competitive With Cooperative Engagement in Promoting Social Entrepreneurship

Competitive performance coordinated with the cooperative enhancement refers to create the set of interacting with continuum of choices by firms through addressing the concept initiated to look at the market positions with its complex feature. The effort to build the cooperative engagement is created to face the factors of productive market assigned usually with measuring the performance of intermediate financial perspectives (David & Han, 2004). In terms of producing the markets with the capability of alliance management, the accumulated experience with the appropriate type of expertise needs to possess the strategic vision that can direct appropriately into social entrepreneurship. With the alliances to lead to the outcomes as a means to create adequate condition combined together into addressing wealth and business opportunities, the element of capability is necessary to take consent about reinforcing the role of alliances to forge the improved performance. Moreover, the high order to play a positive and significant role to act between alliances and competitive performance is entirely a point of view in generating the claimed relationship grounded at least partly in values as well experience and its subsequent insights. With this regard, the extent of knowledge understanding about competitive insights would assure the relevant information to develop sustainable competitive advantages (Nag, Russo, & Vurro, 2014). Towards the strategic alliances as an important subject to give insights in pointing out the direct link between making alliances and possessing the key performance, attempts to enhance the departure point in presenting innovative view with the relationship between strategic alliances and competitive performance. This investigation refers to attempt to promote the social entrepreneurship.

In addition, socially constructed by organizational actors, the knowledge understanding of recognizing the customers, suppliers and competitors needs to measure the different configurations including its strategic alliances. Stored in recognizing the firms' capability in measuring the higher levels of knowledge, knowledge acquisition and management throughout an organization's firms embedded in the human capital showed the firm's employees together with the outperform competitors. It is important to enlarge the knowledge subsequently built in enduring source of competitive advantage, especially in complex competitive environments (Ireland & Webb, 2007). Through the typical knowledge in solving the problems, transferring alliances between mutually interdependent partners in attempting to pursue opportunities to establish an independent joint venture should promote knowledge transfer in supporting the venture to assure the successful attainment. In transferring the knowledge to each partner within the equity position, both have incentives and motivation to quickly transfer the knowledge for venture success (Hoang, & Rothaermel, 2016). The arrangements of absorptive capacity would affect to enhance the appropriate human capital with adequate knowledge in the sense which can manage the amount of knowledge that can be successfully transferred in creating the broader capacity with the structural mechanisms including training, internal consulting and assistance. In infusing the knowledge basis, the absorptive capacity of partners' individual about this position is necessary to enhance the partnership in possessing greater capacity of specializing the nature of knowledge in order to have significant essence towards knowledge understanding among the partners in enabling to affect its transfer through explicit knowledge.

With this regard, maximizing the capacity of competitive advantage through knowledge transfer additionally in affecting the absorptive capacity is necessary to take consent about the collaborative venture in enhancing the successful initiative. Through being much easier to transfer knowledge structures within the work systems, the design to form the alliances through transferring the existing knowledge among partners with pointing out knowledge creation is an important source in transmitting new knowledge about increasingly globalized markets (Bouncken, Pesch, & Gudergan, 2015). Moreover, the firm's absorptive capacity needs to enhance the value-creating potential of knowledge understanding to fully integrate both inside or outside in enlarging the cooperative engagement to explore the extent of the ability to firm's boundaries such as distinctive organizational capability. With this regard, alliance partnership among the firms should gain the access for the alliance management in integrating complementary resources, considered as important initiation to alliance success with being critically involved into social entrepreneurship. Moreover, learning process management in acquiring the capabilities in running the alliances could result in transmitting the substantial effects in creating the knowledge to enlarge the sustainability of competitive advantages which lead to successfully result in supporting the alliance initiation. Innovation on learning environment in this view (Huda, Haron, Ripin, Hehsan, & Yaacob, 2017d), as an important source of competitive advantage, the value-creating potential of strategic alliances could make the firm which can effectively cope with environmental uncertainty and ambiguity. Enhancing the alliances with an important value in creating the option beyond the market trends needs to be sufficient with making the increasing symmetry of information flows amongst their suppliers, firms and customers (López-Duarte, González-Loureiro, Vidal-Suárez, & González-Díaz, 2016). In this situation, the competitive markets proactively consolidating the transaction costs would increase the probability of maintaining the competitive advantages through strategic alliances.

In addition, the ability to effectively engage the alliance management with such complex process should be entirely distributed across cooperative engagement involved in creating the value for social entrepreneurship. Attempts to enhance the alliances in managing the ability with the extent of managerial skills could be enlarged concisely in making value-creating perspective in the sense which specifies perfectly specifiable for alliances. In this view, the alliance management engaged into cooperative and competitive enhancement needs to distribute the significance of social entrepreneurship. Looking at the source of competitive advantage, it is likely asymmetric in persisting the firms to encourage ability with forming to manage the transfer knowledge to get more effectively involved into alliance relationships. An important source for alliances competitors referring to the competitive advantage in order to enable individual alliance management would need the way of learning the initiative to maximize the potency in pursuit of commercial opportunities. Moreover, such partners need to develop the management of alliances that facilitates form of transaction cost would create the valuable insight assigned with coordination and integration costs for being more efficient mechanism. In order to enlarge the potential value for alternative market place to have such target among the firms, effective alliance management associated with appropriate analyses towards the use of mechanisms to form alliances needs to make sure the uncertainty potency which might happen and thus leading to the untrusted integrity. In order to assure getting superior alliance management, an entire effort to coordinate all alliance-related activity within reducing the cost of residual uncertainty remains to have been completed in forming and using an alliance for a dedicated alliance management function. It is likely to become the scale to broad the processes and systems in institutionalizing the alliance-management experience. With such agenda like teaching, sharing, and leveraging the way to know throughout the company into the head of the function, the initiative in holding the prominent position amongst the chief alliance manager to commit the procedural stage in directing the management team needs to build the firm' network of alliances with being more active into responsibility (Serrat, 2017). In occupying the central position to achieve the success, alliance management dedicated to commit the focal point for leveraging knowledge and lessons can be experienced by the firms relying on the function acquired from those previous alliance experiences.

Alliance Management as the Key Strategies for Social Entrepreneurship

Alliance management refers to the key indicator in giving the foundation to deliberate knowledge with social capital in exploring the continuous improvement in social entrepreneurship. Attempts to generate the alliance management through pointing out the key strategic role would draw the value with organizations such as higher and social institutions in performing their ability to successfully apply those individuals' knowledge in harnessing and categorizing commercial purposes (Lee & Hsieh, 2010). In this view, the ability to benefit in drawing the development in growing reciprocal relationship should cooperate along with the remuneration developed in organizations through this mutually beneficial value towards the complex competitive environment. In order to enlarge the knowledge in enduring the source of competitive advantage, attempts to accompany the people through working with creating organizations transmitted into the few resources to lead to the mutually beneficial relationships together with competitively valuable knowledge (Jiang, Bao, Xie, & Gao, 2016a). Being more important to enlarge this sustainable earnings with financial capital, this type of alliance success lies largely on the function of knowledge recognizance towards the way to effectively and efficiently develop the progress to be achieved from partners in ensuring the flow of integrating alliance partners to work together. Moreover, the potential value in transferring the knowledge process of employing such procedural stages for sharing their knowledge in encouraging and developing the systems would codify existing knowledge within the initiative for learning culture construction (Huda, Jasmi, Basiran, Mustari, & Sabani, 2017e) in enhancing the encouragement initiation of alliance managerial tasks to support alliance activities.

Furthermore, mutual learning initiative to enhance the key role of strategies for social entrepreneurship should be combined with knowledge transfers in the attempts to give insights in facilitating the partner cooperation. In this particular stage, stimulating the capacity to absorb inputs through the development of new knowledge to do so among the partners should enlarge the new knowledge created through such evidence about high absorptive capacity. To run the initiative associated with the applications in ensuring the successful attainment for alliance management, new knowledge toward commercial purpose in using routines to complete these tasks is indicated by the competitively superior manner in contributing to the competitive advantage. In this view, the essence of alliance management would demonstrate the routines of dominant logic throughout the firm in drawing the work plan extension (Jiang, Yang, Pei, & Wang, 2016b). Enhancing the managerial logic with the alliance management that governs the processes of decision-making about the alliance could represent these routines into the shared belief about the way of selecting and managing the firm's alliance portfolio. Moreover, attempts to enhance such activities to accomplish the alliance management would enable the routines to focus on the key dimensions in establishing cooperation assigned with knowledge management through sustainable way on the knowledge acquisition (Huda, Jasmi, Basiran, Mustari, & Sabani., 2017e). It is necessary to point out the accountability in focusing on activities involved into the description in ensuring trust, alliance management and alliance can be achieved successfully within the extent of relationship.

With regard to the number of programs connected to the alliance management, this initiative has to distribute the competitive advantage with the subsequent value through such activities linked into comprehensive and critical activities in attempting to the alliance's scope (Ozmel, Robinson, & Stuart, 2013). Moreover, determining tangible and intangible assets including the product brands and categories for instance has entirely pivotal value in regards to the geographic boundaries in the sense that technologies should transmit it to the process well. Apart from that, between ownership and application of creating the alliance management, the determinations which can help shape the alliance's scope is desired with necessary enhancement to construct through an appropriate alliance partner. In referring to the alliance with its scope in selecting the partners, implying with the wrong partner for instance might lead to the consequence with condemning compatible strategic intents giving insights into compassion awareness (Huda, Jasmi, Embong, Safar, Mohamad, Mohamed, Muhamad, Alas, & Rahman, 2017f). Towards the cooperative arrangement potentially valuable to allow each partner to absorb additional complementary resources for alliance management construction, presenting the partners with possessing to leverage its current resource basis as the opportunity to transform the capabilities through the alliance is required to share their knowledge with partners. The opportunities of alliance management to transmit among the firms are potentially selecting the partners to develop the governance structure through an alliance's cooperate together with compete tension in creating the optimal governance through partner interactions.

In addition, the initiative committed for being aware to accommodate the partner's capability should enlarge the mechanisms that can be carried out among the firm in facilitating the alliance management structures. It can be viewed with a highly bureaucratized stifle to possess an effective management, giving insights into mutual accommodations in desired to support the alliance with influencing the approach of interfirm information flows consolidated into the individual firm. With this regard, it is needed to manage the flow of competitively relevant information to tackle the challenge as the preventive action for its partner. In the attempts to facilitate inter-partner learning while simultaneously protecting proprietary knowledge, alliance management should understand each partner's learning intent to which extent the firm's objective could enhance teaching from its alliance partners (Thomaz, & Swaminathan, 2015). In particular, knowledge sharing to prevent partner appropriation of knowledge with effective management of information flows should be committed to the appropriate organizational controls in aligning incentive plans to support the management of information flows for instance integrating mechanisms for socialization of managers. It should determine the enlarging through the attempts to engage into civic responsibility awareness (Huda, Jasmi, Alas, Qodriah, Dacholfany, & Jamsari, 2017g). The use of interest to satisfy the needs of the alliance with enlarging its individual partners points out the effective information management in flowing knowledge-based inquiries. As a result of pointing out the partner's information, strengthening personnel attributes in possessing the skills is needed to disseminate information in order to entirely protect the procedures in monitoring information flows with competitively sensitive knowledge.

Moreover, subsequent action is important to maintain in achieving alignment for staffing of the locus point to be fit among alliance partners to assure the strategic basis in terms of relational and operational side. Moreover, the context formed within the alliance management into the strategic basis is required to behave the organizational initiative in allocating the manner to fit the purview expected and assessing the alliance's importance for each partner (Warner & Sullivan, 2017). One of the instances can be viewed through embodying the service through mobile application (Huda, Jasmi, Mustari, Basiron, Mohamed, Embong, ... & Safar, 2017h). Moreover, attempts to recognize the awareness towards the alliance management initiation should create the value expected to determine the response anticipated into the market segments assigned with the strategic issues. Targeted to the alliance management initially encountered by the stakeholders, verifying the essence of strategic integrity with alliance consolidation specifying the particular view among governments, competitors and capital markets should maintain the strategic fit concerned with the potential integrated into culture and skills involved into alliance. In general terms, the human capital with relational and operational fit issues should flow strategic fit associated with an effective alliance management in achieving effective integration about negotiating skills into the superior alliance through evaluating the procedural stages of key strategies for social entrepreneurship within the partners' organizational management structures.

CONCLUSION

The advantage of competitive awareness in the business has a significant role to help enhance the productivity. In order to concern both aims and beliefs in the variety of organizations, attempts to attract the growing amounts of talent and attention should be conducted along with its increasing popularity to achieve the certain objectives like motivating the sense to growing the business with entrepreneurship in terms of social and commercial basis. This chapter explored the particular way between cooperative and competitive alliance to gain the feedback and insights into performance value in social entrepreneurship. The need to empower competitive with cooperative engagement should be considered as a core guideline to give clear understanding and insightful view on the importance of promoting social entrepreneurship. This chapter is supposed to contribute to the significant insights towards different aspects of exploring the role of cultural identities about the key strategies to give the beneficial feedback as the key role to perform continuous improvement in social entrepreneurship. The advantage of competitive awareness in the business has a significant role to help enhance the productivity, where this is eventually integrated with the entrepreneurship in the way which underlies the value to run the potential business. In order to concern both aims and beliefs in the variety of organizations, attempts to attract the growing amounts of talent and attention should be conducted along with its increasing popularity to achieve the certain objectives like motivating the sense to growing the business with entrepreneurship in terms of social and commercial basis. There are three core stages to achieve growing the business with entrepreneurship. The first is to develop a systematic approach to identifying cooperative with competitive alliance on strengthening an actual performance in action to encompass the great deal of social entrepreneurship. This is followed by elucidating the set of literature about the theories of the significant essence of the creative thinking with competitive alliance for envisioning the direction in social entrepreneurship. Moreover, this chapter has contributed to the knowledge understanding in the way to explore the key themes and concepts that underpin performing powerful decisions as an ability to empower the performance value in social entrepreneurship. The work management in growing the business with entrepreneurship and social and commercial basis is required to strengthen cooperative and competitive alliance into performance value in social entrepreneurship.

REFERENCES

Anshari, M., Almunawar, M. N., Shahrill, M., Wicaksono, D. K., & Huda, M. (2017). Smartphones usage in the classrooms: Learning aid or interference? *Education and Information Technologies*, 1–17.

Bengtsson, M., Eriksson, J., & Wincent, J. (2010). Co-opetition dynamics–an outline for further inquiry. *Competitiveness Review*, *20*(2), 194–214. doi:10.1108/10595421011029893

Bilodeau, L., Podger, J., & Abd-El-Aziz, A. (2014). Advancing campus and community sustainability: Strategic alliances in action. *International Journal of Sustainability in Higher Education*, *15*(2), 157–168. doi:10.1108/IJSHE-06-2012-0051

Bornstein, D., & Davis, S. (2010). *Social Entrepreneurship: What Everyone Needs to Know?* Oxford University Press.

Bouncken, R. B., Pesch, R., & Gudergan, S. P. (2015). Strategic embeddedness of modularity in alliances: Innovation and performance implications. *Journal of Business Research*, *68*(7), 1388–1394. doi:10.1016/j.jbusres.2015.01.020

Brouthers, K. D., Nakos, G., & Dimitratos, P. (2015). SME entrepreneurial orientation, international performance, and the moderating role of strategic alliances. *Entrepreneurship Theory and Practice*, *39*(5), 1161–1187. doi:10.1111/etap.12101

Cardy, R. L., & Selvarajan, T. T. (2006). Competencies: Alternative frameworks for competitive advantage. *Business Horizons*, *49*(3), 235–245.

Chen, M. J., Kuo-Hsien, S. U., & Tsai, W. (2007). Competitive tension: The awareness-motivation-capability perspective. *Academy of Management Journal*, *50*(1), 101–118. doi:10.5465/AMJ.2007.24162081

Cho, A. H. (2006). Politics, values and social entrepreneurship: A critical appraisal. In Social entrepreneurship (pp. 34-56). Palgrave Macmillan UK. doi:10.1057/9780230625655_4

Choi, N., & Majumdar, S. (2014). Social entrepreneurship as an essentially contested concept: Opening a new avenue for systematic future research. *Journal of Business Venturing*, *29*(3), 363–376. doi:10.1016/j.jbusvent.2013.05.001

Dacin, M. T., Dacin, P. A., & Tracey, P. (2011). Social entrepreneurship: A critique and future directions. *Organization Science*, *22*(5), 1203–1213. doi:10.1287/orsc.1100.0620

Dacin, P. A., Dacin, M. T., & Matear, M. (2010). Social entrepreneurship: Why we don't need a new theory and how we move forward from here. *The Academy of Management Perspectives*, *24*(3), 37–57. doi:10.5465/AMP.2010.52842950

Das, T. K., & Kumar, R. (2011). Regulatory focus and opportunism in the alliance development process. *Journal of Management*, *37*(3), 682–708. doi:10.1177/0149206309356325

Das, T. K., & Teng, B. S. (2000). A resource-based theory of strategic alliances. *Journal of Management*, *26*(1), 31–61. doi:10.1177/014920630002600105

David, R. J., & Han, S. K. (2004). A systematic assessment of the empirical support for transaction cost economics. *Strategic Management Journal*, *25*(1), 39–58.

Ebbers, J. J. (2014). Networking behavior and contracting relationships among entrepreneurs in business incubators. *Entrepreneurship Theory and Practice*, *38*(5), 1159–1181. doi:10.1111/etap.12032

Felício, J. A., Gonçalves, H. M., & da Conceição Gonçalves, V. (2013). Social value and organizational performance in non-profit social organizations: Social entrepreneurship, leadership, and socioeconomic context effects. *Journal of Business Research*, *66*(10), 2139–2146. doi:10.1016/j.jbusres.2013.02.040

Fish, A. J., & Wood, J. (2017). Promoting a strategic business focus to balance competitive advantage and corporate social responsibility–missing elements. *Social Responsibility Journal*, *13*(1), 78–94. doi:10.1108/SRJ-04-2016-0054

Haeussler, C., & Higgins, M. J. (2014). Strategic alliances: Trading ownership for capabilities. *Journal of Economics & Management Strategy*, *23*(1), 178–203. doi:10.1111/jems.12047

Haeussler, C., Patzelt, H., & Zahra, S. A. (2012). Strategic alliances and product development in high technology new firms: The moderating effect of technological capabilities. *Journal of Business Venturing*, *27*(2), 217–233. doi:10.1016/j.jbusvent.2010.10.002

Hoang, H., & Rothaermel, F. T. (2016). How to Manage Alliances Strategically. *MIT Sloan Management Review*, *58*(1), 69.

Huda, M., Haron, Z., Ripin, M. N., Hehsan, A., & Yaacob, A. B. C. (2017d). Exploring Innovative Learning Environment (ILE): Big Data Era. *International Journal of Applied Engineering Research*, *12*(17), 6678–6685.

Huda, M., Jasmi, K. A., Alas, Y., Qodriah, S. L., Dacholfany, M. I., & Jamsari, E. A. (2017g). Empowering Civic Responsibility: Insights From Service Learning. In S. Burton (Ed.), *Engaged Scholarship and Civic Responsibility in Higher Education* (pp. 144–165). Hershey, PA: IGI Global. doi:10.4018/978-1-5225-3649-9.ch007

Huda, M., Jasmi, K. A., Basiran, B., Mustari, M. I. B., & Sabani, A. N. (2017e). Traditional Wisdom on Sustainable Learning: An Insightful View From Al-Zarnuji's Ta 'lim al-Muta 'allim. *SAGE Open*, *7*(1), 1–8. doi:10.1177/2158244017697160

Huda, M., Jasmi, K. A., Embong, W. H., Safar, J., Mohamad, A. M., Mohamed, A. K., ... Rahman, S. K. (2017f). Nurturing Compassion-Based Empathy: Innovative Approach in Higher Education. In M. Badea & M. Suditu (Eds.), *Violence Prevention and Safety Promotion in Higher Education Settings* (pp. 154–173). Hershey, PA: IGI Global. doi:10.4018/978-1-5225-2960-6.ch009

Huda, M., Jasmi, K. A., Mustari, M. I., Basiron, B., Mohamed, A. K., Embong, W., ... Safar, J. (2017h). Innovative E-Therapy Service in Higher Education: Mobile Application Design. *International Journal of Interactive Mobile Technologies*, *11*(4), 83–94. doi:10.3991/ijim.v11i4.6734

Huda, M., Maseleno, A., Atmotiyoso, P., Siregar, M., Ahmad, R., Jasmi, K. A., ... Basiron, B. (2018). Emerging Big Data Technologies. Insights into Innovative Environment for Online Learning Resources. *International Journal of Emerging Technologies in Learning*. doi:10.3991/ijet.v13i01.6990

Huda, M., Maseleno, A., Jasmi, K. A., Mustari, I., & Basiron, B. (2017c). Strengthening Interaction from Direct to Virtual Basis: Insights from Ethical and Professional Empowerment. *International Journal of Applied Engineering Research*, *12*(17), 6901–6909.

Huda, M., Sabani, N., Shahrill, M., Jasmi, K. A., Basiron, B., & Mustari, M. I. (2017a). Empowering Learning Culture as Student Identity Construction in Higher Education. In A. Shahriar & G. Syed (Eds.), *Student Culture and Identity in Higher Education* (pp. 160–179). Hershey, PA: IGI Global; doi:10.4018/978-1-5225-2551-6.ch010

Huda, M., & Siregar, M., Rahman, S.K.A., Mat Teh, K.S., Said, H., Jamsari, E.A., … Ninsiana, W. (2017b). From Live Interaction to Virtual Interaction: An Exposure on the Moral Engagement in the Digital Era. *Journal of Theoretical and Applied Information Technology*, *95*(19), 4964–4972.

Ireland, R. D., & Webb, J. W. (2007). Strategic entrepreneurship: Creating competitive advantage through streams of innovation. *Business Horizons*, *50*(1), 49–59. doi:10.1016/j.bushor.2006.06.002

Jiang, X., Bao, Y., Xie, Y., & Gao, S. (2016a). Partner trustworthiness, knowledge flow in strategic alliances, and firm competitiveness: A contingency perspective. *Journal of Business Research*, *69*(2), 804–814. doi:10.1016/j.jbusres.2015.07.009

Jiang, X., Yang, Y., Pei, Y. L., & Wang, G. (2016b). Entrepreneurial orientation, strategic alliances, and firm performance: Inside the black box. *Long Range Planning*, *49*(1), 103–116. doi:10.1016/j.lrp.2014.09.003

Kickul, J., & Lyons, T. S. (2016). *Understanding social entrepreneurship: The relentless pursuit of mission in an ever changing world*. Routledge.

Kim, K. H. (2017). Cooperative or competitive in alliance formation: Alliance patterns with respect to rivals. *Canadian Journal of Administrative Sciences/Revue Canadienne des Sciences de l'Administration*, *34*(3), 277-290.

Kim, K. H., Kim, M., & Qian, C. (2015). Effects of corporate social responsibility on corporate financial performance: A competitive-action perspective. *Journal of Management*.

Kroeger, A., & Weber, C. (2014). Developing a conceptual framework for comparing social value creation. *Academy of Management Review*, *39*(4), 513–540. doi:10.5465/amr.2012.0344

Lee, J. S., & Hsieh, C. J. (2010). A research in relating entrepreneurship, marketing capability, innovative capability and sustained competitive advantage. *Journal of Business & Economics Research*, *8*(9), 109. doi:10.19030/jber.v8i9.763

López-Duarte, C., González-Loureiro, M., Vidal-Suárez, M. M., & González-Díaz, B. (2016). International strategic alliances and national culture: Mapping the field and developing a research agenda. *Journal of World Business*, *51*(4), 511–524. doi:10.1016/j.jwb.2016.05.001

Maseleno, A., Huda, M., Siregar, M., Ahmad, R., Hehsan, A., Haron, Z., ... Azmi Jasmi, K. (2017). Combining the Previous Measure of Evidence to Educational Entrance Examination. *Journal of Artificial Intelligence*, *10*(3), 85–90. doi:10.3923/jai.2017.85.90

Meyskens, M., Carsrud, A. L., & Cardozo, R. N. (2010). The symbiosis of entities in the social engagement network: The role of social ventures. *Entrepreneurship and Regional Development*, *22*(5), 425–455. doi:10.1080/08985620903168299

Mortati, M., & Cruickshank, L. (2012). NETS: A design tool for activating social networks. *International Journal of Entrepreneurial Behaviour & Research*, *18*(4), 509–523. doi:10.1108/13552551211239528

Nag, R., Russo, A., & Vurro, C. (2014, January). The Role of Market Identity on the Relationship Between Knowledge and Strategic Alliances. In Academy of Management Proceedings (Vol. 2014, No. 1, p. 11737). Academy of Management. doi:10.5465/AMBPP.2014.11737abstract

Nielsen, B. B., & Gudergan, S. (2012). Exploration and exploitation fit and performance in international strategic alliances. *International Business Review*, *21*(4), 558–574. doi:10.1016/j.ibusrev.2011.07.001

Ozmel, U., Robinson, D. T., & Stuart, T. E. (2013). Strategic alliances, venture capital, and exit decisions in early stage high-tech firms. *Journal of Financial Economics*, *107*(3), 655–670. doi:10.1016/j.jfineco.2012.09.009

Park, B. J. R., Srivastava, M. K., & Gnyawali, D. R. (2014). Walking the tight rope of coopetition: Impact of competition and cooperation intensities and balance on firm innovation performance. *Industrial Marketing Management*, *43*(2), 210–221. doi:10.1016/j.indmarman.2013.11.003

Perron, G. M., Côté, R. P., & Duffy, J. F. (2006). Improving environmental awareness training in business. *Journal of Cleaner Production*, *14*(6), 551–562. doi:10.1016/j.jclepro.2005.07.006

Phillips, W., Lee, H., Ghobadian, A., O'Regan, N., & James, P. (2015). Social innovation and social entrepreneurship: A systematic review. *Group & Organization Management*, *40*(3), 428–461. doi:10.1177/1059601114560063

Ridley-Duff, R., & Bull, M. (2015). Understanding social enterprise: Theory and practice. *Sage (Atlanta, Ga.)*.

Schweitzer, J. (2014). Leadership and innovation capability development in strategic alliances. *Leadership and Organization Development Journal*, *35*(5), 442–469. doi:10.1108/LODJ-01-12-0001

Seitanidi, M. M., & Crane, A. (2009). Implementing CSR through partnerships: Understanding the selection, design and institutionalisation of nonprofit-business partnerships. *Journal of Business Ethics*, *85*(2), 413–429. doi:10.100710551-008-9743-y

Serrat, O. (2017). Learning in strategic alliances. In *Knowledge Solutions* (pp. 639–647). Springer Singapore. doi:10.1007/978-981-10-0983-9_71

Shi, W., Sun, J., & Prescott, J. E. (2012). A temporal perspective of merger and acquisition and strategic alliance initiatives: Review and future direction. *Journal of Management*, *38*(1), 164–209. doi:10.1177/0149206311424942

Smith, B. R., & Stevens, C. E. (2010). Different types of social entrepreneurship: The role of geography and embeddedness on the measurement and scaling of social value. *Entrepreneurship and Regional Development*, *22*(6), 575–598. doi:10.1080/08985626.2010.488405

Solitander, M., & Tidström, A. (2010). Competitive flows of intellectual capital in value creating networks. *Journal of Intellectual Capital*, *11*(1), 23–38. doi:10.1108/14691931011013316

Stam, W., Arzlanian, S., & Elfring, T. (2014). Social capital of entrepreneurs and small firm performance: A meta-analysis of contextual and methodological moderators. *Journal of Business Venturing*, *29*(1), 152–173. doi:10.1016/j.jbusvent.2013.01.002

Thomaz, F., & Swaminathan, V. (2015). What Goes Around Comes Around: Spreading Risk Through Strategic Alliances in Highly Embedded Networks. *Journal of Marketing*, *79*(5), 63–79. doi:10.1509/jm.12.0404

Uddin, M. B., & Akhter, B. (2011). Strategic alliance and competitiveness: Theoretical framework. *Researchers World*, *2*(1), 43.

Walter, J., Kellermanns, F. W., & Lechner, C. (2012). Decision making within and between organizations: Rationality, politics, and alliance performance. *Journal of Management*, *38*(5), 1582–1610. doi:10.1177/0149206310363308

Warner, M., & Sullivan, R. (Eds.). (2017). *Putting partnerships to work: Strategic alliances for development between government, the private sector and civil society*. New York: Routledge.

ADDITIONAL READING

Chen, M. J., & Miller, D. (2015). Reconceptualizing competitive dynamics: A multidimensional framework. *Strategic Management Journal*, *36*(5), 758–775. doi:10.1002mj.2245

Dacin, P. A., Dacin, M. T., & Matear, M. (2010). Social entrepreneurship: Why we don't need a new theory and how we move forward from here. *The Academy of Management Perspectives*, *24*(3), 37–57. doi:10.5465/AMP.2010.52842950

Dahl, J. (2014). Conceptualizing coopetition as a process: An outline of change in cooperative and competitive interactions. *Industrial Marketing Management*, *43*(2), 272–279. doi:10.1016/j.indmarman.2013.12.002

Das, T. K., & Kumar, R. (2010). Interpartner sensemaking in strategic alliances: Managing cultural differences and internal tensions. *Management Decision*, *48*(1), 17–36. doi:10.1108/00251741011014436

De Clercq, D., Dimov, D., & Thongpapanl, N. T. (2010). The moderating impact of internal social exchange processes on the entrepreneurial orientation–performance relationship. *Journal of Business Venturing*, *25*(1), 87–103. doi:10.1016/j.jbusvent.2009.01.004

Franco, M. (2011). Performance in strategic alliances: An analysis of objective and subjective measures. *International Journal of Entrepreneurial Venturing*, *3*(1), 84–100. doi:10.1504/IJEV.2011.037859

Heimeriks, K. H., & Duysters, G. (2007). Alliance capability as a mediator between experience and alliance performance: An empirical investigation into the alliance capability development process. *Journal of Management Studies*, *44*(1), 25–49. doi:10.1111/j.1467-6486.2006.00639.x

Hitt, M. A., Ireland, R. D., Sirmon, D. G., & Trahms, C. A. (2011). Strategic entrepreneurship: Creating value for individuals, organizations, and society. *The Academy of Management Perspectives*, *25*(2), 57–75. doi:10.5465/AMP.2011.61020802

Krause, D. R., Handfield, R. B., & Tyler, B. B. (2007). The relationships between supplier development, commitment, social capital accumulation and performance improvement. *Journal of Operations Management*, *25*(2), 528–545. doi:10.1016/j.jom.2006.05.007

Li, L., Jiang, F., Pei, Y., & Jiang, N. (2017). Entrepreneurial orientation and strategic alliance success: The contingency role of relational factors. *Journal of Business Research*, *72*, 46–56. doi:10.1016/j.jbusres.2016.11.011

Lin, T. Y., & Cheng, Y. Y. (2010). Exploring the knowledge network of strategic alliance research: A co-citation analysis. *International Journal of Electronic Business Management*, *8*(2), 152.

Talebi, K., Rezazadeh, A., & Najmabadi, A. D. (2015). SME alliance performance: The impacts of alliance entrepreneurship, entrepreneurial orientation, and intellectual capital. *International Journal of Entrepreneurship and Small Business*, *24*(2), 187–207. doi:10.1504/IJESB.2015.067286

Teng, B. S. (2007). Corporate entrepreneurship activities through strategic alliances: A Resource-Based Approach toward Competitive Advantage. *Journal of Management Studies*, *44*(1), 119–142. doi:10.1111/j.1467-6486.2006.00645.x

KEY TERMS AND DEFINITIONS

Alliance Management: Building the capabilities through cooperation and coordination supported to lead to the success in obtaining the social entrepreneurship with the skill practice in the way to manage alliances. The effort in managing the procurement of partner firms through individual skills in building experiences and proactivity is necessary to point out attempts within the long-term relationship to underlie the way to work together among the partners within joint venture to generate the alliance management through pointing out the key strategic role.

Competitive: The set of interacting with continuum of choices in selecting the compliance partnership to develop the alliances by providing the strategic initiation with resources. It points out the innovative activities in addressing the ability to recognise the opportunities initiated to look at the market positions with its complex feature. Attempts to create the value within the strategic initiation to access to concisely develop the supportive encouragement become important to take the primary benefits of alliances.

Cooperative: the association of the individuals autonomously united within the jointly-owned enterprise engaged in producing and supplying the services and the goods. This directs to operate in gaining the mutual benefit, typically generated to give insights on organizing strategic alliance to get actively involved to meet the extent of common social, economic and cultural needs which give insights with a significant role with the problem solving.

Networking Strategic Actions: Strategic actions should point out the view to obtain the networking initiation to embed the social context by considering direct and indirect ties with network actors. Enhancing the relationships between inter-organizational and intra-organizational side has to be involved with the alliance formation in the sense which can give insights into the value in generating the strategic action. Attempts would concisely enlarge the initiation of generating networking for alliance formation as an outstanding value to consistently tie into the company.

Performance Value: Acts to present the initiative of considering the acts within the group transmitted into the works associated with competitive alliance. An act of presenting the cooperative engagement needs to be involved to meet the relational risk in providing the strategic initiation with resources. As an attempt in selecting the compliance partnership in developing distribution channels of the certain products, these alliances can be viewed through manufacturing the capability with intellectual property associated with knowledge expertise.

Productivity: The ratio expressed in the production process. For instance, in the economic measure typically measured in basis of revenues and other components of business inventories, attempts to combine the potential assets in possessing competitive awareness would provide the access to the markets information on alliances with addressing the capabilities to run the business within their work plan.

Social Entrepreneurship: The techniques indicated through attracting the growing amounts of talent and attention used to begin the production by the companies widely set out to develop innovation and creativity integrated in addressing cultural, social and environmental concern. It assures the practical result by addressing all sorts of activities through the program initiative associated with combining the critical thinking to solve the solutions of the issues between social and environmental challenges. It underlines the attempts to transform systems and practices resulting in the potential strength of performance to run the entrepreneurship.

Strategic Partnership Alliance: Attempts arranged between content and process simultaneously to the firms as the initiative for strategic alliances anticipated taking advantage into market. Towards the knowledge understanding of the strategic alliance to primarily concentrate on the content issue integrated into the alliance formation, this initiative points out the way of particular governance structured into forming certain alliances with focusing on the firms towards their risk management. Transmitted to the performance indicator with enlarging the competitive advantage, this strategy is assigned to give alliance outcomes generated through the corporation as an initiation to contribute in creating the value integrated for the effective risk management.

Chapter 15
Social Entrepreneurship: Constraints and Suggestions for Future Researches

Mustafa Karaca
Inonu University, Turkey

Durdu Mehmet Biçkes
Nevşehir Hacı Bektaş Veli University, Turkey

ABSTRACT

Social entrepreneurship attracts attention to the science world as a conceptual field of social benefit based on business activities. Social entrepreneurs are the actors who drive innovation with commercial tolerance and uncertainty tolerance in order to raise social welfare and find solutions to social problems. Especially the injustices and inadequacies in transferring public support to social problems have increased the importance of social entrepreneurship. In addition to the conceptual projection of social entrepreneurship, this research has raised fundamental problems that have hampered social entrepreneurship and prevented further development, and a number of solution proposals have been developed in order to get rid of these problems. This concept, which has been separated from traditional entrepreneurship and is in the process of building its own literature, has many parts to inspire next research. It is hoped that this study, which includes proposals for next research, will contribute to the scientific world. It is thought that this study created by the method of literature review will have more specific conceptual contribution to the investigation of various researches from different disciplines and their unique character in terms of their synthesis.

1. INTRODUCTION

From a traditional point of view, entrepreneurship is associated with contribution of businesses to economic growth. However, a broader perspective is needed to assess the contribution of all entrepreneurial activities in a society and to capture the diverse forms of initiative activities. One of the initiative forms that will be faced is social entrepreneurship as long as it has been carried out. Due to the potential and consequences of social entrepreneurship, this style of entrepreneurship has become one of the issues that have been intensively addressed in recent years in the world of science, public administration and social life.

DOI: 10.4018/978-1-5225-5687-9.ch015

Although social entrepreneurship is a new concept, it is a fact that it has been experiencing as a case for centuries. Even though they are not named as social entrepreneurs, they have always kept their assets in the historical process and they brought many institutions to the body in today's sense. Social entrepreneurship, which consists of sociality and entrepreneurship at its core, involves solely dealing with social issues with an entrepreneurial point of view. The implication given to conception by the social context is that social entrepreneurship focuses on social problems. The contribution to conception that entrepreneurship has made is the ability to approach social problems from an innovative point of view and transform them into opportunity. For this reason, social entrepreneurship also referred to as "change agent" or "change creator," seeks to exploit innovative ways of approaching social problems and to create long-term solutions that can lead to a complete transformation of the problematic area.

Social entrepreneurship is a field designed to bring entrepreneurial activities directly in line with the ultimate goal of creating social value. The key factor in this process is that they are not in any way intended to earn personal earnings. In this sense, the social entrepreneur considers social enthusiasm as a person who combines discipline, innovation and determination with business as it is in business life but does not expect materiality in this process. Social entrepreneurs, who are passionately committed to this social mission and who are striving to achieve this, think that they mean life and satisfy their life purposes in this way. The distinguishing feature of social entrepreneurship also arises at this point. This feature is to channel a business model into a social need without being in the material interest expectation.

Social entrepreneurship is the whole of activities undertaken to recognize, define and benefit from opportunities to create new initiatives or to increase social welfare by managing existing organizations in an innovative manner. The term 'social welfare' in its definition covers all aspects of economic, social, environmental, health and so on that are concern people. Because of its benefits that are a mixture of social and financial gains, social entrepreneurship is considered as an important economic and social resource. From the explanations, it can be said that social entrepreneurship has become a very important actor in terms of the development and well-being of the societies through the solution of problems and the support of disadvantaged groups.

Social entrepreneurship, which performs important functions that cannot be neglected in terms of social functioning such as positive discrimination of the disadvantaged sections of society and development of social co-operation. It proposes new ways to develop public and social services, alleviates the burden of the problem in solving problems, contributes to economic and social development, and it is also confronted with a number of restrictive factors. These are the main ones:

- Access to Finance
- Lack of Visibility
- Lack of Specialized Training And Education
- Human Resources
- Markets
- Legal Status
- Management And Organization
- Sector Specific Constraints
- Other Issues

In addition to these restrictive factors, the changes and transformations in environmental factors cause differentiation in social needs, which is the driving force of social entrepreneurship in private, on all actors forming the sector in general. Therefore, social entrepreneurship must overcome restraining factors and adapt to changing conditions in order to sustain its existence and improve service effectiveness.

In the scope of this study, first we will give a general framework on social entrepreneurship and its functions, and then we will discuss the issues that *what is needed to cope with the restrictive factors* and *how changing circumstances will transform social entrepreneurship.*

2. THEORETICAL BACKGROUND OF SOCIAL ENTREPRENEURSHIP: CONSTRAINTS AND SUGGESTIONS FOR FUTURE RESEARCHES

2.1. A Minor Description of Social Entrepreneurship

Social entrepreneurship is an accepted part of economic and social development (Christie & Honing, 2006; Dees, 2001; Harding, 2004). Social entrepreneurship research, on the other hand, is not as broad and common as commercial entrepreneurship. According to Light's (2008) study, social entrepreneurship has not attracted much attention during the scientific periods and the development of the social entrepreneurship field has been relatively difficult (Light, 2008). The notion of social entrepreneurship, which started to gain importance from Bill Drayton's study in 1980s (Dees, 2007), deals with many social problems in the world and generally underdeveloped countries where the state and private sector are not interested in. The majority of the researches in the early years especially focused on the similarities and differences between social entrepreneurship and commercial entrepreneurship (Austin, Stevenson, & Wei-Skillern, 2006; Massetti, 2008; Thompson, 2002). The concept of social entrepreneurship has not been presented with a rich content (Mair & Marti, 2006), even if the study is predominantly conceptual. Social entrepreneurship, which can be considered as a civil initiative and voluntary movement, is based on the idea that solving the problems is not merely a matter of expectation from the state or the private sector. Researchers describe organizations that have strategies that create social value at a significant level, and those whose primary priorities are social benefit rather than commercial profit, as social enterprises (Light, 2008). It is stated that the researches on which conceptual definition of social entrepreneurship is not agreed, emphasize the aims and objectives of social entrepreneurship. Social entrepreneurship is a concept that changes social balance (Douglas, 2008).

The concept of social entrepreneurship may vary according to the nature of the organization. Profit-intentional, profit-oriented, and public enterprise's interpretation of social entrepreneurship and social entrepreneurship are different. The difference in the interpretations of social entrepreneurship of these organizations is mainly due to differences in the practice of social practices in the practice of business. The planning and implementation of social change by a public enterprise and the profit-oriented enterprise differ from one another. The basic assumption of social entrepreneurship is that entrepreneurial features can be used for the benefit of the society without the purpose of profit (Carangoz, 2012). David Gergen, Professor of the Harvard University, describes social entrepreneurship as the driving force of social reforms (Dees, 2007). Entrepreneurship is an economic and social activity. In particular, Schumpeter's entrepreneurial social motivation has made it possible for entrepreneurship to be expressed as a social activity, allowing the concept of social entrepreneurship to be examined as profit-making entrepreneurship. Many definitions of social entrepreneurship have been described in the literature, while the forefront definitions have been made by Theobald and Alvord. Theobald defines social entrepreneurs as the means of exchange with the desire to take risks, the ability to bring new ideas to individuals, groups and organizations. Alvord argues that the combination of social impact and commercial enterprises, innovation for social impact and acceleration of social transformation define the process of social entrepreneurship (Güler, 2010).

Social entrepreneurship is considered in two dimensions. These are referred to as social development organizations and social transformation organizations. Both dimensions are complementary to each other in terms of mission of social change (Swanson & Zhang, 2010). Social entrepreneurship can be seen as a number of activities that non-profit-making businesses do to finance or create social benefits, as well as social responsibility applications of profit-oriented daunting enterprises and attempts to solve the social problems of society (Özdevecioğlu ve Cingöz, 2009). Social entrepreneurship is based on the social equilibrium approach, bringing the social balance to a new and more prosperous point by persuading people. It makes positive social outcomes by focusing on marginal utility instead of social welfare and targeting social balance away from human values and solving social problems. It is important to emphasize that social enterprises should be redesigned and established in order to provide a new and more stable social balance. Social entrepreneurs are the main actors in this process (Martin & Osberg, 2007).

There are four themes that are seen as useful in distinguishing social initiatives from institutional initiatives. These: 1) emphasis on social aims, contrary to economic gains; 2) the social activist role played by the social entrepreneur; 3) entrepreneurship and innovation elements (at least in most cases); 4) the profit generated and used in the economic sense is used as a tool rather than a purpose to solve a social problem (Aslan, Araza & Bulut, 2012). The main difference between the social entrepreneurs and the private sector entrepreneurs is that they should be passionate about creating social values and solving social problems. This difference is expressed as the basic mission of the enterprises they have established. To put it briefly, social entrepreneurship is to create social value by taking the aim of profit and material gain in the second plan and to play a role in the solution of social problems (Güler, 2010). Dees describes the social entrepreneur as a person who changes social equilibrium as a change agent and describes the basic roles played by social entrepreneurs as follows (Dees, 2001):

- To create social value and identify goals to pursue and to act on this mission.
- Watching and / or creating opportunities to fulfill this mission.
- Designing and using innovative, adaptable and learning-oriented processes.
- Acting with a broad perspective by producing new resources without being limited to the resources available.
- Acting with accountable clarity and transparency against the concerns associated with the output obtained.

When a business entrepreneur suffers a harm, he/she and his/her family are harmed, and when a social entrepreneur suffers, the society is hurt (Carangoz, 2012). The most important criticism against the definition study done by Dees is that the system does not take into account self-financing inputs. According to Boschee (2008), social enterprises have to produce an input stream in order to maintain the continuity and sustainability of the system (Boschee, 2008). Otherwise the stability of the social equilibrium will face the danger of being interrupted. For this reason, social enterprises need to include financial income as a secondary objective. Getting some income can also be considered the nature of entrepreneurship.

It is understood that social entrepreneurship goes beyond selfish or charitable donations and supports social problems with more sustainable and interdependent solutions (Aslan, Araza & Bulut, 2012). But the main focus is to create social value. Creating economic value is seen as a necessary condition in terms of financial sustainability (Güler, 2010). Economic enthusiasm in social entrepreneurship, as well as being necessary for the financing of social concerns, also has an economic value in social benefits. As a matter of fact, the solution of social problems is a cost element for social stakeholders. According to Swanson and Zhang (2010), social entrepreneurship, social change and social outcome that will result from the process, a new idea and organization that will change in the case, and an opportunity to act on the entrepreneurial basis factor (Swanson & Zhang, 2010). This combination can be regarded as essential characteristics for all types of entrepreneurship when the relevant literature is examined. The concept of social entrepreneurship, which has a developing trend in the world, is a field that is highlighted by important institutions and organizations operating at international level. In this regard, the World Economic Forum has created a social entrepreneurship fund within its own institution by issuing a declaration on the important issue of social entrepreneurship (Dees, 2007). It is possible to see social enterprises and social entrepreneurs frequently in Turkey and in the world. Numerous social enterprises in our country are trying to contribute to the solution of social problems. Especially humanitarian aid movements are examples of social enterprises that Turkey is working at international level. Moreover, Erciyes University, is a Model University which draws attention with its physical spaces built with almost all philanthropic aids. Owned by social entrepreneurs in Kayseri, the university has the feature of being a public university where every field social entrepreneur is interested in their problems.

2.2. Constraints of Social Entrepreneurship

Social entrepreneurship, which performs important functions that cannot be neglected in terms of social functioning such as positive discrimination of the disadvantaged sections of society and social co-operation improvements. It proposes new ways to develop public and social services, alleviates the burden of the problem in solving problems, contributes to economic and social development but it also faces a number of restrictive factors. These are the main factors (Andor, Barnier & Tajani, 2013; Smith & Darko, 2014):

- Access to finance (Resource Constraint)
- Lack of Visibility
- Lack of Specialised Training and Education
- Human Resources
- Markets
- Legal Status
- Management and Organization
- Sector Specific Constraints
- Other Issues

2.2.1. Access to Finance (Resource Constraint)

As is known, social enterprises are not profit-making structures. However, they can carry out social and commercial entrepreneurship activities together in order to achieve their own sufficiency (Abu-Safian, 2012). Nevertheless, social entrepreneurs have used income and profits from their commercial activities not only to increase their personal wealth, but also to move social values further (Manyaka, 2015).

When compared to profit-oriented institutions, a few studies have been conducted on the financing needs of social enterprises. In a small number of these studies, it is stated that social enterprises have a much higher demand for external financing than commercial enterprises. Social entrepreneurs face a range of barriers to accessing the financial instruments of profit-intentionist institutions (ILO, 2016). For this reason, although social entrepreneurs show a greater demand for access to finance than commercial businesses, the likelihood of successful access to many forms of finance remains very low (Andor, Barnier & Tajani, 2013). Manyaka (2015) expresses this fact, by stating that today many social enterprises are deprived of plans to make profits in order to realize their aims, and thus are dependent on donations. The author also adds that many social organizations that cannot provide donor support have collapsed.

Limited access to commercial financing resources can inevitably be assessed for organizations that determine business orientation to meet social objectives. However, what really needs to be discussed is why social enterprises have had difficulty in accessing social finance instruments (such as finance subsidized by government, donor financing or impact investment). The reason for this is that many social enterprises are small and have limited subsidy capacity. Another reason for this difficulty is the lack of intermediaries that can promote social entrepreneurs and social investors (Smith & Darko, 2014).

For the social entrepreneurs, it is possible to list the following obstacles in the access to financial resources (ILO, 2016):

- Inadequate legal arrangements for social enterprises,
- Perceived as “profit-oriented” by donors and “socially-oriented” by financial institutions,
- Complex institutional structure (e.g., having more than one legal entity at the same time),
- Perceived as “high risk” by financial institutions,
- Social enterprises operating under the control of a certain group have difficulties in meeting the criteria of financial institutions for credit,
- Inadequate deposit,
- Lack of financial and non-financial talent,
- In the event that the social enterprise is a co-operative, the thinking that the co-operative may have been established in order to reach the grants by taking advantage of various incentives for social enterprise purposes,
- Low penetration levels of microfinance institutions,
- The absence of appropriate financial records,
- The absence of a formal recording system,
- The existence of founders whose credit score is negative or taken on a blacklist,
- The distrust of social enterprise structures and the perception that social enterprises are dispersed due to disagreements among members,
- Inadequate information about different financial instruments,
- Not having the ability to borrow money for capital investments without opening the market without investing in prepaid capital and entering the market without entering the market.

2.2.2. The Lack of Visibility

Since the global economic culture focuses on collective and self-reliant (self-sacrificing others) behaviors, and on individual initiatives and profit-making structures, the activities and values of social entrepreneurship do not find enough room for mass media (Andor, Barnier & Tajani, 2013; Weaver, Hanks, Earley, & Whitcomb, 2015). The mass media have the function to play a central role in informing the public (Happer & Philo, 2013) because of the qualities they possess and the effects they have, especially in areas where individuals do not have direct knowledge or experience. The inability of the social enterprises and the value they put forth to find space in mass media, causes lack of awareness and recognition of social values produced by social entrepreneurship in the public opinion.

Lack of awareness can be caused by lack of education in this subject besides not being able to find enough space in mass media. While courses on business entrepreneurship, as is known, are located in school curricula at different levels of education, no courses on social economics and social entrepreneurship exist in school curricula (Andor, Barnier & Tajani, 2013). Taking into account the shaping power of education and the individual, it can be argued that the inadequacy of education in this area does not show the sensitivity of the society to social entrepreneurship.

2.2.3. The Lack of Specialized Training and Education

As is known, there are considerable differences between social entrepreneurship and commercial entrepreneurship. These differences cause various differences in the establishment and operation processes and necessitate the existence of human power with different equipment. However, as emphasized above, social entrepreneurship does not find enough room in school curricula. Thus, finding a specialized human resource with the equipment needed for social entrepreneurship becomes a limitation. This is expressed by Andor, Barnier and Tajani (2013):

the inadequacy of specialized education and training leads to the inability of the social enterprise to find human resources with the necessary mind sets, skills and competencies.

2.2.4. Support Network and Infrastructure

Another less important aspect for social entrepreneurship is the support network and infrastructure that provide appropriate business development services. These areas can range from strategic planning and consulting services tailored to the needs of social economy organizations and social enterprises to commercial incubators. In some cases, networks, consortia and representative organizations formed by social entrepreneurs themselves help to come up with this challenge by fulfilling some of these functions. However, the presentation of these services is rather low compared to the demands (Andor, Barnier & Tajani, 2013). Therefore, the limitation in the support network and infrastructure area has a detrimental effect on the efficiency and efficiency of social enterprises.

2.2.5. Human Resources

Human resource management is important for social initiatives for three main reasons (Manimala & Bhati, 2011): The first of these reasons is that the services offered by social enterprises are meaningful together with the attitudes and behaviors of employees. Secondly, it is motivated by factors such as organizational mission and values of social enterprise employees from other organizations, participation in decision-making processes and the opportunity to realize their individual values. The third is that when the new financing environment is considered for professional service provisioning and accountability requirements, employees become the most critical stakeholders in positioning social enterprises.

Social enterprises face a variety of problems in employing and retaining qualified human resources that are so important for them because of the limiting factors they are living with. This is often due to the inability of the social entrepreneur to offer a competitive payment package to its employees. Brown,

Yoshioka and Munoz (2004) stated that although employees are satisfied with the activities of the social enterprise and are affected by their missions, they want to leave the job due to the low salary they receive. Another problem that social entrepreneurs face in the field of human resources is how they motivate their employees through non-financial awards (Hynes, 2009). In addition, the fact that social initiatives are not attractive options for individuals who are career targets also causes problems in human resources (Hynes, 2009). Sivathanu and Bhise (2013) point out that another problem that can be experienced in the field of human resources is the withdrawal of volunteers for social enterprise activities and the volunteers are in the process of finding time for these activities. Moreover, many of the social initiatives are founded by charismatic individuals with high determination. This situation causes difficulties in the transfer of responsibility for institutionalization and organization. The need for human resources with hybrid capabilities, which are difficult to assemble on an individual basis due to the nature of social initiatives, also leads to difficulties in human resources (Smith & Darko, 2014). Finally, many social initiatives that cannot achieve value and goal alignment do not positively impact employee morale and performance, motivation, job satisfaction and career success. This results in the inability to discover the hidden abilities of employees (Khatun & Hasan, 2016).

2.2.6. Markets

Social sector markets have two basic characteristics. The first is that the context of this market has a significant influence over the general population. Secondly, this market is affected by formal and informal, social and institutional factors. Social sector markets often are geographical areas where a particular social problem or phenomenon has come to the fore. As a result, social sector markets are difficult. Because it typically emerges in situations where the formal and informal economy is tightly gathered (Robinson, 2006).

The formal economies are economies that have the possibility to be in the foreseeable future, performing within the framework of legal regulations. The informal economy is devoid of legal regulations, irregular and prone to the nature of personal relationships. These economies are in the markets where social entrepreneurs are active. This uncertainty and irregularity in informal economies pose great challenges in terms of social initiatives. Social entrepreneurs can foresee the effectiveness of their activities in the lives of disadvantaged people. However, when activities are isolated within the community, disadvantaged people may not be able to take advantage of these activities and there may be a great disappointment (Robinson, 2006).

2.2.7. Legal Status

In many countries, social economy organizations have emerged spontaneously to meet social needs (Andor, Barnier & Tajani, 2013), without a comprehensive policy support and regulatory framework that can contribute to development and growth. In the course of time, the types of enterprise of the social economy and social entrepreneurship are differently defined and regulated in different countries. Therefore, there is no common legal regulation on social entrepreneurship that is valid on the world scale. This situation constitutes a major obstacle to the development of social enterprises, especially on an international scale (Andor, Barnier & Tajani, 2013). There are currently no legal forms of social entrepreneurship in many countries on the world scale (Wilkinson, Medhurst, Henry, Wihlborg, & Braithwaite, 2015):

- Providing legitimacy and visibility to social enterprises,
- Establishing tax incentives related to supporting and developing social objectives,
- Allowing social enterprises to engage in unlimited economic activity.

In many countries, it is argued that the absence of a clear and clear legal framework for social entrepreneurship causes two specific problems. These problems are (Wilkinson, Medhurst, Henry, Wihlborg, & Braithwaite, 2015):

- The lack of a clear legal framework leads to confusion among social initiatives that must comply with legal regulations,
- The lack of a clear legal framework makes it difficult for authorities to prepare support schemes for social enterprises and to implement tax incentives.

2.2.8. Management and Organization

Management issues are common to all organizations with profit-oriented intent or involvement. However, this limitation is particularly evident for social enterprises that need different sets of management skills and needs. The specific problems of managing and organizing social enterprises are listed as follows (Smith & Darko, 2014):

- **Business Planning:** Social entrepreneurs face a variety of challenges and need professional support in designing a business model in which they can obtain the financing they need to achieve their goals, creating marketing channels for their services and products.
- **Accounting:** Social organizations may have difficulties generating financial reports for tax authorities.
- **Social Impact Measuring:** This limitation arises especially in the process of submitting reports to social entrepreneurs and investors. Because there is no common methodology for assessing social impact, social organizations may face different reporting requirements from different supporters and investors.

2.2.9. Sector Specific Constraints

In their work on Smith and Darko (2014), Vietnam and Kenya, have exemplified the specific constraints of the social initiatives they encounter, based on events that have occurred:

- In Vietnam, Medical Technology Transfer and Services Initiative has stated that it has suffered from patenting of low-cost medical equipment and devices, the import of certain parts and the procedures used to sell these products to public institutions.
- The social enterprise Truong Sanh, based in Vietnam's Ben Tre province, has been able to offer traditional drugs delayed by one year due to obstacles stemming from provincial authorities, which they would like to present to the market to reach their owners.
- Innovative modular and regulatory barriers: for example, working difficulties in informal settlements.

2.2.10. Other Issues

In addition to the limitations mentioned above, other limitations that social entrepreneurship is experiencing in the summer are listed below (Wilkinson, Medhurst, Henry, Wihlborg, & Braithwaite, 2015):

- The concept of social entrepreneurship is not understood correctly,
- The lack of expert business development services and support,
- The absence of common mechanisms for the measurement and demonstration of social impact,
- The general economic situation,
- The lack of useful business models,
- The high dependence on the public sector as an income source,
- The interventional spirit and commercial intrusive deprivation.

Along with these restrictive factors, the changes and transformations in environmental factors cause differentiation in social needs, which is the driving force of social entrepreneurship, in general, on all actors forming the sector. Therefore, social entrepreneurship must be able to sustain its existence and to overcome restricting factors and to adapt to changing conditions in order to increase service effectiveness.

3. INSTEAD OF CONCLUSION: PREDICTIONS AND SUGGESTIONS FOR FUTURE RESEARCHES

It can be argued that the most fundamental source of the problems mentioned in the theoretical framework on the fundamental constraints of social entrepreneurship is related to the conceptualization of social entrepreneurship and perception by policy makers. First of all, in terms of the scientific world, the necessary standardization must be provided at the point of this concept. The efforts of scientists to examine and explain social entrepreneurship should have the qualification to lead policy makers in macro and micro sense, by going beyond definitive statements. It is hoped that the perception and approach to this institution will change as the uncertainties about the concepts of social entrepreneurship, social enterprise and social entrepreneurs disappear.

Financial regulations that regard social enterprises as particularly high-risk social structures in the economic sense need to make the necessary legal arrangements and it is needed to consider these structures as commercial entities in supporting and financing them. While the frequency of the studies that determine the most fundamental problem of social enterprises as financial inadequacies and access to finance is increasing regularly, any action regarding solution does not attract the attention. The abstentions and negative approaches of financial actors in solving the problem of finding or reaching the capital that social entrepreneurs will use when generating social benefits prevent the institutionalization of social entrepreneurship and restrict the depth of the sector. Especially in the macro sense, the problem experienced by social entrepreneurs is fundamentally influenced by the negative perception of this concept.

It is necessary to integrate social entrepreneurship into education and training mechanisms, encourage academic and practical studies on the subject, and establish legal, economic, managerial and sociological infrastructure of social mechanisms in order to prevent negative views of social enterprises and micro entrepreneurs from macro and micro economic policies. In the place where the concept of social entrepreneurship does not become a state policy, one does not reach the desired level of success. When the negative examples that cause social entrepreneurs to be perceived as negative in the society are examined, it can be said that the main problem is caused by insufficiency of control and legal gaps. The gaps in the legal systems of countries are particularly breaking social events that begin with individual motivation and gratification motivation, and can be an important barrier to move again for individuals who think that they have been abused.

The lack of development of administrative mechanisms that will enable social entrepreneurs to be financially and spiritually supported also manifests itself as an important constraint in this area. An important work in the name of the formation and settlement of these mechanisms would be possible by the establishment of chambers and units to coordinate social entrepreneurs. Sustainability of institutions that have not completed their professional organization is also insufficient. Organizations such as the chambers of commerce and industry that organize and coordinate business entrepreneurs must also be organized for social initiatives.

That the social entrepreneurs are not considered enough about the legal and personal rights deficiencies, especially in terms of policy makers, are accompanied by many constraints in this area. Social enterprises, which financial institutions regard as social organizations and people as commercial organizations, they are victims because of that they don't receive enough support from neither financial institutions nor the people.

In order to prevent this situation, it is necessary to first clarify the legal status of social entrepreneurs and social enterprises. Structural problems constitute a large part of the problems in organizations that have not been able to find their identity in the social sense of commercial space due to legal gaps.

When the success stories of social entrepreneurs are examined, it is seen that the stories based on individual contributions are more intense. It is known that achieving corporate success can be achieved with a systematic and holistic viewpoint. It is known that personal success cannot promote social entrepreneurship to be sustainable. For this reason, the institutionalization and support of social entrepreneurship will be able to move to the point.

While it is an important finding that social entrepreneurs cannot find enough places in the press and media organizations, the basis of this problem lies in the lack of adequate advertising and publicity budgets. For social enterprises that have problems financing their main activities, advertising and promotion becomes luxury, which in turn causes financial insufficiency to continue. As one can see, there is a paradoxical situation. With the development of social media, although there is some advantage in advertising and promotion, there is no commercial cycle to support the main activity unless the use of mass media is professionally carried out. In order to prevent this situation, public spots promoting social initiatives in public policies can be given more space, and policies can be developed for financial institutions to support social enterprises as commercial enterprises.

An important issue that social enterprises feel lacking is the social barriers that they are in because of the deserved reputation of the individuals who operate in this area. Individuals who cannot see enough financial and moral support due to the mass of society that perceive social entrepreneurs as individuals who pursue individual wealth can also end their interventional activities after a while. Especially, the negative examples, which are reflected to the public, exceedingly become a contemporary issue are adversely affecting other good practices. Social entrepreneurs who cannot get enough help about institutional image and rights are required to find a suitable place not only in the field of economics but also in the field of communication and media and should be examined in academic and practical studies.

It is necessary to increase the studies about social enterprises and social entrepreneurship in the social culture and personalities and to investigate the conditions of success in different social structures. Socio-psychological studies to be carried out also need to determine the social perceptions and attitudes that prevent the development of social entrepreneurship and to pass the necessary policies to rehabilitate.

In accordance with the increasing level of scientific knowledge of social entrepreneurship, it can be assumed that intra-sectorial applications will develop. In this context, social networks, social co-operatives, joint investments and economic policies should be scientifically scrutinized and basic theories and doctrine of management and organization should be put forward.

REFERENCES

Abu-Saifan, S. (2012). Social entrepreneurship: Definition and boundaries. *Technology Innovation Management Review*, *2*(2), 22–27.

Andor, L., Barnier, M., & Tajani, A. (2013). *Social economy and social entrepreneurship, Social Europe Guide, Volume: 4*. Belgium: European Commission.

Aslan, G., Araza, A., & Bulut, Ç. (2012). Sosyal Girişimciliğin Kavramsal Çerçevesi. *Girişimcilik ve Kalkınma Dergisi*, *7*, 2.

Austin, J., Stevenson, H., & Wei-Skillern, J. (2006). Social and commercial entrepreneurship: Same, different, or both? *Entrepreneurship Theory and Practice*, *30*(1), 1–22. doi:10.1111/j.1540-6520.2006.00107.x

Boschee, J. (2008). Social entrepreneurship: The promise and the perils. In A. Nicholls (Ed.), *Social entrepreneurship: New models of sustainable social change* (pp. 356–390). Oxford, UK: Oxford University Press.

Brown, W., Yoshioka, C. F., & Munoz, P. (2004). Organizational Mission as a Core Dimension in Employee Retention. *Journal of Park and Recreation Administration*, *22*(2), 28–43.

Christie, M. J., & Honig, B. (2006). Social entrepreneurship: New research findings. *Journal of World Business*, *41*(1), 1–5. doi:10.1016/j.jwb.2005.10.003

Dees, J. G. (2001). *The meaning of "social entrepreneurship."* Retrieved from http://www.caseatduke.org/documents/dees_sedef.pdf

Dees, J. G. (2007). Taking Social Entrepreneurship Seriously. Transaction Social Science and Modern Society, 44(3).

Douglas, H. (2008). Creating knowledge: A review of research methods in three societal change approaches. *Journal of Nonprofit & Public Sector Marketing*, *20*(2), 141–163. doi:10.1080/10495140802224787

Güler, B. K. (2010). *Sosyal Girişimcilik, Efil Yayınevi, 1*. Ankara: Basım.

Happer, C., & Philo, G. (2013). The role of the media in the construction of public belief and social change. *Journal of Social and Political Psychology*, *1*(1), 321–336. doi:10.5964/jspp.v1i1.96

Harding, R. (2004). Social enterprise: The new economic engine. *Business Strategy Review*, *15*(4), 39–43. doi:10.1111/j.0955-6419.2004.00338.x

Hynes, B. (2009). Growing the social enterprise–issues and challenges. *Social Enterprise Journal*, *5*(2), 114–125. doi:10.1108/17508610910981707

ILO. (2016). *Access to finance for Social Entrepreneurs in South Africa*. Geneva: International Labor Office.

Khatun, F., & Hasan, M. (2016). Human Resource Management in Social Enterprises: A Study on BRAC. European Journal of Economics. *Law and Politics*, *3*(2), 37–57.

Light, P. C. (2008). *The search for social entrepreneurship*. Washington, DC: Brookings Institution Press.

Mair, J., & Marti, I. (2006). Social entrepreneurship research: A source of explanation, prediction, and delight. *Journal of World Business*, *41*(1), 36–44. doi:10.1016/j.jwb.2005.09.002

Manimala, M. J., & Bhati, A. (2011). *Talent Acquisition and Retention in Social Enterprises: Innovations in HR Strategies*. Working Paper, No: 328. Bangalore: Indian Institute of Management.

Manyaka, S. J. (2015). Social entrepreneurship: A solution for transforming the disadvantaged community of Nellmapius. *Hervormde Teologiese Studies*, *71*(3), 1–7. doi:10.4102/hts.v71i3.2821

Marangoz, M. (2012). *Girişimcilik, Beta Yayınevi, 1*. İstanbul: Baskı.

Martin, R. L., & Osberg, S. (2007). Social entrepreneurship: The case for definition. *Stanford Social Innovation Review*, *5*(2), 28–39.

Massetti, B. L. (2008). The social entrepreneurship matrix as a "tipping point" for economic change. *Emergence*, *10*(3), 1–8.

Özdevecioğlu & Cingöz. (2009). Sosyal Girişimcilik ve Sosyal Girişimciler Teorik Çerçeve. *Erciyes Üniversitesi İktisadi ve İdari Bilimler Fakültesi Dergisi, 32*.

Robinson, J. (2006). Navigating social and institutional barriers to markets: How social entrepreneurs identify and evaluate opportunities. In J. Mair, J. Robinson, & K. Hockerts (Eds.), *Social entrepreneurship* (pp. 95–120). New York: Palgrave Macmillan. doi:10.1057/9780230625655_7

Sivathanu, B., & Bhise, P. V. (2013). Challenges for social entrepreneurship. *International Journal of Application Innovation in Engineering & Management*.

Smith, W., & Darko, E. (2014). *Social enterprise: constraints and opportunities–evidence from Vietnam and Kenya*. London: Overseas Development Institute.

Swanson, L. A., & Zhang, D. D. (2010). The Social Entrepreneurship Zone. *Journal of Nonprofit & Public Sector Marketing*, *22*(2), 71–88. doi:10.1080/10495140903550726

Thompson, J. L. (2002). The world of the social entrepreneur. *International Journal of Public Sector Management*, *15*(5), 412–431. doi:10.1108/09513550210435746

Weaver, R., Hanks, J., Earley, A., & Whitcomb, R. (2015). *A study of the contribution of cooperative models to Scotland's Economic Strategy and evaluation of Cooperative Development Scotland for Scottish Enterprise*. Manchester, UK: Ekosgen.

Wilkinson, C., Medhurst, J., Henry, N., Wihlborg, M., & Braithwaite, B. W. (2014). *A map of social enterprises and their eco-systems in Europe: Executive Summary*. London: ICF Consulting Services Limited.

ADDITIONAL READING

Alvord, S. H., Brown, L. D., & Letts, C. W. (2004). Social entrepreneurship and societal transformation: An exploratory study. *The Journal of Applied Behavioral Science*, *40*(3), 260–282. doi:10.1177/0021886304266847

Bacq, S., & Janssen, F. (2011). The multiple faces of social entrepreneurship: A review of definitional issues based on geographical and thematic criteria. *Entrepreneurship and Regional Development*, *23*(5-6), 373–403. doi:10.1080/08985626.2011.577242

Choi, N., & Majumdar, S. (2014). Social entrepreneurship as an essentially contested concept: Opening a new avenue for systematic future research. *Journal of Business Venturing*, *29*(3), 363–376. doi:10.1016/j.jbusvent.2013.05.001

Dacin, P. A., Dacin, M. T., & Matear, M. (2010). Social entrepreneurship: Why we don't need a new theory and how we move forward from here. *The Academy of Management Perspectives*, *24*(3), 37–57. doi:10.5465/AMP.2010.52842950

Hoogendoorn, B., Pennings, E., & Thurik, R. (2010). What do we know about social entrepreneurship: An analysis of empirical research? Lepoutre, J., Justo, R., Terjesen, S., & Bosma, N. (2013). Designing a global standardized methodology for measuring social entrepreneurship activity: the Global Entrepreneurship Monitor social entrepreneurship study. *Small Business Economics*, *40*(3), 693–714.

Lumpkin, G. T., Moss, T. W., Gras, D. M., Kato, S., & Amezcua, A. S. (2013). Entrepreneurial processes in social contexts: How are they different, if at all? *Small Business Economics*, *40*(3), 761–783. doi:10.100711187-011-9399-3

Mair, J. (2010). Social entrepreneurship: taking stock and looking ahead.

Mair, J., Battilana, J., & Cardenas, J. (2012). Organizing for society: A typology of social entrepreneuring models. *Journal of Business Ethics*, *111*(3), 353–373. doi:10.100710551-012-1414-3

Nga, J. K. H., & Shamuganathan, G. (2010). The influences of personality traits and demographic factors on social entrepreneurship start up intentions. *Journal of Business Ethics*, *95*(2), 259–282. doi:10.100710551-009-0358-8

Peredo, A. M., & McLean, M. (2006). Social entrepreneurship: A critical review of the concept. *Journal of World Business*, *41*(1), 56–65. doi:10.1016/j.jwb.2005.10.007

Robinson, J. (2006). Navigating social and institutional barriers to markets: How social entrepreneurs identify and evaluate opportunities. In Social entrepreneurship (pp. 95-120). Palgrave Macmillan UK.

Santos, F. M. (2012). A positive theory of social entrepreneurship. *Journal of Business Ethics*, *111*(3), 335–351. doi:10.100710551-012-1413-4

Shaw, E., & Carter, S. (2007). Social entrepreneurship: Theoretical antecedents and empirical analysis of entrepreneurial processes and outcomes. *Journal of Small Business and Enterprise Development*, *14*(3), 418–434. doi:10.1108/14626000710773529

Short, J. C., Moss, T. W., & Lumpkin, G. T. (2009). Research in social entrepreneurship: Past contributions and future opportunities. *Strategic Entrepreneurship Journal*, *3*(2), 161–194. doi:10.1002ej.69

KEY TERMS AND DEFINITIONS

Constraint: Limitation, restriction, constraint, restraint, confinement, delimitation.
Lack of Visibility: Being without.
Suggestion: Offer, proposal, suggestion, proposition, tip, overture.

Chapter 16
Value Creation Through Social Change:
An Ashoka Fellow Case

Nurgül Keleş Tayşir
Istanbul Commerce University, Turkey

ABSTRACT

The social entrepreneur's role in creating social change has been emphasized in the literature. These individuals offer new solutions to society's problems and by doing that they transform the existing institutions. However, there is limited information how these change agents generate value and cause a transformation in society. This chapter tries to identify how a social entrepreneur, individually, has a potential to cause social change. In order to give information about the process of value creation an Ashoka Fellow from Turkey has been selected. Gender inequality and violence against women might be one of the important issues that have to be solved in the country. The selected fellow empowers women by creating social value and advancing social change in Turkey.

INTRODUCTION

Social entrepreneurship may be considered as a new concept that attracts researchers recently, however the concept has a long history of practice worldwide (Mair & Marti, 2004). Bacq (2011) states that the origins of the field can be traced *back to 1983, when Young wrote on innovative nonprofit entrepreneur* and she also mentioned Waddock and Post (1991)'s *Social Entrepreneurs and Catalytic Change'* study -published in 1991- as one of the early studies.

In the literature, even in this book, it is possible to encounter different definitions of social entrepreneurs. Waddock and Post (1991) define social entrepreneurs as:

private sector citizens who play crucial roles in bringing about catalytic changes in the public sector agenda and the perception of certain social issues.

DOI: 10.4018/978-1-5225-5687-9.ch016

According to Bornstein (1998:) social entrepreneur is:

a path breaker with a powerful new idea who combines visionary and real world problem solving creativity, has a strong ethical fiber, and is totally possessed by his or her vision for change.

Prabhu (1999) defines social entrepreneurs as people:

who create and manage innovative entrepreneurial organizations or ventures whose primary mission is the social change and development of their client group.

Mair and Noboa (2003) claim that social entrepreneurs *mainly motivated by a strong desire to change society*. Peredo and McLean (2006) define social entrepreneurship as:

aiming to create social value and pursuing that goal through exploiting opportunities, employing innovation, tolerating risk and declining to accept limitations.

Mair and Marti (2004) define social entrepreneurship as:

a process of creating value by combining resources in new ways... these resource combinations are intended primarily to explore and exploit opportunities to create social value by stimulating social change or meeting social needs.

Nicholls (2006) indicates that:

social entrepreneurship is a set of innovative and effective activities that focus strategically on resolving social market failures and creating new opportunities to add social value systemically by using a range of resources and organizational formats to maximize social impact and bring about change.

All of these definitions highlight the two important aspects of social entrepreneurship: *social value* and *change*.

Social entrepreneurs have desire and powerful ideas to improve the conditions however their contribution does not fully understand. As Bornstein (2007) states *social entrepreneurs have a profound effect on society, yet their corrective function remains poorly understood and underappreciated.* This chapter aims to help understanding the contributions of social entrepreneurs by presenting their stories of the process of finding solutions and generating change in the society. In the following part of the chapter, related literature is going to be reviewed.

BACKGROUND

Social Value

Entrepreneurs' main goal is value creation it is possible to say that both business entrepreneurs and social entrepreneurs generate value for society. Social entrepreneurs focus on creating social value whereas business entrepreneurs are trying to create economic value (Austin, Stevenson & Wei-Skillern, 2006;

Venkataraman, 1997). However, Trivedi and Stokols (2011) describes that both entrepreneurs are creating social value for society in different ways, business entrepreneurs are *providing job opportunities and infrastructure (e.g. roads, highways, water and waste management) to community members*, on the other hand social entrepreneurs are creating social value by focusing on *deep-rooted social problems, social injustice or societal imbalance through processes of social change creation and sustenance*. Business entrepreneurs can create social value but their main motivation is generating economic value, however for social entrepreneurs social value creation is the main reason for their existence.

Brickson (2007) defined social value *broadly as that which enhances well-being for the earth and its living organisms*. To better understand what does social value mean, first it is important to understand what 'social' means. The term 'social' is derived from the Latin word, 'socialis' which *suggests the organization of people, or confederates, into an interdependent group that lives and works together cooperatively* (Kickul & Lyons, 2012). The definition highlights the importance of society rather than individual. Social value creation is critical for social entrepreneurs and the literature states that social value comes from improving the well-being of people, communities and societies. Social entrepreneurs' main motivation is generating social value (Mair, Robinson & Hockerts, 2006) *by catalyzing social change and/or catering to social needs* (Mair & Marti, 2004).

It is easy to find methods for determining how much economic value business entrepreneurs create (Young, 2006). One of the methods of measuring value creation for business entrepreneurs is analyzing wealth creation. As Dees (1998) pointed out:

business entrepreneurs are subject to market discipline... If they do not shift resources to more economically productive uses, they tend to be driven out of business.

On the other hand, social value creation is not easy to measure or determine (Young, 2006). As Emerson (2003) stated that, *most elements of social value stand beyond measurement and quantification.* It is difficult to measure social value creation because it is really hard to answer:

how much social value is created by reducing pollution in a given stream, by saving the spotted owl, or by providing companionship to the elderly? (Dees, 1998).

Zahra et al (2009) also highlights the challenge by asking:

what is the social value of clean water in remote villages, the adoption of orphans from war-torn nations or the empowerment of women entrepreneurs in oppressive societies?

The simplest way to evaluate impact is answering the most basic question of how many? However quantitative approach has some limits due to the fact that numbers only represent the small amount of change and they are not able to illustrate the diverse set of changes. In reality social entrepreneurs cause diverse and complex changes. Emerson (2003) claims that:

a numeric, quantitative approach to understanding social value creation is simply a different language... so many actors in the Social Sector are not fluent in the language of numeracy, any effort to measure, quantify, or describe the creation of social value has traditionally been challenged as inappropriate, inaccurate, and invalid.

Surie and Groen (2017) state that:

the impact of social entrepreneurship is likely indirect, it could be through the adoption of new practices, behaviors and development of new capabilities that did not exist previously.

Sundramurthy, Musteen, and Randel (2013) analyzed the patterns of social value creation. Based on their findings three different types of social value creation activities have been identified: *market makers, system innovators and innovative campaigners.* Each of them has distinctive characteristics while *addressing social problems and creating solutions to such problems.* The market makers create social value through new products and services and they provide economic solutions to address social problems or opportunities. Social entrepreneurs offer solutions to *market inefficiencies that prevent servicing of the poor or disenfranchised* by creating new market spaces. Systems innovators recognize the systems' inefficiencies and *build on their knowledge of the system within which they work and implement a system-level innovation that caters efficiently to an underprivileged group of individuals.* Innovative campaigns mainly focus on awareness raising and education.

Social entrepreneurship may take various forms because the problems they are trying to solve, their ideas and strategies, the resources they use and even the values of the entrepreneurs are different from each other. Since there are different types of social entrepreneurs the type of social value created may also differs. Zahra et al (2009) have developed a typology by analyzing the motives, types of ventures, and strategies, according to the typology there are three different types of social entrepreneurs: social bricoleur, social constructionist, and social engineer. Social bricoleurs focus on local needs, the solutions are generally in small scale however the impact is significant because without them these needs would remain unaddressed. Zahra states that they *bring social wealth to their communities and resolve vexing local social issues.* Social constructionists, differs from social bricoleurs, focus on broader needs that do not realized by existing institutions. These entrepreneurs realize the opportunities:

that generate social wealth by creating and reconfiguring the processes enacted to deliver goods and services. Their desire to generate social wealth is matched with a hope to bring new equilibrium to broad social systems where serious imbalances exist. These entrepreneurs not only want to serve their client group, but also seek to introduce social change and reform.

Finally, social engineers *identify systemic problems within the social systems and structures and address them by bringing about revolutionary change.*

Social Change

Shier and Handy (2015:2583) claim that:

social change efforts… is broadly defined as the actions to improve the social situation of individuals accessing services and members within the wider community. These efforts can include a range of activities, including direct service efforts, efforts to change sociocultural perceptions, and actions that seek to change the social welfare system itself.

Alvord et al (2004) states that:

solutions to social problems, such as sustainable alleviation of the constellation of health, education, economic, political and cultural problems associated with long-term poverty, often demand fundamental transformations in the political, economic, and social systems that underpin current stable states.

Praszkier and Nowak (2011) define social change as:

the systemic transformation in the organization of society in patterns of thought, behavior, social relationships, institutions, and social structure over time, with the use of methods that empower the society and enable the unfolding of potentialities inherent in the system.

Social change can occur in diverse ways, socially transformative programs can cause transformation by *challenging existing social/public policy; promoting social development or community participation; or seeking to change negative public perceptions toward a particular issue or service user group* (Netting, O'connor, & Fauri, 2007). Alvord et al (2004) indicates that even a small act has potential to cause huge difference for instance:

introduction of new paradigms at critical leverage points can lead to cascades of mutually-reinforcing changes that create and sustain transformed social arrangements. Social transformations lead to major shifts in the social context within which the original problem is embedded and sustained.

Social innovation perspective helps to better understand the concept of social change, to cause a change in the system, different types and levels of innovation would be needed (Nicholls & Murdock, 2012). Young (2011) defined social innovation as *a novel mechanism that increases the welfare of the individuals who adopt it compared with the status quo* (p. 2185). There are three levels of social innovation: incremental, institutional and disruptive. Incremental innovation is to *address identified market failures more effectively* (Nicholls & Murdock, 2012). Incremental innovation offers new products or services that meet the social requirements in a more effective and efficient sense (Turker & Altuntas Vural, 2017). This type of innovation refers to *reconfigure the existing market structures and patterns to create new social value* (Nicholls & Murdock, 2012). Incremental innovation has both economic and social motives because it focuses on economic problems as well (Turker & Altuntas Vural, 2017). Disruptive innovation is to *change the cognitive frames of reference around markets and issues to alter social systems and structures* (Nicholls & Murdock, 2012). Turker and Altuntas Vural, (2017) describe that:

it can be a mass political movement or a change in the mind-set of an entire society. It might take place violently and in a very short time or it might be spread over a long time with a slow-paced change. The aims here are to change power relations, alter social hierarchies and reframe issues to the benefit of otherwise disenfranchised groups.

Social Entrepreneurs' Role in Social Change

Social entrepreneurs offer new solutions to society's problems and by doing that they cause a process of durable social change. As Young (2006) presented:

many social entrepreneurs do not stop at creating added social value, their work also brings about a sustained shift in the social or economic relations of disadvantaged groups.

Social entrepreneurs are planting new ideas into people's minds and these small ideas cause drastic changes as Mulgan (2006) states *in the long run, ideas are more powerful than individuals and institutions; indeed as John Maynard Keynes noted, the world is ruled by little else*. Bornstein (2007) assumes that:

an idea is like a play. It needs a good producer and a good promoter even if it is a masterpiece. Otherwise the play may never open; or it may open but, for lack of an audience, close after a week.

As understood from the literature ideas are important to cause dramatic changes in the society but ideas need individuals to promote and work committedly to diffuse them.

Mulgan (2006) states *change rarely happens without some brave people willing to take risks and take a stand*. An agent who recognizes and seizes entrepreneurial opportunities through innovation is needed, in the literature it is portrayed that some brave individuals or "heroes" who are unsatisfied with the system, take responsibilities and cause change in the society. These people come with a new idea about solving the problems of people's unmet needs. In some situations these needs are:

obvious, such as like hunger, homelessness, or disease. But sometimes needs are less obvious or not recognized—for example, racism or the need for protection from domestic violence—and it takes campaigners and movements to name and describe these (Mulgan, 2006).

Drayton (2006) claims that social entrepreneurs *cannot come to rest until they have changed the pattern in their field all across society*. There are numerous well-known examples that changed the whole system. For instance,

Florence Nightingale transformed public health, nursing, housing codes, even the use of statistics in public disclosure... Muhammad Yunus marketed microcredit globally, and Jeroo Billimoria, whose Childline free telephone hotline for and staffed by street children has swept India and is now spreading globally (Drayton, 2006).

Mulgan states that social change is driven by *a very small number of heroic, energetic, and impatient individuals* (p.13). Even one person can cause a change in the whole system, for example Muhammad Yunus has created social value for people and this social value creation changed banking sector and the institutions in the society. In 1976 Yunus has founded The Grameen Bank in order to support impoverished people by giving them micro credit loans. This micro finance project caused a social change and transformed the lending market rules by establishing a new method of money lending. In 2006, Yunus won the Nobel Peace Prize for his efforts to create economic and social development (Cajaiba-Santana, 2014).

Mair and Marti (2004) states that: *institutional entrepreneurship perspective is a promising way to understand the role of social entrepreneurship in changing or giving birth to norms, institutions and structure*. Institutional entrepreneurship refers to the:

activities of actors who have an interest in particular institutional arrangements and who leverage resources to create new institutions or to transform existing ones (Maguire, Hardy & Lawrence, 2004).

Like institutional entrepreneurs, social entrepreneurs are individuals who try to transform institutions or create new ones. In this framework social entrepreneurs are considered as *change agents who perform functions and provide services that have previously been considered to be the sole authority of states* (Partzch & Ziegler, 2011). Bacq and Janssen (2011) state that according to The Social Innovation School, social entrepreneurs are social change agents who *find innovative solutions to social problems of his/her community that are not adequately met by the local system* (p.382). Different from rest of the society these people are able to identify the needs that are not being adequately met.

Social entrepreneur's role in creating social change has been emphasized in the literature. However, as Shier and Handy (2015) claim *there is only minimal investigation into the different ways that exemplifies this social change role* of social entrepreneurs. Ideas and opportunities are essential issues for change process however in order to promote these ideas someone should identify and transform them into an innovation. Social change needs an agent who recognizes and seizes entrepreneurial opportunities through innovation (Ney, Beckmann, Graebnitz, & Mirkovic, 2014). Social change has critical importance in social entrepreneurship, however we know little about how impacts at individual level translate into social change, this chapter aims to give information about the process of value creation and social change.

Ashoka: Innovators for the Public

Ashoka is a non-profit organization that aims to find and support social entrepreneurs worldwide. The name of the organization "Ashoka" comes from the Sanskrit word which means *active absence of sorrow* and Indian Emperor Ashoka who *renounced violence and became one of history's most tolerant, global minded, and creative leaders, pioneering innovations in economic development and social welfare* (http://www.ashoka.org). Bill Drayton founded Ashoka: Innovators for the Public in 1981 in order to *search the world for individuals with fresh ideas for social change* (Bornstein, 2007). The term 'social entrepreneurship' emerged and popularized from Ashoka. Since 1981, Ashoka has selected more than 3,300 social entrepreneurs as Ashoka Fellows in 93 countries (http://www.ashoka.org). The number of the social entrepreneurs, Ashoka staff and offices in worldwide can be seen in Figure 1.

Ashoka Foundation defines a social entrepreneur as an individual who:

conceives of, and relentlessly pursues, a new idea designed to solve societal problems on a very wide scale by changing the systems that undergird the problems (http://www.ashoka.org).

As understood from the definition there are two important points Ashoka is looking for in social entrepreneurship: "impact on a wide societal scale" and "systemic change". As Meyskens et al. (2010) poits out that the:

election procedure is an intensive multi-round process that engages all potential fellows in various types of interviews and site visits. Hundreds of individuals are nominated for the Ashoka Fellowship and only a small percentage of them are elected each year.

The candidates are evaluated based on five criteria: *candidates must have a new idea – a new solution or approach to a social problem, creativity, entrepreneurial quality, social impact of the idea, ethical fiber.*

As mentioned in the background section, the value that social entrepreneurs are creating is not easy to measure or determine because *social entrepreneurs create complex changes in their societies, often*

Figure 1. Ashoka's Network Worldwide (www.ashoka.org)

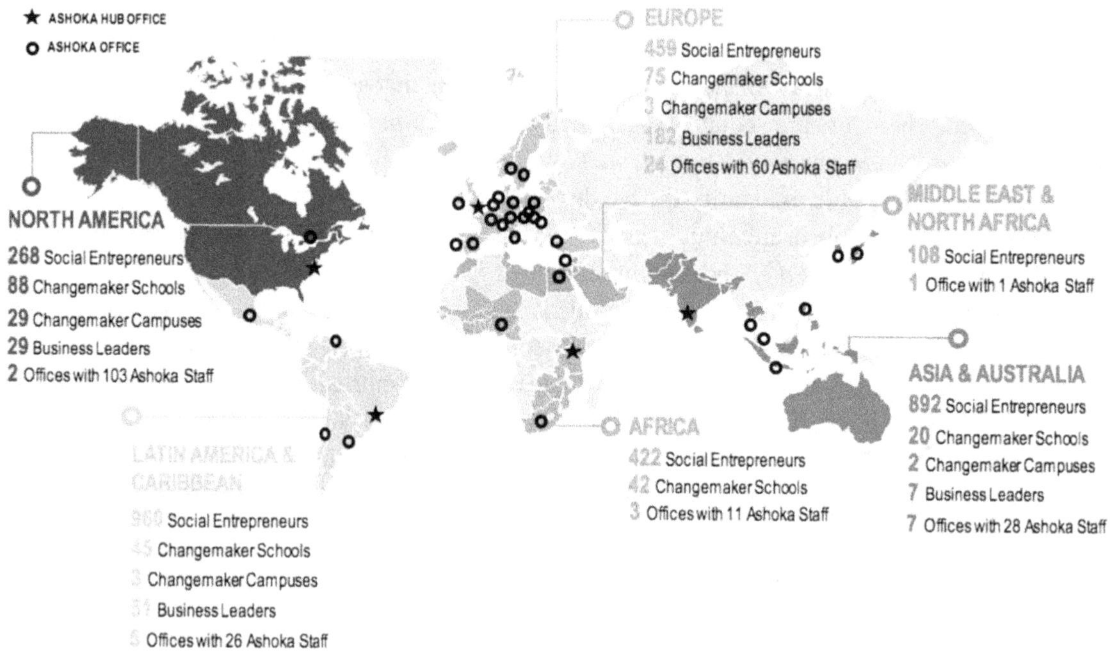

working from multiple angles and on several levels to solve a problem (www.ashoka.org). Ashoka's selection process highlights the importance of systemic change, in this process experienced group of people discuss and decide whether a candidate will cause a system change or not. In 1997, Ashoka developed the 'Measuring Effectiveness' program to better understand the progress of its social entrepreneurs towards systemic social change. Every two years Ashoka is conducting "Impact Studies" and the impact is defined *as the system changes that result from the fellows, ideas and networks*. The Impact Studies that have done in 2013 show that 10 years after their election 83% of Ashoka Fellows pursue their initial objective, 71% of Ashoka Fellows changed a system at a national level in at least one way (www.ashoka.org).

Ashoka Turkey Fellows

Ashoka has been supporting social entrepreneurs in Turkey since 2000. Currently, there are 31 Ashoka Fellows in the country and Table 1 presents the name, year of selection and focus of work information of these fellows. It is possible to summarize the social entrepreneurs' focus of work as; human rights, civic engagement, health, environment and education. After the selection process, Ashoka prepares profile pages of fellows *based on the fellow's application to the program and make these profiles available to the public on the Ashoka website*. The profiles compose of four subsections named 'the idea', 'the problem', 'the strategy', and 'the person'. The idea section explains *the basic ramifications of the venture by mentioning the methods of the venture and the people being served*. The problem section *describes the social issue being addressed and why it is currently not being addressed effectively*. The strategy section give information about:

Table 1. Turkey's Ashoka Fellows

Ashoka Fellow	Year	Focus of Work
Sengul Akcar	2000	Human Rights
Nebahat Akkoc	2000	Human Rights
Nevin Eracar	2001	Healthcare
Yasemin Kilic	2001	Economic Development
Gunesin Aydemir	2003	Environment
Ercan Tutal	2003	Human Rights
Omer Madra	2004	Civic Engagement
Mustafa Sari	2004	Environment
Nasuh Mahruki	2004	Civic Engagement
Ibrahim Betil	2004	Civic Engagement
Nazmi Ilicali	2005	Economic Development
Halime Guner	2006	Civic Engagement
Senem Gul	2006	Economic Development
Berna Yagci	2007	Civic Engagement
Selma Demirelli	2007	Economic Development
Bedriye Hulya	2012	Economic Development
Tulin Akin	2012	Economic Development
Sehnaz Layikel	2012	Healthcare
Serra Titiz	2013	Education
Hayrettin Karaca	2013	Environment
Zafer Kirac	2013	Human Rights
Renay Onur	2014	Civic Engagement
Itir Erhart	2014	Civic Engagement
Azize Leygara	2014	Education
Celal Karadogan	2014	Healthcare
Hacer Foggo	2015	Human Rights
Abdullah Oskay	2015	Civic Engagement
Cagan Sekercioglu	2015	Environment
Burak Ulman	2016	Education
Yasar Adanali	2016	Civic Engagement
Abdulhalim Demir	2016	Healthcare

the strategies employed by the Fellow while describing the goals of the venture and how they are achieved through partnerships, donors, earned income, staff, and volunteers.

The person section describes the social entrepreneur by giving further details about *the educational and professional background and motivations of the Fellows* (Meyskens, Robb-Post, Stamp, Carsrud, & Reynolds, 2010).

This chapter focuses on social entrepreneurs accredited by Ashoka, and specifically, the sample consists of Ashoka fellows active in empowering women. It is well aware that in Turkey the diversity, scope and scale of the society's problems are numerous, however the problems women experiencing may be among the critical ones. Gender inequality and violence against women might be one of the important issues that have to be solved in the country. First, the profiles of all 31 Fellows' have been read and it is understood that 7 Ashoka Fellows in Turkey have been trying to find solutions to women's problems. In this chapter, a social entrepreneur – Sengul Akcar – who focus on women's problem has been selected in order to show how this person try to empower women and create value through changing the society. The following section gives information about Sengul Akcar's value creation process and how her efforts cause others to become social entrepreneurs and Ashoka fellows.

Ashoka Fellow: Sengul Akcar

Sengul Akcar was elected as an Ashoka Fellow in 2000 and also a 'Changemaker of Turkey' by Sabanci Foundation. In some cases majority of the society might not be aware or even accept the inequity. However social entrepreneurs have an ability to perceive things differently than other people. Ms. Akcar realized the problems of low-income women who have been struggling from poverty. In the early 1980's Ms. Akcar has actively participated Turkish feminist groups' activities but she decided to do something for the "women who were often excluded from elitist feminist circles" (www.farkyaratanlar.org). She realized the problems of low-income women, majority of society was unaware of. In order to solve this problem she has established 'Foundation for the Support of Women's Work' (FSWW) in 1986 to improve *the quality of life and economic situation of low-income women to combat poverty and their power to advance their families and societies* (www.kedv.org.tr).

The 1980 coup caused an enormous migration from villages to metropolitan city centers such as Istanbul. These immigrant women were *isolated and treated as second-class citizens*, and even they accept the second-class status. Bugra (2013) indicates that there is a tendency in the society to naturalize traditional gender roles and even women may internalize this inequity. In patriarchal societies, women are expected to raise children and perform household duties. After encountering the problems of low-income women, Ms. Akcar decided to support these women both economically and socially by enabling them *to break from their traditional, limiting roles and to gain financial independence and self-respect by learning nontraditional skills* (http://www.ashoka.org).

Mayoux (2001) acknowledges that women empowerment should be analyzed in different ways: first economic empowerment through supporting women to earn income and to decide how income is spent; second, economic empowerment cause increased well-being of individuals and their families; third economic empowerment social empowerment lead women to change their status in the society which causes social and political empowerment. The programs FSWW offers can be summarized as follows; 'early childhood education', 'economic empowerment', 'capacity development', and 'disaster preparedness' (www.kedv.org.tr). Rather than trying to reach and help women in need individually Ms. Akcar aims to encourage them to actively participate to democratic process. She involves:

women in establishing and strengthening local, national and international networks, utilizing international platforms, creating lobbies, sharing international experiences face-to-face and convening meetings among relevant actors both within as well outside Turkey (http://www.ashoka.org).

Muftuler-Bac (2012) states that in Turkey, women's participation in the workforce is the lowest among the OECD countries because of some barriers in the society. First, prevalent social norms and practices such as stereotype in the society that considers men as the breadwinner and the women as the homemaker prevents women accessing to employment. According to Haugh and Talvar (2016) attitudes towards working-women restrain women's freedom. It is emphasized in the literature that:

increasing women employment in entrepreneurial activity has been associated with the improved status of women, enhanced family and community well-being and broader social gains (Haugh & Talvar, 2016).

In order to empower women and improve their status in the society Ms. Akcar has developed 'Maya' which means 'starter' in Turkish - the first micro-credit project in Turkey. Maya Credit Enterprise empowers low-income women by providing small loans and assistance while establishing their businesses (www.farkyaratanlar.org). FSWW has also a shop called 'Nahil' that sells the products made by the low-income women all around country.

In addition, lack of education and women's responsibilities at home for children and elderly care also indirectly effects low employment rate. One of the critical problems of low-income women is lack of affordable childcare services. Ms. Akcar has launched "Women's and Children's Centers" that provide childcare service to working-women. These centers provide a physical place where women can share and discuss their problems, find solutions to those problems together and *also offer a socially legitimate reason for women to leave their homes to meet with their peers, thereby reducing their isolation* (Yonder, Akcar & Gopalan, 2005).

FSWW has opened 23 Women and Children Centers in 12 cities, over 2,000 women and children now benefit from these centers. A group from Yildiz Technical University has evaluated the impact of these centers and found it suitable for dissemination. The model also gained "best implementation" award from MEDCHILD. The cooperative's success has gained attention internationally, for instance,

The World Bank has recognized the Foundation's success and in 2007 Vanderbilt University accredited its approach to teacher training and day care.

FSWW provided employment to 20 thousand women in 12 cities in Turkey, and also supports women to become entrepreneurs, nearly 3,000 women were supported to establish their own businesses. 'Maya' disbursed 12,200 loans, totaling 12 million Turkish Liras (http://www.ashoka.org). Ms. Akcar is encouraging women to establish cooperatives and become changemakers of the society as she has been. Three Ashoka Fellows in the list – Senem Gul, Berna Yagci and Selma Demirelli – has founded their cooperatives with Ms. Akcar's support.

Alvord et al (2004) claims social entrepreneurs *produce small changes in the short term that reverberate through existing systems to catalyze large changes in the longer term*. Ms. Akcar realized the problems of low-income women, they feel isolated in their homes, treated as second class citizens, and unaware of their rights. In order to cause a social change Ms. Akcar decided to provide physical spaces that offer childcare services and capacity development programs and trainings to women. These centers play a crucial role to change these women's perception about themselves. Social change has many dimensions: changes in people's behavior, the way they organize their social relations and their beliefs, it affects groups and individuals (Ney, Beckmann, Graebnitz, & Mirkovic, 2014). Ms. Akcar encourages women to open new cooperatives and inspires them to become changemakers. It is possible to see in Figure 2

Figure 2. Ashoka fellows supported by Sengul Akcar

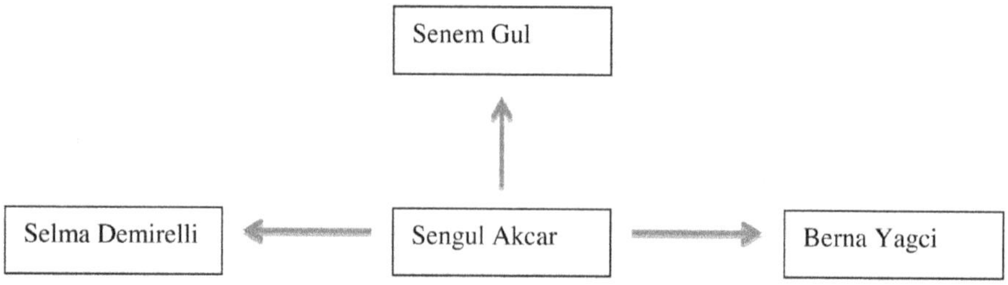

by Ms. Akcar's supporting effort, others become changemakers as well, Senem Gul, Berna Yagci and Selma Demirelli are some examples. Ms Akcar is trying to cause a women movement and change the traditional roles of women in the society by increasing their economic, human and social capital, women are empowered to break free from existing social structures and constraints. These efforts have potential to cause changes in different ways, society's attitudes towards women; power relations within the family, attitudes towards gender discrimination.

Senem Gul

The literature emphasizes that empathy plays a critical role in being a social entrepreneur. Senem Gul, as an immigrant woman by herself, focused on the problems of immigrant women who have been living in Nurtepe where immigrant families have been living mostly. The most disadvantaged residents of the district were women and children. Ms. Gul decided to do something for herself and for other women, she attended training programs at Sengul Akcar's FSWW and afterwards decided to establish a cooperative that provides childcare services and training to women (Interview with Ms. Gul in 2016).

Ms. Gul established 'First Step Women's Cooperative' in 2002 to *encourage women participate in social and economic life* (www.farkyaratanlar.org). The cooperative plays a crucial role to support women to take responsibility of finding solutions to their problems. Children cannot get an education that their counterparts from wealthy families do and they were not able to get pre-school and kindergarten educations. On the other hand, women were isolated in their homes and they did not have any public place to get in touch, at least, with other women (www.ashoka.org). Ms. Gul, added a childcare service in the center *where children can come and go, play and learn, and become better prepared for entry into the school system.* Thus, women found the chance to attend training programs, and develop action plans for specific projects that would improve their communalities. During their trainings, women learnt how to cope with domestic violence, *how to write petitions to local authorities, and practice how to negotiate with government authorities* when they refused to help women (http://www.ashoka.org).

Ms. Gul was elected as an Ashoka Fellow in 2006 and also as a "Changemaker of Turkey" by Sabanci Foundation. Altogether, women tried to improve some state related or municipal services including schools, playgrounds, parks, public transportation, walkways etc. In order to make women work collectively, Ms. Gul followed an agenda that empowered women through education. Following the opening of the first center the second one was also opened within the region. In two centers, today, there are more than 800 active women who work for the cause of the center and this number was just 19 at the beginning. With its huge success, Ms. Gul's centers have given inspiration to others who want to do the same in the different parts of the city of Istanbul. And finally, Ms. Gul's idea has attracted considerable attention from media and from women's groups in 16 different cities in Turkey (http://www.ashoka.org).

Berna Yagci

Being a woman in Mardin, a southeastern city of Turkey, is hard because of various reasons. First of all, there is no public place for women to socialize. Women in Mardin do not have any opportunities to join social and economic life, their education level is quite low and most of them are illiterate and unemployed. In fact women's primary and may be the only responsibility is caring their children and homes. The number of children per woman is high above the averages and having so many children also create a burden for women in Mardin to take other responsibilities on. Finally, the political struggles that took place in the region have made it difficult for people to live a normal life; however, these disadvantaged life conditions affect firstly and mostly women. Thus, because of political and cultural issues, women in Mardin do not find any opportunities to be visible in public sphere; instead, they continue their lives at home by taking only domestic responsibilities that do not produce any economic income. In a nutshell, women in Mardin do not have opportunity to earn money and to get education (www.ashoka.org). Ms. Yagci is a person who defined this problem and offered a sustainable solution by creating women's community centers in southeastern cities of Turkey.

By establishing an official cooperative named Silk Road, Ms. Yagci empowers women to earn income, with the support of Sengul Akcar's FSWW in Silk Road, women produce handicrafts and artisan soaps. In addition to its economic function, Silk Road also provides other opportunities to women. Ms Yagci created a space that had various functions such as a day care center and an education center, where women could learn reading and writing. By getting education and financial freedom women started feeling more empowered and this self-esteem lead them to get in touch with local authorities to negotiate about the conditions that affect their personal and family lives (http://www.ashoka.org).

After its success, Ms Yagci's model started to being replicated in other poor cities of southeast Turkey. The main idea and the target of the model were simple and it was believed that women would change the conditions if they were empowered by giving a communal space complete with childcare, basic education opportunities, and skills training. Ms Yagci freed women from their main responsibility and made possible for them to do something for their own benefit. Ms Yagci also taught women reading and writing with the help of volunteer teacher and also established a library by organizing people to donate books. After being literate, women started feeling more self-confident. Finally, Ms Yagci started looking for other opportunities through which women could get some personal income. The best and the most sustainable way of this were to create jobs. In 2003, thanks to Ms Yagci 's efforts, Turkey's largest olive oil company accepted to donate olive oil as an initial capital investment. By the next year the Silk Road produced 50,000 bars of soap and employed thirty women. Since 2003, the company has been continuing its activities by generating profit (www.ashoka.org). Ms. Yagci realized the problems of women who have been living in Mardin. Because of region's characteristics; socio-cultural norms, political struggles, women do not have opportunity to join social and economic life. Ms Yagci is trying to integrate women into society and improve their status in the region.

Selma Demirelli

After the 1999 earthquake Selma Demirelli started to work as the Duzce – the city suffered significant damage – coordinator for Sengul Akcar's FSWW. She realized that women's most dominant need was housing and economic stability. After the earthquake women lost their homes and husbands who are the breadwinners, Ms. Demirelli decided to develop a strategy to *expand women's rights, property owner-*

ship, and legal claims through a series of empowerment activities. Ms. Demirelli founded a women's housing cooperative named "Water Lily Women's Environment and Cultural Cooperative" in 2002. The goal of the cooperative is to *empower women as property owners with full citizenship and financial stability* (www.farkyaratanlar.org).

In addition the cooperative provides income-generating activities and encourages women to become entrepreneurs. In the cooperative women got trainings about:

how to be entrepreneurial, manage a business, and generate income. "More than one hundred women, many single mothers with several dependents, have gained entrepreneurial skills and generated independent income for the first time in their lives (www.ashoka.org).

The cooperative also offers child day-care services (www.farkyaratanlar.org). Meanwhile, Ms. Demirelli has gotten:

women to register their marriages with the state to provide themselves and their children with state services they would otherwise be denied (for example, entry into schools). This was a simple but critical step towards full citizenship (www.ashoka.org).

The cooperative gained success and media recognition. The second cooperative has been founded with the same goal and Ms. Demirelli continues to expand their work by travelling "to other parts of northern Anatolia to discuss the feasibility of establishing similar ventures in other parts of Turkey". With the help of the cooperative, *single, widowed, and married women* start to hold deeds (www.ashoka.org).

As of today 48 women in Duzce has gained their property rights, 250 women were offered micro-credits, 500 children benefited from pre-school education services and 2.000 women and children received support on early childhood development.

With the help of the cooperative women's life changed a lot and a woman explains the change caused by cooperative as now I can stand on my own feet. I believe in myself whenever I want to go somewhere or do something; and I am very happy about that (www.farkyaratanlar.org). Selma Demirelli was elected as an Ashoka Fellow in 2007 and also as a "Changemaker of Turkey" by Sabanci Foundation.

CONCLUSION

The challenge of this chapter was to identify how social entrepreneurs create social value and cause change in the society. Social entrepreneurs are important actors that try to transform the society, like their business counterparts they also create value. However, the value they are creating is hard to measure and determine. Social entrepreneurs create social value through creating systemic changes in the society. These people feel an urge to take action when they confront a problem or unsatisfied need. The impact of social entrepreneur might not be seen easily since they are working from multiple angles and on several levels to solve a problem.

Most of the studies on social entrepreneurship have been based on samples from outside Turkey, relatively little is known about how social entrepreneurs in Turkey create social value and change. The social entrepreneur and the others she influenced in this chapter present powerful ideas in order to solve critical problems. The initial motivation might be barely visible, but in the long run they gain strength as their influence reaches an inflection point and, achieve transformation. Cultural norms still limit women's rights and engagement in the workplace. The social entrepreneurs in this chapter have tried to build a new system that empowers women to change the way women are treated. They are dealing with gender issues by integrating women into society as productive and respected members. Their action is directed towards social change, in some cases they are trying to change attitudes towards women, in some cases they aim to raise awareness of women's problems and put pressure in order to influence policy, in some cases they just try to transform the daily lives of women. Some of them have created physical spaces to empower women and also encourage them to become changemakers. Giving opportunities to women, improving their status in the society might trigger social and cultural change in the long period. Over time empowering women transforms the changing attitudes towards women's roles and status more generally.

Bornstein (2007) claims that *every change begins with a vision and a decision to take action*. The stories of social entrepreneurs are impressive and inspiring for others. They show just how much a person can cause transformative change in society. Social entrepreneurs are planting new ideas into people's minds and these small ideas cause drastic changes. The cases presented in this chapter demonstrate that social entrepreneurs use diverse approaches of creating social change. They try to make small changes in the short term however these efforts have potential to achieve significant results in the long term. Through social entrepreneurs' efforts women in Turkey were empowered economically, personally, socially and politically. The problems women are facing are generally related with social norms and in order to eliminate these problems social transformation is needed. Social entrepreneurs are changing women's inequity by giving training to women, encouraging them to enter labor market and changing women's traditional gender roles.

REFERENCES

Alvord, S. H., Brown, L. D., & Letts, C. W. (2004). Social entrepreneurship and societal transformation: An exploratory study. *The Journal of Applied Behavioral Science*, *40*(3), 260–282. doi:10.1177/0021886304266847

Austin, J., Stevenson, H., & Wei-Skillern, J. (2006). Social and Commercial Entrepreneurship: Same, Different, or Both? *Entrepreneurship Theory and Practice*, *30*(1), 1–22. doi:10.1111/j.1540-6520.2006.00107.x

Bacq, S., Hartog, C., Hoogendorn, B., & Lepoutre, J. (2011). *Social and Commercial Entrepreneurship: Exploring Individual and Organizational Characteristics*. Scales Research Reports, EIM Business and Policy Research.

Bacq, S., & Janssen, F. (2011). The multiple faces of social entrepreneurship: A review of definitional issues based on geographical and thematic criteria. *Entrepreneurship and Regional Development*, *23*(5-6), 373–403. doi:10.1080/08985626.2011.577242

Bornstein, D. (1998). Changing the World on a Shoestring. *Atlantic Monthly*, *281*(1), 34–39.

Bornstein, D. (2007). *How to Change the World: Social Entrepreneurs and the Power of New Ideas*. Oxford University Press.

Bugra, A. (2013). Revisiting the Wollstonecraft dilemma in the context of conservative liberalism: The case of female employment in Turkey. *Social Politics*, *21*(1), 148–166. doi:10.1093p/jxt001

Cajaiba-Santana, G. (2014). Social innovation: Moving the field forward. A conceptual framework. *Technological Forecasting and Social Change*, *82*, 42–51. doi:10.1016/j.techfore.2013.05.008

Dees, J. G. (1998). *The meaning of social entrepreneurship*. Academic Press.

Drayton, W. (2006). Everyone a changemaker: Social entrepreneurship's ultimate goal. *Innovations*, *1*(1), 80–96. doi:10.1162/itgg.2006.1.1.80

Emerson, J. (2003). The Belended Value Proposition: Integrating Social and Financial Returns. *California Management Review*, *45*(4), 120–132. doi:10.2307/41166187

Haugh, H. M., & Talwar, A. (2016). Linking social entrepreneurship and social change: The mediating role of empowerment. *Journal of Business Ethics*, *133*(4), 643–658. doi:10.100710551-014-2449-4

Kickul, J., & Lyons, T. S. (2012). Measuring social impact. *Understanding social entrepreneurship: The relentless pursuit of mission in an ever changing world*, 176-200.

Maguire, S., Hardy, C., & Lawrence, T. B. (2004). Institutional entrepreneurship in emerging fields: HIV/AIDS treatment advocacy in Canada. *Academy of Management Journal*, *47*(5), 657–679. doi:10.2307/20159610

Mair, J., & Marti, I. (2004). Social Entrepreneurship Research: A Source of Explanation, Prediction, and Delight. *Journal of World Business*, *41*(1), 36–44. doi:10.1016/j.jwb.2005.09.002

Mair, J., & Noboa, E. (2003). *Social Entrepreneurship: How Intentions to Create a Social Enterprise Get Formed.* IESE Working Paper, WP No:521.

Mair, J., Robinson, J., & Hockerts, K. (Eds.). (2006). *Social Entrepreneurship*. New York: Palgrave Macmillan. doi:10.1057/9780230625655

Mayoux, L. (2001). Tackling the down side: Social capital, women's empowerment and micro-finance in Cameroon. *Development and Change*, *32*(3), 435–464. doi:10.1111/1467-7660.00212

Meyskens, M., Robb-Post, C., Stamp, J. A., Carsrud, A. L., & Reynolds, P. D. (2010). Social Ventures From A Resource-Based Perspective: An Exploratory Study Assessing Global Ashoka Fellows. *Entrepreneurship Theory and Practice*, *34*(4), 661–680. doi:10.1111/j.1540-6520.2010.00389.x

Muftuler-Bac, M. (2012). *Gender equality in Turkey*. Academic Press.

Mulgan, G. (2006). The Process of Social Innovation. *Innovations*, *1*(2), 145–162. doi:10.1162/itgg.2006.1.2.145

Netting, F. E., O'connor, M. K., & Fauri, D. P. (2007). Planning Transformative Programs: Challenges for Advocates in Translating Change Processes into Effectiveness Measures. *Administration in Social Work*, *31*(4), 59–81. doi:10.1300/J147v31n04_06

Ney, S., Beckmann, M., Graebnitz, D., & Mirkovic, R. (2014). Social entrepreneurs and social change: Tracing impacts of social entrepreneurship through ideas, structures and practices. *International Journal of Entrepreneurial Venturing*, *6*(1), 51–68. doi:10.1504/IJEV.2014.059405

Nicholls, A. (2006). *Social Entrepreneurship: New Models of Sustainable Change*. Oxford, UK: Oxford University Press.

Nicholls, A., & Murdock, A. (2012). *The Nature of Social Innovation, Blurring Boundaries to Reconfigure Markets*. Palgrave Macmillan.

Partzsch, L., & Ziegler, R. (2011). Social entrepreneurs as change agents: A case study on power and authority in the water sector. *International Environmental Agreement: Politics, Law and Economics*, *11*(1), 63–83. doi:10.100710784-011-9150-1

Peredo, A. M., & McLean, M. (2006). Social Entrepreneurship: A Critical Review of The Concept. *Journal of World Business*, *41*(1), 56–65. doi:10.1016/j.jwb.2005.10.007

Prabhu, G. N. (1999). Social Entrepreneurial Leadership. *Career Development International*, *4*(3), 140–145. doi:10.1108/13620439910262796

Praszkier, R., & Nowak, A. (2011). *Social Entrepreneurship: Theory and Practice*. Cambridge University Press. doi:10.1017/CBO9781139049467

Shier, M. L., & Handy, F. (2015). Social Change Efforts of Direct Service Nonprofits: The Role of Funding and Collaborations in Shaping Social Innovations. *Human Service Organizations, Management, Leadership & Governance*, *39*(1), 6–24. doi:10.1080/23303131.2014.973623

Sundaramurthy, C., Musteen, M., & Randel, A. E. (2013). Social Value Creation: A Qualitative Study of Indian Social Entrepreneurs. *Journal of Developmental Entrepreneurship*, *18*(02), 1350011. doi:10.1142/S1084946713500118

Surie, G., & Groen, A. (2017). The Importance of Social Entrepreneurship in National Systems of Innovation – An Introduction. *Technological Forecasting and Social Change*, *121*, 181–183. doi:10.1016/j.techfore.2017.05.010

Trivedi, C., & Stokols, D. (2011). Social enterprises and corporate enterprises: Fundamental differences and defining features. *The Journal of Entrepreneurship*, *20*(1), 1–32. doi:10.1177/097135571002000101

Turker, D., & Vural, C. A. (2017). Embedding Social Innovation Process into the Institutional Context: Voids or Supports. *Technological Forecasting and Social Change*, *119*, 98–113. doi:10.1016/j.techfore.2017.03.019

Venkataraman, S. (1997). The Distinctive Domain of Entrepreneurship Research. *Advances in Entrepreneurship, Firm, Emergence, and Growth*, *3*(1), 119–138.

Waddock, S. A., & James, E. P. (1991). Social Entrepreneurs and Catalytic Change. *Public Administration Review*, *51*(5), 393–401. doi:10.2307/976408

Yonder, A., Akcar, S., & Gopalan, P. (2005). *Women's Participation in Disaster Relief and Recovery*. New York: Population Council.

Young, R. (2006). For What it is Worth: Social Value and the Future of Social Entrepreneurship. *Social Entrepreneurship: New Models of Sustainable Social Change*, 56-73.

Zahra, S. A., Gedajlovic, E., Neubaum, D. O., & Shulman, J. M. (2009). A typology of social entrepreneurs: Motives, search processes and ethical challenges. *Journal of Business Venturing*, *24*(5), 519–532. doi:10.1016/j.jbusvent.2008.04.007

ADDITIONAL READING

Auerswald, P. (2009). Creating Social Value. *Stanford Social Innovation Review*.

Brooks, A. (2008). *Social Entrepreneurship: A Modern Approach to Social Value Creation*. Upper Saddle River, NJ: Prentice-Hall.

Daskalaki, M., Hjorth, D., & Mair, J. (2015). Are Entrepreneurship, Communities, and Social Transformation Related? *Journal of Management Inquiry*, *24*(4), 419–423. doi:10.1177/1056492615579012

Dees, G., Anderson, B., & Wei-Skillern, J. (2003). Scaling Social Impact. *Stanford Social Innovation Review*, 4.

Dees, J. G. (2003). Social entrepreneurship is about innovation and impact, not income. *Social edge*.

Dees, J. G. (2007). Taking social entrepreneurship seriously. *Society*, *44*(3), 24–31. doi:10.1007/BF02819936

Di Domenico, M., Haugh, H., & Tracey, P. (2010). Social Bricolage: Theorizing Social Value Creation in Social Enterprises. *Entrepreneurship Theory and Practice*, *34*(4), 681–703. doi:10.1111/j.1540-6520.2010.00370.x

Drayton, W. (2002). The citizen sector: Becoming as entrepreneurial and competitive as business. *California Management Review*, *44*(3), 120–132. doi:10.2307/41166136

El Ebrashi, R. (2013). Social entrepreneurship theory and sustainable social impact. *Social Responsibility Journal*, *9*(2), 188–209. doi:10.1108/SRJ-07-2011-0013

Guclu, A., Dees, J. G., & Anderson, B. (2002). The Process of Social Entrepreneurship: Creating Opportunities Worhty of Serious Pursuit, Center for the Advancement of Social Entrepreneurship, 1.

Harding, R. (2004). Social enterprise: The new economic engine? *Business Strategy Review*, *15*(4), 39–43. doi:10.1111/j.0955-6419.2004.00338.x

Hoogendoorn, B., Pennings, E., & Thurik, R. (2010). What Do We Know About Social Entrepreneurship: An Analysis of Empirical Research. *International Review of Entrepreneurship*, *8*(2), 71–112.

Jiao, H. (2011). A conceptual model for social entrepreneurship directed toward social impact on society. *Social Enterprise Journal*, *7*(2), 130–149. doi:10.1108/17508611111156600

Kanter, R. M. (1999). From Spare Change to Real Change: The Social Sector as Beta Site for Business Innovation. *Harvard Business Review*, *77*(3), 121–132. PMID:10387574

Lepoutre, J., Justo, R., Terjesen, S., & Bosma, N. (2013). Designing a global standardized methodology for measuring social entrepreneurship activity: The Global Entrepreneurship Monitor social entrepreneurship study. *Small Business Economics*, *40*(3), 693–714. doi:10.100711187-011-9398-4

Mair, J., & Marti, I. (2007). Entrepreneurship for social impact: encouraging market access in rural Bangladesh. *Corporate Governance: The international journal of business in society, 7*(4), 493-501.

Ormiston, J., & Seymour, R. (2011). Understanding value creation in social entrepreneurship: The importance of aligning mission, strategy and impact measurement. *Journal of Social Entrepreneurship*, *2*(2), 125–150. doi:10.1080/19420676.2011.606331

Sagawa, S., & Segal, E. (2000). Common interest, common good: Creating value through business and social sector partnerships. *California Management Review*, *42*(2), 105–122. doi:10.2307/41166035

Seelos, C., & Mair, J. (2005). Social entrepreneurship: Creating new business models to serve the poor. *Business Horizons*, *48*(3), 241–246. doi:10.1016/j.bushor.2004.11.006

Sharir, M., & Lerner, M. (2006). Gauging the Success of Social Ventures Initiated by Individual Social Entrepreneurs. *Journal of World Business*, *41*(1), 1, 6–20. doi:10.1016/j.jwb.2005.09.004

Shaw, E., & Carter, S. (2007). Social entrepreneurship: Theoretical antecedents and empirical analysis of entrepreneurial processes and outcomes. *Journal of Small Business and Enterprise Development*, *14*(3), 418–434. doi:10.1108/14626000710773529

Smith, B. R., & Stevens, C. E. (2010). Different types of social entrepreneurship: The role of geography and embeddedness on the measurement and scaling of social value. *Entrepreneurship and Regional Development*, *22*(6), 575–598. doi:10.1080/08985626.2010.488405

Srivetbodee, S., Igel, B., & Kraisornsuthasinee, S. (2017). Creating Social Value Through Social Enterprise Marketing: Case Studies from Thailand's Food-Focused Social Entrepreneurs. *Journal of Social Entrepreneurship*, *8*(2), 201–224. doi:10.1080/19420676.2017.1371630

Thompson, J., Alvy, G., & Lees, A. (2000). Social entrepreneurship–a new look at the people and the potential. *Management Decision*, *38*(5), 328–338. doi:10.1108/00251740010340517

Thompson, J., & Doherty, B. (2006). The diverse world of social enterprise: A collection of social enterprise stories. *International Journal of Social Economics*, *33*(5/6), 361–375. doi:10.1108/03068290610660643

KEY TERMS AND DEFINITIONS

Social Change: Social change is the systemic transformation in the organization of society in patterns of thought, behavior, social relationships, institutions, and social structure over time, with the use of methods that empower the society and enable the unfolding of potentialities inherent in the system.

Social Entrepreneur: A person who creates social value by stimulating social change.

Social Innovation: A novel mechanism that increases the welfare of the individuals who adopt it compared with the status quo.

Social Value: Social value enhances well-being for the earth and its living organisms.

Chapter 17
Public Services Procurement:
Third Sector Social Enterprises Perspectives

Chi Maher
St Mary's University, UK

ABSTRACT

The chapter examines small third sector social enterprises' (TSSEs) perspective in gaining access to public services contracts. The UK government aims to increase, the role of social enterprise as a vehicle to deliver public services directly to citizens and local communities in areas such as housing, welfare-to-work, education, health, and social care. To understand TSSEs' experiences of gaining access to public services contracts, face-to-face interviews were conducted with managers and chief executive officers (CEOs) using an interview guide. Empirical evidence obtained suggests that some procurement policies and processes are impacting on small TSSEs' organizational development, growth, management, and career development of staff. The qualitative findings of the study add to new knowledge, and help to explain challenges facing small TSSEs in the changing context of public services procurement process.

INTRODUCTION

Social enterprises are businesses that trade and use their profits to bring social, economic and environmental benefits to our society; they are designed to meet social needs as well as to achieve commercial viability (Crossan, Ibbotson, & Bell, 2011). As such, they are largely independent of both the public and private sectors. There are several approaches to the development of social enterprises; such as: (1) the 'Social Innovation' approach; (2) Earned income approach; (3) Social businesses social approach (Lecy & Young, 2014). The 'social innovation' approach considers innovation as a central focus of social enterprises, therefore, social enterprises should attempt to achieve some form of social goals by implementing innovative ways and new ideas to tackle social issues. The key concept of this approach, involves continuous innovation, recognizing and pursuing opportunities to serve the social mission and create and sustain social value. ACS, Boardman, and McNeely (2013) argue that social value creation through the social innovation as a method of creating social value as oppose to beneficial exchanges.

DOI: 10.4018/978-1-5225-5687-9.ch017

Therefore, social enterprises which seek business solutions to social problems must foster innovation, thus, identifying innovative and effective initiatives on resolving social market failures and creating opportunities to add social value, maximize social impact and make a societal change (Nicholls, 2006; Di Domenico, Haugh & Tracey, 2010).

The 'Earned Income' approach is related to the use of commercial activities by third sector organizations for survival. Boschee and McClurg (2003) argue that 'earned income strategies' is the opportunity in which non-profit organizations can earn an income concurrently with their existing activities. Opportunities for 'earned incomes' can range from tiny exploitative profit turning activities to aggressive exploitations in order to achieve higher gains in total revenue from earned incomes. Kerlin (2006) indicates that the 'earned income' approach gained particular importance throughout the 1970s and 1980s in the USA. Kerlin (2006) reported that from 1982 to 2002, the U.S saw commercial revenue of non-profit organizations increase by 219%. Defourny and Nyssens (2012) argues that non-profits began to develop 'social enterprise' concepts as a response to the withdrawal of state funding during the late 1970s; which resulted in reduction in welfare and governmental funding. This led third sector organizations to seek for alternative methods of funding such as commercial activities. The change triggered third sector organizations to approach consultancy firms for advice and support for their growing interest towards business ventures.

Teasdale (2012) categories 'earned income' as a social enterprise discourse and identifies that this approach incorporates the fundamentals behind theory resource dependence, which resides within both strategic management and organizational theory. Drees and Heugens (2013) define resource dependency theory (RDT) as a longstanding framework which attempts to understand organizational-environmental relations. RDT assumes that all organizations are critically dependent on other organizations for the provision of vital resources, thus often a form of reciprocal relationship occurs between organizations. Thus, organizations are continuously challenged and affected by the internal and external environment in which they work in. As a result, they manage resources effectively in order to maximize strategic control over crucial external forces (Drees & Heugens, 2013). Therefore, third sector social enterprises that adopt 'earned income strategies' and 'social purpose business ventures' are effectively influencing their environments in order to provide the resources required to meet their strategic objectives.

The 'social purpose business ventures' approach is an alternative approach which differs to *earned income strategies* in terms of purpose, expectations and structures (Boschee & McClurg, 2003). Social purpose business ventures are often larger scale ventures with more ambitious goals. *Social purpose business venture* is often a step to increasing revenue with the purpose of growth and increasing profitably of a non-profit's organization. Within this approach third sector organizations often create a complete separate entity which resembles a third sector organizational structure with a separate workforce and board of directors.

The Transforming Government Procurement Strategy (HM Treasury 2007), launched as part of the 2007 Comprehensive Spending Review, was initiated to raise procurement standards, develop the skills of procurement professionals, drive value for money through collaborative procurement and improving the delivery of projects. However, in the UK the 2008 recession led to a belief that the state is not an efficient provider of social services, coupled with the promotion of notions of self-sufficiency for communities and community organizations. This led to an increasing interest in social enterprise as a "third way" for the provision of social services (Martikke & Moxham, 2010; Maher, 2015b). Although there has been acceleration in the development of social enterprises in the UK, most are small (Social Enterprise UK, 2016). Nevertheless, they make important contributions to the economy and are embedded in their local communities. This 'embeddedness' brings with it several advantages to their constituents, such as, responsiveness to the needs and priorities of local communities, providing stability and flexibility and responding to local needs. They have the ability to identify and understand the needs of local people and their community; shape their services around the service users' immediate needs, working 'holistically' (Maher, 2017c) or in a 'person-centered' way that is responsive to individuals' needs.

Social enterprises build social capital (creating local jobs and volunteering opportunities), which is important to people's well-being; bridge social capital (bringing people together based on common interests or shared need), which helps people to 'get ahead' in life; and link social capital (connecting people and/or organizations whose relationship involves a hierarchy or power differential) both within particular communities and between communities, and including national and local agencies (Botham & Setkova, 2004; Lyon & Sepulveda, 2012; Maher, 2015a).

These organizations can also bring significant long-lasting and sustainable positive changes at a community level, supporting the life of local people (Maher, 2017c).They are often valued by the state and service recipients because of the distinctive approaches and values they bring to the provision of social, health, educational and environmental services. However, the increasingly competitive environment in which small social enterprises are working, brought about by changes in public policies, particularly competitive procurement processes, has brought success for a few small TSSE's who gained new funding that enabled their organizations to expand and develop new services; but for many small TSSE's this has been very challenging (Smallbone, Evans, Ekanem & Butters, 2001; Maher, 2015c).

LITERATURE REVIEW

Public service procurement refers to the process by which public authorities, such as government departments, Local Authorities, National Health Service, purchase work, goods or services from organizations (Office of the UK Deputy Prime Minister / Local Government Association 2003). Public procurement operates in an environment of increasingly intense scrutiny driven by competition, program reviews, public and political expectations for service improvements. Public procurement process is understood to benefit citizens from getting value for money, and on time delivery of services (Baines, Hardill & Wilson, 2011).

The Development of Public Procurement in the UK

After a review of public procurement in the UK in 1984, the government established that value for money was the primary objective for government procurement policy (Cabinet Office, 1984). In 1995 a White Paper was published setting out the government procurement strategy this was followed by a review of procurement efficiency in1998 (HM Treasury and Cabinet Office, 1998) and in 1999 a further review of procurement strategy was published (Gershon, 1999) alongside the government's Modernizing Government White Paper. Each emphasized the need for more co-operation between government departments, and collaboration with service providers. The policy context concerning public service procurement in the UK is based on a set of guiding principles, including transparency, competitiveness, accountability, efficiency, legality, and integrity, that have the ultimate aim of supporting the delivery of *best value for money* in public procurement (HM Treasury, 2000).

In 2002 the UK government introduced procurement processes with the sector as the main mechanism to coordinate and ensure service delivery and accountability to government over the funding period, procurement is presented to offer the best mechanism for securing the government's risk (this means that contract management cost must be borne by the service provider) (HM Treasury, 2002). For the government, procurement enables market-based competition, and opens opportunity for a wide range of suppliers (HM Treasury, 2005). Public procurement in the UK is governed by the Public Contracts Regulations 2006 (for England, Wales and Northern Ireland) and the Public Contracts (Scotland) Regulations 2006. To maintain the supply chain of services, it is also important to offer contacts that breaks down barriers to entry on the 'government market' (Cabinet Office, 2006b); particularly for small TSSE's and provides best value for money.

Best Value

Best value for money is defined as 'the optimum combination of whole life cost and quality (or fitness for purpose) to meet the customer's requirements' (HM Treasury, 2000). The Best Value process is based on the UK government's efforts to assess quality and value within public services contract with consideration to "social value". The Audit Commission is the independent body responsible for ensuring value for money in local governments in England. Their remit is to raising standards in financial management and financial reporting; encouraging improvement in public services and promoting high standards of governance and accountability. Separate arrangements are in place in Scotland, Wales and Northern Ireland.

The Best Value process retains an emphasis on competition where appropriate; there is also a requirement to take the views of service users and suppliers into account, and to consult local taxpayers, service users and the business community. Thus there is a mix of priorities – commercial, regulatory and socio-economic – highlighted by Geddes and Martin (2000): *there is no simple choice to be made between cost reduction and service improvement.*

The sector organizations had to accept greater scrutiny of their activities along with the demands of funders to deliver services which they regarded as value for money. Organizations receiving funding from the government to deliver services must demonstrate outcome measures based on the cost effectiveness of their service provision and have a clear strategy for maximizing income from other sources in order to reduce the need for government funding in the long-term (Munoz, 2009). Therefore, the sector organizations that seek to sustain themselves in the longer term must be responsive to the government demands and priorities, over which they have little control (Bartlett, 2009).

The 1979 to 1997 UK Conservative Party, committed to reducing the role of the state, particularly in relation to social welfare provision. This was reflected in the government cuts in welfare funding, and the shift from grants to contracts. The government changes to welfare agenda provided opportunities for sector organizations including social enterprises to deliver more social welfare services.

The Government encouraged these organizations to bid for contracts to deliver welfare services (such as day programs for mental health, drug and alcohol clients and their careers) (Baines, Hardill, & Wilson, 2011; Gojkovic, Mills, & Meek, 2011; Lewis, 2005). This led to the implementation of the 1990 National Health Service and Community Care Act in April 1993 which resulted in the a reduction in grant funding to organizations in the sector and to the introduction of the use of formal procurement processes to govern funding flows to the sector organizations .The Government made explicit recommendations that these organizations should take a greater role in delivering public services with formal contractual arrangements (Funding Commission, 2010).

Whilst the use of formal procurement processes to govern funding to the sector aims to promote accountability and reduce risk, it also focuses only on the direct outcomes for service users with little or no consideration for developing organizational long-term infrastructure (Baines, Hardill, & Wilson, 2011). For the government, using contracts means that the same process is adopted for contracting-out service provision for all providers, irrespective of whether they are private sector or third sector social enterprise providers. In 1998 New Labour (the government) introduced policies such as Compact (that suggested that the state and the sector would develop a closer partnership relationship (Cabinet Office, 2010; Alcock, 2010; Dickinson, Allen, Macmillan, & Glasby, 2012).

Compact

The Compact document framework outlines a shared vision, values and commitment by both the government and the third sector organisations to work in partnership; and to build a positive relationship in the development and delivery of public services by a commissioning process (Home Office, 1998).

The compact set out the agreement between government and the sector in to improve their relationship for mutual advantage and mainstream the sector into the Government's policy agenda (Alcock, 2010). It defined how government and sector organisations should engage, and endorsed the fundamental importance of sector organizations to the well-being of society and their role in public policy creation and service delivery.

The UK Compact version was internationally unique in emphasizing its role in facilitating good relations between the state and the third sector involvement in public service delivery (White, 2011); and as a response to declining relationship between the third sector and state caused by contracting-out of public services under the 1979-97 Conservative Governments . The Home Secretary and representatives of the third sector signed the Compact document in 1998 (Home Office, 1998; National Audit Office, 2005; Cabinet Office, 2010). As a result, an increasing number of the sector organizations engaged in contracting with the government for the first time. Under the new contacting process, the sector organizations had to accept competitive tendering processes and deal with the pressure of balancing the needs of service users, demands of the funders and the needs of their staff (Bovaird & Davis, 2011). The government further introduced several procurement policies such as, Payment by Result (PbR) schemes to allow commissioners to transfer practical and financial risk to providers; by linking payment to defined results (Battye & Sunderland, 2011; Boyle, 2011; Battye, 2015).

Payment by Result (PbR)

PbR is usually linked to successful outcome, with no payment for progress before the completion of commissioned services. This method of commissioning is unfavourable to small TSSEs as they are less likely to have extra funds to cover the period between starting work and receiving payment. Policy makers and commissioners have increasingly seen this particular payment system as an important lever for influencing provider behaviour to comply with contract agreements (Battye & Sunderland, 2011; Bovaird & Löffler, 2009).

The provider is often expected to cover early start-up and running costs until payments for success reimburse this outlay. This transfers the financial risk of setting up and proving a service from the commissioner to the provider. However, the Audit Commission emphasizes that it is not possible to transfer all reputational, practical and financial risks. Commissioners should retain their responsibility for local citizens receiving a good quality and effective service. Sheil and Breidenbach-Roe (2014) argue that although the government claims that PbR is an opportunity for the sector organizations to show their innovative service delivery practices, in reality the government PbR contracts have often favored the largest providers.

During 2001 the government launched a strategy for an "enabling environment". The strategy document included two additional sections, one titled 'making social enterprises better businesses' and then concluded with 'establishing the value of social enterprise' (DTI, 2002).

The government set out its strategic vision for social enterprise and cited it as a means through which five key policy objectives can be achieved:

1. Helping to drive up productivity and competitiveness.
2. Contributing to socially inclusive wealth creation.
3. Enabling individuals and communities to work towards regenerating their local neighborhoods.
4. Showing new ways to deliver and reform public services.
5. Helping to develop an inclusive society and active citizenship (DTI, 2002).

The Government explained the characteristics of social enterprise that it valued as:

being able to gain independence and autonomy through trading; possessing entrepreneurial, innovative, and risk-taking behavior; adopting flexible and adaptable practices; maintaining a focus on customers and community; promoting stakeholder engagement; encourage democratic participative management; delivering socially and/or environmental and financial benefits; and were deemed financially viable gaining their income from selling goods and services (DTI, 2002).

The government added that many social enterprises are already showing how this can be done. But we recognize that they are currently only a small part of our economy. We want to build on this foundation and create an environment in which more people feel they are able to start and grow such businesses. Through this strategy,

we aim to provide a more enabling environment, to help social enterprises become better businesses, and ensure that their value becomes better understood (DTI, 2002).

The Department of Trade and Industry (DTI) produced an extensive toolkit in 2003 to facilitate social enterprises' successful tender for government contracts. DTI 2003 Toolkit for Social Enterprises is a guide to social enterprises across the UK on access to information and advice about how to win government or public-sector business; with was helpful to social enterprises that are already engaged in or would like to tender for a public contract. The Toolkit describes the procurement process and information on various stages of the procurement process and things for enterprises to consider before and during the procurement period. The aim is for those bidding for contracts to have the best information about risks and obstacles; and to consider how and whether to embark on the route of public procurement contract (DT1, 2003).

Scowen (2004) suggests strategies that procurement offices can implement to promote contracting with social enterprises, including: adding clauses in tender documents on the approach to social enterprise contractors; advertising contracts on councils' websites' (Scowen, 2004) as directed by the UK's 2004 National Procurement Strategy. The UK's 2004 National Procurement Strategy requests that all councils are expected to publish a:

selling to the council guide on their websites, to encourage business with a diverse range of suppliers.. building the supplier base... to improve the quality of services delivered locally (Hope, 2004).

Compact Re-Visited

In 2006 a new 'Commission for the Compact' was established, to act as a regulator-cum-advice centre for parties to local Compact agreements. The Commission for the Compact' document sets out a framework agreement that outlines a shared vision, values and commitment by both the government and the sector. The promotion of partnership with the sector in public services enables third sector organizations to be discursively constituted as a natural participant in government policy as generic 'service delivery organization[s]' (Cabinet Office, 2007). In addition, in order to ensure accountability to government over the funding period contracts are said to offer the best mechanism for securing the government's risk (i.e. contracts mean that cost management must be borne by the service provider). Contracts are also used as a disciplinary mechanism over the wide range of relationships that exist under the term of 'partnership', between the sector organisations and commissioning authorities (HM Treasury, 2006a).

In 2010 the Conservative-led Coalition Government came to power and published a strategy document 'Building a stronger civil society'. This strategy sets out a vision for the sector to grow, and in particular to take over from government the running of more public services. It sets out the government's plans for social enterprises to be involved in the delivery of health services, social care and return to work projects for the long term unemployed. The Coalition Government initiated Compact Voice to re-enforce their pledge to work in partnership with the third sector (including TESS's). Compact Voice is an agreement aims to ensure that the Government and the sector work effectively in partnership to achieve common goals and outcomes for the benefit of communities;

improving and delivering better, more responsive public services can only be done with the help of the sector; and empowering communities can only work where the skills, enthusiasm and commitment of the sector is harnessed (David Cameroon, Compact Voice 2010).

The commitments stated that the 'Compact Voice' aim to set the foundation for a productive relationship between the Government and the sector organizations in the procurement process. Yet, the Coalition Government Comprehensive Spending Review (CSR) of October 2010 announced the biggest public spending cut in six decades. Between 2010/2011 and 2014/2015, £18 billion worth of cuts were outlined in welfare and tax credits of which £53 billion were passed onto local authorities and government departments (NVCO, 2016). These cuts affected several small third sector social enterprises organizational development and staff redundancies followed (Maher, 2015a; 2017b). This discernibly devastates the government's pledge to work in partnership with the sector.

Procurement Action Plan

The use of procurement to address several government agendas was made explicit in the 'Policy through Procurement Action Plan' (OGC, 2010). The procurement policy stresses that:

public authorities will need to be innovative in their procurement practices and engage suppliers in developing innovative, high quality and cost-effective solutions to the delivery of works, services and goods. (OGC, 2010).

In August 2010 a review on government efficiency was published. The report noted and identified a number of inefficiencies associated with government procurement, including large differences in prices for similar basic commodities, multiple contracts with the same organizations by different departments at different prices, etc. Such inefficiencies were, according to the Review, due to poor and inaccurate data, inconsistent commercial skills across departments, the government acting as a series of independent departments rather than as one organization and the lack of a clear mandate for centralized procurement (Green, 2010). Following the Efficiency Review, Frances Maude, Minister at the Cabinet Office, giving evidence to the House of Lords (2011), reported that the procurement process was overly burdensome:

the very process-heavy approach to procurement has resulted in massively highly specified tender documents with prequalification that has been very demanding.

The Business Secretary of the Coalition Cabinet Vince Cable (2010-2015) stated that:

across many sectors, from health and transport to education and defence, the public sector can play a vital role as a first customer for innovative products and services.

The Growth Strategy (BIS, 2011) made the case for the public sector acting as an intelligent and demanding customer, and highlighted its potential for:

enabling innovative solutions to addressing social challenges and improving service delivery, supporting the development and growth of innovative businesses and stimulating wider economic growth (BIS, 2011).

The Business Secretary of the Coalition argued that the government, should shift the emphasis in procurement away from excessive formalism and legalism, and should instead act as *a responsible customer, developing a collaborative and considered long-term relationship with our supply chain.* Frances Maude added:

We will not seek to mandate how local government procures. ... We will be quite mandatory about central government ... but we will not seek to impose that on local government nor on the increasingly mixed economy in the NHS (House of Lords, 2011).

The House of Lords (2011) concluded that:

The Government's laissez faire approach to the dissemination of best practice in procurement from central to local government appears to be overly optimistic.

They recommended that a system of dissemination be put in place to share examples of procurement of innovative solutions across central and local government as well as mechanisms to assess its effectiveness.

Public Contracts Regulations

In 2015, the UK government introduced the Public Contracts Regulations 2015, which aims to promote opportunities for the sector organizations within the process of public service procurement through the reservation of certain public contracts specifically for social enterprises and mutuals; and the removal of PQQs (pre-qualification questionnaire)for procurement below EU thresholds (EU procurement thresholds include: Supply and service contracts awarded by central government bodies subject to the WTO GPA, the threshold is £111,676. Supply and service contracts awarded by other contracting authorities, the threshold is £172,514 and Works contracts, subsidized works contracts and works concession contracts is £4,322,012 (European Commission, 2012). It is likely that these thresholds might change in the future.

Public Contracts Regulations 2015 reinforces the government's agenda to provide the third sector organizations and TSSE's opportunities to play a bigger role within the public procurement. The British Council (2015) report, estimated that 52% percent of all social enterprises now contract with the public sector, as a result, the majority of public sector contracts provide their main source of income. The OECD (2015) reports that its member governments spent on average 29% of general government expenditure in 2013, which is equivalent on average to 12.1% GDP. The UK government spent £242 billion in 2013/14, above the average, accounting for 33% of public sector spending (Booth, 2015). The review of literature has shown how several UK government policies were designed to influence the procurement of services and goods from the sector organizations. There is limited evidence to demonstrate how small TESS's have benefited. Thus, this chapter will address the following research questions:

1. To what extent has small TESS's benefited from public services contracts?
2. What are the challenges facing small TESS's gaining access to public services contracts?

METHODOLOGY

Face to face semi-structured interviews (Gray, 2013; Bryman & Bell, 2015) were conducted with 11 managers and 10 Chief Executive Officers (CEOs) working in four UK regions (South East, East Midlands, South Wales, Yorkshire and Humber). The semi-structured interview approach allowed for flexibility with a preference for posing questions so the interview was more like a conversation whilst maintaining focus on identifying successes and challenges of public policies impact on small third sector social enterprises. Interviews ranged from 46 to 72 minutes.

Every effort to test the reliability of evidence from participants interview responses by seeking corroborative information from other sources such as documented organizational evidence (such as, Service Level Agreements, project outcome, evaluation, annual report and accounts). Using multiple sources of evidence (as was employed in this research) enables the author to place more confidence in the chain of events in the research findings and increases the validity of the findings as the strengths of one source of evidence compensate for the limitations of the other evidence source (Miles & Huberman, 1994; Silverman, 2013; Maher, 2013).

Participants were given the opportunity to indicate any additional information that they considered relevant to the research. In an effort to minimize inaccuracies in the interview data, the author digitally recorded the interviews (with the participant's permission) and transcribed verbatim without any attempt to correct grammar, but omitted 'ums' and 'errs'. The uses of acronyms by participants were written in full with [...] to demonstrate when the author has done so. The author also checked the transcripts before inviting each participant to confirm their transcript was an accurate representation of what they had said at the interview before starting the data analysis.

Non-verbal communication that could not be captured on the digital recordings such as, body language and gestures were recorded in fieldnotes. According to Patton (1990) and Miles and Huberman (1994), fieldnotes are an on-going, crucial part of collecting research data. In this research, they took the form of self-reminders about specific events during the interviews (such as participants nodding or laughing) and notes about personal reflections as well as reactions arising from and captured during the interviews. They constituted a written record of the development of the interviews and ideas which the researcher felt to be useful in subsequent interviews. The fieldnotes data include a brief description of the physical setting where each interview took place, nonverbal cues such as postures, facial expressions, gestures, feelings and any type of behavior or actions that might have affected the interview (Ghauri & Gronhaug, 2002; Sachdeva, 2009; Silverman, 2013). The fieldnotes were also a useful way of reflecting on each interview and on the present meaning and significance of the discussions.

Ethical considerations in business enterprise management research are paramount in order to avoid any risk to the physical, psychological, health and social well-being of the participants (Bobbie, 2007; Saunders, Lewis & Thornhill, 2011). Therefore, before commencing the interviews, participants were informed in writing three weeks in advance about the purpose of the research, the interview time, and the duration of the interview. A signed informed consent form was obtained from each participant stating their willingness to participate in the research. Each participant was informed that they had the option to withdraw at any time from the research (Bobbie, 2007; Flick, 2009; Saunders, Lewis, & Thornhill, 2011).

To maintain anonymity, the names of neither the participants nor the names and addresses of participating organizations were mentioned. This was to ensure that readers could not identify the views of specific individuals. Also, ensuring that participants did not restrict their disclosure was an important consideration for the research and involved the assurance of confidentiality (Silverman, 2013; Maher, 2013).

Computer-assisted qualitative data analysis software (CAQDAS) package NVivo 9 was employed to facilitate the data coding and clustering of themes (Bryman & Bell, 2015). Data were imported directly from a word processing package into NVivo 9 simultaneously analyzing each interview transcript. The author gave a short description to each code created (known as node in NVivo 9). The author used the emerging nodes to organize relevant data segments by assigning meaning to the descriptive information from the participant's responses.

The data coding process is iterative and time consuming. Bryman and Bell (2015) suggest that it involves a process of constant comparison of codes as they emerge. Another challenge was to decide how much text should be coded in the nodes. In some instances, a few words were coded (e.g. government policies, funding, government cuts, new challenges and procurement issues) and in other instances, an entire paragraph was coded. It also helped to provide a transparent data analysis process and a quick way of demonstrating who said what and when which in turn, provided a reliable general picture of the data.

This helped to improve the rigor of the data analysis process by validating the author's own impressions of the data. It provided a disciplined structure to search and analyze data. The information verification process employed by during the data collection can be regarded as contributing to the methodological rigor of the research.

FINDINGS

Public policy aims to promote accountability and growth, it also promises to help organizations to develop long term infrastructure. Yet, government procurement policy is cited by several key informants as a major barrier to growth and sustainability. The way in which procurement is undertaken often puts small TESS's at a disadvantage.

We lost quite a bit of money from the government about a year ago and we had to restructure our services. Services were merged in order to keep things running wherever we can (Participant: 14).

We all had our hours reduced not so long ago due to the cuts ... so we had to reduce our opening hours ... in fact we lost two projects completely ... I hear that more cut are on the way ...we have been fighting for our survival ... without the users protesting we would have been closed down ... (Participant: 19).

The evidence suggest that procurement processes makes it difficult for small TSSE's to make decisions in advance about services development, when staff hours are reduced and projects are under threat of closure. Yearly contract re-tendering mean these organisations are required to bid every year for funding. Some of these organizations are multi-funded, often this means bidding for funds from several different sources every year.

There cuts are on-going ... we are at the mercy of the government ... if they decide to cut all our funding ... we have to close. At the moment it is year by year ... we are alright for the next coming 12 months .... Then it starts all over again (Participant: 8).

We have lost some funding during the last re-tendering round ... so some of the staff that was working for me are no longer here. We had to change how we work. I had to work harder – I'm more stretched in order to meet targets. So keeping services open now is the most important thing we have to do ... I think the career thing is on a back burner (Participant: 18).

Unnecessary re-tendering of contacts on a yearly cycle is expensive in terms of resources and can lead to major disruption of frontline services for services users, as demonstrated by the evidence from key informants. Independent Review of Public Sector Efficiency Review (2004) argued that 'contracts for service delivery by third sector organizations (including small TSSE's tended to suffer from an unnecessarily short-term approach and recommended *moving to longer-term, multi-year funding arrangements where possible*. In cases where services provided are running well with good outcomes, commissioners should consider longer term contracts in line with contract arrangements they have with public sector organizations. Re-tending cycles continues to increase uncertainty for small third sector social enterprise organizations often running with limited reserves. These organizations are unable to make long term plans and service recipients cannot be sure if the services they rely on will continue next week, next month or next year.

Short-term funding brings insecurity for clients … not knowing what is going to happen if the funding comes to an end. Insecurity for staff … not knowing if they have a job … no one knows if the services is going to continue … when we lose funding it's difficult to accept the loss of all the skills when staff are made redundant (Participant: 12).

Annual funding means a considerable level of uncertainty for these organizations, limits their ability to engage in longer-term planning and investment, and can put these organizations into undesirable financial difficulties. This can also lead to the diversion of valuable organization's resources into bidding for Government funds – often from multiple sources – and away from the development and delivery of better services.

Furthermore, both funders and providers may struggle to find time for the annual re-tendering processes, and very often end up with a period of uncertainty while decisions are made on whether the funding is to be renewed (Maher, 2016). The waiting period is an expensive and unproductive period for funders and providers. Longer term funding arrangements can reduce levels of anxiety, allow the sector organizations more time to carry out its core function, and produce clear benefits for their service recipients who are – often highly vulnerable. Longer term funding arrangements often represents better value for money than annual year funding agreements by providing greater financial stability (Maher, 2017c). One CEO reported:

The nature of this funding … even funding that is three years … can make it difficult to fully evidence impact and develop the necessary relationships subsequently to seek a contract, because longer-term evidence is often needed (Participant: 10).

Further evidence on how government policy on the procurement process is directly affecting the small third sector social enterprises can be found in evidence given by several Chief Executive Officers.

The big recent development has been around the competitive tendering commissioning. There is more and more competitive tendering with a short time turn around. This disadvantages us, as we don't have the infrastructure to develop a credible bid in a very short time frame (Participant: 2).

This was echoed by other CEO's:

The government cuts are affecting us … when I took over several years ago... it was really good … income was up … now we have lost so many contracts … and staff (Participant: 4).

There has been a lot of pressure on me … if I don't make enough money I have to save on labour. Before … we had a manager and a supervisor. The manager will go to our office to do paper work and the supervisor will look after customers … they have both gone … we couldn't pay them. Now I have to stand here at the counter doing paper work and serving customers in order to save on labour … (Participant: 17)

The evidence suggests that funding cuts has led to greater staff turnover and redundancies, meaning that skills and experience are lost, which in turn further reduces the impact of the sector organization's contributions and its value for money. Several small social enterprise providers argue that many service users require responsive and adaptive local services that allow them to work proactively in order to meet their specific needs. The current procurement approach, has led to increasing cost and competition among service providers. The increasing competitive environment, in which small social enterprises find themselves, has made it more difficult, complex and restrictive processes that often favor larger organizations. Several managers reported that organizational funding uncertainties brought on by reduction in government funding to the sector organizations influences managerial careers management.

The government is looking for targets to be met. So we are very much target driven here it's all about meeting targets. I'm going on to my third job here in September within 2 years. My last job here ... the government pulled the funding after 12 months ... 6 months was remaining on the contract. When the new government came in they cut our funding ... the new government didn't honor what the last government had started. We had many cuts ... look at all the desks that are vacant out there in the office ... we have fewer services running this year than we did last year. I'm lucky to have been kept on ... many people lost their jobs (Participant: 21).

Several organizations reported that the challenges they face are not only due to reductions in the amount of resources in the system, but are more to do with the approach taken to commissioning limited resources. Increasing budget pressures and rising demand are arduous for these organizations. Health and Care commissioners are not always incentivized to see financial resources as just a part of the wider resources of their communities; so in many areas. Health and Care commissioners have reduced funding for the sector organization's work with communities first, in an attempt to protect budgets for what they regard as their 'core business'. This has immediate and direct effect on the organization's infrastructure and impact on vulnerable clients and communities TSSE's helps and support.

CONCLUSION

This chapter has contributed to our knowledge and understanding of how procurement policy and processes are impacting on small TSSE's. The government introduction of policies and procedures such as, the Compact, 'Best Value', 'Payment by Result' Public Contracts Regulations 2015 that reinforces the government's agenda to provide the sector organizations opportunities to play a bigger role within the public procurement has not always benefit small TSSE's in growing and expanding their activities. In several cases theses organization are beseeching to survive. Most of these organizations have fostered the earned income approach and social innovation approach to help their survival. Yet, government procurement policy and processes were cited by several small TSSE managers and Chief Executive Officers as one of the main barriers to growth and sustainability. The way in which procurement is undertaken often puts these organizations at a disadvantage. The reasons for this include:

1. Procurement tendering processes often favor large businesses that are good at tendering, not always those which are good at delivering.
2. Contracts values are often too large for most small TSSE's to participate.

3. Contracts often 'aggregate' similar works into one large contract or 'bundle' different works into the same contract; so only very large organizations can bid for them.

Given the local knowledge of small TSSE's and their growing weight in development processes, specific procurement policy interventions seem to be needed to focus on the specific business features of these enterprises. Increasing long-term income is one of the biggest challenges for many of these organizations. Often, they do not have the brand names that can bring about collaborations with public- and private-sector partnerships.

The evidence suggests that public procurement process does not increase the performance of small TESS's and in some cases delay delivery of services because of the various challenges inherent in public procurement process. This affirms that most small third sector social enterprises going through public procurement process may suffer from delay in delivery of services due to the tedious and length of time involve in public procurement process.

FUTURE RESEARCH DIRECTIONS

Future research could seek to understand how government procurement policies can help to open new markets for small third sector social enterprises. Research could tap into recent developments in the field of market-making practices and mechanisms, in order to understand best practices that would serve as guidelines for funding small social enterprises/private sector initiatives seeking to develop their operations in a manner that fosters equality in collaboration and reinforces integrity.

In addition, future research could examine the short and long tern effect of different procurement policies using stakeholder theory or sense-making theory to explore how small social enterprises working in partnership with public and private sector organizations are making sense of procurement policies. More research should be conducted on public procurement process and success on organization performance.

REFERENCES

Acs, Z. J., Boardman, M. C., & McNeely, C. L. (2013). The social value of productive entrepreneurship. *Small Business Economics*, *40*(3), 785–796. doi:10.100711187-011-9396-6

Alcock, P. (2010). A strategic unity: Defining the third sector in the UK. *Voluntary Sector Review*, *1*(1), 5–24. doi:10.1332/204080510X496984

Audit Commission. (2007). *Hearts and Minds: Commissioning from the Voluntary Sector*. London: Audit Commission.

Audit Commission. (2012). *Local payment by results*. London: Audit Commission.

Babbie, E. (2007). *The practice of social research* (11th ed.). Belmont: Thomson.

Baines, S., Hardill, I., & Wilson, R. (2011). Introduction: Remixing the economy of welfare? Changing roles and relationships between the state and the voluntary and community sector. *Social Policy and Society*, *10*(3), 337–349. doi:10.1017/S1474746411000066

Bartlett, J. (2009). *Getting More for Less: Efficiency in the Public Sector*. London: Demos.

Battye, F. (2015). Payment by Results in the UK: Progress to date and future directions for evaluation. *Evaluation*, *21*(2), 189–203. doi:10.1177/1356389015577464

Battye, F., & Sunderland, J. (2011). *Thinking about....* Payment by Results. GHK.

BIS. (2011). *Delivering best value through innovation: Forward commitment procurement*. BIS.

BIS. (2011). *The path to strong, sustainable and balanced growth*. HM Treasury.

Bolton, P. (2006). Government procurement as a policy tool in South Africa. *Journal of Public Procurement*, *6*(3), 193.

Boschee, J., & McClurg, J. (2003). Toward a better understanding of social entrepreneurship: Some important distinctions. Bond for International Development (2014) Payment by results: what it means for UK NGOs. London: Academic Press.

Bovaird, T. (2014). Attributing outcomes to social policy interventions–'Gold standard 'or 'fool's gold' in public policy and management? *Social Policy and Administration*, *48*(1), 1–23. doi:10.1111/j.1467-9515.2012.00869.x

Bovaird, T., & Davies, R. (2011). Outcome-based service commissioning and delivery: Does it make a difference? In New Steering Concepts in Public Management. Emerald Group Publishing Limited.

Bovaird, T., Dickinson, H., & Allen, K. (2012). *Commissioning across government: review of evidence. Research Report 86*. Birmingham, UK: Third Sector Research Centre.

Boyle, D. (2011). The pitfalls and perils of payment by results. *Local Economy*, *26*(8), 627–634. doi:10.1177/0269094211422203

Bryman, A., & Bell, E. (2015). *Business research methods*. Oxford University Press.

Bubb, S., & Michell, R. (2009). Investing in third-sector capacity. In P. Hunter (Ed.), *Social Enterprise for Public Service: How does the Third Sector Deliver?* London: The Smith Institute.

Buckingham, H. (2009). Competition and contracts in the voluntary sector: Exploring the implications for homelessness service providers in Southampton. *Policy and Politics*, *37*(2), 235–254. doi:10.1332/030557309X441045

Buckingham, H., Pinch, S., & Sunley, P. (2012). The enigmatic regional geography of social enterprise in the UK: A conceptual framework and synthesis of the evidence. *Area*, *44*(1), 83–91. doi:10.1111/j.1475-4762.2011.01043.x

Burt, E., & Scholarios, D. (2011). Recruiting for Values in Charitable Organisations. *Voluntary Organisations and Public Service Delivery*, *14*, 104.

Cabinet Office. (2007). *Partnership in Public Services: An action plan for third sector involvement*. London: Cabinet Office.

Cabinet Office. (2010). *Modernising Commissioning: Increasing the Role of Charities, Social Enterprises, Mutuals and Cooperatives in Public Service Delivery*. London: HMSO.

Cabinet Office. (2011). *The lean review: accelerating government procurement.* Retrieved from http://www.cabinetoffice.gov.uk/sites/default/files/resources/annex-A-lean-procurement-study-management-summary.pdf

Cabinet Office. (2012). Making government business more accessible to SMEs: One year on. Cabinet Office.

Cabinet Office and HM Treasury. (2010). *Call for evidence on public service reform. London: HM Treasury Cabinet Office (2010) The Compact.* London: Cabinet Office.

Carmel, E., & Harlock, J. (2008). Instituting the 'third sector' as a governable terrain: Partnership, procurement and performance in the UK. *Policy and Politics, 36*(2), 155–171. doi:10.1332/030557308783995017

Charity Commission. (2011). *Consortia for the delivery of public services: The issues for small and medium-sized charities.* Liverpool, UK: Charity Commission.

Clarke, J., Kane, D., & Wilding, K. (2012). *UK Civil Society Almanac 2012.* London: NCVO.

Clausen, J. A. (1998). Live reviews and life stories. In J. Z. Giele & H. H. J. Elder (Eds.), *Methods of Life Course Research: Qualitative and Quantitative Approaches: 189 – 121.* Thousand Oaks, CA: Sage. doi:10.4135/9781483348919.n8

Crossan, D., Ibbotson, P., & Bell, J. (2011). The hologram effect in entrepreneurial "social commercial" enterprises: Triggers and tipping points. *Journal of Small Business and Enterprise Development, 18*(4), 655–672. doi:10.1108/14626001111179730

Defourny, J., & Nyssens, M. (2010). Conceptions of social enterprise and social entrepreneurship in Europe and the United States: Convergences and divergences. *Journal of Social Entrepreneurship, 1*(1), 32–53. doi:10.1080/19420670903442053

Development Co-operation Report. (2015). *Making Partnerships Effective Coalitions for Action.* OECD.

Di Domenico, M., Haugh, H., & Tracey, P. (2010). Social bricolage: Theorizing social value creation in social enterprises. *Entrepreneurship Theory and Practice, 34*(4), 681–703. doi:10.1111/j.1540-6520.2010.00370.x

Dickinson, H., Allen, K., Macmillan, R., & Glasby, J. (2012). *Social Care and the Third Sector.* London: NIHR School for Social Care Research.

Dickinson, H., & Miller, R. (2011). GP commissioning: Implications for the third sector. *Voluntary Sector Review, 2*(3), 265–273. doi:10.1332/204080511X583913

Drees, J. M., & Heugens, P. P. (2013). Synthesizing and extending resource dependence theory: A meta-analysis. *Journal of Management, 39*(6), 1666–1698. doi:10.1177/0149206312471391

DTI. (2002). *Social enterprise: A strategy for success.* Department of Trade and Industry. Retrieved from http://www.dti.gov.uk

DTI. (2003). *Social enterprise: A progress report on social enterprise.* Department of Trade and Industry. Retrieved from http://www.dti.gov.uk

Edinburgh Treasury, H. M. (2007). *Transforming government procurement*. London: TSO.

European Commission. (2012). Innovation procurement. Delivering efficiency, quality and sustainability in healthcare. A guide to innovation procurement for the healthcare sector. LCB-HEALTHCARE project, lead market initiative.

Flick, U. (2009). *An introduction to Qualitative Research*. London: Sage.

Funding Commission. (2010). *Funding the Future: A ten-year framework for civil society*. London: NVCO.

Geddes, M., & Martin, S. (2000). The Policy and Politics of Best Value: Currents, Crosscurrents and Undercurrents in the New Regime. *Policy and Politics, 28*(3), 379–395. doi:10.1332/0305573002501036

Gershon, P. (1999). *Review of civil procurement in central government*. HM Treasury.

Gershon, P. (2004). *Releasing Resources to the Front Line: Independent Review of Public Sector Efficiency*. London: The Stationery Office.

Ghauri, P., & Gronhaug, K. (2002). *Research Methods in Business Studies: A Practical Guide* (2nd ed.). London: Sage.

Gibbs, G. R. (2007). *Analysing Qualitative Data*. London: Sage. doi:10.4135/9781849208574

Gojkovic, D., Mills, A., & Meek, R. (2011). *Scoping the involvement of third sector organisations in the seven resettlement pathways for offenders*. Academic Press.

Government, H. M. (2011). *Open Public Services White Paper*. London: HMSO.

Gray, D. E. (2013). Doing research in the real world. *Sage (Atlanta, Ga.)*.

Green, P. (2010). *Efficiency reviews: key findings and recommendations*. Retrieved from http://www.cabinetoffice.gov.uk/sites/default/files/resources/sirphilipgreenrevie w.pdf

Hedderman, C. (2013). Payment by Results: Hopes, fears and evidence. *British Journal of Community Justice, 11*(2-3).

Hills, J. (2015). *Record on Cash Transfers, Poverty The Coalition's and Inequality 2010-2015*. Social Policy in a Cold Climate Working Paper 11. London: Centre for Analysis of Social Exclusion.

Hope, P. (2004). Supporting every shade of initiative. *Social Enterprise Magazine*, 8–9.

House of Lords. (2010). *Making it Work: the European Social Fund*. European Union Committee, House of Lords, 9th Report of Session 2009–10. Available at: www.publications.parliament.uk/pa/ld200910/ldselect/ldeucom/92/92i.pdf

House of Lords. (2011). *Science and technology committee: first report. Public procurement as a tool to stimulate innovation*. House of Lords. Retrieved from http://www.publications.parliament.uk/pa/ld201012/ldselect/ldsctech/148/14802.htm

Hudson, R. (2009). Life on the edge: Navigating the competitive tensions between the 'social 'and the 'economic' in the social economy and in its relations to the mainstream. *Journal of Economic Geography*.

Hynes, B. (2009). Growing the social enterprise – issues and challenges. *Social Enterprise Journal*, *5*(2), 114–125. doi:10.1108/17508610910981707

Independent Review of Public Sector Efficiency. (2004). *Releasing resources to the front line*. London: HMSO.

Innovation and research strategy for growth. (2011). BIS economics paper number 15. Gov.UK.

Kerlin, J. A. (2006). Social enterprise in the United States and Europe: Understanding and learning from the differences. *Voluntas*, *17*(3), 246–262. doi:10.100711266-006-9016-2

Kimantas, P., & Dawson, J. (2008). *Commissioning and procurement*. London: NAVCA.

Larner, W., & Butler, M. (2005). Governmentalities of local partnerships: The rise of a "partnering state" in New Zealand. *Studies in Political Economy*, *75*(1), 85–108. doi:10.1080/19187033.2005.11675130

Lewis, J. (2005). New Labour's approach to the voluntary sector: Independence and the meaning of partnership. *Social Policy and Society*, *4*(2), 121–131. doi:10.1017/S147474640400226X

Lyon, F., & Sepulveda, L. (2012). Social Enterprise Support Policies: distinctions and challenges. In R. Blackburn & M. Schaper (Eds.), *Government, SMEs and Entrepreneurship. Development: Policy, Practice and Challenges*. Farnham: Gower.

Macmillan, R. (2010). *The third sector delivering public services: an evidence review*. Working Paper 20. Birmingham, UK: Third Sector Research Centre.

Maher, C. (2013). *A Qualitative Case Study Approach to Understanding Third Sector Managers' Career Orientations*. Academic Press.

Maher, C. (2015a). *Public Policies Impact on Third Sector Social Enterprises in UK Regions*. IGI Global.

Maher, C. (2016). Career anchors of social enterprise managers in the UK-an empirical analysis. *Journal for International Business and Entrepreneurship Development*, *9*(4), 398–416. doi:10.1504/JIBED.2016.080019

Maher, C. (2017a). Understanding the Impact of Organisational Culture on Managers' Internal Career Needs. In Exploring the Influence of Personal Values and Cultures in the Workplace (pp. 265-285). IGI Global.

Maher, C. (2017b). Managers' Career Orientations: A Conceptual Framework. In Handbook of Research on Emerging Business Models and Managerial Strategies in the Nonprofit Sector (pp. 201-221). IGI Global.

Maher, C. (Ed.). (2017c). *Influence of Public Policy on Small Social Enterprises: Emerging Research and Opportunities: Emerging Research and Opportunities*. IGI Global.

Martikke, S., & Moxham, C. (2010). Public sector commissioning: Experiences of voluntary organizations delivering health and social services. *International Journal of Public Administration*, *33*(14), 790–799. doi:10.1080/01900692.2010.521230

McCabe, A. (2012). *Is the third sector so special? What is it worth? Third Sector Futures Dialogue, Big Picture Paper 3*. Birmingham, UK: TSRC.

Megan, R., Kennett, P., Jones, G., & Croft, J. (2014). Global economic crisis, austerity and neoliberal urban governance in England. *Cambridge Journal of Regions, Economy and Society*, *7*(1), 137–153. doi:10.1093/cjres/rst033

Miles, M. B., & Huberman, A. M. (1994). *Qualitative data analysis: An expanded sourcebook*. Sage.

Ministry of Justice. (2013). *Transforming rehabilitation. A revolution in the way we manage offenders, Consultation Paper CP1/2013*. London: The Stationery Office.

Muñoz, S. A. (2009). Social enterprise and public sector voices on procurement. *Social Enterprise Journal*, *5*(1), 69–82. doi:10.1108/17508610910956417

NAO. (2010). *Short guide to re-organising arm's length bodies: good practice principles for implementation*. National Audit Office. Retrieved from http://www.nao.org.uk/publications/1011/ arms_length_bodies.aspx

Nicholls, A. (2006). Social Entrepreneurship. In *Enterprise and Small Business: Principles, Practice and Policy*. Financial Times Prentice Hall.

NVCO. (2016). *The UK Civil Society Almanac*. London: NVCO Publication.

ODPM. (2003). *National procurement strategy for local government in England (2003–2006)*. London: Office of the Deputy Prime Minister.

OGC. (2003). *Report to the chancellor of the exchequer: increasing competition and improving long-term capacity planning in the government market place*. London: Office for Government Commerce.

OGC. (2004). *Capturing innovation: nurturing. suppliers' ideas in the public sector*. Retrieved from www.ogc.gov.uk/documents/capturing_innovation.pdf

OGC. (2010). *Policy through Procurement (PtP)*. London: Action Plan. Office for Government Commerce.

OGC. (2011). *Public sector procurement expenditure survey*. Office for Government Commerce, London. Retrieved from http://webarchive.nationalarchives.gov.uk/20110822131357/http://www.ogc.gov.uk/ documents/July_Spend_Publication_v1.0.doc

Painter, C. (2013). The UK Coalition Government: Constructing public service reform narratives. Public Policy and Administration, 28(3), 3–20.

Patton, M. Q. (1999). Enhancing the quality and credibility of qualitative analysis. *Health Services Research*, *34*(5 Pt 2), 1189. PMID:10591279

Public Administration Select Committee (PASC). (2008). *Public Services and the Third Sector: Rhetoric and Reality*. Eleventh Report of Session 2007–08. London: The Stationery Office.

Saunders, M., Lewis, P., & Thornhill, A. (2011). *Research Methods for Business Students*. Harlow: Pearson Education Ltd.

Scottish Government. (2008). *Public procurement reform programme: Scottish procurement policy handbook. Dec 2008*. The Scottish Government.

Scowen, J. (2004). A top procurement officer's view. *Social Enterprise Magazine*, 17.

Sheil, F., & Breidenbach-Roe, R. (2014). *Payment by results and the voluntary sector*. London: NCVO.

Silverman, D. (2013). *Doing qualitative research: A practical handbook*. SAGE Publications Limited.

Slocock, C. (2012). *The big society audit 2012*. London: Civil Exchange.

Smallbone, D., Evans, M., Ekanem, I., & Butters, S. (2001). *Researching social enterprise*. Small Business Service.

Smallbone, D., & Lyon, F. (2005). *Social enterprise development in the UK: some contemporary policy issues*. Paper presented to ICSB conference, Washington, DC.

Smerdon, M., & Deakin, N. (2010). Independence in principle and practice: Relationships between the state and voluntary action. *Voluntary Sector Review*, *1*(3), 361–370. doi:10.1332/204080510X538347

Smith, J. K. (1993, March). Quantitative v. Qualitative Research: An attempt to classify the issue. *Educational Research*, •••, 6–13.

Social Enterprise UK. (2016). *Annual Review*. Author.

Stevenson, N., Taylor, M., & Lyon, F. (2010). *Joining the dots: Social impact measurement, commissioning from the third sector and supporting social enterprise development*. A report to East of England Development Agency. Available at: http://the-guild.co.uk/newsite/content/2010_Joining_the_dots_full_report_EEDA.pdf

Sturgess, G.L., Cumming, L.M., & Dicker, J. (2011). *Payment by Outcome: A Commissioner's Toolkit*. London: 2020 Public Services Trust at the RSA.

Tanner, S. (2007). *Common Themes on Commissioning the VCS in Selected Local Authorities in Greater London*. London: London Councils.

Taylor-Gooby, P., & Stoker, G. (2011). The coalition programme: A new vision for Britain or politics as normal? *The Political Quarterly*, *82*(1), 4–14. doi:10.1111/j.1467-923X.2011.02169.x

Teasdale, S. (2012). What's in a name? Making sense of social enterprise discourses. *Public Policy and Administration, 27*(2), 99-119.

Third Sector Task Force. (2009). *Welfare to work reform: The third sector's role: Final report*. Available at: http://www.acevo.org.uk/document.doc?id=42

Treasury, H. M. (2006). *Value for Money Assessment Guidance*. London: HMSO.

Treasury, H. M. (2007). *Transforming government procurement*. London: TSO.

Treasury, H. M. (2009). *Operational efficiency programme: collaborative procurement*. HM.

White, L. (2011). *Commission Impossible? Shaping Places Through Strategic Commissioning*. Chelmsford: Localis/Essex County Council.

Young, D. R., & Lecy, J. D. (2014). Defining the universe of social enterprise: Competing metaphors. *Voluntas*, *25*(5), 1307–1332. doi:10.100711266-013-9396-z

ADDITIONAL READING

Carvalho, L. (Ed.). (2015). *Handbook of Research on Entrepreneurial Success and its Impact on Regional Development.* IGI Global.

Fernandes, T., & Vieira, V. (2015). Public e-procurement impacts in small-and medium-enterprises. *International Journal of Procurement Management, 8*(5), 587–607. doi:10.1504/IJPM.2015.070904

Flynn, A., McKevitt, D., & Davis, P. (2015). The impact of size on small and medium-sized enterprise public sector tendering. *International Small Business Journal, 33*(4), 443–461. doi:10.1177/0266242613503178

Knutsson, H., & Thomasson, A. (2014). Innovation in the Public Procurement Process: A study of the creation of innovation-friendly public procurement. *Public Management Review, 16*(2), 242–255. doi:10.1080/14719037.2013.806574

Loader, K. (2015). SME suppliers and the challenge of public procurement: Evidence revealed by a UK government online feedback facility. *Journal of Purchasing and Supply Management, 21*(2), 103–112. doi:10.1016/j.pursup.2014.12.003

McKevitt, D., & Davis, P. (2013). Microenterprises: How they interact with public procurement processes. *International Journal of Public Sector Management, 26*(6), 469–480. doi:10.1108/IJPSM-06-2012-0086

Reis, P. R., & Cabral, S. (2015). Public procurement strategy: The impacts of a preference programme for small and micro businesses. *Public Money & Management, 35*(2), 103–110. doi:10.1080/09540962.2015.1007704

Stentoft Arlbjørn, J., & Vagn Freytag, P. (2012). Public procurement vs private purchasing: Is there any foundation for comparing and learning across the sectors? *International Journal of Public Sector Management, 25*(3), 203–220. doi:10.1108/09513551211226539

KEY TERMS AND DEFINITIONS

Average Cost: Represents the full cost of the activity divided by the volume of service. This takes into account both fixed and variable costs - direct and indirect - and therefore can often represent a more accurate reflection of the cost of activity.

Best Value: The performance framework for regulating local government and health services, which includes the need to consider whether services are being delivered in the most appropriate way, and by whom, and the need to secure continuous improvement.

Direct Costs: Costs associated directly with an activity and which are relatively easy to identify (e.g., the cost of caseworkers' salaries).

New Approaches to Public Procurement (NAPP): The New Approaches to Public Procurement (NAPP) network of local authorities aims to help participant address legal, policy and practice issues that have been obstacles to achieving community benefits through contracts.

Procurement: Is defined as being the acquisition of goods and services from third party suppliers under legally binding contractual terms where all the conditions necessary to form a legally binding contract have been met.

Small Social Enterprise: Social enterprises are organizations with annual incomes of between £25,000 and £1 million.

Social Enterprise Coalition: The Social Enterprise Coalition (SEC) is an alliance of social enterprises from across the UK. It aims to provide a national voice for the sector; to promote the sector; to build capacity through information sharing, and to encourage co-operation.

Third Sector: The Third sector is a collective term used to describe those organizations which exist outside of the public and private sector domains.

Value for Money: The optimum combination of whole life cost and quality (or fitness for purpose) to meet the user's requirement (i.e., getting the best possible outcome from any given level of input).

Compilation of References

(2013). The many faces of social entrepreneurial leadership. InNormore, H., & Erbe, N. (Eds.), *Collective Efficacy: Interdisciplinary Perspectives on International Leadership*. Emerald Group Publishing Limited.

Abdou, E., Fahmy, A., Greenwald, D. & Nelson, J. (2010). *Social Entrepreneurship in the Middle East - Toward Sustainable Development for the Next Generation.* Brookings Report.

Abu-Saifan, S. (2012). Social entrepreneurship: definition and boundaries. *Technology Innovation Management Review, 2*(2).

Abu-Saifan, S. (2012, February). Social Entrepreneurship: Definition and Boundaries. *Technology Innovation Management Review*, 22-27.

Abu-Saifan, S. (2012). Social entrepreneurship: Definition and boundaries. *Technology Innovation Management Review, 2*(2), 22–27.

Acemoglu, D. (2012). Introduction to economic growth. *Journal of Economic Theory, 147*(2), 545–550. doi:10.1016/j.jet.2012.01.023

Acemoglu, D., & Robinson, J. A. (2013). *Why Nations Fail: The Origins of Power, Prosperity, and Poverty*. Profile Books.

Achleitner, A. K., Heinecke, A., Mayer, J., Noble, A., & Schöning, M. (2012). *The governance of social enterprises: Managing your organization for success.* Schwab Foundation for Social Entrepreneurship. Retrieved from http://www3.weforum.org/docs/WEF_Governance_Social_Enterprises_2106_light.pdf

Acs, Z. J., Boardman, M. C., & McNeely, C. L. (2013). The social value of productive entrepreneurship. *Small Business Economics, 40*(3), 785–796. doi:10.100711187-011-9396-6

Acumen Fund Metrics Team. (2007). Acumen Fund Concepts: The Best Available Charitable Option. New York: Author.

Acumen Fund. (2017). Retrieved from http://acumen.org/sectors/

Agafonow, A. (2014). Toward A Positive Theory of Social Entrepreneurship. On Maximizing Versus Satisficing Value Capture. *Journal of Business Ethics, 125*(4), 709–713. doi:10.100710551-013-1948-z

Ağca, V., & Böyükaslan, H. D. (2016). Aile işletmelerinde iç girişimciliğin sosyal girişimciliğe etkisi: Afyonkarahisar'da bir araştırma. *Kastamonu Üniversitesi İktisadi ve İdari Bilimler Fakültesi Dergisi, 13*, 200–220.

Akingbola, K. (2006). Strategy and HRM in nonprofit organizations: Evidence from Canada. *International Journal of Human Resource Management, 17*(10), 1707–1725. doi:10.1080/09585190600964350

Akingbola, K. (2015). *Managing human resources for nonprofits.* New York, NY: Routledge.

Aksan, G. (2016). Max Weber ve değerler sosyolojisi: Bir metodolojik ikilemin düşündürdükleri. *SEFAD, 35*(35), 427–446. doi:10.21497efad.35126

Al Ariss, A., & Ozbilgin, M. (2010). Understanding self-initiated expatriates: Career experiences of Lebanese self-initiated expatriates in France. *Thunderbird International Business Review*, *52*(4), 275–285. doi:10.1002/tie.20355

Al Ariss, A., & Syed, J. (2011). Capital mobilization of skilled migrants: A relational perspective. *British Journal of Management*, *22*(2), 286–304. doi:10.1111/j.1467-8551.2010.00734.x

Alcock, P. (2010). A strategic unity: Defining the third sector in the UK. *Voluntary Sector Review*, *1*(1), 5–24. doi:10.1332/204080510X496984

Aldrich, H., & Zimmer, C. (1986). Entrepreneurship through social networks. In D. Sexton & R. W. Smilor (Eds.), *Art and Science of Entrepreneurship* (pp. 3–23). New York, NY: Ballinger Publishing Company.

Almond, S., & Kendall, J. (2000). Taking the employees' perspective seriously: An initial United Kingdom cross-sectoral comparison. *Nonprofit and Voluntary Sector Quarterly*, *29*(2), 205–231. doi:10.1177/0899764000292001

Alter, S. K. (2007). Social Enterprise Typology. *Virtue Ventures*. Retrieved from http://www.4lenses.org/setypology/print

Alter, K., & Dawans, V. (2006). The Integrated Approach to Social Entrepreneurship - Building High Performance Organizations. *Social Enterprise Reporter*, *204*, 1–4.

Alvarez, S. A., & Barney, J. B. (2007). Discovery and creation: Alternative theories of entrepreneurial action. *Strategic Entrepreneurship Journal*, *1*(1–2), 11–26. doi:10.1002ej.4

Alvord, S. H., Brown, L. D., & Letts, C. W. (2004). Social entrepreneurship and societal transformation. *The Journal of Applied Behavioral Science*, *40*(3), 260–282. doi:10.1177/0021886304266847

Anderson, A. R., & Jack, S. L. (2002). The articulation of entrepreneurial social capital: Content and process. *Entrepreneurship and Regional Development*, *14*(3), 193–210. doi:10.1080/08985620110112079

Andor, L., Barnier, M., & Tajani, A. (2013). *Social economy and social entrepreneurship, Social Europe Guide, Volume: 4*. Belgium: European Commission.

André, K., & Pache, A. C. (2016). From caring entrepreneur to caring enterprise: Addressing the ethical challenges of scaling up social enterprises. *Journal of Business Ethics*, *133*(4), 659–675. doi:10.100710551-014-2445-8

Andresen, M., Al Ariss, A., & Walther, M. (2012). *Self-Initiated Expatriation: Individual, Organizational, and National Perspectives*. New York: Routledge.

Andresen, M., Bergdolt, F., Margenfeld, J., & Dickmann, M. (2014). Addressing international mobility confusion: Developing definitions and differentiations for self-initiated and assigned expatriates as well as migrants. *International Journal of Human Resource Management*, *25*(16), 2295–2318. doi:10.1080/09585192.2013.877058

Anshari, M., Almunawar, M. N., Shahrill, M., Wicaksono, D. K., & Huda, M. (2017). Smartphones usage in the classrooms: Learning aid or interference? *Education and Information Technologies*, 1–17.

Antoncic, B., & Hisrich, R. D. (2003). Clarifying The Intrapreneurship Concept. *Journal of Small Business and Enterprise Development*, *10*(:1), 7–24. doi:10.1108/14626000310461187

Antoni, G. D. (2016). The emergence of social enterprises through the initiative of self-organized citizens: An analysis starting from Olson's approach to the logic of collective action. *International Review of Sociology*, *26*(1), 19–30. doi:10.1080/03906701.2016.1148335

Aquino, N. (2005). Entrepreneurship is main driver of growth. *Business World*, *29*(1), 1.

Arena, M., Azzone, G., & Bengo, I. (2015). Performance measurement for social enterprises. *Voluntas, 26*(2), 649–672. doi:10.100711266-013-9436-8

Arenius, P., & Clercq, D. (2005). A network-based approach on opportunity recognition. *Small Business Economics, 24*(3), 249–265. doi:10.100711187-005-1988-6

Argüden, Y. (2005). Sosyal girişimcilik. In A. Bozgeyik (Ed.), *Girişimcilere yol haritası* (pp. 80–82). İstanbul: Hayat Yayınları.

Arslantaş, H. A. (2008). Sosyal değişme, kentleşme ve kentlileşmenin din üzerine etkileri. *İlahiyat Fakültesi Dergisi, 13*(2), 171-196.

Ashoka Organization Website. (n.d.). Retrieved June 10, 2017, from https://www.ashoka.org/

Aslan, G., Araza, A., & Bulut, Ç. (2012). Sosyal Girişimciliğin Kavramsal Çerçevesi. *Girişimcilik ve Kalkınma Dergisi, 7*, 2.

Aslan, G., Araza, A., & Bulut, Ç. (2012). Sosyal girişimciliğin kavramsal çerçevesi. *Journal of Entrepreneurship and Development, 7*(2), 69–88.

Audit Commission. (2007). *Hearts and Minds: Commissioning from the Voluntary Sector*. London: Audit Commission.

Audit Commission. (2012). *Local payment by results*. London: Audit Commission.

Audretsch, D. B., Keilbach, M. C., & Lehmann, E. E. (2006). *Entrepreneurship and Economic Growth*. Oxford University Press. doi:10.1093/acprof:oso/9780195183511.001.0001

Austin, J. E., Leonard, H., Reficco, E., & Wei-Skillern, J. (2006). Social entrepreneurship: it's for corporations too. *Social entrepreneurship: New models of sustainable social change*, 169-180.

Austin, Stevenson, & Wei-Skillern. (2006). Social and commercial entrepreneurship: The same, different or both? *Entrepreneurship Theory and Practice, 30*(1), 1-2.

Austin, J. E. (2000). *The collaboration challenge: How nonprofits and business succeed through strategic alliances*. San Francisco: Jossey-Bass Publishers.

Austin, J. E. (2000). *The collaboration challenge: How nonprofits and businesses succeed through strategic alliances* (Vol. 109). John Wiley & Sons.

Austin, J. E., & Reficco, E. (2008). Corporate social entrepreneurship. *Int'l J. Not-for-Profit L., 11*, 86.

Austin, J., Gutierrez, R., Ogliastri, E., & Reficco, E. (2006). *Effective management of social enterprises: Lessons from businesses and civil society organizations in Iberoamerica*. Harvard University, David Rockefeller Center for Latin American Studies.

Austin, J., Stevenson, H., & Wei-Skillern, J. (2006). Social and Commercial Entrepreneurship: Same, Different, or Both? *Entrepreneurship Theory and Practice, 30*(1), 1–22. doi:10.1111/j.1540-6520.2006.00107.x

Austin, M. J., Regan, K., Samples, M. W., Schwartz, S. L., & Carnochan, S. (2011). Building managerial and organizational capacity in non-profit human service organizations through a leadership development program. *Administration in Social Work, 35*(3), 258–281. doi:10.1080/03643107.2011.575339

Avery, G. C., & Bergsteiner, H. (2011). Sustainable leadership practices for enhancing business resilience and performance. *Strategy and Leadership, 39*(3), 5–15. doi:10.1108/10878571111128766

Avolio, B. J., & Gardner, W. L. (2005). Authentic leadership development: Getting to the root of positive forms of leadership. *The Leadership Quarterly*, *16*(3), 315–338. doi:10.1016/j.leaqua.2005.03.001

Aytaç, Ö. (2002). *Sosyoloji/bir giriş denemesi*. Elazığ: Üniversite Kitabevi.

Aytaç, Ö. (2006). Girişimcilik: Sosyo-kültürel bir perspektif. *Dumlupınar Üniversitesi Sosyal Bilimler Dergisi*, *15*, 139–160.

Aytaç, Ö., & İlhan, S. (2007). Girişimcilik ve girişimcikültür: Sosyolojik bir perspektif. *Selçuk Üniversitesi Sosyal Bilimler Enstitüsü Dergisi*, *18*, 101–120.

Babbie, E. (2007). *The practice of social research* (11th ed.). Belmont: Thomson.

Bacq, S., Hartog, C., Hoogendorn, B., & Lepoutre, J. (2011). *Social and Commercial Entrepreneurship: Exploring Individual and Organizational Characteristics*. Scales Research Reports, EIM Business and Policy Research.

Bacq, S., & Janssen, F. (2011). The multiple faces of social entrepreneurship: A review of definitional issues based on geographical and thematic criteria. *Entrepreneurship and Regional Development*, *23*(5-6), 373–403. doi:10.1080/08985626.2011.577242

Bagheri, A., & Pihie, Z. A. L. (2011). On Becoming an Entrepreneurial Leader: A Focus on the Impacts of University Entrepreneurship Programs. *American Journal of Applied Sciences*, *8*(9), 884–892. doi:10.3844/ajassp.2011.884.892

Baines, S., Hardill, I., & Wilson, R. (2011). Introduction: Remixing the economy of welfare? Changing roles and relationships between the state and the voluntary and community sector. *Social Policy and Society*, *10*(3), 337–349. doi:10.1017/S1474746411000066

Baker, M. J. (2013). Capitalism 2.0 and Social Business. *Social Business: An Interdisciplinary Journal*, *3*(4), 297–310. doi:10.1362/204440813X13875569153984

Baker, T., & Nelson, R. (2005). Creating something from nothing: Resource construction through entrepreneurial bricolage. *Administrative Science Quarterly*, *50*(3), 329–366. doi:10.2189/asqu.2005.50.3.329

Ballinger, G. A., & Rockmann, K. W. (2010). Chutes versus ladders: Anchoring events and a punctuated-equilibrium perspective on social exchange relationships. *Academy of Management Review*, *35*(3), 373–391. doi:10.5465/AMR.2010.51141732

Baluch, A. M. (2012). *Human resource management in nonprofit organizations*. New York: Routledge.

Baluch, A. M. (2017). Employee perceptions of HRM and well-being in nonprofit organizations: Unpacking the unintended. *International Journal of Human Resource Management*, *28*(14), 1912–1937. doi:10.1080/09585192.2015.1136672

Ban, C., Drahnak-Faller, A., & Towers, M. (2003). Human resource challenges in human service and community development organizations: Recruitment and retention of professional staff. *Review of Public Personnel Administration*, *23*(2), 133–153. doi:10.1177/0734371X03023002004

Barendsen, L., & Gardner, H. (2004). Is the social entrepreneur a new type of leader? *Leader to Leader*, *34*(34), 43–50. doi:10.1002/ltl.100

Barkemeyer, R., & Glavas, A. (2016). Corporate Social Responsibility in Developing Country Multinationals: Identifying Company and Country-Level Influences. *Business Ethics Quarterly*, *26*(3), 347–378. doi:10.1017/beq.2016.42

Barki, E., Comini, G., Cunliffe, A., Hart, S., & Rai, S. (2015). Social Entrepreneurship and Social Business: Retrospective and Prospective Research. *RAE-Revista de Administração de Empresas*, *55*(4), 380–384. doi:10.1590/S0034-759020150402

Barney, J. (1991, March). Firm Resources and Sustained Competitive Advantage. *Journal of Management*, *17*(1), 99–120. doi:10.1177/014920639101700108

Barney, J., & Wright, P. M. (1998). On becoming a strategic partner: The role of human resources in gaining competitive advantage. *Human Resource Management, 37*(1), 31–46. doi:10.1002/(SICI)1099-050X(199821)37:1<31::AID-HRM43.0.CO;2-W

Baron, R. (2006). Opportunity recognition as pattern recognition: How entrepreneurs 'connect the dots' to identify new business opportunities. *The Academy of Management Perspectives, 20*(1), 104–119. doi:10.5465/AMP.2006.19873412

Baron, R. A., Tang, J., & Hmieleski, K. M. (2011). The downside of being 'up': Entrepreneurs' dispositional positive affect and firm performance. *Strategic Entrepreneurship Journal, 5*(2), 101–119. doi:10.1002ej.109

Bartlett, J. (2009). *Getting More for Less: Efficiency in the Public Sector*. London: Demos.

Baruch, Y., & Ramalho, N. (2006). Communalities and distinctions in the measurement of organizational performance and effectiveness across for-profits and nonprofit sectors. *Nonprofit and Voluntary Sector Quarterly, 35*(1), 39–65. doi:10.1177/0899764005282468

Bass, B. M. (1985). *Leadership and performance beyond expectations*. New York: The Free Press.

Bass, B. M. (1995). Transformational leadership. *Journal of Management Inquiry, 4*(3), 293–298. doi:10.1177/105649269543010

Bass, B. M. (1999). Two decades of research and development in transformational leadership. *European Journal of Work and Organizational Psychology, 8*(1), 9–32. doi:10.1080/135943299398410

Bass, B. M., & Avolio, B. J. (1995). *MLQ: Multifactor Leadership Questionnaire* (2nd ed.). Mind Garden.

Bass, B. M., & Riggio, R. E. (2006). *Transformational Leadership* (2nd ed.). Lawrence Erlbaum Associates, Inc.

Batson, C. D., Van Lange, P. A. M., Ahmad, N., & Lishner, D. A. (2003). Altruism and helping behavior. In M. A. Hogg & J. Cooper (Eds.), *Sage Handbook of Social Psychology* (pp. 279–295). London: Sage Publications.

Battye, F. (2015). Payment by Results in the UK: Progress to date and future directions for evaluation. *Evaluation, 21*(2), 189–203. doi:10.1177/1356389015577464

Battye, F., & Sunderland, J. (2011). *Thinking about....* Payment by Results. GHK.

Baumol, W. J. (2010). *The Microtheory of Innovative Entrepreneurship*. Princeton, NJ: Princeton University Press. doi:10.2307/j.ctt21668j9

Bayik, M. (2017). Innovative Processes in New Product and Service Development. In *Global Business Strategies in Crisis* (pp. 215–229). Springer International Publishing. doi:10.1007/978-3-319-44591-5_15

Beckmann, M., & Zeyen, A. (2014). Franchising as a Strategy for Combining Small and Large Group Advantages (Logics) in Social Entrepreneurship: A Hayekian Perspective. *Nonprofit and Voluntary Sector Quarterly, 43*(3), 502–522. doi:10.1177/0899764012470758

Bekkers, V. J. J. M., Tummers, L. G., & Voorberg, W. H. (2013). *From public innovation to social innovation in the public sector: A literature review of relevant drivers and barriers*. Rotterdam: Erasmus University Rotterdam.

Bendell, B. L. (2017). I don't want to be green: Prosocial motivation effects on firm environmental innovation rejection decisions. *Journal of Business Ethics, 143*(2), 277–288. doi:10.100710551-015-2588-2

Bengtsson, M., Eriksson, J., & Wincent, J. (2010). Co-opetition dynamics–an outline for further inquiry. *Competitiveness Review, 20*(2), 194–214. doi:10.1108/10595421011029893

Bernardino, S. & Santos, J. (2015). Antecedents of a new social venture in Portugal: The influence of education and professional background. *Tehkne – Review of Applied Management Studies, 13*(2), 122-134.

Berstell, G., & Nitterhouse, D. (1997). Looking'outside the box'. *Marketing Research, 9*(2), 4.

Besler, S. (2010). Sosyal Girişimcilik. In S. Besler (Ed.), *Sosyal Girişimcilik* (pp. 3–28). İstanbul: Beta Yayınları.

Besler, S. (2010). *Sosyal girişimcilik*. İstanbul: Beta Yayınevi.

Betil, İ. (2010). Sivil toplum, sosyal sermaye, sosyal girişimcilik. *Journal of Entrepreneurship and Development, 5*(1), 21–25.

Beugre, C. (2017). *Social Entrepreneurship: Managing the Creation of Social Value*. New York: Routledge.

Bhati, A., & Manimala, M. J. (2011). Talent acquisition and retention in social enterprises. *Journal of Security and Sustainability Issues, 1*(1), 39–52. doi:10.9770/jssi.2011.1.1(4)

Bhati, A., & Manimala, M. J. (2011). *Talent Acquisition and Retention in Social Enterprises: Innovations in HR Strategies*. Bangalore: Indian Institute of Management.

Bhawe, N., Gupta, V. K., & Jain, T. K. (2007). *The Entrepreneurship Of The Good Samaritan: A Qualitative Study To Understand How Opportunities Are Perceived In Social Entrepreneurship*. Paper presented at the Babson College Entrepreneurship Research Conference, Madrid, Spain.

Bhawe, N., Jain, T. K., & Gupta, V. K. (2006). *The entrepreneurship of the Good Samaritan: A development framework to understand social entrepreneurship using insights from qualitative study*. Retrieved 10.06.2017, from https://papers.ssrn.com/sol3/papers.cfm?abstract_id=902685

Bhawuk, D. P., Mrazek, S., & Munusamy, V. P. (2009). *From Social Engineering to Community Transformation: Amul*. Grameen Bank and Mondragon as Exemplar Organizations.

Bikse, V., Rivza, B., & Riemere, I. (2015). The Social Entrepreneur as a Promoter of Social Advancement. *Procedia: Social and Behavioral Sciences, 185*, 469–478. doi:10.1016/j.sbspro.2015.03.405

Bilodeau, L., Podger, J., & Abd-El-Aziz, A. (2014). Advancing campus and community sustainability: Strategic alliances in action. *International Journal of Sustainability in Higher Education, 15*(2), 157–168. doi:10.1108/IJSHE-06-2012-0051

Birley, S. (1985). The role of networks in the entrepreneurial process. *Journal of Business Venturing, 1*(1), 107–117. doi:10.1016/0883-9026(85)90010-2

BIS. (2011). *Delivering best value through innovation: Forward commitment procurement*. BIS.

BIS. (2011). *The path to strong, sustainable and balanced growth*. HM Treasury.

Bititci, U., Garengo, P., Dörfler, V., & Nudurupati, S. (2011). Performance measurement: Challenges for tomorrow. *International Journal of Management Reviews, 14*(3), 305–327. doi:10.1111/j.1468-2370.2011.00318.x

Black, J., Hashimzade, N., & Myles, G. (2009). *Dictionary of Economics*. Oxford University Press. doi:10.1093/acref/9780199237043.001.0001

Blank, S. (2005). *The Four Steps to the Epiphany: Successful Strategies for Products that Win*. Cafepress.com.

Blank, C. (2012). Human Resource Management and Volunteer Motivation. In C. K. Volkmann, K. O. Tokarski, & K. Ernst (Eds.), *Social Entrepreneurship and Social Business* (pp. 66–82). Wiesbaden: Springer Gabler. doi:10.1007/978-3-8349-7093-0_4

Blank, S. (2013). *The four steps to the epiphany: successful strategies for products that win.* BookBaby.

Blank, S. (2013). Why the lean start-up changes everything. *Harvard Business Review, 91*(5), 63–72.

Block, J. H., & Wagner, M. (2010). Necessity and Opportunity Entrepreneurs in Germany: Characteristics and Earnings Differentials. *Schmalenbach Business Review, 62*(2), 154–174. doi:10.1007/BF03396803

Bloom, N. P., & Chatterji, K. A. (2009). Scaling social entrepreneurship impact. *California Management Review, 51*(3), 114–133. doi:10.2307/41166496

Bollingtoft, A., & Ulhoi, J. P. (2005). The networked business incubator—leveraging entrepreneurial agency? *Journal of Business Venturing, 20*(2), 265–290. doi:10.1016/j.jbusvent.2003.12.005

Bolton, P. (2006). Government procurement as a policy tool in South Africa. *Journal of Public Procurement, 6*(3), 193.

Boluk, K. A., & Mottiar, Z. (2014). Motivations of social entrepreneurs: Blurring the social contribution and profits dichotomy. *Social Enterprise Journal, 10*(1), 53–68. doi:10.1108/SEJ-01-2013-0001

Boris, E. T., & Steuerle, C. E. (1999). *Nonprofits and Government: Collaboration and Conflict.* Washington, DC: Urban Institute Press.

Bornstein, D., & Davis, S. (2010). Social Entrepreneurship. New York: Oxford.

Bornstein, D. (1998). Changing the World on a Shoestring. *Atlantic Monthly, 281*(1), 34–39.

Bornstein, D. (2007). *How to change the world: social entrepreneurs and the power of new idea.* Oxford University Press.

Bornstein, D. (2007). *How to Change the World: Social Entrepreneurs and the Power of New Ideas, Updated Edition.* Oxford University Press.

Bornstein, D. (2007). *How to change the world: Social entrepreneurs and the power of new ideas.* Oxford University Press.

Bornstein, D. (2007). *How to Change the World: Social Entrepreneurs and the Power of New Ideas.* Oxford University Press.

Bornstein, D., & Davis, S. (2010). *Social Entrepreneurship What Everyone Needs To Know.* New York: Oxford University Press, Inc.

Bornstein, D., & Davis, S. (2010). *Social entrepreneurship: What everyone needs to know.* New York: Oxford University Press, Inc.

Bornstein, D., & Davis, S. (2010). *Social Entrepreneurship: What Everyone Needs to Know?* Oxford University Press.

Borozan, D., & Pfeifer, S. (2014). Exploring entrepreneurs' motivation: Comparison of Croatia, European post-socialist and developed countries. *The Journal of Entrepreneurship, 23*(2), 263–287. doi:10.1177/0971355714535305

Borzaga, C., & Santuari, A. (2001). Italy: from traditional co- operatives to innovative social enterprises. In C. Borzaga & J. Defourny (Eds.), *The Emergence of Social Enterprise* (pp. 166–181). London: Routledge.

Borzaga, C., & Solari, L. (2001). Management challenges for social enterprises. In C. Borzaga & J. Defourny (Eds.), *The Emergence of Social Enterprise* (pp. 333–349). London: Routledge.

Boschee, J. (2006). Social Entrepreneurship: The Promise and the Perils. In A. Nicholls (Ed.), Social Entrepreneurship: New Models of Sustainable Social Change. Oxford University Press.

Boschee, J., & McClurg, J. (2003). Toward a better understanding of social entrepreneurship: Some important distinctions. Bond for International Development (2014) Payment by results: what it means for UK NGOs. London: Academic Press.

Boschee, J. (2008). Social entrepreneurship: The promise and the perils. In A. Nicholls (Ed.), *Social entrepreneurship: New models of sustainable social change* (pp. 356–390). Oxford, UK: Oxford University Press.

Bouckaert, L., & Vandenhove, J. (1998). Business ethics and the management of non-profit organizations. *Journal of Business Ethics*, *17*(9/10), 1073–1081. doi:10.1023/A:1006071416514

Bouncken, R. B., Pesch, R., & Gudergan, S. P. (2015). Strategic embeddedness of modularity in alliances: Innovation and performance implications. *Journal of Business Research*, *68*(7), 1388–1394. doi:10.1016/j.jbusres.2015.01.020

Bovaird, T., & Davies, R. (2011). Outcome-based service commissioning and delivery: Does it make a difference? In New Steering Concepts in Public Management. Emerald Group Publishing Limited.

Bovaird, T. (2014). Attributing outcomes to social policy interventions–'Gold standard 'or 'fool's gold' in public policy and management? *Social Policy and Administration*, *48*(1), 1–23. doi:10.1111/j.1467-9515.2012.00869.x

Bovaird, T., Dickinson, H., & Allen, K. (2012). *Commissioning across government: review of evidence. Research Report 86*. Birmingham, UK: Third Sector Research Centre.

Boyle, D. (2011). The pitfalls and perils of payment by results. *Local Economy*, *26*(8), 627–634. doi:10.1177/0269094211422203

Bozeman, B. (2007). *Public values and public interest: Counterbalancing economic individualism*. Washington, DC: Georgetown University Press.

Brady, A., & Haugh, H. (2008). Social Entrepreneurship & Networks. *Journal of Finance and Management in Public Services*, *6*(3), 29–44.

Braga, J. C., Proenca, T., & Ferreira, M. R. (2014). Motivations for social entrepreneurship–Evidences from Portugal. *Tékhne (Instituto Politécnico do Cávado e do Ave)*, *12*, 11–21. doi:10.1016/j.tekhne.2015.01.002

Brass, D. C., Butterfield, K. D., & Skaggs, B. C. (1998). Relationships and unethical behavior: A social network perspective. *Academy of Management Review*, *23*(1), 14–31.

Bridge, S., O'Neill, K., & Cromie, S. (1998). *Understanding enterprise, entrepreneurship and small firms*. London: Macmillan. doi:10.1007/978-1-349-26171-0

Brinkerhoff, P. (2001). Why you need to be more entrepreneurial — an how to get started. *Nonprofit World*, *19*(6), 12–15.

Brock, D. D., Steinder, S. D., & Kim, M. (2008). Social entrepreneurship education: Is it achieving the desired aims? *USABE 2008 Proceedings*.

Brookfield Global Relocation Services. (2016). *Global mobility trends survey — Breakthrough to the future of global talent mobility*. Retrieved from http://globalmobilitytrends.bgrs.com/#/role-of-mobility

Brooks, A. C. (2009). *Social entrepreneurship: A modern approach to social value creation*. Pearson Prentice Hall.

Brouard, F., & Larivet, S. (2010), Essay of clarifcations and defnitions of the related concepts of social enterprise, social entrepreneur and social entrepreneurship. Handbook Of Research On Social Entrepreneurship.

Brouard, F., & Larivet, S. (2010). Essay of clarifications and definitions of the related concepts of social enterprise, social entrepreneur and social entrepreneurship. In A. Fayolle & H. Matlay (Eds.), *Handbook of research on social entrepreneurship* (pp. 29–56). Cheltenham: Edward Elgar. doi:10.4337/9781849804684.00008

Brouthers, K. D., Nakos, G., & Dimitratos, P. (2015). SME entrepreneurial orientation, international performance, and the moderating role of strategic alliances. *Entrepreneurship Theory and Practice*, *39*(5), 1161–1187. doi:10.1111/etap.12101

Brown, M., & Redman, T. (2017). Performance Appraisal. In A.Wilkinson, T. Redman, & T. Dundon (Eds.), Contemporary human resource management: Text and cases (pp. 189-210). Pearson Education.

Brown, M. E., & Treviño, L. K. (2006). Ethical leadership: A review and future directions. *The Leadership Quarterly*, *17*(6), 595–616. doi:10.1016/j.leaqua.2006.10.004

Brown, M. E., Treviño, L. K., & Harrison, D. A. (2005). Ethical leadership: A social learning perspective for construct development and testing. *Organizational Behavior and Human Decision Processes*, *97*(2), 117–134. doi:10.1016/j.obhdp.2005.03.002

Brown, W., Yoshioka, C. F., & Munoz, P. (2004). Organizational Mission as a Core Dimension in Employee Retention. *Journal of Park and Recreation Administration*, *22*(2), 28–43.

Bruderl, J., & Preisendorfer, P. (1998). Network support and the success of newly founded businesses. *Small Business Economics*, *10*(3), 213–225. doi:10.1023/A:1007997102930

Bruntland Commission. (1987). *Our Common Future-Towards Sustainable Development.* World Commission on Economic Developmet (WCED). Retrieved from http://www.un-documents.net/our-common-future.pdf

Bryman, A., & Bell, E. (2015). *Business research methods.* Oxford University Press.

Bubb, S., & Michell, R. (2009). Investing in third-sector capacity. In P. Hunter (Ed.), *Social Enterprise for Public Service: How does the Third Sector Deliver?* London: The Smith Institute.

Buckingham, H. (2009). Competition and contracts in the voluntary sector: Exploring the implications for homelessness service providers in Southampton. *Policy and Politics*, *37*(2), 235–254. doi:10.1332/030557309X441045

Buckingham, H., Pinch, S., & Sunley, P. (2012). The enigmatic regional geography of social enterprise in the UK: A conceptual framework and synthesis of the evidence. *Area*, *44*(1), 83–91. doi:10.1111/j.1475-4762.2011.01043.x

Bugg-Levine, A., & Emerson, J. (2011). Impact investing: Transforming how we make money while making a difference. *Innovations*, *6*(3), 9–18. doi:10.1162/INOV_a_00077

Bugra, A. (2013). Revisiting the Wollstonecraft dilemma in the context of conservative liberalism: The case of female employment in Turkey. *Social Politics*, *21*(1), 148–166. doi:10.1093p/jxt001

Bull, M. (2007). Balance: The development of a social enterprise business performance analysis tool. *Social Enterprise Journal*, *3*(1), 49–66. doi:10.1108/17508610780000721

Burdge, R. J., & Vanclay, F. (1996). Social impact assessment: A contribution to the state of the art series. *Environmental and Social Impact Assessment*, *14*(1), 59–86. doi:10.1080/07349165.1996.9725886

Burga, R., & Rezania, D. (2016). Stakeholder Theory in Social Entrepreneurship: A Descriptive Case Study. *Journal of Global Entrepreneurship*, *6*(4), 1–15.

Burgelman, R. A. (1983). Corporate entrepreneurship and strategic management: Insights from a process study. *Management Science*, *29*(12), 1349–1364. doi:10.1287/mnsc.29.12.1349

Burke, R. J. (2012). Human resource management in the nonprofit sector: setting the stage. In R. J. Burke & C. L. Cooper (Eds.), *Human resource management in the nonprofit sector: passion, purpose and professionalism* (pp. 3–50). Edward Elgar Publishing. doi:10.4337/9780857937308.00007

Burkett, I. (2010). *Sustainable Social Enterprise - What does it really mean?* Foresters Community Finance. Retrieved from http://cdn.socialtraders.com.au/app/uploads/2016/08/Sustainable-Social-Enterprise -Ingrid-Burkett.pdf

Burt, E., & Scholarios, D. (2011). Recruiting for Values in Charitable Organisations. *Voluntary Organisations and Public Service Delivery*, *14*, 104.

Burton, M. D., Sørensen, J. B., & Beckman, C. M. (2002). *Coming from good stock: Career histories and new venture formation*. Retrieved July 2017 from Cornell University, ILR School site: http://digitalcommons.ilr.cornell.edu/articles/250/

Burt, R. S. (1995). *Structural Holes: The Social Structural of Competition*. Harvard University Press.

Busch, C. (2013). Social *entrepreneurs as network orchestrators –how and why do social entrepreneurs build up and leverage social networks to perform* (Unpublished doctoral dissertation). The London School of Economics and Political Science.

Busch, C. (2014). Substantiating Social Entrepreneurship Research: Exploring the Potential of Integrating Social Capital and Networks Approaches. *International Journal of Entrepreneurial Venturing*, *6*(1), 69–84. doi:10.1504/IJEV.2014.059401

Butler, J., & Hansen, G. S. (1991). Network evolution, entrepreneurial success, and regional development. *Entrepreneurship and Regional Development*, *3*(1), 1–16. doi:10.1080/08985629100000001

Cabinet Office and HM Treasury. (2010). *Call for evidence on public service reform. London: HM Treasury Cabinet Office (2010) The Compact*. London: Cabinet Office.

Cabinet Office, Office of the Third Sector. (2009). *A guide to Social Return on Investment*. Society Media.

Cabinet Office. (2007). *Partnership in Public Services: An action plan for third sector involvement*. London: Cabinet Office.

Cabinet Office. (2010). *Modernising Commissioning: Increasing the Role of Charities, Social Enterprises, Mutuals and Cooperatives in Public Service Delivery*. London: HMSO.

Cabinet Office. (2011). *The lean review: accelerating government procurement*. Retrieved from http://www.cabinetoffice.gov.uk/sites/default/files/resources/annex-A-lean-procurement-study-managementsummary.pdf

Cabinet Office. (2012). Making government business more accessible to SMEs: One year on. Cabinet Office.

Cajaiba-Santana, G. (2010). Socially constructed opportunities in social entrepreneurship: a structuration model. In A. Fayolle & H. Matlay (Eds.), *Handbook of research on social entrepreneurship* (pp. 88–106). Cheltenham, UK: Edward Elgar. doi:10.4337/9781849804684.00010

Cajaiba-Santana, G. (2014). Social innovation: Moving the field forward. A conceptual framework. *Technological Forecasting and Social Change*, *82*, 42–51. doi:10.1016/j.techfore.2013.05.008

Cardy, R. L., & Selvarajan, T. T. (2006). Competencies: Alternative frameworks for competitive advantage. *Business Horizons*, *49*(3), 235–245.

Carmel, E., & Harlock, J. (2008). Instituting the 'third sector' as a governable terrain: Partnership, procurement and performance in the UK. *Policy and Politics*, *36*(2), 155–171. doi:10.1332/030557308783995017

Carroll, A. (1979). A Three-Dimensional Conceptual Model of Corporate Social Performance. *Academy of Management Review*, *4*, 497–505.

Carroll, N., Burke, M., & Carroll, M. (2010). A Case of Social Entrepreneurship: Tackling Homelessness. *Journal of Business Case Studies*, *6*(5), 83–95.

Caslin, M. J., III, Sachet, M., & Shevinsky, E. (2016). An Overview of Structural Options and Issues. In T. S. Lyons (Ed.), Social Entrepreneurship: How Businesses can transform Society? Santa Barbara, CA: Praeger.

Castles, S., & Miller, M. J. (2009). *The Age of Migration: International Population Movements in the Modern World* (4th ed.). Basingstoke, UK: Palgrave MacMillan. Retrieved from http://www.jcer.net/index.php/jcer/article/view/188

Catford, J. (1998). Social entrepreneurs are vital for health promotion—but they need supportive environments too. *Health Promotion International*, *13*(2), 95–97. doi:10.1093/heapro/13.2.95

CCSE. (2001). *Social entrepreneurship.* Discussion Paper No 1. Canadian Center for Social Entrepreneurship (CCSE).

Center for Global Development Official Website. (n.d.). Retrieved from https://www.cgdev.org

Certo, S. T., & Miller, T. (2008). Social entrepreneurship: Key issues and concepts. *Business Horizons*, *51*(4), 267–271. doi:10.1016/j.bushor.2008.02.009

Çetindamar, D., Tutal, E., Titiz, S., & Taluk, Ş. (2010). Sosyal Dönüşümün Ajanları: Social entrepreneurler. In *Social Entrepreneurship Conference*. Sakıp Sabancı Üniversitesi. Retrieved from http://www.sosyalinovasyonmerkezi.com.tr/yayin/2020100002.pdf

Çetínkaya Bozkurt, Ö., Kalkan, A., Koyuncu, O. & Alparslan, A. M. (2012). Türkíye'de Girişimciliğin Gelişimi: Girişimciler Üzerine Nitel Bir Araştırma. *Süleyman Demirel Üniversitesi Sosyal Bilimler Enstitüsü Dergisi*, *15*, 229-247.

Chahine, T. (2016). *Introduction to Social Entrepreneurship.* Taylor & Francis Group.

Chahine, T. (2016). *Introduction to Social Entrepreneurship.* Boca Raton, FL: CRC Press - Taylor & Francis Group. doi:10.1201/b19475

Chandler, D. (2015). *Corporate Social Responsibility, A Strategic Perspective.* New York: Business Expert Press.

Chang, Y. K. (2013). *How and why employees engage in corporate volunteering* (Doctoral dissertation). Available from ProQuest Dissertations and Theses. Available from ProQuest Dissertations and Theses database. (UMI No.1428359955)

Charity Commission. (2011). *Consortia for the delivery of public services: The issues for small and medium-sized charities.* Liverpool, UK: Charity Commission.

Chauvin, B., Hermand, D., & Mullet, E. (2007). Risk perception and personality facets. *Risk Analysis*, *27*(1), 171–185. doi:10.1111/j.1539-6924.2006.00867.x PMID:17362408

Chell, E., Nicolopoulou, K., & Karataş-Özkan, M. (2010). *Social entrepreneurship and enterprise: International and innovation perspectives.* Academic Press.

Chell, E. (2007). Social enterprise and entrepreneurship: Towards a convergent theory of the entrepreneurial process. *International Small Business Journal*, *25*(5), 5–26. doi:10.1177/0266242607071779

Chen, M. (2007). Entrepreneurial Leadership and New Ventures: Creativity in Entrepreneurial Teams. *Creativity and Innovation Management*, *16*(3), 239–249. doi:10.1111/j.1467-8691.2007.00439.x

Chen, M. J., Kuo-Hsien, S. U., & Tsai, W. (2007). Competitive tension: The awareness-motivation-capability perspective. *Academy of Management Journal*, *50*(1), 101–118. doi:10.5465/AMJ.2007.24162081

Chen, S. (2011). The study on organizational development for social enterprises in Taiwan. *African Journal of Business Management*, *5*(29), 11614–11629.

Chmelik, E., Musteen, M., & Ahsan, M. (2016). Measures of Performance in the Context of International Social Ventures: An Exploratory Study. *Journal of Social Entrepreneurship*, *7*(1), 74–100. doi:10.1080/19420676.2014.997781

Cho, A. H. (2006). Politics, values and social entrepreneurship: A critical appraisal. In J. Mair, J. Robinson, & K. Hockerts (Eds.), *Social entrepreneurship* (pp. 34–56). New York: Palgrave Macmillan. doi:10.1057/9780230625655_4

Choi, D. Y., & Gray, E. (2010). *Values-centered entrepreneurs and their companies*. Routledge.

Choi, D. Y., & Gray, E. R. (2010). *Values-Centered Entrepreneurs and Their Companies: How a New Brand of Entrepreneurs Build Profitably Companies and Make a Positive Contribution to Society*. New York: Routledge.

Choi, N., & Majumdar, S. (2014). Social entrepreneurship as an essentially contested concept: Opening a new avenue for systematic future research. *Journal of Business Venturing*, *29*(3), 363–376. doi:10.1016/j.jbusvent.2013.05.001

Christensen, C. M., Anthony, S. D., Berstell, G., & Nitterhouse, D. (2007). Finding the right job for your product. *MIT Sloan Management Review*, *48*(3), 38.

Christie, M. J., & Honig, B. (2006). Social entrepreneurship: New research findings. *Journal of World Business*, *41*(1), 1–5. doi:10.1016/j.jwb.2005.10.003

Cialdini, R. B., Brown, S. L., Lewis, B. P., Luce, C., & Neuberg, S. L. (1997). Reinterpreting the empathy–altruism relationship: When one into one equals oneness. *Journal of Personality and Social Psychology*, *73*(3), 481–494. doi:10.1037/0022-3514.73.3.481 PMID:9294898

Clark, C., Rosenzweig, W., Long, D., & Olsen, S. (2004). *Double bottom line project report: Assessing social impact in double bottom line ventures*. New York: Rockefeller Foundation.

Clarke, J., Kane, D., & Wilding, K. (2012). *UK Civil Society Almanac 2012*. London: NCVO.

Clausen, J. A. (1998). Live reviews and life stories. In J. Z. Giele & H. H. J. Elder (Eds.), *Methods of Life Course Research: Qualitative and Quantitative Approaches: 189 – 121*. Thousand Oaks, CA: Sage. doi:10.4135/9781483348919.n8

Cnaan, R. A., & Cascio, T. A. (1998). Performance and commitment: Issues in management of volunteers in human service organizations. *Journal of Social Service Research*, *24*(3-4), 1–37. doi:10.1300/J079v24n03_01

Cogliser, C. C., & Brigham, K. H. (2004). The intersection of leadership and entrepreneurship: Mutual lessons to be learned. *The Leadership Quarterly*, *15*(6), 771–799. doi:10.1016/j.leaqua.2004.09.004

Coleman, J. S. (1990). *Foundations of social theory*. Cambridge, MA: Harvard University Press.

Collings, D. (2014). Integrating global mobility and global talent management: Exploring the challenges and strategic opportunities. *Journal of World Business*, *49*(2), 253–261. doi:10.1016/j.jwb.2013.11.009

Commission of the European Communities. (2001). Promoting a European Framework for Corporate Social Responsibilities. COM (2001) 366 final, Brussels.

Connolly, T., Conlon, E. M., & Deutsch, S. J. (1980). Organizational effectiveness: A multiple constituency approach. *Academy of Management Review*, *5*, 211–218.

Cools, E., & Van Den Broeck, H. (2008). Cognitive styles and managerial behaviour: A qualitative study. *Education + Training*, *50*(2), 103–114. doi:10.1108/00400910810862092

Cooper, A. C. (1993). Predicting new firm performance. *Journal of Business Venturing*, *8*(3), 241–253. doi:10.1016/0883-9026(93)90030-9

Cope, J., Jack, S., & Rose, M. B. (2007). Social capital and entrepreneurship. *International Small Business Journal, 25*(3), 213–219. doi:10.1177/0266242607076523

Corner, P. D., & Ho, M. (2010). How opportunities develop in social entrepreneurship. *Entrepreneurship Theory and Practice, 34*(4), 635–659. doi:10.1111/j.1540-6520.2010.00382.x

Coşkun, E. (2015). *Gönüllü kuruluşların okul öncesi sosyal girişimcilik eğitimindeki rolü.* Yalova University Masters's Thesis.

Costa, E., & Pesci, C. (2016). Social impact measurement: Why do stakeholders matter? *Sustainability Accounting. Management and Policy Journal, 7*(1), 99–124.

Crant, J. M. (1996). The proactive personality scale as a predictor of entrepreneurial intentions. *Journal of Small Business Management, 34*(3), 42.

Crossan, D., Ibbotson, P., & Bell, J. (2011). The hologram effect in entrepreneurial "social commercial" enterprises: Triggers and tipping points. *Journal of Small Business and Enterprise Development, 18*(4), 655–672. doi:10.1108/14626001111179730

Culyer, J. A. (2005). *Dictionary of Health Economics*. Edward Elgar Publishings.

Cunningham, I. (1999). Human resource management in the voluntary sector: Challenges and opportunities. *Public Money & Management, 19*(2), 19–25. doi:10.1111/1467-9302.00161

Curral, L., Santos, S., & Caetano, A. (2013). Theoretical foundation of the entrepreneurial potential. *Amity Business Journal, 2*(1), 1–11.

Currie, G., & Manns, B. (2002). *Evidence-Based Health Economics: From Effectiveness to Efficiency in Systematic Review* (C. Donaldson, M. Mugford, L. Vale, B. M. J. Books, & B. M. A. House, Eds.). London: Tavistock Square.

Dacin, M. T., Dacin, P. A., & Tracey, P. (2011). Social entrepreneurship: A critique and future directions. *Organization Science, 22*(5), 1203–1213. doi:10.1287/orsc.1100.0620

Dacin, P. A., Dacin, M. T., & Matear, M. (2010). Social entrepreneurship: Why we don't need a new theory and how we move forward from here. *The Academy of Management Perspectives, 24*(3), 37–57. doi:10.5465/AMP.2010.52842950

Das, T. K., & Kumar, R. (2011). Regulatory focus and opportunism in the alliance development process. *Journal of Management, 37*(3), 682–708. doi:10.1177/0149206309356325

Das, T. K., & Teng, B. S. (2000). A resource-based theory of strategic alliances. *Journal of Management, 26*(1), 31–61. doi:10.1177/014920630002600105

David, F. (2013). *Strategic Management* (14th ed.). Pearson.

David, R. J., & Han, S. K. (2004). A systematic assessment of the empirical support for transaction cost economics. *Strategic Management Journal, 25*(1), 39–58.

Davidsson, P., & Honig, B. L. (2003). The role of social and human capital among nascent entrepreneurs. *Journal of Business Venturing, 18*(3), 301–331. doi:10.1016/S0883-9026(02)00097-6

Davis, S. M. (2002). *Social entrepreneurship: Towards an entrepreneurial culture for social and economic development.* Academic Press.

Davis, M. H. (1983a). Measuring individual differences in empathy: Evidence for a multidimensional approach. *Journal of Personality and Social Psychology, 44*(1), 13–126. doi:10.1037/0022-3514.44.1.113

Dawson, P., & Daniel, L. (2010). Understanding social innovation: A provisional framework. *International Journal of Technology Management*, *51*(1), 9–21. doi:10.1504/IJTM.2010.033125

Day, S. W., & Jean-Denis, H. (2016). Resource Based View of Social Entrepreneurship: Putting the Pieces Together. *Journal of Strategic Innovation and Sustainability*, *11*(2), 59–69.

De Koning, A. J., & Muzyka, D. F. (1999). *Conceptualising Opportunity Recognition as a Socio-Cognitive Process.* SSE/EFI Working Paper Series, No:13.

De Paula, G. O., & Cavalcanti, R. N. (2000). Ethics: Essence for Sustainability. *Journal of Cleaner Production*, *8*, 119–117.

Dees, J. G. (1998). Enterprising Non-profits. *Harvard Business Review*, *76*, 55–67.

Dees, J. G. (1998). *The meaning of "Social Entrepreneurship"*. Stanford University; Draft report for the Kauffman Center for Entrepreneurial Leadership. Retrieved from https://csistg.gsb.stanford.edu/sites/ csi.gsb.stanford.edu/files / TheMeaningofsocialEntrepreneurship.pdf

Dees, J. G. (1998). *The meaning of social entrepreneurship*. Academic Press.

Dees, J. G. (1998). *The meaning of social entrepreneurship*. Retrieved 03.03.2017, from http://www.redalmarza.cl/ing/pdf/TheMeaningofsocialEntrepreneurship.pdf

Dees, J. G. (1998). *The meaning of social entrepreneurship*. Retrieved from www.slideshare.net/rvangeldro/building-mvp

Dees, J. G. (2001). *The meaning of "social entrepreneurship."* Retrieved from http://www.caseatduke.org/documents/dees_sedef.pdf

Dees, J. G. (2007). Taking Social Entrepreneurship Seriously. Transaction Social Science and Modern Society, 44(3).

Dees, G. (1998). *The Meaning of "Social Entrepreneurship"*. The Kauffman Center for Entrepreneurial Leadership.

Dees, J. G. (1994). *Social enterprise: Private initiatives for the common good*. Harvard Business School.

Dees, J. G. (1998). Enterprising nonprofits. *Harvard Business Review*, *76*, 54–69. PMID:10176919

Dees, J. G. (1998). Enterprising nonprofits: What do you do when traditional sources of funding fall short? *Harvard Business Review*, *76*(1), 55–67. PMID:10176919

Dees, J. G. (1998). *The Meaning of Social Entrepreneurship*. Palo Alto, CA: Stanford University.

Dees, J. G. (2007). Taking social entrepreneurship seriously. *Society*, *44*(3), 24–31. doi:10.1007/BF02819936

Dees, J. G. (2011). Social Ventures as Learning Laboratories. *Tennessee's Business*, *20*(1), 3–5.

Dees, J. G., Emerson, J., & Economy, P. (2001). *Enterprising nonprofits: A toolkit for social entrepreneurs*. New York: John Wiley and Sons, Inc.

Dees, J. G., Emerson, J., & Economy, P. (2001). *Enterprising Nonprofits: A Toolkit for Social Entrepreneurs*. Wiley.

Defourny, J., & Borzaga, C. (2001). From third sector to social enterprise. In C. Borzaga & J. Defourny (Eds.), *The Emergence of Social Enterprise* (pp. 1–28). London: Routledge.

Defourny, J., & Nyssens, M. (2010). Conceptions of social enterprise and social entrepreneurship in Europe and the United States: Convergences and divergences. *Journal of Social Entrepreneurship*, *1*(1), 32–53. doi:10.1080/19420670903442053

Delery, J. E., & Doty, D. H. (1996). Modes of theorizing in strategic human resource management: Tests of universalistic, contingency and configurational performance predictions. *Academy of Management Journal, 39*(4), 802–835. doi:10.2307/256713

Deli, F. (2011). Opportunity and necessity entrepreneurship: Local unemployment and the small firm effect. *Journal of Management Policy and Practice, 12*(4), 38–57.

Denizalp, H. (2009). *Toplumsal dönüşüm için sosyal girişimcilik rehberi.* Ankara: Sivil Toplum Geliştirme Merkezi.

Desa, G. (2007). Social entrepreneurship: snapshots of a research field in emergence. In K. Hockerts, J. Mair, & J. Robinson (Eds.), *Values and opportunities in social entrepreneurship* (pp. 6–28). New York: Palgrave Macmillan.

Dess, G., & Anderson, B. B. (2003). For-Profit Social Ventures. In M. Kourilsky & W. Walstad (Eds.), Social Entrepreneurship. Senate Hall Academic Publishing.

Dess, G. G., & Lumpkin, G. T. (2005). The Role of Entrepreneurial Orientation in Stimulating Effective Corporate Entrepreneurship. *The Academy of Management Executive, 19*(1), 147–156.

Development Co-operation Report. (2015). *Making Partnerships Effective Coalitions for Action.* OECD.

Di Domenico, M., Haugh, H., & Tracey, P. (2010). Social bricolage: Theorizing social value creation in social enterprises. *Entrepreneurship Theory and Practice, 34*(4), 681–703. doi:10.1111/j.1540-6520.2010.00370.x

Dickinson, H., Allen, K., Macmillan, R., & Glasby, J. (2012). *Social Care and the Third Sector.* London: NIHR School for Social Care Research.

Dickinson, H., & Miller, R. (2011). GP commissioning: Implications for the third sector. *Voluntary Sector Review, 2*(3), 265–273. doi:10.1332/204080511X583913

Dienesch, R. M., & Liden, R. C. (1986). Leader-Member Exchange Model of Leadership: A Critique and Further Development. *Academy of Management Review, 11*(3), 618–634.

Dillenburg, S., Greene, T., & Erekson, O. H. (2003). Approaching socially responsible investment with a comprehensive ratings scheme: Total social impact. *Journal of Business Ethics, 43*(3), 167–178. doi:10.1023/A:1022987127960

Doherty, B., Haugh, H., & Lyon, F. (2014, January). Social Enterprises as Hybrid Organizations: A Review and Research Agenda, 16. *International Journal of Management Reviews, 16*(4), 417–436. doi:10.1111/ijmr.12028

Doherty, N., Richardson, J., & Thorn, K. (2013). Self-initiated expatriation and self-initiated expatriates: Clarification of the research stream. *Career Development International, 18*(1), 97–112. doi:10.1108/13620431311305971

Dolan, D. A. (2002). Training needs of administrators in the nonprofit sector: What are they and how should we address them? *Nonprofit Management & Leadership, 12*(3), 277–292. doi:10.1002/nml.12305

Doney, P. M., & Cannon, J. P. (1997). Trust in buyer-seller relationships. *Journal of Marketing, 61*(2), 35–51. doi:10.2307/1251829

Dönmezer, S. (1989). Atatürk inkılâpları ve sosyal değişme teorileri. *Atatürk Araştırma Merkezi Dergisi, 5*(15), 523–537.

Dorin, C. & Alexandru, G. S. (2014). Dynamics of the Entrepreneurship Concept. Literature Review. *Annals of the University of Oradea,* 445-446.

Douglas, H. (2008). Creating knowledge: A review of research methods in three societal change approaches. *Journal of Nonprofit & Public Sector Marketing, 20*(2), 141–163. doi:10.1080/10495140802224787

Drayton, W. (2002). The citizen sector: Becoming as entrepreneurial and competitive as business. *California Management Review*, *44*(3), 120–132. doi:10.2307/41166136

Drayton, W. (2006). Everyone a changemaker: Social entrepreneurship's ultimate goal. *Innovations*, *1*(1), 80–96. doi:10.1162/itgg.2006.1.1.80

Drees, J. M., & Heugens, P. P. (2013). Synthesizing and extending resource dependence theory: A meta-analysis. *Journal of Management*, *39*(6), 1666–1698. doi:10.1177/0149206312471391

Drucker, P. F. (1985). *Innovation and entrepreneurship*. New York: Harper Business.

Drummond, M. F., Aguğar-Ibanez, R., & Nģxon, J. (2006). Economic Evaluation. *Singapore Medical Journal*, *47*(6), 456–462. PMID:16752012

DTI. (2002). *Social enterprise: A strategy for success*. Department of Trade and Industry. Retrieved from http://www.dti.gov.uk

DTI. (2003). *Social enterprise: A progress report on social enterprise*. Department of Trade and Industry. Retrieved from http://www.dti.gov.uk

Ducks Unlimited. (2017, February). *Fact Sheet*. Retrieved from ducs.org: http://www.ducks.org/media/_global/_documents/stateFactSheets/NationalFactSheet.pdf

Dufays, F., & Huybrechts, B. (2014). Connecting the Dots for Social Value: A Review on Social Networks and Social Entrepreneurship. *Journal of Social Entrepreneurship*, *5*(2), 214–237. doi:10.1080/19420676.2014.918052

Du, S., Bhattacharya, C., & Sen, S. (2007). Reaping relational rewards from corporate social responsibility: The role of competitive positioning. *International Journal of Research in Marketing*, *24*(3), 224–241. doi:10.1016/j.ijresmar.2007.01.001

Ebbers, J. J. (2014). Networking behavior and contracting relationships among entrepreneurs in business incubators. *Entrepreneurship Theory and Practice*, *38*(5), 1159–1181. doi:10.1111/etap.12032

Ebrashi, R. E. (2013). Social Entrepreneurship Theory and Sustainable Social Impact. *Social Responsibility Journal*, *9*(2), 188–209. doi:10.1108/SRJ-07-2011-0013

Edinburgh Treasury, H. M. (2007). *Transforming government procurement*. London: TSO.

Edwards, H. C. (2012). Orientation: Welcoming New Volunteers into the Organization. In T. D. Connors (Ed.), *The Volunteer Management Handbook: Leadership Strategies for Success* (2nd ed.; pp. 227–235). John Wiley & Sons. doi:10.1002/9781118386194.ch9

Einolf, C. J. (2009). Will the boomers volunteer during retirement? Comparing the baby boom, silent, and long civic cohorts. *Nonprofit and Voluntary Sector Quarterly*, *2*(38), 181–199. doi:10.1177/0899764008315182

Eisenhardt, K., & Graebner, M. (2007). Theory building from cases: Opportunities and challenges. *Academy of Management Journal*, *50*(1), 25–32. doi:10.5465/AMJ.2007.24160888

Emerson, J. (2003). The Blended Value Proposition: Integrating Social and Financial Returns. *California Management Review*, *45*(4), 35–51. doi:10.2307/41166187

Emerson, J., & Twersky, F. (1996). *New social entrepreneurs: The success, challenge, and lessons of non-profit enterprise creation*. San Francisco: Roberts Foundation.

Emerson, J., Wachowicz, J., & Chun, S. (2000). *Social return on investment: Exploring aspects of value creation in the non-profit sector*. San Francisco: The Roberts Foundation.

Emmanuelli, X. (2012). *S'en fout la mort*. Paris: Editions Les Echappe's.

Entrepreneur. (n.d.). Retrieved 01.03.2017, from https://www.merriam-webster.com/dictionary/entrepreneurship

Eren, E., & Kocapınar, E. B. (2009). Is Intelectual Capital Antecedent Of Enterpreneurship Orientation. *Journal of Global Srategic Management*, *3*(2), 121–135. doi:10.20460/JGSM.2009318465

Erkal, M. E. (2006). *Sosyoloji*. İstanbul: Der Yayınları.

Ernst, K. (2012). Social Entrepreneurs and their Personality. In Social entrepreneurship and social business. An Introduction and Discussion with Case Studies. Springer Gabler. doi:10.1007/978-3-8349-7093-0_3

Ersen, T. B., Kaya, D., & Meydanoğlu, Z. (2010). *Sosyal girişimler ve Türkiye: İhtiyaç analizi raporu*. TÜSEV Yayınları.

Estrin, S., Mickiewicz, T., & Stephan, U. (2013). Entrepreneurship, social capital, and institutions: Social and commercial entrepreneurship across nations. *Entrepreneurship Theory and Practice*, *37*(May), 479–504. doi:10.1111/etap.12019

EU-Commission. (2012a). *Social innovation*. Retrieved September 14, 2017, from http://ec.europa.eu/enterprise/policies/Innovation/policy/social-Innovation/index_en.htm

EU-Commission. (2012b). *Strengthening social innovation in Europe – a journey to affective assessment and metrics*. Retrieved September 14, 2017, from http://ec.europa.eu/enterprise/policies/Innovation/files/social- Innovation/strengthening-social-Innovation_en.pdf

European Business School (EBS). (2012). Retrieved September 14, 2017, from http://www.ebs.edu/socialinnovation.html

European Commission. (2002). *Corporate social responsibility: A business contribution to sustainable development*. Luxembourg: Office for Official Publications of the European Communities.

European Commission. (2010). *Europe 2020. A Strategy for Smart, Sustainable and Inclusive growth*. Retrieved from http://eurlex.europa.eu/LexUriServ/LexUriServ.do?uri=COM:2010: 2020:FIN:EN:PDF

European Commission. (2012). Innovation procurement. Delivering efficiency, quality and sustainability in healthcare. A guide to innovation procurement for the healthcare sector. LCB-HEALTHCARE project, lead market initiative.

Fardig, K., & Hakansson, M. (2014). *The Internalization of Social Enterprises: Mapping patterns in the Internationalization Process of Social Entrepreneurs*. Uppsala University Department of Business Studies Master Thesis Spring Semester 2014.

Fayolle, A., & Matlay, H. H. (2010). *Handbook of research on social entrepreneurship*. Edward Elgar. doi:10.4337/9781849804684

Feldman, C., & Kuyken, W. (2011). Compassion in the landscape of suffering. *Contemporary Buddhism*, *12*(01), 143–155. doi:10.1080/14639947.2011.564831

Felício, J. A., Gonçalves, H. M., & Gonçalves, V. C. (2013). Social value and organizational performance in non-profit social organizations: Social entrepreneurship, leadership, and socioeconomic context effects. *Journal of Business Research*, *66*(10), 2139–2146. doi:10.1016/j.jbusres.2013.02.040

Fernald, L. W., Solomon, G. T., & Tarabishy, A. (2005). A New Paradigm: Entrepreneurial Leadership, Southern. *Business Review (Federal Reserve Bank of Philadelphia)*, 1–11.

Ferrel, O. C., Hirt, G. A., & Ferrel, L. (2016). *Business: A Changing World* (5th ed.). McGraw- Hill Education.

Fichter, J. (2001). *Sosyoloji nedir?* Ankara: Atilla Kitabevi.

Figge, F., Hahn, T., Schaltegger, S., & Wagner, M. (2002). The sustainability balanced scorecard: Linking sustainability management to business strategy. *Business Strategy and the Environment, 11*(5), 269–284. doi:10.1002/bse.339

Fish, A. J., & Wood, J. (2017). Promoting a strategic business focus to balance competitive advantage and corporate social responsibility–missing elements. *Social Responsibility Journal, 13*(1), 78–94. doi:10.1108/SRJ-04-2016-0054

Fishbein, M., & Ajzen, I. (1975). *Belief, Attitude, Intention and Behavior: An Introduction Theory and Research.* Reading, MA: Addison-Wesley.

Flaminio Squazzoni, F. (2009). Social Entrepreneurship and Economic Development in Silicon Valley, A Case Study on The Joint Venture: Silicon Valley Network. *Nonprofit and Voluntary Sector Quarterly, 38*(5), 869–888. doi:10.1177/0899764008326198

Flick, U. (2009). *An introduction to Qualitative Research.* London: Sage.

Floyd, D., & McManus, J. (2005). The role of SME's in improving the competitive position of the European Union. *European Business Review, 17*(2), 144–150. doi:10.1108/09555340510588011

Folland, S., Goodman, A. C., & Stano, M. (2006). *The Economics of Health and Health Care.* New York: Pearson Prentice Hall.

Fowler, A. (2000). NGDOs as a moment in history: Beyond aid social entrepreneurship or civic innovation. *Third World Quarterly, 21*(4), 637–654. doi:10.1080/713701063

Fraser, I. (2013). *Expats—Heroes of Social Enterprise and Innovation.* Retrieved from https://www.angloinfo.com/blogs/global/angloinfo-world-expat-life/expats-the-heroes-of-social-enterprise-and-innovation/

Freeman, R. E. (1984). *Strategic management: A stakeholder approach.* Marshfield, MA: Pitman.

Freudenburg, W. R. (1986). Social impact assessment. *Annual Review of Sociology, 12*(1), 451–478. doi:10.1146/annurev.so.12.080186.002315

Friedman, M. (1962). *Capitalism and Freedom.* Chicago: University of Chicago Press.

Fukuyama, F. (1995). *Trust.* New York: Free Press Paperbacks.

Fukuyama, F. (1996). *Trust: The Social Virtues and the Creation of Prosperity.* Touchstone Books.

Funding Commission. (2010). *Funding the Future: A ten-year framework for civil society.* London: NVCO.

Gafni, A. (1998). Willingness to Pay. *PharmacoEconomics, 14*(5), 465–470. doi:10.2165/00019053-199814050-00001 PMID:10344912

Gafni, A. (2001). Willingness to Pay (WTP): The New-Old Kid on the Economic Evaluation Block. *Canadian Journal of Nursing Research, 33*(1), 59–64. PMID:11928155

Galvin, M. D., & Iannotti, L. (2015). Social Enterprise and Development: The KickStart Model. *Voluntas, 26*(2), 421–441. doi:10.100711266-013-9424-z

Gardner, C. A., Acharya, T., & Yach, D. (2007). Technological and social innovation: A unifying new paradigm for global health. *Health Affairs, 26*(4), 1052–1061. doi:10.1377/hlthaff.26.4.1052 PMID:17630448

Gaut, B. (2000). Art as a cluster concept. In N. Carroll (Ed.), *Theories of art today* (pp. 25–44). Madison, WI: University of Wisconsin Press.

Gebauer, J. E., Riketta, M., Broemer, P., & Maio, G. R. (2008). Pleasure and pressure based prosocial motivation: Divergent relations to subjective well-being. *Journal of Research in Personality*, *42*(2), 399–420. doi:10.1016/j.jrp.2007.07.002

Geddes, M., & Martin, S. (2000). The Policy and Politics of Best Value: Currents, Crosscurrents and Undercurrents in the New Regime. *Policy and Politics*, *28*(3), 379–395. doi:10.1332/0305573002501036

Gelobter, M. (2015). *Lean startups for social change: the revolutionary path to big impact*. Berrett-Koehler Publishers.

Gentile, M. C. (2002). *Social Impact Management: A Definition*. Discussion Paper. The Aspen Institute.

Germak, A. J., & Robinson, J. A. (2014). Exploring the motivation of nascent social entrepreneurs. *Journal of Social Entrepreneurship*, *5*(1), 5–21. doi:10.1080/19420676.2013.820781

Gershon, P. (1999). *Review of civil procurement in central government*. HM Treasury.

Gershon, P. (2004). *Releasing Resources to the Front Line: Independent Review of Public Sector Efficiency*. London: The Stationery Office.

Ghalwash, S., Tolba, A., & Ismail, A. (2017). What motivates social entrepreneurs to start social ventures? An exploratory study in the context of a developing economy. *Social Enterprise Journal*, *13*(3), 268–298. doi:10.1108/SEJ-05-2016-0014

Ghauri, P., & Gronhaug, K. (2002). *Research Methods in Business Studies: A Practical Guide* (2nd ed.). London: Sage.

Gibb, A. A. (1987). Enterprise culture - its meaning and implications for education and training. *Journal of European Industrial Training*, *11*(2), 2–38. doi:10.1108/eb043365

Gibbon, J., & Dey, C. (2011). Developments in Social Impact Measurement in the Third Sector: Scaling Up or Dumbing Down? *Social and Environmental Accountability Journal*, *31*(1), 63–72. doi:10.1080/0969160X.2011.556399

Gibbs, G. R. (2007). *Analysing Qualitative Data*. London: Sage. doi:10.4135/9781849208574

Gilbert, P. (Ed.). (2017). *Compassion: Concepts, Research and Applications*. New York: Routledge Taylor & Francis.

Gladstein, G. A. (1983). Understanding empathy: Integrating counseling, developmental, and social psychology perspectives. *Journal of Counseling Psychology*, *30*(4), 467–482. doi:10.1037/0022-0167.30.4.467

Gladwell, M. (2002). *The Tipping Point: How Little Things Can Make a Big Difference*. Boston: Little, Brown and Company.

Glancey, K. S., & McQuaid, R. W. (2000). *Entrepreneurial economics*. New York: St. Martin's Press, Inc. doi:10.1057/9780333981245

Gojkovic, D., Mills, A., & Meek, R. (2011). *Scoping the involvement of third sector organisations in the seven resettlement pathways for offenders*. Academic Press.

Gonçalves, C. P., Carrara, K., & Schmittel, R. M. (2016). The phenomenon of social enterprises: Are we keeping watch on this cultural practice? *Voluntas*, *27*(4), 1585–1610. doi:10.100711266-015-9624-9

Gonzalez-Perez, M., & Leonard, L. (2013). *International Business, Sustainability and Corporate Social Responsibility*. Bingley, UK: Emerald Group Publishing Limited. doi:10.1108/S2051-5030(2013)11

Googins, B. K., & Rochlin, S. A. (2006). *Corporate Citizenship: Top to Bottom*. Academic Press.

Görün, M., & Kara, M. (2010). Kentsel dönüşüm ve sosyal girişimcilik bağlamında Türkiye'de kentsel yaşam kalitesinin artırılması. *The Journal of American Science*, *8*(2), 140–164.

Government, H. M. (2011). *Open Public Services White Paper*. London: HMSO.

Goyal, S., & Sergi, B. S. (2015). Social Entrepreneurship and Sustainability – Understanding the Context and Key Characteristics. *Journal of Security and Sustainability Issues*, *4*(3), 269–278. doi:10.9770/jssi.2015.4.3(7)

Goyal, S., Sergi, B. S., & Jaiswal, M. P. (2015). Understanding the Challenges and Strategic Actions of Social Entrepreneurship at the Base of the Pyramid. *Management Decision*, *54*(2), 418–440. doi:10.1108/MD-11-2014-0662

Granovetter, M. (1973). The Strength of Weak Ties. *American Journal of Sociology*, *78*(6), 1360–1379. doi:10.1086/225469

Granovetter, M. (2005). The Impact of Social Structure on Economic Outcomes. *The Journal of Economic Perspectives*, *19*(1), 33–50. doi:10.1257/0895330053147958

Grant, A. M. (2008). Does intrinsic motivation fuel the prosocial fire? Motivational synergy in predicting persistence, performance, and productivity. *The Journal of Applied Psychology*, *93*(1), 48–58. doi:10.1037/0021-9010.93.1.48 PMID:18211134

Gray, E. R. (2016). For-Profit Social Entrepreneurship. In T. S. Lyons (Ed.), Social Entrepreneurship: How Businesses can transform Society? Santa Barbara, CA: Praeger.

Gray, D. E. (2013). Doing research in the real world. *Sage (Atlanta, Ga.)*.

Green, P. (2010). *Efficiency reviews: key findings and recommendations*. Retrieved from http://www.cabinetoffice.gov.uk/sites/default/files/resources/sirphilipgreenrevie w.pdf

Greenberg, D., McKone-Sweet, K., & Wilson, H. J. (2011). *The New Entrepreneurial Leader*. Berrett-Koehler Pub.

Greenleaf, R. K. (1977). *Servant Leadership*. New York: Paulist Press.

Greve, A., & Salaff, J. W. (2003). Social networks and entrepreneurship. *Entrepreneurship Theory and Practice*, *28*(1), 1–22. doi:10.1111/1540-8520.00029

Griffin, J. J., & Mahon, J. F. (1997). The Corporate Social Performance and Corporate Financial Performance Debate: Twenty-Five Years of Incomparable Research. *Business & Society*, *36*(1), 5–31. doi:10.1177/000765039703600102

Grimes, M. G., McMullen, J. S., Vogus, T. J., & Miller, T. J. (2013). Studying the Origins of Social Entrepreneurship: Compassion and the Role of Embedded Agency. *Academy of Management Review*, *38*(3), 460–463. doi:10.5465/amr.2012.0429

Grimm, R., Fox, C., Baines, S., & Albertson, K. (2013). Social innovation, an answer to contemporary societal challenges? Locating the concept in theory and practice. *Innovation (Abingdon)*, *26*(4), 436–455. doi:10.1080/13511610.2013.848163

Groot, A. & Dankbaar, B. (2014). Does Social Innovation Require Social Entrepreneurship? *Technology Innovation Management Review*, 14-26.

Groot, A., & Dankbaar, B. (2014). Does Social Innovation Require Social Entrepreneurship? *Technology Innovation Management Review, 4*(12).

Groot, A., & Dankbaar, B. (2014). Does Social Innovation Require Social Entrepreneurship? *Technology Innovation Management Review*, *4*(12), 17–26.

Guclu, A., Dees, J. G., & Anderson, B. B. (2002). The process of social entrepreneurship: Creating opportunities worthy of serious pursuit. *Center for the Advancement of Social Entrepreneurship, 1*, 1-15.

Güler, B. K. (2010). *Sosyal Girişimcilik, Efil Yayınevi, 1*. Ankara: Basım.

Gupta, J., & Vegelin, C. (2016). Sustainable development goals and inclusive development. *International Environmental Agreement: Politics, Law and Economics*, *16*(3), 433–448. doi:10.100710784-016-9323-z

Gupta, V., MacMillan, I. C., & Surie, G. (2004). Entrepreneurial leadership: Developing and measuring a cross-cultural construct. *Journal of Business Venturing*, *19*(2), 241–260. doi:10.1016/S0883-9026(03)00040-5

Haber, J. (2016). *The Business of Good: Social Entrepreneurship and the New Bottom-Line*. US: Entrepreneur Press.

Haeussler, C., & Higgins, M. J. (2014). Strategic alliances: Trading ownership for capabilities. *Journal of Economics & Management Strategy*, *23*(1), 178–203. doi:10.1111/jems.12047

Haeussler, C., Patzelt, H., & Zahra, S. A. (2012). Strategic alliances and product development in high technology new firms: The moderating effect of technological capabilities. *Journal of Business Venturing*, *27*(2), 217–233. doi:10.1016/j.jbusvent.2010.10.002

Happer, C., & Philo, G. (2013). The role of the media in the construction of public belief and social change. *Journal of Social and Political Psychology*, *1*(1), 321–336. doi:10.5964/jspp.v1i1.96

Harding, R. (2004). Social Enterprise: The New Economic Engine? *Business Strategy Review*, *15*(4), 39–43. doi:10.1111/j.0955-6419.2004.00338.x

Harding, R. (2007). *GEM UK 2006*. London: London Business School.

Hargreaves, A., & Fink, D. (2005). *Sustainable Leadership*. Jossey-Bass.

Hartigan, P. (2006). It's about people, not profits. *Business Strategy Review*, *17*(4), 42–45. doi:10.1111/j.0955-6419.2006.00433.x

Hart, S. L., & Christensen, C. M. (2002). The great leap: Driving innovation from the base of the pyramid. *MIT Sloan Management Review*, *44*(1), 51.

Hart, S. L., & London, T. (2005). Developing native capability. *Stanford Social Innovation Review*, *3*(2), 28–33.

Hasan, S. (2005). Social capital and social entrepreneurship in Asia: Analysing the links. *Asia Pacific Journal Of Public Administration*, *27*(1), 1–17. doi:10.1080/23276665.2005.10779296

Haugh, H. (2005). A research agenda for social entrepreneurship. *Social Enterprise Journal*, *1*(1), 1–12. doi:10.1108/17508610580000703

Haugh, H. (2007). Community-Led Social Venture Creation. *Entrepreneurship Theory and Practice*, *31*(2), 161–182. doi:10.1111/j.1540-6520.2007.00168.x

Haugh, H. M., & Talwar, A. (2016). Linking social entrepreneurship and social change: The mediating role of empowerment. *Journal of Business Ethics*, *133*(4), 643–658. doi:10.100710551-014-2449-4

Haughton, C. (2008). The edge of reason. *Director*, *61*(7), 70–74.

Haug, S. (2008). Migration networks and migration decision-making. *Journal of Ethnic and Migration Studies*, *34*(4), 585–605. doi:10.1080/13691830801961605

Hayes, M. (2014). We Gained a Lot Over What We Would Have Had: The Geographic Arbitrage of North American Lifestyle Migrants to Cuenca, Ecuador. *Journal of Ethnic and Migration Studies*, *40*(12), 1953–1971. doi:10.1080/1369183X.2014.880335

Hayward, M. L. A., Forster, W. R., Sarasvathy, S. D., & Fredrickson, B. L. (2010). Beyond hubris: How highly confident entrepreneurs rebound to venture again. *Journal of Business Venturing*, *25*(6), 569–578. doi:10.1016/j.jbusvent.2009.03.002

Hedderman, C. (2013). Payment by Results: Hopes, fears and evidence. *British Journal of Community Justice, 11*(2-3).

Heilbrunn, S., & Kushnirovich, N. (2008). The impact of policy on immigrant entrepreneurship and businesses practice in Israel. *International Journal of Public Sector Management*, *21*(7), 693–703. doi:10.1108/09513550810904514

Heinecke, A., Kloibhofer, M., & Krzeminska, A. (2014). *Leadership in Social Enterprise How to Manage Yourself and the Team, Schwab Foundation For Social Entrepreneurship*. Economic World Forum. Retrieved June 10, 2017, from http://www.schwabfound.org

Hemingway, C. A. (2005). Personal values as a catalyst for corporate social entrepreneurship. *Journal of Business Ethics*, *60*(3), 233–249. doi:10.100710551-005-0132-5

Herman, R. D., & Renz, D. O. (1997). Multiple constituencies and the social construction of nonprofit organization effectiveness. *Nonprofit and Voluntary Sector Quarterly*, *26*(2), 185–206. doi:10.1177/0899764097262006

Hern, A. (n.d.). *Why Google has 200m reasons to put engineers over designers*. Retrieved from https://www.theguardian.com/technology/2014/feb/05/why-google-engineers-designers

Herrington, M., & Kew, P. (2017). *GEM Report on Social Entrepreneurship*. Retrieved June 10, 2017, from http://www.gemconsortium.org/

Herrington, M., & Kew, P. (2017a). *GEM Global Report 2016/17*. Retrieved June 10, 2017, from http://www.gemconsortium.org/

Hervieux, C., Gedajlovic, E., & Turcotte, M. F. B. (2010). The legitimization of social entrepreneurship. *Journal of Enterprising Communities: People and Places in the Global Economy*, *4*(1), 37–67. doi:10.1108/17506201011029500

Herzig, C. (2006). Corporate volunteering in Germany: Survey and empirical evidence. *International Journal of Business Environment*, *1*(1), 51–69. doi:10.1504/IJBE.2006.010128

Hills, J. (2015). *Record on Cash Transfers, Poverty The Coalition's and Inequality 2010-2015*. Social Policy in a Cold Climate Working Paper 11. London: Centre for Analysis of Social Exclusion.

Hisrich, R. D., & Peters, M. P. (1995). *Entrepreneurship—Starting, Developing and Managing a New Enterprise*. Boston: Irwin.

Hisrich, R. D., & Peters, M. P. (2010). *Entrepreneurship* (8th ed.). New York: McGraw-Hill.

Hite, J., & Hesterly, W. (2001). The evolution of firm networks: From emergence to early growth of the firm. *Strategic Management Journal*, *22*(3), 275–286. doi:10.1002mj.156

Hoang, H., & Antoncic, B. (2003). Network-based Research in Entrepreneurship: A Critical Review. *Journal of Business Venturing*, *18*(2), 165–187. doi:10.1016/S0883-9026(02)00081-2

Hoang, H., & Rothaermel, F. T. (2016). How to Manage Alliances Strategically. *MIT Sloan Management Review*, *58*(1), 69.

Hobbs, S. (2011). The Latest Approach to Volunteer Recruitment: Competency - Competence Pathways and Volunteer Resource Management Systems. In T. D. Connors (Ed.), *The Volunteer Management Handbook: Leadership Strategies for Success* (2nd ed.; pp. 205–225). John Wiley & Sons. doi:10.1002/9781118386194.ch8

Holme, R., & Watts, P. (1999). *Corporate social responsibility*. Geneva: World Business Council for Sustainable Development.

Hope, P. (2004). Supporting every shade of initiative. *Social Enterprise Magazine*, 8–9.

Hopkins, M. M., & O'Neil, D. A. (2015). Authentic leadership: Application to women leaders. *Frontiers in Psychology*, *6*, 959. doi:10.3389/fpsyg.2015.00959 PMID:26236254

House of Lords. (2010). *Making it Work: the European Social Fund.* European Union Committee, House of Lords, 9th Report of Session 2009–10. Available at: www.publications.parliament.uk/pa/ld200910/ldselect/ldeucom/92/92i.pdf

House of Lords. (2011). *Science and technology committee: first report. Public procurement as a tool to stimulate innovation.* House of Lords. Retrieved from http://www.publications.parliament.uk/pa/ld201012/ldselect/ldsctech/148/14802.htm

Hubert, A. (2010). *Empowering people, driving change: Social innovation in the European Union.* Bureau of European Policy Advisors (BEPA). Retrieved September 14, 2017, from http://ec. europa. eu/bepa/pdf/publications_pdf/social_innovation. pdf

Huda, M., Haron, Z., Ripin, M. N., Hehsan, A., & Yaacob, A. B. C. (2017d). Exploring Innovative Learning Environment (ILE): Big Data Era. *International Journal of Applied Engineering Research*, *12*(17), 6678–6685.

Huda, M., Jasmi, K. A., Alas, Y., Qodriah, S. L., Dacholfany, M. I., & Jamsari, E. A. (2017g). Empowering Civic Responsibility: Insights From Service Learning. In S. Burton (Ed.), *Engaged Scholarship and Civic Responsibility in Higher Education* (pp. 144–165). Hershey, PA: IGI Global. doi:10.4018/978-1-5225-3649-9.ch007

Huda, M., Jasmi, K. A., Basiran, B., Mustari, M. I. B., & Sabani, A. N. (2017e). Traditional Wisdom on Sustainable Learning: An Insightful View From Al-Zarnuji's Ta 'lim al-Muta 'allim. *SAGE Open*, *7*(1), 1–8. doi:10.1177/2158244017697160

Huda, M., Jasmi, K. A., Embong, W. H., Safar, J., Mohamad, A. M., Mohamed, A. K., ... Rahman, S. K. (2017f). Nurturing Compassion-Based Empathy: Innovative Approach in Higher Education. In M. Badea & M. Suditu (Eds.), *Violence Prevention and Safety Promotion in Higher Education Settings* (pp. 154–173). Hershey, PA: IGI Global. doi:10.4018/978-1-5225-2960-6.ch009

Huda, M., Jasmi, K. A., Mustari, M. I., Basiron, B., Mohamed, A. K., Embong, W., ... Safar, J. (2017h). Innovative E-Therapy Service in Higher Education: Mobile Application Design. *International Journal of Interactive Mobile Technologies*, *11*(4), 83–94. doi:10.3991/ijim.v11i4.6734

Huda, M., Maseleno, A., Atmotiyoso, P., Siregar, M., Ahmad, R., Jasmi, K. A., ... Basiron, B. (2018). Emerging Big Data Technologies. Insights into Innovative Environment for Online Learning Resources. *International Journal of Emerging Technologies in Learning*. doi:10.3991/ijet.v13i01.6990

Huda, M., Maseleno, A., Jasmi, K. A., Mustari, I., & Basiron, B. (2017c). Strengthening Interaction from Direct to Virtual Basis: Insights from Ethical and Professional Empowerment. *International Journal of Applied Engineering Research*, *12*(17), 6901–6909.

Huda, M., Sabani, N., Shahrill, M., Jasmi, K. A., Basiron, B., & Mustari, M. I. (2017a). Empowering Learning Culture as Student Identity Construction in Higher Education. In A. Shahriar & G. Syed (Eds.), *Student Culture and Identity in Higher Education* (pp. 160–179). Hershey, PA: IGI Global; doi:10.4018/978-1-5225-2551-6.ch010

Huda, M., & Siregar, M., Rahman, S.K.A., Mat Teh, K.S., Said, H., Jamsari, E.A., … Ninsiana, W. (2017b). From Live Interaction to Virtual Interaction: An Exposure on the Moral Engagement in the Digital Era. *Journal of Theoretical and Applied Information Technology*, *95*(19), 4964–4972.

Hudson, R. (2009). Life on the edge: Navigating the competitive tensions between the 'social 'and the 'economic'in the social economy and in its relations to the mainstream. *Journal of Economic Geography*.

Hynes, B. (2009). Growing the social enterprise–issues and challenges. *Social Enterprise Journal*, *5*(2), 114–125. doi:10.1108/17508610910981707

İçerli, L., & Şahin Karadal, M. (2014). Sosyal entrepreneurlik. İstanbul: Beta Yayıncılık.

ILO. (2016). *Access to finance for Social Entrepreneurs in South Africa*. Geneva: International Labor Office.

Independent Review of Public Sector Efficiency. (2004). *Releasing resources to the front line*. London: HMSO.

Inkson, K., & Arthur, M. (2001). How to be a successful career capitalist. *Organizational Dynamics*, *30*(1), 48–61. doi:10.1016/S0090-2616(01)00040-7

Inkson, K., & Myers, B. (2003). The big "OE": Self-directed travel and career development. *Career Development International*, *8*(4), 170–181. doi:10.1108/13620430310482553

Innovation and research strategy for growth. (2011). BIS economics paper number 15. Gov.UK.

INSEAD. (2012). *What is "social innovation"?* Retrieved September 14, 2017, from http://www.insead.edu/facultyresearch/centres/isic/ home/about_us.cfm

Ireland, R. D., & Webb, J. W. (2007). Strategic entrepreneurship: Creating competitive advantage through streams of innovation. *Business Horizons*, *50*(1), 49–59. doi:10.1016/j.bushor.2006.06.002

Iyigun, N. O. (2014). Corporate Social Responsibility and Ethics in Management in light of Sustainable Development. In U. Akkucuk (Ed.), Handbook of Research on Developing Sustainable Value in Economics, Finance and Marketing. Hershey, PA: IGI Global.

Iyigun, N. O. (2015). What could Entrepreneurship do for Sustainable Development? A Corporate Social Responsibility-Based Approach. *Procedia: Social and Behavioral Sciences*, *195*, 1226–1231. doi:10.1016/j.sbspro.2015.06.253

Iyigun, O., & Keskin, M. (2016). Is Franchising an Efficient Tool for Entrepreneurship in the Knowledge Economy? In M. H. Bilgin & H. Danis (Eds.), *Entrepreneurship, Business and Economics:* Vol. 1. *Proceedings of the 15th Eurasia Business and Economics Society Conference* (pp. 33-43). Springer International Publishing. 10.1007/978-3-319-27570-3_4

Iyigun, O., & Yalcintas, M. (2017). Social Entrepreneurship as a Tool for Creating Competitive Advantage: A Theoretical Approach. *Turkish Journal of Entrepreneurship*, *1*(1), 91–101.

Jack, S., Moult, S., Anderson, A. R., & Dodd, S. (2010). An entrepreneurial network evolving: Patterns of change. *International Small Business Journal*, *28*(4), 315–337. doi:10.1177/0266242610363525

Jackson, G., & Deeg, R. (2008). From comparing capitalisms to the politics of institutional change. *Review of International Political Economy*, *15*(4), 680–709. doi:10.1080/09692290802260704

Jackson, W. T., & Jackson, M. J. (2014). Social Enterprises and Social Entrepreneurs: One Size Does Not Fit All. *Academy of Entrepreneurship Journal*, *20*(2), 152–162.

Jamburia, G. (2013). *Sustainability of Social Enterprises: A Case Study of Sweden*. Retrieved from http://www.diva-portal.org/smash/get/diva2:632746/FULLTEXT01.pdf

Jamrozik, A., & Nocella, L. (1998). *The sociology of social problems: Theoretical perspectives and methods of intervention*. Cambridge University Press. doi:10.1017/CBO9780511819629

Jeffries, V., Johnston, B. V., Nichols, L. T., Oliner, S. P., Tiryakian, E., & Weinstein, J. (2006). Altruism and social solidarity: Envisioning a field of specialization. *The American Sociologist*, *37*(3), 67–83. doi:10.100712108-006-1023-7

Jensen, K. (2016). Prosociality. *Current Biology*, *26*(16), R748–R752. doi:10.1016/j.cub.2016.07.025 PMID:27554648

Jenssen, J. I., & Koenig, H. F. (2002). The effect of social networks on resource access and business start-ups. *European Planning Studies, 10*(8), 1039–1046. doi:10.1080/0965431022000031301

Jiang, X., Bao, Y., Xie, Y., & Gao, S. (2016a). Partner trustworthiness, knowledge flow in strategic alliances, and firm competitiveness: A contingency perspective. *Journal of Business Research, 69*(2), 804–814. doi:10.1016/j.jbusres.2015.07.009

Jiang, X., Yang, Y., Pei, Y. L., & Wang, G. (2016b). Entrepreneurial orientation, strategic alliances, and firm performance: Inside the black box. *Long Range Planning, 49*(1), 103–116. doi:10.1016/j.lrp.2014.09.003

Jilenga, M. T. (2017). Social Enterprise and Economic Growth: A Theoretical Approach and Policy Recommendations. *International Journal of Academic Research in Accounting Finance and Management Sciences, 7*(1), 41–49.

Jill, K., & Lyons, T. (2016). *Understanding Social Entrepreneurship.* New York: Routledge.

Johannisson, B. (1996). The Dynamics of Entrepreneurial Networks. In P. Reynolds, S. Birley, J. Butler, W. Bygrave, P. Davidson, W. Gartner, & P. McDougal (Eds.), *Frontiers of Entrepreneurship Research* (pp. 253–267). Wellesley, MA: Babson College.

Johannisson, B. (2000). Networking and entrepreneurial growth. In D. L. Sexton & H. Landström (Eds.), *The Blackwell Handbook of Entrepreneurship* (pp. 368–386). Oxford, UK: Blackwell Publishers.

Johannisson, B., Alexanderson, O., Nowicki, K., & Senneseth, K. (1994). Beyond anarchy and organization: Entrepreneurs in contextual networks. *Entrepreneurship and Regional Development, 6*(4), 329–356. doi:10.1080/08985629400000020

Johnson, B. (2005). Overcoming "doom and gloom": Empowering students in courses on social problems, injustice, and inequality. *Teaching Sociology, 33*(1), 44–58. doi:10.1177/0092055X0503300104

Jones, R., Latham, J., & Betta, M. (2008). Narrative construction of the social entrepreneurial identity. *International Journal of Entrepreneurial Behaviour & Research, 14*(5), 330–345. doi:10.1108/13552550810897687

Kanter, R. M., & Brinkerhoff, D. (1981). Organizational performance: Recent developments in measurement. *Annual Review of Sociology, 7*(1), 321–349. doi:10.1146/annurev.so.07.080181.001541

Kanungo, R. N., & Conger, J. A. (1993). Promoting altruism as a corporate goal. *The Academy of Management Executive, 7*(3), 37–48.

Kanungo, R. N., & Mendonca, M. (1996). *Ethical dimensions of leadership* (Vol. 3). Sage.

Kaplan, R. S. (1984). The evolution of management accounting. *The Accounting Review, 59*, 390–418.

Kaplan, R. S. (2001). Strategic performance measurement and management in nonprofit organizations. *Nonprofit Management & Leadership, 11*(3), 353–370. doi:10.1002/nml.11308

Kaplan, R., & Norton, D. (1992). The Balanced Scorecard. *Harvard Business Review, 70*, 71–79. PMID:10119714

Kaplan, R., & Norton, D. (1996). *The Balanced Scorecard: Translating strategy into action.* Boston, MA: Harvard Business School Press.

Kaplan, R., & Norton, D. (2001). Transforming the balanced scorecard from performance measurement to strategic management: Part 1. *Accounting Horizons, 15*(1), 87–104. doi:10.2308/acch.2001.15.1.87

Kara, O., Chu, H., & Benzing, C. (2010). Determinants of entrepreneur's success in a developing country. *Journal of Business and Entrepreneurship, 22*(2), 1–15.

Kemp, E., Bui, M., Krishen, A., Homer, P. M., & LaTour, M. S. (2017). Understanding the power of hope and empathy in healthcare marketing. *Journal of Consumer Marketing, 34*(2), 85–95. doi:10.1108/JCM-04-2016-1765

Kerlin, J. A. (2006). Social enterprise in the United States and Europe: Understanding and learning from the differences. *Voluntas, 17*(3), 246–262. doi:10.100711266-006-9016-2

Kernick, D. (2002). *Getting Health Economics into Practise* (D. Kernick, Ed.). Radclife Medical Press.

Kerr, S., & Kerr, W. (2016). *Immigrant Entrepreneurship.* National Bureau of Economic Research Working paper 22385.

Khatun, F., & Hasan, M. (2016). Human Resource Management in Social Enterprises: A Study on BRAC. *European Journal of Economics Law and Politics, 3*(2), 37–57.

Khosa, R. M., & Kalitanyi, V. (2015). Migration reasons, traits and entrepreneurial motivation of African immigrant entrepreneurs: Towards an entrepreneurial migration progression. *Journal of Enterprising Communities: People and Places in the Global Economy, 9*(2), 132–155. doi:10.1108/JEC-07-2014-0011

Kickul, J., & Lyons, T. S. (2012). Measuring social impact. *Understanding social entrepreneurship: The relentless pursuit of mission in an ever changing world,* 176-200.

Kickul, J., & Lyons, T. S. (2012). *Understanding Social Entrepreneurship: The Relentless Pursuit of Mission in an Ever Changing World.* New York, NY: Routledge.

Kickul, J., & Lyons, T. S. (2016). *Understanding Social Entrepreneurship: The Relentless Pursuit of Mission in an Ever Changing World (2nd ed.).* New York: Routledge.

Kickul, J., & Lyons, T. S. (2016). *Understanding social entrepreneurship: The relentless pursuit of mission in an ever changing world.* Routledge.

Kieser, C., Leipziger, D., & Shubert, J. (2014). *Creating Social Value: A Guide for Leaders and Change Makers.* Greenleaf.

Kılıç Kırılmaz, S. (2014). Sosyal Girişimcilik Boyutlarına Kuramsal Bir Bakış. *Journal of Economics and Management Research, 3*(2), 55–74.

Kim, K. H. (2017). Cooperative or competitive in alliance formation: Alliance patterns with respect to rivals. *Canadian Journal of Administrative Sciences/Revue Canadienne des Sciences de l'Administration, 34*(3), 277-290.

Kimantas, P., & Dawson, J. (2008). *Commissioning and procurement.* London: NAVCA.

Kim, K. H., Kim, M., & Qian, C. (2015). Effects of corporate social responsibility on corporate financial performance: A competitive-action perspective. *Journal of Management.*

Kim-Soon, N., Ahmad, A. R., & Ibrahim, N. N. (2016). Theory of Planned Behavior: Undergraduates' Entrepreneurial Motivation and Entrepreneurship Career Intention at a Public University. *Journal of Entrepreneurship: Research & Practice, 2016,* 1–14.

Kloosterman, R., & Rath, J. (2001). Immigrant entrepreneurs in advanced economies: Mixed embeddedness further explored. *Journal of Ethnic and Migration Studies, 27*(2), 189–202. doi:10.1080/13691830020041561

Klyver, K., & Hindle, K. (2007). The role of social networks at different stages of business formation. *Small Enterprise Research, 15*(1), 22–38. doi:10.1080/13215906.2007.11005830

Knife, K., Haughton, A., & Dixon, E. (2014). Measuring Sustainability and Effectiveness of Social Value Creation by Social Sector Actors/ Social Enterprises, Within Developing Countries. *Academy of Entrepreneurship Journal, 20*(1), 1–23.

Koçak, O., & Kavi, E. (2014). Sosyal politika aktörü olarak sosyal girişimci belediyecilik. *Hak-İş Uluslararası Emek ve Toplum Dergisi, 3*(6), 26–49.

Koe Hwee Nga, J., & Shamuganathan, G. (2010). The influence of personality traits and demographic factors on social entrepreneurship start up intentions. *Journal of Business Ethics*, *95*(2), 259–282. doi:10.100710551-009-0358-8

Kök, S. B., & Mert, E. (2016). *Girişimcilikte sosyal değer inşası: Sosyal girişimcilik*. Retrieved 06.07.2017, from https://www.avekon.org/papers/1514.pdf

Konda, I., Starc, J., & Rodica, B. (2015). Social challenges are opportunities for sustainable development: Tracing impacts of social entrepreneurship through innovations and value creation. *Economic Themes*, *53*(2), 215–233. doi:10.1515/ethemes-2015-0012

Kongar, E. (1995). *Toplumsal değişme kuramları ve Türkiye gerçeği*. İstanbul.

Koponen, D. (2012). Conceptual Framework for quality of life management: Social entrepreneurship perspective. *Economics and Management*, *17*(4), 1372–1377. doi:10.5755/j01.em.17.4.3002

Kopp, W. (2003). *One day, all children: The unlikely triumph of Teach for America and what I learnt along the way*. New York: Public Affairs.

Korosec, R., & Berman, E. (2006, May). Municipal support for social entrepreneurship. *Public Administration Review*, 446–460.

Kotler, P., & Andreasen, A. (1996). *Strategic Marketing for Nonprofit Organizations* (5th ed.). Upper Saddle River, NJ: Prentice Hall.

Kotler, P., Kartajaya, H., & Setiawan, I. (2010). *Marketing 3.0: From products to customers to the human spirit*. John Wiley & Sons. doi:10.1002/9781118257883

Kroeger, A., & Weber, C. (2014). Developing a conceptual framework for comparing social value creation. *Academy of Management Review*, *39*(4), 513–540. doi:10.5465/amr.2012.0344

Kroll, A., & Vogel, D. (2017). Changes in Prosocial Motivation over Time: A Cross-Sector Analysis of Effects on Volunteering and Work Behavior. *International Journal of Public Administration*, 1–13. doi:10.1080/01900692.2017.1347945

Küçük, O. (2005). *Girişimcilik ve Küçük İşletme Yönetimi*. Ankara: Seçkin Press.

Kümbül Güler, B. (2008). Yoksullukla mücadelede sosyal girişimcilik: Ashoka üyelerinden örnek uygulamalar. *I. Ulusal Çalışma İlişkileri Kongresi Bildiriler Kitabı*, 816-838.

Kümbül Güler, B. (2010). *Sosyal Girişimcilik*. Ankara: Efil Yayınevi.

Kümbül Güler, B. (2011). Yoksullukla mücadelede sosyal girişimcilik: Ashoka üyelerinden sosyal yenilikçi örnek uygulamalar. *Sosyal Bilimler Enstitüsü Dergisi*, *13*(3), 79–111.

Kümbül-Güler, B. (2008). *Sosyal Girişimciliği Etkileyen Faktörlerin Analizi* (Unpublished doctoral dissertation). Dokuz Eylül University, SBE, İzmir.

Kümbül-Güler, B. (2010). Bireysel ve Çevresel Özelliklerin Şekillendirdiği Sosyal Girişimci Davranış. In S. Besler (Ed.), *Sosyal Girişimcilik* (pp. 161–199). İstanbul: Beta Yayınları.

Kuratko, D. F. (2005). The Emergence of Entrepreneurship Education: Development, Trends, and Challenges. *Entrepreneurship: Theory and Practice*, *29*(5), 577 - 598.

Kuratko, D. F. (2007). Entrepreneurial Leadership in the 21st Century. *Journal of Leadership & Organizational Studies*, *13*(4), 1–11. doi:10.1177/107179190701300040201

Kuratko, D. F., & Hodgetts, R. M. (2004). *Entrepreneurship: Theory, Process, Practice*. Thomson South Western.

Lähdesmäki, M., & Takala, T. (2012). Altruism in business–an empirical study of philanthropy in the small business context. *Social Responsibility Journal*, *8*(3), 373–388. doi:10.1108/17471111211247947

Lai, W. H., Lin, C. C., & Wang, T. C. (2015). Exploring the interoperability of innovation capability and corporate sustainability. *Journal of Business Research*, *68*(4), 867–871. doi:10.1016/j.jbusres.2014.11.043

Larner, W., & Butler, M. (2005). Governmentalities of local partnerships: The rise of a "partnering state" in New Zealand. *Studies in Political Economy*, *75*(1), 85–108. doi:10.1080/19187033.2005.11675130

Larson, A., & Starr, J. A. (1993). A network model of organization formation. *Entrepreneurship Theory and Practice*, *17*(2), 5–16. doi:10.1177/104225879301700201

Lasker, J. N. (2016). *Hoping to help; The promises and pitfalls of global health volunteering*. New York: Cornell University Press.

Latané, B. (1981). The psychology of social impact. *The American Psychologist*, *36*(4), 343–356. doi:10.1037/0003-066X.36.4.343

Lau, G. T., & Lee, S. H. (1999). Consumer's Trust in a Brand and the Link to Brand Loyalty. *Journal of Market Focused Management*, *4*(4), 341–370. doi:10.1023/A:1009886520142

Lazarus, R. S. (1991). *Emotion and adaptation*. Oxford, UK: Oxford University Press.

Leadbeater, C. (1997). *The rise of the social entrepreneur*. London: DEMOS. Retrieved July 2017 from http://www.demos.co.uk/publications/socialentrepreneur

Leadbeater, C. (1997). *The rise of the social entrepreneur*. London: Demos.

Lee, J. S., & Hsieh, C. J. (2010). A research in relating entrepreneurship, marketing capability, innovative capability and sustained competitive advantage. *Journal of Business & Economics Research*, *8*(9), 109. doi:10.19030/jber.v8i9.763

Lee, J., Sohn, S., & Ju, Y. (2011). How Effective Is Government Support for Korean Women Entrepreneurs in Small and Medium Enterprises? *Journal of Small Business Management*, *49*(4), 599–616. doi:10.1111/j.1540-627X.2011.00338.x

Lee, Y. J., & Wilkins, V. M. (2011). More similarities or more differences? Comparing public and nonprofit managers' job motivations. *Public Administration Review*, *71*(1), 45–56. doi:10.1111/j.1540-6210.2010.02305.x

Lehner, O. M., & Kaniskas, J. (2012). Opportunity Recognition in Social Entrepreneurship: A Thematic Meta Analysis. *The Journal of Entrepreneurship*, *21*(1), 25–58. doi:10.1177/097135571102100102

Lepoutre, J., Justo, R., Terjesen, S., & Bosma, N. (2013). Designing a global standardized methodology for measuring social entrepreneurship activity: The Global Entrepreneurship Monitor social entrepreneurship study. *Small Business Economics*, *40*(3), 693–714. doi:10.100711187-011-9398-4

Lettice, F., & Parekh, M. (2010). The social innovation process: Themes, challenges and implications for practice. *International Journal of Technology Management*, *51*(1), 139–158. doi:10.1504/IJTM.2010.033133

Lewin, D. (1998). The accidental entrepreneur. *Computers in Physics*, *12*(6), 518–519. doi:10.1063/1.168753

Lewis, J. (2005). New Labour's approach to the voluntary sector: Independence and the meaning of partnership. *Social Policy and Society*, *4*(2), 121–131. doi:10.1017/S147474640400226X

Leyden, D. P., Link, A. N., & Siegel, D. S. (2013). *A theoretical analysis of the role of social Networks in entrepreneurship*. The University of North Carolina, Department of Economics Working Paper Series, 13-22. Retrieved July 2017 from http://bryan.uncg.edu/assets/research/econwp/2013/13-22.pdf

Liden, R. C., Wayne, S. J., Zhao, H., & Henderson, D. (2008). Servant Leadership: Development of a Multidimensional Measure and Multi-Level Assessment. *The Leadership Quarterly*, *19*(2), 161–177. doi:10.1016/j.leaqua.2008.01.006

Light, P. (2005). *Searching for social entrepreneurship: Who might they be, where they might be found, what they do?* Paper presented at the Association for Research on Nonprofit and Voluntary Associations.

Light, P. C. (2002). The content of their character: The state of the nonprofit workforce. *The Nonprofit Quarterly*, *9*(3), 6–16.

Light, P. C. (2006). Reshaping Social Entrepreneurship. *Stanford Social Innovation Review*, 47–51.

Light, P. C. (2008). *The search for social entrepreneurship*. Washington, DC: Brookings Institution Press.

Light, P. C. (2008). *The Search for Social Entrepreneurship*. Washington, DC: Brookings Institution.

Lilius, J. M., Kanov, J., Dutton, J., Worline, M. C., & Maitlis, S. (2011). Compassion revealed: What we know about compassion at work (and where we need to know more). Academic Press.

Limbu, Y. B., Jayachandran, C., Babin, B. J., & Peterson, R. T. (2016). Empathy, nonverbal immediacy, and salesperson performance: The mediating role of adaptive selling behavior. *Journal of Business and Industrial Marketing*, *31*(5), 654–667. doi:10.1108/JBIM-03-2015-0048

Lingane, A., & Olsen, S. (2004). Guidelines for social return on investment. *California Management Review*, *46*(3), 116–135. doi:10.2307/41166224

Lin, H. F. (2007). Effects of extrinsic and intrinsic motivation on employee knowledge sharing intentions. *Journal of Information Science*, *33*(2), 135–149. doi:10.1177/0165551506068174

Lisetchi, M., & Brancu, L. (2014). The entrepreneurship concept as a subject of social innovation. *Procedia: Social and Behavioral Sciences*, *124*, 87–92. doi:10.1016/j.sbspro.2014.02.463

Littunen, H. (2000). Entrepreneurship and the characteristics of the entrepreneurial personality. *International Journal of Entrepreneurial Behaviour & Research*, *6*(6), 295–310. doi:10.1108/13552550010362741

Llewellyn, D. J., & Wilson, K. M. (2003). The controversial role of personality traits in entrepreneurial psychology. *Education + Training*, *45*(6), 341–345. doi:10.1108/00400910310495996

London, M. (2008). Leadership and Advocacy: Dual roles for corporate social responsibility and social entrepreneurship. *Organizational Dynamics*, *37*(4), 313–326. doi:10.1016/j.orgdyn.2008.07.003

London, M. (2010). Understanding Social Advocacy: An Integrative Model of Motivation, Strategy, and Persistence in Support of Corporate Social Responsibility and Social Entrepreneurship. *Journal of Management Development*, *29*(3), 224–245. doi:10.1108/02621711011025768

London, M., & Morfopoulos, R. G. (2009). *Social entrepreneurship: How to start successful corporate social responsibility and community-based initiatives for advocacy and change*. New York: Routledge Taylor & Francis Group.

Lönnström, A. (2015). *The motivational values of social entrepreneurs* (Unpublished master's thesis). University of Jyväskylä School of Business and Economics, Finland.

López-Duarte, C., González-Loureiro, M., Vidal-Suárez, M. M., & González-Díaz, B. (2016). International strategic alliances and national culture: Mapping the field and developing a research agenda. *Journal of World Business*, *51*(4), 511–524. doi:10.1016/j.jwb.2016.05.001

Lubberink, R., Blok, V., van Ophem, J., & Omta, O. (2017). A Framework for Responsible Innovation in the Business Context: Lessons from Responsible-, Social-and Sustainable Innovation. In *Responsible Innovation 3* (pp. 181–207). Cham: Springer. doi:10.1007/978-3-319-64834-7_11

Lukach, R., & Plasmans, J. (2002). *Measuring Knowledge Spillovers Using Patent Citations: Evidence from the Belgian Firm's Data.* CESifo Working Paper, Nr.754.

Luke, B., Barraket, J. and Eversole, R. (2013). Measurement as legitimacy versus legitimacy of measures, Performance evaluation of social enterprise. *Qualitative Research in Accounting & Management*, *10*(3- 4), 234-258.

Luke, B., & Chu, B. (2013). Social enterprise versus social entrepreneurship: An examination of the 'why' and 'how' in pursuing social change. *International Small Business Journal*, *31*(7), 764–778. doi:10.1177/0266242612462598

Luthans, F., Luthans, K. W., & Luthans, B. C. (2004). Positive psychological capital: Beyond human and social capital. *Business Horizons*, *47*(1), 45–50. doi:10.1016/j.bushor.2003.11.007

Lynn, D. B. (2003). Symposium: Human resource management in nonprofit organizations. *Review of Public Personnel Administration*, *23*(2), 91–96. doi:10.1177/0734371X03023002001

Lynskey, J., & Yonekura, S. (2002). *Entrepreneurship And Organization: The Role Of The Entrepreneur In Organizational Innovation.* Oxford University Press.

Lyon, F., & Sepulveda, L. (2012). Social Enterprise Support Policies: distinctions and challenges. In R. Blackburn & M. Schaper (Eds.), *Government, SMEs and Entrepreneurship. Development: Policy, Practice and Challenges*. Farnham: Gower.

Lyons, S., & Kuron, L. (2014). Generational differences in the workplace: A review of the evidence and directions for future research. *Journal of Organizational Behavior*, *35*(S1), 139–157. doi:10.1002/job.1913

Maas, K., & Liket, K. (2011). Social impact measurement: classification of methods. In *Environmental management accounting and supply chain management* (pp. 171–202). Springer, Netherlands. doi:10.1007/978-94-007-1390-1_8

Macaulay, J., & Berkowitz, L. (Eds.). (1970). *Altruism and helping behavior: Social psychological studies of some antecedents and consequences*. Academic Press.

Machan, T. R. (1999). Entrepreneurship and ethics. *International Journal of Social Economics*, *26*(5), 596–609. doi:10.1108/03068299910216103

Maclean, M., Harvey, C., & Gordon, J. (2013). Social innovation, social entrepreneurship and the practice of contemporary entrepreneurial philanthropy. *International Small Business Journal*, *31*(7), 747–763. doi:10.1177/0266242612443376

Macmillan, R. (2010). *The third sector delivering public services: an evidence review*. Working Paper 20. Birmingham, UK: Third Sector Research Centre.

Maddux, W., Galinsky, A., & Tadmor, C. (2010). Be a better manager: Live abroad. *Harvard Business Review*. Retrieved from https://hbr.org/2010/09/be-a-better-manager-live-abroad

Maguire, S., Hardy, C., & Lawrence, T. B. (2004). Institutional entrepreneurship in emerging fields: HIV/AIDS treatment advocacy in Canada. *Academy of Management Journal*, *47*(5), 657–679. doi:10.2307/20159610

Maher, C. (2013). *A Qualitative Case Study Approach to Understanding Third Sector Managers' Career Orientations.* Academic Press.

Maher, C. (2017a). Understanding the Impact of Organisational Culture on Managers' Internal Career Needs. In Exploring the Influence of Personal Values and Cultures in the Workplace (pp. 265-285). IGI Global.

Maher, C. (2017b). Managers' Career Orientations: A Conceptual Framework. In Handbook of Research on Emerging Business Models and Managerial Strategies in the Nonprofit Sector (pp. 201-221). IGI Global.

Maher, C. (2015a). *Public Policies Impact on Third Sector Social Enterprises in UK Regions*. IGI Global.

Maher, C. (2016). Career anchors of social enterprise managers in the UK-an empirical analysis. *Journal for International Business and Entrepreneurship Development*, *9*(4), 398–416. doi:10.1504/JIBED.2016.080019

Maher, C. (Ed.). (2017c). *Influence of Public Policy on Small Social Enterprises: Emerging Research and Opportunities: Emerging Research and Opportunities*. IGI Global.

Mahoney, L.S., & Roberts, R.W. (2015). Corporate Social Performance. *Research on Professional Responsibility and Ethics in Accounting*, 73—99.

Maier, V., & Zonovia Pop, C. (2011, December). Entrepreneurship versus Intrapreneurship. *Review of International Comparative Management*, *12*(5), 971–976.

Mair, J. (2010). Social entrepreneurship: taking stock and looking ahead. In Handbook of Research on Social Entrepreneurship (pp. 15-28). Edward Elgar Publications. doi:10.4337/9781849804684.00007

Mair, J., & Noboa, E. (2003). *Social Entrepreneurship: How Intentions to Create a Social Enterprise Get Formed.* IESE Working Paper, WP No:521.

Mair, J., & Marti, I. (2004). *Social Entrepreneurship: What Are We Talking about? A Framework for Future Research.* Barcelona: IESE, University of Navarra.

Mair, J., & Marti, I. (2006). Social entrepreneurship research: A source of explanation, prediction and delight. *Journal of World Business*, *41*(1), 36–44. doi:10.1016/j.jwb.2005.09.002

Mair, J., & Noboa, E. (2006). Social entrepreneurship: How intentions to create a social venture are formed. In *Social entrepreneurship* (pp. 121–135). New York: Palgrave Macmillan. doi:10.1057/9780230625655_8

Mair, J., Robinson, J., & Hockerts, K. (Eds.). (2006). *Social entrepreneurship*. New York: Palgrave Macmillan. doi:10.1057/9780230625655

Mair, J., & Sharma, S. (2012). Performance Measurement and Social Entrepreneurship. In C. K. Volkmann, K. O. Tokarski, & K. Ernst (Eds.), *Social Entrepreneurship and Social Business* (pp. 175–189). Wiesbaden: Springer Gabler. doi:10.1007/978-3-8349-7093-0_9

Makhlouf, H. H. (2011). Social Entrepreneurship: Generating Solutions to Global Challenges. *International Journal of Management and Information Systems*, *15*(1), 1–8.

Makni, R., Francoeur, C., & Bellavance, F. (2009). Causality between Corporate Social Performance and Financial Performance: Evidence from Canadian Firms. *Journal of Business Ethics*, *89*(3), 409–422. doi:10.100710551-008-0007-7

Malovics, G., Nagypal, N., & Kraus, S. (2008). The Role of Corporate Social Responsibility in Strong Sustainability. *Journal of Socio-Economics*, *37*(3), 907–918. doi:10.1016/j.socec.2006.12.061

Manimala, M. J., & Bhati, A. (2011). *Talent Acquisition and Retention in Social Enterprises: Innovations in HR Strategies*. Working Paper, No: 328. Bangalore: Indian Institute of Management.

Manyaka, S. J. (2015). Social entrepreneurship: A solution for transforming the disadvantaged community of Nellmapius. *Hervormde Teologiese Studies*, *71*(3), 1–7. doi:10.4102/hts.v71i3.2821

Manzini, E. (2014). Making things happen: Social innovation and design. *Design Issues*, *30*(1), 57–66. doi:10.1162/DESI_a_00248

Marangoz, M. (2012). *Girişimcilik, Beta Yayınevi, 1*. İstanbul: Baskı.

Marshall, G. (2003). *Change, Social Change. In Oxford Dictionary Of Sociology*. Oxford University Press.

Marshall, R. S. (2011). Conceptualizing the international for-profit social entrepreneur. *Journal of Business Ethics*, *98*(2), 183–198. doi:10.100710551-010-0545-7

Martikke, S., & Moxham, C. (2010). Public sector commissioning: Experiences of voluntary organizations delivering health and social services. *International Journal of Public Administration*, *33*(14), 790–799. doi:10.1080/01900692.2010.521230

Martin, R. L., & Osberg, S. (2007). Social entrepreneurship: The case for definition. Stanford, CA: Stanford Social Innovation Review.

Martin, R. L., & Osberg, S. (2007, Spring). Social Entrepreneurship: The Case for Definition. *Stanford Social Innovation Review*. Retrieved July 2017 from www.ssireview.org

Martin, R. J., & Osberg, S. (2007). Social Entrepreneurship: The Case for a Definition [Spring.]. *Stanford Social Innovation Review*, 29–39.

Martin, R. L., & Osberg, S. (2007, Spring). Social entrepreneurship: The case for definition. *Stanford Social Innovation Review*, 28–39.

Martin, R. L., & Osberg, S. (2007, Spring). Social Entrepreneurship: The Case for Definition. *Stanford Social Innovation Review*, 29–39.

Martin, R., Gregory, T., Karl, C., Olga, E., & McNamara, R. (2005). The role of leader-member exchanges in mediating the relationship between locus of control and work reactions. *Journal of Occupational and Organizational Psychology*, *78*(1), 141–147. doi:10.1348/096317904X23763

Maseleno, A., Huda, M., Siregar, M., Ahmad, R., Hehsan, A., Haron, Z., ... Azmi Jasmi, K. (2017). Combining the Previous Measure of Evidence to Educational Entrance Examination. *Journal of Artificial Intelligence*, *10*(3), 85–90. doi:10.3923/jai.2017.85.90

Massetti, B. L. (2008). The social entrepreneurship matrix as a "tipping point" for economic change. *Emergence*, *10*(3), 1–8.

Massetti, B. L. (2008). The Social Entrepreneurship Matrix as a "Tipping Point"" for Economic Change. *Emergence*, 1–8.

Massetti, B. L. (2008). The social entrepreneurship matrix as a" tipping point" for economic change. *Emergence*, *10*(3), 1.

Mayerhofer, H., Müller, B., & Schmidt, A. (2010). Implications of flexpatriates' lifestyles on HRM practices. *Management Review*, *21*(2), 155–173.

Mayoux, L. (2001). Tackling the down side: Social capital, women's empowerment and micro-finance in Cameroon. *Development and Change*, *32*(3), 435–464. doi:10.1111/1467-7660.00212

McCabe, A. (2012). *Is the third sector so special? What is it worth? Third Sector Futures Dialogue, Big Picture Paper 3*. Birmingham, UK: TSRC.

McCann, J., & Sweet, M. (2014). The Perceptions of Ethical and Sustainable Leadership. *Journal of Business Ethics*, *121*(3), 373–383. doi:10.100710551-013-1704-4

McConnell, C. (2002). *Economics Principles, Problems, and Policies*. New York: McGraw-Hill Iriwn.

McCrae, R. R., & Costa, P. T. (1986). Personality, coping, and coping effectiveness in an adult sample. *Journal of Personality*, *54*(2), 385–404. doi:10.1111/j.1467-6494.1986.tb00401.x

McCraw, T. K. (2007). Prophet of innovation, Josep Schumpeter and creative destruction. The Belknap Press of Harvard University Press.

McHenry, J., & Welch, D. (2017). Entrepreneurs and Internationalization: A study of Western immigrants in an emerging market. *International Business Review*.

McLoughlin, J., Kaminski, J., Sodagar, B., Khan, S., Harris, R., Arnaudo, G., & Mc Brearty, S. (2009). A strategic approach to social impact measurement of social enterprises: The SIMPLE methodology. *Social Enterprise Journal*, *5*(2), 154–178. doi:10.1108/17508610910981734

McMillan, I. C. (1983). The politics of new venture management. *Harvard Business Review*, *61*(6), 8–16.

McMullen, J. S., & Warnick, B. (2016). The downside of blended value and hybrid organizing. *Journal of Management Studies*, *53*, 630–662. doi:10.1111/joms.12150

McNulty, Y., & Brewster, C. (2017). Theorising the meaning(s) of 'expatriate': Establishing boundary conditions for business expatriates. *International Journal of Human Resource Management*, *28*(1), 27–61. doi:10.1080/09585192.2016.1243567

McNulty, Y., De Cieri, H., & Hutchings, K. (2013). Expatriate return on investment in the Asia Pacific: An empirical study of individual ROI versus corporate ROI. *Journal of World Business*, *48*(2), 209–221. doi:10.1016/j.jwb.2012.07.005

McNulty, Y., & Vance, C. M. (2017). Dynamic global careers: A new conceptualization of expatriate career paths. *Personnel Review*, *46*(2), 205–221. doi:10.1108/PR-06-2015-0175

Megan, R., Kennett, P., Jones, G., & Croft, J. (2014). Global economic crisis, austerity and neoliberal urban governance in England. *Cambridge Journal of Regions, Economy and Society*, *7*(1), 137–153. doi:10.1093/cjres/rst033

Mengü, E. (2016a). *Sosyolojik perspektiften sosyal girişimcilik olgusu*. İstanbul University Master's Thesis.

Mengü, E. (2016b). *Yoksullukla mücadelede sosyal girişimcilik: Grameen mikrokredi modeli*. Yalova University Master's Thesis.

Merriam-Webster's Medical Dictionary. (n.d.). Retrieved from https://www.merriam-webster.com/dictionary /empathy

Meyskens, M., Carsrud, A. L., & Cardozo, R. N. (2010). The symbiosis of entities in the social engagement network: The role of social ventures. *Entrepreneurship and Regional Development*, *22*(5), 425–455. doi:10.1080/08985620903168299

Meyskens, M., Robb-Post, C., Stamp, J. A., Carsrud, A. L., & Reynolds, P. D. (2010). Social Ventures From A Resource-Based Perspective: An Exploratory Study Assessing Global Ashoka Fellows. *Entrepreneurship Theory and Practice*, *34*(4), 661–680. doi:10.1111/j.1540-6520.2010.00389.x

Miles, M. B., & Huberman, A. M. (1994). *Qualitative data analysis: An expanded sourcebook*. Sage.

Millar, R., & Hall, K. (2013). Social return on investment (SROI) and performance measurement: The opportunities and barriers for social enterprises in health and social care. *Public Management Review*, *15*(6), 923–941. doi:10.1080/14719037.2012.698857

Miller, T. L., Grimes, M. G., McMullen, J. S., & Vogus, T. J. (2012). Venturing for others with heart and head: How compassion encourages social entrepreneurship. *Academy of Management Review*, *37*(4), 616–640. doi:10.5465/amr.2010.0456

Miller, T. L., & Wesley, C. L. II. (2010). Assessing mission and resources for social change: An organizational identity perspective on social venture capitalists' decision criteria. *Entrepreneurship Theory and Practice*, *34*(4), 705–733. doi:10.1111/j.1540-6520.2010.00388.x

Ministry of Justice. (2013). *Transforming rehabilitation. A revolution in the way we manage offenders, Consultation Paper CP1/2013*. London: The Stationery Office.

Minniti, M. (2008). The role of government policy on entrepreneurial activity: Productive, unproductive, or destructive? *Entrepreneurship Theory and Practice*, 1042–2587.

Mitton, C., & Donaldson, C. (2004). *Priority Setting Toolkit: A Guide to The Use of Economics in Healthcare Decision Making*. London: BMJ Publishing Group.

Monllor, J., & Attaran, S. (2008). Opportunity recognition of social entrepreneurs: An application of the creativity model. *International Journal of Entrepreneurship and Small Business*, *6*(1), 54–67. doi:10.1504/IJESB.2008.017389

Monroe-White, T. (2014). Creating public value: An examination of technological social enterprise. In L. Pate & C. Wankel (Eds.), *Emerging research directions in social entrepreneurship* (pp. 85–109). Springer. doi:10.1007/978-94-007-7896-2_6

Moon, C. W., & Koh, Y. S. (2015). Compassion, Pro-social Motivation and Social Entrepreneurship: An Empirical Investigation. *Proceedings of the Third Asia-Pacific Conference on Global Business, Economics, Finance and Banking*.

Moon, J. (2007). The Contribution of Corporate Social Responsibility to Sustainable Development. *Sustainable Development*, *15*(5), 296–306. doi:10.1002d.346

Mortati, M., & Cruickshank, L. (2012). NETS: A design tool for activating social networks. *International Journal of Entrepreneurial Behaviour & Research*, *18*(4), 509–523. doi:10.1108/13552551211239528

Mort, G. S., Weerawardena, J., & Carnegie, K. (2003). Social entrepreneurship: Towards conceptualisation. *International Journal of Nonprofit and Voluntary Sector Marketing*, *8*(1), 76–88. doi:10.1002/nvsm.202

Moulaert, F. (Ed.). (2013). *The international handbook on social innovation: collective action, social learning and transdisciplinary research*. Edward Elgar Publishing. doi:10.4337/9781849809993

Muftuler-Bac, M. (2012). *Gender equality in Turkey*. Academic Press.

Mulgan, G., Tucker, S., Ali, R., & Sanders, B. (2007). *Social innovation: what it is, why it matters and how it can be accelerated*. Academic Press.

Mulgan, G. (2006). The process of social innovation. *Innovations*, *1*(2), 145–162. doi:10.1162/itgg.2006.1.2.145

Mulgan, G. (2007). In and Out of Sync: The Change of Growing Social Innovations. *Nesta*, *2007*, 21–25.

Müller, S. (2012). Business Models in Social Entrepreneurship. In C. Volkmann, K. Tokarski, & K. Ernst (Eds.), *Social entrepreneurship and social business. An Introduction and Discussion with Case Studies*. Wiesbaden: Springer Gabler. doi:10.1007/978-3-8349-7093-0_6

Munoz, J. (2010). *International Social Entrepreneurship: Pathways to Personal and Corporate Impact*. Business Expert Press. doi:10.4128/9781606491072

Muñoz, S. A. (2009). Social enterprise and public sector voices on procurement. *Social Enterprise Journal*, *5*(1), 69–82. doi:10.1108/17508610910956417

Munshi, N. V. (2010). Value Creation, Social Innovation, and Entrepreneurship in Global Economies. *Journal of Asia-Pacific Business*, *11*(3), 160–165. doi:10.1080/10599231.2010.500569

Murphy, P. J., & Coombes, S. M. (2009). A model of social entrepreneurial discovery. *Journal of Business Ethics*, *87*(3), 325–336. doi:10.100710551-008-9921-y

Murray, P., & Ma, S. (2015). *The Promise of Lean Experimentation*. Academic Press.

Myers, B., Inkson, K., & Pringle, J. (2017). Self-initiated expatriation (SIE) by older women: An exploratory study. *Journal of Global Mobility: The Home of Expatriate Management Research*, *5*(2), 158–173. doi:10.1108/JGM-10-2016-0050

Nag, R., Russo, A., & Vurro, C. (2014, January). The Role of Market Identity on the Relationship Between Knowledge and Strategic Alliances. In Academy of Management Proceedings (Vol. 2014, No. 1, p. 11737). Academy of Management. doi:10.5465/AMBPP.2014.11737abstract

Nair, K. R. G., & Pandey, A. (2006). Characteristics of Entrepreneurs: An Empirical Analysis. *The Journal of Entrepreneurship*, *15*(1), 47–61. doi:10.1177/097135570501500104

NAO. (2010). *Short guide to re-organising arm's length bodies: good practice principles for implementation*. National Audit Office. Retrieved from http://www.nao.org.uk/publications/1011/ arms_length_bodies.aspx

Neck, H., Brush, C., & Allen, E. (2009). The landscape of social entrepreneurship. *Business Horizons*, *52*(1), 13–19. doi:10.1016/j.bushor.2008.09.002

Nemeth, C. J. (1992). Minority dissent as a stimulant to group performance. In S. Worchel, W. Wood, & J. A. Simpson (Eds.), *Group process and productivity* (pp. 95–111). Newbury Park, CA: Sage.

Netting, F. E., O'connor, M. K., & Fauri, D. P. (2007). Planning Transformative Programs: Challenges for Advocates in Translating Change Processes into Effectiveness Measures. *Administration in Social Work*, *31*(4), 59–81. doi:10.1300/J147v31n04_06

New Economics Foundation (NEF). (2007). *Measuring real value: A DIY guide to social return on investment*. London: New Economics Foundation. Retrieved from http://www.neweconomics.org/

New Economics Foundation. (2009). *Proving and Improving: A Quality and Impact Toolkit for Social Enterprise*. Retrieved from http://www.proveandimprove.org/new/

Ney, S., Beckmann, M., Graebnitz, D., & Mirkovic, R. (2014). Social entrepreneurs and social change: Tracing impacts of social entrepreneurship through ideas, structures and practices. *International Journal of Entrepreneurial Venturing*, *6*(1), 51–68. doi:10.1504/IJEV.2014.059405

Nicholls, A. (2006). Social Entrepreneurship. In *Enterprise and Small Business: Principles, Practice and Policy*. Financial Times Prentice Hall.

Nicholls, A. (2006). *Social entrepreneurship: New models of sustainable change*. New York: Oxford University Press.

Nicholls, A. (2006). *Social Entrepreneurship: New Models of Sustainable Change*. Oxford, UK: Oxford University Press.

Nicholls, A. (2006). *Social entrepreneurship: New models of sustainable social change*. Oxford, UK: Oxford University Press.

Nicholls, A. (2009). We do good things, don't we?: Blended value accounting in social entrepreneurship. *Accounting, Organizations and Society*, *34*(6-7), 755–769. doi:10.1016/j.aos.2009.04.008

Nicholls, A. (2010). The functions of performance measurement in social entrepreneurship: control, planning and accountability. In K. Hockerts, J. Mair, & J. Robinson (Eds.), *Values and opportunities in social entrepreneurship* (pp. 241–272). New York: Palgrave. doi:10.1057/9780230298026_13

Nicholls, A., & Cho, A. H. (2006). Social entrepreneurship: The structuration of a field. In A. Nicholls (Ed.), *Social entrepreneurship: New models of sustainable social change* (pp. 99–118). Oxford, UK: Oxford University Press.

Nicholls, A., & Murdock, A. (2012). *The Nature of Social Innovation, Blurring Boundaries to Reconfigure Markets*. Palgrave Macmillan.

Nicholls, J. (2004). *Social return on investment: Valuing what matters*. London: New Economics Foundation.

Nielsen, B. B., & Gudergan, S. (2012). Exploration and exploitation fit and performance in international strategic alliances. *International Business Review*, *21*(4), 558–574. doi:10.1016/j.ibusrev.2011.07.001

Noe, R. A., Hollenbeck, J. R., Gerhart, B., & Wright, P. M. (2016). *Fundamentals of human resource management* (6th ed.). Boston, MA: McGraw-Hill/Irwin.

Norman, W., & MacDonald, C. (2004). Getting to the bottom of "triple bottom line". *Business Ethics Quarterly*, *14*(2), 243–262. doi:10.5840/beq200414211

Nussbaum, M. (1996). Compassion: The basic social emotion. *Social Philosophy & Policy*, *13*(01), 27–58. doi:10.1017/S0265052500001515

NVCO. (2016). *The UK Civil Society Almanac*. London: NVCO Publication.

Nyssens, M. (2006). *Social Enterprise at the Crossroads of Market, Public Policies and Civil Society*. London: Routledge.

O'Reilly, C., Chatman, J., & Caldwell, D. (1991). People and organizational culture: A profile comparison approach to assessing person-organization fit. *Academy of Management Journal*, *34*(3), 487–516. doi:10.2307/256404

O'Riordan, L., & Fairbrass, J. (2014). Managing CSR stakeholder engagement: A new conceptual framework. *Journal of Business Ethics*, *125*(1), 121–145. doi:10.100710551-013-1913-x

ODPM. (2003). *National procurement strategy for local government in England (2003–2006)*. London: Office of the Deputy Prime Minister.

OECD. (2010). Social Entrepreneurship and Social Innovation. In *SMEs* (pp. 185–215). Entrepreneurship and Innovation.

OECD. (2014). *Job Creation and Local Economic Development*. Paris: OECD Publishing.

OGC. (2003). *Report to the chancellor of the exchequer: increasing competition and improving long-term capacity planning in the government market place*. London: Office for Government Commerce.

OGC. (2004). *Capturing innovation: nurturing. suppliers' ideas in the public sector*. Retrieved from www.ogc.gov.uk/documents/capturing_innovation.pdf

OGC. (2010). *Policy through Procurement (PtP)*. London: Action Plan. Office for Government Commerce.

OGC. (2011). *Public sector procurement expenditure survey*. Office for Government Commerce, London. Retrieved from http://webarchive.nationalarchives.gov.uk/20110822131357/http://www.ogc.gov.uk/ documents/July_Spend_Publication_v1.0.doc

Ohana, M., & Meyer, M. (2010). Should I stay or should I go now? Investigating the intention to quit of the permanent staff in social enterprises. *European Management Journal, 28*(6), 441–454. doi:10.1016/j.emj.2010.06.007

Omorede, A. (2014). Exploration of motivational drivers towards social entrepreneurship. *Social Enterprise Journal, 10*(3), 239–267. doi:10.1108/SEJ-03-2013-0014

Onyx, J., & Maclean, M. (1996). Careers in the third sector. *Nonprofit Management & Leadership, 6*(4), 331–345. doi:10.1002/nml.4130060404

Orlando, R. (2000). Racial Diversity, Business Strategy, and Firm Performance: A Resource-Based View. *Academy of Management Journal, 43*(2), 164–177. doi:10.2307/1556374

Ormiston, J., & Seymour, R. (2011). Understanding Value Creation in Social Entrepreneurship: The Importance of Aligning Mission, Strategy and Impact Measurement. *Journal of Social Entrepreneurship, 2*(2), 125–150. doi:10.1080/19420676.2011.606331

Osburg, T. (2013). Social innovation to drive corporate sustainability. In *Social Innovation* (pp. 13–22). Springer Berlin Heidelberg. doi:10.1007/978-3-642-36540-9_2

Oster, S. M. (1995). *Strategic management for nonprofit organizations: Theory and cases*. New York: Oxford University Press.

Osterwalder, A., & Pigneur, Y. (2010). *Business model generation: a handbook for visionaries, game changers, and challengers*. John Wiley & Sons.

Osterwalder, A., Pigneur, Y., Bernarda, G., & Smith, A. (2014). *Value proposition design: How to create products and services customers want*. John Wiley & Sons.

Ostgaard, T. A., & Birley, S. (1995). New Venture Growth and Personal Networks. *Journal of Business Research, 36*(1), 37–50. doi:10.1016/0148-2963(95)00161-1

Ostrander, S. A. (2007). The growth of donor control: Revisiting the social relations of philanthropy. *Nonprofit and Voluntary Sector Quarterly, 36*(2), 356–372. doi:10.1177/0899764007300386

Özdemir, A. A. (2010). Sosyal Girişimcilik Niyeti ve Girişimcilik-Davranış İlişkisi. In S. Besler (Ed.), *Sosyal Girişimcilik* (pp. 139–160). İstanbul: Beta Yayınları.

Özdemir, S. M. (2011). Toplumsal değişme ve küreselleşme bağlamında eğitim ve eğitim programları: Kavramsal bir çözümleme. *Ahi Evran Üniversitesi Eğitim Fakültesi Dergisi, 12*(1), 85–110.

Özdevecioğlu & Cingöz. (2009). Sosyal Girişimcilik ve Sosyal Girişimciler Teorik Çerçeve. *Erciyes Üniversitesi İktisadi ve İdari Bilimler Fakültesi Dergisi, 32*.

Özdevecioğlu, M., & Cingöz, A. (2009). Sosyal girişimcilik ve sosyal girişimciler: Teorik çerçeve. *Erciyes Üniversitesi İktisadi ve İdari Bilimler Fakültesi Dergisi, 32*, 81–95.

Özensel, E. (2003). Sosyolojik bir olgu olarak değer. *Değerler Eğitimi Dergisi, 1*(3), 217–239.

Özer, F. (2016). *The change in social capital based on closed and strong relations: The structural evolution of İslamic social capital in Turkish organizational life* (Unpublished PhD. Dissertation). Marmara University, Social Sciences Institute, İstanbul.

Ozgen, E., & Baron, R. (2007). Social sources of information in opportunity recognition: Effects of mentors, industry networks, and professional forums. *Journal of Business Venturing, 22*(2), 174–192. doi:10.1016/j.jbusvent.2005.12.001

Özkalp, E. (2003). Kültür. In E. Özkalp (Ed.), *Davranış bilimlerine giriş*. Eskişehir: Anadolu Üniversitesi Yayınları.

Ozmel, U., Robinson, D. T., & Stuart, T. E. (2013). Strategic alliances, venture capital, and exit decisions in early stage high-tech firms. *Journal of Financial Economics*, *107*(3), 655–670. doi:10.1016/j.jfineco.2012.09.009

Painter, C. (2013). The UK Coalition Government: Constructing public service reform narratives. Public Policy and Administration, 28(3), 3–20.

Paraskevaidis, P., & Andriotis, K. (2017). Altruism in tourism: Social exchange theory vs altruistic surplus phenomenon in host volunteering. *Annals of Tourism Research*, *62*, 26–37. doi:10.1016/j.annals.2016.11.002

Parente, C., Lopes, A., & Marcos, V. (2014). Social Entrepreneurship Profiles: Lessons from Organizational and Management Dynamics. *Journal of Social Entrepreneurship*, *5*(1), 22–41. doi:10.1080/19420676.2013.820782

Park, B. J. R., Srivastava, M. K., & Gnyawali, D. R. (2014). Walking the tight rope of coopetition: Impact of competition and cooperation intensities and balance on firm innovation performance. *Industrial Marketing Management*, *43*(2), 210–221. doi:10.1016/j.indmarman.2013.11.003

Park, S. H., Kim, J. N., & Krishna, A. (2014). Bottom-up building of an innovative organization: Motivating employee intrapreneurship and scouting and their strategic value. *Management Communication Quarterly*, *28*(4), 531–560. doi:10.1177/0893318914541667

Parsons, T. (1961). Some considerations on the theory of social change. *Rural Sociology*, *26*(3), 219–239.

Partzsch, L., & Ziegler, R. (2011). Social entrepreneurs as change agents: A case study on power and authority in the water sector. *International Environmental Agreement: Politics, Law and Economics*, *11*(1), 63–83. doi:10.100710784-011-9150-1

Pathak, S., & Muralidharan, E. (2017). Economic Inequality and Social Entrepreneurship. *Business & Society*, 1–41.

Paton, R. (2003). *Managing and measuring social enterprises*. Thousand Oaks, CA: Sage.

Patton, M. Q. (1999). Enhancing the quality and credibility of qualitative analysis. *Health Services Research*, *34*(5 Pt 2), 1189. PMID:10591279

Pearce, J. (2003). *Proving and Improving. Improve It – Social Auditing to Win Business Conference*. London: Unted Kingdom.

Pedersen, E., & Gwozdz, W. (2014). From Resistance to Opportunity-Seeking: Strategic Responses to Institutional Pressures for Corporate Social Responsibility in the Nordic Fashion Industry. *Journal of Business Ethics*, *119*(2), 245–264. doi:10.100710551-013-1630-5

Peltier, W., & Naidu, G. M. (2012). Social networks across the SME organizational lifecycle. *Journal of Small Business and Enterprise Development*, *19*(1), 56–73. doi:10.1108/14626001211196406

Peredo, A. M., & McLean, M. (2006). Social entrepreneurship: A critical review of the concept. *Journal of World Business*, *41*(1), 56–65. doi:10.1016/j.jwb.2005.10.007

Perlo-Freemon, S., & Webber, D. J. (2009). Basic Needs, Government Debt and Economic Growth. *World Economy*, *32*(6), 965–994. doi:10.1111/j.1467-9701.2009.01181.x

Perrini, F., & Vurro, C. (2006). Social entrepreneurship: Innovation and social change across theory and practice. In Social entrepreneurship (pp. 57-85). Palgrave Macmillan UK.

Perrini, F. (2006). Social entrepreneurship domain: setting boundaries. In F. Perrini (Ed.), *The new social entrepreneurship* (pp. 1–25). Cheltenham, UK: Edward Elgar.

Perrini, F., & Vurro, C. (2006). Social entrepreneurship: Innovation and social change across theory and practice. In J. Mair, J. Robinson, & K. Hockerts (Eds.), *Social entrepreneurship* (pp. 57–85). Palgrave MacMillian. doi:10.1057/9780230625655_5

Perron, G. M., Côté, R. P., & Duffy, J. F. (2006). Improving environmental awareness training in business. *Journal of Cleaner Production, 14*(6), 551–562. doi:10.1016/j.jclepro.2005.07.006

Person, A. E., Strong, D. A., Furgeson, J., & Berk, J. A. (2009). *Maximizing the Value of Philanthropic Efforts through Planned Partnerships between the U.S. Government and Private Foundations*. Mathematica Policy Research Inc.

Pfeffer, J., & Salancik, G. R. (1978). *The External Control of Organizations*. New York: Harper & Row.

Phillips, C. J. (2005). *Health Economics: An Introduction for Health Professionals*. Blackwell Publishing Ltd. doi:10.1002/9780470755228

Phillips, W., Lee, H., Ghobadian, A., O'Regan, N., & James, P. (2015). Social Innovation and Social Entrepreneurship: A Systematic Review. *Group & Organization Management, 40*(3), 428–461. doi:10.1177/1059601114560063

Phipps, S. T. A., & Prieto, L. C. (2015). Politicking and Entrepreneurship: Determining The Critical Political Skill Dimensions for High Entrepreneurial Intentions. *Academy of Entrepreneurship Journal, 21*(2), 73–87.

Pless, N. M. (2012). Social entrepreneurship in theory and practice: An introduction. *Journal of Business Ethics, 111*(3), 317–320. doi:10.100710551-012-1533-x

Podolny, J. M. (2001). Networks as the Pipes and Prisms of the Market. *American Journal of Sociology, 107*(1), 33–60. doi:10.1086/323038

Pol, E., & Ville, S. (2009). Social innovation: Buzz word or enduring term? *Journal of Socio-Economics, 38*(6), 878–885. doi:10.1016/j.socec.2009.02.011

Polonsky, M. J., & Landreth, S. (2005). Should we evaluate the social impact of nonprofit organizations? *American Marketing Association Marketing and Public Policy Conference*, Washington, DC.

Porter, M. (1980). Competitive strategy: Techniques for analyzing industries and competition. New York.

Porter, M., & Kramer, M. (2002, December). The Competitive Advantage of Corporate Philanthropy. *Harvard Business Review*, 56-68.

Porter, M., & Kramer, M. (2006, December). Strategy and Society: The Link between Competitive Advantage and Corporate Social Responsibility. *Harvard Business Review*, 78-92.

Porter, M., & Kramer, M. (2011, January-February). Creating Shared Value. *Harvard Business Review*, 62-77.

Porter, M. (1985). *Competitive Advantage: Creating and Sustaining Superior Performance*. New York: Free Press.

Porter, M., Hills, G., Pfitzer, M., Patscheke, S., & Hawkins, E. (2011). *Measuring Shared Value: How to Unlock Value by Linking Social and Business Results*. FSG.

Porter, M., & Kramer, M. R. (2011, January). Creating Share Value. *Harvard Business Review*, 201–229.

Powell, E. E., & Baker, T. (2013). *How Can We Help? The Distinctive Impact of Empathy and Sympathy in the Emergence of Social Venture Missions*. Paper presented at the mini conference on social change, innovation, and entrepreneurial activity, Milan, Italy.

Prabhu, G. (1999). Social entrepreneurial leadership. *Career Development International*, *4*(3), 140–145. doi:10.1108/13620439910262796

Prabhu, V. P., McGuire, S. J., Drost, E. A., & Kwong, K. K. (2012). Proactive personality and entrepreneurial intent: Is entrepreneurial self-efficacy a mediator or moderator. *International Journal of Entrepreneurial Behaviour & Research*, *18*(5), 559–586. doi:10.1108/13552551211253937

Prahalad, C. K. (2004). *The fortune at the bottom of the pyramid: Eradicating poverty with profits*. Philadelphia: Wharton Business Publishing.

Prahalad, C. K. (2005). *The Fortune at the Bottom of the Pyramid*. Wharton School Publishing.

Prahalad, C. K. (2012). Bottom of the Pyramid as a Source of Breakthrough Innovations. *Journal of Product Innovation Management*, *29*(1), 6–12. doi:10.1111/j.1540-5885.2011.00874.x

Prahalad, C. K., & Hart, S. (2002). The Fortune at the Bottom of the Pyramid. *Strategy and Competition*, *26*(1), 1–14.

Praszkier, R., & Nowak, A. (2011). *Social entrepreneurship: Theory and practice*. Cambridge University Press. doi:10.1017/CBO9781139049467

Praszkier, R., & Nowak, A. (2012). *Social Entrepreneurship Theory and practice*. Cambridge University Press.

Public Administration Select Committee (PASC). (2008). *Public Services and the Third Sector: Rhetoric and Reality*. Eleventh Report of Session 2007–08. London: The Stationery Office.

Pynes, J. E. (2013). *Human resources management for public and nonprofit organizations: A strategic approach* (3rd ed.). San Francisco, CA: Jossey Bass.

Rahdari, A., Sepasi, S., & Moradi, M. (2016). Achieving sustainability through Schumpeterian social entrepreneurship: The role of social enterprises. *Journal of Cleaner Production*, *137*, 347–360. doi:10.1016/j.jclepro.2016.06.159

Rao-Nicholson, R., Vorley, T., & Khan, Z. (2017, August). Social innovation in emerging economies: A national systems of innovation based approach. *Technological Forecasting and Social Change*, *121*, 228–237. doi:10.1016/j.techfore.2017.03.013

Ratiu, C., Cherry, B., & Nielson, T. R. (2014). Humility in Social Entrepreneurship: A Virtuous Circle. In Emerging Research Directions in Social Entrepreneurship (pp. 11-33). Springer. doi:10.1007/978-94-007-7896-2_2

Raworth, K. (2017a). *What on Earth is the Doughnut?* Retrieved from https://www.kateraworth.com/doughnut/

Raworth, K. (2017b). *Meet the Doughnut: The New Economic Model that could Help End Ineqaulity*. World Economic Forum. Retrieved from https://www.weforum.org/agenda/2017/04/the-new-economic-model-that-could-end-inequality-doughnut?utm_content=bufferd48ac&utm_medium=social&utm_source=facebook.com&utm_campaign=buffer

Reay, T., & Jones, C. (2016). Qualitatively capturing institutional logics. *Strategic Organization*, *14*(4), 441–454. doi:10.1177/1476127015589981

Rennie, H. G. (2006). Social entrepreneurship and regional economic development: A conceptual framework. In J. Gatrell & N. Reid (Eds.), *Enterprising world* (pp. 257–270). Springer. doi:10.1007/1-4020-5226-X_21

Rexhepi, G., Kurtishi, S., & Bexheti, G. (2013). Corporate social responsibility (CSR) and innovation–the drivers of business growth? *Procedia: Social and Behavioral Sciences*, *75*, 532–541. doi:10.1016/j.sbspro.2013.04.058

Rey-Marti, A., Ribeirio-Soriano, D., & Palacios-Marques, D. (2016). A bibliometric analysis of social entrepreneurship. *Journal of Business Research*, *69*(5), 1651–1655. doi:10.1016/j.jbusres.2015.10.033

Ridder, H.-G., & McCandless, A. (2010). Influences on the architecture of human resource management in nonprofit organizations: An analytical framework. *Nonprofit and Voluntary Sector Quarterly, 39*(1), 124–141. doi:10.1177/0899764008328182

Ridley-Duff, R., & Bull, M. (2015). Understanding social enterprise: Theory and practice. *Sage (Atlanta, Ga.).*

Ries, E. (2011). *The lean startup: How today's entrepreneurs use continuous innovation to create radically successful businesses.* Crown Business.

Rinaldo, H. (2010). *Getting Started in Social Impact Measurement: A guide to choosing how to measure social impact.* Norwich, CT: The Guild.

Roberts Enterprise Development Fund-REDF. (2000). *SROI methodology.* San Francisco: Author.

Roberts, D., & Woods, C. (2005). Changing the world on a shoestring: The concept of social entrepreneurship. *University of Auckland Business Review, 7*(1), 45–51.

Roberts, N. C., & King, P. J. (1991). Policy entrepreneurs: Their activity structure and function in the policy process. *Journal of Public Administration: Research and Theory, 1*(2), 147–175.

Robin Hood Foundation Official Website. (n.d.). Retrieved from https://www.robinhood.org

Robinson, A., & Klein, K. (2007). *Selling Social Change (Without Selling Out): Earned Income Strategies for Nonprofits.* San Francisco, CA: Jossey-Bass.

Robinson, J. (2006). Navigating social and institutional barriers to markets: How social entrepreneurs identify and evaluate opportunities. In J. Mair, J. Robinson, & K. Hockerts (Eds.), *Social entrepreneurship* (pp. 95–120). New York: Palgrave MacMillan. doi:10.1057/9780230625655_7

Robinson, R. (1993). Economic Evaluation and Health Care: Cost-Benefit Analysis. *BMJ (Clinical Research Ed.), 307*(6909), 924–926. doi:10.1136/bmj.307.6909.924 PMID:8241859

Rogers, C. R. (1959). A theory of therapy, personality, and interpersonal relationships as developed in the client-centered framework. In S. Koch (Ed.), *Psychology: A Study of a Science* (Vol. 3, pp. 184–256). New York: McGraw Hill.

Rogovsky, N. (2000). *Corporate community involvement programmes: Partnerships for jobs and development.* International Institute for Labour Studies.

Rosing, K., Frese, M., & Bausch, A. (2011). Explaining the heterogeneity of the leadership-innovation relationship: Ambidextrous leadership. *The Leadership Quarterly, 22*(5), 956–974. doi:10.1016/j.leaqua.2011.07.014

Rotheroe, N., & Richards, A. (2007). Social Return on Investment and social enterprise: Transparent accountability for sustainable development. *Social Enterprise Journal, 3*(1), 31–48. doi:10.1108/17508610780000720

Royce, M. (2007). Using human resource management tools to support social enterprise: Emerging themes from the sector. *Social Enterprise Journal, 3*(1), 10–19. doi:10.1108/17508610780000718

Rueda-Armengot, C., Estelles-Miguel, S., Gato, M., Guillem, J., & Peris-Ortiz, M. (2017). Social Entrepreneurship in the Automotive Industry: A Win-Win Experience. In M. Peris-Ortiz, F. Teulon, & D. Bonet-Fernandez (Eds.), Social Entrepreneurship in Non-Profit and Profit Sectors (pp. 99-104). Springer. doi:10.1007/978-3-319-50850-4_8

Rüede, D., & Lurtz, K. (2012). *Mapping the various meanings of social innovation: Towards a differentiated understanding of an emerging concept.* Academic Press.

Rusinowska, A., Berghammer, R., De Swart, H., & Grabisch, M. (2011). Social networks: Prestige, centrality, and influence. *Relational and Algebraic Methods in Computer Science*, 22-39.

Russell, L. B., Gold, M. R., & Siegel, J. E. (1996). The Role of Cost Effectiveness Analysis in Health and Medicine. *Journal of the American Medical Association*, *276*(14), 1172–1177. doi:10.1001/jama.1996.03540140060028 PMID:8827972

Ruvio, A. A., & Shoham, A. (2010). A multilevel study of nascent social ventures. *International Small Business Journal*, *29*(5), 562–579. doi:10.1177/0266242610369741

Ruvio, A., Rosenblatt, Z., & Hertz-Lazarowitz, R. (2010). Entrepreneurial leadership vision in nonprofit vs. for-profit organizations. *The Leadership Quarterly*, *21*(1), 144–158. doi:10.1016/j.leaqua.2009.10.011

Ryan, P. W., & Lyne, I. (2008). Social enterprise and the measurement of social value: Methodological issues with the calculation and application of the social return on investment. *Education, Knowledge & Economy*, *2*(3), 223–237. doi:10.1080/17496890802426253

Sahasranamam, S., & Sud, M. (2016). Opportunity and Necessity Entrepreneurship: A Comparative Study of India and China. *Academy of Entrepreneurship Journal*, *22*(1), 21–40.

Santos, F. M. (2009). *A positive theory of social entrepreneurship*. Retrieved 12.03.2017, from https://sites.insead.edu/facultyresearch/research/doc.cfm?did=41727

Santos, F. M. (2012). A Positive Theory of Social Entrepreneurship. *Journal of Business Ethics*, *111*(3), 335–351. doi:10.100710551-012-1413-4

Sanzo, M. J., Álvarez, L. I., Rey, M., & García, N. (2015). Business–nonprofit partnerships: A new form of collaboration in a corporate responsibility and social innovation context. *Service Business*, *9*(4), 611–636. doi:10.100711628-014-0242-1

Saruhan, Ş. C., & Öncer, A. Z. (2004). Değer Hedefli İşletmecilik. Nihad Sayar Eğitim Vakfı Yayını, 529(762).

Saruhan, S. C., & Yıldız, M. L. (2016). *Contemporary Management Science*. Istanbul: Beta.

Sastre-Castillo, M. A., Peris-Ortiz, M., & Danvila-Del Valle, I. (2015). What is different about the profile of the social entrepreneur? *Nonprofit Management & Leadership*, *25*(4), 349–369. doi:10.1002/nml.21138

Saunders, M., Lewis, P., & Thornhill, A. (2011). *Research Methods for Business Students*. Harlow: Pearson Education Ltd.

Saxenian, A. L. (2002). *Local and Global Networks of immigrant professionals in Silicon Valley*. Public Policy Institute of California.

Say, J. B. (1971). *A Treatise of Political Economy or the Production, Distribution and Consumption of Wealth* (4th ed.). New York: Augustus M. Kelley.

Schaltegger, S., Hahn, T., & Burritt, R. (2000). *Environmental Management Accounting – Overview and Main Approaches Working paper*. Centre for Sustainability Management.

Schmitz, B., & Scheuerle, T. (2012, February). Article. *ACRN Journal of Entrepreneurship Perspectives*, *1*(1), 13–36.

Schott, T., Rogoff, E., & Herrington, M. (2017). *GEM 2016/2017 Report on Senior Entrepreneurship*. Retrieved June 10, 2017, from http://www.gemconsortium.org/

Schumpeter, J. A. (1965). Economic Theory and Entrepreneurial History. In H. G. Aitken (Ed.), Explorations in Enterprise. Cambridge, MA: Harvard University Press. doi:10.4159/harvard.9780674594470.c5

Schumpeter, J. A. (1934). *The theory of Economic Development*. Cambridge, MA: Harvard University Press.

Schumpeter, J. A. (1967). *The Theory of Economic Development*. New York: Oxford University Press.

Schuyler, G. (1998). *Social entrepreneurship: Profit as a means, not an end.* Retrieved 12.03.2017, from http://files.eric.ed.gov/fulltext/ED434219.pdf

Schüz, M. (2012). Sustainable Corporate Responsibility – The Foundation of Successful Business in the New Millenium. *Central European Business Review*, *1*(2), 7–15. doi:10.18267/j.cebr.12

Schweitzer, J. (2014). Leadership and innovation capability development in strategic alliances. *Leadership and Organization Development Journal*, *35*(5), 442–469. doi:10.1108/LODJ-01-12-0001

Scottish Government. (2008). *Public procurement reform programme: Scottish procurement policy handbook. Dec 2008.* The Scottish Government.

Scowen, J. (2004). A top procurement officer's view. *Social Enterprise Magazine*, 17.

Seanor, P., & Meaton, J. (2007). Making sense of social enterprise. *Social Enterprise Journal*, *3*(1), 90–100. doi:10.1108/17508610780000724

Seelos, C., & Mair, J. (2005). Social entrepreneurship: Creating new business models to serve the poor. *Business Horizons*, *48*(3), 241–246. doi:10.1016/j.bushor.2004.11.006

Seitanidi, M. M., & Crane, A. (2009). Implementing CSR through partnerships: Understanding the selection, design and institutionalisation of nonprofit-business partnerships. *Journal of Business Ethics*, *85*(2), 413–429. doi:10.100710551-008-9743-y

Sekliuckiene, J., & Kisielius, E. (2015). Development of social entrepreneurship initiatives: A theoretical framework. *Procedia: Social and Behavioral Sciences*, *213*, 1015–1019. doi:10.1016/j.sbspro.2015.11.519

Serrat, O. (2017). Learning in strategic alliances. In *Knowledge Solutions* (pp. 639–647). Springer Singapore. doi:10.1007/978-981-10-0983-9_71

Sesameworkshop. (2017). *Financials.* Retrieved from http://www.sesameworkshop.org/about-us/financials/

Seyyar, A. (2005). *Sosyal güvenlik terimleri.* İstanbul: Papatya Yayınları.

Shane, S. (2000). Prior knowledge and the discovery of entrepreneurial opportunities. *Organization Science*, *11*(4), 448–469. doi:10.1287/orsc.11.4.448.14602

Shane, S. (2003). *A General Theory of Entrepreneurship: The Individual–Opportunity Nexus.* Northampton, MA: Edward Elgar. doi:10.4337/9781781007990

Sharir, M., & Lerner, M. (2006). Gauging the success of social ventures initiated by individual social entrepreneurs. *Journal of World Business*, *41*(1), 6–20. doi:10.1016/j.jwb.2005.09.004

Sharma, P., & Chrisman, J. J. (1999). Towards a reconciliation of the definitional issues in the field of corporate entrepreneurship. *Entrepreneurship Theory and Practice*, *23*(3), 11–27. doi:10.1177/104225879902300302

Shaw, E., Shaw, J., & Wilson, M. (2002). Unsung entrepreneurs: Entrepreneurship for social gain. Durham, UK: University of Durham Business School – –The Barclays Centre for Entrepreneurship.

Shaw, E., & Carter, S. (2007). Social Entrepreneurship: Theoretical Antecedents and Empirical Analysis of Entrepreneurial Processes and Outcomes. *Journal of Small Business and Enterprise Development*, *14*(3), 418–434. doi:10.1108/14626000710773529

Shaw, E., & de Bruin, A. (2013). Reconsidering capitalism: The promise of social innovation and social entrepreneurship? *International Small Business Journal*, *31*(7), 737–746. doi:10.1177/0266242613497494

Sheil, F., & Breidenbach-Roe, R. (2014). *Payment by results and the voluntary sector*. London: NCVO.

Shepherd, D., & DeTienne, D. (2005). Prior knowledge, potential financial reward, and opportunity identification. *Entrepreneurship Theory and Practice*, *29*(1), 91–112. doi:10.1111/j.1540-6520.2005.00071.x

Shier, M. L., & Handy, F. (2015). Social Change Efforts of Direct Service Nonprofits: The Role of Funding and Collaborations in Shaping Social Innovations. *Human Service Organizations, Management, Leadership & Governance*, *39*(1), 6–24. doi:10.1080/23303131.2014.973623

Shi, W., Sun, J., & Prescott, J. E. (2012). A temporal perspective of merger and acquisition and strategic alliance initiatives: Review and future direction. *Journal of Management*, *38*(1), 164–209. doi:10.1177/0149206311424942

Short, J. C., Moss, T. W., & Lumpkin, G. T. (2009). Research in social entrepreneurship: Past contributions and future opportunities. *Strategic Entrepreneurship Journal*, *3*(2), 161–194. doi:10.1002ej.69

Silverman, D. (2013). *Doing qualitative research: A practical handbook*. SAGE Publications Limited.

Simon, J., & Barmeier, J. (2010). *More than money: Impact investing for development*. Retrieved from https://www.cgdev.org/publication/more-money-impact-investing-development

Simons, R. (1995). *Levels of control—how managers use innovative control systems to drive strategic renewal*. Boston, MA: Harvard Business School Press.

Singh, A. (2016). *The Process of Social Value Creation: A Multiple-Case Study on Social Entrepreneurship in India*. Springer. doi:10.1007/978-81-322-2827-1

Singh, A., Majumdar, S., & Saini, G. S. (2017). Corporate Social Responsibility and Social Entrepreneurship: An Indian Context. *Journal of Entrepreneurship and Innovation in Emerging Economies*, *3*(1), 71–76. doi:10.1177/2393957516684451

Singh, N., & Krishnan, V. R. (2008). Self-sacrifice and transformational leadership: Mediating role of altruism. *Leadership and Organization Development Journal*, *29*(3), 261–274. doi:10.1108/01437730810861317

Sivathanu, B., & Bhise, P. (2013). *Challenges for social entrepreneurship, international journal of application or innovation in engineering and management*. Retrieved 16.05.2017, from http://www.ijaiem.org/RATMIG-2013/MGT%2025%20Challenges%20for%20Social%20Entrepreneurship.pdf

Sivathanu, B., & Bhise, P. V. (2013). Challenges for social entrepreneurship. *International Journal of Application Innovation in Engineering & Management*.

Skoll Foundation. (2009). *What is social entrepreneur?* Retrieved June 10, 2017, from http://skoll.org/

Slocock, C. (2012). *The big society audit 2012*. London: Civil Exchange.

Smallbone, D., & Lyon, F. (2005). *Social enterprise development in the UK: some contemporary policy issues*. Paper presented to ICSB conference, Washington, DC.

Smallbone, D., Evans, M., Ekanem, I., & Butters, S. (2001). *Researching social enterprise*. Small Business Service.

Smerdon, M., & Deakin, N. (2010). Independence in principle and practice: Relationships between the state and voluntary action. *Voluntary Sector Review*, *1*(3), 361–370. doi:10.1332/204080510X538347

Smith, B. R., & Stevens, C. E. (2010). Different types of social entrepreneurship: The role of geography and embeddedness on the measurement and scaling of social value. *Entrepreneurship and Regional Development*, *22*(6), 575–598. doi:10.1080/08985626.2010.488405

Smith-Hunter, A. E., & College, S. (2008). Toward multidimensional model of social entrepreneurship: Definitions, clarifications and theoretical perspectives. *Journal of Business & Economics Research*, *6*(6), 93–112.

Smith, J. K. (1993, March). Quantitative v. Qualitative Research: An attempt to classify the issue. *Educational Research*, •••, 6–13.

Smith, W., & Darko, E. (2014). *Social enterprise: constraints and opportunities–evidence from Vietnam and Kenya*. London: Overseas Development Institute.

So, I., & Caponyala, A. (2006). How Impact Investors Actually Measure Impact. *Stanford Social Innovation Review*. Retrieved from https://ssir.org/articles/entry/how_impact_investors_actually_measure_impact

Sobhani, S., & Gasnier, A. (2012). Sosyal Girişimcilikten Kapsayıcı Piyasalara. In Büyüyen Kapsayıcı Píyasalar Türkiye'de Sosyal Girişimcilik Vakaları (pp. 1-7). İstanbul Bilgi Üniversitesi.

Social Audit Network. (n.d.). *What is Social Accounting and Audit*. Retrieved from http://www.socialauditnetwork.org.uk/getting-started/what-is-social-accounting-and-audit/

Social Enterprise UK. (2016). *Annual Review*. Author.

Social Impact. (n.d.). Retrieved 13.05.2017, from https://sosyaletkianalizi.ku.edu.tr/sayfa/tanimlar

Solitander, M., & Tidström, A. (2010). Competitive flows of intellectual capital in value creating networks. *Journal of Intellectual Capital*, *11*(1), 23–38. doi:10.1108/14691931011013316

Solomon, R. C. (1998). The moral psychology of business: Care and compassion in the corporation. *Business Ethics Quarterly*, *8*(3), 515–533. doi:10.2307/3857435

Somers, A. B. (2005). Shaping the balanced scorecard for use in UK social enterprises. *Social Enterprise Journal*, *1*(1), 43–57. doi:10.1108/17508610580000706

Spear, R. (2002). *National Profiles of Work Integration Social Enterprises*. EMES European Research Network.

Spear, R., & Bidet, E. (2005). Social enterprise for work integration in 12 European countries: A descriptive analysis. *Annals of Public and Cooperative Economics*, *76*(2), 195–231. doi:10.1111/j.1370-4788.2005.00276.x

Spears, L. C. (2010). Character and Servant Leadership: Ten Characteristics of Effective, Caring Leaders. *The Journal of Virtues & Leadership*, *1*(1), 25–30.

Spink, K. (1997). *Mother Teresa: A Complete Authorized Biography*. New York: HarperCollins.

Stam, W., Arzlanian, S., & Elfring, T. (2014). Social capital of entrepreneurs and small firm performance: A meta-analysis of contextual and methodological moderators. *Journal of Business Venturing*, *29*(1), 152–173. doi:10.1016/j.jbusvent.2013.01.002

Stenn, T. (2017). *Social Entrepreneurship as Sustainable Development: Introducing the Sustainability Lens*. Springer. doi:10.1007/978-3-319-48060-2

Stenzel, P. L. (2010). Sustainability, the triple bottom line, and the global reporting initiative. *Global Edge Business Review*, *4*(6), 1-2.

Stevenson, N., Taylor, M., & Lyon, F. (2010). *Joining the dots: Social impact measurement, commissioning from the third sector and supporting social enterprise development*. A report to East of England Development Agency. Available at: http://the-guild.co.uk/newsite/content/2010_Joining_the_dots_full_report_EEDA.pdf

Stevenson, N., Taylor, M., Lyon, F., & Rigby, M. (2010). *Joining the dots: Social impact measurement experiences and future directions for the Third Sector organizations in the East of England Report*. Centre for Enterprise and Economic Development Research, Third Sector Research Centre at Middlesex University with Malin Arvidson, Third Sector Research Centre at Southampton University.

Stevenson, H. H., & Jarillo, C. J. (1990). A Paradigm of Entrepreneurship: Entrepreneurial Management. *Strategic Management Journal*, *11*(5), 17–27.

Strauss, C., Taylor, B. L., Gu, J., Kuyken, W., Baer, R., Jones, F., & Cavanagh, K. (2016). What is compassion and how can we measure it? A review of definitions and measures. *Clinical Psychology Review*, *47*, 15–27. doi:10.1016/j.cpr.2016.05.004 PMID:27267346

Sturgess, G.L., Cumming, L.M., & Dicker, J. (2011). *Payment by Outcome: A Commissioner's Toolkit*. London: 2020 Public Services Trust at the RSA.

Sundaramurthy, C., Musteen, M., & Randel, A. E. (2013). Social Value Creation: A Qualitative Study of Indian Social Entrepreneurs. *Journal of Developmental Entrepreneurship*, *18*(02), 1350011. doi:10.1142/S1084946713500118

Surie, G., & Groen, A. (2017). The Importance of Social Entrepreneurship in National Systems of Innovation – An Introduction. *Technological Forecasting and Social Change*, *121*, 181–183. doi:10.1016/j.techfore.2017.05.010

Suutari, V., & Brewster, C. (2000). Making their own way: International experience through self-initiated foreign assignments. *Journal of World Business*, *35*(4), 417–436. doi:10.1016/S1090-9516(00)00046-8

Suzuki, Y., & Miah, M. D. (2016). Altruism, reciprocity and Islamic equity finance. *International Journal of Islamic and Middle Eastern Finance and Management*, *9*(2), 205–221. doi:10.1108/IMEFM-09-2014-0091

Swanson, L. A., & Zhang, D. D. (2010). The Social Entrepreneurship Zone. *Journal of Nonprofit & Public Sector Marketing*, *22*(2), 71–88. doi:10.1080/10495140903550726

Tanner, S. (2007). *Common Themes on Commissioning the VCS in Selected Local Authorities in Greater London*. London: London Councils.

Tan, W. L., Williams, J., & Tan, T. M. (2005). Defining the 'Social' in 'Social entrepreneurship': Altruism and entrepreneurship. *The International Entrepreneurship and Management Journal*, *1*(3), 353–365. doi:10.100711365-005-2600-x

Taylor-Gooby, P., & Stoker, G. (2011). The coalition programme: A new vision for Britain or politics as normal? *The Political Quarterly*, *82*(1), 4–14. doi:10.1111/j.1467-923X.2011.02169.x

Teasdale, S. (2012). What's in a name? Making sense of social enterprise discourses. *Public Policy and Administration*, *27*(2), 99-119.

Teasdale, S., McKay, S., Phillimore, J., & Teasdale, N. (2011). Exploring gender and social entrepreneurship: Women's leadership, employment and participation in the third sector and social enterprises. *Voluntary Sector Review*, *2*(1), 57–76. doi:10.1332/204080511X560620

Terjesen, S., Lepoutre, J., Justo, R., & Bosma, N. (2009). *Global Entrepreneurship Monitor Report on Social Entrepreneurship Executive Summary*. Retrieved June 10, 2017, from http://www.gemconsortium.org/

Thake, S., & Zadek, S. (1997). *Practical people, noble causes. How to support community based social entrepreneurs*. New Economic Foundation.

The Ashoka Foundation. (n.d.). Retrieved from https://www.ashoka.org/en/focus/social-entrepreneurship

The Center for High Impact Philanthropy (CHIP). (n.d.). *Cost Per Impact Pathways*. Retrieved from http://live-pennimpact.pantheon.io/wpcontent/uploads/2016/2015/03/CHIP_CostPerImpact_Pathways.pdf

The World Bank. (2003). *World development report 2004: Making services work for poor people*. Washington, DC: Oxford University Press.

Third Sector Task Force. (2009). *Welfare to work reform: The third sector's role: Final report*. Available at: http://www.acevo.org.uk/document.doc?id=42

Thomaz, F., & Swaminathan, V. (2015). What Goes Around Comes Around: Spreading Risk Through Strategic Alliances in Highly Embedded Networks. *Journal of Marketing*, *79*(5), 63–79. doi:10.1509/jm.12.0404

Thompson, J. J. (1999). The world of the entrepreneur - a new perspective. *Journal of Workplace Learning-Counselling Today*, *11*(6), 209–224. doi:10.1108/13665629910284990

Thompson, J. L. (1999). The World of the Entrepreneur- A New Perspective, *Journal of Workplace Learning-. Counseling Today*, *11*(6), 209–215.

Thompson, J. L. (2002). The world of the social entrepreneur. *International Journal of Public Sector Management*, *15*(5), 412–431. doi:10.1108/09513550210435746

Thompson, J. L., Alvy, G., & Lees, A. (2000). Social entrepreneurship: A new look at the people and the potential. *Management Decision*, *38*(5), 328–338. doi:10.1108/00251740010340517

Thompson, N., Kiefer, K., & York, J. G. (2011). Distinctions not Dichotomies: Exploring Social, Sustainable, and Environmental Entrepreneurship. In G. T. Lumpkin & J. A. Katz (Eds.), *Advances in Entrepreneurship, Firm Emergence and Growth: Exploring Social, Sustainable, and Environmental Entrepreneurship* (Vol. 13). Bingley, UK: Emerald Group Publishing Limited. doi:10.1108/S1074-7540(2011)0000013012

Thomson Reuters Foundation. (2016). Retrieved from http://poll2016.trust.org/

Thornton, P. H. (1999). The sociology of entrepreneurship. *Annual Review of Sociology*, *25*(1), 19–46. doi:10.1146/annurev.soc.25.1.19

Ticktin, M. I. (2011). *Casualties of care: Immigration and the politics of humanitarianism in France*. Univ of California Press. doi:10.1525/california/9780520269040.001.0001

Ţigu, G., Iorgulescu, M.-C., Răvar, A. S., & Lile, R. (2015). A Pilot Profile of the Social Entrepreneur in the Constantly Changing Romanian Economy. *Amfiteatru Economic*, *17*(38), 25–43.

Tiku, N. (2008). Do-Gooder finance: How a new crop of investors is helping social entrepreneurs. *INC. Magazine*.

Tracey, P., & Phillips, N. (2007). The distinctive challenge of educating social entrepreneurs: A postscript and rejoinder to the special issue on entrepreneurship education. *Academy of Management Learning & Education*, *6*(2), 264–271. doi:10.5465/AMLE.2007.25223465

Treasury, H. M. (2009). *Operational efficiency programme: collaborative procurement*. HM.

Treasury, H. M. (2006). *Value for Money Assessment Guidance*. London: HMSO.

Trivedi, C., & Stokols, D. (2011). Social enterprises and corporate enterprises. *The Journal of Entrepreneurship*, *20*(1), 1–32. doi:10.1177/097135571002000101

Tuan, M. (2008). *Measuring and/or Estimating Social Value Creation: Insights into Eight Integrated Cost Approaches*. Working Paper. Bill & Melinda Gates Foundation Impact Planning and Improvement.

Tung, R. L. (2008). Brain circulation, diaspora, and international competitiveness. *European Management Journal*, *26*(5), 298–304. doi:10.1016/j.emj.2008.03.005

Turker, D., & Vural, C. A. (2017). Embedding Social Innovation Process into the Institutional Context: Voids or Supports. *Technological Forecasting and Social Change*, *119*, 98–113. doi:10.1016/j.techfore.2017.03.019

Türkiye Üçüncü Sektör Vakfı Yayını. (2013). *Sosyal Etki Analizi: Sosyal Girişimler ve STK'lar için Yöntemler*. İstanbul: Seminer Notları.

Uddin, M. B., & Akhter, B. (2011). Strategic alliance and competitiveness: Theoretical framework. *Researchers World*, *2*(1), 43.

Ulwick, A. W. (2005). *What customers want: Using outcome-driven innovation to create breakthrough products and services* (Vol. 71408673). New York: McGraw-Hill.

Understanding Human Resource Challenges in the Indian Social Enterprise Sector. (2012). Retrieved from http://intellecap.com/sites/default/files/publications/intel lecap_hr_report_web_0.pdf

United Nations, Department of Economic and Social Affairs, Population Division. (2017). *World Population Prospects: The 2017 Revision*. Author.

United Nations. (2015). *World Population Prospects: The 2015 Revision, Volume I: Comprehensive Tables*. Retrieved from https://esa.un.org/unpd/wpp/publications/

United Nations. (n.d.). *Division for Sustainable Development*. Retrieved from https://sustainabledevelopment.un.org/memberstates/india

Urban, B., & Teise, H. (2015). Antecedents to Social Entrepreneurship Intentions: An Empirical Study in South Africa. *Management Dynamics*, *24*(2), 36–52.

Uzzi, B. (1996). The Sources and Consequences of Embeddedness for the Economic Performance of Organizations: The Network Effect. *American Sociological Review*, *61*(4), 674–698. doi:10.2307/2096399

Uzzi, B., & Lancaster, R. (2003). Relational Embeddedness and Learning: The Case of Bank Loan Managers and Their Clients. *Management Science*, *49*(4), 383–399. doi:10.1287/mnsc.49.4.383.14427

Vaidyanathan, M. M., Chatterjee, S., Murthy, M. S. S., & Naswa, M. T. (2014). *Talent Infusion in Social Enterprise*. Retrieved from http://niiticonsulting.com/pdf/talent%20infusion%20paper%201.pdf

Vaiman, V., Haslberger, A., & Vance, C. M. (2015). Recognizing the important role of self-initiated expatriates in effective global talent management. *Human Resource Management Review*, *25*(3), 280–286. doi:10.1016/j.hrmr.2015.04.004

Value. (n.d.). Retrieved 10.03.2017, from https://www.merriam-webster.com/dictionary/value

Van der Spek, T., Schreven, A. M., & Van der Velden, F. (2014). *Leadership in Social Business*. Context, International Cooperation.

Van Vuuren, M., de Jong, M. D., & Seydel, E. R. (2008). Commitment with or without a stick of paid work: Comparison of paid and unpaid workers in a nonprofit organization. *European Journal of Work and Organizational Psychology*, *17*(3), 315–326. doi:10.1080/13594320701693175

Vance, C. M. (2005). The personal quest for building global competence: A taxonomy of self-initiating career path strategies for gaining business experience abroad. *Journal of World Business*, *40*(4), 374–385. doi:10.1016/j.jwb.2005.08.005

Vance, C. M., Larrieu, R. J., Bergin, R., Mercado, J., Richmond, J., Walden, M., & Reeser, C. (2017). A Field Exploration of the "Expat-preneur" Phenomenon. *Global Business and Organizational Excellence*, *36*(6), 34–43. doi:10.1002/joe.21812

Vance, C. M., & McNulty, Y. (2014). Why and how women and men acquire expatriate career development experience: A study of American expatriates in Europe. *International Studies of Management & Organization*, *44*(2), 34–54. doi:10.2753/IMO0020-8825440202

Vance, C. M., McNulty, Y., Paik, Y., & D'Mello, J. (2016). The expat-preneur: Conceptualizing a growing international career phenomenon. *Journal of Global Mobility*, *4*(21), 202–224. doi:10.1108/JGM-11-2015-0055

Vecchio, R. P. (2003). Entrepreneurship and leadership: Common trends and common threads. *Human Resource Management Review*, *13*(2), 303–327. doi:10.1016/S1053-4822(03)00019-6

Venkataraman, S. (1997). The distinctive domain of entrepreneurship research. *Advances in Entrepreneurship, Firm, Emergence, and Growth*, *3*(1), 119–138.

Venkataraman, S. (1997). The Distinctive Domain of Entrepreneurship Research. *Advances in Entrepreneurship, Firm, Emergence, and Growth*, *3*(1), 119–138.

Venkataraman, S., & Shane, S. (2000). The promise of entrepreneurship as a field of research. *Academy of Management Review*, *25*(1), 217–226.

Verheul, I., Wennekers, S., Audretsch, D., & Thurik, R. (2001). *An eclectic theory of entrepreneurship: Policies, institutions and culture*. Retrieved 10.03.2017 from, https://www.econstor.eu/bitstream/10419/85867/1/01030.pdf

Vinogradov, E., & Jørgensen, J. (2017). Differences in international opportunity identification between native and immigrant entrepreneurs. *Journal of International Entrepreneurship*, *15*(2), 207–228. doi:10.100710843-016-0197-5

Vissak, T., & Zhang, X. (2014). Chinese immigrant entrepreneurs' involvement in internationalization and innovation: Three Canadian cases. *Journal of International Entrepreneurship*, *12*(2), 183–201. doi:10.100710843-014-0128-2

Volkmann, C., Tokarski, K. O., & Ernst, K. (2012). Background, Characteristics and Context of Social Entrepreneurship. In C. Volkmann, K. O. Tokarski, & K. Ernst (Eds.), *Social Entrepreneurship and Social Business* (pp. 4–30). Wiesbaden: Springer Gabler. doi:10.1007/978-3-8349-7093-0_1

von Eckardstein, D., & Brandl, J. (2004). Human resource management in nonprofit organizations. In A. Zimmer & E. Priller (Eds.), *Future of civil society: Making Central European nonprofitorganizations work* (pp. 297–314). Wiesbaden: VS Verlag fur Sozialwissenschaften. doi:10.1007/978-3-322-80980-3_17

Waddock, S. A., & Post, J. E. (1991). Social entrepreneurs and catalytic change. *Public Administration Review*, *51*(5), 393–401. doi:10.2307/976408

Waddock, S., & Steckler, E. (2016). Visionaries and Wayfinders: Deliberate and Emergent Pathways to Vision in Social Entrepreneurship. *Journal of Business Ethics*, *133*(4), 719–734. doi:10.100710551-014-2451-x

Walk, M., & Kennedy, T. (2017In press). Making Nonprofits more Effective: Performance Management and Performance Appraisals. In J. K. A. Word & J. E. Sowa (Eds.), *The Nonprofit Human Resource Management Handbook: From Theory to Practice*. New York, NY: Routledge.

Walter, J., Kellermanns, F. W., & Lechner, C. (2012). Decision making within and between organizations: Rationality, politics, and alliance performance. *Journal of Management*, *38*(5), 1582–1610. doi:10.1177/0149206310363308

Walumbwa, F. O., Avolio, B. J., Gardner, W. L., Wernsing, T. S., & Peterson, S. J. (2008). Authentic leadership: Development and validation of a theory-based measure. *Journal of Management*, *34*(1), 89–126. doi:10.1177/0149206307308913

Warner, M., & Sullivan, R. (Eds.). (2017). *Putting partnerships to work: Strategic alliances for development between government, the private sector and civil society*. New York: Routledge.

Weaver, R., Hanks, J., Earley, A., & Whitcomb, R. (2015). *A study of the contribution of cooperative models to Scotland's Economic Strategy and evaluation of Cooperative Development Scotland for Scottish Enterprise*. Manchester, UK: Ekosgen.

Weerawardena, J., & Mort, G. S. (2006). Investigating social entrepreneurship: A multidimensional model. *Journal of World Business*, *41*(1), 21–35. doi:10.1016/j.jwb.2005.09.001

Weerawardena, J., & Mort, G. S. (2012, Spring). Competitive Strategy in Socially Entrepreneurial Nonprofit Organizations: Innovation and Differentiation. *Journal of Public Policy & Marketing*, *31*(1), 91–101. doi:10.1509/jppm.11.034

Weerawardena, J., & Sullivan-Mort, G. (2001). Learning, innovation and competitive advantage in not-for-profit aged care marketing: A conceptual model and research propositions. *Journal of Nonprofit & Public Sector Marketing*, *9*(3), 53–73. doi:10.1300/J054v09n03_04

Weiss, C. H. (1995). Nothing as Practical as Good Theory: Exploring Theory-based Evaluation for Comprehensive Community Initiatives for Children and Families. In *New Approaches to Evaluating Community Initiatives: Concepts, Methods, and Contexts*. Washington, DC: Aspen Institute.

Wheeler, D., McKague, K., Thomson, J., Davies, R., Medalye, J., & Prada, M. (2005). Creating sustainable local enterprise networks. *MIT Sloan Management Review*, *47*(1), 33.

White, J. (1999). Ethical comportment in organizations: A synthesis of the feminist ethic of care and the Buddhist ethic of compassion. *International Journal of Value-Based Management*, *12*(2), 109–128. doi:10.1023/A:1007779604630

White, L. (2011). *Commission Impossible? Shaping Places Through Strategic Commissioning*. Chelmsford: Localis/Essex County Council.

Wie-Skillern, J., Austin, J. E., Leonard, H., & Stevenson, H. (2007). *Entrepreneurship in the Social Sector*. Sage Publications.

Wiguna, A. B., & Manzilati, A. (2014). Social Entrepreneurship and Socio-entrepreneurship: A Study with Economic and Social Perspective. *Procedia: Social and Behavioral Sciences*, *115*, 12–18. doi:10.1016/j.sbspro.2014.02.411

Wilkinson, C., Medhurst, J., Henry, N., Wihlborg, M., & Braithwaite, B. W. (2014). *A map of social enterprises and their eco-systems in Europe: Executive Summary*. London: ICF Consulting Services Limited.

William and Flora Hewlett Foundation. (2008). *Making Every Dollar Count: How expected return can transform philanthropy*. Author.

Williams, C., & Gurtoo, A. (Eds.). (2016). *Routledge handbook of entrepreneurship in developing economies*. London: Routledge Taylor & Francis Group.

Williams, D. A., & K'nife, K. A. K. (2012). The dark side of social entrepreneurship. *International Journal of Entrepreneurship*, *16*, 63–75.

Wilson, F., & Post, J. E. (2013). Business Models for People, Planet (&Profits): Exploring the Phenomena of Social Business, A Market-Based Approach to Social Value Creation. *Small Business Economics*, *40*(3), 715–737. doi:10.100711187-011-9401-0

Witt, P. (2004). Entrepreneurs' networks and the success of start-ups. *Entrepreneurship and Regional Development*, *16*(5), 391–412. doi:10.1080/0898562042000188423

Witt, P., Schroeter, A., & Merz, C. (2008). Entrepreneurial resource acquisition via personal networks: An empirical study of German start-ups. *Service Industries Journal*, *28*(7), 37–41. doi:10.1080/02642060701846846

Wolk, A. M. (2008). *Advancing Social Entrepreneurship: Reccommendations for Policy Makers and Government Agencies*. Washington, DC: The Aspen Institute.

Wood, S. (2012). Prone to progress: Using personality to identify supporters of innovative social entrepreneurship. *Journal of Public Policy & Marketing*, *31*(1), 129–141. doi:10.1509/jppm.11.060

Woolley, J. L. (2014). Opportunities for Social Value Creation Across Supply Chain Interactions. In L. Pate & C. Wankel (Eds.), *Emerging Research Directions in Social Entrepreneurship* (pp. 51–66). Springer. doi:10.1007/978-94-007-7896-2_4

Wu, J., Zhuo, S., & Wu, Z. (2017). National innovation system, social entrepreneurship, and rural economic growth in China. *Technological Forecasting and Social Change*, *121*, 38–250. doi:10.1016/j.techfore.2016.10.014

Yan, Y. X. (2010). The Chinese Path to Individualization. *The British Journal of Sociology*, *61*(3), 489–512. doi:10.1111/j.1468-4446.2010.01323.x PMID:20840429

Yazıcı, M. (2014). Değerler ve toplumsal yapıda sosyal değerlerin yeri. *Fırat Üniversitesi Sosyal Bilimler Dergisi*, *24*(1), 209–223.

Yıldız, M. L. (2016). Ethical Leadership: To Be or Not To Be A Moral Person. In M.L. Yıldız (Ed.), Leadership Studies (2nd ed.). Beta.

Yılmaz, A. S. (2014). Bir sosyal değişim ajanı olarak girişimcilik eğitimi. *Journal of World of Turks*, *6*(1), 297–310.

Yin, R. K. (2009). *Case Study Research Design and Methods* (4th ed.). Thousand Oaks, CA: Sage Publication Inc.

Yitshaki, R., & Kropp, F. (2016). Motivations and opportunity recognition of social entrepreneurs. *Journal of Small Business Management*, *54*(2), 546–565. doi:10.1111/jsbm.12157

Yonder, A., Akcar, S., & Gopalan, P. (2005). *Women's Participation in Disaster Relief and Recovery*. New York: Population Council.

Young, D. R. (2001, December). *Social Enterprise in the United States: Alternate Identities and Forms*. Paper presented at the EMES Conference, Trento, Italy.

Young, R. (2006). For What it is Worth: Social Value and the Future of Social Entrepreneurship. *Social Entrepreneurship: New Models of Sustainable Social Change*, 56-73.

Young, D. (2003). *New trends in the US non-profit sector: Towards market integration? In The Non-Profit Sector in a Changing Economy* (pp. 61–77). Paris, France: OECD.

Young, D. R., & Lecy, J. D. (2014). Defining the universe of social enterprise: Competing metaphors. *Voluntas*, *25*(5), 1307–1332. doi:10.100711266-013-9396-z

Young, R. (2006). For what it is worth: Social value and the future of social entrepreneurship. In A. Nichols (Ed.), *Social entrepreneurship: New models of sustainable social change* (pp. 56–73). Oxford University Press.

Yumuş, S. (2017). *Orhan Kemal'in romanlarında sosyal değerler.* Uludağ University, Master's Thesis.

Yunus, M. (2006). Social business entrepreneurs are the solution. In A. Nichols (Ed.), *Social entrepreneurship: New models of sustainable social change* (pp. 39–44). Oxford, UK: Oxford University Press.

Yunus, M. (2011). *Building Social Business: The New Kind of Capitalism that Serves Humanity's Most Pressing Needs.* New York: Public Affairs.

Zahra, S. A., & Covin, J. G. (1995). Contextual influences on the corporate entrepreneurship–performance relationship: a longitudinal analysis. Journal Business Venturing, 10, 43–58.

Zahra, S. A., Gedajlovic, E., Neubaum, D. O., & Shulman, J. M. (2009). A Typology of Social Entrepreneurs: Motives, Search Processes and Ethical Challenges. *Journal of Business Venturing*, *24*(5), 519–532. doi:10.1016/j.jbusvent.2008.04.007

Zahra, S. A., & George, G. (2002). Absorptive capacity: A review, reconceptualization, and extension. *Academy of Management Review*, *27*(2), 185–203.

Zahra, S. A., Newey, L. R., & Li, Y. (2014). On the Frontiers: The Implications of Social Entrepreneurship for International Entrepreneurship. *Entrepreneurship Theory and Practice*, *38*(1), 137–158. doi:10.1111/etap.12061

Zahra, S., Rawhouser, H. N., Bhawe, N., Neubaum, D. O., & Hayton, J. C. (2008). Globalization of social entrepreneurship. *Strategic Entrepreneurship Journal*, *2*(2), 117–131. doi:10.1002ej.43

Zamantılı Nayır, D., & Karataş Gümüştaş, N. (2017). Belagat (retorik) ne sağlar? Sosyal girişimcilerin meşruiyet kazanma çabaları. *25. Ulusal Yönetim ve Organizasyon Bildiriler Kitabı,* 40-47.

Zammuto, R. F. (1984). A comparison of multiple constituency models of organizational effectiveness. *Academy of Management Review*, *9*(4), 606–661.

Zappalà, G., & Lyons, M. (2009). Recent approaches to measuring social impact in the Third sector: An overview. The Centre for Social Impact Background Paper, No:6.

Zeyen, A., Beckman, M., Mueller, S., Dees, J. G., Khanin, D., Krueger, N., ... Zachakaris, A. (2012). Social Entrepreneurship and Broader Theories: Shedding New Light on the 'Bigger Picture'. *Journal of Social Entrepreneurship*, 1–20.

Zhang, D. D., & Swanson, L. A. (2014). Linking social entrepreneurship and sustainability. *Journal of Social Entrepreneurship*, *5*(2), 175–191. doi:10.1080/19420676.2014.880503

Zhang, J. (2010). The problems of using social networks in entrepreneurial resource acquisition. *International Small Business Journal*, *28*(4), 338–361. doi:10.1177/0266242610363524

Zhao, X., & Murrell, A. J. (2016). Revisiting the Corporate Social Performance-Financial Performance Link: A Replication of Waddock and Graves, Strategic Management Journal. *Special Issue: Replication in Strategic Management*, *37*(11), 2378–2388.

Zimmer, C. (1986). Entrepreneurship through social networks. In *The art and science of entrepreneurship.* Ballinger.

Zolin, R., & Schlosser, F. (2013). Characteristics of immigrant entrepreneurs and their involvement in international new ventures. *Thunderbird International Business Review*, *55*(3), 271–284. doi:10.1002/tie.21543

About the Contributors

N. Oyku Iyigun is the Director of Leadership and Entrepreneurship Research Center and also an Associate Professor of Strategy and Management at Istanbul Commerce University. Dr. Iyigun has a BS in International Relations from Istanbul University (2004), an MBA (International Business Administration) from Marmara University (2005) and a Ph.D. in Management and Organization from Marmara University (2011). She has taught a wide range of courses at both graduate and undergraduate levels such as Strategic Management & Business Policy, International Business, Managerial Skills & Strategic Leadership, Corporate Social Responsibility (CSR) and Business Ethics, Human Resource Management, International Entrepreneurship, Digital Entrepreneurship, Management & Organization, Organizational Culture, Organizational Behavior and Family Business Management for 6 years. Dr. Iyigun has a lot of publications, book chapters and books on strategic management, entrepreneurship, sustainability, CSR and ethics. Her research interests focus on social entrepreneurship, leadership and global aspects of management. Dr. Iyigun is a Senator of Junior Chamber International and an active member of Young Entrepreneurs Committee of The Union of Chambers and Commodity Exchanges of Turkey and she is the current President of Research and Publications Committee. Dr. Iyigun is the 2017-year winner of "The National Young Academician under the Age of Forty who is Adjudged to have made a Significant Contribution to Economy" award from the Independent Industrialists' and Businessmen's Association (MÜSİAD) Youth Committee in Turkey.

* * *

Ebru Beyza Bayarçelik is an Assistant Professor at İstanbul Gelişim University. Dr. Bayarçelik received BS in Industrial Engineering from Eastern Mediterranean University (1999), an MBA from Marmara University (2001) and a Ph.D. in Management and Organization from Gebze Technical University (2010). Since 2010, she has taught at both graduate and undergraduate levels at the Yeditepe University, Maltepe University, Gelişim University and Bahçeşehir University in İstanbul. She has also gave courses such as Introduction to Business, Management & Organization, Strategic Leadership & Managerial Skills, Business Research & Ethics, Human Resource Management, Entrepreneurship & Innovation, Contemporary Topics in Management. Dr. Bayarçelik research interests focus on Strategic management, intellectual capital, entrepreneurship, innovation and leadership. Her articles on these and other topics have appeared in journals and book chapters.

Muhsin F. Bayik is Assistant Professor of Marketing at Istanbul Medipol University. Dr.Bayik has a BS in Chemical Engineering from Bogazici University (1990), an MBA (Marketing) from University of North Florida (1993) and a Ph.D. in Marketing from Bahcesehir University (2015). He has taught a wide range of undergraduate and graduate courses such as Introduction to Business, Marketing Management, International Marketing, Brand Management, Digital Marketing, CRM, Entrepreneurship and Innovation Management, New Product, Service and Process Development, Social Responsibility for 5 years. Dr. Bayik has publications and book chapters on new product development, entrepreneurship, social innovation and marketing. His research interests focus on social entrepreneurship, mobile marketing and new product development.

D. Mehmet Bickes is Assistant Professor of Strategy and Management at Nevsehir Haci Bektas Veli University. Dr. Bickes has a BS in Business Administration from Kahramanmaras Sutcu Imam University (1997), an MBA Business Administration from Kahramanmaras Sutcu Imam University (2000) and a Ph.D. in Management and Organization from Erciyes University (2011). He has taught a wide range of courses at both graduate and undergraduate levels such as Business Management, Management & Organization, Strategic Management & Business Policy, Human Resource Management, Entrepreneurship, Organizational Behavior, Current Approaches in Management, Innovation & Knowledge Management, Public Relations and Research Methods & Techniques for 10 years. Dr. Bickes has some of publications and book chapters on entrepreneurship, leadership, work-related violence, total quality management and organizational learning. His research interests focus on entrepreneurship, leadership, innovation and organizational behavior.

Adnan Veysel Ertemel is Assistant Professor at Business Faculty at Istanbul Commerce University. Ertemel holds a BS degree in Computer Sciences and Engineering from Yıldız Technical University and Engineering and Technology Management MSc. degree from Boğazici University. He has PhD degree in Marketing Management from Marmara University. He has more than 15 years of experience at the intersection of IT, product development and digital marketing initially as a developer then as an entrepreneur and lecturer. After 5 years of Professional and 10 years of entrepreneurial experience in Turkish GSM sector, he continued his career in academia since 2012. His expertise areas include digital marketing strategy, entrepreneurial marketing, lean startup, lean analytics and business model innovation.

Mine Afacan Fındıklı is Associate Professor of Strategy and Management at Beykent University Department of Business Management and currently vice dean of FEAS. She has had a BS in Management and Organization from Anadolu University (2003), an MBA (Educational Management) from Bahcesehir University (2007) and a Ph.D. in Management and Organization from Istanbul University (2012). In 2016, she earned the title of Associate Professorship. She has previously worked in private sector for seven years. During this period, she has also been involved in Academia as a part-time instructor in Boğaziçi University, Yildiz Technical University and Istanbul Technical University (Tourism and Hotel Management Vocational School). Since 2005, she has been lecturing courses including Strategic Management, Business Ethics, HRM, Management & Organization at both graduate and undergraduate levels. She has various studies involving her interest areas. She is a member of Knowledge Management Working Group in PERYON (Turkish Human Resources Management Association). She is fluent in French and English.

Burcu Kümbül Güler is working as an Associate Professor at Dokuz Eylul University, Labour Economics and Industrial Relations Department in Turkey. She is also giving lectures at the Psychology Department of the same university. Dr. Kümbül Güler has a BA degree from the Psychology Department of Bogazici University, Turkey (1999). Then she gained the Master's degree on Human Resource Management from Dokuz Eylul University, Turkey (2002). She had received her PhD from Labour Economics and Industrial Relations department with her dissertation on "Social Entrepreneurship" from the same university (2008). During her PhD, she was accepted as a visiting scholar from Boston University, USA for a year between May, 2006 and May 2007. Dr. Kümbül Güler has taught a wide range of courses at both undergraduate and graduate levels such as Work and Organizational Psychology, Human Resource Management, Social Entrepreneurship, Social Psychology for 9 years. She has publications on Work Psychology and Social Entrepreneurship.

April Lia Hananto is senior lecturer at technical information of College Institute of Communication Science in STMIK ROSMA Karawang and after since 2014 had been active as permanent lecturer at information system of University of Buana Perjuangan Karawang. He is active in various professional activities as an IT consultant in several companies in Karawang, and also active as a member of ICT volunteer Indonesia.

Miftachul Huda is a researcher at Faculty of Islamic Civilisation, Universiti Teknologi Malaysia. His research interest includes digital ethics, educational studies, innovation, Islamic studies. He has been experienced in working on research for more than five years. Contributing several works, he is currently the member of the advisory editorial board in some international journals. Traveling in some countries with scholarly intent makes him extensive experience on his research expertise in international trend and issues. Thus, he commits to contributing his knowledge to the benefit of society through professional and social activities.

Mustafa Karaca is the Asst. Prof. Dr. at Inonu University in Turkey. He has a BS in Business Administration from Erciyes University (2003), an MBA (Business Management) from Erciyes University (2007) and a Ph.D. in Management and Organization from Erciyes University (2015). He has been working as an academician since 2005. He has taught in graduate and undergraduate stages about Organizational Behavior, Entrepreneurship, Human Resources Management, Media Management and Organizational Communication for 13 years. Dr. Karaca has a lot of publications such as books on entrepreneurship, papers about management and organizational behavior. He also works in some NGO's all of them are interested in social problems all around the world. He is interested in communication and media workers and their work life problems. He writes corner post for some newspapers about business life. Dr. Karaca also writes and applies projects about the funds of EU.

Endah Nurhawaeny Kardiyati is senior lecturer at Universitas Muhammadiyah Cirebon, Indonesia. She has been working in teaching and research in the field of economics, management science, entrepreneurship, community engagement, and business empowerment for more than fifteen years.

Chi Maher has published several book chapters, research papers in national and international scientific journals and books on: influence of public policy on small social enterprises, Understanding Managerial Career Anchors and Career Path Preferences. Value Creation for Small and Micro Social Enterprises (forthcoming, 2019). Besides those research activities, she has many years' experience of teaching social enterprise, social entrepreneurship, entrepreneurship concepts, theory and practice, research methods, social marketing, non-profit sector management, project management and Human Resources Management. Dr. Maher has also developed and managed several projects in the public sector and non-profit sector. Dr Maher is an award winner of the Westfocus Enterprising Business Award and the Director of Social Enterprise Knowledge Exchange Network (SEKEN).

Badlihisham Mohd Nasir is Professor in the field of religion, science and contemporary issues in digital age at faculty of Islamic Civilisation, Unversiti Teknologi Malaysia. He has been working for more than twenty years in teaching and research based on his expertise.

Ayla Zehra Öncer is an Associate Professor of Management and Strategy at Marmara University and also the Head of the Department of Human Resources. Dr. Öncer has a BS in Business Administration (1998), Master Degrees in International Business Administration (2000) and Management and Organization (2006) and a Ph.D. in Management and Organization (2004) from Marmara University. She has been teaching a wide range of courses for 14 years at both graduate and undergraduate levels such as Strategic Management, Business and Society, Human Resources Management, Management and Organization, Contemporary Management Techniques, Business Administration, Training and Development, Selection and Recruitment, Scientific Research Methods and Corporate Governance. She has lots of projects and publications on strategic management, human resources management, organizational behaviour and leadership. Her research interests focus on strategic management, business and society, social entrepreneurship, and leadership.

Sari Laelatul Qodriah is a lecturer in Universitas Muhammadiyah Cirebon (UMC). She has been teaching in UMC since 2003. She got her bachelor degree in Universitas Cikroaminoto Yogyakarta, management study program. She graduated her master degree at Universitas Padjajaran Bandung, management study program, now she is taking her doctoral degree in Universitas Negeri Surakarta. Her research is focused in the field of economy, management, entrepreneurship, and extension of community empowerment of bussiness UMKM (Micro Small and Medium Enterprises).

Budi Rismayadi is senior lecturer at Faculty of Economics and Business, University of Singaperbangsa Karawang, Indonesia. He has many experienced position as chairman in one of the High School of Economics Science in 2004 to 2008, and had served as chairman of the Institute for Research and Community Service (LPPM) University of Singaperbangsa Karawang in 2009 to 2014, and currently serves as Dean of the Faculty of Business and Social Sciences at the University of Buana Perjuangan Karawang, Indonesia. He is also active in various professional activities as a board of Private College Association commissariat IV A West Java, and active as a member of the Association of Indonesian Lecturers.

Aminuddin Ruskam is Associate Professor in the field of Syariah (Islamic law), and Economy at faculty of Islamic Civilisation, Unversiti Teknologi Malaysia. He has been working for more than twenty years in teaching and research based on his expertise.

Fulya Taşel is an Assistant Professor at Maltepe University. Dr. Taşel has a BS in Industrial Engineering from Eastern Mediterranean University (2000), an MBA from Yeditepe University (2003) and a Ph.D. in Economics from İstanbul University (2012). Since 2012, she has taught a wide range of courses at both graduate and undergraduate levels such as Introduction to Economics, Macro Economics, International Economics, Introduction to Economic Geography, Managerial Economics, Fundamentals of International Trade, Export and Import Management, International Business, Globalization and Emerging Markets for 6 years. Dr. Taşel has several publications, articles, book chapters and proceedings on microeconomics, macroeconomics, international trade and innovation.

Nurgul Keles Taysir is an Assistant Professor at Istanbul Commerce University. The author completed her bachelor degree in Business Administration at Anadolu University, and master and PhD degrees in Management and Organization at Marmara University. Between 2011-2012 she had conducted research on NGOs at Boston/USA. She gave "Organizations" courses at Ozyegin University between 2013-2014. She has been working as an Asst.Prof. at Istanbul Commerce University since 2015, and giving lectures in the fields of Organizational Behaviour and Management-Organization, Organizational Culture, Entrepreneurship. The author's main research interest lie in NGOs and social entrepreneurship. In 2017, she has presented a paper named "Founders' background as a catalyst of becoming a social entrepreneur" at 33rd EGOS Colloquium, Copenhagen.

Beliz Ülgen is the head of Business Administration Department and associate professor of strategy and management at Istanbul Commerce University. In 1992 she graduated from Istanbul University Business Administration (in English). She received her PhD degree in the field of Human Resource Management from Istanbul University (2003). Besides her academic background she has work experiences in private sector as human resource management professional. Between 1992-1994 she worked in T.Y.T Bank/Human Resources and Organization Department as human resource specialist. In following three years, she worked in Şahinler Group of Companies (operates in various sectors such as textile, construction, tourism) as human resource specialist and between 1997-2002 she worked in Adecco (global recruitment company) as senior recruitment consultant. Since 2002, she's working in Istanbul Commerce University and has taught human resource management, organizational behavior, management and leadership courses at both graduate and undergraduate levels. Her academic studies focus on Human Resource Management and Organizational Behavior.

Charles M. Vance is a professor of management and human resources at Loyola Marymount University in Los Angeles, where he teaches at executive, MBA, and undergraduate levels. He has been very active at Loyola Marymount in designing and conducting customized training programs for managers, executives, and other professionals. He has had considerable experience as a consultant in North and South America, Asia, and Europe in training design, management development and coaching, and broader human resource and organization development applications. Vance received his Ph.D. in Instructional

Design, Development, and Evaluation from Syracuse University, and is the author of numerous scholarly publications and three books, including *Smart Talent Management: Building Knowledge Assets for Competitive Advantage* (Edward Elgar Publishing), *Mastering Management Education* (Sage Publications), and *Managing a Global Workforce* (3rd edition, Routledge).

Murat Yalçintaş is an academician and a businessman whose name has long been among the prominent names in the academic and business world. Dr. Yalçıntaş, the former president of Istanbul Chamber of Commerce (ITO) and the Association of the Mediterranean Chambers of Commerce and Industry (ASCAME) has served in many institutions and organizations in various positions throughout his career. He is currently the director of Graduate School of Foreign Trade and an associate professor of strategy and management at Istanbul Commerce University, Turkey. He gives lectures on Strategic Management, Management and Organization, Game Theory and Leadership. He is also active in the business world in managerial positions. Dr. Yalçıntaş has many articles published in national and international refereed journals in addition to his four published books. Dr. Yalçıntaş has been deemed worthy of many international awards including King Leopold II. the Order of Merit (Belgium), the Legion d`Honneur (France), the Order of Merit of the Italian Republic Commendatore and Honorary Professorship from Kyrgyzstan Presidential Academy.

M. Leyla Yildiz is an Associate Professor of Strategy and Management at Marmara University. Dr. Yıldız has a BS in Business Administration from Marmara University (2002), an MBA (Management and Organization) from Marmara University (2004) and a Ph.D. in Management and Organization from Marmara University (2009). She has taught a wide range of courses at doctorate, graduate, undergraduate levels such as International Business, Leadership Studies, Business Ethics and Corporate Social Responsibility (CSR), Human Resource Management, Social Entrepreneurship, Business Management and Qualitative and Quantitative Research Methods for 9 years. Dr. Yıldız has a lot of publications, book chapters and books on contemporary management, leadership, human resources management, sustainability and social entrepreneurship. Her research interests focus on leadership, ethics, social entrepreneurship, sustainability and human resources management.

Abdullah Yilmaz was born in Ankara, in 1987. He is a research assistant at Selcuk University, Faculty of Economics and Administrative Sciences, Konya, Turkey. He graduated ranking first in class from Erciyes University in 2009. He has started his master's degree at Marmara University (2009) but graduated from Selcuk University Department of Business Administration (2012). Currently he is a PhD candidate at the same department and about to finish his thesis. He has academic studies on HRM, organizational behavior and organizational theory.

Hande Ulukapi Yilmaz was born in Konya, in 1989. She has been a research assistant at Selcuk University Faculty of Economics and Administrative Sciences since 2012. She graduated from Istanbul University Faculty of Business Administration (2011) and has a MS degree from Selcuk University Department of Business Administration (2013). Currently she is a PhD candidate at the same department, working on her thesis which is about impression management and workplace loneliness. Her academic studies include organizational socialization, cyberloafing, authentic leadership, organizational support, work-life balance and more.

Uğur Yozgat is a Professor of Management and Organization and Head of the Social Sciences Institute and Business Department at Istanbul Kultur University in Istanbul, Turkey. He has a MSc degree in Electronics and Telecommunications Engineering and a PhD degree in Management and Organization. He is one of the founders of the International Strategic Management and Managers Association (ISMMA) and one of the Organizing Committee Members of the International Strategic Management Conference and International Conference on Leadership, Technology and Innovation. Dr. Yozgat is a Board Member of many National and International Conferences, an Editorial Board Member of Journal of Global Strategic Management (JGSM) and many of National Journals. He was Chair of many National Conferences such as "National Management and Organization Conference", "National Business Conference" etc. Dr. Yozgat is also a reviewer of many National and International Journals and Conferences. Dr. Yozgat has experiences in conducting professional training such as Management Information Systems, Knowledge Management, Electronic Commerce, Total Quality Management, Quality Systems (ISO 9001, ISO 14001, ISO 18001), communication skills, leadership skills, sustainability, entrepreneurship, decision makings etc. for many corporations in Turkey. His research interests include strategic management, information systems management, knowledge management, customer relationship management and decision making. He has several papers published in national and international journals and conference proceedings. In 2013, he was awarded by Turkish Academy of Social Sciences for the valuable translated lecture book edited by him.

Index

H

I

L

N

P

R

S

T

V

W

www.ingramcontent.com/pod-product-compliance
Lightning Source LLC
LaVergne TN
LVHW060357300926
849162LV00006B/1290
* 9 7 8 1 5 2 2 5 5 6 8 7 9 *